Biomedical Image Synthesis and Simulation

THE ELSEVIER AND MICCAI SOCIETY BOOK SERIES

Advisory Board

Titles

MICCAI

Biomedical Image Synthesis and Simulation

Methods and Applications

Edited by

Ninon Burgos

David Svoboda

ACADEMIC PRESS

An imprint of Elsevier

For information on all Academic Press publications
visit our website at https://www.elsevier.com/books-and-journals

Publisher: Mara Conner
Acquisitions Editor: Tim Pitts
Editorial Project Manager: Ivy Dawn Torre
Production Project Manager: Anitha Sivaraj
Designer: Christian J. Bilbow

Typeset by VTeX

Working together
to grow libraries in
developing countries

www.elsevier.com • www.bookaid.org

Contents

PART 2 Applications

Contributors

Oscar Acosta
Univ Rennes, CLCC Eugène Marquis, INSERM, LTSI - UMR 1099, Rennes, France

Simon Arridge
Centre for Medical Image Computing, UCL, London, United Kingdom
Department of Computer Science, UCL, London, United Kingdom

Anais Barateau
Univ Rennes, CLCC Eugène Marquis, INSERM, LTSI - UMR 1099, Rennes, France

Riccardo Barbano
Department of Medical Physics, UCL, London, United Kingdom
Centre for Medical Image Computing, UCL, London, United Kingdom

Julien Bert
LaTIM, INSERM, UMR1101, Brest, France
Brest University Hospital Center, Brest, France

Ninon Burgos
Sorbonne Université, Institut du Cerveau - Paris Brain Institute - ICM, CNRS, Inria, Inserm, AP-HP, Hôpital de la Pitié-Salpêtrière, Paris, France

Hu Chen
College of Computer Science, Sichuan University, Chengdu, China

Kevin T. Chen
Department of Biomedical Engineering, National Taiwan University, Taipei, Taiwan

Xiaoran Chen
Computer Vision Lab, ETH Zürich, Zürich, Switzerland

Li Cheng
ECE, University of Alberta, Edmonton, AB, Canada

Jae Hyuk Choi
University of Newcastle, Callaghan, New South Wales, Australia

Hilda Chourak

Univ Rennes, CLCC Eugène Marquis, INSERM, LTSI - UMR 1099, Rennes, France

Walter J. Curran Jr.

Department of Radiation Oncology and Winship Cancer Institute, Emory University, Atlanta, GA, United States

Renaud de Crevoisier

Univ Rennes, CLCC Eugène Marquis, INSERM, LTSI - UMR 1099, Rennes, France

Srijay Deshpande

Tissue Image Analytics Centre, Department of Computer Science, University of Warwick, Coventry, United Kingdom

Blake E. Dewey

Department of Electrical and Computer Engineering, Johns Hopkins University, Baltimore, MD, United States

Jason Dowling

CSIRO Health and Biosecurity, Herston, Queensland, Australia

Ivana Drobnjak

Centre for Medical Image Computing (CMIC) and Department of Computer Science, University College London, London, United Kingdom

Jan Ehrhardt

Institute of Medical Informatics, University of Lübeck, Lübeck, Germany

Dennis Eschweiler

Institute of Imaging and Computer Vision, RWTH Aachen University, Aachen, Germany

Alejandro F. Frangi

Centre for Computational Imaging and Simulation Technologies in Biomedicine (CISTIB), School of Computing, University of Leeds, Leeds, United Kingdom
Leeds Institute for Cardiovascular and Metabolic Medicine (LICAMM), School of Medicine, University of Leeds, Leeds, United Kingdom

Mark Graham

School of Biomedical Engineering and Imaging Sciences, King's College London, London, United Kingdom

Peter Greer

University of Newcastle, Callaghan, New South Wales, Australia
Calvary Mater Newcastle Hospital, Waratah, New South Wales, Australia

Shuo Han

Department of Biomedical Engineering, Johns Hopkins University, Baltimore, MD, United States

Yufan He

Department of Electrical and Computer Engineering, Johns Hopkins University, Baltimore, MD, United States

Juan Eugenio Iglesias

Center for Medical Image Computing (CMIC), University College London, London, United Kingdom

Martinos Center for Biomedical Imaging, Massachusetts General Hospital and Harvard Medical School, Boston, MA, United States

Computer Science and Artificial Intelligence Laboratory (CSAIL), Massachusetts Institute of Technology, Cambridge, MA, United States

Mark Jenkinson

FMRIB, University of Oxford, Oxford, United Kingdom

Bangti Jin

Department of Computer Science, UCL, London, United Kingdom

Wenchi Ke

College of Computer Science, Sichuan University, Chengdu, China

Charles Kervrann

EPC Serpico, Inria Rennes, CNRS-UMR144, Institut Curie, PSL Research, Rennes Cedex, France

Ender Konukoglu

Computer Vision Lab, ETH Zürich, Zürich, Switzerland

Violeta Kovacheva

Grid Edge, Birmingham, United Kingdom

Claes N. Ladefoged

Department of Clinical Physiology and Nuclear Medicine, Rigshospitalet, Copenhagen, Denmark

Ina Laube

Institute of Imaging and Computer Vision, RWTH Aachen University, Aachen, Germany

Yang Lei

Department of Radiation Oncology and Winship Cancer Institute, Emory University, Atlanta, GA, United States

Andrea Leo
Department of Translational Research on New Technologies in Medicine and Surgery, University of Pisa, Pisa, Italy

Bowen Li
Department of Computer Science, Johns Hopkins University, Baltimore, MD, United States
PAII Inc, Bethesda, MD, United States
Department of Health Sciences Informatics, Johns Hopkins University, Baltimore, MD, United States

Huiqi Li
Beijing Institute of Technology, Beijing, China

Tian Liu
Department of Radiation Oncology and Winship Cancer Institute, Emory University, Atlanta, GA, United States

Yihao Liu
Department of Electrical and Computer Engineering, Johns Hopkins University, Baltimore, MD, United States

Matteo Mancini
Department of Neuroscience, Brighton and Sussex Medical School, University of Sussex, Brighton, United Kingdom
Cardiff University Brain Research Imaging Centre (CUBRIC), Cardiff University, Cardiff, United Kingdom
NeuroPoly Lab, Polytechnique Montreal, Montreal, QC, Canada

Fayyaz Minhas
Tissue Image Analytics Centre, Department of Computer Science, University of Warwick, Coventry, United Kingdom

Tereza Nečasová
CBIA, Faculty of Informatics, Masaryk University, Brno, Czech Republic

Dong Nie
University of North Carolina at Chapel Hill, Chapel Hill, NC, United States

Jean-Claude Nunes
Univ Rennes, CLCC Eugène Marquis, INSERM, LTSI - UMR 1099, Rennes, France

Laura O'Connor
University of Newcastle, Callaghan, New South Wales, Australia
Calvary Mater Newcastle Hospital, Waratah, New South Wales, Australia

Ilkay Oksuz

Computer Engineering Department, Istanbul Technical University, Istanbul, Turkey

School of Biomedical Engineering & Imaging Sciences, King's College London, United Kingdom

Anders B. Olin

Department of Clinical Physiology and Nuclear Medicine, Rigshospitalet, Copenhagen, Denmark

Jerry L. Prince

Department of Electrical and Computer Engineering, Johns Hopkins University, Baltimore, MD, United States

Richard L.J. Qiu

Department of Radiation Oncology and Winship Cancer Institute, Emory University, Atlanta, GA, United States

Nasir Rajpoot

Tissue Image Analytics Centre, Department of Computer Science, University of Warwick, Coventry, United Kingdom

Parnesh Raniga

CSIRO Health and Biosecurity, Herston, Queensland, Australia

Nishant Ravikumar

Centre for Computational Imaging and Simulation Technologies in Biomedicine (CISTIB), School of Computing, University of Leeds, Leeds, United Kingdom

Leeds Institute for Cardiovascular and Metabolic Medicine (LICAMM), School of Medicine, University of Leeds, Leeds, United Kingdom

Samuel W. Remedios

Department of Computer Science, Johns Hopkins University, Baltimore, MD, United States

Pekka Ruusuvuori

Institute of Biomedicine, University of Turku, Turku, Finland

Faculty of Medicine and Health Technology, Tampere University, Tampere, Finland

David Sarrut

CREATIS, CNRS UMR5220, INSERM U1294, Villeurbanne, France

Université de Lyon, INSA-Lyon, Villeurbanne, France

Centre Léon Bérard, Lyon, France

Johannes Stegmaier

Institute of Imaging and Computer Vision, RWTH Aachen University, Aachen, Germany

Institute for Automation and Applied Informatics, Karlsruhe Institute of Technology, Karlsruhe, Germany

David Svoboda

CBIA, Faculty of Informatics, Masaryk University, Brno, Czech Republic

Ryutaro Tanno

Centre for Medical Image Computing, UCL, London, United Kingdom

Healthcare Intelligence, Microsoft Research Cambridge, Cambridge, United Kingdom

Sotirios A. Tsaftaris

School of Engineering, University of Edinburgh, Edinburgh, United Kingdom

Vladimír Ulman

IT4Innovations, VSB – Technical University of Ostrava, Ostrava, Czech Republic

Gabriele Valvano

IMT School for Advanced Studies Lucca, Lucca, Italy

School of Engineering, University of Edinburgh, Edinburgh, United Kingdom

Tonghe Wang

Department of Radiation Oncology and Winship Cancer Institute, Emory University, Atlanta, GA, United States

Xuyun Wen

Nanjing University of Aeronautics and Astronautics, Nanjing, China

David Wiesner

Centre for Biomedical Image Analysis, Masaryk University, Brno, Czech Republic

Matthias Wilms

Department of Radiology, University of Calgary, Calgary, AB, Canada

Yan Xia

Centre for Computational Imaging and Simulation Technologies in Biomedicine (CISTIB), School of Computing, University of Leeds, Leeds, United Kingdom

Leeds Institute for Cardiovascular and Metabolic Medicine (LICAMM), School of Medicine, University of Leeds, Leeds, United Kingdom

Xiaofeng Yang

Department of Radiation Oncology and Winship Cancer Institute, Emory University, Atlanta, GA, United States

Greg Zaharchuk

Department of Radiology, Stanford University, Stanford, CA, United States

Hui Zhang

Centre for Medical Image Computing (CMIC) and Department of Computer Science, University College London, London, United Kingdom

Yi Zhang

College of Computer Science, Sichuan University, Chengdu, China

Can Zhao

NVIDIA, Santa Clara, CA, United States

He Zhao

Beijing Institute of Technology, Beijing, China

Lianrui Zuo

Department of Electrical and Computer Engineering, Johns Hopkins University, Baltimore, MD, United States

Preface

In 1979, Judith M. S. Prewitt published an innovative paper focused on modeling histology patterns based on graph theory and utilizing Dirichlet tessellation. The created graph, where individual Dirichlet domains corresponded to cells in tissue and edges to the cellular communication pathways, was further used for the comparison, grading, and classification of tissues. With this work, the basic principles of biomedical image modeling were introduced. However, due to the limits of concurrent hardware, it remained a rather theoretical concept. At that time, a manipulation with larger or even higher-dimensional images was hardly reachable for the general public, and even for scientists. In her paper, Judith M. S. Prewitt admitted that the basic image processing tasks were solved with the kind support of Jet Propulsion Laboratory in Caltech, where sufficiently powerful hardware was accessible. Therefore, the modeling and synthesis had to wait for a suitable time point in the next few years.

The change occurred in the early 1990s with the rapid development of particular computer components. First, these were the processors and memory modules, but later highly parallel graphical processing units were constructed and brought hitherto unsuspected possibilities in all the disciplines where high computational power and memory requirements were required. The development of hardware was tightly followed by the methods that had been "sleeping" so far. In particular, the concept of neural networks had been known for many years, but has found its wide use at the beginning of the new century with the boom of highly parallelized computing and its availability to broad masses.

The development was going on, and in October 2016, the first international workshop on Simulation and Synthesis in Medical Imaging (SASHIMI) was organized by Sotirios A. Tsaftaris, Ali Gooya, Alejandro F. Frangi, and Jerry L. Prince as a satellite event of the International Conference on Medical Image Computing and Computer Assisted Intervention. Thanks to its success, the workshop is still active, and more than 80 articles have been published in its proceedings. The workshop attracts the attention of researchers from academia, as well as industry, and in many cases it is the starting point for doing quality research in the field of image synthesis. It is no secret that the SASHIMI workshop, which slowly became the platform for sharing knowledge and experience in the field of image synthesis in medical imaging, was a starting point for writing this book.

David Svoboda
Ninon Burgos

Introduction to medical and biomedical image synthesis

1

David Svoboda[a] **and Ninon Burgos**[b]

[a]*CBIA, Faculty of Informatics, Masaryk University, Brno, Czech Republic*
[b]*Sorbonne Université, Institut du Cerveau - Paris Brain Institute - ICM, CNRS, Inria, Inserm, AP-HP, Hôpital de la Pitié-Salpêtrière, Paris, France*

*The human brain is the best **image synthesizer** ever!*

> When storing our photos using the most popular image file format called *jpeg*, a vast amount of information in the image, to be compressed, is intentionally thrown away to markedly reduce the file size. Afterwards, when viewing the compressed image, the missing parts are surprisingly not disturbing us as those are either too tiny for our eyes or automatically completed by the human brain due to our previous experience with real world scenes.

***Image synthesis** is nothing more than an attempt to mystify human visual perception!*

> Each image synthesis process is naturally followed by an obvious, and often obligatory, question whether the artificially generated image is plausible enough or whether the difference between the artificial and real image is so small or negligible that the human eye is not able to recognize it. Answering "no" to this question clearly shows that our eyes do not accept the generated image as the naturally acquired one.

Every day, millions of images are created using various acquisition devices starting from the smallest ones like smartphones or compact cameras and ending with the large ones, typically including expensive imaging devices located in hospitals or observatories. Taking photos is mostly cheap, fast, and repeatable. This is, however, not true in the case of medical imaging where the acquisition process might be long, expensive, dangerous, or too scarce to be repeated if even possible. A simple example

Biomedical Image Synthesis and Simulation. https://doi.org/10.1016/B978-0-12-824349-7.00008-6

of such a real life situation is scanning the patient's body with computed tomography or positron emission tomography. Regardless of the fact that the scanning process is not comfortable, time demanding, and expensive, one should keep in mind that each exposure of the patient to X-rays increases the probability of getting cancer in the future. On the other hand, more scans would bring more information needed for proper diagnosis or prognosis of the illness for which the patient currently undergoes the examination. Here comes the obvious question: how to reduce time, price, and allow repeatability? A similar issue is apparent also in microscopy where, for proper analysis of cells and subsequent diagnosis, one needs to know the correct shape and location of such cells. This is, however, a difficult task as no one knows the exact shape and location of the observed cells and cell compartments, as we are able to observe them only using the optics that naturally introduce some blur and artifacts. One can rely on standard image restoration methods to improve the images to some extent, but the question of possible shift or misalignment still persists.

The discipline that tries to answer the above-mentioned questions has been studied for years by many research groups and is called simply "image synthesis." One can find many adjectives that anticipate this phrase. These might be "medical," "biomedical," "deep learning based," "model-driven," or "data-driven," but all of them have the same objective – to synthesize some image or its part that is missing. One can even complicate the task and try to synthesize time-lapse image sequences, but this is nothing more than increasing the dimensionality of the image that one wants to artificially generate. In this book, we will try to answer the questions that are narrowly connected to challenges in medical and biomedical imaging and how to answer them using image synthesis.

Currently, image synthesis methods in medical and biomedical imaging are able to augment image datasets, increase image resolution, fill missing or incomplete data, derive data in one modality using another modality, prepare perfect annotation, etc. This is definitely not a small amount, and we can expect that the possibilities will rise in the future. All the given use cases listed above (and not only those) are mentioned in the second part of this book which is dedicated to success stories and how individual image synthesis methods were employed in particular situations. The first part of the book, on the other hand, is more theoretical and shows and explains the basic principles of image synthesis methods, how they work and how to implement them. Both parts together form a book that gives the reader insight into the technical background of image synthesis and how it is used, in the particular disciplines of medical and biomedical imaging.

It is not a secret that this book emerged from the narrow cooperation of the experts in the field of image synthesis in medical imaging. Most of them are more or less connected to the international workshop on Simulation and Synthesis in Medical Imaging (SASHIMI), organized as a satellite event of the International Conference on Medical Image Computing and Computer Assisted Intervention – a vivid platform for sharing knowledge and experience in this field.

The aim of this book is to present the already well-established image synthesis approaches as a family of methods that together form a puzzle game where each tile has its own meaning, position, and is unreplaceable. We hope that the reader will find this puzzle game solvable, interesting, and enjoyable. The book is split into two main parts – Methods & Principles and Applications – each consisting of several chapters written by the specialists and experts in the given fields of medical and biomedical imaging. The first chapter that immediately follows this introduction is focused on traditional systematic modeling, which is also called model-driven approach. We consider this chapter and its position at the very beginning of the book as important because it presents the basic principles of image synthesis that were valid before deep learning appeared and became a de facto standard. Currently, the deep learning approaches dominate, but before we start enjoying their strength, we should understand the cornerstones that are not visible at first sight but still form the fundamentals on which the deep learning methods are also built. The first part of the book thus presents the methods that have been developed for image synthesis in chronological order: first systematic modeling, including parametric modeling, Monte Carlo simulations, and image synthesis methods using segmentation and registration, and then data-driven machine learning approaches including dictionary learning, convolutional neural networks, generative adversarial networks and (variational) autoencoders. The second part of the book is dedicated to the applications of image synthesis, first to medical and then to biomedical imaging. The medical applications start with a chapter dedicated to the use of a framework that simulates magnetic resonance images relying on the acquisition physics principles, i.e., the simulated image is not obtained from another image as will be the case in the following. This chapter precedes a series of modality-agnostic chapters covering image harmonization and enhancement, and how these can help subsequent image processing steps. Follow applications specific to a task, e.g., anomaly detection, or a modality, e.g., positron emission tomography. After the medical applications, the focus is put on biomedical applications, covering different scales, from single cells to whole histological slices, both static and changing in time. The book ends with a third part on perspectives that includes three chapters. The first summarizes the different options that exist and should be considered when validating image synthesis approaches. The second explains the crucial role that uncertainty quantification plays in medical image synthesis. The last concludes the book with research directions that should be worth exploring in the future.

Methods and principles

Parametric modeling in biomedical image synthesis

Pekka Ruusuvuori[a,b]

[a]*Institute of Biomedicine, University of Turku, Turku, Finland*
[b]*Faculty of Medicine and Health Technology, Tampere University, Tampere, Finland*

2.1 Introduction

Simulation and modeling have been widely used to generate synthetic data across multiple disciplines of biomedical sciences, including multiple different imaging modalities and applications. Depending on the imaging modality, on the targeted model object, and on the purpose of the synthesized data, the modeling naturally differs in various aspects. It is clear that medical imaging of macro-level objects, such as magnetic resonance imaging of brains and positron emission tomography of animal models, differs from microscope imaging of cell populations of tissue samples. Even within microscopy, the abundance of imaging modalities, let alone the differences in objects and samples that can be imaged, makes a general approach for covering biomedical image simulation almost impossible. Here, we focus on presenting the typical phases in parametric modeling-based simulation of microscopy images with cells and cellular structures as the objects of interest.

Despite the focus set in a certain application area, the simulation process shares some general principles. The goal of the modeling process is to capture essential characteristics of the underlying phenomenon or physical objects, and then it attempts to mimic the image acquisition device through which we capture the distorted images of the true objects. In more detail, the process can be divided into two steps. First, an ideal, undistorted image of the imaged object is generated. This is done using a model for the objects of interest, which may include prior knowledge on the physical properties of the objects, domain knowledge from biology or medicine, as well as ad-hoc modeling based on visual properties. The result, an ideal object representation, is then fed to the second phase of simulation process, which is the modeled measurement system. This phase aims at distorting the ideal object representation with aberrations and errors caused by the image acquisition process into an image which resembles realistic data obtained from imaging devices.

One way to categorize the simulation approaches is the division into parametric modeling and learning-based modeling approaches [1]. The former category, parametric modeling, is a widely used approach where a simplified, explicitly defined

Biomedical Image Synthesis and Simulation. https://doi.org/10.1016/B978-0-12-824349-7.00009-8

model controlled by user-defined parameters is used for generating shapes and image properties which, to a useful level, resemble the images of real objects. For example, defining a fluorescence-labeled object as a 2D Gaussian surface and its movement over time with a deterministic random walk can be used for simulating time-lapse images using parametric models. The approach enables efficient control over the properties of the simulated image properties, making it well suited for creating synthetic experiments for testing automated image analysis algorithms under various conditions. The latter, learning-based modeling, presents an approach where the model properties are learned from training examples, enabling including the natural variation in generated shapes through the inclusion of representative samples in the training data.

Here, we focus on simulation processes generating synthetic images using parametric modeling. In particular, we discuss parametric modeling of the cellular objects in 2D, both as a generic random shape model and as cell-type specific ad-hoc models. We will also discuss the modeling of microscopy measurement and image acquisition systems. We limit to using the SIMCEP simulation framework [2,3] and its refined versions for specific use cases [4,5] as an example implementation. Finally, we provide example use cases for simulated images generated through parametric modeling, and discuss potential future directions.

2.2 Parametric modeling paradigm

Parametric modeling enables control over the simulated image characteristics, enabling generation of unconstrained quantities of synthetic data with desired properties. In the context of microscopy images of cell populations, some of the obvious characteristics are related to the number of objects, their spatial arrangement in the images, and shape & appearance of the objects. Further, when generating simulated images with realistic appearance for validating image analysis tools, the image acquisition process and other sources of noise and variation also need to be modeled.

In the parametric modeling simulation paradigm, each property is in principle controlled through specific parameters defining, e.g., the attributes of the statistical model from which the generated instance is drawn. Modeling complex biological objects and underlying phenomena, biochemical process, and physical properties of the measurement system can be done by using practical approximations providing coarse representations or using representations tailored to carefully correspond to realistic visual appearance by detailed parameterization of the model. While offering unlimited possibilities for adding properties in the simulation model through introducing more parameters, the complexity of the parameter space is also a shortcoming of the parametric modeling paradigm.

2.2.1 Modeling of the cellular objects

A cell, as the fundamental functional unit in biology, is a very challenging object for modeling with its versatile phenotypes and functionality, despite being extensively studied using different microscopy imaging platforms. Incorporating all the knowledge on various cell types that has been accumulated for decades would be practically impossible using parametric modeling approaches. Instead of fully realistic modeling, the aim is typically to provide simulated images with realistic enough appearance from the perspective of image processing tasks. Further, modeling objects imposes different challenges and limitations when considering modeling of 2D microscopy or temporal 2D modeling, where instead of generating instances from a random model, the model parameters need to incorporate temporal similarity to enable dependency between time points as evolving shapes and spatial appearance. Further, modeling is also dependent on the targeted modality, for example, 2D vs. 3D object generation poses limitations in object placement: overlap in 2D projections is not actual overlap in 3D space. Here, we focus on describing the typical steps in modeling cellular objects in 2D microscopy, which can be considered as a less complex task compared to temporal 2D, 3D, or temporal 3D simulation.

2.2.1.1 Generic parameter-controlled shape modeling: random shape model for nucleus and cell body

Parametric shape modeling enables efficiently controlling the shape of the simulated objects. By modifying the model parameters, it is possible to adjust the object shape and appearance in a fully controlled manner. Parametric random models for generic cell shapes have been introduced in, e.g., [2,3] and [6]. The former, SIMCEP cell simulator, proposed a generic shape model, which can be used for generating various combinations of random shapes with varying degrees of complexity. The model is based on a polygon with randomly dislocated vertices, and a smooth contour fit between the vertices, representing the shape outline.

As presented in [3], a polygon with regular vertices can be generated by equidistantly sampling a circle, and by dislocating the vertices into random spatial locations. The parametric shape model then becomes a random polygon with scale r, generated using a uniform distribution $U(\cdot, \cdot)$ as follows:

$$
\begin{aligned}
x(\theta_i) &= r[U(-\alpha, \alpha) + \cos(\theta_i + U(-\beta, \beta))], \\
y(\theta_i) &= r[U(-\alpha, \alpha) + \sin(\theta_i + U(-\beta, \beta))].
\end{aligned}
\tag{2.1}
$$

The key parameters towards generating varying shapes are the range defining parameter β, which can be used for controlling the randomness of vertex sampling, and the object radius randomness controlled with parameter α, which adds a random constant in the scale of the object. The final outline of the object is obtained by interpolating a cubic spline between the vertices. This contour forms a smooth outline for the parameter-controlled random shape.

In Fig. 2.1, an example of the shape generation is illustrated. The key property of the parameter-controlled random shape is its versatility – through setting the parameter values controlling the object radius (α) and vertex randomness (β), the same

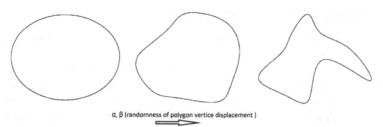

α, β (randomness of polygon vertice displacement)

FIGURE 2.1

Shape complexity controlled through parameters α and β, controlling the randomness of object radius and vertice sampling. Increasing the values from $\alpha = \beta = 0$ on the left creates shapes with increasing complexity. Adapted from [3].

model can be used for generating objects with varying shapes. For example, cell nucleus (relatively round, moderate variation between cells) and cell body (more complex shape with significant variation between cells) can be generated using the same basic model.

Several other parametric random shape models have been presented in the literature. To provide a few examples, in [7] the nucleus shape was modeled using a truncated Fourier series for randomized radius for the nucleus outline, and in [6] the object surface was generated as a deformable model implemented as a fast level-set method with artificial noise as the speed function. In [8], the nuclei shapes (in 3D) were generated using level-set deformed Voronoi diagrams while in [7] the Voronoi diagrams were used for generating cell body outlines.

2.2.1.2 Cell-type specific parametric shape models

The shapes generated using the relatively simple parametric model, however, are limited to generic random outlines and cannot produce shapes of any particular cell type. From the analysis perspective, capability to capture differences (and similarity) between cell phenotypes and to characterize properties related to the appearance in terms of shape and intensity are fundamental requirements for an image analysis algorithm. Thus, as when modeling synthetic images, capability to generate objects (cells) with distinctive phenotypic characteristics is a desired feature. When modeling shapes outside the range of the generic parametric model described above, for example, when aiming towards generating shapes typical for specific cells, the model needs to be defined specifically for this purpose.

Several studies in the literature have proposed cell-type specific parametric models to generate shapes representing certain cell types, or to enable generating different cell types flexibly as in [9]. For example, in [4], ad-hoc parameter-controlled models for five bacteria types with distinctive shapes were presented. Table 2.1 summarizes the shape models, controlled with simple range restricting parameters setting the object lengths. In [7], the cervical cells in Pap smears were modeled using a combination of random parametric models for nuclei and Voronoi tessellation for cell body. In [10], more cell-type specific models were introduced (bacilli as simple linear shapes and white blood cells using the parametric model derived from Eq. (2.1)). In [11], a model-based approach for simulating cells with filopodial protrusions was presented, and used for generating simulated images of lung cancer cells of two phenotypes.

Table 2.1 Examples of simple shapes generated with cell-type specific parametric models corresponding to bacterial cells. Modified from [5].

Target cell type (bacteria)	Sim. shape	Description
E. coli	�	Elongated shape with length drawn from random distribution.
Staphylococcus	●	Roundish shape, e.g., using the basic shape model in Eq. (2.1).
T. pallidum	➛	Curved shape obtained using a randomly sampled sinus curve.
C. coccoides	●	Elliptical, roundish shape, e.g., using the basic shape model in Eq. (2.1).
C. cocleatum	ℰ	Curved, horseshoe-like shape obtained using a randomly sampled sinus curve.

2.2.1.3 Modeling appearance: texture and subcellular organelle models

In cell microscopy, the intensity profile and texture of the cells are fundamental characteristics for the object, but also often carry crucial information about the studied phenomenon. Especially in fluorescence microscopy, the staining can be used for obtaining detailed readout from cell status and function, as well as to reveal the role and function of various subcellular organelles. Thus, modeling the appearance of cells as their intensity distribution and texture forms a complex and challenging task but also offers possibilities for introducing biologically relevant content on a cellular level.

Despite the possibilities, the parametric modeling of appearance is typically guided by visual similarity rather than biologically driven insight. In fact, the texture is often modeled as noise, to be more precise, as multiscale random texture generator, the so-called Perlin noise [12]. The texture, denoted below as t, generated in a spatial coordinate (x, y), is defined as

$$t(x, y) = B + \sum_{i=0}^{n-1} p^i \eta_{xy}(2^i),$$

(2.2)

which forms the texture as a multifrequency noise by taking a weighted sum of n octaves of basic noise function $\eta_{xy}(\cdot)$. The parameter B defines the bias term for texture intensity, and p, which is the persistence parameter, controls the scale of the summed noise functions. As for the generic random shape, the texture synthesis allows generating versatile appearances by controlling only a few parameters. In Fig. 2.2, an example object with multiple realizations of the parametric noise model is illustrated, showing varying levels in detail as the object texture.

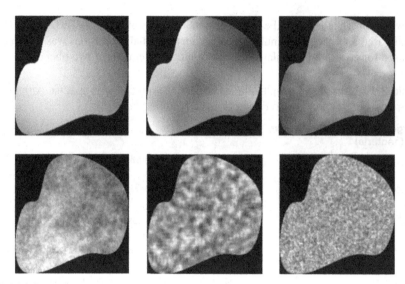

FIGURE 2.2

Texture generation using multiscale noise model. By controlling the noise model scale, texture with different frequency components can be generated. Low frequency components are visible on the top left and high frequency components on the bottom right.

After its introduction in SIMCEP, the multiscale noise generator has been used in many other studies for texture synthesis. As an exception, in SimuCell [9] the modeling of multimarker cell instances includes possibility to guide the marker intensity through, e.g., spatial micro-environment and through marker codependency, providing enhanced opportunities for more biologically guided simulation of cell appearance. Further, in [13], the fluorescence pattern forming the cell texture is modeled using a fluorescence cluster generator, forming a cloud of point-like spots on varying focal levels around the nucleus shape. Some simulators also allow generating bright spots into additional image channels, representing fluorescence labeling of specific small subcellular organelles [14].

2.2.1.4 Modeling spatial distribution and populations

The spatial distribution and quantity of objects in the image are among the key properties when characterizing microscopy images. In reality, there are numerous factors affecting the spatial distribution of cells in a population, including the properties of the cells to the environment of the experiment and many more. In some cases the cells tend to grow rather evenly spaced on a plate, while in others there exists clustering or grouping of cells on varying degrees. The tendency to overlap also varies.

In order to enable generating images representing such characteristics at a population level, the spatial locations need to be controlled at the population level. One possibility is to define the locations as random spatial coordinates with uniform distribution, but with an additional parameter p_c for controlling the probability for a cell

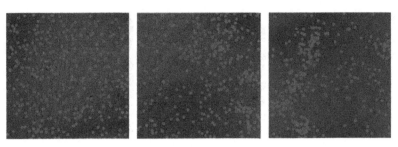

FIGURE 2.3

Modeling population-level differences in spatial locations of cells (from [14]). The probability p_c of a cell to belong in a cluster ranges from 0 on the left, 0.30 in the middle, to 0.60 on the right, whereas the number of objects remains constant.

to belong to a cluster. Thus, with probability $1 - p_c$, a cell is placed randomly in the image, and with probability p_c it is placed within one of the N_c clusters, which is a user-defined number. The maximum allowed overlap of generated objects can be controlled through a parameter with values ranging between [0, 1], where zero means no overlap is allowed and one would allow full overlap. By tuning these handful of parameter values, the simulation process can be set to generate images with varying population-level characteristics. Fig. 2.3 illustrates how the overall image appearance can be efficiently altered through the parameters controlling the spatial arrangement of cells. The spatial appearance, and also the challenge posed to, for instance, cell segmentation algorithms, is adjusted through the probability of clustering (p_c) of a cell.

So far we have considered the spatial organization of cells in the context of cultured cell populations. Tissue micro-environment presents another natural context where cell organization is highly complex and highly regulated. Parametric population models for spatial organization of cells in tissue have also been proposed for various tissue types. For example, in [15], colonic crypt micro-environments were generated through defining clusters as elliptic crypts, while maintaining the simulation framework otherwise similar as presented here. In [8], 3D images representing simulated human colon tissue were generated by placing simulated nuclei on toroid-shaped clusters, representing villi in colon tissue.

2.2.2 Modeling microscopy and image acquisition: from object models to simulated microscope images

Referring to the two-step simulation process, where first an ideal representation of the physical objects is generated, and then this ideal image is distorted by a process mimicking the image formation in optical system and digital image acquisition, the latter part can in general be modeled in more detail using existing knowledge on the process. For example, several technical characteristics of microscopy imaging systems, such as optical aberrations, effect of out-of-focus, background intensity, and

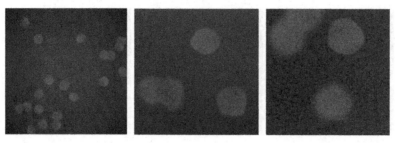

FIGURE 2.4

Modeling unidealities introduced by microscopy and image acquisition process: (left) uneven background illumination, seen as a slowly-varying background intensity in the simulated image; (middle) zoom-in showing blurring caused by the optical system and between-object focus differences; (right) zoom-in showing noise introduced by the imaging device and implemented with an additive noise model. Adapted from [3].

detector noise are well-known features and error sources in microscopy. Thus, their modeling can be more directly based on known physical limitations than modeling of the object appearance.

Uneven background illumination is a visually striking feature often present in microscopy images, and one of the common properties complicating automated analysis. Thus, when generating simulated images sharing realistic characteristics, uneven illumination needs to be included. A common approximation is to use a 2D quadratic function to model the additive background intensity, with control over the strength of the intensity profile and potentially additional parameters to control shift from image center. More accurate models, with two separate factors of additive and multiplicative intensity profiles, have also been proposed. Effectively, they still produce a visual effect clearly visible in Fig. 2.4 (left).

Another typical error source from microscopy is the blur from the optical system. As deconvolution has been intensively studied in microscopy, it is in principle possible to build a fully realistic model of optical blurring based on the point spread function (PSF). However, approximations are also useful here, and an obvious choice is to model the blurring using a Gaussian kernel representing the PSF. A common property of microscopy images is the limited depth focus, causing objects outside the in-focus plane appearing blurred in the image. Thus, to model optical blurring by taking into account objects appearing on different focal planes, in [3] a spatially varying PSF was presented, where the objects were assigned into varying depth levels affecting the width of the Gaussian kernel used for blurring. In Fig. 2.4 (middle), an example of the effect of blurring using varying Gaussian kernel of the approximated PSF is shown.

As the final phase in imaging devices, the continuous signal arriving through the optical system is captured into discrete digital images. In reality, this is done using detectors, which are sensor arrays (e.g., CCD/CMOS) converting the flood of photons arriving through the optical system into voltage differences which are then discretized and converted into a representation suitable for computers. While discrete representation is of course built in the simulation process, the acquisition process also introduces sensor noise. Finally, the acquired image is stored as an image file, where potentially lossy compression is used, introducing the last artifacts to the image. Thus, the image acquisition process can be modeled by a combination of photon shot noise and additive Gaussian noise, and optionally applied lossy compression [1]. Fig. 2.4 (right) illustrates a result from an implementation of such noise model into a simulated microscopy image.

2.3 On learning the parameters

Parametric modeling usually refers to the kind of ad-hoc defined models with experimentally defined values described in this chapter. It is, however, also possible to define the parameter values and their range in a data-driven, learning-based manner. In such modeling, either the parameter values or the whole model is defined by learning the representation from training samples. This is especially useful when considering the shape, appearance, and also population and spatial arrangement of objects, for which it is more challenging to define well-grounded models than for the technical measurement and image acquisition process.

Examples of learning-based models include the approaches by [16,17] for learning subcellular localization models, [4] for learning bacterial cell shapes, [10] for squamous intermediate cell modeling using Fourier shape descriptors and [18] for urothelial cell modeling. Using learning-based modeling, the modeling is largely controlled through the samples included in the training data.

The subcellular localization models in [16] showcase the learning-based parametric modeling approach. The localization models were built to facilitate capturing protein localization patterns and regenerating their natural variation. Such learning-based automated modeling can be used for the purposes of generating statistically accurate simulations covering various biological phenomena in a systematic manner. The model parameters were learned from real microscope images to capture the parameters for a nested conditional model of medial axis for nucleus shape, nucleus texture, and cell shape, and Gaussian mixture models for the protein localization patterns.

Considering learning-based modeling of object classes with distinct shapes, such as different bacteria types, a deformable shape model was proposed in [4]. The model learns shapes from training objects, extracted from segmented microscope images representing shapes characteristic of particular cell types – in this case bacteria with clearly separable round and longish shapes were used as training and target objects. In Fig. 2.5, examples of real (upper row) bacteria with round (left) and longish (right) shapes are shown, and the shapes generated by the deformable shape models trained with the two object classes are illustrated in the lower row. Despite the somewhat successful learning-based modeling approaches referred to here, the representative

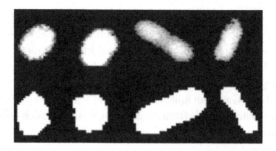

FIGURE 2.5

Learning-based shape simulation using a deformable shape model for two object classes, with parameters learned from real microscope images of two bacteria types: (upper row) examples of real bacteria with round (left) and longish (right) shapes; (lower row) shapes generated by the deformable shape models. Adapted from [4].

power of such models falls short from that of modern generative machine learning-based approaches.

2.4 Use cases

2.4.1 SIMCEP: parametric modeling framework aimed for generating and understanding microscopy images of cells

The SIMCEP simulation framework, with the basic framework presented in [2–4], was developed during the era when biomedical imaging was quickly developing from visual inspection and low-throughput manual analysis into a high-throughput quantitative field, with an effort to interpret image data and the underlying biomedical phenomenon at the level of computational systems [19,20]. The SIMCEP simulation framework follows the workflow described in the schema of Fig. 2.6. First an ideal version of the simulated objects and their spatial arrangement in the population present in the image field-of-view is generated, which also serves as the ground truth for the objects vs. background classification task at the pixel level. Second, the image is distorted with several error sources, emulating aberrations, noise and unidealities introduced in a typical microscope measurement.

The simulation framework had two goals. The first was to provide means for validating automated image analysis algorithms, tools, and software with large volumes of image data in various, controlled, scenarios without the need for manual annotation. This goal has been clearly met, with the simulator being actively used and further developed as of today. One key to this success has been the freely available open source implementation of the SIMCEP framework [3] as well as the benchmark image set [14] generated using it, both of which have been popular resources for the community. The second goal was to create a framework for modeling cells and the microscopy measurement system in a comprehensive manner, possibly later enabling

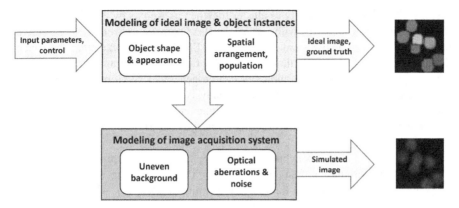

FIGURE 2.6

Simulation workflow of the SIMCEP framework. The process is controlled through input variables, allowing incorporating prior knowledge of the studied samples of conditions, and provides the possibility to generate desired characteristics in the output. The first part generates an ideal image of the underlying sample by generating objects, their appearance, and spatial locations in the image. The second part distorts the ideal image with various sources of errors, resembling the effect of a typical microscope image acquisition.

simulation-based experiments by connecting biology-driven models. This would require feeding genomic or protein level information controlling the appearance of cells directly into the image simulation framework. In [21], a somewhat similar approach was proposed for a different measurement platform, where gene regulatory networks were used as a basis for generating data based on which artificial microarray images were generated. Connecting similar regulatory information into cell appearance is obviously a significantly more complex task. To reach this ambitious goal, the feedback loop, from our understanding of cells and their function at the molecular level to the modeling of cells as images, still needs to be strengthened. Here, the modern deep learning-based approaches are likely to provide a stronger computational basis than the simple parametric models covered in this chapter.

In the previous sections, we described the two basic steps in parametric modeling, generating ideal representation of the underlying objects and modeling the measurement system, using the SIMCEP framework as an example implementation. The SIMCEP approach sets some limitations, for example, we do not cover extensively time-lapse simulations or 3D simulations. Also, the provided examples and alternative approaches do not represent a systematic review of all available approaches.

2.4.2 Simulated data for benchmarking

One of the main benefits of parametric modeling is the control over the simulated image characteristics. Parametric modeling enables generating large quantities of simulated image data with desired properties. For example, by controlling the number of cells and their probability to cluster together, as well as by enabling the cells to overlap, different scenarios with varying levels of complexity from the perspective of automated image analysis can be generated. Similarly, by controlling the shape through the size and especially through the shape randomness parameters, image data with varying levels of shape complexity can be generated. Such property becomes useful when analyzing how different image analysis algorithms handle specific tasks, such as the under-/over-segmentation of touching and overlapping cells, or quantification of the cell properties by extracting numerical descriptors on a population or single cell level.

For example, in [14], a benchmark dataset was generated for surpassing the need for running the simulation framework in order to get access to synthetic validation data. The idea stems from the machine learning community, where benchmark datasets are a popular way to validate and compare algorithms. The simulated benchmark dataset offers possibility to evaluate various attributes in image analysis algorithms, such as cell counting, spot counting, shape descriptors, background noise removal. The obvious downside of a fixed dataset is naturally the lack of control in the simulation process – thus also the parameter setting files were provided to enable easy modification for tailored dataset generation. Similarly, several other publications have presented simulated benchmark datasets for various purposes, see, e.g., [22], where images simulated with methods presented in [6,23] were used alongside real time-lapse experiments for evaluating the performance of cell tracking algorithms. Simulated images have also been accepted in bioimage benchmark collections [24].

As an example use case of how cell-type specific parametric models can be used for validating algorithms for phenotype prediction, in [5] a simulated dataset of bacterial colony images was generated for testing a shape-based classifier. The simulated images of bacterial colonies with a varying concentration of three artificial bacterial types with distinctive shapes were generated, representing a time-lapse experiment where the population dynamics (relative fraction of each cell type at a given time point) varies over time.

2.5 **Future directions**

Recent years have witnessed the deep neural networks conquering practically all computational data analysis and modeling application areas, also within biomedical imaging. The unprecedented accuracy obtained using deep learning-based methods in numerous areas suggests these methods will be increasingly used also in biomedical image synthesis tasks, shifting the focus from traditional parametric modeling towards data-driven modeling.

The modern deep learning-based modeling, however, creates extremely complex, difficult to interpret models. As a result, explainable artificial intelligence is used for gaining insight into the complex machine learning models [25]. This approach is increasingly gaining interest in biomedicine where many applications traditionally require human experts. Also in simulation there remains value in representing the samples and processes in a simple, human-interpretable, and controllable manner. One predictable future direction is the combination of computationally transcendent deep learning models and simple parametric models. Another remaining challenge is to move towards system-level modeling, where the modeling process is driven by the underlying biological phenomenon instead of ad-hoc parameter tuning.

2.6 Summary

Parametric modeling enables efficient incorporation of prior knowledge into the modeled object shape, appearance and distribution, as well as knowledge of the physical measurement system. With full control on the simulation process through the user-defined parameters, such modeling approach offers a flexible tool for simulating images of complex biological samples, such as of cells and tissue, with realistic characteristics. Some of the pioneering simulation frameworks widely used in the biomedical image analysis community, such as, e.g., SIMCEP [3], PAPsynth [7], SimuCell [9], MitoGen [23], CytoPacq [26], rely heavily on parametric modeling.

These tools, and many more, have played an important role in validating automated image analysis algorithms for various tasks. In biomedicine, validation with extensive datasets representing the characteristics and variation of the underlying sample distribution is particularly crucial, and at the same time, ground truth is often expensive and tedious to obtain. Thus, biomedical imaging applications, such as microscopy imaging of cells, has been one of the pioneering fields of simulating synthetic and realistic images of the samples and image acquisition system.

Through increased information on biological processes, and through rapidly improving capability to computationally model complex targets, simulation can be expected to become an integral part of quantitative bioimaging in the future – and the parametric modeling paradigm has its role as the basis of explainable models characterizing the samples and underlying phenomena.

Acknowledgments

The author would like to thank Dr. Antti Lehmussola and Dr. David Svoboda for their helpful comments and input to this chapter.

References

[1] V. Ulman, D. Svoboda, M. Nykter, M. Kozubek, P. Ruusuvuori, Virtual cell imaging: a review on simulation methods employed in image cytometry, Cytometry. Part A 89 (12) (2016) 1057–1072.

[2] A. Lehmussola, J. Selinummi, P. Ruusuvuori, A. Niemisto, O. Yli-Harja, Simulating fluorescent microscope images of cell populations, in: 2005 IEEE Engineering in Medicine and Biology 27th Annual Conference, IEEE, 2006, pp. 3153–3156.

[3] A. Lehmussola, P. Ruusuvuori, J. Selinummi, H. Huttunen, O. Yli-Harja, Computational framework for simulating fluorescence microscope images with cell populations, IEEE Transactions on Medical Imaging 26 (7) (2007) 1010–1016.

[4] A. Lehmussola, P. Ruusuvuori, J. Selinummi, T. Rajala, O. Yli-Harja, Synthetic images of high-throughput microscopy for validation of image analysis methods, Proceedings of the IEEE 96 (8) (2008) 1348–1360.

[5] P. Ruusuvuori, J. Seppala, T. Erkkila, A. Lehmussola, J.A. Puhakka, O. Yli-Harja, Efficient automated method for image-based classification of microbial cells, in: 2008 19th International Conference on Pattern Recognition, IEEE, 2008, pp. 1–4.

[6] D. Svoboda, M. Kozubek, S. Stejskal, Generation of digital phantoms of cell nuclei and simulation of image formation in 3d image cytometry, Cytometry. Part A 75 (6) (2009) 494–509.

[7] P. Malm, A. Brun, E. Bengtsson, Papsynth: simulated bright-field images of cervical smears, in: 2010 IEEE International Symposium on Biomedical Imaging: From Nano to Macro, IEEE, 2010, pp. 117–120.

[8] D. Svoboda, O. Homola, S. Stejskal, Generation of 3d digital phantoms of colon tissue, in: International Conference Image Analysis and Recognition, Springer, 2011, pp. 31–39.

[9] S. Rajaram, B. Pavie, N.E. Hac, S.J. Altschuler, L.F. Wu, Simucell: a flexible framework for creating synthetic microscopy images, Nature Methods 9 (7) (2012) 634.

[10] P. Malm, A. Brun, E. Bengtsson, Simulation of bright-field microscopy images depicting pap-smear specimen, Cytometry. Part A 87 (3) (2015) 212–226.

[11] D.V. Sorokin, I. Peterlík, V. Ulman, D. Svoboda, T. Nečasová, K. Morgaenko, L. Eiselleová, L. Tesařová, M. Maška, Filogen: a model-based generator of synthetic 3-D time-lapse sequences of single motile cells with growing and branching filopodia, IEEE Transactions on Medical Imaging 37 (12) (2018) 2630–2641.

[12] K. Perlin, An image synthesizer, ACM Siggraph Computer Graphics 19 (3) (1985) 287–296.

[13] J. Ghaye, G. De Micheli, S. Carrara, Simulated biological cells for receptor counting in fluorescence imaging, BioNanoScience 2 (2) (2012) 94–103.

[14] P. Ruusuvuori, A. Lehmussola, J. Selinummi, T. Rajala, H. Huttunen, O. Yli-Harja, Benchmark set of synthetic images for validating cell image analysis algorithms, in: 2008 16th European Signal Processing Conference, IEEE, 2008, pp. 1–5.

[15] V.N. Kovacheva, D. Snead, N.M. Rajpoot, A model of the spatial microenvironment of the colonic crypt, in: 2015 IEEE 12th International Symposium on Biomedical Imaging (ISBI), IEEE, 2015, pp. 172–176.

[16] T. Zhao, R.F. Murphy, Automated learning of generative models for subcellular location: building blocks for systems biology, Cytometry. Part A 71 (12) (2007) 978–990.

[17] V.N. Kovacheva, D. Snead, N.M. Rajpoot, A model of the spatial tumour heterogeneity in colorectal adenocarcinoma tissue, BMC Bioinformatics 17 (1) (2016) 1–16.

[18] M. Scalbert, F. Couzinie-Devy, R. Fezzani, Generic isolated cell image generator, Cytometry. Part A 95 (11) (2019) 1198–1206.

[19] H. Peng, Bioimage informatics: a new area of engineering biology, Bioinformatics 24 (17) (2008) 1827–1836.

[20] R. Murphy, The quest for quantitative microscopy, Nature Methods 9 (2012) 627.

[21] M. Nykter, T. Aho, M. Ahdesmäki, P. Ruusuvuori, A. Lehmussola, O. Yli-Harja, Simulation of microarray data with realistic characteristics, BMC Bioinformatics 7 (1) (2006) 1–17.

[22] M. Maška, V. Ulman, D. Svoboda, P. Matula, P. Matula, C. Ederra, A. Urbiola, T. España, S. Venkatesan, D.M. Balak, et al., A benchmark for comparison of cell tracking algorithms, Bioinformatics 30 (11) (2014) 1609–1617.

[23] D. Svoboda, V. Ulman, Mitogen: a framework for generating 3D synthetic time-lapse sequences of cell populations in fluorescence microscopy, IEEE Transactions on Medical Imaging 36 (1) (2016) 310–321.

[24] V. Ljosa, K.L. Sokolnicki, A.E. Carpenter, Annotated high-throughput microscopy image sets for validation, Nature Methods 9 (7) (2012) 637.

[25] A. Adadi, M. Berrada, Peeking inside the black-box: a survey on explainable artificial intelligence (XAI), IEEE Access 6 (2018) 52138–52160.

[26] D. Wiesner, D. Svoboda, M. Maška, M. Kozubek, CytoPacq: a web-interface for simulating multi-dimensional cell imaging, Bioinformatics 35 (21) (2019) 4531–4533.

Monte Carlo simulations for medical and biomedical applications

Julien Bert[a,b] **and David Sarrut**[c,d,e]

[a]*LaTIM, INSERM, UMR1101, Brest, France*
[b]*Brest University Hospital Center, Brest, France*
[c]*CREATIS, CNRS UMR5220, INSERM U1294, Villeurbanne, France*
[d]*Université de Lyon, INSA-Lyon, Villeurbanne, France*
[e]*Centre Léon Bérard, Lyon, France*

3.1 Introduction

3.1.1 A brief history

Monte Carlo methods refer to calculation algorithms based on random numerical simulation that makes it possible to simulate complex physical phenomena, for example, the transport of particles through matter. The first reference in history of the use of a random process to determine the outcome of a phenomenon was provided by the Comte de Buffon in 1733. At that time, he was studying the probability of winning or losing in the "Franc-Carreau" game. This French game has been practiced since the Middle Ages and consists in tossing a coin on a tiled floor and betting on the final position of the coin: you win if the coin does not overlap with any edges of the tile, otherwise you loose. Georges Louis Leclerc de Buffon studied the probability to win the Franc-Carreau game by randomly and repetitively tossing needle on the floor. This was the first stochastic sampling and known as the Buffon's needle problem.

Modern Monte Carlo method, as known today, appeared at the same time as computer science, during World War II, for the needs of the Manhattan Project, in order to model the process of a nuclear explosion. The first numerical simulation in theoretical physics was the Fermi–Pasta–Ulam virtual experiment in 1953 [1]. Much latter than Buffon's needle problem, Ulam and von Neumann were working on particle transport simulation, and published an abstract about a method combining stochastic and deterministic processes [2]. The name of Monte Carlo method appeared for the first time several years later, in 1949, with an article of Metropolis and Ulam [3]. This name referred to the famous gambling casinos Monte Carlo located in Monaco. The Monte Carlo method was not the only ingredient to successfully transport particles through matter, the development of quantum theory, which furnished cross-section data for the interaction of radiation with matter, was the keystone to implement the

Biomedical Image Synthesis and Simulation. https://doi.org/10.1016/B978-0-12-824349-7.00010-4

method in nuclear physics. Nowadays, Monte Carlo simulation is a general method of estimating a numerical quantity that uses random numbers. The method has the capability to explore large configuration spaces in order to extract information, and solve a very wide range of problems (finance, biology, mathematics, physics, etc.) with the advantage of being easy to use.

A couple of years later, the developments of Monte Carlo method to transport particles whose energy is much lower than those involved in thermonuclear application was investigated. Within this context, the simulation of photon transport in matter was essentially solved by Kahn [4] in 1956. The pioneering article [5] published in 1963 by Berger reviews all necessary methods to transport electron using Monte Carlo method. At the same period, Zerby in 1963 used a Monte Carlo calculation to estimate the response of a gamma-ray scintillation counters [6]. The early 1970s marked the rise of Monte Carlo simulations for medical physics applications. From that time their evolution never ceased to extend, following the improvements in computing and discoveries in nuclear physics.

The use of Monte Carlo in the field of biomedical physics consists of (1) modeling imaging systems, in particular in nuclear medicine, (2) characterizing beam and particle accelerators in radiation therapy, and (3) computing absorbed dose in patients. Nowadays, all nuclear imaging systems and all treatment planning systems in radiation therapy use Monte Carlo simulations during several parts of their research and development. As an example, the next generation total-body PET projects (Explorer at UC Davis, PennPET in Pennsylvania, PET20.0 in Ghent or J-PET in Krakow) rely on Monte Carlo simulation to design, control, and test instrumentation, but also to perform research in image reconstruction. All treatment planning systems use Monte Carlo to characterize photon/particle beams, to compute dose point kernels for analytical dose engines, or directly absorbed dose in patients. This is particularly true for new promising radiotherapy protocols, such as hypo-fractionated schedule, "Flash" radiotherapy, proton/hadron therapy, which are mainly oriented towards very high-dose-rate treatment and thus require extremely precise dose distributions.

Nowadays several referent Monte Carlo codes can be used for realistic medical physics applications, which is the result of a legacy of more than half a century of work in the field. The most widely-used are Geant4 [7,8], Penelope [9], MCNP [10], EGSnrc [11], FLUKA [12,13], etc. Most of them are generic codes, however, there are also GAMOS [14] and Gate [15,16], which extend Geant4 code to propose solution fully dedicated to medical application targeting both imaging and particle therapy applications.

3.1.2 Monte Carlo method and biomedical physics

Monte Carlo simulation (MCS) is widely used in the field of biomedical physics. It has many advantages: with the same method, any nuclear imaging model can be simulated, such as computer tomography (CT), cone beam CT, direct digital radiography, positron emission tomography (PET), single-photon emission computed tomography

(SPECT), gamma camera, etc. Additionally, to recover image raw data, MCS makes it possible to estimate dose within the imaged subject, allowing as well dosimetry studies. Imaging systems which are not based on particle transport through matter, such as magnetic resonance imaging (MRI) or ultrasound, cannot be handled directly by MCS. Even if a Monte Carlo method can be applied to electromagnetic signal or wave propagation, here the term of MCS is related to the use of Monte Carlo method in particle physics domains.

MCSs are well-known to produce medical nuclear image synthesis with an extreme realism. This is achieved by the fact that the complete acquisition physics processes from the particle emission to their detection are simulated. For example, standard deterministic synthetic image simulators mostly simulate the noise by using a constant and simple additive model everywhere on the image, which is an approximation. MCSs have the capability to simulate and obtain a realistic noise similar to real data. Another advantage is the ability to derive real clinical data to perform simulation. For example, the MRI and CT image from a patient or a small animal can be used to build a digitized phantom (digital twin of the real object) to achieve realistic simulation. Similarly, radiotracer distribution can be derived from real clinical data to achieve realistic emission tomography simulation [17].

The MCS is also used for its capability to evaluate new system design and new image detector. One more benefit of MCS is the full knowledge of the object to image since it was specified by the user. With this ground truth, it is easy to evaluate and compare new protocols or new reconstruction algorithms. Indeed, MCS results are raw data directly collected on the image detector. Therefore, a 2D/3D reconstruction step is necessary to obtain an exploitable image. This disadvantage for some is a crucial advantage in the field of tomographic reconstruction. Direct digital radiography, histogram, sinogram, or list mode data are easily obtained from MCS, which is mostly not possible from real clinical systems.

The validity domain of a standard particle physics MCS is at the scale of the tissue, i.e., human body and small animal simulations. Paradigm and physics models were originally designed for this scale. Even if 3D cellular models exist [18], MCSs are not capable yet to perform a particle simulation at the cell scale, this is a limitation of the current models. Some effort to extend physics processes for the modeling of biological damage induced by ionizing radiation at the DNA scale was proposed with Geant4-DNA [19]. Although promising results were obtained, single cell and single molecule simulations are quite limited to fundamental work. Bridging the gap between cell and tissue scale into a same simulation remains a major challenge in medical physics MCS.

However, since Monte Carlo method is a generalized concept, it has been used in diverse domains especially in computational biology. Such applications use Monte Carlo method to simulate any biological process, for example, cell population behavior, cell cycle, molecular folding, tumor growing, etc. A few details and application examples will be provided at this end of this chapter.

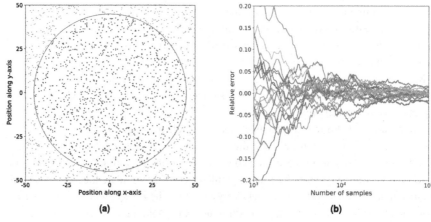

(a)   **(b)**

FIGURE 3.1

Random sampling process of the Monte Carlo method. (a) A circle with a known radius is inscribed in a square with a known dimension. By repeatedly and independently adding points within the square with a uniform random position, the area of the disk can be estimated by using the ratio of points that are inside the circle (green dots – dark gray dots in print version) compared to the total number of points (green + red dots – dark gray + mid gray dots in print version). Subsequently, the value of π by using the formula for a disk area can be estimated and (b) the associated relative error according to the number of points used for the sampling calculated. Here the relative error is illustrated for several independent realizations.

3.2 Underlying theory and principles

In general, Monte Carlo methods are algorithms that consist in estimating an approximate value using a random sampling process. A very simple example to understand the method is to numerically estimate an approximate value of π. Let us consider a circle with a radius r inscribed in a square of dimension l (Fig. 3.1(a)). Then, within this square, we repeatedly and independently add points inside with a uniform random position. This corresponds to the random sampling process of the Monte Carlo method. After a certain number of random draws N, we can calculate the ratio q of points that are inside the circle N_o, compared to the total number N. Knowing the area of the square, we can deduce an approximate value of the area of the disk and therefore, by using the formula for the disk area (πr^2), estimate an approximate value of π. This principle of estimation by a stochastic process is the main essence of the Monte Carlo method.

The uncertainty of the estimated value is conditioned by the number of random draws. It follows the law of large numbers and decreases with a form in $1/\sqrt{N}$. This is illustrated in Fig. 3.1(b), where the relative error between the estimated and real values is plotted as a function of the number of random draws and this is repeated for several independent realizations. The estimated value, at a given number of draws, is different for each new realization due to the statistical uncertainty, but all converge to the same expected value (π). The greater the number of random draws, the closer to the real value the estimation will be.

The strength of the Monte Carlo method is its capability to achieve an estimate with a high precision by using a simple method, even in the cases where the problems are very complex and cannot be resolved with classical methods. For example, in Fig. 3.1(a), if we replace the simple circle shape by a complex shape without known description, the Monte Carlo method will be easy and straightforward to estimate its area. This is not the case with conventional integration methods. However, the main drawback of the method is the correlation between accuracy and number of random draws. A high precision requires a very large number of draws.

Monte Carlo method can be used to solve nonlinear, stochastic, multi-dimensional, and complex problems. This method is used to estimate image synthesis in nuclear medical imaging. The aim is to simulate the most realistic image as possible. For this context, the Monte Carlo principle remains the same as for estimating the value of π, but here the estimated value is a 2D image, resulting from the transport of particles in the patient's body. Each random realization is the path of a particle from the radioactive source to its contribution to the image detector. In this context, we speak of random walk, because the transport of the particle undergoes physical interactions that are determined by stochastic processes as well. Each Monte Carlo draw is summarized by simulating the transport of a particle through matter.

3.3 Particle transport through matter

There are different models of particle transport through medium, but most of them remain similar and are based on the same common work proposed in the early 1970s. For the next sections, we will mostly focus on models from the Geant4 toolkit [8] because this library is the foundation of the GATE software [16,15] which is dedicated to medical applications, and one of the major platform in the field of emission and transmission tomography simulations. As explained, the following models and methods in this chapter remain similar and equivalent to most of Monte Carlo codes for medical physics. Since most of the simulations for conventional nuclear imaging systems are mostly related to photon particles transport, we will mostly focus on this particle. In addition, photon interactions are discrete processes, meaning there are not considered as interacting continuously along the trajectory as charged particle (electron, positron), but only at specific points. Therefore, the principle of particle navigation in Monte Carlo simulation is easier to describe and understand while considering only photons.

3.3.1 Photon physics effects

The photon navigation is driven by the physical effects that occur within the medium. For example, the photoelectric absorption is an interaction that absorbs the photon

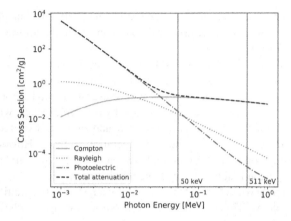

FIGURE 3.2

Liquid water cross-sections for Compton and Rayleigh scattering and photoelectric absorption as a function of particle energy. The total attenuation is plotted as well. Each effect is more or less preponderant over the others, depending on the energy. For example, Compton scattering is less predominant at 50 keV than at 511 keV.

within the matter and could emit an electron. Compton scattering is an elastic scattering that occurs when an incident photon collides with a free electron within the medium. The electron is ejected from the atom and the incident photon is scattered. There is also Rayleigh scattering, which is inelastic scattering, i.e., without energy loss, where only the incident photon is scattered. Photon can also undergo an effect called pair production, which produces an electron–positron pair. This effect is not used for simulation in conventional medical imaging because it only occurs when the photon energy involved exceeds 1.022 MeV (sum of the rest mass energies of an electron and positron). There are different kinds of interactions for each particle type as well. For further reading on radiation interaction in medical physics, please refer to [20,21].

3.3.2 Cross-section and mean free path

Each physical effect has a probability of occurring depending on the energy of the particle and the surrounding environment. The measure that expresses the probability to interact with matter for a given effect is called the cross-section σ (Fig. 3.2). The mean free path $\bar{l}$ is another important measure in Monte Carlo simulation. It corresponds to the average distance between two successive interactions along the path of the particle. It is obtained by the inverse of the cross-section and the density of the material. For example, for a 50 keV photon in a volume of liquid water with a density of 1 g/cm^3, the cross-section of the photoelectric effect is 5.453×10^{-2} cm^2/g (see Fig. 3.2), value obtained from the National Institute of Standards and Technol-

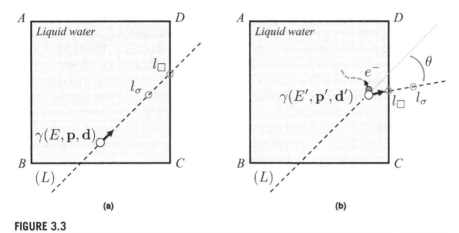

FIGURE 3.3

Basic scheme of the photon navigation through an analytical box of liquid water (a) before defining the next interaction, and (b) after resolving the selected interaction.

ogy (NIST).[1] This leads to a mean free path of 18.3 cm. This means that a 50 keV photon will be absorbed on average at a distance of 18 cm in a tank of water (without considering the other effects). Each effect is more or less preponderant over the others, depending on the energy and medium. For example, Compton scattering is less predominant in CT imaging than in PET imaging (see cross-section at 511 keV in Fig. 3.2).

3.3.3 Models

For each physics effect used in medical imaging synthesis, there are well-validated numerical models to calculate cross-section and resolve the effect. Some of them are based on analytical solutions, for example, the Klein–Nishina model [22] for the Compton scattering. Some others are based on experimental data fitting, for example, in [23] to calculate the cross-section on the photoelectric absorption. There is a panel of models for the physics effects with different accuracy, numerical efficiency, and validity according to the range of the energy used. Most of them are provided in different Monte Carlo codes [8–11].

3.3.4 Particle transport

In MCS the method that handles the particle transport within a given environment is called a particle navigator. Its main role consists in determining and resolving the next interaction according to geometries and physics properties. Let us consider the 2D case with a box ($ABCD$) in Fig. 3.3(a), and a photon γ defined by its position

---

[1] https://physics.nist.gov.

p, energy E, and direction **d**. According to the particle state and medium properties of the current primitive geometry, the next interaction distances l_σ along the particle path L are determined based on the photon physics processes. The Monte Carlo method implies that the next interaction has to be selected randomly. However, this stochastic process must follow the law of physics. If there is a predominant effect for a given medium and energy, this effect has to be selected most often that the other. This is done by first calculating the cross-section σ_i for every physics process i according to particle energy E and the crossed medium. Then, the mean free path $\overline{l_i}$ is estimated for each interaction i and the associated next interaction distance l_i sample using a random number $\xi \in [0, 1[$ as follows:

$$l_i = -\overline{l_i} \log(\xi). \tag{3.1}$$

This method allows randomly sampling different distance values by respecting the expected value provided by the mean free path $\overline{l_i}$. From all of these distances, the shortest value l_σ is selected and the corresponding physics effect will be the next interaction to consider. The free path distance value expresses the probability that an interaction occurs, then the shortest distance corresponds to the highest probability. Subsequently, the next volume boundary distance $l_\square$ along the path L is considered. This boundary distance is obtained using a raytracing method by considering the particle path as a ray that intersects a geometry primitive, here a 2D box. According to the primitive, different intersection algorithms have to be used; more details can be found in Section 3.4.2.2.

Cross-section, mean free path, and the next interaction distance are related to the medium crossed by the particle. Therefore, if this particle escapes the current geometry, each of these physics' variables has to be recalculated. The boundary distance is used for this purpose and allows calculating if the particle will escape the current geometry or not. If the value of l_σ is smaller than $l_\square$, the particle moves to the distance l_σ and the MCS resolves the discrete process. This consists in, according to the physics effect, sampling a new state for the particle (energy and direction). For example, for the Compton scattering, the photon will be scattered with an angle θ and a new secondary electron will be sampled (see Fig. 3.3(b)). If l_σ is larger, the particle moves to the next boundary without interacting with the medium. This mechanism allows considering the change of the medium along the particle path. If a physics process occurs in an other medium than that considered, the cross-section has to be recalculated. In this case, particles are transported at the border of this new material and the particle tracking restarts. These steps are repeated until all particles are either absorbed or escape from the phantom. Each released secondary particle has to be navigated as well. For example, any electron sampled from photon interactions or from electron interactions will be tracked. The complete particle cascade will be handled by the MCS by tracking one by one each particle.

Charged particles have also a dedicated method to simulate their transport within matter. However, since the model is more complex than for photons, especially because they are interacting and losing energy continuously along their trajectories, it will not be presented here. For more reading on electron tracking, please refer to [24].

3.4 **Monte Carlo simulation structure**

A photon is the simplest particle to simulate within a medium and the main component of an MCS in medical imaging. However, in practice, this is not sufficient to simulate a complete medical or biomedical system. Other elements must be considered, such as the emission source, the phantom definition, the detector properties, etc. The next sections will describe all the elements, structures and mechanisms used to achieve a complete MCS within the context of image synthesis. GATE software [16], which is one of the major software dedicated to MCS of medical imaging [15], was selected as reference for the next sections. However, numerous other MCS packages (Penelope [9], MCNP [10], EGSnrc [11], FLUKA [12,13], etc.) follow the same concepts and any equivalent of the presented elements can be found.

The structure of the simulation in nuclear imaging can be simplified in three basic simulation elements. There is at least a source, a phantom and a detector (except for some special cases out of interest here). The particle source manages the emission of new particles to track. The phantom represents numerically a virtual object to interact with, such as the patient or any element of the environment (collimator, couch, etc). The detector is a particular phantom where every interaction is stored during the simulation. The aim is to recover a final image based on the collected raw data. By mixing different types of sources, phantoms and detectors, it is possible within the same software architecture to simulate a large variety of biomedical imaging systems.

3.4.1 **Particle source model**

A source is a particle generator, which is in charge of randomly emitting a particle with a certain energy distribution, spatial distribution, angular distribution, and following a certain activity, potentially defined by a decay factor. Any type of source can be simulated using a mathematical model.

3.4.1.1 *Analytical source*

The most basic models are analytical sources. They are described with a single analytical shape as a point, or a surface or a volume (see Fig. 3.4(a)). The type of the particle may be produced using a radioisotope or a given particle type. Similarly, the chosen energy may be provided by an energy spectrum (see Fig. 3.4(c)) or for a given constant energy value. The activity distribution within an analytical source is considered as homogeneous, which implies that the random emission point within the source follows a uniform distribution. It is also possible to emit the particle with a given angle distribution, in order to produce isotropic source or with an oriented aperture.

3.4.1.2 *Voxelized source*

Instead of primitive analytical geometry, voxelized sources can be used to simulate complex shape and heterogeneous distribution activities. Similar to a 3D image, the source is composed of voxels, where each of them contains a different activity value.

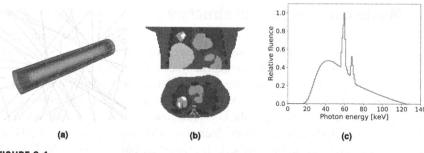

FIGURE 3.4

Example of the main type of particle source models employ in MCS: (a) I^{125} source represented by thin layers inside nested cylinder, green rays (light gray in print version) indicate trajectories of emitted photon particles; (b) voxelized source model of a thorax with a lung tumor where each voxel contains a particle activity value, the different colors indicate the radioactivity level; and (c) example of photon energy spectrum used for CT simulation, here the tube voltage is 120 kVp and the filter equivalent to 2 mm aluminium.

This distribution can be derived from real clinical image data. Each voxel is an analytical volume where the activity inside is considered uniform. A voxelized source is typically used to simulate emission imaging, as illustrated in Fig. 3.4(b), where it is possible to give different activities in each organ and tumor.

3.4.1.3 Cumulative density function

A particle generator must emit a new random state for each emitted particle. This is obtained using energy, activity or spatial distribution (see Fig. 3.4). The mechanism to select randomly a value based on a distribution, consists in converting the nD distribution into a 1D normalized cumulative density function (CDF). A new sample is achieved by first getting a random number. Subsequently, a search algorithm is used to find the bin density of the CDF that corresponds to the random number. The physical value (energy, activity, etc.) corresponding to this bin is used to define the state of the particle to emit.

3.4.1.4 Time management

Another import mechanism in MCS is the time management. For some applications that use a radioisotope, each emitted particle has to be set with a timestamp. This is particularly useful, for example, in PET imaging, where the coincidences are defined based on gamma pairs detected within the same time window. This is implemented by keeping in memory a global clock time t_n and the total value of the source activity A_{t_0} at time t_0 and the one A_{t_n} at time t_n. The timestamp t_e for each emitted particle is calculated by first calculating the random lapse time dt_n between this particle emission and the previous one, by using a random number ξ and the total activity at time t_n,

$$dt_n = -\frac{\log(\xi)}{A_{t_n}}. \tag{3.2}$$

Subsequently, the clock time is updated as $t_{n+1} = t_n + dt_n$. This new clock time will be used to define the timestamp for the particle to emit. Finally, the total activity value has to be updated as well according to the decay factor λ,

$$A_{t_{n+1}} = A_{t_0} \exp\left(-\frac{(t_0 - t_n)}{\lambda}\right). \tag{3.3}$$

3.4.1.5 Phase space

For a realistic source simulation with a reasonable computation time, a pre-simulation with the source alone can be used. Resulting emitted particles are stored into a data file, named phase space file, in order to be reused for other simulations. This file stores for each particle its type, energy, position, and direction. One major drawback of this solution is the need to store a large number of particles to avoid any statistical bias from reusing several times the same particles in the file. This implies that phase space can quickly reach extremely large file sizes with several GB of data. This issue may slow down the MCS due to the over read access to large data on the hard drive. For some applications, where uncorrelated probability distribution of the particle state can be found, the phase space can be parametrized, decreasing drastically the size of data to be stored [25,26]. Recent works use artificial intelligence, more specifically generative adversarial network, to produce compact source models based on phase space [27].

3.4.2 Digitized phantom

A phantom is a kind of digital twin of an object from the real environment that needs to be simulated, for example, any part of the imaging system, patient, bed, etc. The phantom physically represents matter in the simulation. Its geometry and composition are used by the navigator to make the particles evolve in this virtual environment. Designing a simulation requires determining the elements that will have a direct influence on the results. The aim is reducing the complexity of the simulation as much as possible. Then, each object is created and placed within the scene with the real dimension and the real material composition. Objects of the scene are hierarchically organized allowing placing any object inside another. Similarly to the sources, there is a multitude of phantom types that can be simulated in MCS. The most common phantom in nuclear imaging simulation will be presented in the next sections.

3.4.2.1 Matter composition

A common property of any phantom is the material composition. Since phantoms are mimicking real objects they have to be defined with a given medium. The exact composition and density of this medium will be exploited by the different physic

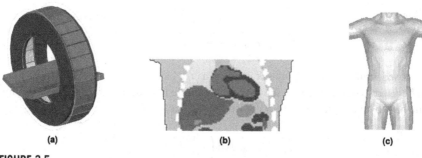

(a)   (b)   (c)

FIGURE 3.5

Example of the main types of phantom models used in MCS: (a) PET scanner described with analytical geometries which include couch, shielding, detector modules, and crystals; (b) thorax voxelized geometry derived from a patient CT (each color is a different medium); and (c) tessellated geometry, which is composed of several triangles to model a body. Nest meshes can also be used to model the different organs.

processes to compute cross sections and resolve interactions. For example, the mixture of the bone tissue has to be defined following the proportion of each atomic element that composes this tissue, such as, hydrogen, carbon, nitrogen, oxygen, etc. The density and the total atom density have to be also defined. In practice, a material database is built in order to avoid repeating the definition of the same material. Each phantom is assigned to a medium that points to this material database. For more complex phantoms, especially for patient and small animal phantoms where mediums are heterogeneous, the medium assignment can be derived from a CT image [28]. This is obtained by labeling the image into medium based on the Hounsfield unit. Different institutions provide the composition and the properties of various material for MCS, such as the International Commission on Radiation Units and Measurements (ICRU), International Commission on Radiological Protection (ICRP), National Institute of Standards and Technology (NIST), etc. A reference for human tissue composition in MCS is the ICRU report 46 [29]. Another report that gathers body tissues from different institutes and non-human material can be found in [30].

3.4.2.2 Analytical geometry

The environment can be composed of different analytical geometry primitives such as spheres, torus, boxes, etc. For example, a complete PET scan can be modeled with such primitive as shown in Fig. 3.5(a). The medium of a geometry primitive is considered as homogeneous. Since the particle navigator requires geometric information from each primitive contained in the scene, such as the next boundary distance, every primitive type (sphere, box, etc.) has to be described using ray-tracing functions considering the different primitives' geometrical specificities.

In the case of a 2D box, for example, as illustrated in Fig. 3.3(b), the distance to the box boundary $l_\square$ along the path L is determined by an efficient ray/box intersection algorithm [31]. This method considers the particle as a ray defined by a parametric equation $\mathbf{R} = \mathbf{p} + l\mathbf{d}$, where l is the distance between the particle along the path L and the 2D box, which is considered as an axis-aligned bounding box (AABB). The interaction point between the ray and AABB is determined by considering each intersection of the ray with lines that compose the AABB. Every distance between the ray and the lines is calculated using their respective line equations. The final intersection distance $l_\square$ with the box is given by the minimum positive value between all line distance intersections. In the more general case, a 3D oriented bounding box (OBB) is considered. In this case the intersections are calculated using plans instead of lines. For a better computation efficiency, the reference frame of the OBB is changed to an AABB during the calculation of each intersection.

Efficient ray-tracing functions for numerous geometry primitives can be found in [32]. The efficiency of the method used to estimate the intersection between the particle path and a geometry primitive is very important, since it will be called a very large number of times during the simulation to track the particle within the environment.

3.4.2.3 Voxelized geometry

Similarly to the voxelized particle source, a voxelized phantom is used to simulate a geometry that contains heterogeneous medium. In medical applications, voxelized phantoms are derived from patient anatomical CT images or based on anthropomorphic numerical models (see Fig. 3.5(b)). Each voxel within such phantom may represent different media allowing the simulation of tissue heterogeneity. For computational efficiency purposes, a voxelized geometry in MCS is considered as a parameterized geometry. Instead of simulating millions of voxels that compose the phantom, only a single analytical box (AABB) representing a voxel is used in the simulation. The voxel position (box vertices) is updated according to the voxel index that contains the particle using its position $\mathbf{p}$ and the voxel size (S_u, S_v, S_w). Subsequently, using this information the navigator determines the medium crossed by the particle and the associated interaction distances along the particle path L. For this kind of phantom, particle navigation is simple to implement and subsequently optimize considering that a regular grid of voxels is used [33–35]. For example, a classical optimization consists in skipping voxels with same medium or grouping voxels that have the same material [36].

3.4.2.4 Tessellated geometry

Voxelized geometry is associated with limitations for certain medical applications. Finite voxel sizes do not allow the incorporation of fine details and complex surfaces, such as curve and round objects. A potential solution consists of using smaller voxels to model complex objects, however, this dramatically increases computational run times and data volumes to be handled by the simulation. Alternatively, complex analytical geometries may be handled using B-splines, non-uniform rational B-spline and Bezier. However, intersection calculations remain complex and time consuming with such geometries. In addition, they are not easy to manipulate and visualize. On the other hand, tessellated geometry is a volume where the surface is sampled by using a basic shape primitive.

Triangular mesh is the most common and simple tessellated geometry used in biomedical applications (see Fig. 3.5(c)). One major drawback of this phantom is the assumption that the mesh volume is composed of a homogeneous medium, leading to significant approximations since heterogeneity cannot be modeled. Similarly to the voxelized geometry with the number of voxels, the numbers of triangles impact the level of details of the represented phantom. There is a trade-off between the level of details on the mesh and the quantity of data to be stored for this mesh. As previously shown in [37,38], a mesh is able to represent any kind of object, ranging from simple ones (boxes, spheres, etc.) to complex objects obtained using computer-aided design modeling and medical image segmentation. Similarly to the voxelized geometry, the tessellated requires a ray-tracing function to determine the distance to the volume boundary. The mesh intersection is achieved by using an efficient algorithm of ray/triangle intersection [39].

The mesh boundary distance requires more calculations compared to a simple voxel since a ray-tracing approach is needed between the particle path and every triangle Δ_i that composes the primitive. A partitioning data structure method [40] may be used to avoid this exhaustive research over all triangles. This will be described with more details in the Section 3.4.2.6.

3.4.2.5 Mixed geometry

Certain applications require the use of fine detailed objects, like a tessellated geometry volume, within a voxelized geometry, i.e., a patient phantom. This is the case when simulation includes artificial implants (screws, hip replacements, etc.) or anatomical details derived from other imaging modalities, such as, for example, MRI of the arteries, spinal cord, atheroma, etc. A good example is in coronary angiography presented in Fig. 3.6. The simulation of nested basic primitives is easy to handle by the navigator, since their borders do not overlap. This is not the case with voxelized volumes where voxels are partially overlapping with other parts of a tessellated phantom.

A solution is the use of a parallel world concept first introduced by [42] as part of the electron gamma shower code [43,11]. The basic concept is the use of overlapping worlds containing the geometry of different scenes. This concept was also subsequently implemented in Geant4 [44] for scoring dose within analytical volume applications. In this case only the main world contains physical material properties and is concerned by particle interactions. Subsequently, [45] extended this concept with the layered mass geometry where each of the two worlds contains material properties, providing an appropriate solution to the combined voxelized/analytical simulation issue. On the other hand, within layered mass geometry each parallel world requires its own navigator and geometry, with the particle stepping driven by the smaller step associated with one of these navigators. In addition, running several navigators within the same simulation may hamper computational efficiency. Finally, the implementation within a dedicated MCS of such a navigation mechanism may require significant changes on the MCS code itself. Another solution consists

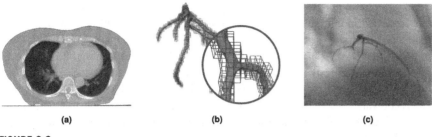

(a)   (b)   (c)

FIGURE 3.6

Example of mixed geometry in the field of coronary angiography using fluoroscopy [41]. This is a typical application requiring the combination of a voxelized phantom derived from a thoracic patient CT (a) and a mesh phantom segmented from a coronary patient MRI (b), where the coronary mesh and the BVH structure for leaves that contains at least one triangle is illustrated (see Section 3.4.2.6). (c) The final transmission angiography image recovered from this simulation using a iodine dilution within the blood artery.

of using a hybrid voxelized/analytical primitive proposed in [41], that combines both voxelized and analytical object descriptions into a same object without the need to simultaneously run two parallel simulations or modify the underlying MC navigation code.

3.4.2.6 Hierarchical geometry and space partitioning data structure

Every phantom in an MCS scene has to be hierarchically organized as if they were nested inside each other. This is not only a requirement for improving the readability of a simulation, but it plays a key role on the simulation run time. For example, there is a difference in simulating, on the one hand, 27 648 boxes as crystals in PET imaging simulation and in simulating, on the other hand, one cylinder as detector head that includes 192 boxes as block detectors, that themselves include 144 boxes as crystals. After each particle step the navigator will check every box in the scene to test and compute the intersection with the particle. In the first case, 27 648 collision tests will be necessary to determine which crystal will be reached by a particle. In the second case, with a hierarchical organization, only 337 collision tests will be necessary for each particle step. The number of tests is reduced because a single test will be used to check the intersection with the cylinder detector head. Subsequently, the tracking will determine which block detectors will be crossed by the particle (192 tests). And finally, the crystal that will interact with the particle is defined by testing only the crystals contained by the considered block detector (144 tests).

In this simple example, organizing the PET design into different levels of hierarchical geometry is easy and can be specified manually by defining which object is nested with another. However, for more complex scenes, an automatic solution using a space partitioning data structure can be used. The most common method is the bounding volume hierarchy (BVH) concept [40]. Such methods are used for real-time rendering in computer graphics. The aim is to automatically organize a scene containing different objects in a hierarchical tree structure, consisting of root, internal nodes, and leaves. This allows testing the bounding box of each group of objects before testing the objects themselves, similarly to the block detectors and crystals, but here in an automatic way. Regular bounding boxes may also be used to split a scene. This is equivalent to a voxelized volume where each voxel is a tree leaf that contains objects to test during the particle tracking. See the previous example in coronary angiography simulation in Fig. 3.6(b), where such regular BVH was used to optimize the navigation within the coronary mesh. More complex BVH methods can be used for a better efficiency, such as the octree method [46]. Each node of this BVH has exactly eight children (octree) that split the 3D space into $2 \times 2 \times 2$ regular cells. Each of these children are sub-divided following the same rule if there are containing an object. This recursive data tree structure is capable to adapt the bounding box size according to the level of subdivision. For example, large empty volumes will be enclosed by large bounding boxes while small objects will be contained in small bounding boxes. This drastically reduces the number of testing collisions including bounding box border during the particle tracking. Octrees are often used in 3D graphics and game engines, especially to handle triangular-based mesh objects. Octree is also used in MCS to handle mesh objects avoiding testing every triangle after each particle step.

3.4.3 Particle detector

The last major element in MCS is the simulation of particle detectors. From the simulation point of view, a particle detector is more or less a phantom where details of the particle interactions, such as position, energy, and dose deposition or time-of-flight, are recorded and stored.

Such a phantom is sometimes named "sensitive" phantom. Any detector from medical imaging devices may be simulated, for example, PET crystals, X-ray flat panel, or CT curve multi-detectors. The different layers or elements that constitute a particle detector are designed on the simulation. The sensitive phantom is only reserved for the volume that should in the real system record the particle detection, as for example the amorphous silicon layer in the X-ray detector case.

MCSs are very computationally demanding which limits therefore their capability to simulate the complete part of the detection. For example, optical photon propagation within the PET crystal can be simulated, but the electronic part of the detection including photo-multiplier are mostly not simulated. Therefore alternative solutions have to be employed to simulate mostly off-line the post processing to recover the digitized information. Analytical functions can be used to mimic the analog/digitizer part of an imaging system. Detected photons can be sorted to define timed coincidences in PET simulation. Diverse processing may be applied to simulate delay time, energy cut-off, etc.

3.5 **Running a Monte Carlo simulation**

Before running a simulation several questions have to be answered: How many particles are needed? How long my simulation will take? Generally, the number of particles is defined according to the application. For example, in a CT simulation, a number of counts per pixel is expected in order to obtain a realistic image. By testing different numbers of particles, the ratio between primary photons from the source and the number of particles detected may be estimated. This ratio can be used to define the final number of particles according to the number of counts per pixel desired. In addition, most MCS codes provide statistical uncertainty for each pixel based on the variance of the number of interactions [47]. This may help to define a realistic level of noise on the recovered data from the simulation. This is different in emission tomography, such as in PET or SPECT. Since an isotope is used, an acquisition time can be specified. The simulation will emit particles until the global clock time reaches the required simulation time.

The underlying question with the number of particles is to choose the pseudorandom number generator (PRNG). Indeed, the heart of the MCS is the sampling of random numbers. A PRNG is characterized by a period indicating the number of values that can be generated before a cycle appears. This is important to avoid any statistical bias in MCS. Existing criteria may be used to safely define the period $\mathcal{P}$ of a PRNG. For example, Knuth [48] suggested a limit as $\frac{\mathcal{P}}{1000}$ number of values allowed, while Ripley [49] defines a limit as $\frac{1}{200}\sqrt{\mathcal{P}}$, and there are some suggestions that in extreme cases an even safer limit might be $\sqrt[3]{\mathcal{P}}$. A standard transmission or emission tomography simulation requires 10^9 to 10^{12} particles. Using the safer Ripley criterion, the minimum period of the PRNG should be $\mathcal{P} > 10^{36}$. Although some PRNGs are not so far from this period, such as the KISS generator [50] with a $\mathcal{P} = 10^{37}$, most of them are safe to use in MCS, such as the Brent generator [51] ($\mathcal{P} = 10^{77}$) or the widely-used Mersenne-Twister generator [52] ($\mathcal{P} = 10^{600}$). A PRNG with a large period requires more data to store the state of the generator and more computation time to draw a new random number. This may play a role in the total time of an MCS.

Some simulations need days of computation, users have to be aware of the expected run time before starting a simulation. Generally, time computation of an MCS is mostly linear to the number of particles. Therefore, by simulating a small but sufficient number of particles, and measuring the run time, the total time for the complete simulation may be easily obtained by extrapolation. In MCS parallel execution is easily implemented, especially targeted cluster computing. Since there are no interactions between particles, the simulation can be split into several independent simulations. Therefore, the number of particles or the time period has to be chosen according to each sub-simulation. The PRNG starting state has to be different for each run in order to have real independent simulations. Results will be gathered by concatenation or by addition in order to obtain the final data. According to the simulated system, raw data can be 2D projections, histograms, sinograms, or list mode data. Examples of what is expected in terms of data and image in MCS are presented in Fig. 3.7. Sinogram data from PET simulation and PET image after reconstruction

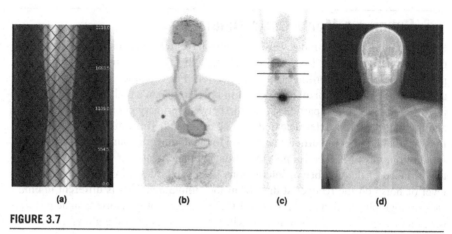

FIGURE 3.7

Examples of results obtained by MCS: (a) sinogram raw data from ^{18}F-FDG thorax PET simulation using Gate software, (b) reconstructed ^{18}F-FDG PET image recovered from realistic simulation using patient CT and the Gate software, (c) whole-body planar ^{111}In SPECT simulation [53], and (d) body radiography directly recovered from MCS using patient CT and the GGEMS software [54].

are illustrated in this figure. A simple direct digital radiography is also presented with a whole body simulation in SPECT imaging.

3.6 Improving Monte Carlo simulation efficiency

MCS has evolved steadily along with computer power. Despite Moore's law (the number of transistors in a dense integrated circuit doubles about every two years), this is not enough and algorithmic methods are constantly being developed in order to drastically improve the computation time in MCS. The long execution time of MCS remains the major issue preventing their use in routine clinical practice, and limiting some applications in research. The objective is to push forward the simulation limit and get simulated data very close to real clinical data, but also to be able to deploy such simulation in a clinical context. This requires integrating complexity from new features, detectors, and new kind of information without increasing the simulation time.

A potential solution to the intensive computational issues of MCS can be based on the use of computer clusters, although this solution may be less realistic within a routine clinical environment or for a small research group given the associated cost and logistic issues (necessary space and informatics infrastructures). On the other hand, numerous methods to speed up the simulations exist. They are based on algorithmic techniques, such as variance reduction technique or on the use of graphics processing units accelerated hardware. Nowadays, the new trend in artificial intelligence is expected to contribute significantly in MCS domain. This section is dedicated to presenting past and recent methods that are essential to improve simulation efficiency.

3.6.1 Woodcock tracking

The Woodcock tracking (WT) method [55] is one of the most widely used variance reduction techniques in medical MCS due to an associated improvement in the navigation through CT images' voxelized volumes. The WT method is limited to discrete processes, e.g., gamma particles. For example, electrons cannot be handled by such a method due to their electric charge that induces continuous effects during their displacements.

The main advantage of WT is avoiding ray-tracing calculations on the voxel boundaries while particles cross different media. WT is associated with an oversampling of the particle step when the phantom contains high density tissue. This is typically the case in medical applications, where a CT image contains mainly soft tissues and for some small regions bones and metal implants (dental amalgams, for example). This was resolved in [56] by introducing the concept of Super-Voxels. This consists of grouping voxels, without merging their materials, into virtual subvolumes called Super-Voxels, where each of them uses a local Woodcock tracking. This new Super-Voxel-WT version reduces this oversampling issue and speeds up particle navigation.

Within the context of particle tracking, a promising proof of concept in [57] was proposed to model, by using a generative adversarial network, the distribution of particles exiting a patient during MCS of emission tomography imaging devices. The resulting compact artificial neural network is then able to generate particles exiting the patient, going towards the detectors, avoiding costly particle tracking within the patient.

3.6.2 GPU

Graphics processing units (GPUs) are in many different domains, especially in medical physics, a low cost alternative solution for the acquisition of high computation power. Within this context different MCS codes have been used and implemented on GPUs targeting specific applications. Most of them are focused on dose calculation, and few of them on CT imaging applications [58–60], PET imaging [61], and SPECT [62]. Each of these codes has different implementation strategies and is dedicated to one application. Only one modular simulation platform GGEMS from [54,41] proposes hardware-adapted solutions for the different components of MCS with advanced mechanisms allowing numerous medical applications (PET, SPECT, CT imaging). GGEMS was successfully used in PET scattering correction [63] and sped up SPECT simulation [53]. The acceleration factor, reaching two orders of magnitude, is provided by the use of the many parallel cores embedded within a GPU. The proposed solutions are still limited to some specific applications and they are not easily generalizable.

3.6.3 Fixed force detection

For some MCS applications a very small fraction of photons contributes to the desired results. This is the case, for example, in X-ray scattering calculation or in SPECT imaging, where simulations are very slow to converge due to the solid angle of the detector and the loss of photons in the collimator. In order to decrease the computation time, several variance reduction techniques have been developed [64]. The geometrical importance sampling [65] approach uses particle splitting and Russian roulette that consists in generating additional photons with a multiplicity value depending on the particle position, with the idea that the particles close to the detector have larger contributions than others. Within this context a fixed forced detection, initially presented in [66], can be applied to speed up simulation. Fixed forced detection is based on an MCS, but forces the detection of a photon in each detector pixel weighted by the probability of emission (or scattering) and transmission to this pixel. This method was successfully used for X-ray imaging scattering calculation [66] and fast SPECT simulation [67].

3.6.4 Angular response functions

A common approach in SPECT imaging is the use of angular response functions which replaces the explicit photon tracking in the imaging head by a tabulated model of the collimator-detector response function [68,69] estimated from MC simulations. Although this approach may be adapted to voxelized phantoms, the complexity level of the multidimensional probability distribution remains too high to be tabulated. A recent study in condensed matter domain has demonstrated the feasibility to learn an effective model by using deep Artificial Neural Networks [70]. Furthermore, the feasibility to learn the angular response function of an SPECT collimator-detector system was shown [71] with a neural network, from a learning dataset of millions of particles generated by conventional MC simulations.

Therefore, deep neural networks have demonstrated their capability to learn the complex model of response functions and open a new paradigm that consists in bypassing the standard step-by-step particle tracking by a response function. Although this is a major breakthrough in MC simulations, those approaches that predict how particles are globally transported through a phantom or a detector are still in their infancy, especially to obtain generalizable models where statistical properties and limitations are still unknown and require further investigation.

3.7 Examples of Monte Carlo simulation applications in medical physics

MCSs are useful for various applications since they allow recovering raw data and estimating unmeasurable information using a virtual system. The aim of MCS is to help designing imaging systems, investigating quantitative imaging, understanding confounding physical effects, optimizing acquisition protocols, or developing new image reconstruction algorithms. A numerical physics simulation allows for a perfect control on the chain that acquires the images. In addition, it is possible to recover information that is not possible to measure on real systems. This opens a large perspective of studies and evaluations for different systems or methods. Any concept of unconventional systems can be evaluated and studied without having to build it. In the same way, new clinical image acquisition protocols or image reconstruction methods can be studied by using realistic simulations without the use of real patients.

By combining the different elements from the structure of a Monte Carlo simulation (sources, phantoms, and detectors), it is possible to obtain a multitude of applications, whether in medical imaging or in particle therapy. Each of these elements are placed together within a same main mother volume called "world." This volume, that simulates the environment, allows transporting the particles between the different parts of the simulated system (scanner, patient, detectors, etc.). The world is most of the time filled with air material. Since a large number of applications can be used in image synthesis with MCS, only a few typical applications in emission and transmission imaging are presented in this section. All of them use the standard elements provided by a MCS structure as detailed in Section 3.4.

There are a large number of applications in emission imaging. Most of the commercial PET or SPECT scanners have been already modeled for MCS and validated using experimental data [15]. For example, a PET scanner can be easily simulated by combining a voxelized source (distribution of the radioactive tracer) with a voxelized phantom (patient anatomy). The scanner itself (gantry, shielding, couch, camera, etc.) can be modeled using simple geometry primitives or tessellated objects from computer-aided design software. The same configuration can be adapted for an SPECT scanner. The difference lies in the arrangement of the crystals for obtaining a planar gamma camera. The collimator in the front of the camera is modeled by using analytical phantoms. One or several cameras can be used statically or in rotation around the patient in order to recover tomographic data. Prototyping cameras in emission imaging, such as Compton cameras or prompt gamma camera for hadron therapy, can be studied using MCS [15]. Preclinical imaging systems can also be simulated. The scanner with the correct dimensions is modeled and a phantom of a small animal, such as a mouse, for example, is used. An MCS with optical photon effects opens the possibility to simulate applications in bioluminescence and fluorescence [72].

Similarly, most of the transmission imaging systems can be simulated by combining the different elements of a Monte Carlo simulation. For example, a medical X-ray source is easily simulated by considering the real specifications (focal point, aperture, beam shape, spectrum, collimator, etc.) [16]. By adding a voxelized phantom to model the patient anatomy, this provides the basis for any MCS in X-ray imaging, such as CT, cone-beam CT, fluoroscopic imaging, etc. The main difference between such systems lies on the design of the particle detector. For example, cone-beam CT and fluoroscopic imaging use a flat panel detector to recover 2D image projection [73], while a CT system has a curved-shape detector.

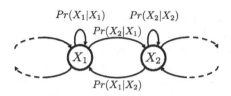

FIGURE 3.8

Examples of Markov chain, where X_1 and X_2 are different states of a system. Each state has a probability density function Pr to move to another state or to stay at the same state. In practice, a state can be any particular configuration that simulate a biological process, like, for example, growth of cell population, cell cycle, molecular folding, etc.

In addition, it is also possible to simulate unconventional transmission imaging systems such as dual energy CT systems [74], where photons are emitted following two different spectrums, spectral or photon-counting CT systems [75], which are able to count the number of incoming photons and measure photon energy, or megavolt cone beam-CT imaging, which involves acquiring the irradiation beam of a linear accelerator used in external beam radiation therapy [76]. By using additional physical effects like refraction, reflection, and Fresnel diffraction, it is also possible to simulate phase-contrast X-ray imaging [77]. There are also applications in proton CT imaging where proton particles are used instead of photons to image a subject [78].

3.8 Monte Carlo simulation for computational biology
3.8.1 Generalization of the Monte Carlo method

Monte Carlo methods have become widespread in many fields, such as physical sciences, engineering, finance, computer graphics, computational biology, etc. In particle physics, the method involves randomly sampling the path of particles passing through matter. The probability function to get the path history of a particle $Pr(\Omega)$ cannot be sampled directly, due to its complexity and high dimensionality.

Therefore, this is solved by decomposing the problem into N problems using a Markov chain traversed by a method of random walk. This strategy is part of a class of algorithms named Markov chain Monte Carlo methods and can be generalized and applied in many different domains, especially in computational biology. A particle that crosses matter and changes direction and energy can be seen as a change from a state X_1 to a state X_2. This sequential change of state is considered as a Markov chain (see Fig. 3.8) which is a stochastic model describing a possible sequence of events with a certain probability. For example, the probability to move from the state X_1 to the state X_2 is defined by the probability density function $Pr(X_2|X_1)$. By posing the problem as a probability of state change, it is possible to model many stochastic problems, especially in the field of computational biology, like the state change of cell cycle [79], for example.

The Markov chain Monte Carlo method randomly draws a sequence of states $\{X_0, X_1, \dots\}$. For each sequence, a first starting random state is selected X_0. Then, the Markov chain is randomly traversed (by random walk) until reaching an end state. One main property of Markov chains is that the next state X_{n+1} only depends on the current state X_n and the associated probability $Pr(X_{n+1}|X_n)$. The complexity and the dimensionality of the probability density function to change from a state to another is lower compared to $Pr(\Omega)$. This allows sampling to be performed by a Monte Carlo method. However, the final probability density function for a large number of sampled sequences converges at the end to the original targeted probability function $Pr(\Omega)$.

Different algorithms can be used to perform the random walk. If the probability density function between the states is simple, the cumulative density function can be used to draw with a single random number a new state (see Section 3.4.1.3). For more complex functions with low dimensionality, for example, where there are discontinuities, or functions whose cumulative probability density (integral) is too difficult to obtain, a rejection method can be used.

This method is closely related to calculating an integral using a Monte Carlo method. In the case of a 2D function, two random variables are used and placed in the space of the probability density function. If the points formed by the two random variables (ξ_x, ξ_y) do not meet the condition $\xi_y < Pr(\xi_x)$, meaning that the point is above the curve, the sample is rejected. The procedure is repeated until a sample that validates the condition $\xi_y < Pr(\xi_x)$ is accepted. This is equivalent to the method presented at the beginning of this chapter for estimating the value of π (Section 3.2, Fig. 3.1) by using the samples that were drawn within the circle. The final sampled distribution with a very large number of values is identical to the original targeted probability density function.

In the general case, where the probability density function is complex and highly multidimensional, the Metropolis–Hasting algorithm [3,80] is used. This algorithm is able to determine the acceptance of a candidate state by calculating an acceptance rate based on the probability density function of the current and candidate states. The most probable state candidate compared to the current state will be always accepted, while the least probable state will be most often rejected. This corresponds to obtaining a random walk which tends to preferentially visit the regions of the space of states where the density of probabilities is higher but occasionally visit regions of low density.

To conclude, the Markov chain Monte Carlo method is a generalized method, applicable directly or conceptually to different problems especially in computational biology. In practice, a state can be any particular configuration that simulates a biological process, for example, cell population behavior, cell cycle or molecular folding.

3.8.2 **Examples of computational biology applications**

The first example in computational biology that uses Monte Carlo method is the cell cycle simulation [79]. Each event of the cell cycle incorporates a variability by using a Monte Carlo approach. There are also MC simulations of plasmid replication [81], DNA replication [82], or DNA lesion simulation [83] under irradiation.

Markov chain Monte Carlo methods are also used to study the change of protein configurations. For example, in [84] the authors have used MCS to study the folding of a small protein and in [85] to study the localization of transmembrane fragments in membrane proteins. Ion transport in cell membrane channels [86] were also simulated, and in [87] the simulation of intercellular interfaces, which serve to convey information between cells, was performed.

In addition to cells, tissue can also be simulated, especially using the cellular Potts model [88]. It is used to simulate individual and collective cell behavior, such as cell migration, growth, division, and cell signaling. This enables the theoretical study of vasculogenesis and angiogenesis [89], morphogenesis, tumor development, etc. The dynamics of cells are directly governed by a function that minimizes the energy of the cell configuration. For this, an adaptation of the Metropolis–Hasting method (random walk) is used to accept or reject states. An implementation of the cellular Potts model can be found in the CompuCell3D software [18].

There exists another stochastic model of tissue or tumor cell growth, in particular with a modified version of the Gompertz model [90] or in the work proposed in [91] where a multiscale model to assess the impact of radiotherapy on the development of the tumor is used. Most of these models use the concept of Markov chain Monte Carlo [92] to evolve the cell population based on local cell behaviors governed by probability density functions. A direct simulation at the tissue or tumor level would not have been possible due to the multidimensionality and complexity of the problem to achieve a global behavior.

3.9 Summary

In general, Monte Carlo methods are algorithms that consist in estimating an approximate value using a random sampling process. The method has the capability to explore large configuration spaces in order to extract information, and solve a very wide range of problems with the advantage of being easy to use. Combining Monte Carlo method with particle physics model allows solving particle transport within matter. Such simulations are widely used in the field of biomedical physics. With the same method, any nuclear imaging model can be simulated, such as CT, cone beam CT, direct digital radiography, PET, SPECT, gamma camera, etc. This method has many advantages, such as achieving very realistic image synthesis, allowing the evaluation of new system designs, new image detectors, as well as evaluating and comparing new protocols and new reconstruction algorithms. Results from Monte Carlo simulations are raw data directly recorded from the image detector. This capability allows producing different kinds of raw data (sinogram, projection, list mode, etc.), which is mostly not possible on real imaging systems. This is also a drawback, since a 2D/3D reconstruction step is therefore necessary to obtain an exploitable image. In addition, MCSs make it possible to recover information that is not possible to measure on real systems, such as particle scatter, dose to organs, etc. MCSs are computationally demanding, since billions of particles have to be transported through matter, which limits their applicability in clinic but also in research. However, recent advances in variance reduction techniques, on the use of GPU architectures, or on deep learning approaches tend to reduce more and more the calculation time in MCS. Monte Carlo approaches can also be used in computational biology. The basic concept of Markov chain Monte Carlo method is used to simulate cell cycle, tumor growing, etc.

References

[1] T. Dauxois, M. Peyrard, S. Ruffo, The Fermi–Pasta–Ulam "numerical experiment": history and pedagogical perspectives, European Journal of Physics 26 (2005) S3–S11.

[2] S.M. Ulam, J. von Neumann, On combination of stochastic and deterministic processes, Bulletin of the American Mathematical Society 53 (1947).

[3] N. Metropolis, S.M. Ulam, The Monte Carlo method, Journal of the American Statistical Association 44 (247) (1949) 335–341.

[4] H. Kahn, Use of different Monte Carlo sampling techniques, in: Symposium on Monte Carlo Methods, 1956, pp. 146–190.

[5] M.J. Berger, Monte Carlo calculation of the penetration and diffusion of fast charged particles, Methods in Computational Physics 1 (1963) 135–215.

[6] C.D. Zerby, A Monte Carlo calculation of the response of gamma-ray scintillation counters, Methods in Computational Physics 1 (1963) 89–134.

[7] R. Brun, M. Hansroul, J.C. Lassalle, Geant user's guide, Tech. Rep., CERN Report DD/EE/82, 1982.

[8] J. Allison, K. Amako, J. Apostolakis, H. Araujo, P. Arce Dubois, M. Asai, G. Barrand, R. Capra, S. Chauvie, R. Chytracek, G. Cirrone, G. Cooperman, G. Cosmo, G. Cuttone, G. Daquino, M. Donszelmann, M. Dressel, G. Folger, F. Foppiano, J. Generowicz, V. Grichine, S. Guatelli, P. Gumplinger, A. Heikkinen, I. Hrivnacova, A. Howard, S. Incerti, V. Ivanchenko, T. Johnson, F. Jones, T. Koi, R. Kokoulin, M. Kossov, H. Kurashige, V. Lara, S. Larsson, F. Lei, O. Link, F. Longo, M. Maire, A. Mantero, B. Mascialino, I. McLaren, P. Mendez Lorenzo, K. Minamimoto, K. Murakami, P. Nieminen, L. Pandola, S. Parlati, L. Peralta, J. Perl, A. Pfeiffer, M. Pia, A. Ribon, P. Rodrigues, G. Russo, S. Sadilov, G. Santin, T. Sasaki, D. Smith, N. Starkov, S. Tanaka, E. Tcherniaev, B. Tome, A. Trindade, P. Truscott, L. Urban, M. Verderi, A. Walkden, J. Wellisch, D. Williams, D. Wright, H. Yoshida, Geant4 developments and applications, IEEE Transactions on Nuclear Science 53 (1) (2006) 270–278, https://doi.org/10.1109/TNS.2006.869826.

[9] F. Salvat, J. Fernandez-Varea, J. Sempau, Penelope – a code system for Monte Carlo simulation of electron and photon transport, Tech. Rep., Workshop Proceedings Issy-les-Moulineaux, France, 2001.

[10] X-5 Monte Carlo Team, MCNP — a general Monte Carlo n-particle transport code, Tech. Rep., LA-CP-03-0284, 2003.

[11] I. Kawrakow, D.W.O. Rogers, The EGSnrc code system: Monte Carlo simulation of electron and photon transport, Tech. Rep., NRCC Report PIRS-701, 2003.

[12] T.T. Böhlen, F. Cerutti, M.P.W. Chin, A. Fasso, A. Ferrari, P.G. Ortega, A. Mairani, P.R. Sala, G. Smirnov, V. Vlachoudis, The FLUKA code: developments and challenges for high energy and medical applications, Nuclear Data Sheets 120 (2014) 211–214.

[13] A. Ferrari, P.R. Sala, A. Fasso, J. Ranft, FLUKA: a multi-particle transport code, Tech. Rep., CERN-2005-10, INFN/TC_05/11, SLAC-R-773, 2005.

[14] P. Arce, J. Ignacio Lagares, L. Harkness, D. Pérez-Astudillo, M. Cañadas, P. Rato, M. de Prado, Y. Abreu, G. de Lorenzo, M. Kolstein, A. Díaz, Gamos: a framework to do Geant4 simulations in different physics fields with an user-friendly interface, Nuclear Instruments and Methods in Physics Research Section A: Accelerators, Spectrometers, Detectors and Associated Equipment 735 (2014) 304–313.

[15] D. Sarrut, M. Bała, M. Bardiès, J. Bert, M. Chauvin, K. Chatzipapas, M. Dupont, A. Etxebeste, L.M. Fanchon, S. Jan, G. Kayal, A.S. Kirov, P. Kowalski, W. Krzemien, J. Labour, M. Lenz, G. Loudos, B. Mehadji, L. Ménard, C. Morel, P. Papadimitroulas, M. Rafecas, J. Salvadori, D. Seiter, M. Stockhoff, E. Testa, C. Trigila, U. Pietrzyk, S. Vandenberghe, M.-A. Verdier, D. Visvikis, K. Ziemons, M. Zvolský, E. Roncali, Advanced Monte Carlo simulations of emission tomography imaging systems with GATE, Physics in Medicine and Biology 66 (10) (2021), https://doi.org/10.1088/1361-6560/abf276.

[16] S. Jan, D. Benoit, E. Becheva, T. Carlier, F. Cassol, P. Descourt, T. Frisson, L. Grevillot, L. Guigues, L. Maigne, C. Morel, Y. Perrot, N. Rehfeld, D. Sarrut, D.R. Schaart, S. Stute, U. Pietrzyk, D. Visvikis, N. Zahra, I. Buvat, GATE V6: a major enhancement of the GATE simulation platform enabling modelling of CT and radiotherapy, Physics in Medicine and Biology 56 (4) (2011) 881–901, https://doi.org/10.1088/0031-9155/56/4/001.

[17] A. Le Maitre, W.P. Segars, S. Marache, A. Reilhac, M. Hatt, S. Tomei, C. Lartizien, D. Visvikis, Incorporating patient-specific variability in the simulation of realistic whole-body ^{18}F-FDG distributions for oncology applications, Proceedings of the IEEE 97 (12) (2009) 2026–2038, https://doi.org/10.1109/JPROC.2009.2027925.

[18] M.H. Swat, G.L. Thomas, J.M. Belmonte, A. Shirinifard, D. Hmeljak, J.A. Glazier, Multi-scale modeling of tissues using CompuCell3D, Methods in Cell Biology 110 (2012) 325–366, https://doi.org/10.1016/B978-0-12-388403-9.00013-8.

[19] S. Incerti, I. Kyriakou, M.A. Bernal, M.C. Bordage, Z. Francis, S. Guatelli, V. Ivanchenko, M. Karamitros, N. Lampe, S.B. Lee, S. Meylan, C.H. Min, W.G. Shin, P. Nieminen, D. Sakata, N. Tang, C. Villagrasa, H.N. Tran, J.M.C. Brown, Geant4-DNA example applications for track structure simulations in liquid water: a report from the Geant4-DNA project, Medical Physics 45 (8) (2018) e722–e739, https://doi.org/10.1002/mp.13048.

[20] C. Leroy, P.-G. Rancoita, Principles of Radiation Interaction in Matter and Detection, World Scientific Publishing Co. Pte. Ltd., 2009.

[21] E.B. Podgorsak, Radiation Physics for Medical Physicists, Springer, 2006.

[22] A. Klein, Y. Nishina, Über die Streuung von Strahlung durch freie Elektronen nach der neuen relativistischen Quantendynamik von Dirac, Zeitschrift für Physik 52 (1929) 853–868.

[23] F. Biggs, R. Lighthill, Analytical approximations for X-ray cross-sections III, Tech. Rep., Sandia National Labs, USA, 1988, https://doi.org/10.2172/7124946.

[24] T.M. Jenkins, W.R. Nelson, A. Rindi, A.E. Nahum, D.W.O. Rogers, Monte Carlo Transport of Electrons and Photons, Physical Sciences, vol. 38, Plenum Press, United States, 1988.

[25] M. Zhang, W. Zou, T. Chen, L. Kim, A. Khan, B. Haffty, N.J. Yue, Parameterization of brachytherapy source phase space file for Monte Carlo-based clinical brachytherapy dose

calculation, Physics in Medicine and Biology 59 (2) (2014) 455–464, https://doi.org/10.1088/0031-9155/59/2/455.

[26] G. Bootsma, H. Nordström, M. Eriksson, D. Jaffray, Monte Carlo kilovoltage S-ray tube simulation: a statistical analysis and compact simulation method, Physica Medica 72 (2020) 80–87, https://doi.org/10.1016/j.ejmp.2020.03.015.

[27] D. Sarrut, N. Krah, J.M. Létang, Generative adversarial networks (GAN) for compact beam source modelling in Monte Carlo simulations, Physics in Medicine and Biology 64 (21) (2019) 215004, https://doi.org/10.1088/1361-6560/ab3fc1.

[28] W. Schneider, T. Bortfeld, W. Schlegel, Correlation between CT numbers and tissue parameters needed for Monte Carlo simulations of clinical dose distributions, Physics in Medicine and Biology 45 (2) (2000) 459–478.

[29] ICRU46, Photon, electron, proton and neutron interaction data for body tissues, Tech. Rep., International Commission on Radiation Units and Measurements, Report 46, 1992.

[30] R.J. McConn, C.J. Gesh, R.T. Pagh, R.A. Rucker, R.G. Williams, Compendium of material composition data for radiation transport modeling, Tech. Rep., Pacific Northwest National Laboratory, 2011, PNNL-15870.

[31] B. Smits, Efficient bounding box intersection, in: Ray Tracing News, vol. 15, 2002.

[32] C. Ericson, Real-Time Collision Detection, Morgan Kaufmann Publishers, Elsevier, 2005.

[33] V. Hubert-Tremblay, L. Archambault, D. Tubic, R. Roy, L. Beaulieu, Octree indexing of DICOM images for voxel number reduction and improvement of Monte Carlo simulation computing efficiency: octree indexing of DICOM CT images, Medical Physics 33 (8) (2006) 2819–2831, https://doi.org/10.1118/1.2214305.

[34] P. Arce, J. Apostolakis, G. Cosmo, A technique for optimised navigation in regular geometries, in: 2008 IEEE Nuclear Science Symposium Conference Record, IEEE, Dresden, Germany, 2008, pp. 857–859, https://doi.org/10.1109/NSSMIC.2008.4774537.

[35] J. Schümann, H. Paganetti, J. Shin, B. Faddegon, J. Perl, Efficient voxel navigation for proton therapy dose calculation in TOPAS and Geant4, Physics in Medicine and Biology 57 (11) (2012) 3281–3293, https://doi.org/10.1088/0031-9155/57/11/3281.

[36] D. Sarrut, L. Guigues, Region-oriented CT image representation for reducing computing time of Monte Carlo simulations, Medical Physics 35 (4) (2008) 1452–1463, https://doi.org/10.1118/1.2884854.

[37] A. Badal, I. Kyprianou, D.P. Banh, A. Badano, J. Sempau, *penMesh* – Monte Carlo radiation transport simulation in a triangle mesh geometry, IEEE Transactions on Medical Imaging 28 (12) (2009) 1894–1901, https://doi.org/10.1109/TMI.2009.2021615.

[38] R. Said, J. Chang, P. Young, G. Tabor, S. Coward, Image-based meshing of patient-specific data: converting medical scans into highly accurate computational models, in: 2008 2nd International Conference on Bioinformatics and Biomedical Engineering, IEEE, Shanghai, China, 2008, pp. 1672–1676, https://doi.org/10.1109/ICBBE.2008.747.

[39] T. Moller, B. Trumbore, Fast, minimum storage ray-triangle intersection, Journal of Graphics Tools 2 (1997) 21–28.

[40] H.J. Haverkort, Results on geometric networks and data structures, Tech. Rep., PhD Thesis, Utrecht University, 2004.

[41] J. Bert, Y. Lemaréchal, D. Visvikis, New hybrid voxelized/analytical primitive in Monte Carlo simulations for medical applications, Physics in Medicine and Biology 61 (9) (2016) 3347–3364, https://doi.org/10.1088/0031-9155/61/9/3347.

[42] G. Yegin, A new approach to geometry modeling for Monte Carlo particle transport: an application to the EGS code system, Nuclear Instruments and Methods in Physics Re-

search Section B: Beam Interactions with Materials and Atoms 211 (3) (2003) 331–338, https://doi.org/10.1016/S0168-583X(03)01318-1.

[43] W.R. Nelson, H. Hirayama, D.W.O. Rogers, The EGS4 code system, Tech. Rep., SLAC-265, 1985.

[44] J. Apostolakis, M. Asai, G. Cosmo, A. Howard, V. Ivanchenko, M. Verderi, Parallel geometries in Geant4: foundation and recent enhancements, in: IEEE Nucl. Sci. Symp. and Med. Imaging Conf. Rec., 2008, pp. 883–886.

[45] S.A. Enger, G. Landry, M. D'Amours, F. Verhaegen, L. Beaulieu, M. Asai, J. Perl, Layered mass geometry: a novel technique to overlay seeds and applicators onto patient geometry in Geant4 brachytherapy simulations, Physics in Medicine and Biology 57 (19) (2012) 6269–6277, https://doi.org/10.1088/0031-9155/57/19/6269.

[46] D. Meagher, Octree encoding: a new technique for the representation, manipulation and display of arbitrary 3-d objects by computer, Tech. Rep., Rensselaer Polytechnic Institute, 1980, Technical Report IPL-TR-80-111.

[47] B.R.B. Walters, I. Kawrakow, D.W.O. Rogers, History by history statistical estimators in the BEAM code system, Medical Physics 29 (12) (2002) 2745–2752, https://doi.org/10.1118/1.1517611.

[48] D. Knuth, The Art of Computer Programming, vol. 2: Seminumerical Algorithms, 3rd ed., Addison-Wesley Longman Publishing Co., Inc., 1997.

[49] B. Ripley, Thoughts on pseudorandom number generators, Journal of Computational and Applied Mathematics 31 (1) (1990) 153–163, https://doi.org/10.1016/0377-0427(90)90346-2.

[50] R. Christian, G. Casella, Monte Carlo Statistical Methods, Springer, 2013.

[51] R.P. Brent, Fast and reliable random number generators for scientific computing, in: Applied Parallel Computing. State of the Art in Scientific Computing, 2006, pp. 1–10.

[52] M. Matsumoto, T. Nishimura, Mersenne twister: a 623-dimensionally equidistributed uniform pseudo-random number generator, ACM Transactions on Modeling and Computer Simulation 8 (1) (1998) 3–30, https://doi.org/10.1145/272991.272995.

[53] M.-P. Garcia, J. Bert, D. Benoit, M. Bardiès, D. Visvikis, Accelerated GPU based SPECT Monte Carlo simulations, Physics in Medicine and Biology 61 (11) (2016) 4001–4018, https://doi.org/10.1088/0031-9155/61/11/4001.

[54] J. Bert, H. Perez-Ponce, Z.E. Bitar, S. Jan, Y. Boursier, D. Vintache, A. Bonissent, C. Morel, D. Brasse, D. Visvikis, Geant4-based Monte Carlo simulations on GPU for medical applications, Physics in Medicine and Biology 58 (16) (2013) 5593–5611, https://doi.org/10.1088/0031-9155/58/16/5593.

[55] E. Woodcock, T. Murphy, P. Hemmings, S. Longworth, Techniques used in the GEM code for Monte Carlo neutronics calculations in reactors and other systems of complex geometry, in: Proc. Conf. Applications of Computing Methods to Reactor Problems, vol. 557, 1965.

[56] A. Behlouli, D. Visvikis, J. Bert, Improved Woodcock tracking on Monte Carlo simulations for medical applications, Physics in Medicine and Biology 63 (22) (2018) 225005.

[57] D. Sarrut, A. Etxebeste, N. Krah, J.M. Létang, Modeling complex particles phase space with GAN for Monte Carlo SPECT simulations: a proof of concept, Physics in Medicine and Biology 66 (5) (2021) 055014, https://doi.org/10.1088/1361-6560/abde9a.

[58] J. Lippuner, I.A. Elbakri, A GPU implementation of EGSnrc's Monte Carlo photon transport for imaging applications, Physics in Medicine and Biology 56 (22) (2011) 7145–7162, https://doi.org/10.1088/0031-9155/56/22/010.

[59] X. Jia, H. Yan, L. Cervino, M. Folkerts, S.B. Jiang, A GPU tool for efficient, accurate, and realistic simulation of cone beam CT projections, Medical Physics 39 (12) (2012) 7368–7378, https://doi.org/10.1118/1.4766436.

[60] K. Kim, T. Lee, Y. Seong, J. Lee, K.E. Jang, J. Choi, Y.W. Choi, H.H. Kim, H.J. Shin, J.H. Cha, S. Cho, J.C. Ye, Fully iterative scatter corrected digital breast tomosynthesis using GPU-based fast Monte Carlo simulation and composition ratio update, Medical Physics 42 (9) (2015) 5342–5355, https://doi.org/10.1118/1.4928139.

[61] Y. Lai, Y. Zhong, A. Chalise, Y. Shao, M. Jin, X. Jia, Y. Chi, gPET: a GPU-based, accurate and efficient Monte Carlo simulation tool for PET, Physics in Medicine and Biology 64 (24) (2019) 245002, https://doi.org/10.1088/1361-6560/ab5610.

[62] T. Rydén, J. Heydorn Lagerlöf, J. Hemmingsson, I. Marin, J. Svensson, M. Båth, P. Gjertsson, P. Bernhardt, Fast GPU-based Monte Carlo code for SPECT/CT reconstructions generates improved 177Lu images, EJNMMI Physics 5 (1) (2018) 1, https://doi.org/10.1186/s40658-017-0201-8.

[63] B. Ma, M. Gaens, H. Xu, J. Bert, M. Lenz, U. Pietrzyk, N.J. Shah, L. Caldeira, P. Lohmann, L. Tellmann, C. Lerche, J. Scheins, E. Rota Kops, Scatter correction based on GPU-accelerated full Monte Carlo simulation for brain PET/MRI, IEEE Transactions on Medical Imaging 39 (1) (2020) 140–151, https://doi.org/10.1109/TMI.2019.2921872.

[64] D.R. Haynor, R.L. Harrison, T.K. Lewellen, The use of importance sampling techniques to improve the efficiency of photon tracking in emission tomography simulations, Medical Physics 18 (5) (1991) 990–1001, https://doi.org/10.1118/1.596615.

[65] J. De Beenhouwer, S. Staelens, S. Vandenberghe, J. Verhaeghe, R. Van Holen, E. Rault, I. Lemahieu, Physics process level discrimination of detections for GATE: assessment of contamination in SPECT and spurious activity in PET, Medical Physics 36 (4) (2009) 1053–1060, https://doi.org/10.1118/1.3078045.

[66] A. Colijn, F. Beekman, Accelerated simulation of cone beam X-ray scatter projections, IEEE Transactions on Medical Imaging 23 (5) (2004) 584–590, https://doi.org/10.1109/TMI.2004.825600.

[67] T. Cajgfinger, S. Rit, J.M. Létang, A. Halty, D. Sarrut, Fixed forced detection for fast SPECT Monte-Carlo simulation, Physics in Medicine and Biology 63 (5) (2018) 055011, https://doi.org/10.1088/1361-6560/aa9e32.

[68] X. Song, W.P. Segars, Y. Du, B.M.W. Tsui, E.C. Frey, Fast modelling of the collimator-detector response in Monte Carlo simulation of SPECT imaging using the angular response function, Physics in Medicine and Biology 50 (8) (2005) 1791–1804, https://doi.org/10.1088/0031-9155/50/8/011.

[69] P. Descourt, T. Carlier, Y. Du, X. Song, I. Buvat, E.C. Frey, M. Bardies, B.M.W. Tsui, D. Visvikis, Implementation of angular response function modeling in SPECT simulations with GATE, Physics in Medicine and Biology 55 (9) (2010) N253–N266, https://doi.org/10.1088/0031-9155/55/9/N04.

[70] H. Shen, J. Liu, L. Fu, Self-learning Monte Carlo with deep neural networks, Physical Review B 97 (20) (2018), https://doi.org/10.1103/PhysRevB.97.205140.

[71] D. Sarrut, N. Krah, J.N. Badel, J.M. Létang, Learning SPECT detector angular response function with neural network for accelerating Monte-Carlo simulations, Physics in Medicine and Biology 63 (20) (2018) 205013, https://doi.org/10.1088/1361-6560/aae331.

[72] V. Cuplov, I. Buvat, F. Pain, S. Jan, Extension of the GATE Monte-Carlo simulation package to model bioluminescence and fluorescence imaging, Journal of Biomedical Optics 19 (2) (2014) 026004, https://doi.org/10.1117/1.JBO.19.2.026004.

[73] L. Goertz, P. Tsiamas, A. Karellas, E. Sajo, P. Zygmanski, Monte Carlo simulation of a prototypical patient dosimetry system for fluoroscopic procedures, Physics in Medicine and Biology 60 (15) (2015) 5891–5909, https://doi.org/10.1088/0031-9155/60/15/5891.

[74] C. Remy, A. Lalonde, D. Béliveau-Nadeau, J.-F. Carrier, H. Bouchard, Dosimetric impact of dual-energy CT tissue segmentation for low-energy prostate brachytherapy: a Monte Carlo study, Physics in Medicine and Biology 63 (2) (2018) 025013, https://doi.org/10.1088/1361-6560/aaa30c.

[75] A. Makeev, M. Clajus, S. Snyder, X. Wang, S.J. Glick, Evaluation of position-estimation methods applied to CZT-based photon-counting detectors for dedicated breast CT, Journal of Medical Imaging 2 (2) (2015) 023501, https://doi.org/10.1117/1.JMI.2.2.023501.

[76] S. Benhalouche, J. Bert, N. Boussion, A. Autret, O. Pradier, D. Visvikis, GATE Monte-Carlo simulation of an MV-CBCT flat panel for synergistic imaging and dosimetric applications in radiotherapy, IEEE Transactions on Radiation and Plasma Medical Sciences 1 (5) (2017) 444–451, https://doi.org/10.1109/TRPMS.2017.2718545.

[77] M. Langer, Z. Cen, S. Rit, J.M. Létang, Towards Monte Carlo simulation of X-ray phase contrast using GATE, Optics Express 28 (10) (2020) 14522, https://doi.org/10.1364/OE.391471.

[78] R. Rescigno, C. Bopp, M. Rousseau, D. Brasse, A pencil beam approach to proton computed tomography, Medical Physics 42 (11) (2015) 6610–6624, https://doi.org/10.1118/1.4933422.

[79] J.D. Keasling, H. Kuo, G. Vahanian, A Monte Carlo simulation of the Escherichia coli cell cycle, Journal of Theoretical Biology 176 (3) (1995) 411–430, https://doi.org/10.1006/jtbi.1995.0209.

[80] W.K. Hastings, Monte Carlo sampling methods using Markov chains and their applications, Biometrika 57 (1) (1970) 97–109, https://doi.org/10.1093/biomet/57.1.97.

[81] H. Kuo, J.D. Keasling, A Monte Carlo simulation of plasmid replication during the bacterial division cycle, Biotechnology and Bioengineering 52 (6) (1996) 633–647.

[82] W.C. Dewey, N. Albright, Developing a model of DNA replication to be used for Monte Carlo calculations that predict the sizes and shapes of molecules resulting from DNA double-strand breaks induced by X irradiation during DNA synthesis, Radiation Research 148 (5) (1997) 421–434.

[83] B. Brzozowska, A. Tartas, A. Wojcik, Monte Carlo modeling of DNA lesions and chromosomal aberrations induced by mixed beams of alpha particles and X-rays, Frontiers in Physics 8 (2020) 567864, https://doi.org/10.3389/fphy.2020.567864.

[84] P. Ojeda, M.E. Garcia, A. Londoño, N.-Y. Chen, Monte Carlo simulations of proteins in cages: influence of confinement on the stability of intermediate states, Biophysical Journal 96 (3) (2009) 1076–1082, https://doi.org/10.1529/biophysj.107.125369.

[85] M. Milik, J. Skolnick, Insertion of peptide chains into lipid membranes: an off-lattice Monte Carlo dynamics model, Proteins 15 (1) (1993) 10–25, https://doi.org/10.1002/prot.340150104.

[86] T. van der Straaten, G. Kathawala, A. Trellakis, R. Eisenberg, U. Ravaioli, BioMOCA—a Boltzmann transport Monte Carlo model for ion channel simulation, Molecular Simulation 31 (2–3) (2005) 151–171, https://doi.org/10.1080/08927020412331308700.

[87] Y. Neve-Oz, J. Sajman, Y. Razvag, E. Sherman, InterCells: a generic Monte-Carlo simulation of intercellular interfaces captures nanoscale patterning at the immune synapse, Frontiers in Immunology 9 (2018) 2051, https://doi.org/10.3389/fimmu.2018.02051.

[88] N. Graner, N. Glazier, Simulation of biological cell sorting using a two-dimensional extended Potts model, Physical Review Letters 69 (13) (1992) 2013–2016, https://doi.org/10.1103/PhysRevLett.69.2013.

[89] S.E.M. Boas, Y. Jiang, R.M.H. Merks, S.A. Prokopiou, E.G. Rens, Cellular Potts model: applications to vasculogenesis and angiogenesis, in: P.-Y. Louis, F.R. Nardi (Eds.), Probabilistic Cellular Automata, in: Emergence, Complexity and Computation, vol. 27, Springer International Publishing, Cham, 2018, pp. 279–310.

[90] C.F. Lo, A modified stochastic Gompertz model for tumour cell growth, Computational & Mathematical Methods in Medicine 11 (1) (2010) 3–11, https://doi.org/10.1080/17486700802545543.

[91] S. Apeke, L. Gaubert, N. Boussion, P. Lambin, D. Visvikis, V. Rodin, P. Redou, Multiscale modeling and oxygen impact on tumor temporal evolution: application on rectal cancer during radiotherapy, IEEE Transactions on Medical Imaging 37 (4) (2018) 871–880, https://doi.org/10.1109/TMI.2017.2771379.

[92] D. Drasdo, R. Kree, J.S. McCaskill, Monte Carlo approach to tissue-cell populations, Physical Review E 52 (6) (1995) 6635–6657, https://doi.org/10.1103/PhysRevE.52.6635.

Medical image synthesis using segmentation and registration

4

Ninon Burgos

Sorbonne Université, Institut du Cerveau - Paris Brain Institute - ICM, CNRS, Inria, Inserm,
AP-HP, Hôpital de la Pitié-Salpêtrière, Paris, France

4.1 Introduction

Many of the early works on medical image synthesis had for objective to improve subsequent image processing steps such as segmentation or registration. In 2005, van de Kraats et al. [1] presented a new method to register (preoperative) magnetic resonance (MR) images to (intraoperative) X-ray images. MR-to-X-ray registration is very challenging because of the different underlying contrast mechanisms. A consequence of these differences is that several tissues, especially bone, have dissimilar appearances on both modalities, which makes it difficult to directly apply gradient- or intensity-based registration methods. Their idea was thus to convert multispectral MR images into computed tomography (CT) images by constructing a look-up table, and to then register the synthetic CT to X-ray, which is an easier task as both modalities have the same underlying contrast mechanisms. They showed that registering synthetic CTs to X-ray data using a gradient-based approach outperformed direct registration from the MR data. Five years later, Roy et al. [2] investigated whether lesions could be detected in the absence of an appropriate lesion-distinguishing MR sequence (a FLAIR) by synthesizing a FLAIR from other sequences (T1-weighted and T2-weighted) using a patch-based approach (see Chapter 5), and showed that it was indeed the case. Other examples are described in Chapter 10.

In both these examples, image synthesis was used to improve segmentation or registration. Instead, what will be described in this chapter is how segmentation and registration can be used to synthesize medical images of a particular modality from images of another modality. The use case throughout the chapter will be the synthesis of CT from MR images as almost all the works reported target two very concrete applications: attenuation correction of positron emission tomography (PET) data, particularly for PET/MR scanners, and radiotherapy treatment planning from MRI only (more details are provided in Chapters 19 and 20).

One of the factors limiting the widespread use of PET/MR scanners is probably the imperfect attenuation correction, leading to a bias of the PET activity, particularly in the brain. Before the emergence of PET/CT scanners, attenuation cor-

Biomedical Image Synthesis and Simulation. https://doi.org/10.1016/B978-0-12-824349-7.00011-6

rection was mostly based on transmission measurements. However, because of the restricted space and the strong magnetic field, installing a rotating radiation source in a PET/MR scanner is challenging. With PET/CT systems, the attenuation coefficients are derived from CT scans. However, in contrast to CT images, MR image intensities do not directly provide information about the tissue attenuation properties.

The aim of radiotherapy treatment planning (RTP) is to optimize the therapeutic ratio by delivering an optimal dose of radiation over the tumorous area while sparing the normal tissues. RTP first requires contouring the tumor and organs at risk. Once these volumes have been defined, the attenuation properties of the different tissues are used as parameters in an optimization process calculating the optimal dose distribution to treat the tumor. Most radiotherapy treatments are planned using a CT scan of the patient as its acquisition is fast and tissue attenuation coefficients can easily be derived from the CT intensity values in Hounsfield units. However, CT images have a low soft-tissue contrast, which can lead to large organ delineation errors, particularly when located in the brain, head and neck, or pelvic regions. MRI is often preferred over CT as a structural imaging modality, mainly for its excellent soft-tissue contrast. Although MRI is increasingly used in clinical practice, its role in RTP is limited by the fact that it does not readily provide tissue attenuation properties, hampering the calculation of dose distributions. This is a critical limitation for the clinical deployment of the MR-linac devices combining an MR scanner and a linear accelerator—the machine delivering the radiation dose.

To solve these two problems, numerous methods have been proposed. Both the general principles and particular examples of segmentation- and registration-based image synthesis approaches will be described. The reasons why these two families of methods have almost exclusively been applied to the MR-to-CT synthesis task and why they have been supplanted by other methods will then be discussed.

4.2 Segmentation-based image synthesis

Segmentation-based approaches can generally be decomposed into two components: the first consists in segmenting the source image and the second consists in assigning intensity values to the different tissue classes obtained to generate the desired image. The segmentation can be manual or automatic, and the intensities can be assigned in bulk (i.e., predefined values are assigned to each tissue class) or in a subject-specific manner. This process is illustrated in Fig. 4.1. Note that segmentation-based image synthesis can also be called classification-based image synthesis [3].

4.2.1 Segmentation approaches

4.2.1.1 Manual segmentation

Manual segmentation is not uncommon in domains such as RTP [4–6]. In their early work on the use of MRI for RTP, Jonsson et al. [4] manually segmented the patient outline, bones, lungs, and air cavities. An example of a pelvis MRI and synthetic CT,

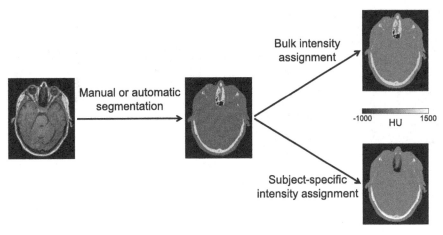

FIGURE 4.1

Segmentation-based approaches can be decomposed into two parts: the first consists in segmenting, manually or automatically, the source image (here an MR image) and the second consists in assigning intensity values to the different tissue classes obtained to generate the target image (here a CT image in Hounsfield units [HU]). Intensities can be assigned in bulk (i.e., predefined values assigned to each tissue class) or in a subject-specific manner.

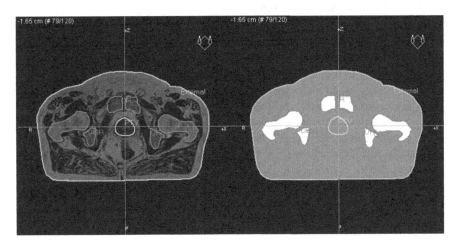

FIGURE 4.2

Example of a manually segmented MR image (left) and the resulting synthetic CT with assigned mass densities (right) [4]. *Jonsson et al. 2010 Radiat. Oncol. 5 62, https:// doi.org/ 10.1186/ 1748-717X-5-62 © 2010, Jonsson et al.; licensee BioMed Central Ltd.*

overlaid with patient outline and bone contours, is shown in Fig. 4.2. Body and bone outlines were also contoured in [5] and bone and air in [6]. Manual segmentation is

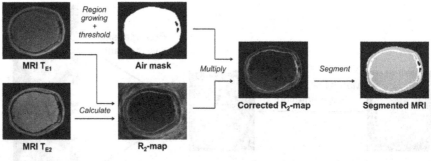

FIGURE 4.3

Automatic segmentation of dual ultra-short echo time (UTE) images using a thresholding approach [11]. The uncorrected R2 map is calculated from the UTE images acquired at echo times TE_1 and TE_2. The R2 map is masked with an air mask derived from the first-echo image to generate the corrected R2 map. The corrected R2 map can be segmented into bone, soft-tissue, and air. *Keereman et al. 2010 J. Nucl. Med. 51(5) 812, https:// doi.org/ 10.2967/ jnumed.109.065425.*

very time-consuming and thus automatic segmentation methods have naturally been employed.

4.2.1.2 Automatic segmentation

Segmenting MR images for PET attenuation correction was already a topic of interest in the 1990s: Le Goff et al. [7] segmented brain T1-weighted (T1w) MR images based on thresholding and mathematical morphology tools. Later, Martínez-Möller et al. [8] used thresholding to segment the body into four classes: background, lungs, fat and soft-tissues. They relied on a specific MRI sequence, the Dixon method, which exploits the fact that water and fat protons have slightly different resonance frequencies. By acquiring images when their spins are in and out of phase with each other, water and fat images can be derived [9]. In this work [8], a threshold was applied to the water and fat images to separate soft-tissue and fat from the background. Connected-component analysis of the air in the inner part of the body was used to define the lung class. The tissue/air classification was refined using a morphologic closing filter. Catana et al. [10] and Keereman et al. [11] also used a particular MRI sequence to segment head images into three classes (bone, soft-tissue, and air), the ultra-short echo time (UTE) sequence. Two images, UTE_1 and UTE_2, were acquired at different echo times, TE_1 and TE_2, respectively, such that the bone signal is present in UTE_1 but not in UTE_2, while the signals from other tissues are similar in both images. In [10], a head mask was first obtained by applying a morphologic closing operation to the UTE_2 image. Bone tissue was segmented from a combination of the two UTE images $\left(\frac{UTE_1 - UTE_2}{UTE_2{}^2}\right)$ using an empirically determined threshold. The air cavities were segmented in the same way but from another combination of the UTE images $\left(\frac{UTE_1 + UTE_2}{UTE_1{}^2}\right)$. Finally, the voxels included in the head mask that were not identified as bone or air were classified as soft-tissue. From the two UTE images, in [11] the R2* value, which is the inverse of the T2* relaxation time, was first calculated for each voxel as follows: $R2* = \frac{\ln UTE_1 - \ln UTE_2}{TE_2 - TE_1}$. It was then possible to distinguish between cortical bone, which is expected to have high R2* values, from soft-tissue, expected to have low R2* values. The distinction between air and tissue is, however, more difficult because of possible artifacts or noise in the UTE images. To overcome this problem, a binary air mask was created from the first-echo image (UTE_1) and applied to the R2* map. Finally, the corrected R2* map was segmented into three tissue classes (bone, soft-tissue, and air) using thresholds. The method is illustrated in Fig. 4.3. Refinements for the R2* map segmentation were later proposed [12]. Combining cortical bone segmentation and water–fat decomposition, Berker et al. [13] proposed a 4-class (bone, soft-tissue, fat, and air) segmentation technique using a UTE triple-echo sequence. The combination of the first and third echoes, both in-phase, was used to segment cortical bone, while the combination of the second echo, out-of-phase, with the in-phase echoes enabled the separation of the fat and water signals and the calculation of the water–fat fraction. Bone was then segmented using an empirically determined threshold.

The fuzzy c-means (FCM) algorithm was implemented in several works. This unsupervised method generalizes the k-means algorithm by allowing each data point to belong to multiple clusters with varying degrees of membership [14]. This is, for example, the case of Zaidi et al. [15], who applied the FCM algorithm on T1w spin-echo images to segment air, brain tissue, skull, nasal sinuses, and scalp. Some manual intervention of the operator was required to refine the segmentation of the skull. Later, Hsu et al. [16] applied it to segment a set of MR images (T1w, T2w, Dixon, and UTE) into five tissue classes (fluid, fat, white matter, gray matter, and bone). Su et al. [17] followed a similar idea but reduced the inputs to a single acquisition UTE-mDixon sequence. The three images derived from this sequence (fat, water, and R2*) were used as inputs for an FCM algorithm aiming at identifying five clusters (air, brain, fat, fluid, and bone). They later extended the approach to thorax synthetic CT generation [18]. Instead of the UTE sequence, Khateri et al. [19] proposed to use a short echo time sequence, combined with a Dixon sequence, to segment the head in four tissue classes using FCM. Active learning-based classification was proposed in [20] to refine segmentations obtained with fuzzy clustering.

Other segmentation approaches have also been used. A knowledge-based segmentation approach consisting of three steps was proposed in [21]. First, tissues were segmented using a supervised neural network-based classification. The brain and extracerebral region were then separated based on anatomical knowledge: it is known that the brain soft-tissue is surrounded by cerebrospinal fluid which is in turn surrounded by the extracerebral region, while the extracerebral region is surrounded by the background region. Anatomical knowledge was finally used to segment the extracerebral region into the mastoid process, craniofacial cavities, bone, and soft-tissue, based, for example, on the fact that air-filled cavities are compact and connected by small junctions, while bone regions are narrow and elongated. Schulz et al. [22] based their 3-class (air, soft-tissue, and lung) segmentation method on a T1w sequence. The body was first extracted from the background using slice-wise region growing with an automatically determined threshold, and another region growing was performed to segment the lungs. Instead of segmenting MR images, the use of non-attenuation corrected (NAC)-PET images was investigated in [23]. The 3-class segmentation consisted of segmenting the NAC-PET to derive a first attenuation map, using this map to correct the raw PET data for attenuation, and refining the segmentation using the newly reconstructed PET image. This process was repeated to first segment the body contour, then segment the lungs, and finally refine the lung segmentation. Instead of segmenting the skull in image space, Yang et al. [24] proposed a skull segmentation method for T1w MR images via a multiscale bilateral filtering processing of MRI sinogram data in the Radon domain. This segmentation method was combined with a multiscale FCM approach to classify the other tissues. In [25], air, bone, and soft-tissue were segmented from brain UTE images using a multi-phase level-set approach. This active contour strategy allows segmenting images with more than two regions [26]. Finally, a 3D deep convolutional neural network (DeepMedic [27]) was trained in [28] to segment air, water, fat, and bone from T2w and Dixon images of the pelvis.

4.2.2 Intensity assignment approaches

Once the input image has been segmented, meaningful intensities must be assigned to each tissue class in order to obtain the synthetic image of interest.

4.2.2.1 Segmentation methods with bulk assignment

The simplest way to obtain a synthetic image from a segmented image is to assign predefined intensity values to each tissue class. This can be easily done when generating CT images as their voxels are displayed in terms of relative radiodensity expressed in Hounsfield units (HU). For example, air has an attenuation of -1000 HU, fat between -120 and -90 HU, water of 0 HU, and cortical bone between 500 and 1900 HU. In their work illustrated in Fig. 4.2, Jonsson et al. [4] assigned mass densities of 1.33 g/cm^3 to femoral bone, 1.025 g/cm^3 to soft-tissue and 0.001 g/cm^3 to air.

4.2.2.2 Segmentation methods with subject-specific assignment

The main drawback of assigning predefined values to the different tissue classes is that subject variability is not taken into account, which limits synthesis accuracy. This is particularly important in the MRI-to-CT image synthesis scenario for the bone region as it is known that several factors, such as age, can affect bone density [29, 30]. To overcome this limitation, several groups explored the possible existence of a mapping between the CT HU and MRI intensities, particularly R2* values in the bone region. If the ability of CT imaging to determine bone mineral content has been known for a long time [31], several studies showed that MR imaging could also provide some useful information. It was, for example, demonstrated using the UTE

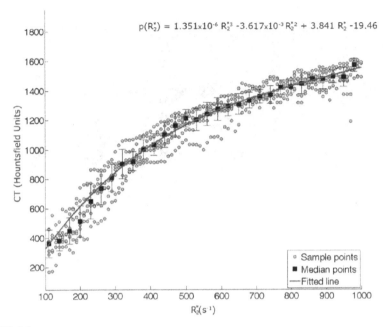

FIGURE 4.4

Illustration of how MR intensity values can be converted into CT Hounsfield units (HU) for subject-specific intensity assignment [33]. R2* versus HU scatter plot with sampled points are shown for each of the ten patients in gray. Every third median bin-value is shown with black squares. Standard deviation to the mean value is shown with black error bars. A 3rd-order polynomial fit to the median points is shown with the blue (dark gray in print version) line (goodness of fit $r^2 = 0.93$). *Ladefoged et al. 2015 Phys. Med. Biol. 60 8047, https://doi.org/10.1088/0031-9155/60/20/8047 © Institute of Physics and Engineering in Medicine. Reproduced by permission of IOP Publishing. All rights reserved.*

sequence that the water bound to the collagen in cortical bone (higher density) has a shorter spin–spin relaxation time T2 than the water present in the porous regions of cortical bone (lower density) [32]. As T2* includes T2 relaxation, it is expected that changes in R2* values (R2* = 1/T2*) would reflect changes in bone density.

Kapanen et al. [34] exploited in-phase images from a Dixon sequence to model the relation between MR intensity and HU within bone by fitting a second order polynomial. Pseudo-CTs were generated by manually contouring the MR images, converting MR intensity values into HU within bone, and assigning to the other tissue classes a value of 0 HU.

Juttukonda et al. [35] acquired dual UTE and Dixon sequences from which they derived R2*, fat, water, and UTE$_1$ images used to segment bone, fat, soft-tissue, and air, respectively, based on simple thresholding. Predefined linear attenuation co-efficients were then assigned to the air, fat, and soft-tissues classes, while tissues

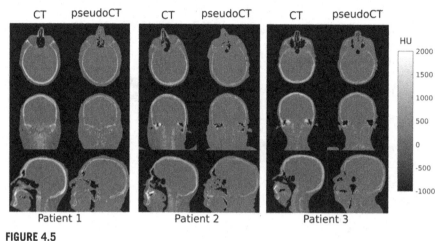

FIGURE 4.5

Three examples of CT images and ZTE-based pseudo-CTs generated using the segmentation algorithm and the linear relationship between normalized ZTE intensity and CT density in Hounsfield units (HU) described in [38]. *Khalifé et al. 2017 Phys. Med. Biol. 62 7814, https://doi.org/10.1088/0031-9155/60/20/8047 © Institute of Physics and Engineering in Medicine. Reproduced by permission of IOP Publishing. All rights reserved.*

classified as bone were converted to HU using a regression model between the R2* values and HU. Several steps were necessary to obtain this model. First, the CT and R2* images of several subjects were aligned, and bone was segmented in both modalities using thresholds. To reduce noise, the R2* values were divided into bins. The mean R2* values and HU were then computed and plotted for each bin. Finally, a sigmoid model was fit to the data.

Ladefoged et al. [33] also acquired and used UTE images to extract a continuous bone signal for each patient and map R2* values to HU. The model was, however, different as a third-order polynomial was fit instead of a sigmoid, see Fig. 4.4. This could be explained by the lower threshold chosen for included bone and the different formula used to compute the R2* map. In addition to the R2*-to-HU mapping, they proposed to improve the attenuation map generation using regional masks to separately treat complex areas with mixed air and tissue. These regional masks, defined on an atlas, were transported to the subject's space and used, in combination with the R2* values, to assign predefined attenuation coefficients to the frontal sinus, nasal septa and ethmoidal sinus, mastoid process, and skull base.

Other sequences have been exploited to convert MR intensities into CT HUs, mainly the zero echo-time (ZTE) sequence that allows capturing bone density variations [36–39]. A linear regression was used to convert ZTE-normalized to HU values in the skull [38] while a two-segment piecewise linear model was used in pelvic bone regions [39]. Examples of brain pseudo-CT images obtained with this approach are shown in Fig. 4.5.

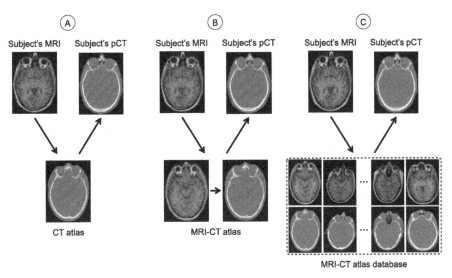

FIGURE 4.6

Registration-based approaches for image synthesis: direct multimodal (A) and indirect uni-modal (B) single-atlas registration, and (C) multi-atlas registration. The atlas is composed of (A) a single CT image, (B) a pair of MRI and CT images, and (C) multiple pairs of MRI and CT images.

4.3 Registration-based image synthesis

In registration-based methods, an atlas is deformed to match the subject's anatomy using non-rigid registration. If we keep as use case MRI-to-CT image synthesis, the atlas can be composed of a single CT image, of a pair of MR and CT images, or of multiple pairs of MR and CT images, as illustrated in Fig. 4.6. The principle was first introduced in 1993 by Miller et al. [40].

4.3.1 Single-atlas registration approaches

4.3.1.1 Direct multimodal registration

When the atlas is composed of only one image of the target modality, a synthetic image is generated by directly registering the atlas to the source image of the subject of interest. The registration is thus multimodal. Schreibmann et al. [41] developed a multimodality optical flow deformable model mapping a representative CT template directly to the subject's MR image, thus generating a simulated CT image that matches the patient's anatomy. Multimodal inter-subject being the most challenging registration scenario, very few studies implemented a direct registration image synthesis approach.

4.3.1.2 Indirect unimodal registration

The majority of single-atlas registration approaches use an atlas composed of a pair of images: an image of the source contrast/modality and an image of the target contrast/modality. The source atlas image is registered to the subject's source image and the resulting transformation is applied to the target atlas image to generate the subject's target image. The atlas can be obtained from a single individual but is most often obtained by averaging the images of multiple individuals. Long before the introduction of PET/MR scanners, researchers were already developing image synthesis approaches for attenuation correction. Huang et al. [42] did so in 1997 using a pair of transmission and emission scans as atlas. They proposed an inter-subject registration method to align the emission scan of the atlas to that of the target subject. The resulting transformation was then used to align the transmission scan of the atlas and generate a transmission scan for the subject under investigation.

Ten years later, Kops et al. [43] built a transmission-MRI atlas from the transmission and MR images of normal volunteers that were spatially normalized and averaged using the Statistical Parametric Mapping version 2 (SPM2)[1] software. To generate the subject's transmission image, the MRI atlas was registered to the subject's MR image and the same transformation was applied to the transmission atlas. With this method, it is possible to take into account morphological differences related to gender using female and male templates [44]. Downling et al. [45] proposed to generate a pseudo-CT image by registering an MRI atlas, result of a groupwise registration, to the subject's MR image and applying the same transformation to a CT atlas aligned to the MRI atlas. Izquierdo-Garcia et al. [46] generated attenuation maps using the SPM8 software. The initial step of the method consisted of creating MRI and CT atlases. To do so, T1w MR images were first segmented into six tissue classes (gray matter, white matter, cerebrospinal fluid, bone, soft-tissue, and air) using SPM. The segmented images were then non-rigidly co-registered using Dartel [47] to form the MRI atlas. The same transformations were applied to the CT images, previously affinely aligned with the T1w images, and the CT atlas was created by averaging the co-registered CT images. To generate a pseudo-CT, the MR image of the subject of interest is segmented into six tissue classes and non-rigidly registered to the MRI atlas. The associated CT atlas is finally mapped into the subject's space by applying the inverse transformation.

4.3.2 Multi-atlas registration approaches

The methods described in the previous section rely on a single atlas and strongly depend on the accuracy of the mapping between the atlas and subject spaces and on the representativeness of the atlas. A possible solution to improve the representativeness of the atlas and limit the consequences of mis-registrations is to use multiple atlases.

The multi-atlas methods reported below rely on a database of CT and MRI pairs. Each pair is created by registering the CT and MR images of a subject. To generate

---

[1] http://www.fil.ion.ucl.ac.uk.

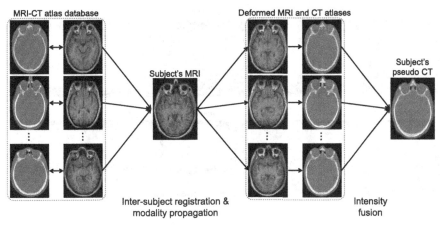

FIGURE 4.7

Multi-atlas registration approach to generate a pseudo-CT from an MR image. All the MR images in the atlas database are registered to the subject's MR image. The CTs in the atlas database are then mapped using the same transformation to the subject's MR image. The subject's pseudo-CT image is obtained by fusing the deformed atlas CT images.

a pseudo-CT from the subject's MR image, the MR images from the database are non-rigidly registered to the subject's MRI. The CTs in the database are then mapped to the target subject using the transformation that maps the subject's corresponding MRI in the atlas database to the subject's MRI. A final step consists in fusing the deformed CT images. The approach is illustrated in Fig. 4.7.

To fuse the deformed CTs, Sjolund et al. [48] proposed an iterative registration to the mean. The consistency of the deformed CTs was improved by iteratively forming their voxelwise mean, registering each deformed CT to the mean, and creating a new mean estimate. However, it appeared that better results were reached by directly taking the voxelwise median of the deformed CTs. Instead of computing the voxelwise median, Burgos et al. [49] obtained a pseudo-CT by computing a weighted-average of the deformed CTs. The weights were derived from a local similarity measure computed between the MR image of the subject of interest and the MR images of the atlases. This image similarity measure reflects the morphological similarity, meaning that more weight is given to the atlases that are the most similar in terms of morphology to the subject of interest. This approach can generate pseudo-CT images from a single [49] or multiple [50] MRI contrasts in the brain [49,50], head & neck [6,51], and pelvic [6] regions; see the examples in Fig. 4.8. A similar approach was implemented in [52]. Merida et al. [53] looked at the probability of a voxel in the subject space to belong to a certain tissue class. Three tissue classes (air, soft-tissue, and bone) were defined by intensity thresholding the deformed CTs. The intensity value of the pseudo-CT was determined by averaging for each voxel the CT intensities of the atlases belonging to the maximum probability class.

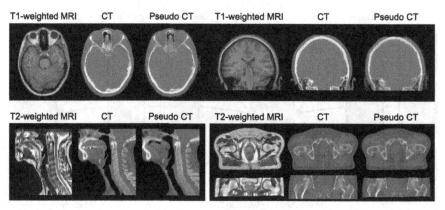

FIGURE 4.8

Examples of pseudo-CT images obtained from MR images with a multi-atlas registration approach [6,49,51] in the brain (top), head & neck (bottom left), and pelvis (bottom right).

4.3.3 Combination of registration and regression approaches

To increase synthesis accuracy, several groups proposed to combine multi-atlas registration and regression approaches.

In the seminal work of Hofmann et al. [54], local information derived from a supervised learning technique and global information obtained from multi-atlas registration were combined to predict a pseudo-CT image: multi-atlas registration was used as prior knowledge for a Gaussian process regression. The global step of the method consisted of non-rigidly registering the MR images from the training dataset to the subject's MR image and applying the same transformations to the corresponding CT images in the training dataset. The local step aimed at determining a mapping between MR image patches centered at a voxel of interest and the real CT HU values using Gaussian process regression. Training pairs comprising the position of the voxel in the subject coordinate system and the patch surrounding it were extracted from the deformed images in the training dataset. Prior knowledge from the atlas registration was included by setting the mean function of the Gaussian process to the average value of the registered CT images. For an unseen patch, Gaussian process regression returned a Gaussian-distributed predictive distribution for the mapping of the MR patches to the CT HU. Finally, to predict a pseudo-CT image for a new subject, for each voxel of the MR image a surrounding patch was extracted and the mean of the Gaussian-distributed predictive distribution was defined as the estimated CT value. The method was also adapted to whole-body attenuation correction [55].

A similar approach combining intensity and geometry information into a unifying probabilistic Bayesian framework was later proposed [56]. The method implemented in [57] relies on a database of co-registered T1w MR images, CT images, and air masks segmented from the CT images using k-means clustering. Pseudo-CT generation required three steps. First, each atlas was non-rigidly registered to the subject's MR image. A probabilistic air mask was then computed as the percentage of the aligned CT atlases that labeled a voxel as air, and refined using a hidden Markov random field segmentation on the T1w MR image. Each voxel labeled as air was assigned the mean value of the atlas CTs belonging to the air mask. For the rest of the tissues, small neighborhoods centered around each voxel were defined in the target. Patches of the same size were defined in the atlases in the vicinity of the central voxel. Sparse regression was then used to select the most similar patches, in terms of intensity, among all the atlas patches within the search window. Finally, the sparse coefficients were applied to combine the atlas CTs and generate the pseudo-CT. More details on the use of dictionary learning for image synthesis can be found in Chapter 5.

4.4 Hybrid approaches combining segmentation and registration

The methods described in this section combine both image segmentation and registration to generate synthetic images.

Bezrukov et al. [58] proposed a method combining segmentation, multi-atlas registration and supervised learning techniques, which relied on the subject's Dixon images and on an atlas database. Each atlas comprised a 5-tissue class segmentation (outer air, lung, fat tissue, non-fat tissue, and fat/non-fat tissue mix), a map of potential artifact locations extracted from regions with low MR intensity and differentiated into air-filled regions not part of the lungs and soft-tissue regions, a CT image, and a bone location map. After segmentation of the subject's MR image into five tissue classes, the segmented MR images from the atlas database were registered to the subject's image and the resulting transformations were applied to the images forming the atlases. A subject-specific map of potential artifact locations was created by averaging the atlas artifact maps. This map was used to classify the low MRI intensity regions as inside air or soft-tissue masked by artifacts. Predefined linear attenuation coefficients were assigned to the segmented regions of the MR image to create an intermediate attenuation map. For the prediction of bone tissue, a map of potential bone locations was created from the atlas CT images by combining the individual bone location maps. This map determined the areas where Gaussian process regression was applied. For each voxel within these areas, a pseudo-CT value was computed from the CT atlases and converted to linear attenuation coefficients using a piecewise linear transformation. The final attenuation map was created by augmenting the intermediate attenuation map with the predicted bone linear attenuation coefficients.

Combining the segmentation of an MR image and the use of a CT image database, Marshall et al. [59] proposed a method where the subject's MR image was compared to an atlas database of CT images using a set of 19 similarity metrics such as gender, age, and body, lung, and bone geometries. The most similar CT image was selected and non-rigidly aligned to the subject's MR image. Bones from the registered CT

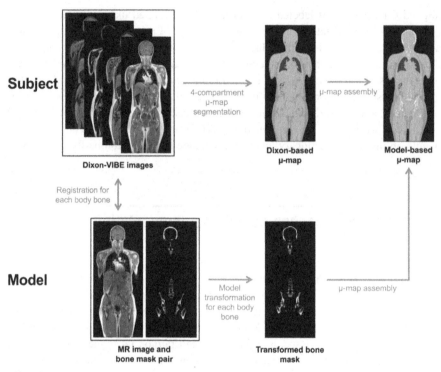

FIGURE 4.9

Schematic drawing of the hybrid segmentation/registration-based approach for considering bone in whole-body PET/MR attenuation correction [63]. The subject-specific attenuation map (μ-map) is generated by first segmenting the subject's Dixon images into four classes (air, lung, soft-tissue, and fat). The bone class is then added by registering the MR model to the subject for each bone individually and applying the same transformation to the bone mask. *Paulus et al. 2015 J. Nucl. Med. 56 1061, https://doi.org/10.2967/jnumed.115.156000.*

image were then added to the MR image previously segmented into four tissue classes (air, lung, fat and lean tissue).

Exploiting multiple MRI sequences, Anazodo et al. [60] proposed to overlay a bone mask to the attenuation map obtained from the segmentation of Dixon images [8]. The bone mask was created by segmenting a T1w MR image using the *New Segment* function from SPM8 [61]. SPM has also been used in [62].

The method implemented by Paulus et al. [63], illustrated in Fig. 4.9, was based on a regular 4-class segmentation from a Dixon sequence and atlas-based bone segmentation algorithm. The atlas was composed of pairs of pre-aligned MR image and bone mask (containing bone densities) for each major bone in the body, including left and right upper femur, left and right hip, spine, and skull. To generate a subject-specific attenuation map, the subject's Dixon images were first segmented into four classes (air, lung, soft-tissue, and fat). The bone class was then added by registering the MR model to the subject for each bone individually and applying the same transformation to the bone mask. The method was then validated in the brain region [64].

In their work, Arabi et al. [65] combined multi-atlas segmentation and synthesis with the aim to improve the synthesis of CT images from MRI in the bone region. Their framework consisted of two steps. In the first, bone was segmented using multi-atlas segmentation. In the second, a pseudo-CT was generated using a multi-atlas approach, the atlases being fused based on the resemblance of both the bone map obtained at the first step and the morphological similarity to the MR image of the subject being analyzed.

4.5 Future directions and research challenges

In this chapter, we covered image synthesis approaches that rely on well-established image processing techniques, namely segmentation and registration. The vast majority of these approaches have been applied to the synthesis of CT from MR images. This can be explained by two reasons. First, these image synthesis approaches were developed to answer particular needs: that of accurate electron density estimation when only MR images are available, which occurs in the context of both PET/MR attenuation correction (see Chapter 19) and MRI-only RTP (see Chapter 20). The second reason is that their accuracy appears limited on other tasks, which is why they have been supplanted by better performing methods.

The development of MR-to-CT image synthesis approaches followed the development of new technologies. Regarding attenuation correction, even though first attempts of synthesizing attenuation maps date back to the 1990s [42], many works have accompanied the release of PET/MR scanners (2010 for Philips and Siemens Healthineers, 2011 for GE Healthcare). Prototypes of MR-Linac date back to the same period [66]. These technological developments led to new problems, namely the fact that MR image intensities do not directly provide information about the tissue attenuation properties, to which image synthesis was proposed as a solution.

Segmentation-based methods essentially rely on the subject's MR images. This explains why specific sequences such as the Dixon, UTE, or ZTE, often only acquired for the purpose of image synthesis, have been employed. Various segmentation strategies have been implemented: manual segmentation, mainly in the context of RTP and/or as proof of concept, and a large range of automatic methods that include mainly intensity thresholding and fuzzy c-means. Initially, once segmented, predefined values were often assigned to each tissue class, but subject-specific assignments have shown their superiority, especially in bone regions. A limitation of segmentation methods is the difficulty in delineating tissues in regions with air/tissue and air/bone interfaces. Another one is their susceptibility to MR image artifacts.

Registration-based methods rely on both the subject's MR images and on an atlas or database of atlases. The first methods developed relied on a single atlas to generate a subject-specific attenuation map. Their accuracy was limited as a single template can hardly be representative of all the potential patients, even if they do not present morphological abnormalities. These methods also strongly depend on the accuracy of the registration used to map the atlas to the target subject. A solution to both improve the representativeness of the atlas and reduce the impact of registration inaccuracies has been to use a database of atlases. However, this comes with the price of having to run multiple, time-consuming, non-rigid registrations. Another limitation is the limited ability of these methods to handle anatomical abnormalities (e.g., unusual bone density).

The second reason that can explain the use of segmentation and registration-based approaches to only MR-to-CT image synthesis is that their accuracy appears limited on other tasks. Jog et al. [67], for example, compared a multi-atlas registration approach with their random forest regression method for the synthesis of T2w from T1w MR images and of FLAIR from T1-, T2-, and proton density-weighted MR images, and observed that the multi-atlas registration approach led to blurrier images from which lesions were barely visible. Multi-atlas registration has, nonetheless, successfully been used to generate pseudo-healthy PET images from T1w MR images [68,69]. Many techniques have now supplanted segmentation and registration-based approaches, starting with patch-based methods that do not require non-rigid alignment between the training and target subjects (more in Chapter 5) until the nowadays highly predominant deep learning approaches (more in Chapters 6, 7 and 8).

Interested readers can find further information in several reviews and comparison articles. In the context of RTP, approaches that exist to generate synthetic CT images have been reviewed, for example, in [70–72] while their performance has been compared in [73,74]. Several reviews have been published over the years regarding image synthesis for attenuation correction [75–80], and Ladefoged et al. [81] published a multi-center study aiming at evaluating the performance of various attenuation correction methods, including five segmentation-based [8,10,12,33,35], three atlas-based [46,49,53], and two hybrid approaches combining segmentation and use of an atlas [60,64].

4.6 Summary

Even though medical image synthesis can be used to improve subsequent image processing techniques such as segmentation or registration, in this chapter we saw how segmentation and registration could themselves be used for image synthesis. Segmentation-based approaches consist in segmenting the source image, either manually or automatically, and assigning intensity values to the different tissue classes obtained, using bulk or subject-specific assignment, to generate the desired image. Registration-based methods consist in deforming an atlas, composed of a single image, a pair of images or multiple pairs, to match the subject's anatomy using non-rigid registration. Most segmentation- and registration-based image synthesis approaches have been used to synthesize CT from MR images in the context of PET(/MR) attenuation correction and MRI-only radiotherapy treatment planning. Even though these techniques helped answer concrete needs, they have now been supplanted by deep learning methods.

Acknowledgments

Funding has been received from the French government under management of Agence Nationale de la Recherche as part of the "Investissements d'avenir" programme reference ANR-10-IAIHU-06 (Agence Nationale de la Recherche-10-IA Institut Hospitalo-Universitaire-6).

References

[1] E.B. van de Kraats, G.P. Penney, T. van Walsum, W.J. Niessen, Multispectral MR to X-ray registration of vertebral bodies by generating CT-like data, in: J.S. Duncan, G. Gerig (Eds.), Medical Image Computing and Computer-Assisted Intervention – MICCAI 2005, in: Lecture Notes in Computer Science, Springer, 2005, pp. 911–918.

[2] S. Roy, A. Carass, N. Shiee, D.L. Pham, J.L. Prince, MR contrast synthesis for lesion segmentation, in: 2010 IEEE International Symposium on Biomedical Imaging: From Nano to Macro, 2010, pp. 932–935.

[3] J.L. Prince, A. Carass, C. Zhao, B.E. Dewey, S. Roy, D.L. Pham, Image synthesis and superresolution in medical imaging, in: S.K. Zhou, D. Rueckert, G. Fichtinger (Eds.), Handbook of Medical Image Computing and Computer Assisted Intervention, Academic Press, 2020, pp. 1–24.

[4] J.H. Jonsson, M.G. Karlsson, M. Karlsson, T. Nyholm, Treatment planning using MRI data: an analysis of the dose calculation accuracy for different treatment regions, Radiation Oncology 5 (2010) 62.

[5] J. Korhonen, M. Kapanen, J. Keyriläinen, T. Seppälä, M. Tenhunen, A dual model HU conversion from MRI intensity values within and outside of bone segment for MRI-based radiotherapy treatment planning of prostate cancer, Medical Physics 41 (1) (2014) 011704.

[6] F. Guerreiro, N. Burgos, A. Dunlop, K. Wong, I. Petkar, C. Nutting, K. Harrington, S. Bhide, K. Newbold, D. Dearnaley, N.M. deSouza, V.A. Morgan, J. McClelland, S. Nill, M.J. Cardoso, S. Ourselin, U. Oelfke, A.C. Knopf, Evaluation of a multi-atlas CT synthesis approach for MRI-only radiotherapy treatment planning, Physica Medica 35 (2017) 7–17.

[7] R. Le Goff-Rougetet, V. Frouin, J.-F. Mangin, B. Bendriem, Segmented MR images for brain attenuation correction in PET, in: Medical Imaging 1994, 1994, pp. 725–736.

[8] A. Martinez-Möller, M. Souvatzoglou, G. Delso, R.A. Bundschuh, C. Chefd'hotel, S.I. Ziegler, N. Navab, M. Schwaiger, S.G. Nekolla, Tissue classification as a potential approach for attenuation correction in whole-body PET/MRI: evaluation with PET/CT data, Journal of Nuclear Medicine 50 (4) (2009) 520–526.

[9] W.T. Dixon, Simple proton spectroscopic imaging, Radiology 153 (1) (1984) 189–194.

[10] C. Catana, A. van der Kouwe, T. Benner, C.J. Michel, M. Hamm, M. Fenchel, B. Fischl, B. Rosen, M. Schmand, A.G. Sorensen, Toward implementing an MRI-based PET attenuation-correction method for neurologic studies on the MR-PET brain prototype, Journal of Nuclear Medicine 51 (9) (2010) 1431–1438.

[11] V. Keereman, Y. Fierens, T. Broux, Y. De Deene, M. Lonneux, S. Vandenberghe, MRI-based attenuation correction for PET/MRI using ultrashort echo time sequences, Journal of Nuclear Medicine 51 (5) (2010) 812–818.

[12] J. Cabello, M. Lukas, S. Förster, T. Pyka, S.G. Nekolla, S.I. Ziegler, MR-based attenuation correction using ultrashort-echo-time pulse sequences in dementia patients, Journal of Nuclear Medicine 56 (3) (2015) 423–429.

[13] Y. Berker, J. Franke, A. Salomon, M. Palmowski, H.C.W. Donker, Y. Temur, F.M. Mottaghy, C. Kuhl, D. Izquierdo-Garcia, Z.A. Fayad, F. Kiessling, V. Schulz, MRI-based attenuation correction for hybrid PET/MRI systems: a 4-class tissue segmentation technique using a combined ultrashort-echo-time/Dixon MRI sequence, Journal of Nuclear Medicine 53 (5) (2012) 796–804.

[14] J.C. Bezdek, Pattern Recognition with Fuzzy Objective Function Algorithms, Advanced Applications in Pattern Recognition, Springer US, 1981.

[15] H. Zaidi, M.-L. Montandon, D.O. Slosman, Magnetic resonance imaging-guided attenuation and scatter corrections in three-dimensional brain positron emission tomography, Medical Physics 30 (5) (2003) 937–948.

[16] S.-H. Hsu, Y. Cao, K. Huang, M. Feng, J.M. Balter, Investigation of a method for generating synthetic CT models from MRI scans of the head and neck for radiation therapy, Physics in Medicine and Biology 58 (23) (2013) 8419.

[17] K.-H. Su, L. Hu, C. Stehning, M. Helle, P. Qian, C.L. Thompson, G.C. Pereira, D.W. Jordan, K.A. Herrmann, M. Traughber, R.F. Muzic, B.J. Traughber, Generation of brain pseudo-CTs using an undersampled, single-acquisition UTE-mDixon pulse sequence and unsupervised clustering, Medical Physics 42 (8) (2015) 4974–4986.

[18] K.-H. Su, H.T. Friel, J.-W. Kuo, R.A. Helo, A. Baydoun, C. Stehning, A.N. Crisan, M.S. Traughber, A. Devaraj, D.W. Jordan, P. Qian, A. Leisser, R.J. Ellis, K.A. Herrmann, N. Avril, B.J. Traughber, R.F. Muzic, UTE-mDixon-based thorax synthetic CT generation, Medical Physics 46 (8) (2019) 3520–3531.

[19] P. Khateri, H.S. Rad, A.H. Jafari, A.F. Kazerooni, A. Akbarzadeh, M.S. Moghadam, A. Aryan, P. Ghafarian, M.R. Ay, Generation of a four-class attenuation map for MRI-based attenuation correction of PET data in the head area using a novel combination of STE/Dixon-MRI and FCM clustering, Molecular Imaging and Biology 17 (6) (2015) 884–892.

[20] P. Qian, Y. Chen, J. Kuo, Y. Zhang, Y. Jiang, K. Zhao, R.A. Helo, H. Friel, A. Baydoun, F. Zhou, J.U. Heo, N. Avril, K. Herrmann, R. Ellis, B. Traughber, R.S. Jones, S. Wang, K. Su, R.F. Muzic, mDixon-based synthetic CT generation for PET attenuation correction on abdomen and pelvis jointly using transfer fuzzy clustering and active learning-based classification, IEEE Transactions on Medical Imaging 39 (4) (2020) 819–832.

[21] G. Wagenknecht, E.R. Kops, L. Tellmann, H. Herzog, Knowledge-based segmentation of attenuation-relevant regions of the head in T1-weighted MR images for attenuation correction in MR/PET systems, in: Nuclear Science Symposium Conference Record, NSS'09, 2009, IEEE, 2009, pp. 3338–3343.

[22] V. Schulz, I. Torres-Espallardo, S. Renisch, Z. Hu, N. Ojha, P. Börnert, M. Perkuhn, T. Niendorf, W.M. Schäfer, H. Brockmann, T. Krohn, A. Buhl, R.W. Günther, F.M. Mottaghy, G.A. Krombach, Automatic, three-segment, MR-based attenuation correction for

whole-body PET/MR data, European Journal of Nuclear Medicine and Molecular Imaging 38 (1) (2011) 138–152.

[23] T. Chang, R.H. Diab, J.W. Clark Jr., O.R. Mawlawi, Investigating the use of nonattenuation corrected PET images for the attenuation correction of PET data, Medical Physics 40 (8) (2013) 082508.

[24] X. Yang, B. Fei, Multiscale segmentation of the skull in MR images for MRI-based attenuation correction of combined MR/PET, Journal of the American Medical Informatics Association 20 (6) (2013) 1037–1045.

[25] H.J. An, S. Seo, H. Kang, H. Choi, G.J. Cheon, H.-J. Kim, D.S. Lee, I.C. Song, Y.K. Kim, J.S. Lee, MRI-based attenuation correction for PET/MRI using multiphase level-set method, Journal of Nuclear Medicine 57 (4) (2016) 587–593.

[26] L.A. Vese, T.F. Chan, A multiphase level set framework for image segmentation using the Mumford and Shah model, International Journal of Computer Vision 50 (3) (2002) 271–293.

[27] K. Kamnitsas, C. Ledig, V. Newcombe, J. Simpson, A. Kane, D. Menon, D. Rueckert, B. Glocker, Efficient multi-scale 3D CNN with fully connected CRF for accurate brain lesion segmentation, Medical Image Analysis 36 (2017) 61–78.

[28] T.J. Bradshaw, G. Zhao, H. Jang, F. Liu, A.B. McMillan, Feasibility of deep learning-based PET/MR attenuation correction in the pelvis using only diagnostic MR images, Tomography 4 (3) (2018) 138–147.

[29] A.M. Fehily, R.J. Coles, W.D. Evans, P.C. Elwood, Factors affecting bone density in young adults, The American Journal of Clinical Nutrition 56 (3) (1992) 579–586.

[30] C. Schulte-Geers, M. Obert, R. Schilling, S. Harth, H. Traupe, E. Gizewski, M. Verhoff, Age and gender-dependent bone density changes of the human skull disclosed by high-resolution flat-panel computed tomography, International Journal of Legal Medicine 125 (3) (2011) 417–425.

[31] N.E. Reich, F.E. Seidelmann, R. Tubbs, W.J. Mac Intyre, T. Meaney, R. Alfidi, R. Pepe, Determination of bone mineral content using CT scanning, American Journal of Roentgenology 127 (4) (1976) 593–594.

[32] R.A. Horch, J.S. Nyman, D.F. Gochberg, R.D. Dortch, M.D. Does, Characterization of ^{1}H NMR signal in human cortical bone for magnetic resonance imaging, Magnetic Resonance in Medicine 64 (3) (2010) 680–687.

[33] C.N. Ladefoged, D. Benoit, I. Law, S. Holm, A. Kjær, L. Højgaard, A.E. Hansen, F.L. Andersen, Region specific optimization of continuous linear attenuation coefficients based on UTE (RESOLUTE): application to PET/MR brain imaging, Physics in Medicine and Biology 60 (20) (2015) 8047.

[34] M. Kapanen, M. Tenhunen, T1/T2*-weighted MRI provides clinically relevant pseudo-CT density data for the pelvic bones in MRI-only based radiotherapy treatment planning, Acta Oncologica 52 (3) (2013) 612–618.

[35] M.R. Juttukonda, B.G. Mersereau, Y. Chen, Y. Su, B.G. Rubin, T.L. Benzinger, D.S. Lalush, H. An, MR-based attenuation correction for PET/MRI neurological studies with continuous-valued attenuation coefficients for bone through a conversion from R2* to CT-Hounsfield units, NeuroImage 112 (2015) 160–168.

[36] F. Wiesinger, L.I. Sacolick, A. Menini, S.S. Kaushik, S. Ahn, P. Veit-Haibach, G. Delso, D.D. Shanbhag, Zero TE MR bone imaging in the head, Magnetic Resonance in Medicine 75 (1) (2016) 107–114.

[37] C. Huang, J. Ouyang, T. Reese, Y. Wu, G. El Fakhri, J. Ackerman, Continuous MR bone density measurement using water-and fat-suppressed projection imaging (WASPI) for

PET attenuation correction in PET-MR, Physics in Medicine and Biology 60 (20) (2015) N369.

[38] M. Khalifé, B. Fernandez, O. Jaubert, M. Soussan, V. Brulon, I. Buvat, C. Comtat, Subject-specific bone attenuation correction for brain PET/MR: can ZTE-MRI substitute CT scan accurately?, Physics in Medicine and Biology 62 (19) (2017) 7814.

[39] A.P. Leynes, J. Yang, D.D. Shanbhag, S.S. Kaushik, Y. Seo, T.A. Hope, F. Wiesinger, P.E.Z. Larson, Hybrid ZTE/Dixon MR-based attenuation correction for quantitative uptake estimation of pelvic lesions in PET/MRI, Medical Physics 44 (3) (2017) 902–913.

[40] M.I. Miller, G.E. Christensen, Y. Amit, U. Grenander, Mathematical textbook of deformable neuroanatomies, Proceedings of the National Academy of Sciences 90 (24) (1993) 11944–11948.

[41] E. Schreibmann, J.A. Nye, D.M. Schuster, D.R. Martin, J. Votaw, T. Fox, MR-based attenuation correction for hybrid PET-MR brain imaging systems using deformable image registration, Medical Physics 37 (5) (2010) 2101.

[42] C.-L. Huang, W.-T. Chang, L.-C. Wu, J.-K. Wang, Three-dimensional PET emission scan registration and transmission scan synthesis, IEEE Transactions on Medical Imaging 16 (5) (1997) 542–561.

[43] E.R. Kops, H. Herzog, Alternative methods for attenuation correction for PET images in MR-PET scanners, in: Nuclear Science Symposium Conference Record, vol. 6, NSS'07, 2007, IEEE, 2007, pp. 4327–4330.

[44] E.R. Kops, H. Herzog, Template based attenuation correction for PET in MR-PET scanners, in: Nuclear Science Symposium Conference Record, NSS'08, 2008, IEEE, 2008, pp. 3786–3789.

[45] J.A. Dowling, J. Lambert, J. Parker, O. Salvado, J. Fripp, A. Capp, C. Wratten, J.W. Denham, P.B. Greer, An atlas-based electron density mapping method for magnetic resonance imaging (MRI)-alone treatment planning and adaptive MRI-based prostate radiation therapy, International Journal of Radiation Oncology, Biology, Physics 83 (1) (2012) e5–e11.

[46] D. Izquierdo-Garcia, A.E. Hansen, S. Förster, D. Benoit, S. Schachoff, S. Fürst, K.T. Chen, D.B. Chonde, C. Catana, An SPM8-based approach for attenuation correction combining segmentation and nonrigid template formation: application to simultaneous PET/MR brain imaging, Journal of Nuclear Medicine 55 (11) (2014) 1825–1830.

[47] J. Ashburner, A fast diffeomorphic image registration algorithm, NeuroImage 38 (1) (2007) 95–113.

[48] J. Sjölund, D. Forsberg, M. Andersson, H. Knutsson, Generating patient specific pseudo-CT of the head from MR using atlas-based regression, Physics in Medicine and Biology 60 (2) (2015) 825.

[49] N. Burgos, M.J. Cardoso, K. Thielemans, M. Modat, S. Pedemonte, J. Dickson, A. Barnes, R. Ahmed, C.J. Mahoney, J.M. Schott, J.S. Duncan, D. Atkinson, S.R. Arridge, B.F. Hutton, S. Ourselin, Attenuation correction synthesis for hybrid PET-MR scanners: application to brain studies, IEEE Transactions on Medical Imaging 33 (12) (2014) 2332–2341.

[50] N. Burgos, M.J. Cardoso, K. Thielemans, M. Modat, J. Dickson, J.M. Schott, D. Atkinson, S.R. Arridge, B.F. Hutton, S. Ourselin, Multi-contrast attenuation map synthesis for PET/MR scanners: assessment on FDG and Florbetapir PET tracers, European Journal of Nuclear Medicine and Molecular Imaging 42 (9) (2015) 1447–1458.

[51] N. Burgos, M.J. Cardoso, F. Guerreiro, C. Veiga, M. Modat, J. McClelland, A. Knopf, S. Punwani, D. Atkinson, S.R. Arridge, B.F. Hutton, S. Ourselin, Robust CT synthesis for radiotherapy planning: application to the head & neck region, in: Medical Image Computing and Computer-Assisted Intervention – MICCAI 2015, 2015, pp. 476–484.

[52] J.A. Dowling, J. Sun, P. Pichler, D. Rivest-Hénault, S. Ghose, H. Richardson, C. Wratten, J. Martin, J. Arm, L. Best, S.S. Chandra, J. Fripp, F.W. Menk, P.B. Greer, Automatic substitute computed tomography generation and contouring for magnetic resonance imaging (MRI)-alone external beam radiation therapy from standard MRI sequences, International Journal of Radiation Oncology, Biology, Physics 93 (5) (2015) 1144–1153.

[53] I. Mérida, A. Reilhac, J. Redouté, R.A. Heckemann, N. Costes, A. Hammers, Multi-atlas attenuation correction supports full quantification of static and dynamic brain PET data in PET-MR, Physics in Medicine and Biology 62 (7) (2017) 2834.

[54] M. Hofmann, F. Steinke, V. Scheel, G. Charpiat, J. Farquhar, P. Aschoff, M. Brady, B. Schölkopf, B.J. Pichler, MRI-based attenuation correction for PET/MRI: a novel approach combining pattern recognition and atlas registration, Journal of Nuclear Medicine 49 (11) (2008) 1875–1883.

[55] M. Hofmann, I. Bezrukov, F. Mantlik, P. Aschoff, F. Steinke, T. Beyer, B.J. Pichler, B. Schölkopf, MRI-based attenuation correction for whole-body PET/MRI: quantitative evaluation of segmentation-and atlas-based methods, Journal of Nuclear Medicine 52 (9) (2011) 1392–1399.

[56] M.S.R. Gudur, W. Hara, Q.-T. Le, L. Wang, L. Xing, R. Li, A unifying probabilistic Bayesian approach to derive electron density from MRI for radiation therapy treatment planning, Physics in Medicine and Biology 59 (21) (2014) 6595.

[57] Y. Chen, M. Juttukonda, Y. Su, T. Benzinger, B.G. Rubin, Y.Z. Lee, W. Lin, D. Shen, D. Lalush, H. An, Probabilistic air segmentation and sparse regression estimated pseudo CT for PET/MR attenuation correction, Radiology 275 (2) (2015) 562–569.

[58] I. Bezrukov, H. Schmidt, F. Mantlik, N. Schwenzer, C. Brendle, B. Schölkopf, B.J. Pichler, MR-based attenuation correction methods for improved PET quantification in lesions within bone and susceptibility artifact regions, Journal of Nuclear Medicine 54 (10) (2013) 1768–1774.

[59] H.R. Marshall, J. Patrick, D. Laidley, F.S. Prato, J. Butler, J. Théberge, R.T. Thompson, R.Z. Stodilka, Description and assessment of a registration-based approach to include bones for attenuation correction of whole-body PET/MRI, Medical Physics 40 (8) (2013) 082509.

[60] U.C. Anazodo, J.D. Thiessen, T. Ssali, J. Mandel, M. Günther, J. Butler, W. Pavlosky, F.S. Prato, R.T. Thompson, K.S.S. Lawrence, Feasibility of simultaneous whole-brain imaging on an integrated PET-MRI system using an enhanced 2-point Dixon attenuation correction method, Frontiers in Neuroscience 8 (2015) 434.

[61] J. Ashburner, K.J. Friston, Unified segmentation, NeuroImage 26 (3) (2005) 839–851.

[62] J. Teuho, J. Linden, J. Johansson, J. Tuisku, T. Tuokkola, M. Teräs, Tissue probability-based attenuation correction for brain PET/MR by using SPM8, IEEE Transactions on Nuclear Science 63 (5) (2016) 2452–2463.

[63] D.H. Paulus, H.H. Quick, C. Geppert, M. Fenchel, Y. Zhan, G. Hermosillo, D. Faul, B. Fernando, K. Friedman, T. Koesters, Whole-body PET/MR imaging: quantitative evaluation of a novel model-based MR attenuation correction method including bone, Journal of Nuclear Medicine 56 (7) (2015) 1061–1066.

[64] T. Koesters, K.P. Friedman, M. Fenchel, Y. Zhan, G. Hermosillo, J. Babb, I.O. Jelescu, D. Faul, F.E. Boada, T.M. Shepherd, Dixon sequence with superimposed model-based bone compartment provides highly accurate PET/MR attenuation correction of the brain, Journal of Nuclear Medicine 57 (6) (2016) 918–924.

[65] H. Arabi, N. Koutsouvelis, M. Rouzaud, R. Miralbell, H. Zaidi, Atlas-guided generation of pseudo-CT images for MRI-only and hybrid PET–MRI-guided radiotherapy treatment planning, Physics in Medicine and Biology 61 (17) (2016) 6531.

[66] J.J. Lagendijk, B.W. Raaymakers, A.J. Raaijmakers, J. Overweg, K.J. Brown, E.M. Kerkhof, R.W. van der Put, B. Hårdemark, M. van Vulpen, U.A. van der Heide, MRI/linac integration, Radiotherapy and Oncology 86 (1) (2008) 25–29.

[67] A. Jog, A. Carass, S. Roy, D.L. Pham, J.L. Prince, Random forest regression for magnetic resonance image synthesis, Medical Image Analysis 35 (2017) 475–488.

[68] N. Burgos, M.J. Cardoso, A. Mendelson, J.M. Schott, D. Atkinson, S.R. Arridge, B.F. Hutton, S. Ourselin, Subject-specific models for the analysis of pathological FDG PET data, in: Medical Image Computing and Computer-Assisted Intervention – MICCAI 2015, 2015, pp. 651–658.

[69] N. Burgos, M.J. Cardoso, J. Samper-González, M.-O. Habert, S. Durrleman, S. Ourselin, O. Colliot, Anomaly detection for the individual analysis of brain PET images, Journal of Medical Imaging 8 (2) (2021) 024003.

[70] J.M. Edmund, T. Nyholm, A review of substitute CT generation for MRI-only radiation therapy, Radiation Oncology 12 (2017) 28.

[71] E. Johnstone, J.J. Wyatt, A.M. Henry, S.C. Short, D. Sebag-Montefiore, L. Murray, C.G. Kelly, H.M. McCallum, R. Speight, Systematic review of synthetic computed tomography generation methodologies for use in magnetic resonance imaging-only radiation therapy, International Journal of Radiation Oncology, Biology, Physics 100 (1) (2018) 199–217.

[72] J.A. Dowling, J. Korhonen, MR-only methodology, in: G. Liney, U. van der Heide (Eds.), MRI for Radiotherapy: Planning, Delivery, and Response Assessment, Springer, 2019, pp. 131–151.

[73] H. Arabi, J.A. Dowling, N. Burgos, X. Han, P.B. Greer, N. Koutsouvelis, H. Zaidi, Comparative study of algorithms for synthetic CT generation from MRI: consequences for MRI-guided radiation planning in the pelvic region, Medical Physics 45 (11) (2018) 5218–5233.

[74] A. Largent, A. Barateau, J.-C. Nunes, C. Lafond, P.B. Greer, J.A. Dowling, H. Saint-Jalmes, O. Acosta, R. de Crevoisier, Pseudo-CT generation for MRI-only radiation therapy treatment planning: comparison among patch-based, atlas-based, and bulk density methods, International Journal of Radiation Oncology, Biology, Physics 103 (2) (2019) 479–490.

[75] M. Hofmann, B. Pichler, B. Schölkopf, T. Beyer, Towards quantitative PET/MRI: a review of MR-based attenuation correction techniques, European Journal of Nuclear Medicine and Molecular Imaging 36 (S1) (2009) 93–104.

[76] I. Bezrukov, F. Mantlik, H. Schmidt, B. Schölkopf, B.J. Pichler, MR-based PET attenuation correction for PET/MR imaging, Seminars in Nuclear Medicine 43 (1) (2013) 45–59.

[77] V. Keereman, P. Mollet, Y. Berker, V. Schulz, S. Vandenberghe, Challenges and current methods for attenuation correction in PET/MR, Magnetic Resonance Materials in Physics, Biology and Medicine 26 (1) (2013) 81–98.

[78] G. Wagenknecht, H.-J. Kaiser, F.M. Mottaghy, H. Herzog, MRI for attenuation correction in PET: methods and challenges, Magnetic Resonance Materials in Physics, Biology and Medicine 26 (1) (2013) 99–113.

[79] D. Izquierdo-Garcia, C. Catana, MR imaging-guided attenuation correction of PET data in PET/MR imaging, PET Clinics 11 (2) (2016) 129–149.

[80] A. Mehranian, H. Arabi, H. Zaidi, Vision 20/20: magnetic resonance imaging-guided attenuation correction in PET/MRI: challenges, solutions, and opportunities, Medical Physics 43 (3) (2016) 1130–1155.

[81] C.N. Ladefoged, I. Law, U. Anazodo, K.St. Lawrence, D. Izquierdo-Garcia, C. Catana, N. Burgos, M.J. Cardoso, S. Ourselin, B. Hutton, I. Mérida, N. Costes, A. Hammers, D. Benoit, S. Holm, M. Juttukonda, H. An, J. Cabello, M. Lukas, S. Nekolla, S. Ziegler, M. Fenchel, B. Jakoby, M.E. Casey, T. Benzinger, L. Højgaard, A.E. Hansen, F.L. Andersen, A multi-centre evaluation of eleven clinically feasible brain PET/MRI attenuation correction techniques using a large cohort of patients, NeuroImage 147 (Supplement C) (2017) 346–359.

Dictionary learning for medical image synthesis

Ilkay Oksuz[a,b]

[a]*Computer Engineering Department, Istanbul Technical University, Istanbul, Turkey*
[b]*School of Biomedical Engineering & Imaging Sciences, King's College London, United Kingdom*

5.1 Introduction

Image synthesis is a vital task in medical image understanding and analysis. Image synthesis is necessary in many situations such as multi-institution studies, rapid emergency scans, and population studies, where the images of a desired modality or protocol are missing for a given down-stream image analysis algorithm. Moreover, a specific contrast that is essential for an algorithm might be missing in one acquisition. The remedy for such clinical scenarios is threefold. First, the clinicians can just rely on the existing images and utilize their image processing algorithm on available images, which in-turn results in a sub-optimal solution. Second, they can discard the data of the patients with inadequate/missing image data from the cohort study. Finally, they can choose to use a new image analysis framework that will perform at par on the same data. Image synthesis offers an alternative solution: to generate an image with the desired modality, tissue contrast, and/or intensity profile utilizing the database of images and additional priors.

To generate medical images of the desired contrast, early works focused on histogram matching [1]. Contrast synthesis has been utilized for enabling better registration and segmentation (more in Chapter 10). This family of methods suffer when pathology (e.g., brain tumors, hypertrophic cardiomyopathy, etc.) is present. To overcome such challenges, there has been some work to initially segment the structures and then apply histogram matching, which in turn generates additional problems due to the inaccuracies of the initial segmentation [2]. A second approach to generate images is to acquire images of the subject with a set of predefined parameters [3]. This approach can suffer from some major drawbacks such as: (i) approximations made during the mathematical formulations of image acquisitions, (ii) influence of artifacts on the mathematical inversion, and (iii) difficulty to stick to pre-defined mechanisms in clinical scenarios. Example-based approaches defined on patches address these shortcomings by generating a dictionary of image patches. By generating a sparse representation of patch space from different modalities, the synthetic image can be accurately generated. There are two fundamental advantages of using sparsity in image synthesis. First, to reconstruct a synthetic image (patch), we desire to use training patches that are close in intensity, so it would not be optimal to pick a lot of patches,

Biomedical Image Synthesis and Simulation. https://doi.org/10.1016/B978-0-12-824349-7.00012-8

which can have adversarial influence on the final tissue contrast. Second, if too many similar training patches are part of the reconstruction, the corresponding contrast image (patch) might be too smooth due to the cumulative effects of small mismatches in each patch.

The remainder of the chapter is organized as follows. First, we describe the theory of sparse representations and dictionary learning. Then, we provide an overview of methods that utilize dictionary learning for medical image synthesis. Finally, we describe the advantages and shortcoming of dictionary learning for medical image synthesis.

5.2 Sparse coding

The definition of sparsity can be summarized as representing some phenomenon with as few variables as possible [4]. In statistics and machine learning, the sparsity principle is used to perform model selection, which aids in selecting the optimal model from a variety of alternatives. To capture the concise and compact representation in visual data, a popular way is to adopt dictionary learning to achieve sparse representation using only a few active code elements for representing images.

In signal processing, sparse coding has received a lot of interest in representing data with limited linear combinations of dictionary elements [5]. Sparse coding is a technique that is originally developed to explain the early visual processing in the brain [6]. In a pioneer exploratory experiment, Olshausen et al. [6] demonstrated that dictionary learning could easily discover underlying structures in natural image patches. Subsequently, the corresponding tools have been utilized on many tasks including image denoising, image compression computer vision, and audio processing. In particular, we focus on applications where the dictionary is learned and adapted to data, generating a compact representation that is useful in various contexts.

Fig. 5.1 illustrates an example of the sparse coding process. Given a set of basis vectors (atoms) $D \in \mathbb{R}^{m \times K}$, a signal (a column of Y defined as y_i) can be represented as linear combination of atoms in D. The dictionary D can be predefined or learnt from the data itself. In the setting of medical image synthesis, signals (Y) can be considered as image patches to be synthesized and the dictionary D is composed of patches that are coming from the desired tissue contrast and/or modality. Sparse representation of the signal can be represented as

$$Y = DX. \tag{5.1}$$

Here each column $x_i \in \mathbb{R}^{K \times 1}$ is the coding coefficient vector. There is no unique solution for X in sparse setting, since $K > m$ creates an under-determined system. This means that the number of unknown parameters is larger than the number of equations. There are multiple optimization schemes to approach this under-determined system imposing prior information over coefficients. The fundamental assumption in medical image synthesis is that for each image patch, a small number of relevant and

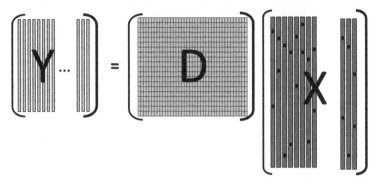

FIGURE 5.1

Sparse Coding Process. The signals in Y are represented by a linear combination of a given dictionary D with coding coefficient matrix X (adopted from [5]). The signals Y represent the image patches from testing images, where dictionary D is the learnt mapping or patches from training images; X is the sparse coefficient matrix, where black color indicates the sparse codes and red color (dark gray in print version) highlights the zero entries.

similar examples can always be found from a rich and over-complete patch dictionary D, which has the same contrast (and assembled into patch vectors in the same order) as y_i column vector. It is unlikely that a single patch will form a perfect match, but it is quite likely that an optimal linear combination of a small number of patches will yield a very close approximation.

5.2.1 Orthogonal matching pursuit

The orthogonal matching pursuit (OMP) algorithm [7] is a methodology to solve NP-hard sparsity problems. OMP (illustrated in Algorithm 1) builds a sparse solution to a given signal by iteratively building up an approximation; the vector y (usually patches in image synthesis) is approximated as a linear combination of a few atoms (the columns d_j) of D (representative patterns), where the active set of atoms to be used is built atom by atom in a greedy fashion. The support $\mathcal{L}$ is defined as the indices of non-zero components in x. At each iteration, a new atom that best correlates with the current residual is added to the active set. Initially, the sparse coefficient is equal to zero $x = 0$ and iteratively a k-term approximation to the signal y is approximated by maintaining a set of active atoms (initially empty), and expanding the set by one additional atom at each iteration. Each iteration stops until a pre-defined number of atoms in the active set is reached by the sparsity level. The entire process stops when a residual error threshold (ϵ) is reached. The term D^+ stands for matrix pseudo-inversion which can be computed as $D^+ = (D^T D)^{-1} D^T$.

If the equation is sufficiently sparse, the l_0-norm can be replaced with the l_1-norm:

$$\hat{x} = \min_x \|x\|_1 \quad \text{subject to} \quad y = Dx, \tag{5.2}$$

Algorithm 1 OMP Algorithm.

Input:

    vector $\ldots y = (y_1, y_2, \ldots, y_m)$
    dictionary $\ldots D \in \mathbb{R}^{m \times K}$
    initial support (index set) $\ldots \mathcal{L} = \emptyset$
    error threshold $\ldots \epsilon$

Output:

    sparse coefficient $\ldots x$

1: **Initialization:**

    $x = 0$ (initial solution)
    $r^{(0)} = y$ (initial residual)
    $it = 1$ (iteration)

2: **while** $\|r^{(it-1)}\|_2 > \epsilon$ **do**

3:     $\forall j \in \{1, \ldots, K\} : t_j = \dfrac{(d_j^T r^{(it-1)})^2}{\|d_j\|_2^2}$ $\triangleright$ Compute correlations

4:     $idx = \underset{k \notin \mathcal{L}}{\operatorname{argmax}}\, t_k$ $\triangleright$ Find an atom in D with maximum correlation

5:     $\mathcal{L} = \mathcal{L} \cup \{idx\}$ $\triangleright$ Support update

6:     $x(\mathcal{L}) = D(\mathcal{L})^+ y$ $\triangleright$ Sparse coefficient update

7:     $r^{(it)} = y - D(\mathcal{L})x(\mathcal{L})$ $\triangleright$ Residual update

8:     $it = it + 1$

9: **end while**

---

or

$$\hat{x} = \min_{x} \|x\|_1 \quad \text{subject to} \quad \|y - Dx\|_2 < \varepsilon, \tag{5.3}$$

where Eq. (5.3) is a relaxed version of Eq. (5.2). If the constrained problem is relaxed with Lagrangian multipliers then

$$\hat{x} = \min_{x} \|y - Dx\|_2^2 + \lambda \|x\|_1, \tag{5.4}$$

where λ is a Lagrangian multiplier to control the sparsity. The second term refers to the sparsity level and the first term reflects the reconstruction error in Eq. (5.4).

5.3 Dictionary learning

In medical image analysis, some applications aim to learn the dictionary D directly from data [8] instead of utilizing a pre-defined set of bases (e.g., Fourier transforms, wavelets, and/or curvelets). Given a set of training signals $Y = [y_1, y_2, \ldots, y_N] \in \mathbb{R}^{m \times N}$, a dictionary D can be defined to represent each signal (patch) in Y sparsely with the equation

$$\langle \hat{D}, \hat{X} \rangle = \underset{D,X}{\mathrm{argmin}} \|Y - DX\|_2^2 \quad \text{subject to} \quad \|X\|_0 \leq L, \tag{5.5}$$

where L is the sparsity parameter and columns x_i of $X \in \mathbb{R}^{K \times N}$ represent sparse coding coefficients. Since the optimization of Eq. (5.5) is defined over D and X, this problem can be solved iteratively by changing the fixed parameter. This optimization strategy starts with initializing the dictionary by using randomly selected training signals. One drawback of this approach is the inability to reach the global optimal solution. The K-SVD algorithm is an alternative approach to ensure a solution to the dictionary learning problem.

The K-SVD algorithm resembles k-means clustering [9]. The K-SVD follows an iterative two-step process (e.g., k-means) to learn the dictionary and find the sparse solutions. After initializing the dictionary D, the solution of the sparse coefficients is found by keeping D fixed, followed by a second stage searching for a better dictionary. The K atoms in the dictionary are updated separately in the dictionary update stage. This is a direct generalization of the k-means algorithm, in which K clusters are also updated separately.

The major difference between the K-SVD and other dictionary learning methods is that the sparse coding coefficients X are not fixed in the dictionary update step. In the K-SVD algorithm, an atom in D and its corresponding row in X are updated simultaneously. This accelerates the convergence of the learning process, which makes the K-SVD a state-of-the-art dictionary learning solution. The major drawback of the K-SVD algorithm is the requirement to calculate SVD at each iteration K times, which in turn adds additional computational complexity.

5.4 Medical image synthesis with dictionary learning

Image synthesis in computer vision could be formulated as a transfer of styles between a given image s_a, on to a corresponding image s_b acquired on the same scene. If there is a mapping $f()$ from A to B, $b = f(a)$, which can convert all s_a from space A to all s_b from space B, and if this mapping is invertible, the mapping can generate any transform between a and b. However, generally this mapping is difficult to learn directly. An assumption on the existence of a mapping space can be made, since both images reflect the same scene. Image synthesis can be performed with the pair of dictionaries and the mapping between the styles.

In the medical image analysis research, the algorithms on data-oriented synthesis can be described as example-based methods. Example-based methods are capable to learn a mapping from a limited number of image pairs by utilizing multiple extracted image patches from the source image. The fundamental assumption for synthesis is

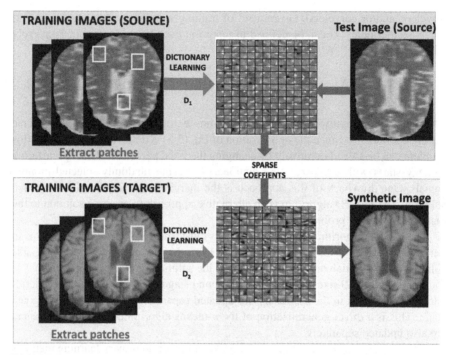

FIGURE 5.2

General flowchart of example-based sparsity induced image synthesis. There are two components: (1) dictionary learning, which is learning multi-modal dictionaries for training images from source and target domains (indicated with blue arrows – mid gray arrows in print version); and (2) sparse coding, which is computing sparse coefficients for the learned dictionaries to reconstruct the source image while at the same time using the same coefficients to transfer the source image to another modality (indicated with red arrows – dark gray arrows in print version).

the shared sparse codes between source and target modality image spaces. The general framework of dictionary learning for image synthesis is illustrated in Fig. 5.2. There are two components of the medical image synthesis pipeline. Dictionary learning, where patch-based dictionaries are learnt for training images from target (D_1) and atlas (D_2) domains, respectively. The second component consists of computing sparse coefficients for the learned dictionaries to reconstruct the source image while at the same time using the same coefficients to transfer the source image to another modality.

The primary aim of medical image synthesis is to synthesize an image of the desired tissue contrast and/or resolution. In general in example-based image synthesis, target contrast dictionary (D_1) and source contrast dictionary (D_2) are composed of 1D column vectors composed of information gathered from 2D or 3D patches extracted from a set of co-registered atlas and subject images. The sparse coefficients

X are learnt utilizing Eq. (5.1) from the source domain. Finally, the learnt sparse coefficients are utilized for generating image patches, and thus the image in the target domain (indicated as synthetic image in Fig. 5.2). The sparsity is enforced utilizing a sparsity term in Eq. (5.4). The dictionary can also be learnt from the data instead of utilizing a set of patches. Huang et al. proposed a methodology to learn a joint dictionary for the target and source domains using the K-SVD algorithm, which can increase the data fidelity of the dictionary [10]. Some example applications with additional constraints for dictionary learning are provided below.

An early work of example-based image synthesis is for converting the multimodal image registration problem into mono-modal registration in correlative microscopy images [11]. There has been increasing interest in sparse representations that aim to learn two separate dictionaries from registered image pairs and synthesize the target magnetic resonance imaging (MRI) modality data from the patches of the source MRI modality [12]. In their pioneering work, Roy et al. [12] utilized sparse coding for MR contrast synthesis with the assumption that patch pairs from different modalities have the same representations and can be directly used for training dictionaries to estimate the contrast of the target modality. For the purpose of registration and segmentation, Iglesias et al. [13] utilized a patch matching algorithm for T1-weighted image synthesis. Bahrami et al. utilized the sparsity constraint to generate 7T MR images utilizing 3T brain MRI images [14].

A group of example-based models are built on the assumption that a large database is available with source–target image pairs. These methodologies have employed a variety of techniques to learn the dictionaries. Ye et al. [15] presented an idea to measure the similarity between test and training data in the same modality with iterative refinement on patches. Using the nearest neighbor to the input patch in source images, the target modality patch is synthesized as illustrated in Fig. 5.3. Vemulapalli et al. [16] first generate multiple target modality candidate values for each voxel. Then they select the best candidate values jointly for all the voxels. Their technique aims to maximize a local consistency function to improve the quality of the synthesized images across different modalities. Huang et al. [10] proposed to first align weakly-supervised data and then generate super-resolution cross-modality data simultaneously using a joint convolutional sparse coding scheme. In a follow-up work, Huang et al. [17] integrated paired and unpaired training data by constructing correspondences across different modalities and leveraging weakly-coupled data.

Wang et al. relied on the idea of sparse representation for reconstructing low dose positron emission tomography (PET) images [18]. They utilized a mapping strategy to ensure the information from multi-sequence MR is incorporated with the sparse coefficients and low-count PET images could be applied to the prediction of full dose PET images. An et al. suggested a multi-level sparsity based method applied to PET data [19]. Their fundamental assumption is the difference in between the low- and full-count data relationships. They argue against the application of the learned sparse coefficients from one dictionary to the other one and propose the multi-level scheme accordingly. Wang et al. highlighted the fact that super-resolution can only be possible with a complete dictionary and coupled training [20]. However, the multi-

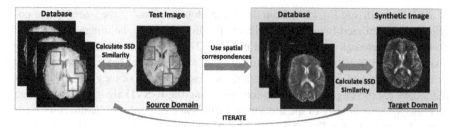

FIGURE 5.3

Flowchart of the patch-based image synthesis via modality propagation described in [15]. First, patches are extracted from source domain images in the database and source images. The nearest neighbor patch is searched in a restricted space within the population database. In the second stage, to incorporate information from the target domain, the initially generated synthetic image is refined utilizing a similar nearest neighbor search principle in the target domain. The result images are adopted from [15] for iterations 1 and 3.

sequence MR images are not present in the training data for PET reconstruction, due to the difficulty of collecting such data. Therefore, they proposed to use an semi-supervised tripled dictionary learning methodology to benefit from the entire training data (including incomplete) to estimate the full-count PET.

5.5 Future directions and research challenges

The sparse-learning-based methods covered in this chapter include several steps such as patch extraction, encoding, and reconstruction. One major drawback is this serial process, which would be time-consuming for testing. In clinical practice, being able to extract patches optimizing the encoding and to reconstruct the image in a serial way can give birth to practical concerns. Moreover, the outputs of the aforementioned methods are likely to be over-smooth, given the fact that they are done with patch-based processing. This is further concerning for the clinical usability in fine structure detection. For instance, over-smoothing on MR images can generate adverse effects on down-stream tasks (e.g., segmentation, registration, etc.) and introduce issues with signal-to-noise ratio on the pathology region and hinder automatic detection.

Although the dictionary learning-based methods showed good synthesis capability, they suffer from the hand-crafted feature design. The utilized features (hand-crafted features) usually have limited ability to capture meaningful image information. The complex optimization problems are time-consuming for applying on new test datasets. In addition, the patch size can cause blurred regions and loss of texture information, which are vital for detecting anatomy and pathology. In contrast, deep learning-based methods can learn representative features directly from the training datasets. Moreover, the computational complexity is a serious concern in comparison to fast processing of deep learning methods (in the order of milliseconds).

5.6 Summary

We have summarized the principles of dictionary learning and its application on medical image synthesis with this chapter. The dictionary learning based methods have been utilized for image synthesis in early 2010s, due to their success, which lies in sparsity. In dictionary-based design, a patch can be generated with a small set of dictionary atoms (patches). Therefore, dictionary learning gives a more adjustable representation of the database and has the capability to map important features sparsely from the original data space. However, the success of deep learning methods for generative tasks caused a decrease in the techniques utilizing dictionary learning. In the future, the sparse representation can play a key role in extracting information in deep learning setups for medical image synthesis.

Acknowledgments

Ilkay Oksuz has benefitted from the 2232 International Fellowship for Outstanding Researchers Program of TUBITAK (Project No. 118C353). However, the entire responsibility of the chapter belongs to the owner of the chapter. The financial support received from TUBITAK does not mean that the content of the publication is approved in a scientific sense by TUBITAK.

References

[1] C.A. Cocosco, V. Kollokian, R.K.-S. Kwan, G.B. Pike, A.C. Evans, Brainweb: online interface to a 3D MRI simulated brain database, in: NeuroImage, Citeseer, 1997.

[2] X. Han, B. Fischl, Atlas renormalization for improved brain MR image segmentation across scanner platforms, IEEE Transactions on Medical Imaging 26 (4) (2007) 479–486.

[3] R. Deichmann, C. Good, O. Josephs, J. Ashburner, R. Turner, Optimization of 3-D MP-RAGE sequences for structural brain imaging, NeuroImage 12 (1) (2000) 112–127.

[4] H. Lee, A. Battle, R. Raina, A.Y. Ng, Efficient sparse coding algorithms, in: B. Schölkopf, J.C. Platt, T. Hofmann (Eds.), Advances in Neural Information Processing Systems 19, Proceedings of the Twentieth Annual Conference on Neural Information Processing Systems, Vancouver, British Columbia, Canada, December 4–7, 2006, MIT Press, 2006, pp. 801–808.

[5] J. Mairal, F.R. Bach, J. Ponce, Sparse modeling for image and vision processing, Foundations and Trends in Computer Graphics and Vision 8 (2–3) (2014) 85–283, https://doi.org/10.1561/0600000058.

[6] B.A. Olshausen, D.J. Field, Emergence of simple-cell receptive field properties by learning a sparse code for natural images, Nature 381 (6583) (1996) 607–609, https://doi.org/10.1038/381607a0, https://ui.adsabs.harvard.edu/abs/1996Natur.381..607O.

[7] J.A. Tropp, A.C. Gilbert, Signal recovery from random measurements via orthogonal matching pursuit, IEEE Transactions on Information Theory 53 (12) (2007) 4655–4666, https://doi.org/10.1109/TIT.2007.909108.

[8] R. Rubinstein, A.M. Bruckstein, M. Elad, Dictionaries for sparse representation modeling, Proceedings of the IEEE 98 (6) (2010) 1045–1057, https://doi.org/10.1109/JPROC.2010.2040551.

[9] M. Aharon, M. Elad, A.M. Bruckstein, K-SVD: An algorithm for designing overcomplete dictionaries for sparse representation, IEEE Transactions on Signal Processing 54 (11) (2006) 4311–4322, https://doi.org/10.1109/TSP.2006.881199.

[10] Y. Huang, L. Shao, A.F. Frangi, Simultaneous super-resolution and cross-modality synthesis of 3D medical images using weakly-supervised joint convolutional sparse coding, in: 2017 IEEE Conference on Computer Vision and Pattern Recognition, CVPR 2017, Honolulu, HI, USA, July 21–26, 2017, IEEE Computer Society, 2017, pp. 5787–5796, https://doi.org/10.1109/CVPR.2017.613.

[11] T. Cao, C. Zach, S. Modla, D. Powell, K. Czymmek, M. Niethammer, Multi-modal registration for correlative microscopy using image analogies, Medical Image Analysis 18 (6) (2014) 914–926, https://doi.org/10.1016/j.media.2013.12.005.

[12] S. Roy, A. Carass, J.L. Prince, Magnetic resonance image example-based contrast synthesis, IEEE Transactions on Medical Imaging 32 (12) (2013) 2348–2363, https://doi.org/10.1109/TMI.2013.2282126.

[13] J.E. Iglesias, E. Konukoglu, D. Zikic, B. Glocker, K. Van Leemput, B. Fischl, Is synthesizing MRI contrast useful for inter-modality analysis?, in: K. Mori, I. Sakuma, Y. Sato, C. Barillot, N. Navab (Eds.), Medical Image Computing and Computer-Assisted Intervention – MICCAI 2013, Springer, Berlin, Heidelberg, 2013, pp. 631–638.

[14] K. Bahrami, F. Shi, X. Zong, H.W. Shin, H. An, D. Shen, Hierarchical reconstruction of 7T-like images from 3T MRI using multi-level CCA and group sparsity, in: N. Navab, J. Hornegger, W.M. Wells, A. Frangi (Eds.), Medical Image Computing and Computer-Assisted Intervention – MICCAI 2015, Springer International Publishing, Cham, 2015, pp. 659–666.

[15] D.H. Ye, D. Zikic, B. Glocker, A. Criminisi, E. Konukoglu, Modality propagation: coherent synthesis of subject-specific scans with data-driven regularization, in: International Conference on Medical Image Computing and Computer-Assisted Intervention, Springer, 2013, pp. 606–613.

[16] R. Vemulapalli, H. Van Nguyen, S.K. Zhou, Unsupervised cross-modal synthesis of subject-specific scans, in: 2015 IEEE International Conference on Computer Vision (ICCV), 2015, pp. 630–638, https://doi.org/10.1109/ICCV.2015.79.

[17] Y. Huang, L. Shao, A.F. Frangi, Cross-modality image synthesis via weakly coupled and geometry co-regularized joint dictionary learning, IEEE Transactions on Medical Imaging 37 (3) (2018) 815–827, https://doi.org/10.1109/TMI.2017.2781192.

[18] Y. Wang, P. Zhang, L. An, G. Ma, J. Kang, F. Shi, X. Wu, J. Zhou, D.S. Lalush, W. Lin, et al., Predicting standard-dose PET image from low-dose PET and multimodal MR images using mapping-based sparse representation, Physics in Medicine and Biology 61 (2) (2016) 791.

[19] L. An, P. Zhang, E. Adeli, Y. Wang, G. Ma, F. Shi, D.S. Lalush, W. Lin, D. Shen, Multi-level canonical correlation analysis for standard-dose PET image estimation, IEEE Transactions on Image Processing 25 (7) (2016) 3303–3315, https://doi.org/10.1109/TIP.2016.2567072.

[20] D. Wang, Y. Huang, A.F. Frangi, Region-enhanced joint dictionary learning for cross-modality synthesis in diffusion tensor imaging, in: S.A. Tsaftaris, A. Gooya, A.F. Frangi, J.L. Prince (Eds.), Simulation and Synthesis in Medical Imaging – Second International

Workshop, SASHIMI 2017, Held in Conjunction with MICCAI 2017, Québec City, QC, Canada, September 10, 2017, Proceedings, in: Lecture Notes in Computer Science, vol. 10557, Springer, 2017, pp. 41–48.

Convolutional neural networks for image synthesis

6

Dong Nie[a] and Xuyun Wen[b]

[a]*University of North Carolina at Chapel Hill, Chapel Hill, NC, United States*
[b]*Nanjing University of Aeronautics and Astronautics, Nanjing, China*

6.1 Convolutional neural networks for image synthesis

Deep learning models can learn a hierarchy of features, i.e., high-level features built upon low-level features. Convolutional neural network (CNN) [1,2] is one popular type of deep learning models, in which trainable filters and local neighborhood pooling operations are applied in an alternating sequence starting with the raw input images. When trained with appropriate regularization, CNN can achieve superior performance on visual object recognition and image classification tasks compared with traditional learning-based methods [3]. However, most CNNs are designed for 2D natural images. They are not well suited for medical image analysis, since most medical images are 3D volumetric images, such as magnetic resonance imaging (MRI), computerized tomography (CT), and positron emission tomography. Compared to 2D CNN, 3D CNN can better model the 3D spatial information due to the use of 3D convolution operations which preserve the spatial neighborhood of 3D image. As a result, 3D CNN can solve the discontinuity problem across slices, which are problematic for 2D CNN.

CNN. A typical CNN is stacked by several convolutional + batch normalization + activation function layers, max pooling layers, and fully connected layers [4]. A CNN can be used for classification and regression, which mainly depends on the tasks and designation of the loss functions. A classical scenario is that a CNN takes an image (patch) as input and then outputs a single value which represents the classified category or regressed value for this image (patch).

Structured CNN - FCN. The output of a conventional CNN is a single target value, which is unable to preserve neighborhood information in the output space. Researchers propose to use a fully convolutional network (FCN) to produce the structured output [5–8]. Instead of predicting the target modality voxel by voxel (each voxel of the target modality is predicted by a CNN), FCNs are used to estimate the target images in a patch-by-patch manner (a source image is partitioned into overlapped patches, each patch is fed into the network, and then the outputs for the patches

Biomedical Image Synthesis and Simulation. https://doi.org/10.1016/B978-0-12-824349-7.00013-X

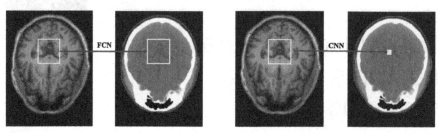

FIGURE 6.1

Illustration of the difference between fully convolutional network (FCN) and convolutional neural network (CNN). The left column shows MR slices, and the right one shows corresponding CT slices.

are recombined as an entire prediction target image), as shown in Fig. 6.1. Compared to using CNN for voxel-wise prediction, using FCN for patch-wise prediction has several obvious advantages. First, the neighborhood information can be preserved in each predicted patch. Second, the prediction efficiency can be greatly improved since an entire patch can be predicted by a single pass of forward propagation in the neural network.

In the following paragraphs, the details of network architecture of FCN used in the source-to-target prediction will be described. Compared to the conventional CNN, the pooling layers are not used in this application. This is because the pooling layers often reduce the spatial resolution of feature maps. Although this property is desirable for tasks, such as image classification, since the pooling over local neighborhood could enhance invariance to certain image distortions, it is not desired in the task of image prediction, where subtle image distortions need to be precisely captured in the prediction process.

3D FCN for estimating target images from source data. FCNs are widely used for segmentation and reconstruction in both computer vision and medical image analysis fields [9–14,5], because they can preserve spatial information in a local neighborhood of the image space and are also much faster compared to CNNs at the testing stage since FCNs can output a patch at a time while CNNs output a voxel. Researchers adopt FCNs to work as image generator. A typical 3D FCN (as shown in Fig. 6.2) is proposed to perform the medical image synthesis task. It is worth noting that the convolution operations used are without pooling, since pooling could potentially lead to loss of resolution and feature misalignment. To increase the receptive field and context information, researchers design large filters and also use dilated convolutions (dilated convolution is a type of convolution that "inflates" the kernel by inserting holes between the kernel elements [15]) as shown in Fig. 6.2.

3D UNet for estimating target images from source data. As mentioned above, pooling could cause loss of resolution and fine-grained details. However, pooling is one of the most efficient approaches to increase the receptive field and decrease the computational cost. To safely use pooling, researchers introduced UNet for segmentation and reconstruction in both computer vision and medical image analysis

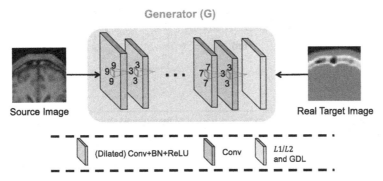

FIGURE 6.2

The 3D FCN architecture for estimating a target image from a source image. Conv + BN + ReLU: convolutional + batch normalization + rectified linear unit layers; GDL: image gradient difference loss.

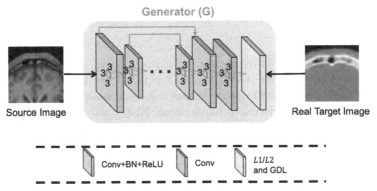

FIGURE 6.3

The 3D UNet architecture for estimating a target image from a source image. Conv + BN + ReLU: convolutional + batch normalization + rectified linear unit layers; GDL: image gradient difference loss.

fields [16], because it designs long-range skip connections between encoder and decoder to correct the errors in pooling and upsampling operations. A typical 3D UNet is shown in Fig. 6.3 to perform the medical image synthesis task.

6.2 Neural network building blocks

6.2.1 Neuron

The neuron is the basic building block of the networks. Each neuron receives some inputs, performs a dot product, and optionally follows it with a non-linearity. Note that

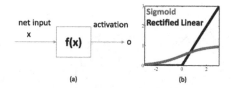

(a)   (b)

FIGURE 6.4

Panel (a) shows an activation function in neural networks and (b) displays typical activation functions.

neurons have weights and biases which can be learned. Let us take a 3D-convolution based neuron as an example.

Mathematically, the 3D convolution operation is given by

$$
a_{ij}(x, y, z)
$$
$$
= f\left(\sum_{c=1}^{C} \sum_{p=0}^{P_i-1} \sum_{q=0}^{Q_i-1} \sum_{r=0}^{R_i-1} W_{ijc}(p,q,r)a_{(i-1)c}(x - p - \delta_p, y - q - \delta_q, z - r - \delta_r) \right),
$$
$$(6.1)$$

where x, y, z denote the 3D voxel position, W is a 3D filter, a is a 3D feature map from the previous $(i-1)$th layer. Initially, a is the input patch, c and C are the index and number of feature maps in the previous layer, while i and j are the layer index and filter index, respectively. Furthermore, P_i, Q_i, and R_i are the dimensions of the ith filter in 3D space, respectively; $\delta_p = (P_i - 1)/2$, $\delta_q = (Q_i - 1)/2$, and $\delta_r = (R_i - 1)/2$; f is an activation function that encodes the non-linearity in the CNN.

6.2.2 Activation function

The activation function is one of the most important building blocks in neural networks, which is put at the end of or in-between neural networks to help decide if the neuron should fire or not as shown in Fig. 6.4(a). The activation function is a non-linear transformation that we do over the input signal. There are several widely used activation functions, such as sigmoid (Eq. (6.2)), Rectified Linear Unit (denoted as ReLU) [17] (Eq. (6.3)), tanh (Eq. (6.4)), and so on:

$$
\text{sigmoid}(x) = 1/\left(1 + e^{-x}\right), \tag{6.2}
$$

$$
\text{ReLU}(x) = \max(0, x), \tag{6.3}
$$

$$
\tanh(x) = \frac{2}{1 + e^{-2x}} - 1. \tag{6.4}
$$

The sigmoid used to be a frequent activation function but ReLU has recently been more frequently adopted in CNNs (shown in Fig. 6.4(b)), because ReLU can alleviate the gradient vanishing or gradient explosion problems which often occur using a sigmoid activation function [18] (see Section "Vanishing gradient"). Some activation functions are also proposed to further improve the ReLU, such as LeakyReLU [19] (Eq. (6.5)), Parametric Rectified Linear Unit (denoted as PReLU) [20] (Eq. (6.6), note that θ is a learned vector which has the same size as x), exponential linear unit (denoted as elu) [21] (Eq. (6.7)), and so on:

$$\text{LeakyReLU}(x) = \begin{cases} \alpha x, & x < 0, \\ x, & x \geq 0, \end{cases} \tag{6.5}$$

$$\text{PReLU}(x) = \begin{cases} \theta x, & x < 0, \\ x, & x \geq 0, \end{cases} \tag{6.6}$$

$$\text{elu}(x) = \begin{cases} \alpha(e^x - 1), & x < 0, \\ x, & x \geq 0. \end{cases} \tag{6.7}$$

When it comes to medical image synthesis with CNNs, we usually set ReLU as activation functions in the intermediate layers [22,7,8]. While there are various choices for the last convolution (fully connected) layer, ReLU, tanh, sigmoid, or void (without activation function) are the most widely used ones.

6.2.3 Generator layer details

Details of layers in FCN. A typical architecture of an FCN-based generator network G is showed in Fig. 6.2, where the numbers indicate the filter sizes. This network takes a source image as the input, and tries to generate the corresponding target image. Specifically, it has nine layers containing convolution, batch normalization, and ReLU operations. The kernel sizes are 9^3, 3^3, 3^3, 3^3, 9^3, 3^3, 3^3, 7^3, and 3^3, respectively. The numbers of filters for all the layers are $32, 32, 32, 64, 64, 64, 32, 32$, and 1, respectively, for the individual layers. The last layer only includes one convolutional filter, and its output is considered as the estimated target image. Regarding the architecture, pooling operation is not used since it will reduce the spatial resolution of the feature maps. Considering the fact that the traditional convolution operations of the generator in Fig. 6.2 cannot guarantee a sufficiently effective receptive field [23], the dilation convolution is adopted as an alternative [15] so that enough receptive field can be achieved. The dilation for the first and last convolution layers of the generator in Fig. 6.2 is 1, and 2 for all the other convolution layers.

Details of layers in UNet. A typical architecture of a UNet-based generator is shown in Fig. 6.3. In the UNet, the convolution filter sizes are all set to $3 \times 3 \times 3$. The channels of convolution blocks in the encoder are set to $32, 64, 64, 128, 128, 256, 512$, and the channels of the decoder convolution blocks are symmetrically set. Note that the number of channels of the last block is 1. There are three pooling layers in the encoder phase and three stridden convolutions in the decoder phase. For each convolutional block except the last, convolutional + batch normalization + ReLU layers used. The last block is made simply of a convolutional layer.

6.3 Training a convolutional neural network

6.3.1 Loss functions

Various loss functions are adopted to train the deep models, such as the cross-entropy, L_1 or L_2 losses. Typically, a reconstruction loss (i.e., L_1 or L_2) is used to train the synthesis model as in

$$L_p(Y, \hat{Y}) = \left\| Y - \hat{Y} \right\|^p, \tag{6.8}$$

where Y is the ground-truth target image, and $\hat{Y}$ is the predicted target image by the generator network. It is the L_2-loss if $p = 2$ and the L_1-loss if $p = 1$. The L_1-loss is more robust than the L_2-loss in medical image synthesis tasks since the L_1-loss is not as sensitive to outlier voxels as the L_2-loss. Also, the L_1-loss does a better job in producing less blurry images since the L_2-loss tends to make the generated images blurry. However, we can obtain more stable reconstruction results by using the L_2-loss than the L_1-loss. More importantly, the networks can usually converge faster with the L_2-loss since the gradient of the L_1-loss is constant.

If using the L_2-loss, we can consider using the gradient difference loss to alleviate the blurriness issues.

Image gradient difference loss. We usually incorporate the L_p-loss term of Eq. (6.8) as a data fitting term in the loss of the generator, aiming at generating a target image from its corresponding source image. However, as the L_p-loss may result in blurry images, we propose to use an image gradient difference loss ("GDL") as an additional term to alleviate the blurriness. It is defined as

$$L_{GDL}(Y, \hat{Y}) = \left\| |\nabla Y_x| - |\nabla \hat{Y}_x| \right\|^2 + \left\| |\nabla Y_y| - |\nabla \hat{Y}_y| \right\|^2 + \left\| |\nabla Y_z| - |\nabla \hat{Y}_z| \right\|^2, \tag{6.9}$$

where Y is the ground-truth target image, and $\hat{Y}$ is the predicted target by the generator network. This loss tries to minimize the difference of the magnitudes of the gradients between the ground-truth target image and the synthetic target image. In this way, the synthetic target image will try to keep the regions with strong gradients (i.e., edges) for an effective compensation of the L_2 reconstruction term. By combining all losses above, the generator can thus be modeled to minimize the loss function given by

$$L_{total} = L_p + \lambda L_{GDL}. \tag{6.10}$$

6.3.2 Back propagation

The medical image synthesis networks are optimized by back propagation. Assuming the reconstruction loss L and the network parameters θ, we compute the gradient back propagated at layer l as

$$\frac{\partial L}{\partial \theta_{ij}^{(l)}} = \delta_i^{(l+1)} a_j^{(l)}, \tag{6.11}$$

where a is the neuron value computed by Eq. (6.1) and δ is the "error," which we refer to as an "error" term to send back the error from the output throughout the network, propagated to layer l. Correspondingly, we compute the "error" at layer l as

$$\delta_j^{(l)} = f'\left(a^{(l)}\right) \sum_{i=1}^{n} \delta_i^{(l+1)} \theta_{ij}^{(l)}. \tag{6.12}$$

Following Eqs. (6.11) and (6.12), we can propagate "errors" back to all the layers throughout the network, thus, the entire network could be updated.

6.3.3 Image synthesis accuracy

For medical image synthesis tasks, the mean absolute error (MAE), peak signal-to-noise ratio (PSNR), and structural similarity (SSIM) index [24] are the widely used evaluation metrics to quantitatively measure the performance. Suppose I is the ground-truth image with size of $m \times n$, and J is the synthesized image. Then

$$MAE\,(I, J) = \frac{1}{mn} \sum_{i=0}^{m-1} \sum_{j=0}^{n-1} |I\,(i, j) - J\,(i, j)|, \tag{6.13}$$

$$PSNR\,(I, J) = 10\log_{10}\left(\frac{MAX_I^2}{MSE\,(I, J)}\right), \tag{6.14}$$

where MAX_I is the maximum possible pixel value of the image, and MSE is the mean squared error:

$$MSE\,(I, J) = \frac{1}{mn} \sum_{i=0}^{m-1} \sum_{j=0}^{n-1} (I(i, j) - J(i, j))^2, \tag{6.15}$$

$$SSIM\,(I, J) = \frac{(2\mu_I\mu_J + C_1)(2\sigma_{IJ} + C_2)}{\left(\mu_I^2 + \mu_J^2 + C_1\right)\left(\sigma_I^2 + \sigma_J^2 + C_2\right)}, \tag{6.16}$$

where μ_I and μ_J are the mean of image I and J, respectively; σ_I and σ_J are the variance of I and J, respectively; σ_{IJ} is the covariance between I and J; C_1 and C_2 are two variables to stabilize the division with weak denominator, with $C_1 = (k_1 L)^2$ and $C_2 = (k_2 L)^2$, where L is the dynamic range of the pixel-values; typically, this is $2^n - 1$ where n is the number of bits per pixel, $k_1 = 0.01$ and $k_2 = 0.03$. Note that it will return a local SSIM map when using Eq. (6.16), and a further average step should be applied to obtain a global SSIM (scalar).

6.4 Practical aspects

6.4.1 Pooling layers

A pooling operation is designed to downsample the feature maps, that is, if there are N input feature maps, then there will be exactly N corresponding output feature maps with downsampled size. Pooling layers are periodically inserted in-between successive convolution layers in CNNs, with the purpose of progressively reducing the spatial size of the representation so that we can reduce the amount of parameters and computation cost in the network, and hence to also control overfitting to some extent. Formally,

$$x_j^l = f\left(\beta_j^l \text{down}\left(x_i^{l-1}\right) + b_j^l\right), \tag{6.17}$$

where $\text{down}(\cdot)$ represents a sub-sampling function. The widely used ones are max and average pooling.

6.4.2 Convolutional versus fully connected neural networks

Deep learning models can learn a hierarchy of features, i.e., high-level features building on low-level ones. The CNNs [3,4,25] are a type of deep models, in which trainable filters and local neighborhood pooling operations are applied in an alternating sequence starting with the raw input images. This results in a hierarchy of increasingly complex features. One property of CNNs is that they can capture highly non-linear mappings between inputs and outputs [3]. A typical fully connected network consists of a series of fully connected layers that connect each neuron in one layer to all neurons in the other layer. The CNNs assume the input of the network is structure data, for example, images; in contrast, the fully connected neural networks can accept broader input data. However, fully connected neural networks result in many more network parameters compared to CNNs since CNNs share weight parameters in each layer. As a result, fully connected neural networks demand much more data to achieve comparable performance as CNNs. Accordingly, CNNs, and especially FCNs, are the main choices for medical image synthesis.

6.4.3 Vanishing gradient

As more layers using certain activation functions (for example, sigmoid) are added to neural networks, the gradient of the loss function approaches zero (or explosive) because of the chain-rule-based back propagation, making the network hard to train. Indeed, gradients of neural networks are found using back-propagation, which finds the derivatives of the network by moving layer by layer from the final layer to the initial one; by the chain rule, the derivatives of each layer are multiplied down the network, from the final layer to the initial, to compute the derivatives of the initial layers.

There are several solutions to this phenomenon. At first, using suitable activation functions, for example ReLU, can largely alleviate this issue. Secondly, residual net-

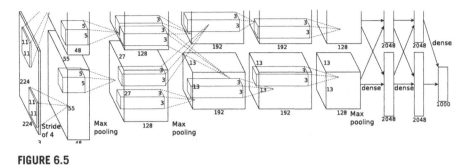

FIGURE 6.5

Illustration of famous AlexNet. The chart is directly from the original paper [4].

works are another solution, as they provide residual connections straight to earlier layers. Finally, batch normalization layers can also resolve the issue. Batch normalization reduces this problem by simply normalizing the input so the input does not reach the outer edges of the sigmoid function (where the derivative is not too small).

6.5 **Commonly known networks**

With years of development, numerous network architectures have been proposed for different applications, in which AlexNet [4], VGGNet [26], Inception [27], ResNet [28], and DenseNet [29] are the milestone architectures that inspire the computer vision field to move forward. We briefly cover three of them: AlexNet, UNet, and Inception network.

6.5.1 **AlexNet**

AlexNet [4] is the name of a convolutional neural network which has had a huge impact on the field of machine learning, specifically in the application of deep learning to computer vision. It was famous for winning the 2012 ImageNet LSVRC-2012 competition (achieving the state-of-the-art performance on image recognition challenges at that time) by a large margin (15.3% vs 26.2% (second place) error rates). AlexNet was the most representative CNN architecture in the early stage, which had a very similar architecture as LeNet [30] but was deeper and wider (i.e., with more filters per layer), and with stacked convolutional layers, as shown in Fig. 6.5. It consisted of 11×11, 5×5, 3×3, convolutions, max pooling, dropout [31], data augmentation, ReLU activations, and stochastic gradient descent (SGD) with momentum [32]. It attached ReLU activations after every convolutional and fully-connected layer. AlexNet was trained for six days simultaneously on two Nvidia

Geforce GTX 580 GPUs, which is the reason for why this network is split into two pipelines.

Apart from deeper and wider layers, AlexNet has the following characteristics that revolutionized neural networks:

- ReLU activation function is used instead of Tanh or sigmoid to add non-linearity, which largely alleviates the vanishing gradient phenomenon. As a result, the training of the network is accelerated by six times with the same accuracy.
- Dropout, which randomly drops out nodes in the network, is adopted instead of regularization to deal with overfitting, which largely improves the generalization ability of the networks.
- Overlap pooling is utilized to reduce the size of the network, which can not only make the network smaller but also reduce the top-1 and top-5 error rates by 0.4% and 0.3%, respectively.

6.5.2 UNet

In encoder–decoder-based synthesis networks, downsampling (i.e., pooling) and upsampling (e.g., bilinear interpolation or transpose convolution) are frequently used. However, such operations could lead to potential misalignment of feature maps and loss of localization accuracy, which would probably result in decrease of performance.

The UNet [16] has been proposed to alleviate the above mentioned issues. A UNet usually includes two paths. The first is a contracting path (encoder) which is used to capture the context in the image. The encoder is just a traditional stack of convolutional and max pooling layers. The second path is the symmetric expanding path (usually called as the decoder) which is used to enable precise localization using transposed convolutions. Lateral connections between the encoder and decoder layers are developed to alleviate this issue by incorporating both high-resolution feature maps and rich-semantic feature maps to increase the localization accuracy. Specifically, at every step of the decoder, skip connections were used to get better precise locations by concatenating the output of the transposed convolution layers with the feature maps from the encoder at the same level.

The original UNet architecture is shown in Fig. 6.6, which consists of five downsampling stages in the encoder and five corresponding upsampling stages in the decoder. The size of the network prediction output is usually the same size as that of the input image (note that in the original UNet the output size is a little smaller than the input size, while in later works researchers usually set the same output size as the input size). Though the UNet was originally developed for medical image segmentation, it is also usually adopted to work as the image generator to perform the medical image synthesis, since it is able to alleviate the loss of spatial details and fine-grained details can be recovered in the dense prediction compared to plain FCN.

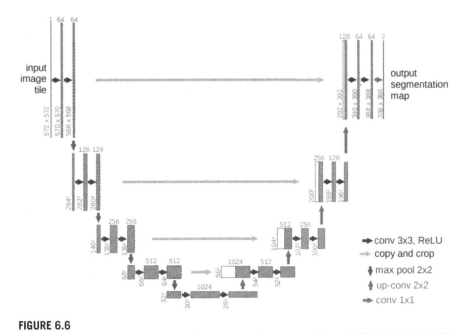

FIGURE 6.6

Illustration of the famous UNet for dense prediction. The chart is directly from the original paper [16].

6.5.3 Inception network

The Inception network [27] is another milestone in image recognition. Considering that naively stacking large convolution operations is computationally expensive and that very deep networks are prone to overfitting, the researchers in [27] proposed to make the network "wider" rather than "deeper" by utilizing "wider" network components, i.e., they build filters (as basic components) with multiple sizes operating on the same level, as shown in Fig. 6.7. In particular, a naive inception module (Fig. 6.7(a)) is designed to perform convolution on an input, with three different sizes of filters (1×1, 3×3, 5×5). Additionally, max pooling is also performed as an extra branch. The outputs of the four branches are merged and sent to the next inception module. The concatenation of the output of the pooling layer with the outputs of the convolutional layers would lead to an inevitable increase in the number of channels from stage to stage, which would lead to a computational blow up within a few stages for the network.

Reducing dimension wherever the computational cost has a huge increase is a proposed solution to the above-mentioned issue. The idea is based on the success of embeddings: even low-dimensional embeddings might contain sufficient information to capture a relatively large image patch. In particular, 1×1 convolutions are used to compute reductions before the expensive 3×3 and 5×5 convolution operations.

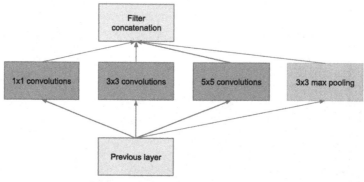

(a) Inception module, naive version.

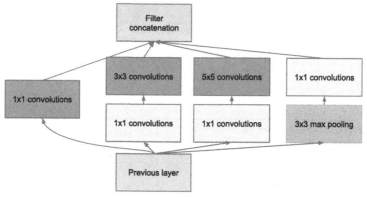

(b) Inception module with dimension reductions.

FIGURE 6.7

Illustration of the famous Inception modules. The chart is directly from the original paper [27].

Besides being used as reductions, they also include the use of ReLU. The entire Inception module is depicted in Fig. 6.7(b).

The Inception network is composed of the sequential stacking of 22 layers. The layers consists of convolutional operations, max pooling operations, Inception modules, as well as a final linear projection. For details, please refer to [27]. The evolution Inception-v3 [26] proposes even "cheaper" Inception modules by decomposing an $n \times n$ convolution filter into two convolution filters, $1 \times n$ and $n \times 1$.

6.6 Conclusion

In this chapter, we introduced deep learning based medical image synthesis. In particular, we firstly introduced basic deep learning concepts to understand a synthesis network, such as building blocks, various deep learning layers, back propagation, and so on. Then we presented classic CNNs for medical image synthesis, as well as the evaluation metrics. Finally, we demonstrated the commonly know networks which play important roles in image synthesis.

References

[1] X. Glorot, Y. Bengio, Understanding the difficulty of training deep feedforward neural networks, in: International Conference on Artificial Intelligence and Statistics, 2010, pp. 249–256.

[2] Y. LeCun, Y. Bengio, G. Hinton, Deep learning, Nature 521 (7553) (2015) 436–444.

[3] Y. LeCun, et al., Gradient-based learning applied to document recognition, Proceedings of the IEEE 86 (11) (1998) 2278–2324.

[4] A. Krizhevsky, I. Sutskever, G.E. Hinton, ImageNet classification with deep convolutional neural networks, in: Advances in Neural Information Processing Systems, 2012, pp. 1097–1105.

[5] D. Nie, X. Cao, Y. Gao, L. Wang, D. Shen, Estimating CT image from MRI data using 3D fully convolutional networks, in: International Workshop on Large-Scale Annotation of Biomedical Data and Expert Label Synthesis, Springer, 2016, pp. 170–178.

[6] D. Nie, R. Trullo, J. Lian, C. Petitjean, S. Ruan, Q. Wang, D. Shen, Medical image synthesis with context-aware generative adversarial networks, in: International Conference on Medical Image Computing and Computer-Assisted Intervention, Springer, 2017, pp. 417–425.

[7] H.-C. Shin, N.A. Tenenholtz, J.K. Rogers, C.G. Schwarz, M.L. Senjem, J.L. Gunter, K.P. Andriole, M. Michalski, Medical image synthesis for data augmentation and anonymization using generative adversarial networks, in: International Workshop on Simulation and Synthesis in Medical Imaging, Springer, 2018, pp. 1–11.

[8] Q. Yang, P. Yan, Y. Zhang, H. Yu, Y. Shi, X. Mou, M.K. Kalra, Y. Zhang, L. Sun, G. Wang, Low-dose CT image denoising using a generative adversarial network with Wasserstein distance and perceptual loss, IEEE Transactions on Medical Imaging 37 (6) (2018) 1348–1357.

[9] J. Long, E. Shelhamer, T. Darrell, Fully convolutional networks for semantic segmentation, in: Proceedings of the IEEE Conference on Computer Vision and Pattern Recognition, 2015, pp. 3431–3440.

[10] D. Nie, L. Wang, Y. Gao, D. Shen, Fully convolutional networks for multi-modality isointense infant brain image segmentation, in: Biomedical Imaging (ISBI), 2016 IEEE 13th International Symposium on, IEEE, 2016, pp. 1342–1345.

[11] D. Nie, L. Wang, E. Adeli, C. Lao, W. Lin, D. Shen, 3-D fully convolutional networks for multimodal isointense infant brain image segmentation, IEEE Transactions on Cybernetics 49 (3) (2019) 1123–1136.

[12] C. Dong, C.C. Loy, K. He, X. Tang, Image super-resolution using deep convolutional networks, IEEE Transactions on Pattern Analysis and Machine Intelligence 38 (2) (2016) 295–307.

[13] K. Bahrami, F. Shi, I. Rekik, D. Shen, Convolutional neural network for reconstruction of 7T-like images from 3T MRI using appearance and anatomical features, in: International Workshop on Large-Scale Annotation of Biomedical Data and Expert Label Synthesis, Springer, 2016, pp. 39–47.

[14] X. Han, MR-based synthetic CT generation using a deep convolutional neural network method, Medical Physics 44 (4) (2017) 1408–1419.

[15] F. Yu, V. Koltun, Multi-scale context aggregation by dilated convolutions, arXiv preprint, arXiv:1511.07122.

[16] O. Ronneberger, P. Fischer, T. Brox, U-Net: convolutional networks for biomedical image segmentation, in: International Conference on Medical Image Computing and Computer-Assisted Intervention, Springer, 2015, pp. 234–241.

[17] V. Nair, G.E. Hinton, Rectified linear units improve restricted Boltzmann machines, in: Proceedings of the 27th International Conference on Machine Learning (ICML-10), 2010, pp. 807–814.

[18] B. Xu, N. Wang, T. Chen, M. Li, Empirical evaluation of rectified activations in convolutional network, arXiv preprint, arXiv:1505.00853.

[19] A.L. Maas, A.Y. Hannun, A.Y. Ng, Rectifier nonlinearities improve neural network acoustic models, in: Proc. ICML, vol. 30, 2013, p. 3.

[20] K. He, X. Zhang, S. Ren, J. Sun, Delving deep into rectifiers: surpassing human-level performance on ImageNet classification, in: Proceedings of the IEEE International Conference on Computer Vision, 2015, pp. 1026–1034.

[21] D.-A. Clevert, T. Unterthiner, S. Hochreiter, Fast and accurate deep network learning by exponential linear units (elus), arXiv preprint, arXiv:1511.07289.

[22] D. Nie, H. Zhang, E. Adeli, L. Liu, D. Shen, 3D deep learning for multi-modal imaging-guided survival time prediction of brain tumor patients, in: International Conference on Medical Image Computing and Computer-Assisted Intervention, Springer, 2016, pp. 212–220.

[23] W. Luo, Y. Li, R. Urtasun, R. Zemel, Understanding the effective receptive field in deep convolutional neural networks, in: Advances in Neural Information Processing Systems, 2016, pp. 4898–4906.

[24] Z. Wang, A.C. Bovik, H.R. Sheikh, E.P. Simoncelli, Image quality assessment: from error visibility to structural similarity, IEEE Transactions on Image Processing 13 (4) (2004) 600–612.

[25] J. Bouvrie, Notes on convolutional neural networks, Tech. Rep., 2006.

[26] K. Simonyan, A. Zisserman, Very deep convolutional networks for large-scale image recognition, arXiv preprint, arXiv:1409.1556.

[27] C. Szegedy, W. Liu, Y. Jia, P. Sermanet, S. Reed, D. Anguelov, D. Erhan, V. Vanhoucke, A. Rabinovich, Going deeper with convolutions, in: Proceedings of the IEEE Conference on Computer Vision and Pattern Recognition, 2015, pp. 1–9.

[28] K. He, X. Zhang, S. Ren, J. Sun, Deep residual learning for image recognition, in: Proceedings of the IEEE Conference on Computer Vision and Pattern Recognition, 2016, pp. 770–778.

[29] G. Huang, Z. Liu, L. Van Der Maaten, K.Q. Weinberger, Densely connected convolutional networks, in: Proceedings of the IEEE Conference on Computer Vision and Pattern Recognition, 2017, pp. 4700–4708.

[30] Y. LeCun, B. Boser, J.S. Denker, D. Henderson, R.E. Howard, W. Hubbard, L.D. Jackel, Backpropagation applied to handwritten zip code recognition, Neural Computation 1 (4) (1989) 541–551.

[31] N. Srivastava, G. Hinton, A. Krizhevsky, I. Sutskever, R. Salakhutdinov, Dropout: a simple way to prevent neural networks from overfitting, Journal of Machine Learning Research 15 (1) (2014) 1929–1958.

[32] Y.E. Nesterov, A method for solving the convex programming problem with convergence rate $o(1/k^2)$, Doklady Akademii Nauk SSSR 269 (1983) 543–547.

Generative adversarial networks for medical image synthesis

Yang Lei, Richard L.J. Qiu, Tonghe Wang, Walter J. Curran Jr., Tian Liu, and Xiaofeng Yang

Department of Radiation Oncology and Winship Cancer Institute, Emory University, Atlanta, GA, United States

7.1 Introduction

Image synthesis is the process that generates synthetic/pseudo images in the target image modality/domain (named as target domain) from the inputs of source images that reside in a different image modality/domain (named as source domain). The aim of image synthesis is to bypass a certain imaging procedure and use the synthetic images instead [1]. The motivation could be multifold: the specific image acquisition is infeasible; it bears additional labor and cost; some imaging procedures add ionizing radiation exposure to patients; uncertainties could be introduced from the image registration between different modalities. In recent years, research in image synthesis has gained great interest in radiation oncology, radiology and biology [2]. The presumed benefits have intrigued several investigations in a number of potential clinical applications such as magnetic resonance imaging (MRI)-only radiation therapy treatment planning [3–9], positron emission tomography (PET)/MRI scanning [10,11], proton stopping power estimation [12–15], synthetic image-aided auto-segmentation [16–22], low dose computerized tomography (CT) denoising [23–25], image quality enhancement [26–29], reconstruction [30,12], high resolution visualization [31], etc.

Historically, image synthesis methods have been investigated for decades. The conventional machine learning methods, such as random forest-based methods or dictionary learning-based methods, usually rely on models with explicit manually designed principles about the conversion of images from one modality to another [7,9,32–39]. Therefore, the conventional methods are usually application-specific and can be complicated [40].

Unlike conventional machine learning, deep learning does not rely on hand-crafted features given by humans [2,40–42]. It utilizes neural networks (NNs) or convolutional NNs (CNNs) with several hidden layers containing a large number of neurons or convolutional kernels to automatically learn the way of extracting informative features. As a result, deep learning has been widely adopted in the medical

Biomedical Image Synthesis and Simulation. https://doi.org/10.1016/B978-0-12-824349-7.00014-1

imaging and biomedical imaging fields in the past several years [43]. For image synthesis tasks, the workflow of deep learning-based methods usually consists of two stages: a training stage for the network to build the mapping between the source and target image domain; and an inference stage to generate the synthetic image, called synthetic target image, from a newly arrived source image. Various networks and architectures have been proposed for better performance on different tasks. In this literature survey, a class of network architectures, called generative adversarial networks (GANs), especially the conditional GANs (cGANs) [44] and cycle-consistent GANs (Cycle-GANs), are introduced and explained. The emerging GAN-based methods and applications geared for medical and biomedical image synthesis are systematically reviewed and discussed. As compared to cGANs and Cycle-GANs, GAN models are only supervised by adversarial and discriminator losses without the image loss that is calculated between synthetic and ground-truth image. Thus, the spatial arrangement of the synthetic images generated by a GAN model may be incorrect or partially correct, but the generator manages to convince the discriminator that the image is real. Namely, for GAN models, the synthetic image structural details may be inconsistent. Finding out such inconsistencies would be difficult for medical and biomedical image synthesis applications. This difference between GANs and both cGANs and Cycle-GANs makes the cGANs and Cycle-GANs more popular. Thus, in this chapter, we plan to focus more on cGANs and Cycle-GANs. In short, we aim to:

- Summarize the latest network architecture designs of cGAN and Cycle-GAN.
- Summarize the latest medical and biomedical image synthesis applications of cGAN and Cycle-GAN.
- Highlight important contributions and identify existing challenges.

7.2 Generative adversarial networks

The GAN, introduced by Ian J. Goodfellow et al. [45], is a developed approach of "generative modeling" using a flexible unsupervised deep learning architecture. Generative modeling uses unsupervised or semi-supervised learning to learn a distribution from a training dataset and can then be used to generate data that mimic the training data. Its ability of creating massive realistic contents makes it extremely popular and useful, gaining tremendous success in the field of computer vision.

7.2.1 Network architecture

A GAN consists of two competing networks, a generator and a discriminator. The generator uses a noise vector as input. The generator is trained to generate artificial data that approximate the target data distribution. The discriminator is trained to distinguish the artificial data from the true data. The discriminator encourages the generator to predict realistic data by penalizing unrealistic predictions. While a discriminator tries to differentiate between real samples and those generated by the generator, the generator tries to fool the discriminator by minimizing this loss. The two networks compete in a zero-sum game. The adversarial loss could be considered as a trainable network-based loss term. The loss to supervise the generator of GAN is called adversarial loss. More details regarding the adversarial loss are introduced in Section 7.2.2.2.

Generally, the generator of a GAN is implemented via a CNN, which consists of several convolutional layers followed by fully connected layers to perform regression or classification. The discriminator of a GAN can also be implemented via a CNN. The output of the discriminator can be a scalar, where 1 represents "real" and 0 represents "fake". To achieve this, tanh or soft-max operator with thresholding is implemented at the end of the discriminator.

7.2.1.1 Deep convolutional GANs

Deep convolutional GANs produce better and more stable training results when a fully connected layer is replaced by a convolutional layer [46]. The architecture of the generator in DCGANs is illustrated in the work of [47]. In the core of the framework, pooling layers were replaced with fractional-stride convolutions, which allowed it to learn from a random input noise vector by spatial upsampling to generate an image from it.

7.2.2 Loss function

As described above, GANs rely on the continuous improvement of both the generator and the discriminator. The performance of these networks is directly dependent on the design of their loss functions.

7.2.2.1 Discriminator loss

The binary cross-entropy (BCE) loss is often used to supervise the discriminator network(s) [48]. Since the goal of the discriminator is to judge the authenticity of a generated image, the discriminator should improve its ability to identify a synthetic image as not real and an original image as real. For example, given the input noise vector I_n, the corresponding generator F_G learned from a previous iteration, the corresponding discriminator F_D, its target original/ground-truth image I_{tar}, and the generated synthetic image from input noise $F_G(I_n)$, the loss of the discriminator measured by BCE can be expressed as follows:

$$F_D = \arg\min_{F_D} \{BCE(F_D(I_{tar}), 1) + BCE(F_D(F_G(I_n)), 0)\}, \qquad (7.1)$$

where 1 denotes real and 0 denotes fake.

7.2.2.2 Adversarial loss

The loss function of the generator is often composed of several losses for different purposes/constraints. Here we first discuss the adversarial loss. As introduced above, the goal of the generator is to fool the discriminator, i.e., let the discriminator think a synthetic image is real. Thus, given the previously learned discriminator F_D, source noise I_n, ground-truth target image I_{tar}, and generator F_G, the adversarial loss measured by BCE can be expressed as follows:

$$L_{adv} = BCE\left(F_D\left(F_G\left(I_n\right)\right), 1\right), \qquad (7.2)$$

which means that by minimizing the loss term of Eq. (7.2), the synthetic image $F_G(I_n)$ would be close to real for the discriminator F_D.

7.2.3 Challenges of training GANs

GANs have gained a lot of interest in medical image processing due to their ability of data generation without explicitly modeling the probability density function. GANs have been shown to be useful in many biomedical and medical image applications, such as image reconstruction [49], image enhancement [48,50], segmentation [51, 52], classification and detection [53], augmentation [54], and cross-modality image synthesis [55].

GANs can improve the realism of generated results thanks to the adversarial supervision introduced. However, a "basic" GAN-based network can be difficult to train since the generator and discriminator need to be trained simultaneously to reach Nash equilibrium. Binary classifications of the results as fake or real provide stepped and unsmooth gradients, which makes it difficult to train the discriminator. To alleviate this problem, the Wasserstein GAN (WGAN) [56] was proposed to use Earth-Mover distance based metrics to replace the binary classification to improve the gradient back-propagation during discriminator training.

There were two important changes adopted to modify the architecture of early GANs, which were batch normalization and leaky ReLU. Batch normalization [57] was used for regulating the poor initialization to prevent the deep generator from mode collapse, which was a major drawback in the early GAN framework. Leaky ReLU [58] activation was introduced at the place of maxout activation [45] for all layers of a discriminator, which improved the resolution of the output image.

7.3 Conditional GANs

Initially, GANs were trained with no restrictions on data generation. Later, they were updated by using conditional image constraints to derive synthetic images with desired properties, coined as cGANs. CGANs have been extensively used in medical image synthesis studies thanks to their capability of data generation without explicitly modeling the probability density function. Paired images are used to train cGANs. The adversarial loss brought by the discriminator provides a clever way of incorporating unlabeled samples into training and imposing a higher order of consistency. One major difference between GANs and cGANs is that GANs take a noise vector as input, whereas the cGANs take a source image as input. This difference is shown in Fig. 7.1 (see (a) *vs.* (b)).

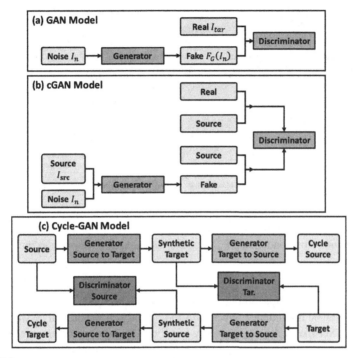

FIGURE 7.1

An illustration of GAN (a), cGAN (b), and Cycle-GAN (c) frameworks. The difference between GAN and cGAN is the input for generator and discriminator. The difference between cGAN and Cycle-GAN is that the Cycle-GAN needs two generators and two discriminators to build cycle loops and inverse mappings.

7.3.1 **Network architecture**

A cGAN is composed of a generative network and a discriminative network. The generative network is trained to generate synthetic images, and the discriminative network is trained to judge whether an input image is real or synthesized. The training goal of a cGAN is to train the generative network to produce synthetic images that are realistic enough to fool the discriminator, and train the discriminative network to distinguish the synthetic images from real images. As the two networks play a zero-sum game, the performance of each one increases when they compete against each other until both networks reach their maximum potential. This conflict goal explains the name of "adversarial." After the model is trained, the synthetic image of a new source image can be obtained via feeding it into the trained generator network.

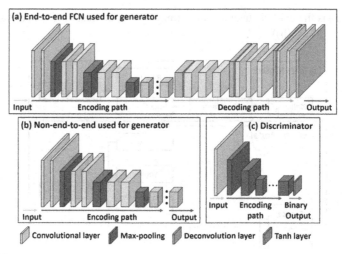

FIGURE 7.2

Illustrations of cGAN network architectures: (a) shows an end-to-end FCN used for generator; (b) shows a non-end-to-end FCN used for generator; (c) shows a discriminator architecture.

Fig. 7.2 shows example architectures of cGANs. Basically, the generator network of a cGAN can be implemented by an end-to-end fully convolutional network (FCN), such as a U-Net-like architecture as shown in Fig. 7.2(a), or be implemented by a non-end-to-end FCN as shown in Fig. 7.2(b). FCNs use convolutional neural networks (CNNs) to transform image pixels to pixel classes or synthetic pixel values. Unlike the CNNs that we encountered earlier for image classification or object detection, an FCN transforms the height and width of intermediate feature maps back to those of the input image: this is achieved by the transposed convolutional layer, also called deconvolution layer. As a result, the classification output and the input image have a one-to-one correspondence at the pixel level: the channel dimension at any output pixel holds the classification result for the input pixel at the same spatial position. In this book, we relax the definition of FCN compared with the CNN and consider U-Net-like architectures as FCNs, even though they include pooling layers.

The end-to-end FCN can generate an output of the same size as the input. The non-end-to-end FCN, on the other hand, can generate different sized outputs. The end-to-end FCN is often composed of an encoding path and a decoding path, where the encoding path down-samples the feature map size and the decoding path up-samples the feature map size to perform an end-to-end output. The encoding path is composed of either several convolutional layers with stride size larger than 1 or several convolutional layers with stride size of 1 followed by max-pooling layers to reduce the feature map's size. The decoding path is composed of several deconvolution layers to obtain the end-to-end mapping, several convolution layers, and maybe a tanh layer to perform the regression. There may be several residual blocks [50] or dense blocks [55] used as short skip connections between the encoding path and the decoding path. Residual blocks are frequently used to learn the residual information between source and target image domains. Dense blocks are used to capture multi-scale or multi-level image features. For some applications, a long residual block is used as a long skip connection [59], which bypasses the feature maps from the first convolution layer to the last convolution layer, to guide all the hidden layers of the generator focusing on learning the difference between input source and target domain images. Some works integrated attention gates into the long skip connection of the generator architecture to capture the most relevant semantic contextual information without enlarging the receptive field [17]. The feature maps extracted from the coarse scale were used in gating to disambiguate irrelevant and noisy responses in long skip connections. This was performed immediately prior to the concatenation operation to merge only relevant activations. Additionally, attention gates filter the neuron activations during both the forward pass and the backward pass.

The non-end-to-end FCN is commonly composed of an encoding path and maybe followed by several fully connected layers for the prediction task. The discriminator is often composed of several convolutional layers and max-pooling layers, and followed by a sigmoid or soft-max layer to perform the binary classification.

7.3.2 Loss function

As described above, to derive synthetic images with the desired properties, differently from GANs, cGANs need to be supervised not only in terms of the minimization of the adversarial and discriminator losses, but also in terms of the minimization of the conditional loss $L_{condition}$ that can describe the desired properties. Thus, the total loss to supervise generator and discriminator is as follows:

$$F_G = \arg\min_{F_G} \{L_{condition}\left(F_G\left(I_{src}\right), I_{tar}\right) + \mu L_{adv}\}, \qquad (7.3)$$

where μ denotes the balancing parameter of adversarial loss, and

$$F_D = \arg\min_{F_D} \{BCE\left(F_D\left(I_{tar}\right), 1\right) + BCE\left(F_D\left(F_G\left(I_{src}\right)\right), 0\right)\}. \qquad (7.4)$$

7.3.2.1 Image distance loss

Several image distance losses exist to measure the difference between synthetic and target images. Two kinds of widely used losses are the pixel-wise loss and the structural loss. The mean square error (MSE) is often used as pixel-wise loss for image synthesis tasks [2,60]. Some other works used the l_p-norm ($p \in (1, 2)$) as pixel-wise loss [55]. As the l_p-norm regularization has fewer solutions than the l_2-norm optimization (MSE), over-smoothing results (i.e., blurry regions) are reduced. On the other hand, it is demonstrated that the optimization solution under l_p-norm regularization has more solutions than the l_1-norm optimization (MAE). It means the misclassification situations (the solution on ± 1, such as misclassification of bone-to-air in MRI-only synthetic CT estimation) are minimized by averaging several solutions obtained by similar samples (the solution around ± 1).

The second component of the image distance loss function is the gradient difference loss (GDL), which measures the structural similarity between synthetic and ground-truth target images. Between any two images X and Y, the GDL is defined as

$$GDL(X, Y) = \sum_{i,j,k} \left\{ \begin{array}{l} \left(|X_{i,j,k} - X_{i-1,j,k}| - |Y_{i,j,k} - Y_{i-1,j,k}| \right)^2 \\ + \left(|X_{i,j,k} - X_{i,j-1,k}| - |Y_{i,j,k} - Y_{i,j-1,k}| \right)^2 \\ + \left(|X_{i,j,k} - X_{i,j,k-1}| - |Y_{i,j,k} - Y_{i,j,k-1}| \right)^2 \end{array} \right\}, \quad (7.5)$$

where i, j, and k represent pixels in the x-, y-, and z-axis, respectively.

7.3.2.2 Histogram matching loss

To force the synthetic image to reach a similar histogram distribution as that of the ground truth image, Lei et al. proposed a histogram matching loss, also called Max-Info loss [61]. The MaxInfo loss is a measure of mutual dependency between two probability distributions,

$$\text{MaxInfo}(X, Y) = \sum_{i,j,k} p\left(X_{i,j,k}, Y_{i,j,k}\right) \log \frac{p\left(X_{i,j,k}, Y_{i,j,k}\right)}{p\left(X_{i,j,k}\right) \cdot p\left(Y_{i,j,k}\right)}, \quad (7.6)$$

where $p(X, Y)$ is the joint probability function of X and Y; $p(X)$ and $p(Y)$ are the marginal probability functions of X and Y.

7.3.2.3 Perceptual loss

The challenge of some synthesis tasks is that the structure/edge boundary would be blurred due to residual anatomical mismatches between the training deformed source image and ground-truth target image [61]. If only the image distance loss is used (e.g., MSE or GDL), GAN-based methods could not produce sharp boundaries as mismatches between source and target images are mixed during training. Indeed, even with accurate registration, a small mismatch between the source and target image in a training pair still exists. The perceptual loss is often used to enhance the boundary contrast and sharpness. The main idea of perceptual supervision [62] is that feeding forward networks (i.e., generator(s)) could generate a high-confidence fooling image (i.e., synthetic image) by using a perceptual loss that measures the perceptual and semantic differences between synthetic and ground-truth images.

The perceptual loss is defined by a feature difference on high-level feature maps. These high-level feature maps are extracted from both the target and synthetic target images, via a network named feature pyramid network. Many pre-trained networks have been trained on ImageNet [62]. Such networks can also be trained on other datasets. For example, for lung CT synthesis tasks, the feature pyramid network can be pre-trained using the dataset of thoracic CT images and paired lung contours obtained from 2017 AAPM Thoracic Auto-segmentation Challenge [52,63].

The feature pyramid network, denoted by F_s, extracted multi-level feature maps from the ground-truth target image (X) and the synthetic image (Y), respectively, i.e., $f_X = \bigcup_{i=1}^{N} F_s^i(X)$ and $f_Y = \bigcup_{i=1}^{N} F_s^i(Y)$, where N is the number of pyramid levels. The perceptual loss is defined as the Euclidean distance between the two feature maps, and calculated as

$$L_p(f_X, f_Y) = \sum_{i=1}^{N} \frac{\omega_i}{C_i \cdot H_i \cdot W_i \cdot D_i} \left\| F_s^i(X) - F_s^i(Y) \right\|_2^2, \qquad (7.7)$$

where C_i denotes the number of feature map channels at the ith pyramid level; H_i, W_i, and D_i denote the height, width, and depth of that feature map; ω_i is a balancing parameter for feature level i. Since the semantic information of the feature map at higher pyramid levels would be coarse, the weight for that level's perceptual loss should be enlarged, thus it is often set as $\omega_i = p^{i-1}$ with $p \in (1, 2)$ [61].

7.3.3 Variants of cGANs

Many variants of the cGAN framework have been proposed to meet the desired output. In this chapter, we examine some cGAN frameworks that are or can be used for medical or biomedical image synthesis, which includes Pix2pix and InfoGAN.

7.3.3.1 Pix2pix

Pix2pix is a supervised image-to-image translation model proposed by Isola et al. [44]. Pix2pix is a kind of cGAN but in an end-to-end synthesis way. Namely, the network outputs an equal-sized synthetic image from the input source image. It has received a multi-domain user acceptance in the computer vision community for image synthesis, whose merit is to combine the adversarial loss with the l_1-norm minimization loss (or termed as MAE loss) so that the network learns not only the mapping from the input image to the output image but also the loss function to generate an image resembling the ground truth. To train this network, both the adversarial loss of judging the authenticity of synthetic images and the image-based accuracy loss (such as MAE) are used. By using an image-based accuracy loss, the cGAN is trained in a supervised manner, which can be more suitable for the image synthesis task when the learning targets are given. For example, in the image synthesis task of MRI-only radiation therapy, the paired planning CT and corresponding registered MRI are given for training. By training a supervised cGAN, the synthetic CT (sCT) for a new arrival MRI can not only look like a real CT but also has accurate intensity value, i.e., Hounsfield value, which is essential for radiation therapy dose calculation.

7.3.3.2 InfoGAN

For some medical image synthesis tasks, such as cone beam CT (CBCT) scatter correction and PET attenuation correction, the histogram of the generated synthetic image also matters. If only using image intensity value accuracy as loss function, the model then cannot be supervised properly. InfoGAN was developed for computer vision tasks by adding an information-theoretic extension to the cGAN that is able to learn disentangled representations. InfoGAN is a cGAN that also maximizes the mutual information, which forces the image distribution similarity between a small subset of the latent variables and the observation [64]. A lower bound of the mutual information objective was derived that could be optimized efficiently. For example, InfoGAN successfully disentangled writing styles from digit shapes on the modified national institute of standards and technology (MNIST) dataset, pose from lighting of 3D rendered images, and background digits from the central digit on the street view house numbers (SVHN) dataset [64]. It also discovered visual concepts that included hair styles, presence/absence of eyeglasses, and emotions on the CelebFaces attributes dataset. It would be expected that InfoGAN could serve well for medical or biomedical image synthesis in the future. InfoGAN has for example been used to generate 3D CT volume from 2D projection data [61].

7.4 Cycle GAN

As introduced previously, cGANs rely on two sub-networks, a generator and a discriminator, that compete against each other and are optimized sequentially in a zero-sum framework. Namely, the discriminator learns to enhance its ability to differentiate real from fake, and the generator learns to enhance its ability to derive real-looking synthetic images to fool the discriminator. Cycle-GANs double the process of a typical cGAN by enforcing an inverse transformation, i.e., translating a synthetic target image back to the source image domain, called cycle source image [65]. This difference between cGAN and Cycle-GAN is shown in Fig. 7.1(b)–(c). It further constrains the model and can increase the accuracy in the output synthetic target image. Mismatches could exist between source and target image domains in the training set even after good image registration, which would create an ill-posed problem. To address this issue, a Cycle-GANs introduces an additional cycle loop to force the model to be close to a one-to-one mapping.

7.4.1 Network architecture

Fig. 7.1(c) shows an example of traditional Cycle-GAN framework. As can be seen, the Cycle-GAN is composed of two full loops: the first is a mapping from the source image domain to the target image domain and then a mapping from the target image domain back to the source image domain; the second loop is a mapping from the target image domain to the source image domain and then a mapping from the source image domain back to the target image domain. Thus, the Cycle-GAN is composed of two generators, i.e., from the source image domain to the target image domain and from the target image domain to the source image domain. The two generators often share the same network architecture, but with different parameters that are optimized alternately and independently. The framework also includes two discriminators: one is to judge whether the synthetic source image is real or fake; the other is used to judge whether the synthetic target image is real or fake.

7.4.2 Loss function: cycle consistency loss

As compared to cGANs, Cycle-GANs introduce two cycle loops, namely from the source to the target and then from the target to the source (regarded as back to the source, thus, the first cycle loop), and from the target to the source and then from the source to the target (regarded as back to the target, thus, the second cycle loop). These two loops force the trained model to be close to a one-to-one mapping. To achieve this, the cycle consistency loss is introduced. Let $G_{\text{src}-\text{tar}}$ denote the generator of the mapping from the source image domain to the target image domain, $G_{\text{tar}-\text{src}}$ denote the generator of the mapping from the target image domain to the source image domain, I_{src} denote the source image, I_{tar} denote the target image, and L_d denote the image distance loss, which can be the MAE, MSE or GDL as introduced in Section 7.3.2.1. Then, the cycle consistency loss can be represented as follows:

$$L_{cyc}\left(G_{\text{src}-\text{tar}}, G_{\text{tar}-\text{src}}, I_{\text{src}}, I_{\text{tar}}\right) = \begin{array}{l} L_d\left(G_{\text{tar}-\text{src}}\left(G_{\text{src}-\text{tar}}(I_{\text{src}})\right), I_{\text{src}}\right) \\ +L_d\left(G_{\text{src}-\text{tar}}\left(G_{\text{tar}-\text{src}}(I_{\text{tar}})\right), I_{\text{tar}}\right) \end{array}, \quad (7.8)$$

where $G_{\text{tar}-\text{src}}\left(G_{\text{src}-\text{tar}}(I_{\text{src}})\right)$ is the output of first feeding I_{src} into the generator $G_{\text{src}-\text{tar}}$ and then feeding the output into the generator $G_{\text{tar}-\text{src}}$, namely the output of this term denotes the cycle source image. Thus, the optimization of the two generators is obtained by

$$G_{\text{src}-\text{tar}}, G_{\text{tar}-\text{src}} = \underset{G_{\text{src}-\text{tar}}, G_{\text{tar}-\text{src}}}{\arg\min} \left\{ \begin{array}{l} L_{\text{adv}}\left(G_{\text{src}-\text{tar}}(I_{\text{src}})\right) + L_{\text{adv}}(G_{\text{tar}-\text{src}}(I_{\text{tar}})) \\ +L_{cyc}\left(G_{\text{src}-\text{tar}}, G_{\text{tar}-\text{src}}, I_{\text{src}}, I_{\text{tar}}\right) \end{array} \right\}.$$
$$(7.9)$$

Denoting by D_{src} and D_{tar} the two discriminators, the optimization of the two discriminators is obtained by

$$(D_{\text{src}}, D_{\text{tar}}) = \underset{D_{\text{src}}, D_{\text{tar}}}{\arg\min} \left\{ \begin{array}{l} BCE\left[D_{\text{src}}\left(G_{\text{src}-\text{tar}}(I_{\text{src}})\right), 0\right] + BCE\left[D_{\text{src}}\left(I_{\text{src}}\right), 1\right] \\ +BCE\left[D_{\text{tar}}\left(G_{\text{tar}-\text{src}}(I_{\text{tar}})\right), 0\right] + BCE\left[D_{\text{tar}}\left(I_{\text{tar}}\right), 1\right] \end{array} \right\}.$$
$$(7.10)$$

7.4.3 Variants of Cycle GAN

Many variants of the Cycle-GAN framework have been proposed for image synthesis. In this study, we review some Cycle-GAN frameworks that are or can be used for medical or biomedical image synthesis, which includes residual Cycle-GAN [50], dense Cycle-GAN [55], unsupervised image-to-image translation networks [66], Bicycle-GAN [67] and StarGAN [68].

7.4.3.1 Residual Cycle-GAN

For image synthesis tasks, promising results have been accomplished by Cycle-GANs with residual blocks when source and target image modalities shared good similarity, such as between CBCT and CT images [50] or between low dose PET and full dose PET [69]. In these works, several residual blocks were used as short skip connections in generators of Cycle-GANs. Each residual block was constructed with a residual connection and multiple hidden layers, as shown in Fig. 7.3. The input feature map was extracted from the source image and then it bypassed the hidden layers of a residual block via the residual connection, therefore the hidden layers were assigned to learn the differences between source and target images. A residual block was engineered using two convolution layers within residual connection and an element-wise sum operator.

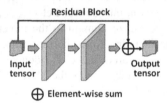

FIGURE 7.3

An illustration of residual block. This block is implemented by two convolutional layers with an element-wise sum operator.

7.4.3.2 Dense Cycle-GAN

When the source image is very different from the target image, the major difficulty in modeling the synthesis is that the location, structure, and shape of the source and target images can vary significantly among different patients. In order to accurately predict each voxel in the anatomic regions, such as soft-tissue and bone structures in the task of mapping MRI to CT, inspired by densely connected CNNs, several dense blocks were introduced to capture multi-scale information (including low- and high-frequency) by extracting features from previous hidden layers and deeper hidden layers [55]. As shown in the generator architecture of Fig. 7.4, the dense block is implemented by five convolutional layers, a concatenation operator, and a convolutional layer to shorten the feature map size. Similar to the residual blocks used in Cycle-GANs, dense blocks are also often used as short skip connections in generators.

7.4.3.3 Unsupervised image-to-image translation networks (UNIT)

Some image synthesis problems such as multi-modal MRI synthesis [70] require mapping multiple image domains rather than mapping only one image domain to another image domain. In computer vision, such tasks were previously solved by unsupervised image-to-image translation networks (UNIT). The UNIT framework aims at learning a joint distribution of images in different domains by using images from the marginal distributions in individual domains. It would be difficult to learn the joint distribution from the arrival source image's marginal distribution without additional assumptions. To address the problem, a shared-latent space assumption

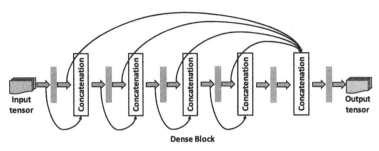

FIGURE 7.4

An illustration of a dense block.

was introduced and an unsupervised image-to-image translation framework based on coupled GANs was proposed [44].

7.4.3.4 Bicycle-GAN

For multi-modal image synthesis, Zhu et al. [67] improved the UNIT by introducing Bicycle-GAN. This network aims to model a distribution of possible outputs in a conditional generative modeling setting. The ambiguity of the mapping is distilled in a low-dimensional latent vector, which can be randomly sampled at test time. A generator learns to map the given input, combined with this latent code, to the output. It was explicitly encouraged that the connection between output and latent code be invertible. This helps prevent a many-to-one mapping from the latent code to the output during training, also known as mode collapse, which produces more diverse results. Zhu et al. explored several variants of this approach by employing different training objectives, network architectures, and methods of injecting the latent code. Bicycle-GAN encouraged bijective consistency between the latent encoding and output modes.

7.4.3.5 StarGAN

StarGAN, also known as Unified GAN, is another variant of Cycle-GAN used for multi-modal image translation [68]. The challenge of multi-modal image synthesis is the limited scalability and robustness in handling more than two domains, since different models should be built independently for every pair of image domains. To address this limitation, StarGAN was proposed to solve the multiple modality image-to-image translations using only a single model. The unified model architecture of StarGAN allows simultaneous training of multiple datasets from different domains within a single network. This leads to superior quality of translated images compared to traditional Cycle-GAN models, as well as the novel capability of flexibly translating an input image to any desired target domain. StarGAN was previously used in computer vision tasks such as a facial attribute transfer and facial expression synthesis tasks [68], and was also used for multi-modal MRI synthesis [70].

7.5 Practical aspects

Raw data from clinical databases are usually not suited for network training. It is important to perform data pre-processing such as cropping, zero-padding or patching based on a setup of network input dimension and size, image normalization and data augmentation prior to network training.

7.5.1 Network input dimension and size

Based on different goals, the networks take either 3D or 2D medical images as input. Depending on the network design and graphics processing unit (GPU) memory limitation, some methods directly use the whole volume as input to train the network [71], while some methods process the 3D image slice by slice, called as 2.5D [60], or use 2D/3D patches [72–74,61]. The 3D-based approaches take 3D patches or the whole volume as input and utilize 3D convolution kernels to extract spatial and contextual information from the input images. Full-sized whole volume training often leads to increasing computational cost and complexity as a larger number of layers are used. Compared to whole volume-based methods, some methods extract 2D small patches from the 3D image by sliding a 2D window across the original images prior to network prediction, and then use patch fusion to obtain the final full-sized result. 2D/3D patch-based methods are less computationally demanding.

7.5.2 Pre-processing

Pre-processing plays an important role in synthesis tasks, since there are intensity, contrast, and noise variations in the images. To ease network training, pre-processing techniques are usually applied beforehand. Typical pre-processing techniques include registration [75–82], bias/scatter/attenuation correction [83,10], voxel intensity normalization [84] and cropping [85].

7.5.3 Data augmentation

Data augmentation is used to reduce over-fitting and increase the amount of training samples. Typical data augmentation techniques include rotation, translation, scaling, flipping, distortion, linear warping, elastic deformation, and noise contamination [86].

7.6 CGAN and Cycle-GAN applications

Conditional GANs and Cycle-GANs have been successfully used for several medical/biomedical applications. In this section, we only briefly summarize some of them as these applications will be discussed in detail in the next few chapters in Part 2 of this book.

7.6.1 Multi-modal MRI synthesis

MRI is widely used in clinical practice thanks to its capability in providing meaningful anatomical and functional information [87]. Through applying different MRI pulse sequences, multi-contrast images can be acquired while scanning the same anatomy. Therefore, integrating the strengths of each sequence can help unveiling rich underlying information of tissue that facilitates diagnosis and treatment management [35,55,88–90]. However, due to limited scan time, inconsistent machine settings, scan artifacts and corruption, and patient allergies to contrast agents, it is difficult to apply a unified group of MRI scan sequences to each individual patient. To tackle this challenge, cGAN and Cycle-GAN frameworks have been investigated for multi-modal MRI synthesis [91–98].

7.6.2 MRI-only radiation therapy treatment planning

MRI has superior soft tissue contrast over CT, allowing for improved organ-at-risk segmentation and target delineation for radiation therapy treatment planning [99]. Since dose calculation algorithms rely on electron density maps generated from CT images for calculating dose, MRIs are typically registered to CT images and used alongside the CT image for treatment planning [100]. Since electron density information and CT images are vital to the treatment-planning workflow, methods which generate electron density and CT images from MRIs, called sCT generation, have been investigated [101–103]. CGANs and Cycle-GANs have been used in the generation of sCT by introducing an additional discriminator to distinguish the sCT from real CT [59,55]. Please, see more details from Chapter 20 "Image synthesis for MRI-only radiotherapy treatment planning" of this book.

7.6.3 Image quality improvement/enhancement

Image quality improvement or enhancement, such as CBCT correction, PET attenuation correction (AC), and low-dose or low-count PET, is essential for medical imaging. The Cycle-GAN framework has been used for CBCT correction thanks to its ability of efficiently converting images between the source domain and the target domain when the underlying structures are similar, even if the mapping between domains is nonlinear [50]. For the PET AC, cGANs and Cycle-GANs are used to directly estimate AC PET from non-AC PET. Dong et al. applied a Cycle-GAN to perform PET AC on whole body for the first time [48]. They also demonstrated the reliability of their method by including sequential scans in their testing datasets to evaluate the PET intensity changes with time on their AC PET, as well as ground truth. Cycle-GAN was applied as a learning-based low-count PET reconstruction method [69], which was performed directly on low-count PET to generate full-count PET. Please, see more details from Chapter 13 "Medical image denoising", Chapter 18 "Image synthesis for low-count PET acquisitions: lower dose, shorter time", and Chapter 19 "PET/MRI attenuation correction" of this book.

7.6.4 Cell synthesis

Cell image synthesis is often considered a three-step approach with the initial generation of cell phantoms, texture synthesis and a final simulation of the imaging system [104]. The morphology can be modeled, e.g., using prior knowledge-based deformations of basic shapes [104], statistical shape models [105], spherical harmonics [106] or using shape spaces derived from diffeomorphic measurements [107]. As a next step, generated phantoms need to be translated to realistically looking images, which can be obtained either conventionally by mathematic description of the texture synthesis, by modeling protein distributions in sub-cellular components or by transfer of real textures to the simulated objects [108].

CGANs and Cycle-GANs excel at realistic image data generation as well. Extensions of the cGAN framework with conditional labels allow generating realistic images that reflect semantic properties provided to the generator [44,67]. These methods have also been used for generating biological images like multi-channel data of human cultured cells [109], protein localization in different cell cycle stages [110] or entire tissues [111]. In addition to the generation of realistic textures, GANs have also been successfully used to mimic the shape of cells in 3D [112]. The simulations are usually finalized by placing synthetic phantoms in a virtual image space and by performing a simulation of the imaging system. This is often accomplished by adding artificial disruptions like dark current, photon shot noise, sensor readout noise, and a point spread function [113] or using more elaborate physically motivated wave-optical simulation approaches [114]. Please, see more details from Chapter 21 "Review of cell image synthesis for image processing."

7.7 Summary and discussion

GANs have been increasingly used in the application of medical/biomedical imaging. As reviewed in this chapter, cGAN- and Cycle-GAN-based image synthesis is an active research field. With developments in both artificial intelligence and computing hardware, more GAN-based methods are expected to facilitate the clinical workflow with novel applications. Compared with conventional model-based methods, GAN-based methods are more generalized since the same network and architecture for a pair of image modalities can be applied to different pairs of image modalities with minimal adjustment. This allows easy extension of the applications using a similar methodology to a variety of imaging modalities for image synthesis. GAN-based methods generally outperform conventional methods in generating more realistic synthetic images with higher similarity to real images and better quantitative metrics. In implementation, depending on the hardware, training a GAN-based model usually takes several hours to days. However, once the model is trained, it can be applied to new patients to generate synthetic images within a few seconds or minutes. Due to these advantages, GAN-based methods have attracted great research and clinical interest in medical imaging and biomedical imaging.

Although the reviewed literature shows the success of GAN-based image synthesis in various applications, there are still some open questions that need to be answered in future studies. Firstly, for the training of GAN-based models, most of the reviewed studies require paired datasets, i.e., the source image and target image need to have pixel-to-pixel correspondence. This requirement poses difficulties in collecting sufficient eligible datasets, as well as demands high accuracy in image registration. As compared to cGANs, it is demonstrated that Cycle-GANs can relax the requirement of the paired datasets to unpaired datasets, which can be beneficial for clinical application in enrolling a large number of patient datasets for training. However, even though the image quality obtained with Cycle-GANs can be better than with cGANs, the numerical performance may not be improved significantly in some synthesis tasks due to the residual mismatch between synthetic image and ground truth target image.

Secondly, although the merits of GAN-based methods have been demonstrated, their performance can be inconsistent under the circumstances that the input images are drastically different from the training dataset. As a matter of fact, unusual cases are generally excluded in most of the reviewed studies. Therefore, these unusual cases, which do happen occasionally in clinical setting, should be dealt with caution when using GAN-based methods to generate synthetic images. For example, some patients have a hip prosthesis, which creates severe artifacts on both CT and MR images. The related effect of its inclusion in the training or testing dataset towards network performance is an important question that has not been studied, yet. There are more unusual cases that could exist in all those imaging modalities and are worth of investigation, for example, all kinds of implants that introduce artifacts, obese patients whose scan has higher noise level than on average, and patients with anatomical abnormalities, just to name a few. To conclude, the research in image synthesis is still wide open. The authors are expected to see more activities in this domain for the years to come.

Disclosures

The authors declare no conflicts of interest.

References

[1] A. Alotaibi, Deep generative adversarial networks for image-to-image translation: a review, Symmetry 12 (2020) 1705.

[2] T. Wang, Y. Lei, Y. Fu, J.F. Wynne, W.J. Curran, T. Liu, X. Yang, A review on medical imaging synthesis using deep learning and its clinical applications, J. Appl. Clin. Med. Phys. 22 (2021) 11–36.

[3] Y. Liu, Y. Lei, Y. Wang, T. Wang, L. Ren, L. Lin, M. McDonald, W.J. Curran, T. Liu, J. Zhou, X. Yang, MRI-based treatment planning for proton radiotherapy: dosimetric

validation of a deep learning-based liver synthetic CT generation method, Phys. Med. Biol. 64 (2019) 145015.

[4] Y. Liu, Y. Lei, T. Wang, O. Kayode, S. Tian, T. Liu, P. Patel, W.J. Curran, L. Ren, X. Yang, MRI-based treatment planning for liver stereotactic body radiotherapy: validation of a deep learning-based synthetic CT generation method, Br. J. Radiol. 92 (2019) 20190067.

[5] Y. Liu, Y. Lei, Y. Wang, G. Shafai-Erfani, T. Wang, S. Tian, P. Patel, A.B. Jani, M. McDonald, W.J. Curran, T. Liu, J. Zhou, X. Yang, Evaluation of a deep learning-based pelvic synthetic CT generation technique for MRI-based prostate proton treatment planning, Phys. Med. Biol. 64 (2019) 205022.

[6] G. Shafai-Erfani, Y. Lei, Y. Liu, Y. Wang, T. Wang, J. Zhong, T. Liu, M. McDonald, W.J. Curran, J. Zhou, H.K. Shu, X. Yang, MRI-based proton treatment planning for base of skull tumors, Int. J. Part. Ther. 6 (2019) 12–25.

[7] Y. Lei, J.J. Jeong, T. Wang, H.K. Shu, P. Patel, S. Tian, T. Liu, H. Shim, H. Mao, A.B. Jani, W.J. Curran, X. Yang, MRI-based pseudo CT synthesis using anatomical signature and alternating random forest with iterative refinement model, J. Med. Imag. 5 (2018) 043504.

[8] Y. Lei, H-K. Shu, S. Tian, T. Wang, T. Liu, H. Mao, H. Shim, W.J. Curran, X. Yang, Pseudo CT estimation using patch-based joint dictionary learning, in: IEEE Engineering in Medicine & Biology Society, 2018, pp. 5150–5153.

[9] X. Yang, Y. Lei, H-K.G. Shu, P. Rossi, H. Mao, H. Shim, W.J. Curran, T. Liu, Pseudo CT estimation from MRI using patch-based random forest, SPIE Med. Imaging 10133 (2017).

[10] X. Yang, T. Wang, Y. Lei, K. Higgins, T. Liu, H. Shim, W.J. Curran, H. Mao, J.A. Nye, MRI-based attenuation correction for brain PET/MRI based on anatomic signature and machine learning, Phys. Med. Biol. 64 (2019) 025001.

[11] X. Yang, B. Fei, Multiscale segmentation of the skull in MR images for MRI-based attenuation correction of combined MR/PET, J. Am. Med. Inform. Assoc. 20 (2013) 1037–1045.

[12] J. Harms, Y. Lei, T. Wang, M. McDonald, B. Ghavidel, W. Stokes, W.J. Curran, J. Zhou, T. Liu, X. Yang, Cone-beam CT-derived relative stopping power map generation via deep learning for proton radiotherapy, Med. Phys. 47 (2020) 4416–4427.

[13] T. Wang, Y. Lei, J. Harms, B. Ghavidel, L. Lin, J. Beitler, M. McDonald, W. Curran, T. Liu, J. Zhou, X. Yang, Learning-based stopping power mapping on dual energy CT for proton radiation therapy, arXiv:Medical Physics, arXiv:2005.12908, 2020.

[14] S. Charyyev, T. Wang, Y. Lei, B. Ghavidel, J. Beitler, M. McDonald, W. Curran, T. Liu, J. Zhou, X. Yang, Learning-based synthetic dual energy CT imaging from single energy CT for stopping power ratio calculation in proton radiation therapy, arXiv: Medical Physics, arXiv:2005.12908, 2020.

[15] S. Charyyev, Y. Lei, J. Harms, B. Eaton, M. McDonald, W.J. Curran, T. Liu, J. Zhou, R. Zhang, X. Yang, High quality proton portal imaging using deep learning for proton radiation therapy: a phantom study, Biomed. Phys. Eng. Express 6 (2020) 035029.

[16] X. Dai, Y. Lei, T. Wang, A. Dhabaan, M. McDonald, J. Beitler, W. Curran, J. Zhou, T. Liu, X. Yang, Synthetic MRI-aided head-and-neck organs-at-risk auto-delineation for CBCT-guided adaptive radiotherapy, arXiv: Medical Physics, arXiv:2010.04275, 2020.

[17] X. Dong, Y. Lei, S. Tian, T. Wang, P. Patel, W.J. Curran, A.B. Jani, T. Liu, X. Yang, Synthetic MRI-aided multi-organ segmentation on male pelvic CT using cycle consistent deep attention network, Radiother. Oncol. 141 (2019) 192–199.

[18] Y. Lei, X. Dong, Z. Tian, Y. Liu, S. Tian, T. Wang, X. Jiang, P. Patel, A.B. Jani, H. Mao, W.J. Curran, T. Liu, X. Yang, CT prostate segmentation based on synthetic MRI-aided deep attention fully convolution network, Med. Phys. 47 (2020) 530–540.

[19] Y. Lei, T. Wang, J. Harms, Y. Fu, X. Dong, W.J. Curran, T. Liu, X. Yang, CBCT-based synthetic MRI generation for CBCT-guided adaptive radiotherapy, in: D. Nguyen, et al. (Eds.), Artificial Intelligence in Radiation Therapy, Springer International Publishing, Cham, 2019, pp. 154–161.

[20] Y. Lei, T. Wang, S. Tian, X. Dong, A.B. Jani, D. Schuster, W.J. Curran, P. Patel, T. Liu, X. Yang, Male pelvic multi-organ segmentation aided by CBCT-based synthetic MRI, Phys. Med. Biol. 65 (2020) 035013.

[21] Y. Liu, Y. Lei, Y. Fu, T. Wang, J. Zhou, X. Jiang, M. McDonald, J.J. Beitler, W.J. Curran, T. Liu, X. Yang, Head and neck multi-organ auto-segmentation on CT images aided by synthetic MRI, Med. Phys. 47 (2020) 4294–4302.

[22] Y. Fu, Y. Lei, T. Wang, S. Tian, P. Patel, A.B. Jani, W.J. Curran, T. Liu, X. Yang, Pelvic multi-organ segmentation on cone-beam CT for prostate adaptive radiotherapy, Med. Phys. 47 (2020) 3415–3422.

[23] J.M. Wolterink, T. Leiner, M.A. Viergever, I. Isgum, Generative adversarial networks for noise reduction in low-dose CT, IEEE Trans. Med. Imaging 36 (2017) 2536–2545.

[24] Y. Lei, D. Xu, Z. Zhou, T. Wang, X. Dong, T. Liu, A. Dhabaan, W.J. Curran, X. Yang, A denoising algorithm for CT image using low-rank sparse coding, SPIE Med. Imaging 10574 (2018).

[25] T. Wang, Y. Lei, Z. Tian, X. Dong, Y. Liu, X. Jiang, W.J. Curran, T. Liu, H.K. Shu, X. Yang, Deep learning-based image quality improvement for low-dose computed tomography simulation in radiation therapy, J. Med. Imag. 6 (2019) 043504.

[26] X. Dai, Y. Lei, Y. Liu, T. Wang, L. Ren, W.J. Curran, P. Patel, T. Liu, X. Yang, Intensity non-uniformity correction in MR imaging using residual cycle generative adversarial network, Phys. Med. Biol. 65 (2020) 215025.

[27] T. Wang, Y. Lei, N. Manohar, S. Tian, A.B. Jani, H.K. Shu, K. Higgins, A. Dhabaan, P. Patel, X. Tang, T. Liu, W.J. Curran, X. Yang, Dosimetric study on learning-based cone-beam CT correction in adaptive radiation therapy, Med. Dosim. 44 (2019) e71–e79.

[28] Y. Lei, X. Tang, K. Higgins, T. Wang, T. Liu, A. Dhabaan, H. Shim, W.J. Curran, X. Yang, Improving image quality of cone-beam CT using alternating regression forest, SPIE Med. Imaging 10573 (2018).

[29] X. Yang, Y. Lei, X. Dong, T. Wang, K. Higgins, T. Liu, H. Shim, W.J. Curran, H. Mao, J.A. Nye, J. Nucl. Med. 60 (2019) 174.

[30] G. Yang, S. Yu, H. Dong, G. Slabaugh, P.L. Dragotti, X. Ye, F. Liu, S. Arridge, J. Keegan, Y. Guo, D. Firmin, J. Keegan, G. Slabaugh, S. Arridge, X. Ye, Y. Guo, S. Yu, F. Liu, D. Firmin, P.L. Dragotti, G. Yang, H. Dong, DAGAN: deep de-aliasing generative adversarial networks for fast compressed sensing MRI reconstruction, IEEE Trans. Med. Imaging 37 (2018) 1310–1321.

[31] Y. Lei, D. Xu, Z. Zhou, K. Higgins, X. Dong, T. Liu, H. Shim, H. Mao, W.J. Curran, X. Yang, High-resolution CT image retrieval using sparse convolutional neural network, SPIE Med. Imaging 10573 (2018).

[32] D. Andreasen, K. Van Leemput, R.H. Hansen, J.A.L. Andersen, J.M. Edmund, Patch-based generation of a pseudo CT from conventional MRI sequences for MRI-only radiotherapy of the brain, Med. Phys. 42 (2015) 1596–1605.

[33] S. Aouadi, A. Vasic, S. Paloor, R.W. Hammoud, T. Torfeh, P. Petric, N. Al-Hammadi, Sparse patch-based method applied to mri-only radiotherapy planning, Phys. Med. 32 (2016) 309.

[34] A. Torrado-Carvajal, J.L. Herraiz, E. Alcain, A.S. Montemayor, L. Garcia-Canamaque, J.A. Hernandez-Tamames, Y. Rozenholc, N. Malpica, Fast patch-based pseudo-CT synthesis from T1-weighted MR images for PET/MR attenuation correction in brain studies, J. Nucl. Med. 57 (2016) 136–143.

[35] Y. Lei, H.K. Shu, S. Tian, J.J. Jeong, T. Liu, H. Shim, H. Mao, T. Wang, A.B. Jani, W.J. Curran, X. Yang, Magnetic resonance imaging-based pseudo computed tomography using anatomic signature and joint dictionary learning, J. Med. Imag. 5 (2018) 034001.

[36] T. Huynh, Y.Z. Gao, J.Y. Kang, L. Wang, P. Zhang, J. Lian, D.G. Shen, A.s.D.N. Initi, Estimating CT image from MRI data using structured random forest and auto-context model, IEEE Trans. Med. Imaging 35 (2016) 174–183.

[37] D. Andreasen, J.M. Edmund, V. Zografos, B.H. Menze, K. Van Leemput, Computed tomography synthesis from magnetic resonance images in the pelvis using multiple random forests and auto-context features, Proc. SPIE 9784 (2016).

[38] X. Yang, Y. Lei, H-K. Shu, P. Rossi, H. Mao, H. Shim, W.J. Curran, T. Liu, A learning-based approach to derive electron density from anatomical MRI for radiation therapy treatment planning, Int. J. Radiat. Oncol. Biol. Phys. (2017) S173–S174, Elsevier.

[39] G. Shafai-Erfani, T. Wang, Y. Lei, S. Tian, P. Patel, A.B. Jani, W.J. Curran, T. Liu, X. Yang, Dose evaluation of MRI-based synthetic CT generated using a machine learning method for prostate cancer radiotherapy, Med. Dosim. 44 (2019) e64–e70.

[40] T. Wang, Y. Lei, Y. Fu, W.J. Curran, T. Liu, J.A. Nye, X. Yang, Machine learning in quantitative PET: a review of attenuation correction and low-count image reconstruction methods, Phys. Med. 76 (2020) 294–306.

[41] S. Momin, Y. Fu, Y. Lei, J. Roper, J. Bradley, W. Curran, T. Liu, X. Yang, Knowledge-based radiation treatment planning: a data-driven method survey, arXiv:Medical Physics, arXiv:2009.07388, 2020.

[42] Y. Fu, Y. Lei, T. Wang, W.J. Curran, T. Liu, X. Yang, Deep learning in medical image registration: a review, Phys. Med. Biol. 65 (2020), https://doi.org/10.1088/361-6560/ab843e.

[43] Y. Lei, Y. Fu, T. Wang, R.L.J. Qiu, W.J. Curran, T. Liu, X. Yang, Deep learning in multi-organ segmentation, arXiv:2001.10619 [abs], 2020.

[44] P. Isola, J. Zhu, T. Zhou, A.A. Efros, Image-to-image translation with conditional adversarial networks, in: 2017 IEEE Conference on Computer Vision and Pattern Recognition (CVPR), 2017, pp. 5967–5976.

[45] I.J. Goodfellow, J. Pouget-Abadie, M. Mirza, B. Xu, D. Warde-Farley, S. Ozair, A.C. Courville, Y. Bengio, Generative adversarial nets, in: NIPS, 2014, pp. 2672–2680.

[46] N. Singh, K. Raza, Medical image generation using generative adversarial networks, arXiv:2005.10687 [abs], 2020.

[47] M. Mehralian, B. Karasfi, RDCGAN: unsupervised representation learning with regularized deep convolutional generative adversarial networks, in: 2018 9th Conference on Artificial Intelligence and Robotics and 2nd Asia-Pacific International Symposium, 2018, pp. 31–38.

[48] X. Dong, Y. Lei, T. Wang, K. Higgins, T. Liu, W.J. Curran, H. Mao, J.A. Nye, X. Yang, Deep learning-based attenuation correction in the absence of structural information for whole-body positron emission tomography imaging, Phys. Med. Biol. 65 (2020) 055011.

[49] X. Ying, H. Guo, K. Ma, J. Wu, Z. Weng, Y. Zheng, X2CT-GAN: reconstructing CT from biplanar X-rays with generative adversarial networks, in: 2019 IEEE/CVF Conference on Computer Vision and Pattern Recognition (CVPR), 2019, pp. 10611–10620.

[50] J. Harms, Y. Lei, T. Wang, R. Zhang, J. Zhou, X. Tang, W.J. Curran, T. Liu, X. Yang, Paired cycle-GAN-based image correction for quantitative cone-beam computed tomography, Med. Phys. 46 (2019) 3998–4009.

[51] W. Dai, N. Dong, Z. Wang, X. Liang, H. Zhang, E.P. Xing, SCAN: structure correcting adversarial network for organ segmentation in chest X-rays, in: Deep Learning in Medical Image Analysis and Multimodal Learning for Clinical Decision Support, 2018, pp. 263–273.

[52] X. Dong, Y. Lei, T. Wang, M. Thomas, L. Tang, W.J. Curran, T. Liu, X. Yang, Automatic multiorgan segmentation in thorax CT images using U-net-GAN, Med. Phys. 46 (2019) 2157–2168.

[53] Q. Zhang, H. Wang, H. Lu, D. Won, S. Yoon, Medical image synthesis with generative adversarial networks for tissue recognition, in: 2018 IEEE International Conference on Healthcare Informatics (ICHI), 2018, pp. 199–207.

[54] C. Han, K. Murao, S.i. Satoh, H. Nakayama, Learning more with less: GAN-based medical image augmentation, arXiv:1904.00838 [abs], 2019.

[55] Y. Lei, J. Harms, T. Wang, Y. Liu, H.K. Shu, A.B. Jani, W.J. Curran, H. Mao, T. Liu, X. Yang, MRI-only based synthetic CT generation using dense cycle consistent generative adversarial networks, Med. Phys. 46 (2019) 3565–3581.

[56] M. Arjovsky, S. Chintala, L. Bottou, Wasserstein GAN, arXiv:1701.07875 [abs], 2017.

[57] S. Ioffe, C. Szegedy, Batch normalization: accelerating deep network training by reducing internal covariate shift, in: Proceedings of the 32nd International Conference on International Conference on Machine Learning, vol. 37, JMLR.org, Lille, France, 2015, pp. 448–456.

[58] A.L. Maas, A.Y. Hannun, A.Y. Ng, Rectifier nonlinearities improve neural network acoustic models, in: ICML Workshop on Deep Learning for Audio, Speech and Language Processing, 2013, p. 3.

[59] D. Nie, R. Trullo, J. Lian, L. Wang, C. Petitjean, S. Ruan, Q. Wang, D. Shen, Medical image synthesis with deep convolutional adversarial networks, IEEE Trans. Biomed. Eng. 65 (2018) 2720–2730.

[60] Y. Lei, T. Wang, Y. Liu, K. Higgins, S. Tian, T. Liu, H. Mao, H. Shim, W.J. Curran, H-K.G. Shu, X. Yang, MRI-based synthetic CT generation using deep convolutional neural network, SPIE Med. Imaging 10949 (2019).

[61] Y. Lei, Z. Tian, T. Wang, K. Higgins, J.D. Bradley, W.J. Curran, T. Liu, X. Yang, Deep learning-based real-time volumetric imaging for lung stereotactic body radiation therapy: a proof of concept study, Phys. Med. Biol. 65 (2020) 235003.

[62] J. Johnson, A. Alahi, L. Fei-Fei, Perceptual losses for real-time style transfer and super-resolution, arXiv:1603.08155 [abs], 2016.

[63] J. Yang, H. Veeraraghavan, S.G. Armato 3rd, K. Farahani, J.S. Kirby, J. Kalpathy-Kramer, W. van Elmpt, A. Dekker, X. Han, X. Feng, P. Aljabar, B. Oliveira, B. van der Heyden, L. Zamdborg, D. Lam, M. Gooding, G.C. Sharp, Autosegmentation for thoracic radiation treatment planning: a grand challenge at AAPM 2017, Med. Phys. 45 (2018) 4568–4581.

[64] X. Chen, Y. Duan, R. Houthooft, J. Schulman, I. Sutskever, P. Abbeel, InfoGAN: interpretable representation learning by information maximizing generative adversarial nets, in: Proceedings of the 30th International Conference on Neural Information Processing Systems, Curran Associates Inc., Barcelona, Spain, 2016, pp. 2180–2188.

[65] Y. Liu, Y. Lei, T. Wang, Y. Fu, X. Tang, W.J. Curran, T. Liu, P. Patel, X. Yang, CBCT-based synthetic CT generation using deep-attention cycleGAN for pancreatic adaptive radiotherapy, Med. Phys. 47 (2020) 2472–2483.

[66] M-Y. Liu, T. Breuel, J. Kautz, Unsupervised image-to-image translation networks, arXiv:1703.00848 [abs], 2017.

[67] J-Y. Zhu, R. Zhang, D. Pathak, T. Darrell, A.A. Efros, O. Wang, E. Shechtman, Toward multimodal image-to-image translation, arXiv:1711.11586 [abs], 2017.

[68] Y. Choi, M. Choi, M. Kim, J. Ha, S. Kim, J. Choo, StarGAN: unified generative adversarial networks for multi-domain image-to-image translation, in: 2018 IEEE/CVF Conference on Computer Vision and Pattern Recognition, 2018, pp. 8789–8797.

[69] Y. Lei, X. Dong, T. Wang, K. Higgins, T. Liu, W.J. Curran, H. Mao, J.A. Nye, X Yang, Whole-body PET estimation from low count statistics using cycle-consistent generative adversarial networks, Phys. Med. Biol. 64 (2019) 215017.

[70] X. Dai, Y. Lei, Y. Fu, W.J. Curran, T. Liu, H. Mao, X. Yang, Multimodal MRI synthesis using unified generative adversarial networks, Med. Phys. 47 (2020) 6343–6354.

[71] X. Yang, T. Wang, Y. Lei, X. Jiang, A. Jani, P. Patel, X. Tang, A. Dhabaan, W.J. Curran, T. Liu, A learning-based method to improve pelvis cone beam CT image quality for prostate cancer radiation therapy, Int. J. Radiat. Oncol. Biol. Phys. (2018) E377–E378, Elsevier.

[72] X. Dong, T. Wang, Y. Lei, K. Higgins, T. Liu, W.J. Curran, H. Mao, J.A. Nye, X. Yang, Synthetic CT generation from non-attenuation corrected PET images for whole-body PET imaging, Phys. Med. Biol. 64 (2019) 215016.

[73] V. Alex, K. Vaidhya, S. Thirunavukkarasu, C. Kesavadas, G. Krishnamurthi, Semisupervised learning using denoising autoencoders for brain lesion detection and segmentation, J. Med. Imag. 4 (2017) 041311.

[74] K. Vaidhya, S. Thirunavukkarasu, V. Alex, G. Krishnamurthi, Multi-modal brain tumor segmentation using stacked denoising autoencoders, in: A. Crimi, et al. (Eds.), Brainlesion: Glioma, Multiple Sclerosis, Stroke and Traumatic Brain Injuries, Springer International Publishing, Cham, 2016, pp. 181–194.

[75] Y. Fu, Y. Lei, T. Wang, W.J. Curran, T.J. Liu, X.J.A. Yang, Deep learning in medical image registration: a review, arXiv:1912.12318 [abs], 2019.

[76] Y. Fu, Y. Lei, T. Wang, K. Higgins, J.D. Bradley, W.J. Curran, T. Liu, X. Yang, LungRegNet: an unsupervised deformable image registration method for 4D-CT lung, Med. Phys. 47 (2020) 1763–1774.

[77] Y. Fu, Y. Lei, T. Wang, P. Patel, A.B. Jani, H. Mao, W.J. Curran, T. Liu, X. Yang, Biomechanically constrained non-rigid MR-TRUS prostate registration using deep learning based 3D point cloud matching, Med. Image Anal. 67 (2021) 101845.

[78] Y. Fu, T. Wang, Y. Lei, P. Patel, A.B. Jani, W.J. Curran, T. Liu, X. Yang, Deformable MR-CBCT prostate registration using biomechanically constrained deep learning networks, Med. Phys. 48 (2021) 253–263.

[79] Y. Lei, Y. Fu, J. Harms, T. Wang, W.J. Curran, T. Liu, K. Higgins, X. Yang, 4D-CT deformable image registration using an unsupervised deep convolutional neural network, in: D. Nguyen, et al. (Eds.), Artificial Intelligence in Radiation Therapy, Springer International Publishing, Cham, 2019, pp. 26–33.

[80] Y. Lei, Y. Fu, T. Wang, Y. Liu, P. Patel, W.J. Curran, T. Liu, X. Yang, 4D-CT deformable image registration using multiscale unsupervised deep learning, Phys. Med. Biol. 65 (2020) 085003.

[81] X. Yang, Q. Zeng, Y. Lei, S. Tian, T. Wang, X. Dong, A. Jani, H. Mao, W. Curran, P. Patel, T. Liu, MRI-US registration using label-driven weakly-supervised learning for multiparametric MRI-guided HDR prostate brachytherapy, Int. J. Radiat. Oncol. Biol. Phys. (2019) E727, Elsevier.

[82] Q. Zeng, Y. Fu, Z. Tian, Y. Lei, Y. Zhang, T. Wang, H. Mao, T. Liu, W.J. Curran, A.B. Jani, P. Patel, X. Yang, Label-driven magnetic resonance imaging (MRI)-transrectal ultrasound (TRUS) registration using weakly supervised learning for MRI-guided prostate radiotherapy, Phys. Med. Biol. 65 (2020) 135002.

[83] Y. Lei, X. Tang, K. Higgins, J. Lin, J. Jeong, T. Liu, A. Dhabaan, T. Wang, X. Dong, R. Press, W.J. Curran, X. Yang, Learning-based CBCT correction using alternating random forest based on auto-context model, Med. Phys. 46 (2019) 601–618.

[84] X-Y. Zhou, G-Z. Yang, Normalization in training U-Net for 2-D biomedical semantic segmentation, IEEE Robot. Autom. Lett. 4 (2018) 1792–1799.

[85] T. Wang, Y. Lei, G. Shafai-Erfani, X. Jiang, X. Dong, J. Zhou, T. Liu, W.J. Curran, X. Yang, H-K.G. Shu, Learning-based automatic segmentation on arteriovenous malformations from contract-enhanced CT images, SPIE Med. Imaging (2019) 10950.

[86] C. Shorten, T.M. Khoshgoftaar, A survey on image data augmentation for deep learning, J. Big Data 6 (60) (2019).

[87] J. Jeong, L. Wang, B. Ji, Y. Lei, A. Ali, T. Liu, W.J. Curran, H. Mao, X. Yang, Machine-learning based classification of glioblastoma using delta-radiomic features derived from dynamic susceptibility contrast enhanced magnetic resonance images: introduction, Quant. Imaging Med. Surg. 9 (2019) 1201–1213.

[88] T. Wang, N. Manohar, Y. Lei, A. Dhabaan, H.K. Shu, T. Liu, W.J. Curran, X. Yang, MRI-based treatment planning for brain stereotactic radiosurgery: dosimetric validation of a learning-based pseudo-CT generation method, Med. Dosim. 44 (2019) 199–204.

[89] T. Wang, R.H. Press, M. Giles, A.B. Jani, P. Rossi, Y. Lei, W.J. Curran, P. Patel, T. Liu, X. Yang, Multiparametric MRI-guided dose boost to dominant intraprostatic lesions in CT-based high-dose-rate prostate brachytherapy, Br. J. Radiol. 92 (2019) 20190089.

[90] Y. Lei, J. Harms, T. Wang, S. Tian, J. Zhou, H.K. Shu, J. Zhong, H. Mao, W.J. Curran, T. Liu, X. Yang, MRI-based synthetic CT generation using semantic random forest with iterative refinement, Phys. Med. Biol. 64 (2019) 085001.

[91] S. Olut, Y.H. Sahin, U. Demir, G. Unal, Generative adversarial training for MRA image synthesis using multi-contrast MRI, in: I. Rekik, et al. (Eds.), PRedictive Intelligence in MEdicine, Springer International Publishing, Cham, 2018, pp. 147–154.

[92] B. Yu, L. Zhou, L. Wang, J. Fripp, P. Bourgeat, in: IEEE 15th International Symposium on Biomedical Imaging (ISBI 2018), 2018, IEEE, 2018, pp. 626–630.

[93] S.U. Dar, M. Yurt, L. Karacan, A. Erdem, E. Erdem, T. Cukur, Image synthesis in multi-contrast MRI with conditional generative adversarial networks, IEEE Trans. Med. Imaging 38 (2019) 2375–2388.

[94] Y. Lei, Y. Liu, T. Wang, S. Tian, X. Dong, X. Jiang, T. Liu, H. Mao, W.J. Curran, H-K.G. Shu, X. Yang, Brain MRI classification based on machine learning framework with auto-context model, SPIE Med. Imaging 10953 (2019).

[95] A. Sharma, G. Hamarneh, Missing MRI pulse sequence synthesis using multi-modal generative adversarial network, IEEE Trans. Med. Imaging (2019).

[96] B. Yu, L. Zhou, L. Wang, Y. Shi, J. Fripp, P. Bourgeat, Ea-GANs: edge-aware generative adversarial networks for cross-modality MR image synthesis, IEEE Trans. Med. Imaging 38 (2019) 1750–1762.

[97] M. Yurt, S.U.H. Dar, A. Erdem, E. Erdem, T. Çukur, mustGAN: multi-stream generative adversarial networks for MR image synthesis, arXiv:1909.11504, 2019.

[98] K. Armanious, C. Jiang, M. Fischer, T. Kustner, T. Hepp, K. Nikolaou, S. Gatidis, B. Yang, MedGAN: medical image translation using GANs, Comput. Med. Imaging Graph. 79 (2020) 101684.

[99] M.A. Schmidt, G.S. Payne, Radiotherapy planning using MRI, Phys. Med. Biol. 60 (2015) R323–R361.

[100] U.A. van der Heide, A.C. Houweling, G. Groenendaal, R.G. Beets-Tan, P. Lambin, Functional MRI for radiotherapy dose painting, Magn. Reson. Imaging 30 (2012) 1216–1223.

[101] R.G. Price, J.P. Kim, W.L. Zheng, I.J. Chetty, C. Glide-Hurst, Image guided radiation therapy using synthetic computed tomography images in brain cancer, Int. J. Radiat. Oncol. Biol. Phys. 95 (2016) 1281–1289.

[102] J.M. Edmund, T. Nyholm, A review of substitute CT generation for MRI-only radiation therapy, Radiat. Oncol. 12 (2017) 28.

[103] E. Johnstone, J.J. Wyatt, A.M. Henry, S.C. Short, D. Sebag-Montefiore, L. Murray, C.G. Kelly, H.M. McCallum, R. Speight, Systematic review of synthetic computed tomography generation methodologies for use in magnetic resonance imaging-only radiation therapy, Int. J. Radiat. Oncol. Biol. Phys. 100 (2018) 199–217.

[104] D. Svoboda, V. Ulman, MitoGen: a framework for generating 3D synthetic time-lapse sequences of cell populations in fluorescence microscopy, IEEE Trans. Med. Imaging 36 (2017) 310–321.

[105] T. Heimann, H.P. Meinzer, Statistical shape models for 3D medical image segmentation: a review, Med. Image Anal. 13 (2009) 543–563.

[106] X. Ruan, R.F. Murphy, Evaluation of methods for generative modeling of cell and nuclear shape, Bioinformatics 35 (2019) 2475–2485.

[107] T. Peng, W. Wang, G.K. Rohde, R.F. Murphy, Instance-based generative biological shape modeling, Proc. IEEE Int. Symp. Biomed. Imaging 5193141 (2009) 690–693.

[108] M. Kozubek, When deep learning meets cell image synthesis, Cytometry, Part A 97 (2020) 222–225.

[109] P. Goldsborough, N. Pawlowski, J.C. Caicedo, S. Singh, A.E. Carpenter, CytoGAN: generative modeling of cell images, bioRxiv (2017) 227645.

[110] A. Osokin, A. Chessel, R.E.C. Salas, F. Vaggi, GANs for biological image synthesis, in: 2017 IEEE International Conference on Computer Vision (ICCV), 2017, pp. 2252–2261.

[111] D. Eschweiler, T. Klose, F.N. Müller-Fouarge, M. Kopaczka, J. Stegmaier, Towards annotation-free segmentation of fluorescently labeled cell membranes in confocal microscopy images, in: N. Burgos, et al. (Eds.), Simulation and Synthesis in Medical Imaging, Springer International Publishing, Cham, 2019, pp. 81–89.

[112] D. Wiesner, T. Nečasová, D. Svoboda, On generative modeling of cell shape using 3D GANs, in: ICIAP, 2019.

[113] J. Stegmaier, J. Arz, B. Schott, J.C. Otte, A. Kobitski, G.U. Nienhaus, U. Strahle, P. Sanders, R. Mikut, Generating semi-synthetic validation benchmarks for embryomics, in: 2016 IEEE 13th International Symposium on Biomedical Imaging (ISBI), 2016, pp. 684–688.

[114] M. Weigert, K. Subramanian, S.T. Bundschuh, E.W. Myers, M. Kreysing, Biobeam-multiplexed wave-optical simulations of light-sheet microscopy, PLoS Comput. Biol. 14 (2018) e1006079.

Autoencoders and variational autoencoders in medical image analysis

8

Jan Ehrhardt[a] and Matthias Wilms[b]

[a]*Institute of Medical Informatics, University of Lübeck, Lübeck, Germany*
[b]*Department of Radiology, University of Calgary, Calgary, AB, Canada*

8.1 Introduction

Autoencoders are neural networks that learn a low-dimensional mapping of high-dimensional input data. They consist of two main parts: an encoder $f(\mathbf{x})$, which maps the input $\mathbf{x} \in \mathbb{R}^d$ to a latent vector $\mathbf{z} \in \mathbb{R}^r$ ($r \ll d$); and a decoder $g(\mathbf{z})$. In a classical setup, the decoder tries to reconstruct the input $\mathbf{x}$ given only $\mathbf{z}$. The mapping to a low-dimensional latent space makes autoencoders suitable for representation learning [1], since it can be assumed that $\mathbf{z}$ contains the information about the major properties of the input data that are most likely also related to the different real factors underlying the problem at hand. Autoencoders are trained in an *unsupervised* manner as their goal is to reproduce the input and thus no ground-truth information like classification labels or object segmentations are required for training. To ensure that $\mathbf{x} \approx g(f(\mathbf{x})) = \mathbf{x}'$, a so-called reconstruction loss is usually used to penalize the differences between the original input $\mathbf{x}$ and its reconstruction $\mathbf{x}'$. Unseen samples can then be mapped to their latent representation through a trained encoder to use the inferred representation as input features for downstream tasks like classification or clustering. Alternatively, the input data can be reconstructed or manipulated by successively sending them through the trained encoder and decoder. Such a setup is typically used for denoising, segmentation, or certain image synthesis tasks. Autoencoders can also be used to generate completely new data by sampling latent vectors $\mathbf{z}$ and sending them through the trained decoder $g(\mathbf{z})$. However, since the distribution of the latent space is generally unknown, new latent vector samples can lie far away from the training data, which leads to unrealistic output images. This problem motivated the introduction of two highly important and influential approaches that aim to control the distribution of the latent variables, namely regularized autoencoders and variational autoencoders.

Regularized autoencoders use additional constraints besides the reconstruction loss to influence the organization of the latent space. These constraints are not necessarily designed to shape the distribution of the $\mathbf{z}$ vectors and only few techniques allow for systematically sampling the latent space and synthesizing new samples.

Biomedical Image Synthesis and Simulation. https://doi.org/10.1016/B978-0-12-824349-7.00015-3

In contrast, variational autoencoders present a general and probabilistic method for jointly learning latent representations and corresponding inference models, eventually enabling the generation of new samples. Variational autoencoders assume that the observed input $\mathbf{x}$ is a random sample of an underlying process with unknown probability distribution $p^*(\mathbf{x})$. The underlying process is approximated by a conditional model with learnable parameters θ and latent variables $\mathbf{z}$ that follow a chosen prior probability distribution $p(\mathbf{z})$. During training, the decoder's probability to reconstruct $\mathbf{x}$ from $\mathbf{z}$ is maximized, which is related to optimizing a reconstruction loss. Additionally, the encoder's probability $q(\mathbf{z}|\mathbf{x})$ is constrained to make sure that it matches the chosen prior. Typically, a normal prior distribution $p(\mathbf{z})$ is used, which leads to efficient implementations and results in a Gaussian mixture representation of the input data. Similar to standard autoencoders, the encoder and decoder parts of a variational autoencoder are trained simultaneously.

Autoencoders and variational autoencoders are powerful tools with widespread applications in biomedical image analysis and synthesis [2–4]. Because of the low-dimensional data representation and the ability to generate new, unseen data, they are ideal tools for image synthesis tasks. The low-dimensional latent space representation can, for example, be utilized to systematically analyze or manipulate certain properties of the input data to aid image reconstruction, data augmentation, or modality transfer.

8.1.1 History of the method

Autoencoders have a long and successful tradition in neural network-based machine learning with their roots dating back at least to the 1980s. Early on, the research was mostly focused on employing them for representation learning and dimensionality reduction for downstream tasks and several similar concepts with different names appeared at the same time. Learning internal data representations with neural networks that only consist of a single hidden layer is, for example, mentioned in [5]. Here, the authors found that for the task of mapping an input to itself – the autoencoding problem –, the network does not necessarily learn a simple identity map via backpropagation, but potentially more complex representations. This idea was further exploited in [6] where stacked autoassociative neural networks were used to capture different levels of abstraction. Internal representations and ways to learn them were also discussed for closely related Boltzmann machines [7].

An early use case of an autoassociative network in image processing can be found in [8]. There, an encoder/decoder network architecture was proposed for image compression that was deemed competitive with data reduction through linear principal components analysis (PCA). In those early years, the relation between autoencoders and PCA was frequently used to explain effects, to propose future research directions, and to motivate novel concepts. For example, in [9], it was explicitly shown that the problem solved by an autoassociative network with only linear activations and an L_2-loss is similar to a PCA, which can be efficiently solved in closed form. The abilities of neural networks with nonlinear activation functions were then utilized in [10] to derive a nonlinear variant of PCA. Since then, general nonlinear dimensionality reduction [11] and nonlinear representation learning [1] have evolved into standard use cases of autoencoders.

Following the general trend of deep learning, autoencoder architectures have also become deeper and more complex over the years [12,13] and several slight modifications or extensions of the general autoencoder framework have been proposed to address specific shortcomings. Key developments were, for example, the use of constraints that force the autoencoder to explicitly learn sparse representations of high-dimensional data [14], ways to organize the latent space in a favorable manner (e.g., contractive autoencoders [15]), and the introduction of so-called denoising autoencoders [16]. While the main idea of denoising autoencoders is to learn image features that are invariant against stochastic variations, they also provide an important step towards generative modeling with autoencoders. Because of their stochastic nature, they enable the sampling of new data from the learned approximation of the data distribution.

For generative modeling with encoder/decoder-like neural networks, the introduction of variational autoencoders in [17,18] was a key moment. Relying on ideas from variational Bayesian inference and by making use of the so-called *reparametrization trick*, variational autoencoders approximately map the potentially complicated distribution of the input data to a simple base distribution (e.g., factorized Gaussian) that can be efficiently sampled. This advancement has already led to numerous new application scenarios while their true potential has not been fully exploited yet.

8.1.2 Autoencoders and variational autoencoders in biomedical image analysis and synthesis

The remarkable increase in the amount of available biomedical image data over the last decades has fueled the demand for automated processing and analysis of these data. Besides workload reduction and decision support for clinicians, gaining new knowledge and insights by uncovering previously unknown relations in high-dimensional, heterogeneous, and complex biomedical data have been key drivers of innovation. Autoencoders are an excellent tool for this purpose since they help to structure data and to shed light on the complex relations between the different factors associated with the process being studied. Moreover, many autoencoder variants such as variational autoencoders are generative models that allow to visualize and verify the learned representations by systematically modifying the learned factors when synthesizing new images.

Consequently, the application of autoencoders and especially variational autoencoders for biomedical image analysis and synthesis tasks has been an exceptional success story in recent years. After the introduction of variational autoencoders in 2014 [17,18], a well-received review article in 2017 [2] wrote about them "There are no peer-reviewed papers applying these methods to medical images yet [...]." In 2020, a review article on applications of variational autoencoders to biomedical data appeared [3], citing over 140 articles with more than 25 articles covering biomedical imaging.

Because of their flexibility and versatility, the potential applications of autoencoders and variational autoencoders in biomedical image analysis and synthesis are numerous. They have been successfully employed for classical image analysis tasks like image segmentation [19], image registration [20–22], unsupervised and semisupervised classification [23–25], representation learning [26–28], shape analysis [29,30,20], and anomaly detection [31–33]. The use of autoencoders and variational autoencoders for image synthesis tasks is especially driven by recent innovations from the machine learning and computer vision communities [34–37] that led to stark improvements in their ability to disentangle factors and to synthesize realistic high resolution images [37,38]. Typical biomedical image synthesis scenarios include image denoising and computed tomography/magnetic resonance image reconstruction [39–44], interslice interpolation [45], image inpainting [46], data augmentation [47], modality transfer [27,48], and simulation of longitudinal processes [28,49,50].

8.1.3 Outline of this chapter and notation

In the following sections, we will thoroughly discuss autoencoders and variational autoencoders. For both, we will first review the theoretical foundations of the standard variants and then present some of their numerous extensions that either address specific shortcomings or have been developed for particular applications (see Fig. 8.1). Finally, in Section 8.4 some applications of variational autoencoders in medical imaging will be discussed.

In what follows, we will primarily focus on *generative modeling*, where the goal usually is to create a model that is able to synthesize new, unseen images that are similar, yet not identical to the images in a given training database. For a general discussion of the underlying theory, images are considered in a vectorized form as observed variables $\mathbf{x} \in \mathbb{R}^d$. We, furthermore, assume that these images are generated by an unknown underlying process with an unobserved continuous *latent variable* $\mathbf{z} \in \mathcal{Z} \subseteq \mathbb{R}^r \, (r \ll d)$.

8.2 Autoencoders

As introduced in Section 8.1, autoencoders are neural networks consisting of an encoder $f_\phi : \mathbb{R}^d \to \mathcal{Z} \, (\mathcal{Z} \subseteq \mathbb{R}^r)$ for mapping the input $\mathbf{x} \in \mathbb{R}^d$ to the latent space and a decoder $g_\theta : \mathcal{Z} \to \mathbb{R}^d$ for reconstructing the input from a latent representation with learnable network parameters ϕ and θ. For a given dissimilarity function or reconstruction loss $\mathcal{L}^{\text{rec}}(\cdot, \cdot)$, the autoencoder problem is to find parameters ϕ and θ that minimize the overall distortion function

$$\min \mathcal{L}(\phi, \theta) = \min_{\phi, \theta} \sum_{i=1}^{N} \mathcal{L}^{\text{rec}} \left(\mathbf{x}_i, g_\theta(f_\phi(\mathbf{x}_i)) \right) \tag{8.1}$$

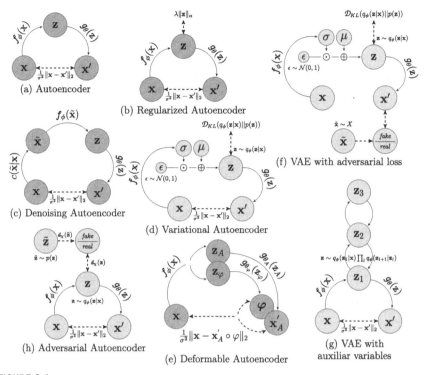

FIGURE 8.1

Sketches of the principal structure of some models of autoencoders (⬤) and variational autoencoders (◯) discussed in this chapter. Solid arrows in this diagram represent mappings implemented by neural networks. Dashed arrows indicate loss functions used for training.

for the given training samples $\mathcal{X} = \{\mathbf{x}_i\}_{i=1}^{N}$. An intuitive dissimilarity function is the L_2-norm $\mathcal{L}^{\text{rec}}(\mathbf{x}, \mathbf{x}') = \left\| \mathbf{x} - \mathbf{x}' \right\|_2^2$, but other measures, such as L_p-norms, cross-entropy, and Hamming distance are also used, depending on the input data (e.g., color or gray value images, label images, or binary data). To minimize the distortion function $\mathcal{L}(\phi, \theta)$, the network parameters $\{\phi, \theta\}$ are jointly learned during training using standard techniques like backpropagation and stochastic gradient descent.

Fig. 8.2 shows the typical structure of an autoencoder. It consists of two networks: the encoder translates the original high-dimensional input into the low-dimensional latent code. The decoder network recovers the data from the latent code, usually with progressively larger output layers. In general, any contracting (resp. expanding) network architecture can be used. For image processing applications, convolutional layers are often combined with a dense layer before and after the latent space. Autoencoders do not make use of skip connections because the image information should be entirely represented in the latent code.

At first, the ability to reconstruct input data does not seem to be of great benefit. However, from an application perspective, two properties of autoencoders are of par-

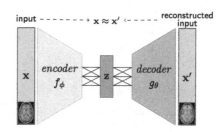

FIGURE 8.2

Typical structure of an autoencoder where the encoder and decoder are implemented as neural networks.

ticular interest: (1) The encoder learns to map the input data to the low-dimensional latent space in a way that essential image features that distinguish training samples are encoded in the latent variables. The variables can then be used for subsequent analyses (e.g., classification, clustering); (2) Since the size of the latent space is restricted, a perfect reproduction of the input image is usually impossible. Thus, the reconstructed output image only contains the most crucial image information (in terms of the loss function) with noise and insignificant image features being suppressed.

The size of the latent space r is the key attribute of autoencoders. Large latent variables allow the network to simply learn the identity function and thus no relevant image features can be extracted. If the latent space has too few dimensions, the capacity to reconstruct the input image is limited, leading to blurred or even unrecognizable results. The ideal autoencoder is sensitive enough to the inputs to create an accurate reconstruction and insensitive enough so that the model does not simply memorize the training data. Unfortunately, no known rule of thumb exists to choose an appropriate latent space size for real world applications. Therefore, the parameter r is usually heuristically determined via some a priori knowledge about the number of underlying factors for the problem at hand or estimated with grid search strategies.

8.2.1 Regularized autoencoders

From a generative modeling perspective, the decoder network can be used to synthesize new images with features predefined by their latent codes. However, in Eq. (8.1), no restrictions are imposed on the latent space $\mathcal{Z}$ aside from the predefined dimension r, and the latent variables $\mathbf{z} = f_\phi(\mathbf{x})$, therefore, exhibit an unstructured distribution. This implies that no information is available to sample data in $\mathcal{Z}$ to generate images close to the training set because of the unknown valid value range of the latent variables, gaps in the latent space, and a lack of separability with respect to different image properties.

To structure the latent space, several regularization techniques have been proposed, which are summarized here under the term *regularized autoencoders* (see Fig. 8.1(b)). A general and rather obvious idea, is to add an explicit *regularizer of the latent variables* to the cost function to be minimized:

$$\min \mathcal{L}(\phi, \theta) = \min_{\phi, \theta} \sum_{i=1}^{N} \mathcal{L}^{\text{rec}}\left(\mathbf{x}_i, g_\theta(f_\phi(\mathbf{x}_i))\right) + \lambda \mathcal{L}^{\text{reg}}(\mathbf{z}_i). \tag{8.2}$$

Here, λ acts as a scaling parameter to adjust the trade-off between reconstruction quality and latent space regularization. Depending on the chosen regularization term $\mathcal{L}^{\text{reg}}(\mathbf{z})$, different shortcomings of autoencoders can be addressed. For example, the use of the squared L_2-norm for $\mathcal{L}^{\text{reg}}(\mathbf{z}) = \|\mathbf{z}\|_2^2$ forces the latent variables to be close to zero.

8.2.1.1 Sparse autoencoders

Sparse autoencoders impose a sparsity constraint on the latent variables and force the autoencoder to learn only a sparse set of features even for high-dimensional latent spaces. This effectively alleviates the problem of having to choose an optimal value for r as it forces the autoencoder to extract only few prominent features in the images while setting all others to zero. A simple strategy to achieve this, is regularization utilizing the L_1-norm $\mathcal{L}^{\text{reg}}(\mathbf{z}) = \|\mathbf{z}\|_1$. Other approaches enforce the average activation of each component of the latent space to match a predefined sparsity level ρ, i.e., $\mathbb{E}[|z_i|] \approx \rho$, $i = 1 \ldots, r$ [51,52,23]. Sparse autoencoders have advantages in the context of representation learning, however they do not allow a consistent sampling of the latent space and are therefore not suitable for image synthesis tasks.

8.2.1.2 Contractive autoencoders

In autoencoders and sparse autoencoders, there is no guarantee that very similar inputs $\mathbf{x}$ result in similar latent representations $\mathbf{z}$. As this is a desirable property when working with those representations, the model can be explicitly trained to map similar inputs to similar parts of the latent space by forcing the derivative of the latent variables with respect to the input to be small. Hence, small changes to the input should result in very similar encodings. This leads to

$$\mathcal{L}^{\text{reg}}(\mathbf{z}) = \|\nabla_{\mathbf{x}} \mathbf{z}\|^2. \tag{8.3}$$

Note that since the derivative with respect to the input is already determined during backpropagation of the network, the regularization term in Eq. (8.3) can be very efficiently implemented.

Since we explicitly encourage our model to learn an encoding in which similar inputs have similar encodings, we essentially force the model to learn how a neighborhood of inputs can be *contracted* into a smaller neighborhood of outputs. Thus, we impose a structure on the latent space. There is a strong link between contracting autoencoders and denoising autoencoders (see Section 8.2.1.3): Both approaches enforce an insensitivity to small perturbations of the input [53].

8.2.1.3 Denoising autoencoders

A completely different approach to regularize autoencoders and to increase their robustness are denoising autoencoders [16]. Denoising autoencoders are not primarily meant to generate denoised images, but to learn robust image features that are independent of stochastic image variations. Instead of a direct regularization of the latent variables, they learn to reconstruct the original data from randomly corrupted inputs $\tilde{\mathbf{x}}_i \sim c(\tilde{\mathbf{x}}|\mathbf{x}_i)$ (see Fig. 8.1(c)). Here, $c(\tilde{\mathbf{x}}|\mathbf{x})$ is a conditional distribution generating corrupted samples of $\mathbf{x}$, e.g., by adding Gaussian noise or other stochastic perturbations. The learning process of the autoencoder now uses the non-autoassociative reconstruction loss $\mathcal{L}^{\text{rec}}\left(\mathbf{x}_i, g_\theta(f_\phi(\tilde{\mathbf{x}}_i))\right)$ with random samples $\tilde{\mathbf{x}}_i$, demanding the encoder to produce very close mappings $\mathbf{z}_i = f_\phi(\tilde{\mathbf{x}}_i)$ for different realizations of $\tilde{\mathbf{x}}_i \sim c(\tilde{\mathbf{x}}|\mathbf{x}_i)$. This prevents the autoencoder from simply learning an identity mapping, but requires it to undo the corruptions.

Denoising autoencoders can also be trained when no clean data is available. This is especially important in biomedical image analysis where the acquisition of noise-free image data is impossible. The objective function $\mathcal{L}^{\text{rec}}\left(\tilde{\mathbf{x}}', g_\theta(f_\phi(\tilde{\mathbf{x}}_i))\right)$ is now changed so that both the inputs $\tilde{\mathbf{x}}$ and the targets $\tilde{\mathbf{x}}'$ are drawn from a corrupted distribution (not necessarily the same). As long as the added noise has zero-mean – or, more generally, as long as $\mathbb{E}_{c(\tilde{\mathbf{x}}|\mathbf{x})}[\tilde{\mathbf{x}}] = \mathbf{x}$ – this does not change what the network learns [54].

An interesting property of denoising autoencoders is their ability to implicitly estimate the underlying data distribution. Based on this property, a trained denoising autoencoder can be used as a generative model by a two-step Markov chain approach:

$$\tilde{\mathbf{x}}_{t-1} \sim c(\tilde{\mathbf{x}}|\mathbf{x}_{t-1}) \qquad \text{(generate corrupted sample),} \qquad (8.4\text{a})$$

$$\mathbf{x}_t \sim p_{\phi,\theta}(\mathbf{x}|\tilde{\mathbf{x}}_{t-1}) \qquad \text{(generate network output).} \qquad (8.4\text{b})$$

The conditional distribution $p_{\phi,\theta}(\mathbf{x}|\tilde{\mathbf{x}})$ is defined by the encoder–decoder network using the corrupted input $\tilde{\mathbf{x}}$. As shown in [55], under certain conditions for the distributions $c(\tilde{\mathbf{x}}|\mathbf{x})$ and $p_{\phi,\theta}(\mathbf{x}|\tilde{\mathbf{x}})$, the distribution of the generated sequence of samples $\mathbf{x}_0, \ldots, \mathbf{x}_t, \ldots, \mathbf{x}_n$ from Eq. (8.4) converges to the underlying data distribution $p^*(\mathbf{x})$ for $n \to \infty$. For a wide range of corrupting distributions, denoising autoencoders thus provide a means for generating data by a simple Markov chain that alternately takes samples from the corruption process and from the denoising model.

Although these properties provide deeper insights into how denoising autoencoders learn and how the structure of the underlying data manifolds is captured, they are rarely used in practical applications. Sampling with Markov chains is costly in practical applications, since many samples must be generated to produce sufficiently diverse data. Instead of defining the data distribution implicitly by a Markov process, a direct sampling from this distribution is also of high interest. A possibility for this is offered by variational autoencoders, which will be discussed next.

8.2.2 Summary

Autoencoders are neural networks capable of finding structure within data to create a compact representation of the input. During training, they learn a potentially complex nonlinear mapping from the input to a compressed latent representation (encoder) and a mapping from the latent representation back to the input (decoder). Classical autoencoders do not constrain the organization of the latent space, due to the use of a simple reconstruction loss. This results in a lack of interpretability and regularity. Thus, the main difficulty in working with autoencoders is to enforce the learning of a meaningful and generalizable representation of the latent space.

There are several variants of the general autoencoder architecture with the goal of ensuring meaningful latent representations for the task at hand. Some regularized versions, such as contracting or denoising autoencoders, estimate local properties of the data-generating distribution and can be used for generative modeling [53]. Other variants, like sparse or quantized autoencoders [56], are designed to learn more informative and concise latent representations. Another common strategy to enforce latent representations useful for an actual classification task is to first pretrain the autoencoder in a self-supervised manner on unlabeled data, followed by supervised fine-tuning of the encoding function with a smaller amount of labeled data [23].

The flexibility and adaptability of autoencoders contribute significantly to the success of these models and enable a wide range of applications in medical imaging, from denoising, image inpainting, and modality transfer to classification, segmentation, and anomaly detection (see Section 8.1.2). Difficulties in the implementation and use of autoencoders result from the fact that the size of the latent space has to be defined in advance and a suitable balance between the capacity of the decoder and the size of the latent space has to be found.

8.3 Variational autoencoders

The mathematical basis of variational autoencoders differs significantly from classical autoencoders. In Section 8.2, we have seen that autoencoders map a given input to a latent vector in the encoding step and to the reconstructed output in the decoding step. This is a deterministic process, and in general, sampling from the latent space of classical autoencoders is not reasonable. In contrast, variational autoencoders directly describe the observations in a probabilistic manner and aim to approximate the unknown data distribution $p^*(\mathbf{x})$ in dependence of latent variables $\mathbf{z}$. The objective of variational autoencoders is to maximize the integral

$$p^*(\mathbf{x}) \approx p_\theta(\mathbf{x}) = \int p_\theta(\mathbf{x}|\mathbf{z})p(\mathbf{z})d\mathbf{z} \tag{8.5}$$

with respect to the network parameters θ for the given training data $\mathcal{X} = \{\mathbf{x}_i\}_{i=1}^{N}$. Here, $p_\theta(\mathbf{x}|\mathbf{z})$ is the decoder's probability to reconstruct $\mathbf{x}$ from latent representation $\mathbf{z}$ while $p(\mathbf{z})$ denotes a chosen prior distribution for the latent space. Similar to classical autoencoders, variational autoencoders also use self-supervised learning and a similar network architecture. The later aspect seems surprising at first, since in Eq. (8.5) only latent variable and decoder function are present. However, the optimization of Eq. (8.5) using variational Bayesian inference leads to an encoder–decoder structure that is very similar to classical autoencoders.

The core problem in Bayesian statistics is to draw conclusions about unknown quantities from observed data by calculations about the underlying posterior probability densities. For many problems in machine learning, posterior densities are intractable and efficient methods to approximate them are needed. Variational inference is a set of techniques to approximate complicated probability distributions by optimization over a family of approximate densities [57].

In the context of image synthesis or generative modeling, we consider a collection of high-dimensional, independently, and identically distributed (i.i.d.) samples $\mathcal{X} = \{x_i\}_{i=1}^N$, e.g., images, drawn from an unknown distribution $x \sim p^*(x)$. The aim of generative modeling with variational autoencoders is to learn an approximate conditional model $p_\theta(x|z)$ with parameters θ and latent variables z to draw new samples by

$$z_{new} \sim p(z) \quad \text{and} \quad x_{new} \sim p_\theta(x|z_{new}), \tag{8.6}$$

where $p(z)$ is a posit prior probability distribution over the latent variables. To find the optimal parameters of the model, we aim to maximize the log-likelihood of the observed data given the model parameters.[1] Under the i.i.d. assumption, the probability assigned to the data by the model is

$$\log p_\theta(\mathcal{X}) = \sum_{x \in \mathcal{X}} \log p_\theta(x), \tag{8.7}$$

with $p_\theta(x) = \int p_\theta(x|z)p(z)dz$ as given in Eq. (8.5). The difficulty of this optimization is that the integral has no analytical solution or efficient estimator. Due to this intractability, $p_\theta(x)$ cannot be differentiated with respect to the parameters and no gradient-based optimization is possible. Note that $p_\theta(x|z)$ and $p(z)$ are both tractable, and that the intractability results from the integration. The densities are further related through Bayes' theorem by

$$p_\theta(x) = \frac{p_\theta(x|z)p(z)}{p_\theta(z|x)}, \tag{8.8}$$

and Eq. (8.8) shows that the intractability of $p_\theta(x)$ results from the intractability of the posterior conditional probability of the latent variables given the observations $p_\theta(z|x)$ (and vice versa).

The goal of variational inference is to approximate the exact conditional $p(z|x)$ by a density functions $q^*(z) \in \mathfrak{S}$, where $\mathfrak{S}$ is a predefined family of densities over

---

[1] Note that $p_\theta(x)$ is short-hand for $p(x|\theta)$, i.e., the likelihood with respect to the model parameters, which is the marginal likelihood (or evidence) with respect to the latent variable.

the latent variables. The approximation problem is formulated by minimizing the Kullback–Leibler divergence[2]

$$q^*(\mathbf{z}) = \arg\min_{q \in \mathfrak{S}} \mathcal{D}_{KL}\left(q(\mathbf{z})\|p(\mathbf{z}|\mathbf{x})\right). \tag{8.9}$$

The approximate density q may or may not depend on the data. The key idea behind variational autoencoders is to sample only values of $\mathbf{z}$ that are likely to have produced $\mathbf{x}$, instead of sampling from the whole latent space under the prior $p(\mathbf{z})$. Therefore, we design the approximate density $q_\phi(\mathbf{z}|\mathbf{x})$ as conditional on the given observations and parameterized by ϕ, which here are the parameters of a neural network; $q_\phi(\mathbf{z}|\mathbf{x})$ is represented by the encoder and $p_\theta(\mathbf{x}|\mathbf{z})$ is represented by the decoder of the variational autoencoder.

8.3.1 The evidence lower bound (ELBO)

The objective formulated in Eq. (8.9) is not computable because it requires the computation of the (intractable) model evidence $p_\theta(\mathbf{x})$. To see the connection of Eq. (8.9) with the evidence, consider Eq. (8.8) and expand the Kullback–Leibler divergence to

$$\begin{aligned}
\mathcal{D}_{KL}&\left(q_\phi(\mathbf{z}|\mathbf{x})\|p_\theta(\mathbf{z}|\mathbf{x})\right)\\
&= \mathbb{E}_{q_\phi(\mathbf{z}|\mathbf{x})}\left[\log q_\phi(\mathbf{z}|\mathbf{x}) - \log p_\theta(\mathbf{z}|\mathbf{x})\right]\\
&= \underbrace{\mathbb{E}_{q_\phi(\mathbf{z}|\mathbf{x})}\left[\log q_\phi(\mathbf{z}|\mathbf{x}) - \log p_\theta(\mathbf{x}|\mathbf{z}) - \log p(\mathbf{z})\right]}_{\triangleq -\mathcal{L}(\theta,\phi)\ (\text{ELBO})} + \log p_\theta(\mathbf{x}). \tag{8.10}
\end{aligned}$$

Note that the evidence is independent of q and therefore only the first term of Eq. (8.10) is optimized instead of the KL divergence. The negative of this term is called *the evidence lower bound* (ELBO) and can be rewritten as a sum of the expected log-likelihood of the data and the KL divergence between the prior $p(\mathbf{z})$ and $q_\phi(\mathbf{z}|\mathbf{x})$:

$$\begin{aligned}
\mathcal{L}(\theta,\phi) &= \mathbb{E}_{q_\phi(\mathbf{z}|\mathbf{x})}\left[\log p_\theta(\mathbf{x}|\mathbf{z}) - \log q_\phi(\mathbf{z}|\mathbf{x}) + \log p(\mathbf{z})\right]\\
&= \mathbb{E}_{q_\phi(\mathbf{z}|\mathbf{x})}\left[\log p_\theta(\mathbf{x}|\mathbf{z})\right] - \mathbb{E}_{q_\phi(\mathbf{z}|\mathbf{x})}\left[\log q_\phi(\mathbf{z}|\mathbf{x}) - \log p(\mathbf{z})\right]\\
&= \underbrace{\mathbb{E}_{q_\phi(\mathbf{z}|\mathbf{x})}\left[\log p_\theta(\mathbf{x}|\mathbf{z})\right]}_{\text{decoder}} - \underbrace{\mathcal{D}_{KL}\left(q_\phi(\mathbf{z}|\mathbf{x})\|p(\mathbf{z})\right)}_{\text{encoder}}. \tag{8.11}
\end{aligned}$$

Eq. (8.11) depends on the parameters of $p_\theta(\mathbf{x}|\mathbf{z})$ and $q_\phi(\mathbf{z}|\mathbf{x})$ and has an encoder–decoder structure. Both components are now tractable, and maximizing $\mathcal{L}(\theta,\phi)$

---

[2] The Kullback–Leibler divergence is an information-theoretic measure of proximity between two densities, defined by $\mathcal{D}_{KL}(q(x)\|p(x)) = \mathbb{E}_{q(x)}\left[\log q(x) - \log p(x)\right]$. It is always nonnegative ($\mathcal{D}_{KL}(q\|p) \geq 0$), asymmetric ($\mathcal{D}_{KL}(q\|p) \neq \mathcal{D}_{KL}(p\|q)$), and only zero if both densities are identical $\mathcal{D}_{KL}(q\|p) = 0 \Leftrightarrow q(\cdot) = p(\cdot)$.

(ELBO) is the optimization criterion of variational autoencoders. In order to discover what exactly is optimized by ELBO, we reformulate Eq. (8.10):

$$\log p_\theta(\mathbf{x}) - \mathcal{D}_{KL}\left(q_\phi(\mathbf{z}|\mathbf{x}) || p_\theta(\mathbf{z}|\mathbf{x})\right)$$

$$= \underbrace{\mathbb{E}_{q_\phi(\mathbf{z}|\mathbf{x})}\left[\log p_\theta(\mathbf{x}|\mathbf{z})\right] - \mathcal{D}_{KL}\left(q_\phi(\mathbf{z}|\mathbf{x}) || p(\mathbf{z})\right)}_{=\mathcal{L}(\theta,\phi)} \qquad (8.12)$$

$$\leq \log p_\theta(\mathbf{x}).$$

Due to $\mathcal{D}_{KL}(\cdot||\cdot) \geq 0$, ELBO is a lower bound of the log-evidence, and maximizing $\mathcal{L}(\theta, \phi)$ with respect to the parameters θ and ϕ optimizes two concurrent goals: (1) the model evidence $p_\theta(\mathbf{x})$ is maximized, which means that the generative model better adapts to the data, and (2) the KL divergence is minimized, whereby the true posterior distribution $p_\theta(\mathbf{z}|\mathbf{x})$ is better approximated by $q_\phi(\mathbf{z}|\mathbf{x})$. It can also be seen from Eq. (8.12) that the achievable reconstruction quality depends on how well q_ϕ can adapt to the true posterior $p(\mathbf{z}|\mathbf{x})$, i.e., what capacity q_ϕ has.

8.3.2 Implementation and optimization of variational autoencoders

Section 8.3.1 derives the optimization criterion of variational autoencoders and now the question arises how this criterion can be implemented and optimized using neural networks. On the right-hand side of Eq. (8.11), encoder and decoder are represented as conditional probability densities. First, we define a (deterministic) decoder function $g_\theta : \mathcal{Z} \to \mathbb{R}^d$ represented by a multilayer neural network with parameters θ to map the latent values $\mathbf{z}$ to an output image $\mathbf{x}'$. The choice of the likelihood $p_\theta(\mathbf{x}|\mathbf{z})$ depends on the type of the processed data. For gray value images a Gaussian $\mathcal{N}(\mathbf{x}|g_\theta(\mathbf{z}), \sigma^2 \cdot I)$ is often used, where σ^2 is a hyperparameter reflecting the assumed noise in the data. The log-likelihood in Eq. (8.11) corresponds to the reconstruction loss for classical autoencoders (see Eq. (8.1)), for the assumed Gaussian this would correspond to the L_2 norm

$$\log p_\theta(\mathbf{x}|\mathbf{z}) = -\frac{1}{2\sigma^2}\|\mathbf{x} - g_\theta(\mathbf{z})\|^2 + \text{const.} \qquad (8.13)$$

Other choices are possible, e.g., the Laplacian distribution would correspond to the L_1-norm, or a Bernoulli distribution can be used for binary data.

Common choices to define the encoder are a normal prior $p(\mathbf{z}) \sim \mathcal{N}(\mathbf{z}|0, I)$ and a factorized Gaussian $q_\phi(\mathbf{z}|\mathbf{x}) \sim \mathcal{N}(\mathbf{z}|\boldsymbol{\mu}_\phi(\mathbf{x}), I\sigma_\phi^2(\mathbf{x}))$ as approximate distribution. These choices allow easy sampling of the latent variable $\mathbf{z}$, offer a flexible approximating distribution q_ϕ and most importantly allow the calculation of the KL divergence $\mathcal{D}_{KL}\left(q_\phi(\mathbf{z}|\mathbf{x}) || p(\mathbf{z})\right)$ in closed form. The KL divergence is obtained in this case by

$$\mathcal{D}_{KL}\left(\mathcal{N}(\mu, \Sigma) || \mathcal{N}(0, I)\right) = \frac{1}{2}\left(\mu^T \mu + \text{tr}(\Sigma) - k - \log|\Sigma|\right), \qquad (8.14)$$

where k is the dimensionality of the distribution and $\Sigma = \text{diag}(\sigma^2)$ is in our case a diagonal matrix. The functions $\mu_\phi(\cdot), \sigma_\phi(\cdot) : \mathcal{X} \to \mathbb{R}^r$ are estimated by the (deterministic) neural network encoder function $f_\phi(\mathbf{x}) = \left(\mu_\phi(\mathbf{x}), \log \sigma_\phi^2(\mathbf{x}) \right)^T$. Note that the network output is $\log \sigma_\phi^2$ to increase numerical stability, since sigma must be positive and tends to be less than 1, and $\log \sigma_\phi^2$ is needed anyway to calculate the KL divergence.

In order to optimize the network parameters θ, ϕ during the training process, the gradients $\nabla_{\theta,\phi} \mathcal{L}(\theta, \phi)$ must be calculated. However, we cannot directly backpropagate gradients through the random variable $\mathbf{z}$ and this prevents the learning of the encoder parameters ϕ. The *reparametrization trick* [17] expresses the latent variable $\mathbf{z}$ as a deterministic and differentiable function of ϕ and $\mathbf{x}$ and a newly introduced random variable ϵ:

$$\mathbf{z} = \mu_\phi(\mathbf{x}) + \sigma_\phi(\mathbf{x}) \odot \epsilon \quad \text{with } \epsilon \sim \mathcal{N}(0, \mathbf{I}). \tag{8.15}$$

Here, $\odot$ denotes the Hadamard product. Given the reparametrization of $\mathbf{z}$, the derivation of the loss function is reformulated in the following way:

$$\begin{aligned} \nabla_{\theta,\phi} \mathcal{L}(\theta, \phi) &= \nabla_{\theta,\phi} \left(\mathbb{E}_{q_\phi(\mathbf{z}|\mathbf{x})} \left[\log p_\theta(\mathbf{x}|\mathbf{z}) \right] - \mathcal{D}_{KL} \left(q_\phi(\mathbf{z}|\mathbf{x}) || p(\mathbf{z}) \right) \right) \\ &= \nabla_{\theta,\phi} \left(\mathbb{E}_{\epsilon \sim \mathcal{N}(0, \mathbf{I})} \left[\log p_\theta(\mathbf{x}|\mu_\phi + \sigma_\phi \odot \epsilon) \right] \right. \\ &\quad \left. - \nabla_{\theta,\phi} \mathcal{D}_{KL} \left(q_\phi(\mathbf{z}|\mathbf{x}) || p(\mathbf{z}) \right) \right), \end{aligned} \tag{8.16}$$

where the second term in Eq. (8.16) is directly computed by differentiating Eq. (8.14), and the expectation in the first term is now independent of the parameters ϕ. A Monte Carlo method can be used to estimate the gradient of the likelihood:

$$\begin{aligned} \nabla_{\theta,\phi} \mathbb{E}_{q_\phi(\mathbf{z}|\mathbf{x})} \left[\log p_\theta(\mathbf{x}|\mathbf{z}) \right] &= \nabla_{\theta,\phi} \mathbb{E}_{\epsilon \sim \mathcal{N}(0, \mathbf{I})} \left[\log p_\theta(\mathbf{x}|\mu_\phi + \sigma_\phi \odot \epsilon) \right] \\ &\approx \nabla_{\theta,\phi} \left(\frac{1}{K} \sum_{k=1}^{K} \log p_\theta(\mathbf{x}|\mu_\phi + \sigma_\phi \odot \epsilon^{(k)}) \right) \tag{8.17} \\ &\quad \text{with } \epsilon^{(k)} \sim \mathcal{N}(0, \mathbf{I}). \end{aligned}$$

This estimator converges for $K \to \infty$, but Kingma and Welling [17] argue that $K = 1$ can be used as long as the minibatch size is large in the stochastic gradient-based optimization.

Fig. 8.3 shows the resulting structure of a neural network to implement variational autoencoders with Gaussian priors. Comparing with Fig. 8.2, we see that the encoder f_ϕ now estimates the mean and standard deviation, and the latent code $\mathbf{z}$ is generated by the reparametrization trick using a random sample $\epsilon \sim \mathcal{N}(0, \mathbf{I})$. Encoders and decoders can be implemented as convolutional or fully connected neural networks with capacities adapted to the problem. As discussed for autoencoders, we need to predefine the size of the latent space in balance with the capacity of the decoder.

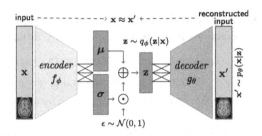

FIGURE 8.3

Typical structure of a neural network-based variational autoencoder with a Gaussian prior $p(\mathbf{z})$. See also Fig. 8.2 for comparison.

Given the encoder f_ϕ and decoder g_θ, the training of variational autoencoders can be summarized as given in Algorithm 1.

Input : Data set $\mathcal{X}$; DecoderNet$_\theta$ and EncoderNet$_\phi$
Result: Learned parameters θ, ϕ

$(\theta, \phi) \longleftarrow$ initialize
while *Stochastic gradient descent not converged* **do**
    $\mathcal{M} \sim \mathcal{X}$ (sample minibatch of data)
    for $\mathbf{x}_i \in \mathcal{M}$ **do**
        $(\boldsymbol{\mu}, \log \boldsymbol{\sigma}^2) \longleftarrow f_\phi(\mathbf{x})$ (encoder)
        $\boldsymbol{\epsilon} \sim \mathcal{N}(0, \boldsymbol{I})$ (sample random noise)
        $\mathbf{z} = \boldsymbol{\mu} + \boldsymbol{\sigma} \odot \boldsymbol{\epsilon}$
        $\mathbf{x}'_i \longleftarrow g_\theta(\mathbf{z})$ (decoder)
        Compute the loss function from Eqs. (8.13) and (8.14)
        $\mathcal{L}_i \longleftarrow \log p_\theta(\mathbf{x}_i|\mathbf{z}) + \mathcal{D}_{KL}(\mathcal{N}(\boldsymbol{\mu}, \boldsymbol{\sigma})|\mathcal{N}(0, \boldsymbol{I}))$
    end
    Compute stochastic gradient (using Eq. (8.17))
    $\nabla_{\theta,\phi}\tilde{\mathcal{L}} = \nabla_{\theta,\phi}\left(\frac{1}{|\mathcal{M}|}\sum_i \mathcal{L}_i\right)$
    Update network parameters by backpropagation
    $(\theta, \phi) \longleftarrow$ Stochastic gradient descent optimizer
end
Algorithm 1: Training algorithm for variational autoencoders in pseudocode.

8.3.3 Advantages and challenges of variational autoencoders

Variational autoencoders (VAEs) provide a general way to estimate the data distribution of a given training set. Unlike standard autoencoders, they describe latent attributes in probabilistic terms, resulting in continuous and compact latent representations. This is visualized in Fig. 8.4, where the 2D latent space encodings learned

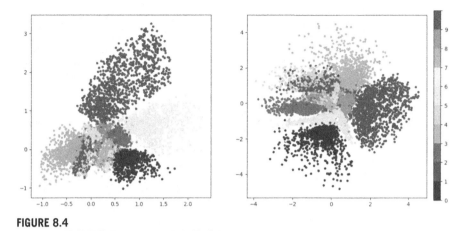

FIGURE 8.4

Visualization of the 2-dimensional latent space of an autoencoder (left) and a variational autoencoder (right) trained on the MNIST data set of handwritten digits $0, 1, \ldots, 9$.

from the MNIST dataset are shown. The autoencoder's latent space is less structured and the encoded vectors are grouped in clusters corresponding to different data classes. There are large gaps between clusters that are not associated with any data points, which prevents the latent space from being sampled efficiently and systematically. In contrast, the latent variables of the VAE are organized according to a normal distribution and although the data classes are also arranged in clusters, there are barely any gaps between these clusters. Moreover, in addition to the probabilistic sampling mechanism, the VAE's decoder has also learned to generate images from a continuous latent space. This provides an easy way to generate new samples and enables applications like interpolation between data points, reconstruction of corrupted images or allow semantic operations with latent vector arithmetic, e.g., to query visual analogies or to generate images from visual attributes (see Fig. 8.5 and [58,36,59]).

Another generative modeling approach that has attracted much attention in recent years are generative adversarial networks (GANs, see Chapter 7). One reason for their popularity is their ability to synthesize photo-realistic images. Their adversarial training approach is also easier to understand than the rather complex theoretical basis of VAEs (probabilistic model and variational inference). However, there are a number of advantages that VAEs provide over GANs: despite their complex theoretical basis, VAEs are easier to train and rarely suffer from the major problems of GAN models such as nonconvergence or diminished gradients. Since the evidence in Eq. (8.5) is maximized over all examples in the training set, VAE models also cover all modes of the data, and do not suffer from the problems of mode collapse and lack of diversity often seen in GANs. In addition, standard GAN models do not have an encoder and are, therefore, incapable of mapping a given input to a latent representation.

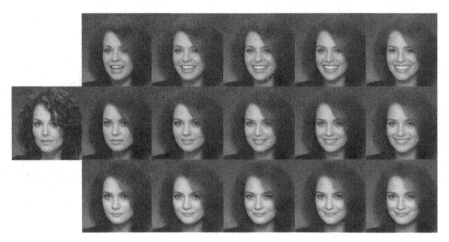

FIGURE 8.5

Exemplary decoupling of attribute vectors in a variational autoencoder model. Here, smiling (from left to right) and mouth opening effects (top to bottom) are disentangled, which allows for a systematic manipulation of the original image (left). In this example, it can also be seen that this variational autoencoder introduces a regular pattern visible in all generated images. Image source: Tom White [59] under CC BY 4.0 license.

8.3.3.1 Current challenges of variational autoencoders

A major drawback of variational autoencoders is the blurriness of generated samples. This is especially evident when compared to photo-realistic images generated by GANs. The reason for this is currently not fully understood and has motivated a number of research efforts. Essentially, three possible causes for this phenomenon are currently being discussed: (1) The asymmetric behavior of the KL divergence in the ELBO criterion leads to the preference of higher variances in the generated data over a sufficient mapping of the training set. (2) The true posterior distribution can only be inadequately approximated by the mostly used factorized Gaussian distribution as prior distribution, which prevents a tight fit of the ELBO to the true evidence $\log p_\theta(\mathbf{x})$. (3) Variational autoencoders usually have a Gaussian distribution as likelihood term, which is equivalent to training with an L_2-loss that has a tendency to ignore features that occupy few pixels or cause only small intensity changes.

The first cause can be explained by considering the empirical data distribution of the training set $q_\chi = \frac{1}{N}\sum_i \delta_i(\mathbf{x}_i)$, where δ_i is the Dirac distribution centered at $\mathbf{x}_i$. The ELBO criterion in Eq. (8.11) can be reformulated as (see [60] for a derivation)

$$\mathcal{L}(\theta, \phi) = -\mathcal{D}_{KL}\left(q_\phi(\mathbf{z}|\mathbf{x})q_\chi(\mathbf{x})||p_\theta(\mathbf{x}|\mathbf{z})p(\mathbf{z})\right) + \text{const}$$
$$= -\mathcal{D}_{KL}\left(q_{\chi,\phi}(\mathbf{x},\mathbf{z})||p_\theta(\mathbf{x},\mathbf{z})\right) + \text{const}. \tag{8.18}$$

Here, $\text{const} = -\mathcal{H}(q_\chi(\mathbf{x}))$ is the entropy of the training set. When a perfect fit between $p_\theta(\mathbf{x},\mathbf{z})$ and $q_{\chi,\phi}(\mathbf{x},\mathbf{z})$ is not possible, the asymmetry of the KL divergence causes the variance of $p_\theta(\mathbf{x}, \mathbf{z})$ to be larger than the variance of $q_{\chi,\phi}(\mathbf{x}, \mathbf{z})$. Consequently, the reconstructed data $p_\theta(\mathbf{x}|\mathbf{z})p(\mathbf{z})$ contains samples that differ from the training data. Causes (1) and (2) are both related to an insufficient approximation of the posterior distribution by $q_\phi(\mathbf{z}|\mathbf{x})$ and can be alleviated by choosing a sufficiently flexible encoder and prior distribution $p(\mathbf{z})$ (see discussion in Section 8.3.6). However, the relationship in Eq. (8.18) provides an explanation for why VAEs are not prone to mode collapse and prefer generating deviant samples to incompletely mapping the diversity in the training set. In this sense, explanation (3) shows why the model favors blurring over other divergent features in the generated samples. This can be countered by increasing the capacity of the decoder and alternative likelihood terms. Some possible solutions are discussed in Section 8.3.5.

Another frequently observed problem in VAEs is posterior collapse [61,62,56,63], where some dimensions of the latent space represent the prior that does not contain information about the data, i.e., $\exists i : \forall \mathbf{x}\, q_\phi(z_i|\mathbf{x}) \approx p(z_i)$. This reduces the capacity of the generative model and prevents the decoder network to use the information content of all latent dimensions

Some works assume that the posterior collapse is caused by a mismatch of prior and posterior distributions [64,65]. Other works assume that local maxima in the optimization criterion of the VAE are the cause and, therefore, propose an annealing process during optimization [61,34,62,66] or an alternative optimization criterion [67–69].

8.3.4 Disentanglement of the latent space

While imposing a prior during optimization leads to a better organization of a VAE's latent space than in standard autoencoders, the latent variables still do not necessarily carry an interpretable meaning or directly represent isolated true factors of data variation. Therefore, and similar to autoencoders (see discussion in Section 8.2.2), different extensions of the vanilla VAE method exist to disentangle the latent variables. Popular, general variants for unsupervised latent variable disentanglement are β-VAEs [34] and FactorVAEs [70]. In β-VAEs, the standard loss in Eq. (8.11) is augmented with an additional β hyperparameter that allows putting more weight on the KL divergence term by choosing $\beta > 1$:

$$\mathcal{L}(\theta, \phi) = \mathbb{E}_{q_\phi(\mathbf{z}|\mathbf{x})}\left[\log p_\theta(\mathbf{x}|\mathbf{z})\right] - \beta \mathcal{D}_{KL}\left(q_\phi(\mathbf{z}|\mathbf{x})\|p(\mathbf{z})\right). \qquad (8.19)$$

As outlined in [71], for a factorized Gaussian prior, this encourages the β-VAE to better disentangle the latent variables, which eventually leads to an improved isolation of the underlying factors of the data. However, while large β values will lead to a better disentanglement, they also negatively impact the reconstruction quality. This is, for example, addressed in FactorVAEs [70] where the optimization objective is augmented with an additional term that explicitly penalizes correlations between latent variables through a discriminator.

Many downstream tasks in medical image analysis require the disentanglement of shape and appearance of the anatomical or pathological structures visible in an image.

Deforming autoencoders [72] provide a way to achieve this by splitting the latent representation of an image into appearance and shape features (see Fig. 8.1(e)). Here, shape information is represented by a smooth spatial transformation with respect to a template space. The transformation can then be utilized to warp a deformation-free appearance template to a specific shape configuration (see also Section 8.4.3). While initially being proposed for computer vision applications and based on a standard autoencoder architecture, VAE-based variants for medical images were proposed in [20,73] where spatial transformations are represented by diffeomorphisms. This line of research is related to previous probabilistic generative models for shape modeling with diffeomorphic transformations like [74].

In addition to purely unsupervised or semisupervised disentanglement as discussed above, approaches also exist that perform disentanglement in a supervised way or that directly couple the generative modeling process with a downstream task. For example, [28] presents a VAE whose latent space is mapped to a single variable to directly perform regression within the generative model.

8.3.5 Alternative reconstruction objectives

As already addressed in Section 8.3.2, the choice of log-likelihood $p_\theta(\mathbf{x}|\mathbf{z})$ determines the distance measure used to evaluate the similarity between training data and generated samples. This is directly related to the reconstruction loss used in autoencoders (see Eq. (8.1)) and the discussion in this section consequently applies to autoencoders as well.

Commonly used probability distributions, such as the Gaussian, Laplace, or Bernoulli distributions, lead to pixel-wise, intensity-based distance measures. In particular, the widely used squared Euclidean distance (see Eq. (8.13)) often yields blurry results. Some works therefore propose to use distance measures that assess the perceptual similarity of images [75,36,76–79]. A popular perceptual image similarity metric is the structural similarity metric (SSIM) [80], which compares the local statistics of image patches, and several works use this metric for VAEs to generate less blurred images [79]. Other approaches propose to compare learned image features, e.g., high-level features extracted from pre-trained networks, as a perceptual similarity measure for generative tasks [76,75].

An interesting line of research is the use of adversarial training in combination with a VAE [36]. Here, an encoder and a decoder are learned together with a discriminator, where encoder and decoder generate image data and the discriminator judges the image quality, i.e., serves as a reconstruction objective (see Fig. 8.1(f)). Since adversarial training is unstable and sensitive to hyper-parameter values, this approach is often combined with an additional pixel-wise intensity difference, e.g., L_1- or L_2-loss, to stabilize the training [75]. As can be seen from Fig. 8.6, the adversarial loss leads to a significant improvement in the visual quality of the generated images. This example, therefore, shows that it is possible to improve the generative capabilities of a model considerably through appropriate, image-focused reconstruction objectives that go well beyond routinely chosen quadratic terms. However, recent research also

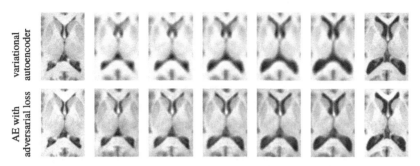

variational
autoencoder

AE with
adversarial loss

FIGURE 8.6

Synthesizing new images by linear interpolation between two original T1 brain MR images (first/last column) in the latent space of a variational autoencoder (VAE) (top row; quadratic loss used for training) and an autoencoder (AE) trained with an adversarial loss (bottom row). It can be seen that applying the adversarial loss considerably improves the quality of the generated images, which are less blurry and better preserve important anatomical details when compared to the images produced by the standard VAE.

suggests that similar improvements are also possible by careful design and increasing the flexibility of the model even with standard losses [37,38].

8.3.6 Improving the flexibility of the model

8.3.6.1 Alternative priors and auxiliary variables

As seen in Eq. (8.12) and discussed in Section 8.3.3, increasing the match of the approximate distribution $q_\phi(\mathbf{z}|\mathbf{x})$ with respect to the true posterior $p_\theta(\mathbf{z}|\mathbf{x})$, improves the tightness of the variational bound (ELBO) to the true evidence $\log p_\theta(\mathbf{x})$. Provided that the encoder function has enough capacity, this accuracy is determined by the prior. Choosing a prior that is too simple could, therefore, lead to over-regularization.

A number of papers suggest alternative prior distributions to the often used mean field inference via factorized Gaussian. For example, Kingma and Welling [17, 60] mention a number of other distributions that can be implemented via the reparametrization trick, including Laplace, Logistic, or full-covariance Gaussian distributions. Tomczak and Welling (2018) [81] propose a flexible mixture distribution (e.g., a mixture of Gaussians) with components given by variational posteriors conditioned on learnable pseudoinputs, the "variational mixture of posteriors" prior:

$$p(\mathbf{z}) = \frac{1}{K} \sum_{k=1}^{K} q_\psi(\mathbf{z}|\boldsymbol{u}_k), \qquad (8.20)$$

where q_ψ is implemented as a network with parameters ψ, and $\boldsymbol{u}_k$ are learnable *pseudoinputs*.

The introduction of auxiliary latent variables is another way to increase the expressiveness of variational autoencoders [18,62,82,37]. Here, the observed variable $\mathbf{x}$

depends on a hierarchy of stochastic latent variables $\mathbf{z}_1, \ldots, \mathbf{z}_L$,

$$p_\theta(\mathbf{x}, \mathbf{z}_1, \ldots, \mathbf{z}_L) = p_\theta(\mathbf{x}|\mathbf{z}_1) p(\mathbf{z}_L) \prod_{l=1}^{L-1} p(\mathbf{z}_l|\mathbf{z}_{l+1}), \qquad (8.21)$$

and the approximate variational distribution is factorized as $q_\phi(\mathbf{z}_1, \ldots, \mathbf{z}_L|\mathbf{x}) = q_\phi(\mathbf{z}_1|\mathbf{x}) \prod_{l=1}^{L-1} q_\phi(\mathbf{z}_{l+1}|\mathbf{z}_l)$ so that each latent variable is conditioned on the variable below in the hierarchy (see Fig. 8.1(g)). A hierarchy of latent stochastic variables leads to a more expressive model, but latent variables deeper in the hierarchy may tend to collapse into the prior [62,37]. Eq. (8.21) assumes a Markov independence structure on the latent variables, but other approaches use shortcuts and complex inference models to exploit deeper hierarchies of latent variables while avoiding variable collapse [82,62,37].

8.3.6.2 Importance weighted autoencoder

The importance weighted autoencoder proposed by Burda et al. (2016) [83] uses importance sampling to increase the model's flexibility. From Eq. (8.11), it can be seen that the ELBO criterion can be written as a lower bound

$$\log p_\theta(\mathbf{x}) \geq \mathcal{L}^{VAE}(\theta, \phi) = \mathbb{E}_{q_\phi(\mathbf{z}|\mathbf{x})} \left[\log \left(\frac{p_\theta(\mathbf{x}, \mathbf{z})}{q_\phi(\mathbf{z}|\mathbf{x})} \right) \right]. \qquad (8.22)$$

During optimization, the gradient is estimated via Monte Carlo sampling with $\nabla_{\theta,\phi}\hat{\mathcal{L}}^{VAE} \approx \sum_{k=1}^{K} \frac{1}{K} \nabla_{\theta,\phi} \log \left(\frac{p_\theta(\mathbf{x}, \mathbf{z}_k)}{q_\phi(\mathbf{z}_k|\mathbf{x})} \right)$ (see Section 8.3.2). Then, the importance weighted autoencoder optimizes

$$\mathcal{L}_K^{IWAE}(\theta, \phi) = -\mathbb{E}_{\mathbf{z}_k \sim q_\phi(\mathbf{z}|\mathbf{x})} \left[\log \left(\frac{1}{K} \sum_{k=1}^{K} \frac{p_\theta(\mathbf{x}, \mathbf{z}_k)}{q_\phi(\mathbf{z}_k|\mathbf{x})} \right) \right], \qquad (8.23)$$

for a given sample size $K \geq 1$. It is obvious that $\mathcal{L}^{VAE} = \mathcal{L}_1^{IWAE}$, and Burda et al. (2016) [83] further show that $\mathcal{L}^{VAE} = \mathcal{L}_1^{IWAE} \leq \mathcal{L}_2^{IWAE} \leq \cdots \leq \mathcal{L}_K^{IWAE} \leq \log p_\theta(\mathbf{x})$, which implies a tighter lower bound with increasing sample size converging to $\lim_{K \to \infty} \mathcal{L}_K^{IWAE} = \log p_\theta(\mathbf{x})$. To understand why this approach is called importance weighted autoencoder, we consider the gradient of $\mathcal{L}_K^{IWAE}$:

$$\nabla_{\theta,\phi} \mathcal{L}_K^{IWAE} \approx \sum_{k=1}^{K} \tilde{w}_k \nabla_{\theta,\phi} \log \left(\frac{p_\theta(\mathbf{x}, \mathbf{z}_k)}{q_\phi(\mathbf{z}_k|\mathbf{x})} \right), \quad \text{where } \tilde{w}_k = \frac{\frac{p_\theta(\mathbf{x}, \mathbf{z}_k)}{q_\phi(\mathbf{z}_k|\mathbf{x})}}{\sum_{j=1}^{K} \frac{p_\theta(\mathbf{x}, \mathbf{z}_j)}{q_\phi(\mathbf{z}_j|\mathbf{x})}}. \qquad (8.24)$$

From Eqs. (8.22) and (8.24), we see that the gradient of $\mathcal{L}^{VAE}$ evenly weights the samples, whereas the gradient of $\mathcal{L}_K^{IWAE}$ weights the samples based on their relative importance $\tilde{w}_k$.

8.3.6.3 Adversarial autoencoders

Adversarial autoencoders [84] combine the probabilistic encoding model of a variational autoencoder with the adversarial training framework of generative adversarial networks (see Fig. 8.1(h)). A new discriminative function $d_\chi : \mathcal{Z} \rightarrow [0, 1]$ is introduced, that is trained to discriminate between latent samples drawn from the prior $p(\mathbf{z})$ and the posterior $q_\phi(\mathbf{z}|\mathbf{x})$ generated by the encoder. In this way, the adversarial training replaces the Kullback–Leibler divergence to pull the learned posterior towards the prior distribution. The discriminator is learned by minimizing the cost of misassignment of real or fake samples:

$$\mathcal{L}^{dis}(\chi) = -\frac{1}{N} \sum_{i=1}^{N} \log(d_\chi(\tilde{\mathbf{z}}_i)) - \frac{1}{N} \sum_{j=1}^{N} \log(d_\chi(\mathbf{z}_j)). \tag{8.25}$$

Here, N is the size of a minibatch, $\tilde{\mathbf{z}}_i \sim p(\mathbf{z})$ are samples drawn from the prior distribution, and $\mathbf{z}_j \sim q_\phi(\mathbf{z}|\mathbf{x})$ are samples generated by the encoder. The adversarial autoencoder is trained jointly in two phases – the reconstruction phase and the regularization phase – executed on each minibatch. In the reconstruction phase, the autoencoder updates the encoder and decoder to minimize the reconstruction error and to match the prior:

$$\mathcal{L}^{AAE}(\theta, \phi) = \underbrace{-\mathbb{E}_{q_\phi(\mathbf{z}|\mathbf{x})}\left[\log p_\theta(\mathbf{x}|\mathbf{z})\right]}_{\mathcal{L}^{rec}(\theta,\phi)} + \underbrace{\mathbb{E}_{q_\phi(\mathbf{z}|\mathbf{x})}\left[\log(1 - d_\chi(\mathbf{z}))\right]}_{\mathcal{L}^{prior}(\phi)}. \tag{8.26}$$

In the regularization phase, the network first updates the discriminator by Eq. (8.25) to distinguish true samples from generated samples. Then its generator, which is also the encoder of the autoencoder, is updated by minimizing $\mathcal{L}^{prior}$ to confuse the discriminator.

An important difference to classical VAEs is that the prior distribution does not need to be analytically defined here to compute the KL divergence. In adversarial autoencoders, we only need to sample from the prior distribution. This allows the use of more complicated distributions even without having access to their explicit form.

8.4 Example applications

As already briefly discussed in Section 8.1.2, autoencoders and VAEs have a wide range of applications in medical image processing. Comprehensive overviews of their use can be found in various survey articles, e.g., [2,85,86,3]. In this section, we will focus on three important applications of VAEs: unsupervised pathology detection, explanation of classification results, and decoupled shape and appearance modeling in multimodal image registration.

8.4.1 **Unsupervised pathology detection**

The goal of anomaly detection is to learn a model of the normal data and then to identify the samples that do not match the normal model as anomalies. The use of autoencoders for this task follows the premise that the latent subspace of the normal samples is learned by the autoencoder. Once learned, the result is a low reconstruction error for normal samples and a high reconstruction error for anomalies. When using a VAE, this premise can be further extended to include that the generated latent representations for anomalies do not match the prior distribution $p(\mathbf{z})$.

In medical imaging, anomaly detection can be used to automatically detect and localize pathologies in image databases [31,32,87,88,33]. In contrast to segmentation methods that focus on a specific pathology, anomaly detection works assumption-free: a model is trained on images of the chosen modality, e.g., brain magnetic resonance imaging, which is then used to detect arbitrary pathologies, e.g., hemorrhages, tumors, lesions due to stroke or multiple sclerosis. In [33], a number of autoencoder and VAE architectures are explored for this task, where a segmentation map is generated by thresholding the pixel-wise reconstruction error. They also show the advantages of using VAEs over autoencoders and GAN-based approaches [89], as VAEs combine better detection performance with a simple optimization procedure. Evaluations solely based on the reconstruction error potentially ignore useful information from the latent encoding. Uzunova et al. [32], therefore, introduce a patch-based approach where the relative patch position is passed as a condition to a conditional VAE. To create the segmentation, the pixel-wise reconstruction error is combined with the probability of the latent encoding of this patch. Their results show the usefulness of latent information (see Fig. 8.7). This is supported by findings in [87] where an improved detection performance was achieved when the derivative of $\mathcal{D}_{KL}$ with respect to the input is combined with the reconstruction error.

As expected, the segmentation accuracy achievable with those unsupervised approaches is lower than for current supervised segmentation methods. For example, Dice values of ~ 0.5 are reported for brain tumors in [32] while a recent segmentation approach [90] reports values ~ 0.9. However, unsupervised anomaly detection has the advantage of not requiring any expensive labeled training data and it is fully independent of the type of anomaly.

8.4.2 **Image synthesis for the explanation of black-box classifiers**

In a clinical setting, clinicians and patients need to trust an automated image analysis system. To achieve this, such a system must be able to explain its decisions and predictions in a comprehensible way to a nontechnician [93]. Therefore, several papers address the problem of generating plausible explanations for the predictions of black-box image classifiers, such as machine learning methods. One important class of approaches exploits the gradients of the classification function for this purpose to perform guided backpropagation [91] or to generate gradient-weighted class activation maps (gradCAMs) [92].

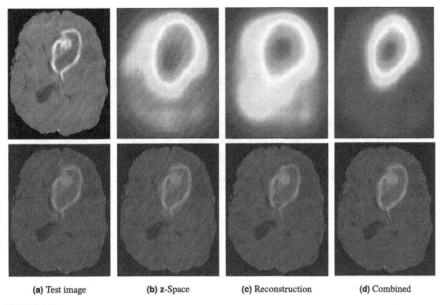

| **(a)** Test image | **(b)** z-Space | **(c)** Reconstruction | **(d)** Combined |

FIGURE 8.7

Unsupervised VAE-based pathology detection of a brain tumor image (a) and resulting anomaly scores (growing values: blue → red (dark gray → light gray in print version)) computed from latent encodings (b), reconstruction error (c), and a combination of both (d). The second row shows ground-truth segmentation and resulting thresholded segmentation maps [32].

Another class of approaches tries to directly identify image regions that change the classification result when manipulated [94,95]. To achieve the most realistic manipulation of image regions in medical image data, an inpainting and image synthesis method based on VAEs is proposed in [96]. Here, in a first step, a VAE is trained on healthy images. For the explanation task, image regions to be manipulated are replaced with their corresponding healthy appearance synthesized by the VAE. An optimization procedure now finds the image regions that are most significant for the classification result.

Fig. 8.8 shows the explanation results for a multilabel classifier trained to detect pathologies in retinal optical coherence tomography (OCT) images. If the classifier is trained correctly, the explanations should approximately match the location of the pathologies in the images. Fig. 8.8, row 1, shows input OCT images with the ground-truth labels of the pathologies. The remaining rows show overlaid explanation maps of different explanation techniques. The VAE-based technique in row 2 shows a clear focus on the pathology. This shows that the trained classifier makes reliable predictions and that the learned VAE model provides suitable perturbations for the image regions to be hidden, compared to replacing them with constant values.

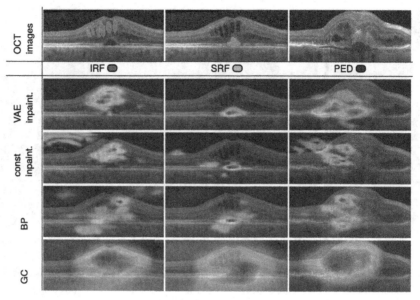

FIGURE 8.8

Comparison of different explanation techniques for a multilabel retinal optical coherence tomography (OCT) classifier. Shown are row-wise: retinal OCT images with ground truth labels IRF (⬤), SRF (◯), and PED (⬤); VAE-based inpainting method; inpainting with constant values (gray); guided backpropagation (BP) [91]; gradCAM (GC) [92]. Columns show an explanation of three pathology labels IRF (intraretinal fluid), SRF (subretinal fluid), and PED (pigment epithelium detachment).

8.4.3 Decoupled shape and appearance modeling for multimodal data

In medical imaging, multiple images of the same subject are often acquired using different imaging modalities. In these cases, the shape of the objects depicted remain the same while their appearance differs between modalities. It would, therefore, be desirable to learn representations where shape and appearance are disentangled. Disentangled shape and appearance variations facilitate discrimination of underlying factors in representation learning, but are also a desirable property in many image synthesis tasks, as they allow for a more controlled generation of certain image properties. For example, modality transfer typically targets appearance modifications while preserving object shapes. Similar examples can be found in the context of cross-modality analysis, image imputation, image inpainting, anomaly detection, and data augmentation.

The deforming autoencoder introduced in [72] interprets an image $\mathbf{x}$ as a composition of two parts: a deformation-free appearance template $\mathbf{x}_A$ and a deformation $\boldsymbol{\varphi}$, such that $\mathbf{x} \approx \mathbf{x}_A \circ \boldsymbol{\varphi}$, with $\circ$ denoting the warping function. Appearance $\mathbf{x}_A$ and

source   interpolated shape   target

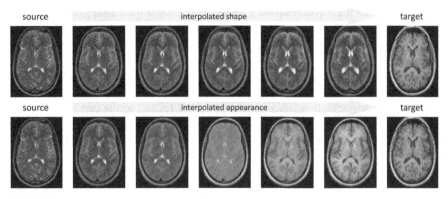

source   interpolated appearance   target

FIGURE 8.9

Visualization of the disentangled latent representations for shape and appearance in a deformable autoencoder [73]. Decoded images from interpolated latent vectors between two images of different modalities (left, T2; right, T1) are shown. (Top) Interpolation is performed in the shape space only. (Bottom) Interpolation is performed in the appearance space only. Note that only the shape (e.g., ventricles) changes in the top row, while in the bottom row the intensities change while the shape is constant.

deformation φ are generated by an autoencoder architecture with a composite latent vector $\mathbf{z} = [\mathbf{z}_A, \mathbf{z}_\varphi]$ and two separate decoders $g_{\theta_A}(\mathbf{z}_A)$ and $g_{\theta_\varphi}(\mathbf{z}_\varphi)$. In population-based studies, it is often desirable to map all images to a common reference frame (a template or atlas). This can be achieved by learning a global appearance template $\mathcal{T}$ over all training samples and defining φ with respect to the template space [20,73]. By using an additive appearance map $\mathbf{\Delta}_A$ that approximates the pixel-wise differences to the template each input image is represented by $\mathbf{x} \approx (\mathcal{T} + \mathbf{\Delta}_A) \circ \varphi$. Note that all components ($\mathcal{T}$, $\mathbf{\Delta}_A = g_{\theta_A}(\mathbf{z}_A)$, $\varphi = g_{\theta_\varphi}(\mathbf{z}_\varphi)$) are learned from the training data. To ensure appropriate learning of the autoencoder's network parameters, additional terms besides reconstruction loss and KL divergence must be included in the optimization objective to ensure smoothness and zero-centering of the deformations (see [73]).

One problem with the deformable autoencoder presented above is that differences between the input image and the reconstructed image are compensated either via spatial deformations or by the creation or elimination of structures in the appearance map. In practice, this requires careful balancing of the capacities of $\mathbf{z}_A$ and $\mathbf{z}_\varphi$ and leads to blurred appearance maps and incomplete decoupling. In [73] filtering techniques are incorporated into the network architecture, to ensure that the appearance map does not change the shape of the template. It has been shown that this approach not only improves the disentanglement of shape and appearance, but also improves the quality of the generated templates and the accuracy of the registration to the template space.

As shown in Fig. 8.9, deformable autoencoders are an excellent tool for synthesizing images with predefined features. Here, images from different modalities (T1-

and T2-weighted magnetic resonance images) were used for training. Shown is the linear interpolation between two images in latent space when only the shape component (top row) or only the appearance component is modified. In this way, topological or appearance properties of the synthesized images can be selectively changed.

Possible applications of deformable autoencoders include modality transfer, data augmentation, and anomaly detection. By mapping into a common template space, they also enable population-based analyses and are related to the concept of image metamorphosis used in computational anatomy [97,98]. In this way, they allow for individualized models of age- or disease-related alteration processes and the identification of better disease markers.

8.5 Future directions and research challenges

The often inadequate quality of images generated by autoencoders or variational autoencoders is a key challenge to be addressed in future research. Promising research directions related to this problem are: (1) increasing the flexibility and capacity of the coding model; here, especially inverse autoregressive flows [35] or complex latent variable models [37] are promising candidates; (2) a stabilization of the learning procedure to avoid local minima in the objective function and posterior collapse [63]; and – related to the previous points – (3) a careful design of the network architecture used [38]. Also, the inclusion of adversarial learning techniques [36] will certainly motivate further developments. Whether a unified network architecture can be established given the wide range of applications for VAEs remains an open question.

Another research direction that has attracted increased attention recently, is the generation of meaningful latent space representations. Here, new task-specific approaches for generating uncorrelated representations of defined attributes similar to deformable autoencoders can be expected and likely more general approaches for disentangling the dimensions of latent space will be developed.

Furthermore, autoencoders and variational autoencoders are excellent starting points for semisupervised and multitask learning applications [99]. Since labeled data is still a limited resource for most medical image analysis problems, the importance of such approaches will continue to grow. It is, therefore, expected that both autoencoders and variational autoencoders will play an essential role in applications where data is scarce.

Recent and anticipated future improvements of the quality of generated images will help to open up new application areas for variational autoencoders. For example, synthetically generated image data could be used for data augmentation and modality transfer, and the encoder–decoder structure together with successful latent variable disentanglement allows for straightforward and systematic manipulation of existing samples.

The application of VAEs for population-based statistical analyses is also an underexplored area at the moment. A systematic investigation and increase of the statistical power of the generated probabilistic models would be of advantage for the detection of demographic or disease-specific relations, to aid biomarker discovery, or to characterize and simulate disease progression.

8.6 Summary

Autoencoders and variational autoencoders are key techniques in learning-based biomedical image analysis and synthesis. Both approaches provide a way to structure high-dimensional data in an unsupervised way by converting them into compact, low-dimensional representations using bottleneck encoder–decoder neural network architectures. The encoder part maps the high-dimensional input to its low-dimensional latent space representation using a learned and potentially highly complex nonlinear function, while the decoder is trained to reverse this process. The latent space serves multiple purposes as it can, for example, be used as a starting point for downstream tasks like classification, to systematically generate new data via sampling techniques, and to manipulate certain properties of mapped inputs, which makes autoencoders and variational autoencoders suitable tools for image synthesis tasks.

From a theoretical point of view, autoencoders and variational autoencoders use different ways to solve the unsupervised learning problem stated above. Autoencoders are setup in a deterministic fashion and their optimization mainly aims at minimizing a data reconstruction error. This allows them to learn complex encoder/decoder functions that effectively compress the data. However, their latent space usually lacks a meaningful structure, which makes it hard to systematically sample new data or manipulate certain aspects of the inputs. To alleviate this shortcoming, several extensions such as sparse, contractive, or denoising autoencoders have been proposed. Those extensions aim at inducing a structure on the latent space by employing different regularization techniques during the optimization process. Even for those regularized versions, the data distribution in the latent space is usually unknown, which prevents autoencoders from effectively being used as probabilistic generative models. Variational autoencoders directly address this aspect by employing tools from Bayesian statistics to define and solve the optimization problem in a probabilistic way. The basic idea is to structure the latent space in a way that the low-dimensional data distribution follows a predefined, simple base distribution like a factorized Gaussian that is easy to sample. While this probabilistic setup already leads to powerful generative models, numerous extensions of this general idea exist that, for example, aim at specifically disentangling different generating factors of the underlying process in the latent space or that propose reconstruction objectives that help the models to synthesize high-quality images.

Autoencoders and variational autoencoders have lately seen an enormous success in biomedical image analysis and synthesis as evidenced by the growing number of research papers that apply them in many different scenarios. This chapter exemplarily showcased their use for unsupervised pathology detection, explanation of image classification results, and decoupled shape and appearance modeling in multimodal image registration approaches. However, due to their flexibility, potential scenarios go well beyond those examples and cover all areas of biomedical image analysis and synthesis such as image segmentation, image registration, image reconstruction, data augmentation, or modality transfer. It can also be assumed that anticipated future methodological advances in this area that, for example, help to improve the visual quality of synthetically generated images, will even increase their applicability.

References

[1] Y. Bengio, A. Courville, P. Vincent, Representation learning: a review and new perspectives, IEEE Trans. Pattern Anal. Mach. Intell. 35 (8) (2013) 1798–1828, https://doi.org/10.1109/TPAMI.2013.50.

[2] G. Litjens, T. Kooi, B.E. Bejnordi, A.A.A. Setio, F. Ciompi, M. Ghafoorian, J.A.W.M. van der Laak, B. van Ginneken, C.I. Sánchez, A survey on deep learning in medical image analysis, Med. Image Anal. 42 (2017) 60–88, https://doi.org/10.1016/j.media.2017.07.005, arXiv:1702.05747.

[3] R. Wei, A. Mahmood, Recent advances in variational autoencoders with representation learning for biomedical informatics: a survey, IEEE Access 9 (2021) 4939–4956, https://doi.org/10.1109/ACCESS.2020.3048309.

[4] C.L. Srinidhi, O. Ciga, A.L. Martel, Deep neural network models for computational histopathology: a survey, Med. Image Anal. 67 (2021) 101813.

[5] D.E. Rumelhart, G.E. Hinton, R.J. Williams, Learning internal representations by error propagation, in: Parallel Distributed Processing: Explorations in the Microstructure of Cognition, Vol. 1: Foundations, MIT Press, Cambridge, MA, USA, 1986, pp. 318–362.

[6] D.H. Ballard, Modular learning in neural networks, in: Proceedings of the Sixth National Conference on Artificial Intelligence – Volume 1, AAAI'87, AAAI Press, Seattle, Washington, 1987, pp. 279–284.

[7] D.H. Ackley, G.E. Hinton, T.J. Sejnowski, A learning algorithm for Boltzmann machines, Cogn. Sci. 9 (1) (1985) 147–169.

[8] G. Cottrel, P. Munro, D. Zipser, Image compression by back propagation: a demonstration of extensional programming, in: Advances in Cognitive Science, vol. 2, Abbex, 1988.

[9] H. Bourlard, Y. Kamp, Auto-association by multilayer perceptrons and singular value decomposition, Biol. Cybern. 59 (4–5) (1988) 291–294.

[10] M.A. Kramer, Nonlinear principal component analysis using autoassociative neural networks, AIChE J. 37 (2) (1991) 233–243.

[11] G.E. Hinton, R.R. Salakhutdinov, Reducing the dimensionality of data with neural networks, Science 313 (5786) (2006) 504–507.

[12] Y. Bengio, P. Lamblin, D. Popovici, H. Larochelle, Greedy layer-wise training of deep networks, Adv. Neural Inf. Process. Syst. 19 (2006) 153–160.

[13] A. Krizhevsky, G.E. Hinton, Using very deep autoencoders for content-based image retrieval, in: ESANN, vol. 1, Citeseer, 2011, p. 2.

[14] M. Ranzato, C. Poultney, S. Chopra, Y. Cun, Efficient learning of sparse representations with an energy-based model, Adv. Neural Inf. Process. Syst. 19 (2006) 1137–1144.

[15] S. Rifai, P. Vincent, X. Muller, X. Glorot, Y. Bengio, Contractive auto-encoders: explicit invariance during feature extraction, in: International Conference on Machine Learning, 2011.

[16] P. Vincent, H. Larochelle, Y. Bengio, P.-A. Manzagol, Extracting and composing robust features with denoising autoencoders, in: Proceedings of the 25th International Conference on Machine Learning, ICML'08, Association for Computing Machinery, New York, NY, USA, 2008, pp. 1096–1103, https://doi.org/10.1145/1390156.1390294.

[17] D.P. Kingma, M. Welling, Auto-encoding variational Bayes, in: International Conference on Learning Representations (ICLR 2014), 2014, arXiv:1312.6114.

[18] D.J. Rezende, S. Mohamed, D. Wierstra, Stochastic backpropagation and approximate inference in deep generative models, in: International Conference on Machine Learning, in: PMLR, 2014, pp. 1278–1286.

[19] A. Myronenko, 3D MRI brain tumor segmentation using autoencoder regularization, in: A. Crimi, S. Bakas, H. Kuijf, F. Keyvan, M. Reyes, T. van Walsum (Eds.), Brainlesion: Glioma, Multiple Sclerosis, Stroke and Traumatic Brain Injuries, in: Lecture Notes in Computer Science, Springer International Publishing, Cham, 2019, pp. 311–320, https://doi.org/10.1007/978-3-030-11726-9_28.

[20] A. Bône, P. Vernhet, O. Colliot, S. Durrleman, Learning joint shape and appearance representations with metamorphic auto-encoders, in: A.L. Martel, P. Abolmaesumi, D. Stoyanov, D. Mateus, M.A. Zuluaga, S.K. Zhou, D. Racoceanu, L. Joskowicz (Eds.), Medical Image Computing and Computer Assisted Intervention – MICCAI 2020, in: Lecture Notes in Computer Science, Springer International Publishing, Cham, 2020, pp. 202–211, https://doi.org/10.1007/978-3-030-59710-8_20.

[21] M. Blendowski, N. Bouteldja, M.P. Heinrich, Multimodal 3D medical image registration guided by shape encoder–decoder networks, Int. J. Comput. Assisted Radiol. Surg. 15 (2) (2020) 269–276, https://doi.org/10.1007/s11548-019-02089-8.

[22] X. Yang, X. Han, E. Park, S. Aylward, R. Kwitt, M. Niethammer, Registration of pathological images, in: S.A. Tsaftaris, A. Gooya, A.F. Frangi, J.L. Prince (Eds.), Simulation and Synthesis in Medical Imaging, Springer International Publishing, Cham, 2016, pp. 97–107.

[23] M. Kallenberg, K. Petersen, M. Nielsen, A.Y. Ng, P. Diao, C. Igel, C.M. Vachon, K. Holland, R.R. Winkel, N. Karssemeijer, M. Lillholm, Unsupervised deep learning applied to breast density segmentation and mammographic risk scoring, IEEE Trans. Med. Imaging 35 (5) (2016) 1322–1331, https://doi.org/10.1109/TMI.2016.2532122.

[24] J.-Z. Cheng, D. Ni, Y.-H. Chou, J. Qin, C.-M. Tiu, Y.-C. Chang, C.-S. Huang, D. Shen, C.-M. Chen, Computer-aided diagnosis with deep learning architecture: applications to breast lesions in US images and pulmonary nodules in CT scans, Sci. Rep. 6 (1) (2016) 24454, https://doi.org/10.1038/srep24454.

[25] M. Chen, X. Shi, Y. Zhang, D. Wu, M. Guizani, Deep features learning for medical image analysis with convolutional autoencoder neural network, IEEE Trans. Big Data 7 (4) (2017) 750–758, https://doi.org/10.1109/TBDATA.2017.2717439.

[26] E. Puyol-Antón, B. Ruijsink, J.R. Clough, I. Oksuz, D. Rueckert, R. Razavi, A.P. King, Assessing the impact of blood pressure on cardiac function using interpretable biomarkers and variational autoencoders, in: M. Pop, M. Sermesant, O. Camara, X. Zhuang, S. Li, A. Young, T. Mansi, A. Suinesiaputra (Eds.), Statistical Atlases and Computational Models of the Heart. Multi-Sequence CMR Segmentation, CRT-EPiggy and LV Full Quantification Challenges, in: Lecture Notes in Computer Science, Springer International Publishing, Cham, 2020, pp. 22–30, https://doi.org/10.1007/978-3-030-39074-7_3.

[27] A. Chartsias, T. Joyce, G. Papanastasiou, S. Semple, M. Williams, D.E. Newby, R. Dharmakumar, S.A. Tsaftaris, Disentangled representation learning in cardiac image analysis, Med. Image Anal. 58 (2019) 101535, https://doi.org/10.1016/j.media.2019.101535.

[28] Q. Zhao, E. Adeli, N. Honnorat, T. Leng, K.M. Pohl, Variational AutoEncoder for regression: application to brain aging analysis, in: International Conference on Medical Image Computing and Computer-Assisted Intervention (MICCAI 2019), vol. 11765, 2019, pp. 823–831, https://doi.org/10.1007/978-3-030-32245-8_91.

[29] B. Gutiérrez-Becker, I. Sarasua, C. Wachinger, Discriminative and generative models for anatomical shape analysis on point clouds with deep neural networks, Med. Image Anal. 67 (2021) 101852, https://doi.org/10.1016/j.media.2020.101852.

[30] H. Uzunova, P. Kaftan, M. Wilms, N.D. Forkert, H. Handels, J. Ehrhardt, Quantitative comparison of generative shape models for medical images, in: T. Tolxdorff, T.M. Deserno, H. Handels, A. Maier, K.H. Maier-Hein, C. Palm (Eds.), Bildverarbeitung für die Medizin 2020, Informatik aktuell, Springer Fachmedien, Wiesbaden, 2020, pp. 201–207, https://doi.org/10.1007/978-3-658-29267-6_45.

[31] N. Pawlowski, M.C.H. Lee, M. Rajchl, S. McDonagh, E. Ferrante, K. Kamnitsas, S. Cooke, S. Stevenson, A. Khetani, T. Newman, F. Zeiler, R. Digby, J.P. Coles, D. Rueckert, D.K. Menon, V.F.J. Newcombe, B. Glocker, Unsupervised lesion detection in brain CT using Bayesian convolutional autoencoders, in: Medical Imaging with Deep Learning (MIDL 2018), 2018.

[32] H. Uzunova, S. Schultz, H. Handels, J. Ehrhardt, Unsupervised pathology detection in medical images using conditional variational autoencoders, Int. J. Comput. Assisted Radiol. Surg. 14 (3) (2019) 451–461, https://doi.org/10.1007/s11548-018-1898-0.

[33] C. Baur, S. Denner, B. Wiestler, N. Navab, S. Albarqouni, Autoencoders for unsupervised anomaly segmentation in brain MR images: a comparative study, Med. Image Anal. 69 (2021) 101952.

[34] I. Higgins, L. Matthey, A. Pal, C. Burgess, X. Glorot, M. Botvinick, S. Mohamed, A. Lerchner, Beta-VAE: learning basic visual concepts with a constrained variational framework, in: ICLR 2017, 2016.

[35] D.P. Kingma, T. Salimans, R. Jozefowicz, X. Chen, I. Sutskever, M. Welling, Improved variational inference with inverse autoregressive flow, Adv. Neural Inf. Process. Syst. 29 (2016) 4743–4751.

[36] A.B.L. Larsen, S.K. Sønderby, H. Larochelle, O. Winther, Autoencoding beyond pixels using a learned similarity metric, in: International Conference on Machine Learning, in: PMLR, 2016, pp. 1558–1566.

[37] L. Maaløe, M. Fraccaro, V. Liévin, O. Winther, BIVA: a very deep hierarchy of latent variables for generative modeling, in: NeurIPS, 2019.

[38] A. Vahdat, J. Kautz, NVAE: a deep hierarchical variational autoencoder, in: Advances in Neural Information Processing Systems, vol. 33, 2020, pp. 19667–19679.

[39] L. Gondara, Medical image denoising using convolutional denoising autoencoders, in: 2016 IEEE 16th International Conference on Data Mining Workshops (ICDMW), 2016, pp. 241–246, https://doi.org/10.1109/ICDMW.2016.0041.

[40] Y. Liu, Y. Zhang, Low-dose CT restoration via stacked sparse denoising autoencoders, Neurocomputing 284 (2018) 80–89, https://doi.org/10.1016/j.neucom.2018.01.015.

[41] H. Chen, Y. Zhang, M.K. Kalra, F. Lin, Y. Chen, P. Liao, J. Zhou, G. Wang, Low-dose CT with a residual encoder-decoder convolutional neural network, IEEE Trans. Med. Imaging 36 (12) (2017) 2524–2535, https://doi.org/10.1109/TMI.2017.2715284.

[42] A. Gomez, V. Zimmer, N. Toussaint, R. Wright, J.R. Clough, B. Khanal, M.P.M. van Poppel, E. Skelton, J. Matthews, J.A. Schnabel, Image reconstruction in a manifold of image patches: application to whole-fetus ultrasound imaging, in: F. Knoll, A. Maier, D. Rueckert, J.C. Ye (Eds.), Machine Learning for Medical Image Reconstruction, in:

Lecture Notes in Computer Science, Springer International Publishing, Cham, 2019, pp. 226–235, https://doi.org/10.1007/978-3-030-33843-5_21.

[43] C. Biffi, J.J. Cerrolaza, G. Tarroni, A. de Marvao, S.A. Cook, D.P. O'Regan, D. Rueckert, 3D high-resolution cardiac segmentation reconstruction from 2D views using conditional variational autoencoders, in: IEEE 16th International Symposium on Biomedical Imaging (ISBI 2019), 2019, pp. 1643–1646, https://doi.org/10.1109/ISBI.2019.8759328.

[44] J. Mehta, A. Majumdar, Rodeo: robust de-aliasing autoencoder for real-time medical image reconstruction, Pattern Recognit. 63 (2017) 499–510.

[45] P. Afshar, A. Shahroudnejad, A. Mohammadi, K.N. Plataniotis, Carisi: convolutional autoencoder-based inter-slice interpolation of brain tumor volumetric images, in: 2018 25th IEEE International Conference on Image Processing (ICIP), 2018, pp. 1458–1462.

[46] R. Ayub, Q. Zhao, M.J. Meloy, E.V. Sullivan, A. Pfefferbaum, E. Adeli, K.M. Pohl, In-painting cropped diffusion MRI using deep generative models, in: I. Rekik, E. Adeli, S.H. Park, M.d.C. Valdés Hernández (Eds.), Predictive Intelligence in Medicine, Springer International Publishing, Cham, 2020, pp. 91–100.

[47] M. Pesteie, P. Abolmaesumi, R.N. Rohling, Adaptive augmentation of medical data using independently conditional variational auto-encoders, IEEE Trans. Med. Imaging 38 (12) (2019) 2807–2820.

[48] A. Chartsias, T. Joyce, M. Giuffrida, S.A. Tsaftaris, Multimodal MR synthesis via modality-invariant latent representation, IEEE Trans. Med. Imaging 37 (3) (2018) 803–814, https://doi.org/10.1109/TMI.2017.2764326.

[49] Q. Zhao, Z. Liu, E. Adeli, K.M. Pohl, Longitudinal self-supervised learning, Med. Image Anal. (2021) 102051.

[50] P. Mouches, M. Wilms, D. Rajashekar, S. Langner, N. Forkert, Unifying brain age prediction and age-conditioned template generation with a deterministic autoencoder, in: Medical Imaging with Deep Learning – MIDL 2021, 2021.

[51] H. Lee, C. Ekanadham, A.Y. Ng, Sparse deep belief net model for visual area V2, in: NIPS, 2007.

[52] A. Ng, et al., Sparse autoencoder, Tech. Rep., Stanford University, 2011.

[53] G. Alain, Y. Bengio, What regularized auto-encoders learn from the data-generating distribution, J. Mach. Learn. Res. 15 (1) (2014) 3563–3593.

[54] J. Lehtinen, J. Munkberg, J. Hasselgren, S. Laine, T. Karras, M. Aittala, T. Aila, Noise2Noise: learning image restoration without clean data, in: International Conference on Machine Learning, in: PMLR, 2018, pp. 2965–2974.

[55] Y. Bengio, L. Yao, G. Alain, P. Vincent, Generalized denoising auto-encoders as generative models, Adv. Neural Inf. Process. Syst. 26 (2013) 899–907.

[56] A. van den Oord, O. Vinyals, K. Kavukcuoglu, Neural discrete representation learning, in: NIPS, 2017.

[57] C.W. Fox, S.J. Roberts, A tutorial on variational Bayesian inference, Artif. Intell. Rev. 38 (2012) 85–95.

[58] X. Yan, J. Yang, K. Sohn, H. Lee, Attribute2Image: conditional image generation from visual attributes, in: B. Leibe, J. Matas, N. Sebe, M. Welling (Eds.), Computer Vision – ECCV 2016, in: Lecture Notes in Computer Science, Springer International Publishing, Cham, 2016, pp. 776–791.

[59] T. White, Sampling generative networks, arXiv:1609.04468.

[60] D.P. Kingma, M. Welling, An introduction to variational autoencoders, Found. Trends Mach. Learn. 12 (4) (2019) 307–392, https://doi.org/10.1561/2200000056, arXiv:1906.02691.

[61] S.R. Bowman, L. Vilnis, O. Vinyals, A.M. Dai, R. Jozefowicz, S. Bengio, Generating sentences from a continuous space, in: International Conference on Learning Representations (ICLR 2016), 2016.

[62] C.K. Sønderby, T. Raiko, L. Maaløe, S.K. Sønderby, O. Winther, Ladder variational autoencoders, Adv. Neural Inf. Process. Syst. 29 (2016) 3738–3746.

[63] J. Lucas, G. Tucker, R. Grosse, M. Norouzi, Understanding posterior collapse in generative latent variable models, in: Deep Generative Models for Highly Structured Data (ICLR 2019 Workshop), 2019.

[64] C. Cremer, X. Li, D. Duvenaud, Inference suboptimality in variational autoencoders, in: International Conference on Machine Learning, in: PMLR, 2018, pp. 1078–1086.

[65] Y. Kim, S. Wiseman, A. Miller, D. Sontag, A. Rush, Semi-amortized variational autoencoders, in: International Conference on Machine Learning, in: PMLR, 2018, pp. 2678–2687.

[66] C.-W. Huang, S. Tan, A. Lacoste, A.C. Courville, Improving explorability in variational inference with annealed variational objectives, in: NeurIPS, 2018.

[67] D.J. Rezende, F. Viola, Taming VAEs, arXiv:1810.00597.

[68] A. Alemi, B. Poole, I. Fischer, J. Dillon, R.A. Saurous, K. Murphy, Fixing a broken ELBO, in: International Conference on Machine Learning, in: PMLR, 2018, pp. 159–168.

[69] B. Dai, D. Wipf, Diagnosing and enhancing VAE models, in: International Conference on Learning Representations, 2018.

[70] H. Kim, A. Mnih, Disentangling by factorising, in: International Conference on Machine Learning, in: PMLR, 2018, pp. 2649–2658.

[71] C.P. Burgess, I. Higgins, A. Pal, L. Matthey, N. Watters, G. Desjardins, A. Lerchner, Understanding disentangling in β-VAE, arXiv:1804.03599.

[72] Z. Shu, M. Sahasrabudhe, R. Alp Güler, D. Samaras, N. Paragios, I. Kokkinos, Deforming autoencoders: unsupervised disentangling of shape and appearance, in: V. Ferrari, M. Hebert, C. Sminchisescu, Y. Weiss (Eds.), Computer Vision – ECCV 2018, vol. 11214, Springer International Publishing, Cham, 2018, pp. 664–680, https://doi.org/10.1007/978-3-030-01249-6_40.

[73] H. Uzunova, H. Handels, J. Ehrhardt, Guided filter regularization for improved disentanglement of shape and appearance in diffeomorphic autoencoders, in: Medical Imaging with Deep Learning (MIDL), 2021.

[74] J. Krebs, H. Delingette, B. Mailhé, N. Ayache, T. Mansi, Learning a probabilistic model for diffeomorphic registration, IEEE Trans. Med. Imaging 38 (9) (2019) 2165–2176, https://doi.org/10.1109/TMI.2019.2897112.

[75] A. Dosovitskiy, T. Brox, Generating images with perceptual similarity metrics based on deep networks, in: Proceedings of the 30th International Conference on Neural Information Processing Systems, 2016.

[76] J. Johnson, A. Alahi, L. Fei-Fei, Perceptual losses for real-time style transfer and super-resolution, in: B. Leibe, J. Matas, N. Sebe, M. Welling (Eds.), Computer Vision – ECCV 2016, in: Lecture Notes in Computer Science, Springer International Publishing, Cham, 2016, pp. 694–711, https://doi.org/10.1007/978-3-319-46475-6_43.

[77] A. Lamb, V. Dumoulin, A. Courville, Discriminative regularization for generative models, arXiv:1602.03220.

[78] M. Mathieu, C. Couprie, Y. LeCun, Deep multi-scale video prediction beyond mean square error, in: 4th International Conference on Learning Representations, ICLR 2016, 2016.

[79] J. Snell, K. Ridgeway, R. Liao, B.D. Roads, M.C. Mozer, R.S. Zemel, Learning to generate images with perceptual similarity metrics, in: 2017 IEEE International Conference on Image Processing (ICIP), 2017, pp. 4277–4281, https://doi.org/10.1109/ICIP.2017.8297089.

[80] Z. Wang, A.C. Bovik, H.R. Sheikh, E.P. Simoncelli, Image quality assessment: from error visibility to structural similarity, IEEE Trans. Image Process. 13 (4) (2004) 600–612, https://doi.org/10.1109/TIP.2003.819861.

[81] J. Tomczak, M. Welling, VAE with a VampPrior, in: International Conference on Artificial Intelligence and Statistics, in: PMLR, 2018, pp. 1214–1223.

[82] I. Gulrajani, K. Kumar, F. Ahmed, A.A. Taiga, F. Visin, D. Vazquez, A. Courville, PixelVAE: a latent variable model for natural images, in: International Conference on Learning Representations (ICLR 2017), 2016.

[83] Y. Burda, R.B. Grosse, R. Salakhutdinov, Importance weighted autoencoders, in: ICLR (Poster), 2016.

[84] A. Makhzani, J. Shlens, N. Jaitly, I. Goodfellow, B. Frey, Adversarial autoencoders, arXiv:1511.05644.

[85] J. Ker, L. Wang, J. Rao, T. Lim, Deep learning applications in medical image analysis, IEEE Access 6 (2018) 9375–9389, https://doi.org/10.1109/ACCESS.2017.2788044.

[86] A.S. Lundervold, A. Lundervold, An overview of deep learning in medical imaging focusing on MRI, Z. Med. Phys. 29 (2) (2019) 102–127, https://doi.org/10.1016/j.zemedi.2018.11.002.

[87] D. Zimmerer, F. Isensee, J. Petersen, S. Kohl, K. Maier-Hein, Unsupervised anomaly localization using variational auto-encoders, in: D. Shen, T. Liu, T.M. Peters, L.H. Staib, C. Essert, S. Zhou, P.-T. Yap, A. Khan (Eds.), Medical Image Computing and Computer Assisted Intervention – MICCAI 2019, in: Lecture Notes in Computer Science, Springer International Publishing, Cham, 2019, pp. 289–297, https://doi.org/10.1007/978-3-030-32251-9_32.

[88] S. You, K.C. Tezcan, X. Chen, E. Konukoglu, Unsupervised lesion detection via image restoration with a normative prior, in: International Conference on Medical Imaging with Deep Learning, in: PMLR, 2019, pp. 540–556.

[89] T. Schlegl, P. Seeböck, S.M. Waldstein, U. Schmidt-Erfurth, G. Langs, Unsupervised anomaly detection with generative adversarial networks to guide marker discovery, in: M. Niethammer, M. Styner, S. Aylward, H. Zhu, I. Oguz, P.-T. Yap, D. Shen (Eds.), Information Processing in Medical Imaging, in: Lecture Notes in Computer Science, Springer International Publishing, Cham, 2017, pp. 146–157, https://doi.org/10.1007/978-3-319-59050-9_12.

[90] K. Kamnitsas, C. Ledig, V.F.J. Newcombe, J.P. Simpson, A.D. Kane, D.K. Menon, D. Rueckert, B. Glocker, Efficient multi-scale 3D CNN with fully connected CRF for accurate brain lesion segmentation, Med. Image Anal. 36 (2017) 61–78, https://doi.org/10.1016/j.media.2016.10.004.

[91] J. Springenberg, A. Dosovitskiy, T. Brox, M. Riedmiller, Striving for simplicity: the all convolutional net, in: ICLR (Workshop Track), 2015.

[92] R.R. Selvaraju, M. Cogswell, A. Das, R. Vedantam, D. Parikh, D. Batra, Grad-CAM: visual explanations from deep networks via gradient-based localization, in: Proceedings of the IEEE International Conference on Computer Vision, 2017, pp. 618–626.

[93] F. Doshi-Velez, B. Kim, Towards a rigorous science of interpretable machine learning, arXiv:1702.08608.

[94] R.C. Fong, A. Vedaldi, Interpretable explanations of black boxes by meaningful perturbation, in: Proceedings of the IEEE International Conference on Computer Vision, 2017, pp. 3429–3437.

[95] M.T. Ribeiro, S. Singh, C. Guestrin, "Why should I trust you?": explaining the predictions of any classifier, in: Proceedings of the 22nd ACM SIGKDD International Conference on Knowledge Discovery and Data Mining, KDD'16, ACM, New York, NY, USA, 2016, pp. 1135–1144, https://doi.org/10.1145/2939672.2939778.

[96] H. Uzunova, J. Ehrhardt, T. Kepp, H. Handels, Interpretable Explanations of Black Box Classifiers Applied on Medical Images by Meaningful Perturbations Using Variational Autoencoders, Medical Imaging 2019: Image Processing, vol. 10949, International Society for Optics and Photonics, 2019, p. 1094911, https://doi.org/10.1117/12.2511964.

[97] A. Trouvé, L. Younes, Metamorphoses through Lie group action, Found. Comput. Math. 5 (2) (2005) 173–198.

[98] M. Niethammer, G.L. Hart, D.F. Pace, P.M. Vespa, A. Irimia, J.D. Van Horn, S.R. Aylward, Geometric metamorphosis, in: G. Fichtinger, A. Martel, T. Peters (Eds.), Medical Image Computing and Computer-Assisted Intervention – MICCAI 2011, in: Lecture Notes in Computer Science, Springer, Berlin, Heidelberg, 2011, pp. 639–646.

[99] V. Cheplygina, M. de Bruijne, J.P.W. Pluim, Not-so-supervised: a survey of semi-supervised, multi-instance, and transfer learning in medical image analysis, Med. Image Anal. 54 (2019) 280–296, https://doi.org/10.1016/j.media.2019.03.009.

Applications

Optimization of the MR imaging pipeline using simulation

Ivana Drobnjak[a,d], **Mark Graham**[b,d], **Hui Zhang**[a], **and Mark Jenkinson**[c]

[a]*Centre for Medical Image Computing (CMIC) and Department of Computer Science, University College London, London, United Kingdom*
[b]*School of Biomedical Engineering and Imaging Sciences, King's College London, London, United Kingdom*
[c]*FMRIB, University of Oxford, Oxford, United Kingdom*

9.1 Overview

High-quality data is an essential prerequisite for many magnetic resonance (MR) studies. Obtaining such data relies on the careful optimization of the full imaging pipeline, from data acquisition in the scanner to computational processing of that data. This optimization process can be challenging; the cost of MR scanning means it is often not feasible to perform the large number of experiments required to carefully optimize pipelines. Furthermore, the complexity of the process means it is often not possible to isolate and investigate a particular aspect of the imaging pipeline, such as the effect of a pulse sequence on a particular artifact. These issues also hinder the development of new imaging pipelines.

Simulation has a key role to play in optimization of the imaging pipelines. A good simulator enables us to circumvent the cost of MR scanning and perform many experiments; it also allows us to deal with the complexity of MR by carefully isolating and studying the effects of interest. In this chapter we describe the process of MR simulation and show many examples of MR imaging applications. In the interest of clarity, we focus on one particular simulation framework, Physics-Oriented Simulated Scanner for Understanding MRI (POSSUM) [1], however, the principles and the process apply similarly to other simulation frameworks. We focus on the simulation of brain images, but the methods described can be adapted for other body areas as well.

The applications cover four broad themes. Firstly, we show how the simulator can be used to carefully evaluate post-processing algorithms, here using the example of correcting movement and other artifacts in both functional MRI (fMRI) and diffusion-weighted MRI (DW-MRI). Secondly, we show how simulation can be used

---

[d] These authors have equal contribution.

to study artifacts: in this case, the susceptibility-by-movement interaction, and quantify their affect on the imaging process. Thirdly, we use a simulator to study, develop, and optimize new techniques for image acquisition by investigating the measurement of transient currents with MRI. Finally, we show how a simulator can be used to provide training data to develop new, machine-learning based techniques for processing data.

9.2 History of MRI simulation

The field of MRI simulation is extremely large and well developed. An excellent, in-depth description of MRI, with a an insightful signal processing angle that is extremely useful for those who develop simulations, was done by Liang and Lauterbur in [2]. Another valuable resource for understanding MRI, and in particular the ins and outs of pulse sequences, which can be extremely useful for all those who want to work on pulse sequence simulation and development, was done by Haacke in [3]. Every simulator is a simplification of the physical environment, and the choices and assumptions made in designing a simulator are typically motivated by the intended application of the system. Here we focus on tools that simulate full MR images as opposed to just radiofrequency (RF) pulses or nuclear magnetic resonance (NMR) signals.

The simplest tools for MR simulation use steady-state solutions of the Bloch equations for the well-known pulse sequences [4–7]. By applying these solutions to an input that describes the spatial variation of MR parameters (T_1, T_2, proton density) in the brain, an output MR image is produced. Whilst computationally very efficient, this approach fails to model the process of image acquisition, involving the recording of a signal in k-space (i.e., the frequency space) which is vital if realistic images and their artifacts are to be simulated.

An early method that made use of k-space signals was the "k-space formalism" [8]. It involves Fourier transforming a high-resolution map of tissue type and proton density to produce a k-space signal, then simulating the acquisition for a given pulse sequence by selecting the relevant elements from this dense k-space signal. Relaxation parameters and simple artifacts such as eddy currents can be taken into account during the k-space selection. This method is fast but precludes the inclusion of more complex artifacts, such as movement of the object during the acquisition of a slice.

Another popular method for simulation analytically relates properties of an input object to the imaged signal. Early work [9,10] focused on finding a closed-form expression for the k-space signal generated from ellipsoids such as those in the famous Shepp–Logan phantom [11]. Guerquin et al. [12] and Ngo [13] extended this work by enabling the simulation of more realistic phantoms. Although allowing very realistic representations of scanner objects, these methods cannot model a number of artifacts such as movement and spin-history effects. In order to realistically model such artifacts, a simulator must solve the Bloch equations.

The simplest Bloch-based simulators solve the equations once for each tissue type—white matter (WM), gray matter (GM), and cerebrospinal fluid (CSF)—and combine the resultant signals in each voxel using proportions determined by a tissue template, as seen in the extremely popular BrainWeb tool [14,15]. This method is fast because the equations need only be solved once per tissue type. However, the method means each spin experiences the same magnetic field history which prevents artifacts such as B_0 and B_1 inhomogeneities being modeled.

Methods that solve the Bloch equations over a grid with spatially varying values of ρ, T_1, and T_2, representing the object being imaged, allow for the most realistic simulations [16–19,1]. They allow reproduction of a range of image artifacts including eddy currents, susceptibility, Gibbs ringing, ghosting, and chemical shift. Some, such as POSSUM, simulate arbitrary movement of the object throughout the acquisition of an image [1]. POSSUM can also calculate susceptibility fields from the input object, taking into account the changing of the susceptibility-induced field with object movement, as well as being able to account for time-varying off-resonance fields, such as those caused by the patient breathing [20].

One of the key challenges for grid-based methods is that an extremely large number of spin isochromats for each grid point must be simulated to accurately capture effects such as intra-voxel dephasing or spin-echoes [21]. One approach to overcome this uses mathematical modeling for T_2^* dephasing effects [17] and spin-echoes, essentially by modifying the magnitude of the magnetization vector as dictated by the spin-echo [19,1]. The second approach is to solve Bloch equations for each of the millions of isochromats per grid point [22–24]. The power of this approach is that it allows simulation of realistic diffusion effects, RF pulses, and even magnetization transfer. However, because of the extremely heavy computational load, they are often used on a single grid point or for very small ROIs. Alternatively, when used for whole images, to be computationally feasible, they dramatically reduce the number of isochromats, often to just one per grid point, which can reduce their accuracy.

9.2.1 Diffusion MRI

Much of the work in Diffusion MRI simulation has focused on providing data that can help assess tractography algorithms [25–32]. One of the key inputs to these simulators is a numerical phantom of white matter bundles ("tractogram") which depending on the approach can vary in its complexity. White matter diffusion contrast is generated either with a simple Diffusion Tensor (DT) model [26], multiple DTs to model crossing fibers [29], CHARMED model [28], or zeppelin model [30,31]. The underlying MRI simulation here is either non-existing (e.g., only diffusion contrast with noise modeling is present [32]) or signal is produced directly in image space using steady-state solutions [4–7] or it is also additionally then converted to k-space where it is further manipulated via k-space formalism [30]. These models rely on an underlying description of WM structures to generate the signal, which means they are unable to produce full-brain images that realistically model the signal in the gray matter and cerebrospinal fluid.

Another line of work focuses on realistic modeling of MR artifacts and supports development and validation of DW-MR artifact removal techniques. Here, the simplest methods simply assign a single value of diffusion-weighting contrast to each of the three tissue types, then combine these signals using probabilistic segmentation to form an image [33,34]. Not only do these methods fail to represent the complexity of the diffusion signal, which cannot be simplified to a single intensity per tissue type, but they do not simulate the process of MR acquisition. Some work has combined this simple model of diffusion contrast with a simulation of the full process of MR acquisition [35]. The most sophisticated simulator in this domain is DW-POSSUM [36] which creates realistic diffusion weighting maps from very high resolution HCP (Human Connectome Project) images and combines these with Bloch equation based simulation of MRI images.

9.3 The POSSUM simulation framework
9.3.1 POSSUM for MRI and functional MRI

The software simulation tool we use as an exemplar in this chapter is called POSSUM (Physics-Oriented Simulated Scanner for Understanding MRI), and forms a part of FSL.[1] The descriptive scheme of the framework of POSSUM is shown in Fig. 9.1.

POSSUM is based on solving the Bloch equation

$$\frac{d\mathbf{M}}{dt} = \gamma \mathbf{M} \times \mathbf{B} - \frac{M_x \hat{\mathbf{x}} + M_y \hat{\mathbf{y}}}{T_2} - \frac{(M_z - M_0)\hat{\mathbf{z}}}{T_1}, \tag{9.1}$$

which describes the time evolution of the magnetization vector $\mathbf{M} = M_x \hat{\mathbf{x}} + M_y \hat{\mathbf{y}} + M_z \hat{\mathbf{z}}$ in the presence of the magnetic field $\mathbf{B} = B_z \hat{\mathbf{z}}$. The constant γ is the gyromagnetic ratio (42.6 MHz/T for hydrogen nuclei), T_1 describes the exponential recovery of the longitudinal component of the magnetization vector $M_z \hat{\mathbf{z}}$ towards its equilibrium value $M_0 \hat{\mathbf{z}}$, and T_2 describes the exponential decay of the transverse component of the magnetization vector $M_x \hat{\mathbf{x}} + M_y \hat{\mathbf{y}}$ to its equilibrium value of zero. The magnetic field is represented in the simulator as

$$\mathbf{B}(\mathbf{r}, t) = B_0 \hat{\mathbf{z}} + B_p(\mathbf{r})\hat{\mathbf{z}} + (\mathbf{G}(t) \cdot \mathbf{r})\hat{\mathbf{z}}, \tag{9.2}$$

where B_0 is the main static magnetic field, $B_p(\mathbf{r})$ is due to off-resonance effects (e.g., induced by susceptibility variation across soft tissue and air/bone boundaries), $\mathbf{G}(t)$ represents the gradient system of the scanner, and $\mathbf{r} = x\hat{\mathbf{x}} + y\hat{\mathbf{y}} + z\hat{\mathbf{z}}$ is the spatial coordinate.

---

[1] FMRIB Software Library, http://www.fmrib.ox.ac.uk/fsl/.

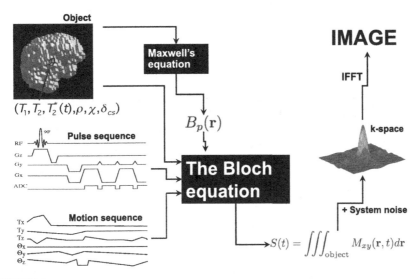

FIGURE 9.1

Descriptive representation of the POSSUM framework. On the left are the inputs to the Bloch equation solver: object, pulse sequence, and motion sequence. The object is a collection of object voxels, and each voxel is a collection of tissues with known relaxation times T_1, T_2, T_2^*, the spin density ρ, and the chemical shift value δ_{cs}. Susceptibility value χ is also defined for each voxel and used to calculate perturbation field B_p via solving Maxwell's equations. The pulse sequence is defined by the values of the gradient field, RF pulse parameters (including the desired flip angle), and read-out timings. The motion sequence is defined by the values of the motion parameters (translations T_x, T_y, T_z, and Euler angles θ_x, θ_y, θ_z characterizing rotations about the center of the volume). The output of the main part of the simulator is the signal $S(t)$. Signal values are calculated at the read-out points and then, after the thermal noise is added to them, are arranged into a k-space at appropriate sampling positions that are calculated from the pulse sequence gradients. The final stage of the simulation process is the image reconstruction, for which POSSUM uses Fast Fourier Transform (FFT). Note that the complex noise-free, non-reconstructed signal $S(t)$ is also available as a direct output and can be passed into any custom reconstruction software.

The MR signal of the object, received by the scanner, is given by the signal equation

$$S(t) = \iiint_{\text{object}} M_{xy}(\mathbf{r}, t) d\mathbf{r} , \tag{9.3}$$

where M_{xy} is the projection of the magnetization vector into the transverse plane, $\mathbf{r}$ is in the object coordinate system, and all the behavior of the magnetization is described in the object coordinate system. As there is no analytical solution for this integral, we write

$$S(t) = \sum_{j \in \Lambda} \sum_{\mathbf{r_0} \in \Omega} s_j(\mathbf{r_0}, t), \qquad (9.4)$$

where Ω is the collection of all of the object voxels, Λ is the collection of all the tissue types in the object, and $s_j(\mathbf{r_0}, t)$ is the signal coming from the jth tissue component of the object voxel centered at $\mathbf{r_0}$.

The input object is modeled by a collection of rectangular volume elements ("object voxels") with physical dimensions of (L_x, L_y, L_z), which have typical values $L_x = L_y = L_z = 1$ mm, but can be made much smaller than the final image voxels for extra accuracy at the cost of run time. Each object voxel is assumed to contain a mixture of tissues, each of which are uniformly distributed across the object voxel spatially. This implies that, for each tissue type, all of the properties (relaxation times T_1, T_2, and the spin density ρ) are constant over the object voxel.

We assume that the excitation period is significantly smaller than the relaxation times T_1 and T_2^*, as it is in most pulse sequences, and therefore model the excitation as happening instantaneously. The actual flip angle for each object voxel is calculated as a proportion of the desired flip angle. This proportion is evaluated from the slice profile by looking at the difference of the angular frequency evaluated at the center of each object voxel $\omega(\mathbf{r_0}, t_{0-}) = \gamma \left(\mathbf{G}(t_{0-}) \cdot \mathbf{r_0} + B_p(\mathbf{r_0}) \right)$ and the center frequency of the RF pulse ω_{RF}, i.e.,

$$\alpha(\mathbf{r_0}, t_{0-}) = W(\omega(\mathbf{r_0}, t_{0-}) - \omega_{RF}), \qquad (9.5)$$

where $W(\cdot)$ is the slice profile function (e.g., windowed-sinc).

POSSUM also simulates T_2^* changes in each input voxel; T_2^* models the effects of physiological changes within the object. Specifically, T_2^* variation in time is used to model the effects of neuronal activation on the MR signal, via the BOLD effect. This model can also include, as additional T_2^* variation, unwanted physiological changes (e.g., low frequency networks – so called "resting states" or respiratory-induced fluctuations). The T_2^* variation is user-defined for every object voxel separately.

9.3.1.1 Modeling artifacts

There is a range of artifacts that can be simulated with POSSUM, below are examples of some of the most common artifacts, together with a description of their implementation in POSSUM.

Susceptibility. In order to evaluate the distortion in the magnetic field due to the susceptibility differences, a perturbation method for solving Maxwell's equations is used [37]. This method requires that the magnetic susceptibility, χ, at each point in the object is known. Note that, due to the major magnetic susceptibility differences between the air and bone/tissue interface, it is important to have a good segmentation of the air spaces within the head.

Motion. To incorporate motion of the object in the scanner, POSSUM uses two coordinate systems: one that is fixed to the scanner and the other that is fixed to the object. POSSUM solves the Bloch equation in the coordinate system of the object in which our object appears static and the scanner moves relative to the object. We assume that the speed of the motion is very small relative to the precessional speed of spins, so that the axis about which the spins are precessing is always the direction of the main static field.

Inhomogeneity in the magnetic field induced by the susceptibility differences between different tissues will also be influenced by motion. When the object is moving, the coordinate systems of the object and the scanner are no longer aligned therefore, in the reference frame of the object, the orientation of the main magnetic field is changing and this in turn changes the B_p values of the perturbed field, which is implemented into the simulation equations.

Chemical shift. An additional B_0 inhomogeneity is introduced that is not dependent on the actual position of the object voxel but on the tissue type (as it depends on the shielding constant δ_{cs}), so there is an additional constant $B_{cs} = \delta_{cs} B_0$ in Eq. (9.2) which does not vary when the brain is moving.

Eddy currents. Unwanted induced currents are produced in the conducting elements of an MR scanner. They arise due to the fast changing fields that occur within the scanner, normally due to rapid switching of applied gradient fields. The effect of the eddy currents is to create additional, unwanted gradient fields which are simulated by superimposing a sum of exponentially decaying terms on to the gradient waveform.

RF field inhomogeneities. Inhomogeneities in the RF field are modeled separately in the simulator for the receiving RF coil and the transmitting RF coil. Inhomogeneity in the receiving RF coil impacts received signal strength and is modeled with an extra multiplier $k_{rec}(\mathbf{r_0})$ in Eq. (9.4):

$$S(t) = \sum_{j \in \Lambda} \sum_{\mathbf{r_0} \in \Omega} k_{rec}(\mathbf{r_0}) s_j(\mathbf{r_0}, t). \tag{9.6}$$

Inhomogeneity in the transmitting RF coil impacts the strength of the flip angle and is modeled with an extra multiplier $k_{tr}(\mathbf{r_0})$ in the equation for the flip angle (9.5):

$$\alpha(\mathbf{r_0}, t_{0-}) = k_{tr}(\mathbf{r_0}) W(\omega(\mathbf{r_0}, t_{0-}) - \omega_{RF}). \tag{9.7}$$

The values of $k_{rec}(\mathbf{r_0})$ and $k_{tr}(\mathbf{r_0})$ range from zero (maximal inhomogeneity) to one (no inhomogeneity). They are specified for every object voxel through user specified files.

Noise. MR scanners, like all measurement devices, are influenced by noise. For instance, thermal noise is present in the object and receiver electronics, which results in fluctuations in the received signal that cover a wide frequency range. This is modeled as additive, independent, white Gaussian noise in both receiver channels within the simulator.

Physiological noise. This is specifically respiratory and cardiovascular noise, modeled by modifying the T_2^* and B_0 variations in time.

POSSUM is written in C++ for a variety of Unix-based platforms (e.g., MacOSX, Linux, Windows subsystem or virtual machine, etc.). More details can be found in [1].

9.3.2 POSSUM for diffusion MRI

Fig. 9.2 presents a conceptual overview DW-POSSUM, which is used to simulate data with realistic diffusion contrast [36]. The DW-POSSUM framework takes four main inputs. The first is a geometric object that specifies the proton density and location of WM, GM, and CSF, along with their T_1 and T_2 values. The second is a representation of diffusion-weighting. The third is a pulsed-gradient spin-echo (PGSE) sequence, detailing RF pulses and gradients. The first two inputs are combined with diffusion parameters extracted from the third (direction and magnitude of diffusion weighting) to produce a geometric object with its proton density reduced by a diffusion attenuation factor – this serves as the new input to POSSUM, and is how diffusion-weighting is introduced into the simulated DWIs. The attenuation factor is defined as $A_b\left(\hat{b}\right) = S_b\left(\hat{b}\right)/S_0$, the ratio between the diffusion-weighted signal $\left(S_b\left(\hat{b}\right)\right)$ and the signal without diffusion weighting (S_0) in a given voxel, defined for a b-value, b, and direction of diffusion weighting, $\hat{b}$. The attenuation factor is a dimensionless quantity that takes values between 0 and 1. The effect of the PGSE sequence is modeled implicitly, through: (1) the introduction of diffusion-weighting through the input object, (2) the introduction of eddy-current artifacts induced by the PGSE gradients, and (3) the use of T_2 rather than T_2^* values in the input object. The fourth input is any detail that will lead to the simulation of artifacts, such as motion parameters. The effects of eddy currents arising from the diffusion gradients are included in the echo-planar imaging (EPI) sequence that is passed to the simulator.

The framework creates two outputs. The first is a DWI. The MR simulator takes the attenuated object, pulse sequence, and details pertaining to artifacts, and solves Bloch's and Maxwell's equations at each point in the object, summing the resultant signal in order to generate the k-space measurements. This is Fourier transformed to produce the output DWI. The second output is a displacement field that describes the mapping of this DWI from a distorted to undistorted space. More information on POSSUM and simulated datasets can be found at https://fsl.fmrib.ox.ac.uk/fsl/fslwiki/POSSUM

9.4 Applications

We will cover a number of ways simulation can be used to optimize the MR imaging pipeline. Firstly, we will discuss assessing motion correction algorithms for fMRI (Section 9.4.1), and movement and eddy-current correction algorithms for DW-MRI (Section 9.4.2). We then cover the use of simulation to examine the susceptibility-by-movement artifact in Section 9.4.3 and to investigating a new type of MR contrast in Section 9.4.4. Finally, in Section 9.4.5, we cover the use of simulation to generate data for training machine learning algorithms.

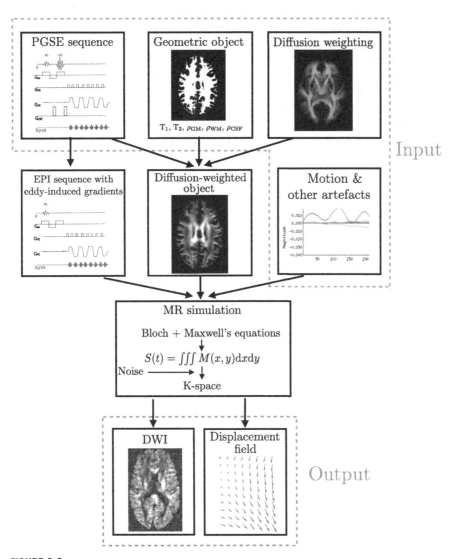

FIGURE 9.2

The pipeline for simulating DWIs. Blue-bounded boxes (light gray-bounded boxes in print version) indicate the required inputs: a geometric object and associated description of diffusion weighting for that object, a PGSE sequence, and description of any artifacts to be simulated. The simulated creates a DWI and an associated displacement field describing how any spatial artifacts may be corrected by mapping into artifact-free space.

9.4.1 **Motion correction algorithms for fMRI**

This section describes how simulations can be used to evaluate the effect of motion artifacts on fMRI images and the effectiveness of the motion correction algorithm in removing those artifacts.

Motion correction is an important issue in fMRI analysis as even the slightest patient motion (1–2 degrees of rotation or a few mm translation) during a scan can mean that a voxel location does not correspond to the same physical point in the volume as the same voxel in a subsequent volume. This can create a range of errors in the results such as false positive or false negative brain activations. Hence, motion correction algorithms are one of the necessary parts of every fMRI data analysis package.

However, most of them are developed and validated using empirically acquired fMRI data, for which the ground truth is not known and therefore the precise accuracy of the methods difficult to estimate (e.g., see [38]). MRI simulations are crucial for creating the ground truth that can be used to evaluate these errors and support development. There are a few simulators that can be used for this. Here we use the POSSUM simulator and quantify the performance of the motion correction algorithm MCFLIRT [39,38].

9.4.1.1 *MCFLIRT algorithm*

The MCFLIRT algorithm is an image-similarity-based motion correction algorithm. In order to correct the motion-corrupted images, first a reference image is chosen from the time series. Which volume is taken to be the reference image is a user-defined option. The two most common options are the middle image (default option in MCFLIRT) and the first image. All of the other images are then registered to the reference image. The registration process is computed by constructing a cost function that quantifies the dissimilarity between the two images and then searches for the transformation that gives the minimum cost value.

The method used in MCFLIRT for the process of minimization is known as golden section search [39]. Searching in each of the 6 parameter directions stops when a specified tolerance has been reached. The default tolerances in MCFLIRT are 0.057 degrees for the rotations and 0.02 mm for the translations. The cost function is selected by the user and can be: mutual information, correlation ratio, normalized correlation (default), normalized mutual information, or least squares. When calculating the dissimilarity between the reference image (I_r) and the image we want to register to the reference image (I), interpolation needs to be applied to I. This is a process that calculates the intensity in the image I at points between the original image voxel points. The interpolation choices in MCFLIRT are trilinear, sinc, and nearest neighbor. Different choices of the interpolation function are used for different stages of the algorithm.

The registration process is done in three stages using trilinear interpolation, from low to high resolution, and from high to low stopping tolerance for the golden search process. These three stages were the default stages of the MCFLIRT algorithm. An extra fourth stage is optional, and is the same as the third stage except that the sinc interpolation method is used instead of the trilinear interpolation method. Once the minimization process is finished and all of the transformation parameters are estimated, a transformation is applied to the image. This transformation can be applied using either trilinear or sinc or the nearest neighbor interpolation method (the default in MCFLIRT is trilinear interpolation).

9.4.1.2 Simulations

The simulations were done using a static magnetic field strength of 3 T and an EPI sequence with parameters: TE = 30 ms, TR = 3 s, flip angle 90°, maximum gradient strength 35 mT/m, rise times 0.2 ms, and crushers of maximum magnitude. The input object was a 3D digital brain phantom introduced by the McConnell Brain Imaging Centre, Montreal Neurological Institute, McGill University [40–42]. The brain phantom consists of a set of 3-dimensional "fuzzy" tissue membership volumes, with nine tissue classes (white matter, gray matter, cerebrospinal fluid (CSF), fat, muscle, glial tissue, bone, skin, and connective tissue), where the voxel values in these volumes reflect the proportion of tissue present in that voxel, in the range [0,1].

MCFLIRT performance is evaluated by measuring the accuracy of the estimated motion parameters and estimating the root mean square error that remains in the images after the corrections occurred. A range of different MCFLIRT options was tested, see Table 9.1. A 3-stage optimization process (the current MCFLIRT default option with trilinear interpolation) was compared to the 4-stage process with an extra optimization step using the sinc interpolation. The comparison was done for two different choices of the reference image: the middle image in the time series (the current default option) and the first image in the time series.

Table 9.1 Eight different combinations of MCFLIRT options that were tested in the experiments for testing the accuracy of the estimated parameters. Each is labeled.

Label	Stages (Interpolation)	Reference	Tolerance	Cost function
TrilF	3 (Trilinear)	First	default	Normalized Correlation
TrilM	3 (Trilinear)	Middle	default	Normalized Correlation
TrilMTol	3 (Trilinear)	Middle	reduced	Normalized Correlation
TrilMCr	3 (Trilinear)	Middle	default	Correlation Ratio
SincF	4 (Sinc)	First	default	Normalized Correlation
SincM	4 (Sinc)	Middle	default	Normalized Correlation
SincMTol	4 (Sinc)	Middle	reduced	Normalized Correlation
SincMCr	4 (Sinc)	Middle	default	Correlation Ratio

9.4.1.3 Results

Fig. 9.3 shows examples of brain images when affected with rotation about the z axis at different times in the sequence. Fig. 9.4 shows the results of motion correction of simulated data. In the top plot the green (light gray in print version) lines represent the results for the case with no B_0 inhomogeneities, while black lines represent the

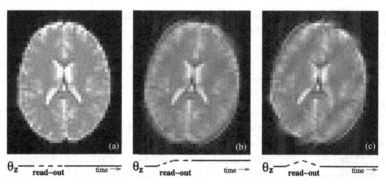

FIGURE 9.3

Example images showing the effects of within-scan motion (rigid-body rotation about the z-axis) on an EPI image: (a) no motion; (b) constant rotation; (c) back and forth rotation. Note that the degree of motion is exaggerated here (9 degrees) to illustrate the effect visually. The line underneath the image represents the angle of rotation as a function of time with the read-out portion of the sequence represented with a dashed line.

case with B_0 inhomogeneities. In all other plots the value of the estimated motion parameter is shown. The true value of motion which was used in the simulations is in blue (dark gray in print version), while each of the other lines represents motion correction done with a combination of options described in the legend.

It can be observed that the overall accuracy of the MCFLIRT estimation of the motion parameters is good – as observed by the closeness between the lines with the blue line (dark gray line in print version). A few differences can be seen between different motion correction options. The motion correction using the correlation ratio cost function does not perform as well as the one using the normalized correlation. This confirms the results of validation done by Bannister [39], and further justifies the use of the normalized correlation cost function in the MCFLIRT algorithm.

Regarding the number of stages in the optimization process, the results suggest considerable improvement when using four stages in the motion correction process. This improvement was stable across all of the different parameters, including the situation when the motion was quite complex, involving a change in all of the parameters. This suggest that MCFLIRT should change its current default option of a 3-stage process to a 4-stage. The results also show that the current default tolerance for the golden section search (0.057 degrees for the rotations and 0.002 mm for the translations) performed as well as the reduced tolerance level (0.0057 degrees for the rotations and 0.0002 mm for the translations). The choice of a reference image did not seem to impact results significantly or in any predictable way. It is possible that the timing and shape of the motion paradigm influences the preferable reference image. It would be interesting to further analyze the relationship between the two.

In addition to the conclusions drawn about the various motion correction options, a significant observation was made regarding the B_0 inhomogeneities. It can be seen

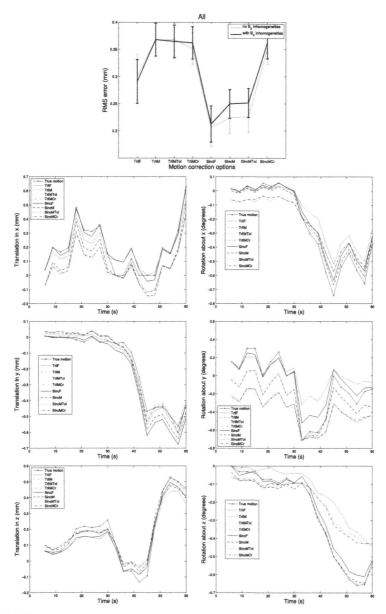

FIGURE 9.4

RMS mean error results for the MCFLIRT motion correction algorithm when applied to data simulated with all of the motion parameters changing. The top plot shows the error bars which indicate the standard error for simulations with no B_0 inhomogeneities (green line – light gray line in print version) versus with B_0 inhomogeneities (black line). Other plots show MCFLIRT estimation of the motion parameters. The ground-truth values are shown with a blue line (dark gray line in print version) in each of the plots.

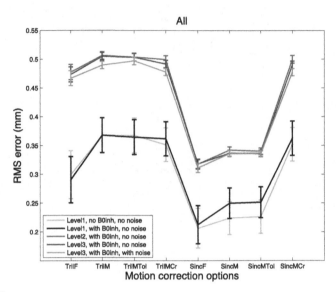

FIGURE 9.5

RMS mean error results for the MCFLIRT motion correction algorithm when applied to simulated data of Group1 (green line – lightest gray line in print version), Group2 (black line), Group3 (red line – mid gray line in print version), Group4 (blue line – dark gray line in print version), and Group5 (magenta line – light gray in print version).

that the presence of the magnetic-susceptibility-induced B_0 inhomogeneities (black lines) did not make a significant difference in the estimation of the motion parameters. This is quite an interesting and new observation. The error did increase in most of the cases, but this increase was not as big as what might be intuitively expected.

The results shown in Fig. 9.4 are based on motion that is instantaneous and uses only rigid body affine transformations. In reality, the subjects move continuously and motion affects the images in a more complex way.

Fig. 9.5 shows how different levels of complexity of motion have different impact on the performance of the correction algorithm. Motion that happens instantaneously between the volume acquisitions (Level1), is the easiest to correct and the root-mean square (RMS) error is the smallest. The presence of B_0 inhomogeneities did create a difference, but this difference is not prominent. Motion that happens instantaneously between the slice acquisitions (Level2), adds an extra motion artifact to the images, namely slice misalignment. Results show that it is the slice misalignment that creates the biggest difference (by a factor of 1.7) in parameter estimation. Motion that happens continuously throughout the image acquisition (Level3), adds (on the top of Level2 motion) an extra motion artifact to the images, namely blurring. From the results, however, it is concluded that blurring does not considerably change the accuracy of parameter estimation. The accuracy does not change much either when noise is added to the images (SNR = 100).

Overall, in addition to finding more accurate choices of some of the existing MCFLIRT options, the results suggested that the main step forward in improving the MCFLIRT algorithm was to include a model for correction of the distortion due to slice misalignment. These conclusions and directions for future work would have been very difficult to find without MRI simulations. For further details about this example, please, see [43].

9.4.2 Motion and eddy-current correction algorithms for diffusion MRI

In this section we demonstrate the application of DW-POSSUM to assess post-processing tools for correcting movement and eddy-current. We evaluate two commonly used tools: the first is the `eddy_correct` function from the FSL software, which performs an affine (12 degrees-of-freedom) registration of each volume in a dataset to a $b = 0$ image in order to simultaneously correct for motion and eddy-current (EC) distortions. We also test a more sophisticated method, FSL's `eddy`, which registers each volume to a model-free prediction of how it should look in undistorted space [44]. The full description of this work can be found in [36].

DW-MRI data was simulated, consisting of two shells, $b = 700/2000$ s/mm^2, 32/64 directions with 12 $b = 0$ images, TR/TE = 7500/109 ms, $72 \times 86 \times 55$ with isotropic voxel size 2.5 mm. All simulations were performed at 3 T. Eddy current gradients were added to the pulse sequence, and movement introduced by selecting a translation along each axis for each volume randomly from the range from -5 to 5 mm, in addition to a rotation about each axis taken from the range of -5 to $5°$. Ground-truth displacement fields, describing the mapping for each volume from distorted to undistorted space, were also produced by DW-POSSUM.

The simulated datasets were corrected using `eddy_correct` and `eddy`. Default settings were used for `eddy_correct`, i.e., correlation ratio as the similarity measure and trilinear interpolation. Default settings were mostly used for `eddy`, i.e., 1000 voxels for estimating the Gaussian process hyperparameter, spline interpolation, quadratic first-level modeling of the EC, and no second-level modeling. However we used 10 iterations rather than the default 5, because we sometimes found 5 was not sufficient to ensure convergence. We also performed correction using `eddy_correct` with normalized mutual information (NMI) as a cost function, to test the claim that it is more robust than other cost-functions [45].

Results for correction of the datasets with EC artefacts are shown in Fig. 9.6, which demonstrates that `eddy_correct` is unable to correct the data well, even for DWIs acquired with $b = 700$ s/mm^2, whilst `eddy` is able to provide good correction across the dataset. Volumes corrected with `eddy_correct` have average errors of one voxel at $b = 700$ s/mm^2, rising to 1.5 voxels at $b = 1000$ s/mm^2. This seems to be caused by the increasing contrast differences between the DWI and $b = 0$ volumes as b-value is increased, which makes direct registration progressively worse. These findings are in agreement with previous work [33] which found that DWIs can only be successfully corrected by registration to $b = 0$ for $b \leq 300$ s/mm^2. By contrast,

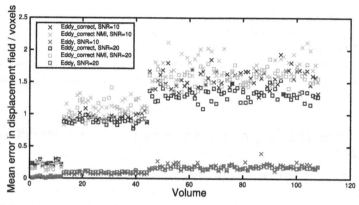

FIGURE 9.6

Mean error in displacement field across the brain. The first 12 volumes are $b = 0$, the next 32 are $b = 700$ s/mm^2 and the remaining 64 $b = 2000$ s/mm^2.

eddy is able to correct with errors of less than 0.2 voxels across the dataset at SNR = 20, and 0.5 voxels at SNR = 10.

This application demonstrates how simulators may be used to provided quantitative evaluations of post-processing tools. Provision of an objective ground-truth, the correct displacement field to map from distorted to undistorted space, allows the tools to be objectively analyzed. In this case, they reveal that eddy_correct systematically overscales high b-value data in order to align the edges of these volumes with the CSF rim of $b = 0$ volumes; something that is difficult to perceive through qualitative inspection. The simulator has been applied, in other words, to more thoroughly study eddy. In [36], the tool is used to better understand the diffusion sampling schemes required to allow the tool to perform well. The simulator has been used to evaluate eddy's ability to correct for slice outlier artifacts [44], intra-volume movement artifacts [46], and the variation of the susceptibility field with movement [47].

9.4.3 Investigating the susceptibility-by-movement artifact

One advantage of simulators is they enable the studying of phenomena that may be difficult to study in real data. These may be difficult to study due to the confounding presence of noise or other variables, or the expense of acquiring such data. One such example of this is the susceptibility-by-movement artefact. The susceptibility artefact is caused by an off-resonance field induced by differences in magnetic susceptibility at the air–tissue interface, which cause geometric distortions when data is acquired with an EPI sequence. If the subject moves in the scanner, then the susceptibility field and, in turn, the distortions alter. Whilst the static case is well characterized and studied in the literature [48], comparatively little work has been done to assess the impact of this dynamic case, when the subject moves, and as a result the artifact is rarely considered when acquiring and processing data. This work first appeared in [49].

POSSUM's ability to model the interaction between the movement and susceptibility artifact makes it a natural test bed to assess the impact of the susceptibility-by-movement artefact. POSSUM can use an air–tissue segmentation to obtain a first-order solution to Maxwell's equations, providing a set of basis functions that describe how the susceptibility field changes with subject movement. We simulated two DW-MRI datasets: one with moderate patient movement, and one with severe movement. A control dataset with simulated movement but a susceptibility field that did not vary with subject movement was also simulated. Each of these datasets was corrected in a way designed to mimic the best correction available using the static susceptibility field assumption: ground-truth displacement fields were calculated from the known movement parameters and static fields, and applied to each volume.

Fig. 9.7 shows the results. We found that a 5° rotation about the y-axis caused changes in the susceptibility field of up to 30 Hz, corresponding to distortions of up to 6 mm for the acquisition protocol used. This is slightly smaller than the field changes measured in real data – [50] found changes of 50 Hz for similar rotations at 3 T – indicating our dynamic distortions are in a realistic range but may slightly underestimate the true size of the effect. Our simulations show a left–right asymmetry in dynamic displacement fields for rotations around y (Fig. 9.7b, Volume 4) and left–right symmetry for rotations around x (Fig. 9.7b, Volume 5) that matches observations made in real data [51]. Further results in [49] demonstrate the effect these dynamic distortions have on downstream processing, such as measuring fractional anisotropy (FA).

These results show how simulation can be invaluable for studying hard-to-isolate features of the real image acquisition process. Whilst existing work had sought to examine the dynamic susceptibility effect in real data [50], it was challenging to examine the effect of this artifact on downstream image processing, and thus difficult to understand the extent to which it affected analysis. The ability to switch off the artifact in simulation, enabled us to carefully study it and conclude that neglecting it could substantially impact results. This in turn assisted the development of new methods to correct the artifact: [47] proposed a technique to correct for the artifact, and was able to use data simulated with DW-POSSUM, alongside real data, to carefully validate the effectiveness of the tool.

9.4.4 Investigating and optimizing image acquisition

A very important area for the use of simulations is investigating new image acquisition techniques and optimizing parameters for maximizing sensitivity to markers we are interested in. Here we will show an example of using simulations in predicting the level of contrast that can be achieved with time-varying magnetic fields.

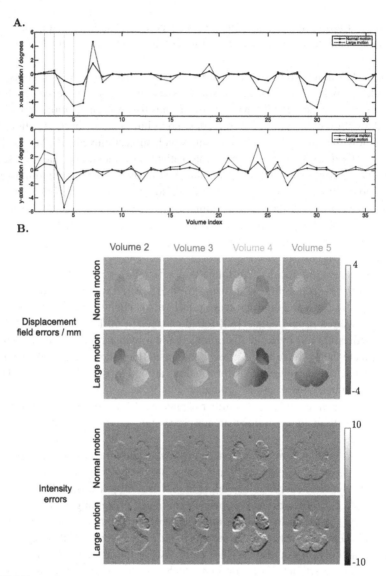

FIGURE 9.7

Susceptibility-movement interaction. A. The x- and y-rotation parameters used for the simulation of the first 36 volumes (z-rotations not shown because they do not contribute to the dynamic susceptibility effect, translations were all 0). The colored vertical lines highlight the motion of the volumes depicted in plot B.

B. Top two rows show the errors in displacement field caused by the dynamic portion of the susceptibility artefact, for volumes 2–5 of the acquisition—the motion these volumes experienced is highlighted with color in plot A. Bottom two rows show the error in intensity of these volumes after they are corrected for motion and the static portion of the susceptibility field, obtained by subtraction from ground truth images.

Time-varying magnetic fields in MR imaging occur in various scanning situations such as gradient fields, eddy currents, physiological changes (respiration, cardiac variation, neuronal activation) or use of MRI contrast agents such as superparamagnetic iron oxides (SPIOs) [52]. The order of magnitude of these magnetic fields can be anything from pT (e.g., neuronal current induced fields) to mT (e.g., gradient fields), or even higher. If not properly taken into account, they result in powerful and unpredictable artifacts that are hard to correct for, and hence understanding them is necessary for optimizing a wide range of MRI and NMR techniques [53–60].

Simulations of time-varying magnetic fields exist in various degrees of complexity [61–64], however, in order to accurately capture all of the effects a sophisticated simulation approach is needed. POSSUM can simulate these effects very precisely, from long to very short events that only affect a few lines of the k-space. This ability turns out to be crucial for accurately reproducing the local spatial structure of the image.

In this section we show in an experiment the impact time-varying magnetic field on images. The phantom used in the experiment was constructed from a hollow glass sphere, filled with SF96/50 silicone oil. A carbon fiber conductor (diameter 0.015 mm) was placed inside the glass sphere and through the conductor the current pulse was applied. Both real scanning images and simulator images are generated.

A series of EPI acquisitions (260 volumes) were taken, each with a different onset time for the 5 ms current pulse with respect to the echo time. Three particular onset timings of the current were considered: A (current pulse was *on* during acquisition of the k-space lines 63–66), B (k-space lines 76–79), and C (k-space lines 88–91). Each of the *on* periods had a duration equivalent to the acquisition of 4 lines in the k-space. The center of the whole k-space acquisition was on line 65 (shown in A).

Fig. 9.8 shows the current effects: A–B–C on the left show results when the current flows thought the conductor into the plane; A–B–C on the right are for the current flowing out of the plane. The images clearly show a very characteristic spatial pattern caused by the changing magnetic field with ringing predominantly in the phase encode direction (left to right). The results show that substantially different patterns of ringing arise for the different current timings. For instance, the frequency is increasing as the timing of the current moves away from the center of the k-space (where A is the most central and C is the furthest).

All of the experiments performed reveal a very good match between the experimental and the simulated results. It would be extremely hard to get such a good match using simulations that do not include a realistic model of the scanner and its environment. For instance, the ringing patterns are critically dependent on modeling the correct image formation (in the k-space) as well as the reconstruction method. In addition, the signal loss (or gain) is highly dependent on getting a good model of the spatial phase dependence (at a sub-voxel level) since this causes the intra-voxel dephasing and hence signal cancellation.

Although the experimental data was available and analyzed, the ringing patterns formed in the proximity of the conducting wire were not initially observed. It was

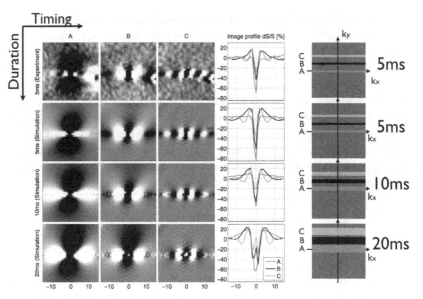

FIGURE 9.8

This figure shows the effects of a current pulse occurring during the acquisition of the center of the k-space (A), further (B), and the furthest (C). Images show the spatial pattern of the signal change in the proximity of the wire. The black regions are negative and the white regions are positive values of the signal change, with the color range the same for all of the images (-3 to 3). Experimental results (actual scanner images) for the 5 ms long current pulse are in the first row. Their corresponding numerical simulations (POSSUM generated images) are in the second row. The third and fourth rows are simulation results for the longer duration of the current pulse, 10 ms (third) and 20 ms (fourth row).

only when the POSSUM simulations were performed that the ringing was discovered and subsequently found in the experimental data. Observing these patterns was more obvious in simulations because the simulated data was noise-free. This example demonstrates again the use and the importance of the simulation models.

There are many other examples of similar research for different applications. Nunes et al. [35] uses POSSUM to find the sequence for the diffusion MRI acquisition that minimizes the effect of eddy currents. Alexander et al. [65] introduced a concept called "Active Imaging" which handles optimization of the diffusion MRI sequences for minimizing variance to the tissue microstructure parameters. Drobnjak et al. [66,67] shows a range of simulations and optimization techniques used for maximizing sensitivity of diffusion MRI signal to axon diameter.

9.4.5 Simulated data for machine learning

In this section we show how we might use simulation to provide training data for machine learning algorithms. Whilst supervised machine learning tools have huge potential application in medical image analysis, they require large, labeled datasets for training. Not only can these be costly to acquire, requiring vast amounts of an expert's time to provide accurate labels, but the labeling can be subjective, with high inter-rater disagreement. Furthermore, datasets need to contain enough examples to sufficiently characterize the domain of interest, which can prove difficult in real datasets where there may be few examples of rare cases. Simulation offers the opportunity to create large, labeled datasets, with known "ground-truth" labels.

Here we demonstrate the application of DW-POSSUM to providing simulated data to produce a quality control (QC) tool for detecting intra-volume movement artifacts. These artifacts are subtle and often hard to observe, requiring very laborious manual QC to spot. Volumes containing these artifacts typically need to be identified in QC so that they can either be removed, or information about them can be used as confounds in later statistical analysis [68]. This work is described more fully in [69].

The work made use of both simulated and real data in this experiment. For the real data, ten subjects were taken from the developing Human Connectome Project [70] (dHCP), which contains MRI data acquired in neonates. These were chosen because neonatal scans tend to contain large amounts of movement. Manual QC was performed by visual inspection, with one rater assigning a label of either acceptable or unacceptable to each volume. The rater classified the whole dataset twice, on two separate occasions, to provide an estimate of intra-rater agreement. Simulated data was designed to be visually similar to the dHCP data. Known motion was injected into the datasets during simulation. The motion traces were designed to produce data with clear signs of intra-volume movement, similar to those seen in the real data, in order to produce a suitable training set for the classifier. This was achieved by synthesizing traces with large, sudden motion spikes, modeling a subject suddenly moving his/her head. The traces describe the object's translations along and rotations about each of the three axes, with movement occurring between the acquisition of each slice. Signal dropout was also simulated as this is often, but not always, present in volumes that show other signs of severe intra-volume movement. A total of 1096 volumes were simulated. Fig. 9.9 compares the real and simulated data. Two simple convolutional neural networks were trained, one on the real and one on the simulated data. Networks were trained on sagittal slices. Testing was performed on three withheld volumes from the real dataset.

Results in Fig. 9.10 show the precision–recall curves for both the real-trained and simulation-trained classifiers. The curve shows the simulation-trained classifier is able to approach the performance of the real-trained classifier, though its performance is sensitive to the choice of classification threshold, due to the domain shift between the real and simulated data. Further results in [69] show that incorporating just a small amount of real labeled data can improve the classifier, enabling it to achieve high performance with a fraction of the labeling required for the fully real-trained classifier.

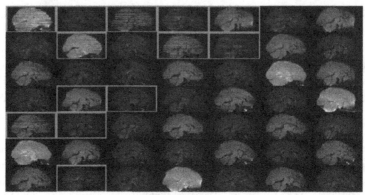

Real data

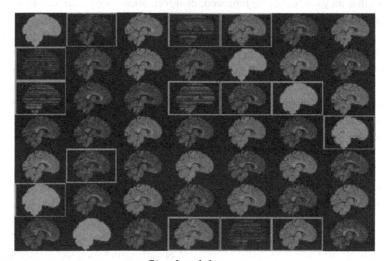

Simulated data

FIGURE 9.9

Real and simulated data. Red (mid gray in print version) bounding boxes indicate the volume was labeled as containing intra-volume movement.

Work such as this suggests that hybrid approaches, combing large amounts of simulated data with smaller amounts of real, labeled data, offer the opportunity to develop performant machine learning tools whilst drastically reducing the need for labeled data. In [71], the authors simulate MR scans with varying sequence parameters in order to develop segmentation tools that are invariant to MR-physics; in [72] simulated data containing extreme contrast variations was used to train modality-agnostic segmentation tools. In [73], the authors show that simulated data with movement artifacts can be used to train networks to remove movement artifacts from data.

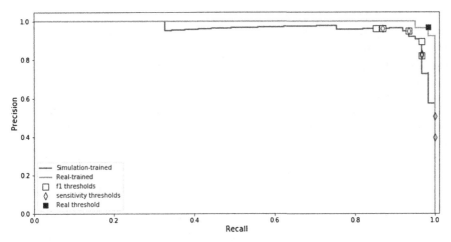

FIGURE 9.10

Precision–recall curve for both classifiers in the test set, consisting of 516 volumes. The threshold for the real-trained classifier of 0.5 is plotted on the curve, as are the seven thresholds determined for both the F1- and sensitivity-based criteria for the simulation-trained classifier.

9.5 Future directions and research challenges

Simulations are a necessary tool for creation, optimization, and validation of every MR imaging pipeline. They are so essential that to a certain degree all developmental pathways have been using some form of simulations or another, from in-house builds to more well known publicly accessible ones. Most simulators and digital phantoms serve their intended purpose for single applications, however plenty of applications remain that are still unable to be addressed, waiting for a simulator that can deliver it all.

So what is an ideal MR simulation system of the future? Although the answer here depends ultimately on the application in question, one would argue that each scientist on the MR imaging pipeline wants a simulation system that can produce realistic anatomical simulated MR images of any area of the body for a variety of different scanning conditions and is fully controllable, accurate, robust, simple to use, fast and easily accessible to all. The development of such a computer system is a very complex task.

The first reason for the complexity of the task is the difficulty of *capturing all of the realistic scanner effects in one model*. There are many factors that influence the generation of MR images: scanner environment, pulse sequence, subject's brain/body structure and MR characteristics, and subject's behavior, which can change from experiment to experiment. Furthermore, one would want to capture realistic respiratory, cardiovascular, physiological, and all other body functions; realistic image related artifacts (e.g., rigid-body motion of the object and magnetic field inhomogeneities);

realistic MR functionality such as spin-echos, gradient echos, RF pulses, diffusion gradients, etc. Many of these effects have been modeled in isolation from one another, and future work will see solutions that try to combine these into one larger aggregated model.

The second reason for the complexity of the simulator development is the *computational demand* of simulators of this kind. Incorporating all of the realistic scanner effects creates a huge demand on the computational memory and time. The input object itself that describes the MR properties of the simulated brain/body can occupy large amounts of memory, and to run a single MRI simulation of the full Bloch equations with all of the features described could take months. These problems are possibly the most pressing and has so far prevented many of the simulators from simulating fully realistic MR images. New developments in GPU programming, and the increasing power of computers will be crucial here in driving future research and developing new ways of parallelizing and speeding up the simulation process.

The third reason for the complexity of the simulator development task is the difficulty in *evaluating software* of this kind. In order to evaluate each of the software features it is crucial to have experimental data to compare the simulated data with. However, it is impossible to fully control the experimental data, which is also noisy and contains many unplanned factors that are part of the scanning process as well as the increasingly sophisticated, and often hidden, reconstruction algorithms. Here, future research will draw on current developments of physical phantoms that could provide ground truth for the validation of the simulation algorithms.

The fourth reason is the need to be *up-to date with the new developments in the field of MR imaging*. MR imaging is evolving rapidly and we are seeing developments such as more powerful hardware systems with extremely strong magnetic fields and strong gradient coils, enabling scanning at much higher resolutions. These developments are pushing the boundaries of the MR imaging field in identifying new contrasts, however, they also bring with them a range of new challenges such as more pronounced or totally new artifacts. Future simulation systems need to be flexible and continually develop in order to keep up with these new developments.

Each of these challenges correspond to a range of potential areas of future research in the field of simulations, some of which we have mentioned above. In the future, which is becoming more and more digital, with increasing sizes of data sets and the use machine learning, with its need for highly controllable large ground truth training data sets, the need for MR simulations will only grow.

References

[1] I. Drobnjak, D. Gavaghan, E. Süli, J. Pitt-Francis, M. Jenkinson, Development of a functional magnetic resonance imaging simulator for modeling realistic rigid-body motion artifacts, Magnetic Resonance in Medicine 56 (2) (2006) 364–380.

[2] Z. Liang, P. Lauterbur, Principles of Magnetic Resonance Imaging: A Signal Processing Perspective, IEEE Press Series in Biomedical Engineering, IEEE Press, Inc., New York, 2000.

[3] E. Haacke, R. Brown, M. Thompson, R. Venkatesan, Magnetic Resonance Imaging, Physical Principles and Sequence Design, Willey-Liss, 1999.

[4] A. Simmons, S.R. Arridge, G.J. Barker, S.C. Williams, Simulation of MRI cluster plots and application to neurological segmentation, Magnetic Resonance Imaging 14 (1) (1996) 73–92.

[5] S.J. Riederer, S. Suddarth, S. Bobman, J. Lee, H. Wang, J.R. MacFall, Automated MR image synthesis: feasibility studies, Radiology 153 (1) (1984) 203–206.

[6] D. Rundle, S. Kishore, S. Seshadri, F. Wehrli, MRI simulator: a teaching tool for radiology, in: SPIE Proceedings, vol. 1234, 1990, pp. 60–65.

[7] T. Hacklnder, H. Mertens, Virtual MRI: a PC-based simulation of a clinical MR scanner, Academic Radiology 12 (1) (2005) 85–96.

[8] J. Petersson, J.-O. Christoffersson, K. Golman, MRI simulation using the k-space formalism, Magnetic Resonance Imaging 11 (4) (1993) 557–568.

[9] C.G. Koay, J.E. Sarlls, E. Özarslan, Three-dimensional analytical magnetic resonance imaging phantom in the Fourier domain, Magnetic Resonance in Medicine 58 (2) (2007) 430–436.

[10] H.M. Gach, C. Tanase, F. Boada, 2D & 3D Shepp–Logan phantom standards for MRI, in: Systems Engineering, 2008. ICSENG'08. 19th International Conference on, IEEE, 2008, pp. 521–526.

[11] L.A. Shepp, B.F. Logan, The Fourier reconstruction of a head section, IEEE Transactions on Nuclear Science 21 (3) (1974) 21–43.

[12] M. Guerquin-Kern, L. Lejeune, K.P. Pruessmann, M. Unser, Realistic analytical phantoms for parallel magnetic resonance imaging, IEEE Transactions on Medical Imaging 31 (3) (2012) 626–636.

[13] T.M. Ngo, G.S. Fung, S. Han, M. Chen, J.L. Prince, B.M. Tsui, E.R. McVeigh, D.A. Herzka, Realistic analytical polyhedral MRI phantoms, Magnetic Resonance in Medicine 76 (2) (2016) 663–678.

[14] R.-S. Kwan, A.C. Evans, G.B. Pike, MRI simulation-based evaluation of image-processing and classification methods, IEEE Transactions on Medical Imaging 18 (11) (1999) 1085–1097.

[15] C.A. Cocosco, V. Kollokian, R.K.-S. Kwan, G.B. Pike, A.C. Evans, BrainWeb: online interface to a 3D MRI simulated brain database, in: NeuroImage, Citeseer, 1997.

[16] R. Summers, L. Axel, S. Israel, A computer simulation of nuclear magnetic resonance imaging, Magnetic Resonance in Medicine 3 (1986) 363–376.

[17] M. Olsson, R. Wirestam, B. Persson, A computer simulation program for MR imaging: application to RF and static magnetic field imperfections, Magnetic Resonance in Medicine 34 (1995) 612–617.

[18] D.A. Yoder, Y. Zhao, C.B. Paschal, J.M. Fitzpatrick, MRI simulator with object-specific field map calculations, Magnetic Resonance Imaging 22 (3) (2004) 315–328.

[19] H. Benoit-Cattin, G. Collewet, B. Belaroussi, H. Saint-Jalmes, C. Odet, The SIMRI project: a versatile and interactive MRI simulator, Journal of Magnetic Resonance 173 (1) (2005) 97–115.

[20] I. Drobnjak, G.S. Pell, M. Jenkinson, Simulating the effects of time-varying magnetic fields with a realistic simulated scanner, Magnetic Resonance Imaging 28 (2010) 1014–1021, https://doi.org/10.1016/j.mri.2010.03.029, http://www.ncbi.nlm.nih.gov/pubmed/20418038.

[21] P. Shkarin, R.G. Spencer, Direct simulation of spin echoes by summation of isochromats, Concepts in Magnetic Resonance. Part A 8 (4) (1996) 253–268.

[22] T. Stöcker, K. Vahedipour, D. Pflugfelder, N.J. Shah, High-performance computing MRI simulations, Magnetic Resonance in Medicine 64 (1) (2010) 186–193.

[23] C.G. Xanthis, I.E. Venetis, A. Chalkias, A.H. Aletras, MRISIMUL: a GPU-based parallel approach to MRI simulations, IEEE Transactions on Medical Imaging 33 (3) (2014) 607–617.

[24] F. Liu, J.V. Velikina, W.F. Block, R. Kijowski, A.A. Samsonov, Fast realistic MRI simulations based on generalized multi-pool exchange tissue model, IEEE Transactions on Medical Imaging 36 (2) (2017) 527–537.

[25] K.H. Maier-Hein, P.F. Neher, J.-C. Houde, M.-A. Côté, E. Garyfallidis, J. Zhong, M. Chamberland, F.-C. Yeh, Y.-C. Lin, Q. Ji, et al., The challenge of mapping the human connectome based on diffusion tractography, Nature Communications 8 (1) (2017) 1349.

[26] A. Leemans, J. Sijbers, M. Verhoye, A. Van der Linden, D. Van Dyck, Mathematical framework for simulating diffusion tensor MR neural fiber bundles, Magnetic Resonance in Medicine 53 (4) (2005) 944–953.

[27] T.G. Close, J.D. Tournier, F. Calamante, L.A. Johnston, I. Mareels, A. Connelly, A software tool to generate simulated white matter structures for the assessment of fibre-tracking algorithms, NeuroImage 47 (2009) 1288–1300.

[28] E. Caruyer, A. Daducci, M. Descoteaux, J.-C. Houde, J.-P. Thiran, R. Verma, Phantomas: a flexible software library to simulate diffusion MR phantoms, 2014.

[29] B. Wilkins, N. Lee, N. Gajawelli, M. Law, N. Leporé, Fiber estimation and tractography in diffusion MRI: development of simulated brain images and comparison of multi-fiber analysis methods at clinical b-values, NeuroImage 109 (2015) 341–356.

[30] P.F. Neher, F.B. Laun, B. Stieltjes, K.H. Maier-Hein, Fiberfox: facilitating the creation of realistic white matter software phantoms, Magnetic Resonance in Medicine 1470 (2013) 1460–1470.

[31] D. Perrone, B. Jeurissen, J. Aelterman, T. Roine, J. Sijbers, A. Pizurica, A. Leemans, W. Philips, D-brain: anatomically accurate simulated diffusion MRI brain data, PLoS ONE 11 (2016) e0149778, https://doi.org/10.1371/journal.pone.0149778.

[32] T. Sarwar, K. Ramamohanarao, A. Zalesky, Mapping connectomes with diffusion MRI: deterministic or probabilistic tractography?, Magnetic Resonance in Medicine 81 (2) (2019) 1368–1384.

[33] M.E. Bastin, Correction of eddy current-induced artefacts in diffusion tensor imaging using iterative cross-correlation, Magnetic Resonance Imaging 17 (1999) 1011–1024.

[34] M.E. Bastin, On the use of the flair technique to improve the correction of eddy current induced artefacts in MR diffusion tensor imaging, Magnetic Resonance Imaging 19 (2001) 937–950, https://doi.org/10.1016/S0730-725X(01)00427-1.

[35] R.G. Nunes, I. Drobnjak, S. Clare, P. Jezzard, M. Jenkinson, Performance of single spin-echo and doubly refocused diffusion-weighted sequences in the presence of eddy current fields with multiple components, Magnetic Resonance Imaging 29 (2011) 659–667, https://doi.org/10.1016/j.mri.2011.02.015.

[36] M.S. Graham, I. Drobnjak, H. Zhang, Realistic simulation of artefacts in diffusion MRI for validating post-processing correction techniques, NeuroImage 125 (2016) 1079–1094.

[37] M. Jenkinson, J.L. Wilson, P. Jezzard, Perturbation method for magnetic field calculations of nonconductive objects, Magnetic Resonance in Medicine 52 (2004) 471–477, https://doi.org/10.1002/mrm.20194.

[38] M. Jenkinson, P. Bannister, J. Brady, S. Smith, Improved optimisation for the robust and accurate linear registration and motion correction of brain images, NeuroImage 17 (2) (2002) 825–841.

[39] P. Bannister, Motion correction for functional magnetic resonance images, PhD thesis, University of Oxford, 2003.

[40] D. Collins, A. Zijdenbos, V. Kollokian, J. Sled, N. Kabani, C. Holmes, A. Evans, Design and construction of a realistic digital brain phantom, IEEE Transactions on Medical Imaging 17 (3) (1998) 463–468.

[41] C. Cocosco, V. Kollokian, R.-S. Kwan, A. Evans, BrainWeb: online interface to a 3D MRI simulated brain database, in: Third Int. Conf. on Functional Mapping of the Human Brain, 1997.

[42] R. Kwan, A. Evans, G. Pike, MRI simulation-based evaluation of image-processing and classification methods, IEEE Transactions on Medical Imaging 18 (11) (1999) 1085–1097.

[43] I. Drobnjak, FMRI simulator: Development and applications, PhD thesis, University of Oxford, 2007.

[44] J.L. Andersson, S.N. Sotiropoulos, An integrated approach to correction for off-resonance effects and subject movement in diffusion MR imaging, NeuroImage 125 (2016) 1063–1078.

[45] G.K. Rohde, A.S. Barnett, P.J. Basser, S. Marenco, C. Pierpaoli, Comprehensive approach for correction of motion and distortion in diffusion-weighted MRI, Magnetic Resonance in Medicine 51 (2004) 103–114, https://doi.org/10.1002/mrm.10677.

[46] J.L. Andersson, M.S. Graham, I. Drobnjak, H. Zhang, N. Filippini, M. Bastiani, Towards a comprehensive framework for movement and distortion correction of diffusion MR images: within volume movement, NeuroImage 152 (2017) 450–466.

[47] J.L. Andersson, M.S. Graham, I. Drobnjak, H. Zhang, J. Campbell, Susceptibility-induced distortion that varies due to motion: correction in diffusion MR without acquiring additional data, NeuroImage 171 (2018) 277–295.

[48] D. Le Bihan, C. Poupon, A. Amadon, F. Lethimonnier, Artifacts and pitfalls in diffusion MRI, Journal of Magnetic Resonance Imaging 24 (3) (2006) 478–488.

[49] M.S. Graham, I. Drobnjak, M. Jenkinson, H. Zhang, Quantitative assessment of the susceptibility artefact and its interaction with motion in diffusion MRI, PLoS ONE 12 (10) (2017) e0185647.

[50] P. Jezzard, S. Clare, Sources of distortions in functional MRI data, Human Brain Mapping 8 (1999) 80–85, https://doi.org/10.1002/(SICI)1097-0193(1999)8:2/3<80::AID-HBM2>3.0.CO;2-C.

[51] J.L. Andersson, C. Hutton, J. Ashburner, R. Turner, K. Friston, Modeling geometric deformations in EPI time series, NeuroImage 13 (2001) 903–919, https://doi.org/10.1006/nimg.2001.0746.

[52] R. Weissleder, G. Elizondo, J. Wittenberg, C.A. Rabito, H.H. Bengele, L. Josephson, Ultrasmall superparamagnetic iron oxide: characterization of a new class of contrast agent for MR imaging, Radiology 175 (1990) 489–493.

[53] P.T. Callaghan, J. Stepisnik, Spatially-distributed pulsed gradient spin echo NMR using single-wire proximity, Physical Review Letters 75 (24) (1995) 4532–4535, https://doi.org/10.1103/PhysRevLett.75.4532.

[54] V. Renvall, R. Joensuu, R. Hari, Functional phantom for FMRI: a feasibility study, Magnetic Resonance Imaging 24 (2006) 315–320.

[55] G. Scott, M. Joy, R. Armstrong, R. Henkelman, RF current density imaging in homogenous media, Magnetic Resonance in Medicine 28 (1992) 186–201.

[56] M. Joy, G. Scott, M. Henkelman, In vivo detection of applied electric currents by magnetic resonance imaging, Magnetic Resonance Imaging 7 (1989) 89–94.

[57] G. Pell, D. Abbott, S. Fleming, J. Prichard, G. Jackson, Further steps toward direct magnetic resonance (MR) imaging detection of neural action currents: optimization of MR sensitivity to transient and weak currents in a conductor, Magnetic Resonance in Medicine 55 (5) (2006) 1038–1046.

[58] N. Petridou, D. Plenz, A. Silva, M. Loew, J. Bodurka, A. Bandettini, Direct magnetic resonance detection of neuronal electrical activity, Proceedings of the National Academy of Sciences 103 (43) (2006) 16015–16020.

[59] C. Faber, C. Heil, B. Zahneisen, D. Balla, R. Bowtell, Sensitivity to local dipole fields in the CRAZED experiment: an approach to bright spot MRI, Journal of Magnetic Resonance 182 (2006) 315–324.

[60] R. Bowtell, R. Bowley, Analytic calculations of the E-fields induced by the time-varying magnetic fields generated by the cylindrical gradient coils, Magnetic Resonance in Medicine 44 (2000) 782–790.

[61] J. Bodurka, P. Bandettini, Toward direct mapping of neuronal activity: MRI detection of ultraweak, transient magnetic field changes, Magnetic Resonance in Medicine 47 (2002) 1052–1058.

[62] J. Bodurka, P. Bandettini, EPI magnitude signal formation in the proximity of straight conductor subjected to a weak electric current, in: Proc. Int. Soc. of Magnetic Resonance in Medicine 15, 1976.

[63] A. Cassara, G. Hagberg, M. Bianciardi, M. Migliore, B. Maraviglia, Realistic simulations of neuronal activity: a contribution to the debate on direct detection of neuronal currents in MRI, NeuroImage 39 (2007) 87–106.

[64] D. Konn, P. Gowland, R. Bowtell, MRI detection of weak magnetic fields due to an extended current dipole in a conducting sphere: a model for direct detection of neuronal currents in the brain, Magnetic Resonance in Medicine 50 (1) (2003) 40–49.

[65] J.D. Clayden, Z. Nagy, M.G. Hall, C.A. Clark, D.C. Alexander, Active imaging with dual spin-echo diffusion MRI, in: International Conference on Information Processing in Medical Imaging, Springer, 2009, pp. 264–275.

[66] I. Drobnjak, B. Siow, D.C. Alexander, Optimizing gradient waveforms for microstructure sensitivity in diffusion-weighted MR, Journal of Magnetic Resonance 206 (1) (2010) 41–51.

[67] I. Drobnjak, H. Zhang, A. Ianuş, E. Kaden, D.C. Alexander, PGSE, OGSE, and sensitivity to axon diameter in diffusion MRI: insight from a simulation study, Magnetic Resonance in Medicine 75 (2) (2016) 688–700.

[68] A. Yendiki, K. Koldewyn, S. Kakunoori, N. Kanwisher, B. Fischl, Spurious group differences due to head motion in a diffusion MRI study, NeuroImage 88 (2014) 79–90.

[69] M.S. Graham, I. Drobnjak, H. Zhang, A supervised learning approach for diffusion MRI quality control with minimal training data, NeuroImage 178 (2018) 668–676.

[70] E.J. Hughes, T. Winchman, F. Padormo, R. Teixeira, J. Wurie, M. Sharma, M. Fox, J. Hutter, L. Cordero-Grande, A.N. Price, et al., A dedicated neonatal brain imaging system, Magnetic Resonance in Medicine 78 (2) (2017) 794–804, https://doi.org/10.1002/mrm. 26462.

[71] P. Borges, C. Sudre, T. Varsavsky, D. Thomas, I. Drobnjak, S. Ourselin, M.J. Cardoso, Physics-informed brain MRI segmentation, in: International Workshop on Simulation and Synthesis in Medical Imaging, Springer, 2019, pp. 100–109.

[72] B. Billot, D. Greve, K. Van Leemput, B. Fischl, J.E. Iglesias, A.V. Dalca, A learning strategy for contrast-agnostic MRI segmentation, arXiv:2003.01995.

[73] R. Shaw, C.H. Sudre, T. Varsavsky, S. Ourselin, M.J. Cardoso, A k-space model of movement artefacts: application to segmentation augmentation and artefact removal, IEEE Transactions on Medical Imaging 39 (9) (2020) 2881–2892, https://doi.org/10.1109/TMI.2020.2972547.

Synthesis for image analysis across modalities

10

Matteo Mancini[a,b,c] **and Juan Eugenio Iglesias**[d,e,f]

[a]*Department of Neuroscience, Brighton and Sussex Medical School, University of Sussex, Brighton, United Kingdom*
[b]*Cardiff University Brain Research Imaging Centre (CUBRIC), Cardiff University, Cardiff, United Kingdom*
[c]*NeuroPoly Lab, Polytechnique Montreal, Montreal, QC, Canada*
[d]*Center for Medical Image Computing (CMIC), University College London, London, United Kingdom*
[e]*Martinos Center for Biomedical Imaging, Massachusetts General Hospital and Harvard Medical School, Boston, MA, United States*
[f]*Computer Science and Artificial Intelligence Laboratory (CSAIL), Massachusetts Institute of Technology, Cambridge, MA, United States*

10.1 General motivation

Many problems and applications in medical imaging are inherently multi-modal. Some *in vivo* and *ex vivo* examples, illustrated in Figs. 10.1 and 10.2, include:

- The use of complementary modalities. For example, structural imaging with computerized tomography (CT) and functional imaging with positron emission tomography (PET) are frequently combined in cancer diagnostics [1] or preoperative staging [2] (Fig. 10.1a). Another example would be the combination of *ex vivo* magnetic resonance imaging (MRI) and histology, for 3D histology reconstruction [3] or MR signal modeling purposes [4] (Fig. 10.1b). In such scenarios, it is often desirable to register the two modalities [5], e.g., with visualization purposes. Another possible application is to use segmentation made on one modality to learn how to automatically segment images of the other modality [6].
- The use of different varieties of the same modality. For instance, MRI studies are often multi-modal (Fig. 10.1c), and include different MR contrasts (T1, T2, FLAIR, diffusion), possibly acquired in different orientations (sagittal, axial, coronal). In histology, consecutive sections are often stained with different dyes, e.g., targeting different antigens with immunohistochemistry [7] (Fig. 10.1d). Again, it is often desirable to register these into the same coordinate frame [8], e.g., to evaluate multiple imaging contrasts at the same spatial location.
- Comparing images of the same modality, but acquired on different hardware platforms, e.g., at different sites. For example, MRI scanners from different

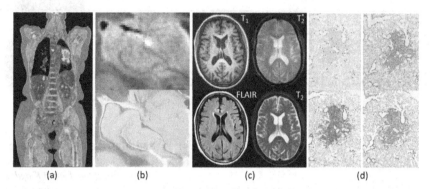

FIGURE 10.1

Multi-modal applications in medical imaging: (a) coronal slices of whole body PET-CT scan from the publicly available Cancer Image Archive (cancerimagingarchive.net); (b) *ex vivo* MRI (top) and luxol fast blue histology (bottom) of the hippocampal head and amygdala, in coronal orientation [11]; (c) four axial slices of scans with different MR contrasts, from a subject from the public ADNI repository (adni-info.org); and (d) four consecutive histological sections, stained with different dyes [8].

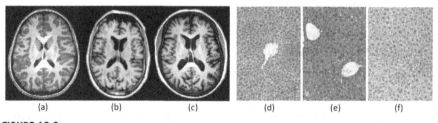

FIGURE 10.2

Examples of images of the same modality acquired on different hardware platforms: (a)–(c) axial slices of T1-weighted MP-RAGE human brain MRI scans, acquired on different 3-Tesla scanners (source: adni-info.org); (d)–(f) H&E stained sections of rat liver tissue (source: ihcworld.com). Harmonization techniques that reduce differences in image appearance are required to minimize the impact of acquisition heterogeneity in subsequent analyses.

vendors have different implementations of the widespread T1-weighted MP-RAGE sequence [9] (Fig. 10.2a–c). In histology, the appearance of the ubiquitous Haemotoxylin and Eosin (H&E) staining will vary across automatic stainers [10] (Fig. 10.2d–f). Image analysis across sites requires accounting for these differences; this is essentially an harmonization problem, discussed in Chapter 11.

One general approach to inter-modality problems is to develop methods that do not depend on the modality of the input data, or that are resilient to variations in the image contrast properties of the input. For example, cost functions based on information theory have been widely used in inter-modality medical image registration [5], since they can model complex nonlinear relationships between image intensities. A good example in segmentation is the widespread use of Bayesian approaches based on generative models in brain MRI [12]. These approaches combine a prior model of neuroanatomy (a deformable probabilistic atlas) with a likelihood model of image appearance (often a Gaussian mixture model, or GMM). By learning the GMM parameters directly from the scans to segment, these methods can adapt to any type of MRI contrast.

While modality-agnostic approaches have been widely used in medical imaging, their performance is lower than their intra-modality counterparts. In registration, nonlinear alignment is much more accurate when images have been acquired on the same platform with the same protocol, and intra-modality cost functions are used, e.g., sum of squared differences or normalized cross-correlation. In segmentation, Bayesian approaches cannot match the performance of convolutional neural networks (CNNs, best represented by the ubiquitous Unet [13]) when there is no domain gap between the training and test data.

In this context, image synthesis provides an attractive alternative. Rather than using inter-modality techniques, which showcase lower performance, can we modify the appearance of the images to turn the analysis at hand into an intra-modality problem? Two opposing factors need to be considered with this approach. On the one hand, image synthesis is not perfect, and inaccuracies in the shape and appearance of the synthetic image will inevitably propagate into subsequent analyses. On the other hand, such analyses are expected to be more accurate than in the original inter-modality scenario. The question is thus: Does this improvement outweigh the mistakes made in the synthesis? In the rest of this chapter we will show that the answer can be yes, in the context of two of the most representative problems in medical image analysis: registration and segmentation.

10.2 **Registration**
10.2.1 **Background**

Image registration [14–16] is the process of bringing two or more images into the same coordinate frame. There is a wide literature of image registration of natural images with applications in, e.g., panoramic stitching [17], stereo vision [18], or satellite imaging [19]. In these applications, registration is needed to compare or integrate information from different images, of the same or different modalities. The medical imaging community has played a very active part in the development of registration techniques (particularly in 3D [20,5,21,22]), as these find many applications in medicine: registering medical scans can be used not only to integrate modalities [23] or stitch panoramas [24] as with natural images, but also provides a solution to tasks that are quite specific to medical imaging. Examples include:

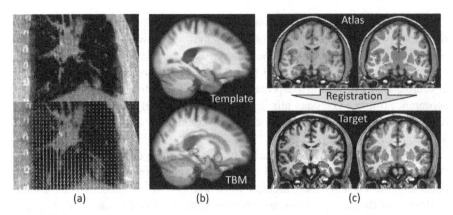

FIGURE 10.3

Example applications of image registration in medical imaging: (a) estimated motion between exhale (top) and inhale (bottom) lung CT scans (source: Cancer Image Archive);
the estimated deformation field is overlaid on the latter, and is particularly strong around
the diaphragm, in the lower part of the image; (b) tensor-based morphometry (TBM) of
50 Alzheimer's subjects vs 50 elderly controls (source: ADNI); (top) unbiased template
from the 100 subjects [34]; (bottom) TBM. The hot regions represent faster expansion in
Alzheimer's (e.g., the ventricles), whereas the cold regions represent faster compression
(atrophy, e.g., on the hippocampal head and tail); (c) Registration-based segmentation: a
brain MR scan ("atlas", top left) is registered to another scan to segment (bottom left), and
the resulting deformation field is used to propagate the labels of the atlas (top right) to the
target space, in order to automatically obtain a segmentation (bottom right). This segmentation is fair for subcortical structures, but poor for the cerebral cortex, due to the difficulty
of volumetrically registering its convoluted surface.

- Quantifying change between scans, often by computing the determinant of the
  Jacobian matrix of the deformation field at each point – values above 1.0 indicate expansion, and values below indicate contraction. These scans can be from
  the same subject, e.g., to analyze deformations of the lung and liver during the
  respiratory cycle [25,26] (Fig. 10.3a), or longitudinal change in disease [27]; but
  also from different subjects, in order to study the variability within a population
  or across groups using tensor-based morphometry [28] (Fig. 10.3b).
- Registration is also a key component of voxel-based morphometry [29], a
  widespread neuroimaging technique for comparing the local concentration of gray
  matter between two groups of subjects.
- Finally, registration has also been widely used in segmentation: if one has one or
  multiple scans with ground truth segmentations (often known as "atlases"), one
  can simply register these scans to a new image, and use the deformation fields to
  propagate the labels to automatically obtain a segmentation (Fig. 10.3c). This approach, particularly the multi-atlas version, has been successfully used in domains
  like brain, cardiac, or lung imaging [30–33].

Most registration algorithms are explicitly cast as optimization problems: given a "fixed" image (also known as "reference", or "target"), and a "moving" image to deform (also known as "floating image"), one seeks to optimize a deformation (parametric or not) with respect to an *ad hoc* similarity metric that measures the resemblance between the fixed and (deformed) moving images, often combined with a regularizer that ensures the smoothness of the deformation – which is a proxy for its plausibility. Registration can be linear or nonlinear. The former seeks to optimize a linear transform, which may be constrained to be rigid (i.e., rotation and translation) or similarity (rigid plus isotropic scaling); or allowed to be fully affine (i.e., with shearing). Linear transforms are sufficient to model the motion of rigid objects, e.g., to align different brain MRI scans of the same subject acquired in the same session. Deformable registration is required to model nonlinear shape changes (e.g., between respiratory cycles, as in Fig. 10.3a; or across different subjects), and is typically initialized with a linear transform.

There are three main components to a registration algorithm. The first one is the optimizer. Classical registration methods are based on numerical optimization using standard techniques, such as gradient descent [35], stochastic gradient descent [36], conjugate gradient descent [37], or the L-BFGS algorithm [38]. More recently, unsupervised deep learning registration methods have used CNNs to predict the deformation field in one shot [39,40], by using an unlabeled dataset to learn how to maximize the same similarity metrics as traditional methods.

The second component is the deformation model; while it is out of the scope of this chapter to survey the vast literature on such models [21], we provide a short summary with examples here. Nonparametric models attempt to optimize a field voxel by voxel, such that the number of parameters is D times the number of voxels (where D is the number of dimensions, typically 2 or 3). This field can represent, e.g., the deformation directly [41]; a stationary velocity field (SVF) one can integrate to obtain a diffeomorphic (and thus invertible) deformation [42]; or an initial velocity field within a Large Deformation Diffeomorphic Metric Mapping framework (LDDMM [43,44]). Parametric models, on the other hand, summarize the nonlinear deformation field (or SVF, initial momentum, etc.) into a lower dimensional set of parameters, e.g., the coefficients for a set of basis functions [45]. The most widespread parametric model is arguably the B-spline model [46], which optimizes a set of D-dimensional vectors located on evenly spaced control points (e.g., 10 voxels apart in each spatial direction), such that the deformation at any location is obtained via interpolation with B-splines.

The third and final component of a registration algorithm, which is the most relevant to this chapter, is the similarity metric, which we cover in the following section below.

10.2.2 Similarity metrics and their limitations

While geometric point matching algorithms have been popular in natural images (e.g., the widespread scale-invariant feature transform, or SIFT [47,48]), medical imaging has largely relied on similarity metrics directly built on dense voxel intensities (often called "iconic"), often complemented by regularizers that prevent deformation fields (in the nonlinear case) from becoming too convoluted and implausible [21]. One simple metric is the sum of squared differences (SSD) across voxels of the fixed and registered images. SSD assumes that, deformations aside, the relationship between the intensities of the two images is additive Gaussian noise. Therefore, this approach only works well when the intensity profiles of the two scans are almost identical, i.e., intra-modality, and with calibrated intensities. Even if this limitation can be ameliorated with contrast matching techniques [49], it still restricts the applicability of SSD to images acquired on the same platform, or from calibrated modalities such as CT – where the voxel intensities correspond to physically meaningful Hounsfield units and are fairly consistent across scanning platforms.

A slightly more flexible metric than SSD is the normalized cross-correlation (NCC), which assumes a linear relationship between the intensities of the two scans, and is thus invariant to changes in brightness and contrast, but still only works well in intra-modality scenarios. A more popular metric, particularly in MRI, is the local NCC (LNCC [50]), which uses a neighborhood around each voxel to estimate local means and covariances. These local statistics are used to compute voxel-wise values of NCC, which are averaged across the image domain. LNCC has the advantage of being highly robust against the intensity inhomogeneities that are present in MRI, as they appear as a smooth multiplicative "bias field", which is approximately constant in a local patch – and therefore barely affects the LNCC, in spite of greatly influencing the global NCC. Still, LNCC is only widely applicable intra-modality.

Across modalities, the registration literature has been dominated by information theoretic metrics, particularly mutual information (MI) and its normalized version (NMI) [51,52,5]. These methods build a joint histogram for the intensities of the fixed and registered images, using binning or kernel density estimation, and try to maximize its MI, i.e., the amount of information obtained about the intensity of a voxel in one modality, when observing the intensity of the (registered) voxel in the other modality. MI can model complex nonlinear relationships between intensities, and also one-to-many correspondences. This flexibility in the model has been crucial to the success of MI in an array of inter-modality registration problems (e.g., PET to MRI, or across MRI contrasts), particularly in linear registration.

Unfortunately, the flexibility of the MI model is also the reason for its failure when the deformation model is also highly flexible. This is because MI can be further increased by convoluted and implausible deformations that produce peaks in the joint histogram. This problem is illustrated in Fig. 10.4, where we have nonlinearly registered the brain scans from two different subjects from the publicly available IXI dataset using different MR modalities and metrics (https://brain-development.org/ixi-dataset). In order to compare metrics in a fair manner, we switched off the regularizer – otherwise one needs to use different regularizer weights for the metrics in an equitable fashion, which is not straightforward. Instead, we used a parametric B-spline model with 5 mm spacing between control points, which implicitly regularizes the deformation.

| (a) Fixed image (T1) | (b) Linear registration NMI: 1.124 | (c) NMI registration NMI: 1.157 | (d) NMI registration Jacobian (log |J|) | (e) LNCC registration NMI: 1.141 | (f) LNCC registration Jacobian (log |J|) |

FIGURE 10.4

Registration with NMI: (a) axial slice of T1 scan of reference subject; (b) corresponding axial slice of T2 scan of moving subject, after linear registration; (c) nonlinearly registered T2, using NMI; (d) corresponding Jacobian determinant map (in logarithmic scale; dark represents compression, bright represents expansion); (e) nonlinearly registered T2, using a deformation field computed with its corresponding T1 scan and LNCC; and (f) corresponding Jacobian determinant map. The NMI of the different deformed volumes with respect to the fixed TI image is displayed under each image.

Fig. 10.4a shows an axial slice of the T1 scan used as fixed image. The linearly registered T2 scan of the moving subject is shown in Fig. 10.4b; the NMI with the fixed image is equal to 1.124 (accounting for the whole volume, not only the axial slice). When NMI is used as a criterion to nonlinearly register the volume, the final value of the metric increases to NMI = 1.157, but the registered image (Fig. 10.4c) has been greatly deformed in order to substitute subcortical gray matter (e.g., putamen and caudate) by white matter, which is more abundant in the histogram and leads to higher NMI. This is clearly reflected in the corresponding Jacobian map (Fig. 10.4d), which showcases neighboring regions of high expansion and compression. When a deformation field is computed from the T1 scans and then applied to the T2 (Fig. 10.4e), the metric is not as high as in the previous case (NMI = 1.141); this is expected, as the NMI was not explicitly optimized. However, the deformation field is much less convoluted (Fig. 10.4f), does not eliminate any structures, and is qualitatively more accurate. Therefore, using NMI as metric may not always be a good idea in nonlinear registration.

10.2.3 Synthesis-based similarity metrics

In our 2013 MICCAI conference paper [53], we showed that the qualitative results from the example above hold in a quantitative and more general fashion when applied to a larger dataset, and when the real T1 is replaced by a synthetic counterpart (in Fig. 10.4 we cheated in the sense that we used the real T1 data corresponding to the T2 moving scan in the registration). The experimental setup was the following: 39 T1-weighted scans (1 mm isotropic resolution) with 36 manually labeled brain structures were independently registered to eight proton density (PD) scans (also 1 mm isotropic) with manual labels for the same set of 36 structures; T1 scans were also available for these eight subjects for evaluation purposes. Six registrations methods were compared, combining two deformation models and three cost functions. The

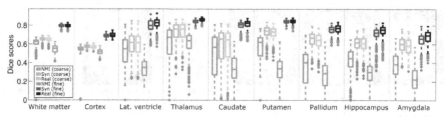

FIGURE 10.5

Boxplot of Dice scores in the registration experiment from [53]. Horizontal box lines indicate the three quartile values. Whiskers extend to the most extreme values within 1.5 times the interquartile range from the ends of the box. Samples beyond those points ("outliers") are marked with crosses.

deformation models were a "coarse" and a "fine" nonlinear registration; the former is a grid of control points with 30 mm spacing and B-spline interpolation; the latter is a nonparametric symmetric diffeomorphic registration method [50] with Gaussian regularization (kernel width 3 mm). The cost functions were: (i) NMI; (ii) LNCC using a synthetic T1 rather the PD scan as fixed image; and (iii) LNCC using the real T1 as fixed image – which represents a ceiling for the performance that the synthesis-based approach may achieve. The synthesis was computed from the paired PD-T1 data in a supervised leave-one-out fashion (i.e., $N = 7$ in training), with a simple exemplar-based method using patches. For evaluation, we used the Dice overlap between the manually labeled structures in the fixed and registered images.

The results for a representative subset of the 36 brain structures are shown in Fig. 10.5. With the coarse deformation model, straight deformation with NMI is almost as good as using the synthetic or real T1s with LNCC for some structures, albeit considerably worse for others (e.g., putamen, pallidum, hippocampus, and amygdala). However, when the high-dimensional nonparametric fine model is used, NMI falters and performs worse than with the coarse model. On the other hand, LNCC with both synthetic and real data takes advantage of the additional flexibility to yield greatly improved Dice scores, compared with the coarse version. This creates a huge gap between the two cost functions in this fine nonlinear deformation setup – over 40 Dice points, in some cases. Remarkably, and even with a simple pre-deep-learning technique, supervised synthesis yields results that are only approximately one Dice point lower than those produced by the real T1 scans.

Similar results have been reported in the literature. For example, Chen et al. [54,55] used probabilistic patch regression to synthesize MR contrasts to improve inter-modality brain MRI registration. As in our work, they also demonstrated an improvement over the use of information theory metrics. Moreover, they showed that additional performance could be obtained by synthesizing in both directions (e.g., T1 from T2, and T2 from T1) and then using intra-modality registration with two channels. More recently, even better results in inter-modality registration of brain MRI have obtained with synthesis techniques based on modern CNNs [56].

10.2.4 **Other applications of synthesis-based registration**

Synthesis-based, inter-modality registration has also found application in other domains. One example is radiation therapy planning: while CT is the modality of choice for dose calculation, MRI is more suitable for delineation of the organs at risk in many body regions. Combining the two modalities requires registration, which can be difficult with mutual information. Synthesis-based registration has been successfully applied in this context, e.g., by Roy et al. [57] in brain imaging (using patch matching), or Cao et al. [58,59] in prostate (using regression trees).

Another appealing application of synthesis is the registration of pre-operative and intra-operative images of different modalities. This scenario is often particularly challenging for mutual information, due to the large deformations of tissue that usually occur in surgical procedures. For example, Onefrey et al. [60] used synthesis based on principal component analysis and dictionary learning to register pre-operative prostate MRI to intra-procedure trans-rectal ultrasound. In the context of liver cancer, Wei et al. [61,62] used adversarial training [63,64] (which enables synthesis with unpaired data) to synthesize CT from pre-operative MRI and register it to intra-operative CT images.

In addition to bridging the domain gap, the synthesis step can also improve registration by removing undesired elements or artifacts from the images. For example, in the aforementioned liver surgery application, Wei et al. inpainted the resection probe in the intra-operative CT to improve the registration to the pre-operative MRI (via the synthetic CT). In a similar fashion, Yang et al. [65] used a deep variational convolutional encoder–decoder network to improve the registration of brain MRI scans of subject with tumors to atlases, by learning a mapping from pathological to quasi-normal images.

Finally, we would like to emphasize that synthesis-based, inter-modality registration is not exclusive to *in vivo* imaging of the human body. For example, Bogovic et al. [66] used boosted decision trees to register microscopy images of *drosophila melanogaster* (fruit fly) brains with genetically encoded calcium indicators to an atlas stained with *nc82* (a monoclonal antibody). Another example is our previous work [67], where we used a simultaneous registration-synthesis framework based on random forests to register histological sections of human brain samples to *ex vivo* MRI scans.

10.3 **Segmentation**

10.3.1 **Background**

Image segmentation is the process of partitioning an image into multiple regions, assigning to them a set of unique labels. Every application in computer vision and collateral fields requires the segmentation process to generalize and therefore to deal with images from multiple sources. In medical imaging, segmentation plays a fundamental role as it is the basis for quantitative assessments (e.g., volumetry) and more advanced processing (e.g., anatomy-constrained tractography). The automation of the procedure is also crucial, as manual labeling of the different biological tissues in a given modality is often a very time-consuming task that requires specific expertise. As a result, research or clinical centers may not have the required expertise, and even where the expertise is available, the manual nature of the task may be problematic in terms of scalability and reproducibility.

Early image segmentation techniques (e.g., histogram-based thresholding [68], clustering-based methods [69], edge detection-based methods [70], region-based methods [71], or graph-based methods [72]) are suitable for simple images, but do not generalize well, and their performance depends heavily on the complexity of the segmentation task. As mentioned in Section 10.1 above, a representative method with reasonable robustness across related modalities has been the combination of probabilistic atlas priors and GMM [12,73] in brain MRI segmentation. This is a flexible approach, capable of being adaptive to different contrasts but also of taking into account specific priors. In addition, it uses a shared coordinate system given by the atlas and therefore allows to achieve spatial correspondence between all the images, with the consequent advantage of being able to analyze variability across the population [29]. For these reasons, it has become almost a standard in neuroimaging [74], despite being at times computationally expensive, at least compared to more recent solutions based on deep learning.

Segmentation is often closely linked to image registration. As explained in the previous section, registration can be used to align two images in order to propagate the labels from the moving image to the target (as in Fig. 10.3c), reducing the segmentation problem to the registration one. If multiple sets of labels (or atlases) are available, this procedure can be extended to the family of approaches called multi-atlas segmentation [25]. The most common of these approaches consists in registering all the available atlases to the target image, propagating the respective labels and then assigning the final labels with a label fusion algorithm [33] (e.g., majority voting, which amounts to selecting the most frequent label for each voxel).

The relationship between registration and segmentation could actually be bidirectional, since it is also possible to use segmentation to aid registration: if the labels for both images are already known, the boundaries defined by the labels can be used to inform the registration process. An example is given by the boundary-based registration technique [75], where white matter boundaries in brain images are used to compute white-gray matter intensity differences that are subsequently maximized to match the interface to a new brain scan.

As a final alternative, segmentation can be approached as a classification problem, where the goal is to assign an appropriate label to each pixel or voxel on the basis of its intensity or texture. Using a training set, a general mapping for the labels can be learned through several machine learning techniques, including support vector machine (SVM) [76], random forests [77], or neural networks. Currently, the most common way to perform segmentation tasks is through CNNs (for a review, see [78]), which have the advantage of being very fast at test time. However, focusing the classification problem on intensity or texture features is not without issues, as we will see shortly.

10.3.2 **Domain gap and synthesis-based solutions**

Here we focus on the machine learning methods that dominate the segmentation literature, and therefore through the lens of voxel classification problems. Regardless of how one approaches the problem, potential issues can arise in both intra- and inter-modality scenarios due to domain gap, i.e., the fact that models fitted to data collected in one domain often generalize poorly to other domains:

- In the intra-modality case, variations in the acquisition protocol could introduce substantial differences in image intensity distributions (as seen in Fig. 10.2) and lead to label misassignments regardless of how the problem is approached. This scenario is common not only in studies across multiple research sites, but also whenever patients with anatomical alterations are involved, where hyper-intensities or hypo-intensities may be present;
- In the inter-modality case, two images have been acquired using different modalities, and the labels defined on one modality (e.g., MRI) are required to segment the other modality (e.g., CT); in this scenario, registration-based segmentation is affected by the issues already discussed for inter-modality registration in Section 10.2, while the classification-based approach is ill-posed given that the target image to segment does not share the same modality with the training set.

Intra-modality variation. Let us first focus on the intra-modality variation issue, and specifically on the problem of segmenting images acquired either with the same modality but potentially different parameters or images acquired with different types of contrast within the same modality (e.g., different MRI sequences). From the brief overview of segmentation approaches, there is already a solution for this problem, and it is probabilistic atlas-based segmentation. There are however two main drawbacks. The first, as mentioned, is time consumption, ranging from 30 minutes (e.g., SPM) to a few hours (e.g., FreeSurfer) of processing. The second is the suitability for specific applications in medical imaging: despite the success in brain segmentation, applications outside the scope of neuroimaging have been explored in the literature with different levels of success. For instance, in abdominal CT there are studies that achieved multi-organ segmentation through a probabilistic atlas [79,80], although again with relatively high computation times (compared with CNNs). The literature is sparser for thoracic imaging, although a study on multi-atlas segmentation for cardiac applications showed that small structures may be challenging [81]. There are then specific applications where atlases would not be appropriate, as histopathology and microscopy.

Modern segmentation approaches are based on CNNs, since they are fast and they can be trained for any specific application in medical imaging [78], from MRI to microscopy. However, their specificity is also a drawback: these approaches cannot usually cope with contrast or intensity variations that were not included in the training set. One simple way to overcome this limitation could be to use transfer learning [82,83], where given a network already trained on a source contrast, additional training is carried out on a set of images with the target contrast, leveraging data augmentation to avoid over-fitting [84]. This approach is not only usually less

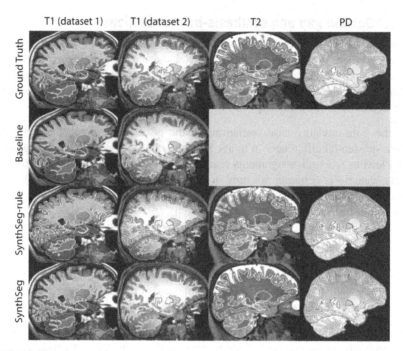

FIGURE 10.6

SynthSeg [86]: segmentation examples for each method and MRI sequence. The baseline consisted in using the segmentation as learned on the first T1 dataset; such baseline is not able to cope with the other sequences.

time- and data-consuming than training a network from scratch, but also can leverage fundamental features already learned in the original training [85]. Unfortunately, one major drawback is still the need for enough data with manually delineated labels for each desired contrast.

A recent approach our group proposed leverages both CNNs and probabilistic generative models to overcome the contrast and intensity dependencies that affect most approaches [86]. This approach is called *SynthSeg*: the general idea is to train a neural network to segment images with random contrast. To generate those images, a set of label maps is deformed and then used to generate an image, where each label is sampled from a different random Gaussian distribution. Blurring and random bias field noise are added to the images to respectively mimic partial volume effects and overall replicate the acquisition process. With this set of label maps and the related synthetic images, a CNN is trained to predict the label map from a given image. In this manner, the overall approach is unsupervised, as it does not require labeled data, but uniquely sets of labels.

We report here some examples of *SynthSeg* on different datasets (Fig. 10.6), including: two different T1-weighted datasets, a T2-weighted dataset, and a skull-stripped, PD-weighted dataset (more details are available in [86]). We also report the related comparisons against: (1) the ground-truth segmentation, (2) supervised segmentation based on only one dataset (baseline), and (3) a different implementation of *SynthSeg* (*SynthSeg-rule*), where the generative model has prior information about the test image intensities. When comparing the segmentation results, one can remarkably see how *SynthSeg* labels resemble the ground truth and how it outperforms segmentation based on a single dataset. Interestingly, *SynthSeg* also performs slightly better than *SynthSeg-rule*: this could appear as a counter-intuitive result, but it seems to indicate that the random contrasts in the generative model allows the CNN to learn to segment unexpected contrasts and therefore being more effective with unseen data.

Inter-modality variation. In this case, the labels are defined on one modality but required for a different modality. This is a harder problem, and the most common solution is the use of inter-modality nonlinear registration as the basis to propagate the labels. A completely different approach would be a synthesis-based one, with the advantage of avoiding registration, especially in those cases where the registration can be challenging (e.g., MRI-CT).

An example of such an approach has been described by Huo et al. [6]. The approach is based on generative adversarial networks (GANs) [63], specifically on cycle-consistent adversarial networks (*CycleGANs*) [64], which are explained in more detail in Chapter 7. Their general application is image translation problems: given two related but unpaired image sets the goal is to find a mapping that associates to each image from one set their correspondent representation in the other, which may not exist (as the sets are unpaired).

As they are based on unpaired data, *CycleGANs* offer an interesting way to tackle problems beyond image translation. The literature has several examples where variations of these networks are used for a wide range of applications, such as domain adaption [87], denoising [88], and data augmentation [89]. In this application to segmentation, Huo et al. [6] extended the *CycleGAN* architecture (two generator networks and two discriminator networks) adding a segmentation network for the target modality and including as an additional input a set of labels for the source modality. This novel architecture (showed in Fig. 10.7) is called *SynSeg-Net*. The training process is happening on the two distinct paths highlighted in Fig. 10.7: on the path starting from the source modality, the image is fed to the related generator to obtain the "translated" one in the target domain; the translated image is then fed to both the segmentation network, the discriminator one and the other generator network. The path starting from the target modality involves instead only the related generator and discriminator networks. In this overall process, one is able to take into account three different components in the overall loss function: as in the original *CycleGAN* architecture, one can minimize differences between the "translated" images and the real ones in the opposite domain (GAN losses), as well as the differences between the images "translated" twice (e.g., source→target→source) and the real ones in the same domain (cycle-consistency losses); in addition, one can also minimize the differences between the output of the segmentation network and the ground-truth labels. It must

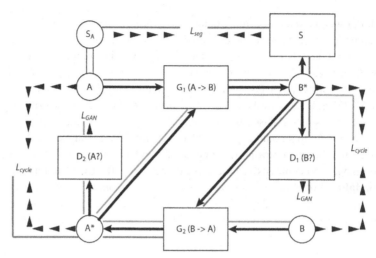

FIGURE 10.7

Schematic architecture of *SynSeg-Net* [6], with highlighted the two training paths: the red (dark gray in print version) path represents the workflow for a real image from the source modality A, while the green (mid gray in print version) path represents the workflow for a real image from the target modality B. The black arrowheads show the contributions to each of the loss function components. This is an example of training path: starting from A (top-left) a given image is fed to the first generator (G1) to obtain the "translated" image in the target domain (B*); B* is then fed to three networks: the segmentation network (S), the first discriminator (D1) and the second generator (G2); G2 gives the image "translated" twice.

be mentioned that for testing purposes, and therefore for the ultimate practical use, the only network needed is the segmentation one.

The specific application here is the segmentation of abdominal CT images while the labels have been defined on MRI images. Their results remarkably show how the Dice similarity coefficient between the *SynSeg-Net* labels and the manually defined ones is comparable to what a CNN could achieve in a supervised setting, with the tremendous advantage of not requiring actual labels in the target domain. It is important to highlight that this is the most representative case for the rationale behind synthesis-based segmentation: the labels are delineated using MRI data as the contrast makes the task easier for a human expert, but depending on the scenario (e.g., emergency-room patients) CT acquisitions will be preferred and would benefit from segmentation as well.

Interestingly, this last approach once again offers us the chance to show how intertwined segmentation and registration can be. In a work we presented in 2019 [90], we used a similar architecture, where in addition to the original *CycleGAN* components we added two segmentation networks, one for each modality, making the architecture symmetric. Although the proof of concept is the same, the application is different: the goal of this network is to actually generate synthetic images to reduce a difficult inter-modality registration problem (histology to MRI) to an intra-modality one, with the segmentation acting as an additional constraint for the learning process. Once completed the training, one of the two generator networks is used to obtain a synthetic image that can then be nonlinearly registered to the respective image in the other domain. Using manually placed landmarks, the results showed lower registration errors compared to direct nonlinear registration.

10.4 Other directions and perspectives

In this last section, we would like to discuss two current research directions related to registration and segmentation where synthesis is a potential game-changer.

The first one is harmonization. We hinted in Section 10.3 at this problem when discussing intra-modality problems where there is significant contrast variation. More in general, harmonization becomes an important factor when data acquired from different centers and with different equipment is pooled together. This is once again not only the case for multi-center studies, but also a recurrent condition when assembling large datasets, for example, for machine learning purposes. There is a growing literature of approaches designed to retrieve a common contrast for images acquired for example on two different MRI scanners. An example based on CNNs is the approach proposed by Dewey et al. [91]. This approach still requires paired training data, that in the scenario of multi-center studies could be challenging to satisfy. Relying once again on cycle-consistency, Modanwal et al. [92] proposed a solution that is able to handle unpaired data and overcome the limitations of the original *CycleGAN* architecture through a patch-focused discriminator. Moving towards generalization, in both the cases of CNNs and adversarial architectures, the design tends to become someway cumbersome if one needs to harmonize three or more datasets, as one would need to train one network for each pair. A possible solution is given by a recent approach called image style transfer [93], where a tailored CNN is able to extract the style (in terms of texture and contrast) from a source image and apply it to a target image, originally for artistic purposes. Using a similar approach, Ma et al. [94] were able to minimize differences in brightness, contrast, and texture in cardiac data from different sources.

The second research direction we would like to discuss is super-resolution, i.e., acquisition or processing techniques that are able to go beyond the maximum spatial resolution of the considered medium [95] (more on super-resolution in Chapter 12). In terms of processing, an emblematic example is exploiting self-similarity properties to learn a mapping between a high resolution image and a down-sampled version of itself, using, for example, random forests [96] or neural networks [97]. As it is the case in this example, the usual assumption in these approaches is that the high-resolution and low-resolution images belong to the same modality. However, an important extension would be the mapping between a high-resolution modality and a different low-resolution one. This is a more common scenario than one would think:

as more data from large-scale microscopy becomes available, it becomes easier to build high-resolution atlases and templates.

For segmentation purposes, as the application of such atlases will be on images with inherently lower-resolution modalities, several limitations arise. A well-known one is the partial volume effect, where a voxel includes contribution from two different tissues (i.e., two different labels in the high-resolution atlas). For this specific problem, one can once again rely on the combination of GMM-based generative models and CNNs, leveraging on the knowledge of just known sets of labels. This approach, similar to *SynthSeg* and called *PV-SynthSeg* [86], serves well the purpose of segmentation. However, the ultimate goal of super-resolution is to provide the actual images and current research is going in this direction: using weakly-supervised or unsupervised approaches, there are already the first successful attempts at synthesize super-resolution medical images from one low-resolution modality to a high-resolution related modality [98,99]. As the availability of paired data is once again a rare case, future studies shall leverage architectures based on adversarial learning and cycle-consistency [100].

To conclude this chapter, it is important to mention that improving registration and segmentation through synthesis plays an important role in the overall landscape of biomedical image analysis, as showed in the considerations on harmonization and super-resolution techniques. The applications presented in the next chapters will leverage the concepts discussed so far and provide a concrete context for synthesis-based approaches, both in terms of specific image modalities and more advanced analyses.

References

[1] R. Bar-Shalom, N. Yefremov, L. Guralnik, D. Gaitini, A. Frenkel, A. Kuten, H. Altman, Z. Keidar, O. Israel, Clinical performance of PET/CT in evaluation of cancer: additional value for diagnostic imaging and patient management, Journal of Nuclear Medicine 44 (8) (2003) 1200–1209.

[2] G. Antoch, J. Stattaus, A.T. Nemat, S. Marnitz, T. Beyer, H. Kuehl, A. Bockisch, J.F. Debatin, L.S. Freudenberg, Non-small cell lung cancer: dual-modality PET/CT in preoperative staging, Radiology 229 (2) (2003) 526–533.

[3] J. Pichat, J.E. Iglesias, T. Yousry, S. Ourselin, M. Modat, A survey of methods for 3D histology reconstruction, Medical Image Analysis 46 (2018) 73–105.

[4] J. Mollink, M. Kleinnijenhuis, A.-M. van Cappellen van Walsum, S.N. Sotiropoulos, M. Cottaar, C. Mirfin, M.P. Heinrich, M. Jenkinson, M. Pallebage-Gamarallage, O. Ansorge, et al., Evaluating fibre orientation dispersion in white matter: comparison of diffusion MRI, histology and polarized light imaging, NeuroImage 157 (2017) 561–574.

[5] J.P.W. Pluim, J.B.A. Maintz, M.A. Viergever, Mutual-information-based registration of medical images: a survey, IEEE Transactions on Medical Imaging 22 (8) (2003) 986–1004.

[6] Y. Huo, Z. Xu, H. Moon, S. Bao, A. Assad, T.K. Moyo, M.R. Savona, R.G. Abramson, B.A. Landman Synseg-net, Synthetic segmentation without target modality ground truth, IEEE Transactions on Medical Imaging 38 (4) (2018) 1016–1025.

[7] A.H. Coons, H.J. Creech, R. Norman Jones, Immunological properties of an antibody containing a fluorescent group, Proceedings of the Society for Experimental Biology and Medicine 47 (2) (1941) 200–202.

[8] J. Borovec, J. Kybic, I. Arganda-Carreras, D.V. Sorokin, G. Bueno, A.V. Khvostikov, S. Bakas, E.I-C. Chang, S. Heldmann, et al., ANHIR: automatic non-rigid histological image registration challenge, IEEE Transactions on Medical Imaging (2020).

[9] J.P. Mugler III, J.R. Brookeman, Three-dimensional magnetization-prepared rapid gradient-echo imaging (3D MP RAGE), Magnetic Resonance in Medicine 15 (1) (1990) 152–157.

[10] B.E. Bejnordi, G. Litjens, N. Timofeeva, I. Otte-Höller, A. Homeyer, N. Karssemeijer, J.A.W.M. van der Laak, Stain specific standardization of whole-slide histopathological images, IEEE Transactions on Medical Imaging 35 (2) (2015) 404–415.

[11] M. Mancini, A. Casamitjana, L. Peter, E. Robinson, S. Crampsie, D.L. Thomas, J.L. Holton, Z. Jaunmuktane, J.E. Iglesias, A multimodal computational pipeline for 3D histology of the human brain, Scientific Reports (2020).

[12] J. Ashburner, K.J. Friston, Unified segmentation, NeuroImage 26 (3) (2005) 839–851.

[13] O. Ronneberger, P. Fischer, T. Brox, U-net: convolutional networks for biomedical image segmentation, in: International Conference on Medical Image Computing and Computer-Assisted Intervention, Springer, 2015, pp. 234–241.

[14] L. Gottesfeld Brown, A survey of image registration techniques, ACM Computing Surveys 24 (4) (1992) 325–376.

[15] B. Zitova, J. Flusser, Image registration methods: a survey, Image and Vision Computing 21 (11) (2003) 977–1000.

[16] R. Szeliski, Computer Vision: Algorithms and Applications, Springer Science & Business Media, 2010.

[17] M. Brown, D.G. Lowe, Automatic panoramic image stitching using invariant features, International Journal of Computer Vision 74 (1) (2007) 59–73.

[18] B.D. Lucas, T. Kanade, et al., An iterative image registration technique with an application to stereo vision, 1981.

[19] C. Nuth, A. Kääb, Co-registration and bias corrections of satellite elevation data sets for quantifying glacier thickness change, The Cryosphere 5 (1) (2011) 271–290.

[20] J.B.A. Maintz, M.A. Viergever, A survey of medical image registration, Medical Image Analysis 2 (1) (1998) 1–36.

[21] A. Sotiras, C. Davatzikos, N. Paragios, Deformable medical image registration: a survey, IEEE Transactions on Medical Imaging 32 (7) (2013) 1153–1190.

[22] M.A. Viergever, J.B.A. Maintz, S. Klein, K. Murphy, M. Staring, J.P.W. Pluim, A survey of medical image registration–under review, Medical Image Analysis 33 (2016) 140–144.

[23] A.P. James, B.V. Dasarathy, Medical image fusion: a survey of the state of the art, Information Fusion 19 (2014) 4–19.

[24] L. Wang, J. Traub, S. Weidert, S.M. Heining, E. Euler, N. Navab, Parallax-free intraoperative X-ray image stitching, Medical Image Analysis 14 (5) (2010) 674–686.

[25] T. Rohlfing, C.R. Maurer Jr, W.G. O'Dell, J. Zhong, Modeling liver motion and deformation during the respiratory cycle using intensity-based nonrigid registration of gated MR images, Medical Physics 31 (3) (2004) 427–432.

[26] Y. Yin, E.A. Hoffman, C.-L. Lin, Mass preserving nonrigid registration of CT lung images using cubic B-spline, Medical Physics 36 (9 Part 1) (2009) 4213–4222.

[27] P.A. Freeborough, N.C. Fox, Modeling brain deformations in Alzheimer disease by fluid registration of serial 3D MR images, Journal of Computer Assisted Tomography 22 (5) (1998) 838–843.

[28] M.K. Chung, K.J. Worsley, T. Paus, C. Cherif, D.L. Collins, J.N. Giedd, J.L. Rapoport, A.C. Evans, A unified statistical approach to deformation-based morphometry, NeuroImage 14 (3) (2001) 595–606.

[29] J. Ashburner, K.J. Friston, Voxel-based morphometry—the methods, NeuroImage 11 (6) (2000) 805–821.

[30] E.M. van Rikxoort, B. de Hoop, M.A. Viergever, M. Prokop, B. van Ginneken, Automatic lung segmentation from thoracic computed tomography scans using a hybrid approach with error detection, Medical Physics 36 (7) (2009) 2934–2947.

[31] P. Aljabar, R.A. Heckemann, A. Hammers, J.V. Hajnal, D. Rueckert, Multi-atlas based segmentation of brain images: atlas selection and its effect on accuracy, NeuroImage 46 (3) (2009) 726–738.

[32] I. Isgum, M. Staring, A. Rutten, M. Prokop, M.A. Viergever, B. van Ginneken, Multi-atlas-based segmentation with local decision fusion—application to cardiac and aortic segmentation in CT scans, IEEE Transactions on Medical Imaging 28 (7) (2009) 1000–1010.

[33] J.E. Iglesias, M.R. Sabuncu, Multi-atlas segmentation of biomedical images: a survey, Medical Image Analysis 24 (1) (2015) 205–219.

[34] S. Joshi, B. Davis, M. Jomier, G. Gerig, Unbiased diffeomorphic atlas construction for computational anatomy, NeuroImage 23 (2004) S151–S160.

[35] R. Fletcher, Practical Methods of Optimization, John Wiley & Sons, 2013.

[36] H. Robbins, S. Monro, A stochastic approximation method, The Annals of Mathematical Statistics (1951) 400–407.

[37] J.R. Shewchuk, et al., An introduction to the conjugate gradient method without the agonizing pain, 1994.

[38] R.H. Byrd, P. Lu, J. Nocedal, C. Zhu, A limited memory algorithm for bound constrained optimization, SIAM Journal on Scientific Computing 16 (5) (1995) 1190–1208.

[39] G. Balakrishnan, A. Zhao, M.R. Sabuncu, J. Guttag, A.V. Dalca, Voxelmorph: a learning framework for deformable medical image registration, IEEE Transactions on Medical Imaging 38 (8) (2019) 1788–1800.

[40] B.D. de Vos, F.F. Berendsen, M.A. Viergever, H. Sokooti, M. Staring, I. Išgum, A deep learning framework for unsupervised affine and deformable image registration, Medical Image Analysis 52 (2019) 128–143.

[41] J.-P. Thirion, Image matching as a diffusion process: an analogy with Maxwell's demons, Medical Image Analysis 2 (3) (1998) 243–260.

[42] V. Arsigny, O. Commowick, X. Pennec, N. Ayache, A log-Euclidean framework for statistics on diffeomorphisms, in: International Conference on Medical Image Computing and Computer-Assisted Intervention, Springer, 2006, pp. 924–931.

[43] M.F. Beg, M.I. Miller, A. Trouvé, L. Younes, Computing large deformation metric mappings via geodesic flows of diffeomorphisms, International Journal of Computer Vision 61 (2) (2005) 139–157.

[44] J. Ashburner, K.J. Friston, Diffeomorphic registration using geodesic shooting and Gauss–Newton optimisation, NeuroImage 55 (3) (2011) 954–967.

[45] K.J. Friston, J. Ashburner, C.D. Frith, J.-B. Poline, J.D. Heather, R.S.J. Frackowiak, Spatial registration and normalization of images, Human Brain Mapping 3 (3) (1995) 165–189.

[46] D. Rueckert, L.I. Sonoda, C. Hayes, D.L.G. Hill, M.O. Leach, D.J. Hawkes, Non-rigid registration using free-form deformations: application to breast MR images, IEEE Transactions on Medical Imaging 18 (8) (1999) 712–721.

[47] D.G. Lowe, Object recognition from local scale-invariant features, in: Proceedings of the Seventh IEEE International Conference on Computer Vision, vol. 2, IEEE, 1999, pp. 1150–1157.

[48] D.G. Lowe, Distinctive image features from scale-invariant keypoints, International Journal of Computer Vision 60 (2) (2004) 91–110.

[49] R.C. Gonzalez, R.E. Woods, S.L. Eddins, Digital Image Processing, Prentice Hall, 2002.

[50] B.B. Avants, C.L. Epstein, M. Grossman, J.C. Gee, Symmetric diffeomorphic image registration with cross-correlation: evaluating automated labeling of elderly and neurodegenerative brain, Medical Image Analysis 12 (1) (2008) 26–41.

[51] W.M. Wells III, P. Viola, H. Atsumi, S. Nakajima, R. Kikinis, Multi-modal volume registration by maximization of mutual information, Medical Image Analysis 1 (1) (1996) 35–51.

[52] F. Maes, A. Collignon, D. Vandermeulen, G. Marchal, P. Suetens, Multimodality image registration by maximization of mutual information, IEEE Transactions on Medical Imaging 16 (2) (1997) 187–198.

[53] J.E. Iglesias, E. Konukoglu, D. Zikic, B. Glocker, K. Van Leemput, B. Fischl, Is synthesizing MRI contrast useful for inter-modality analysis?, in: International Conference on Medical Image Computing and Computer-Assisted Intervention, Springer, 2013, pp. 631–638.

[54] M. Chen, A. Jog, A. Carass, J.L. Prince, Using image synthesis for multi-channel registration of different image modalities, in: Medical Imaging 2015: Image Processing, vol. 9413, International Society for Optics and Photonics, 2015, p. 94131Q.

[55] M. Chen, A. Carass, A. Jog, J. Lee, S. Roy, J.L. Prince, Cross contrast multi-channel image registration using image synthesis for MR brain images, Medical Image Analysis 36 (2017) 2–14.

[56] X. Liu, D. Jiang, M. Wang, Z. Song, Image synthesis-based multi-modal image registration framework by using deep fully convolutional networks, Medical & Biological Engineering & Computing 57 (5) (2019) 1037–1048.

[57] S. Roy, A. Carass, A. Jog, J.L. Prince, J. Lee, MR to CT registration of brains using image synthesis, in: Medical Imaging 2014: Image Processing, vol. 9034, International Society for Optics and Photonics, 2014, p. 903419.

[58] X. Cao, J. Yang, Y. Gao, Y. Guo, G. Wu, D. Shen, Dual-core steered non-rigid registration for multi-modal images via bi-directional image synthesis, Medical Image Analysis 41 (2017) 18–31.

[59] X. Cao, J. Yang, Y. Gao, Q. Wang, D. Shen, Region-adaptive deformable registration of CT/MRI pelvic images via learning-based image synthesis, IEEE Transactions on Image Processing 27 (7) (2018) 3500–3512.

[60] J.A. Onofrey, I. Oksuz, S. Sarkar, R. Venkataraman, L.H. Staib, X. Papademetris, MRI-TRUS image synthesis with application to image-guided prostate intervention, in: International Workshop on Simulation and Synthesis in Medical Imaging, Springer, 2016, pp. 157–166.

[61] D. Wei, S. Ahmad, J. Huo, W. Peng, Y. Ge, Z. Xue, P.-T. Yap, W. Li, D. Shen, Q. Wang, Synthesis and inpainting-based MR-CT registration for image-guided thermal ablation of liver tumors, in: International Conference on Medical Image Computing and Computer-Assisted Intervention, Springer, 2019, pp. 512–520.

[62] D. Wei, S. Ahmad, J. Huo, P. Huang, P.-T. Yap, Z. Xue, J. Sun, W. Li, D. Shen, Q. Wang, SLIR: Synthesis, localization, inpainting, and registration for image-guided thermal ablation of liver tumors, Medical Image Analysis 65 (2020) 101763.

[63] I. Goodfellow, J. Pouget-Abadie, M. Mirza, B. Xu, D. Warde-Farley, S. Ozair, A. Courville, Y. Bengio, Generative adversarial nets, in: Advances in Neural Information Processing Systems, 2014, pp. 2672–2680.

[64] J.-Y. Zhu, T. Park, P. Isola, A.A. Efros, Unpaired image-to-image translation using cycle-consistent adversarial networks, in: Proceedings of the IEEE International Conference on Computer Vision, 2017, pp. 2223–2232.

[65] X. Yang, X. Han, E. Park, S. Aylward, R. Kwitt, M. Niethammer, Registration of pathological images, in: International Workshop on Simulation and Synthesis in Medical Imaging, Springer, 2016, pp. 97–107.

[66] J.A. Bogovic, P. Hanslovsky, A. Wong, S. Saalfeld, Robust registration of calcium images by learned contrast synthesis, in: 2016 IEEE 13th International Symposium on Biomedical Imaging (ISBI), IEEE, 2016, pp. 1123–1126.

[67] J.E. Iglesias, M. Modat, L. Peter, A. Stevens, R. Annunziata, T. Vercauteren, E. Lein, B. Fischl, S. Ourselin, Alzheimer's Disease Neuroimaging Initiative, et al., Joint registration and synthesis using a probabilistic model for alignment of MRI and histological sections, Medical Image Analysis 50 (2018) 127–144.

[68] M.E. Yüksel, M. Borlu, Accurate segmentation of dermoscopic images by image thresholding based on type-2 fuzzy logic, IEEE Transactions on Fuzzy Systems 17 (4) (2009) 976–982.

[69] D. Comaniciu, P. Meer, Mean shift: a robust approach toward feature space analysis, IEEE Transactions on Pattern Analysis and Machine Intelligence 24 (5) (2002) 603–619.

[70] J. Wang, L. Ju, X. Wang, An edge-weighted centroidal Voronoi tessellation model for image segmentation, IEEE Transactions on Image Processing 18 (8) (2009) 1844–1858.

[71] L. Garcia Ugarriza, E. Saber, S.R. Vantaram, V. Amuso, M. Shaw, R. Bhaskar, Automatic image segmentation by dynamic region growth and multiresolution merging, IEEE Transactions on Image Processing 18 (10) (2009) 2275–2288.

[72] Y. Boykov, O. Veksler, R. Zabih, Fast approximate energy minimization via graph cuts, IEEE Transactions on Pattern Analysis and Machine Intelligence 23 (11) (2001) 1222–1239.

[73] K. Van Leemput, F. Maes, D. Vandermeulen, P. Suetens, Automated model-based tissue classification of MR images of the brain, IEEE Transactions on Medical Imaging 18 (10) (1999) 897–908.

[74] J. Ashburner, SPM: a history, NeuroImage 62 (2) (2012) 791–800.

[75] D.N. Greve, B. Fischl, Accurate and robust brain image alignment using boundary-based registration, NeuroImage 48 (1) (2009) 63–72.

[76] H.-Y. Yang, X.-Y. Wang, Q.-Y. Wang, X.-J. Zhang, LS-SVM based image segmentation using color and texture information, Journal of Visual Communication and Image Representation 23 (7) (2012) 1095–1112.

[77] V. Lempitsky, M. Verhoek, J.A. Noble, A. Blake, Random forest classification for automatic delineation of myocardium in real-time 3D echocardiography, in: International Conference on Functional Imaging and Modeling of the Heart, Springer, 2009, pp. 447–456.

[78] S.M. Anwar, M. Majid, A. Qayyum, M. Awais, M. Alnowami, M.K. Khan, Medical image analysis using convolutional neural networks: a review, Journal of Medical Systems 42 (11) (2018) 226.

[79] H. Park, P.H. Bland, C.R. Meyer, Construction of an abdominal probabilistic atlas and its application in segmentation, IEEE Transactions on Medical Imaging 22 (4) (2003) 483–492.

[80] C. Chu, M. Oda, T. Kitasaka, K. Misawa, M. Fujiwara, Y. Hayashi, Y. Nimura, D. Rueckert, K. Mori, Multi-organ segmentation based on spatially-divided probabilistic atlas from 3D abdominal CT images, in: International Conference on Medical Image Computing and Computer-Assisted Intervention, Springer, 2013, pp. 165–172.

[81] R. Finnegan, J. Dowling, E.-S. Koh, S. Tang, J. Otton, G. Delaney, V. Batumalai, C. Luo, P. Atluri, A. Satchithanandha, et al., Feasibility of multi-atlas cardiac segmentation from thoracic planning CT in a probabilistic framework, Physics in Medicine and Biology 64 (8) (2019) 085006.

[82] S.J. Pan, Q. Yang, A survey on transfer learning, IEEE Transactions on Knowledge and Data Engineering 22 (10) (2009) 1345–1359.

[83] G. Litjens, T. Kooi, B.E. Bejnordi, A.A.A. Setio, F. Ciompi, M. Ghafoorian, J.A. van der Laak, B. van Ginneken, C.I. Sánchez, A survey on deep learning in medical image analysis, Medical Image Analysis 42 (2017) 60–88.

[84] C. Shorten, T.M. Khoshgoftaar, A survey on image data augmentation for deep learning, Journal of Big Data 6 (1) (2019) 60.

[85] D. Soekhoe, P. van der Putten, A. Plaat, On the impact of data set size in transfer learning using deep neural networks, in: International Symposium on Intelligent Data Analysis, Springer, 2016, pp. 50–60.

[86] B. Billot, D. Greve, K. Van Leemput, B. Fischl, J.E. Iglesias, A.V. Dalca, A learning strategy for contrast-agnostic MRI segmentation, in: MIDL, 2020.

[87] J. Hoffman, E. Tzeng, T. Park, J.-Y. Zhu, P. Isola, K. Saenko, A. Efros, T. Darrell, Cycada: cycle-consistent adversarial domain adaptation, in: International Conference on Machine Learning, in: PMLR, 2018, pp. 1989–1998.

[88] D. Engin, A. Genç, H.K. Ekenel, Cycle-dehaze: enhanced CycleGAN for single image dehazing, in: Proceedings of the IEEE Conference on Computer Vision and Pattern Recognition Workshops, 2018, pp. 825–833.

[89] V. Sandfort, K. Yan, P.J. Pickhardt, R.M. Summers, Data augmentation using generative adversarial networks (CycleGAN) to improve generalizability in CT segmentation tasks, Scientific Reports 9 (1) (2019) 1–9.

[90] M. Mancini, Y. Huo, B. Landman, J.E. Iglesias, Segmentation-aware adversarial synthesis for registration of histology to MRI, in: Proceedings of the International Society Magnetic Resonance in Medicine, 2019.

[91] B.E. Dewey, C. Zhao, J.C. Reinhold, A. Carass, K.C. Fitzgerald, E.S. Sotirchos, S. Saidha, J. Oh, D.L. Pham, P.A. Calabresi, et al., Deepharmony: a deep learning approach to contrast harmonization across scanner changes, Magnetic Resonance Imaging 64 (2019) 160–170.

[92] G. Modanwal, A. Vellal, M. Buda, M.A. Mazurowski, MRI image harmonization using cycle-consistent generative adversarial network, in: Medical Imaging 2020: Computer-Aided Diagnosis, vol. 11314, International Society for Optics and Photonics, 2020, p. 1131413.

[93] L.A. Gatys, A.S. Ecker, M. Bethge, Image style transfer using convolutional neural networks, in: Proceedings of the IEEE Conference on Computer Vision and Pattern Recognition, 2016, pp. 2414–2423.

[94] C. Ma, Z. Ji, M. Gao, Neural style transfer improves 3D cardiovascular MR image segmentation on inconsistent data, in: International Conference on Medical Image Computing and Computer-Assisted Intervention, Springer, 2019, pp. 128–136.

[95] Z. Wang, J. Chen, S.C.H. Hoi, Deep learning for image super-resolution: a survey, IEEE Transactions on Pattern Analysis and Machine Intelligence (2020).

[96] D.C. Alexander, D. Zikic, A. Ghosh, R. Tanno, V. Wottschel, J. Zhang, E. Kaden, T.B. Dyrby, S.N. Sotiropoulos, H. Zhang, et al., Image quality transfer and applications in diffusion MRI, NeuroImage 152 (2017) 283–298.

[97] S.B. Blumberg, R. Tanno, I. Kokkinos, D.C. Alexander, Deeper image quality transfer: training low-memory neural networks for 3d images, in: International Conference on Medical Image Computing and Computer-Assisted Intervention, Springer, 2018, pp. 118–125.

[98] Y. Huang, L. Shao, A.F. Frangi, Simultaneous super-resolution and cross-modality synthesis of 3D medical images using weakly-supervised joint convolutional sparse coding, in: Proceedings of the IEEE Conference on Computer Vision and Pattern Recognition, 2017, pp. 6070–6079.

[99] T. Zheng, H. Oda, T. Moriya, T. Sugino, S. Nakamura, M. Oda, M. Mori, H. Takabatake, H. Natori, K. Mori, Multi-modality super-resolution loss for GAN-based super-resolution of clinical CT images using micro CT image database, in: Medical Imaging 2020: Image Processing, vol. 11313, International Society for Optics and Photonics, 2020, p. 1131305.

[100] Y. Yuan, S. Liu, J. Zhang, Y. Zhang, C. Dong, L. Lin, Unsupervised image super-resolution using cycle-in-cycle generative adversarial networks, in: Proceedings of the IEEE Conference on Computer Vision and Pattern Recognition Workshops, 2018, pp. 701–710.

Medical image harmonization through synthesis

11

Blake E. Dewey, Yufan He, Yihao Liu, Lianrui Zuo, and Jerry L. Prince
Department of Electrical and Computer Engineering, Johns Hopkins University, Baltimore, MD,
United States

11.1 Introduction

Medical imaging is crucial to the monitoring and investigation of many disorders of the human body. However, differences in hardware/software implementation and acquisition technique can cause undesired contrast variations in images, producing inconsistent results during analysis [1]. This is especially important in modern image analysis, which focuses heavily on machine learning-based methods, where it is assumed that the testing data are similar to the training data. Consider the example shown in Fig. 11.1, which shows two optical coherence tomography (OCT) acquisitions of the same human retina (left, top two rows) acquired on two different OCT scanners (Spectralis and Cirrus). Even to the untrained eye, these images appear to be of different quality, though they do appear to be depicting the same general anatomy. Given these differences, one can see why a machine learning model, for example, trained on Spectralis images may not be accurate when used (without retraining or fine-tuning) on a Cirrus image. Because of these differences, many methods that are shown to be accurate on a given dataset may not be reliably used on another dataset without significant effort to retrain. We can see this effect by comparing the segmentation of the retinal layers by a deep network trained on Spectralis data, when it is applied to the Cirrus scan in Fig. 11.1 (third row, right side). When compared to the ground-truth segmentation for the Cirrus scan (second row, right side), we can see that there is a clear breakdown in the segmentation results. These segmentations would be unusable in a calculation of relevant biomarkers such as retinal layer thickness. This motivates the need for image harmonization, where test images are "harmonized" to the training data to produce more consistent results.

The concept of harmonization has evolved over many years [2,3], often borrowing from image synthesis [4,5] or statistical concepts in other fields [6,7]. Some of the earliest work on harmonization used histogram equalization, where the input image intensities are altered to make its image histogram match the histogram of a target image (e.g., training data) [8]. Different matching strategies have been proposed, but

Biomedical Image Synthesis and Simulation. https://doi.org/10.1016/B978-0-12-824349-7.00018-9

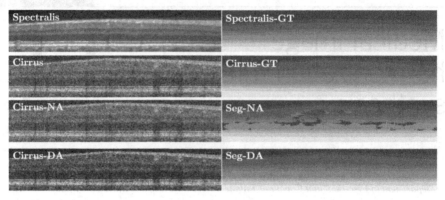

FIGURE 11.1

Cropped macular B-scan images from OCT and corresponding segmentations for a single subject from two different OCT scanners (Cirrus and Spectralis). Rows 1 and 2 show the original images and ground-truth segmentations (GT) from each scanner. Row 3 shows the same Cirrus scan and a naive application (NA) of a deep segmentation network trained on Spectralis data. The bottom row shows the domain-adapted (DA) Cirrus image and the corresponding segmentation.

the entire premise of this approach falls apart when images of significantly different anatomies or those containing pathology are considered [6]. In such cases, matched histograms may not be representative of differences in the image contrast alone and subsequent analysis would potentially be inaccurate. In a different way, statistical modeling has also been considered as a harmonization technique [7,1,9]. In these approaches, volumes of specific segmented regions can be harmonized using mixed-effects or batch effect mitigation techniques, which remove confounding effects like acquisition differences. However, if the initial segmentation is grossly inaccurate, as in the third row of Fig. 11.1, these methods are less effective. In light of the difficulties of global and statistical methods, we turn to image synthesis methods, which are capable of providing a viable solution that generates intensity transformations without depending on any global measures such as histograms or segmentations that are derived before harmonization.

Broadly, medical image synthesis takes input images and uses a model to produce a different contrast or modality based on the input anatomy. Medical image synthesis has its origins in patch-matching and dictionary-based approaches, where exemplar contrast features are learned by the model and used to predict the appearance of a medical image under different conditions. This was commonly used in magnetic resonance imaging (MRI), for example, to create images of missing or corrupted contrasts or even a completely different modality such as computed tomography (CT) [10–12]. Some early synthesis-based harmonization used these more traditional methods [5], but the variety of contrast features quickly stretched the ability of more traditional models to accurately create details of medical images with the fidelity required. Over recent years, synthesis has moved from these methods to deep learning models which are much more capable of accurately producing realistic medical images [13–15]. With modern deep learning approaches, we now commonly see approaches that produce accurate representations of CT or positron emission tomography (PET) images from MRI, for example [16].

It is straightforward to see how image synthesis can be used for harmonization. Suppose, for example, that we have two sets of data acquired in different ways, e.g., two different OCT scanners like in Fig. 11.1, and would like to harmonize Set #2 to Set #1. We can then reframe this as a simple cross-modality synthesis problem and train a model to generate images that mimic Set #1 from the images in Set #2. After harmonization, these images can then be used as inputs to downstream processing (such as segmentation) to produce more reliable results. A key challenge in realizing such a harmonization algorithm is how to train the method. If images of a subset of subjects can be found within both sets, then we can draw on the extensive literature of supervised synthesis and train a model using these overlapping subjects; otherwise, we must look to unsupervised or semi-supervised methods to provide adequate training. Regardless of the training strategy, synthesis-based harmonization allows for accurate, locally-adapted harmonized images to use for downstream processing, yielding consistent results even from inconsistent sources [17,18].

11.2 Supervised techniques

In the context of image synthesis, images of the same subject acquired from both the source and target domains (contrast or modality) provide fully-supervised training data. This is a great benefit, as we can directly train our model using examples with voxel to voxel correspondence. Knowing this, we first describe how synthesis-based harmonization works in this ideal case. Supervised synthesis techniques are essentially regression models that take an input image of a certain modality and generate an image of the same anatomy matching the target modality. The goal of supervised harmonization is the same: we want to take an input image that is acquired in a certain way and produce an image of the same anatomy as if it were acquired in a different way. In contrast to full modality synthesis, harmonization most often requires only subtle changes to the contrast, which might be challenging to produce accurately. With sufficient training data, however, such differences in acquisition should be well represented, even in the presence of pathology, allowing state-of-the-art deep learning architectures to properly recreate them. Additionally, when multiple views from each domain are available, such as in multi-contrast MRI, we can leverage complementary data to create a more comparable output. While there will continue to be increasing use of synthesis in the world of harmonization, we will focus on DeepHarmony [2] as an example that highlights some of the strengths and pitfalls of supervised harmonization methods.

11.2.1 Architecture and training

Unlike the world of computer vision where many diverse network architectures are in widespread use, medical image analysis has mainly focused on two main structures, the U-Net and the ResNet [19,20]. Both are deep, multi-level architectures that are well tested in the literature, especially in image synthesis applications [21]. As well, these architectures have many variants that can be tuned to particular tasks for better performance [22]. For the sake of brevity, we will focus on the U-Net, which is used in a large proportion of medical image synthesis papers to date. The U-Net structure allows for multi-resolution information to be incorporated without suffering from loss of information by using skip connections to bring information from the encoding path to the decoding path [19]. This is critically important in synthesis and harmonization tasks as multi-resolution features have been shown to be important even prior to deep learning methods, especially in difficult to predict areas such as outside of the brain in head MRI [12,23].

The U-Net has a number of variants in medical imaging synthesis that provide improvements on the base structure. Many of these variants, such as the addition of residual connections, and the use of 3D information have shown improvement in segmentation results and are commonly used in synthesis models. One variant that has particular utility in harmonization is the addition of a skip connection bringing the input image to the final steps of the network [2]. This turns the classic U-Net structure into a kind of residual network, where instead of reconstructing a completely new image, the network only needs to produce the difference between the input and the target. In Fig. 11.2, we show an example of this in the network architecture of Deep-Harmony, where the input image is concatenated to the final feature map and a 1×1 convolution is used to produce the final image. Since the targets in harmonization tend to be very similar, this allows the network to focus on how the images are different instead of how they are the same. We can take this a step further by initializing the network as an identity transform, so the very first loss is the difference between the two (input and target) images [24]. By grounding our harmonization method in state-of-the-art synthesis architectures, we can produce similar images with high fidelity and realistic appearance.

After defining the synthesis architecture, we must choose a loss function to optimize. The simplest and most effective first component of the loss is to directly compare the pixel values of the network output with the training data. Using l_2- or l_1-loss between pixels will tend to produce consistent results to our input image. This is crucial in synthesis of medical images, as minor changes to the appearance of medical images can lead to misinterpretation [25]. This differs from natural image analysis, where artifacts may not change the interpretation of the image. These losses, however, have limitations and normally lead to overly smooth synthetic images, as a smooth inconsistency tends to have a lower loss on average than a sharp difference. This is not desirable in a harmonization setting, since we want to use harmonized images along with images from the target set [12]. There are a number of ways to overcome these limitations and produce consistent results from both sets. For instance, if the network does not overly smooth the image so much to remove important features,

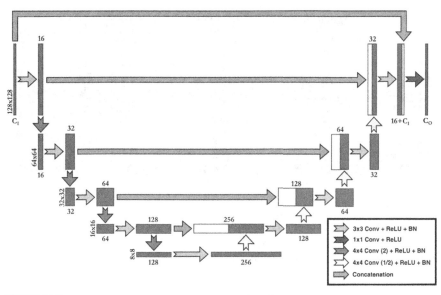

FIGURE 11.2

The modified U-Net structure used by the DeepHarmony model. Notable differences include additional concatenation (topmost green arrow – light gray in print version) and strided convolution/deconvolution.

the reduced noise may be an added benefit, so it might be preferred to also put the target images through the harmonization framework. The DeepHarmony [2] method trained an auxiliary network for this task because of the explicit directionality of the model, but it is also possible in other models (e.g., CycleGAN or StarGAN) without such additions, as synthesis between different sources and targets is inherent in the structure [26,27]. Regardless of the implementation, these methods will create harmonized images from all domains and so will share traits common to the synthetic images.

Even if all images are synthetic and therefore consistent for processing, we may want them to look realistic. To do this, we can incorporate additional loss terms such as adversarial losses and/or perceptual losses [28], both of which use additional network layers (either optimized with the generative network or pretrained, respectively) to give a loss based on a spatial scale of information that is larger than a voxel. These losses are commonly used to increase the "realness" of synthetic images, but are limited by deterministic networks. As medical imaging has some component of randomness involved, adversarial losses and other more complex losses may try to replicate random noise and complex, but ultimately incorrect, shading patterns. This can be corrected by injecting a small amount of randomness into the network, giving the network the ability to produce more realistic results [14]. Each of these additional losses can be used in harmonization tasks to more realism, allowing for reuse of algorithms or networks that were trained on real images.

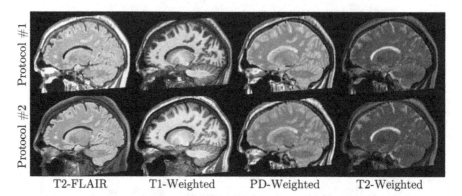

FIGURE 11.3

Example slices of four MRI contrasts acquired using two different acquisition protocols on the same subject. Differences are notable in contrast between the two T2-FLAIR images and in the gray matter/white matter contrast of the T1-weighted images.

11.2.2 Using more information

While many modalities are limited to a single image type, MRI is commonly acquired with multiple tissue contrasts in a single scanning session. This is highly beneficial to synthesis and thus harmonization, as many times images from the source set may not have enough information to accurately predict harmonized images of the target contrast [2]. One excellent example is T1-weighted MR images, where contrast between gray and white matter can be very different based on the acquisition strategy, as shown in Fig. 11.3. We can see that it might be difficult to predict the edges of the gray matter accurately using only the T1-weighted images. DeepHarmony, for example, demonstrated significant improvement in multiple metrics when multiple input images were used to predict the output images.

We can also see in Fig. 11.3 that resolution can be an important factor in harmonization. Even with preprocessing steps such as registration and super-resolution, there are still differences in images that are acquired at different resolutions, as can be seen in the T2-FLAIR images in the first column of this figure. Without knowledge of how the high resolution features of the anatomy should look, the network can only do so much. However, by providing additional images at different resolutions (acquired during the same scanning session), the network can more accurately predict what an image should look like in a higher resolution target domain. This would be especially true in a particularly difficult harmonization task where resolution is a large component. Consider an example where we would like to harmonize the high-resolution T1-weighted image for a brain segmentation task but we find it was acquired at a much lower resolution than our target domain and only one high resolution image was acquired, say a T2-weighted FLAIR image. A sample protocol that depicts this example is shown in Fig. 11.4. In this case, we can use the high-resolution T2-weighted FLAIR along with the other acquired images to accurately

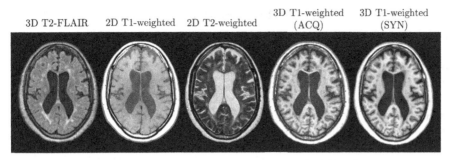

3D T2-FLAIR   2D T1-weighted   2D T2-weighted   3D T1-weighted (ACQ)   3D T1-weighted (SYN)

FIGURE 11.4

Multi-contrast synthesis experiment showing a synthetic high-resolution, 3D-acquired, T1-weighted image. In this example, we used the left three images (3D-acquired FLAIR and two 2D-acquired images) to create a synthetic 3D-acquired T1-weighted image (SYN). This result shows a strong similarity to the acquired T1-weighted image (ACQ) even though no similarly acquired image was used as input.

predict the high-resolution T1-weighted image. Multiple inputs can also provide fault tolerance for a method, such as in the paper by Chartias et al. [29], where multiple inputs were used to produce a common latent space that can be fused together. This kind of fault tolerant synthesis can be very useful in harmonization, where missing information is always possible due to malfunctions or data loss. In this way, harmonization and synthesis come even closer together as we see that in some instances harmonization of two multi-contrast MRI datasets might include the synthesis of a missing contrast for use in a specific analysis method, e.g., a segmentation method that requires T2-weighted imaging for accurate quantification of volume of the entire skull cavity [30].

11.3 Unsupervised techniques

As described above, harmonization is relatively straightforward when overlapping and multi-contrast images are available, but when (more commonly) overlapping data are not available, we must look to other techniques to train an appropriate model. Again, we can look to synthesis methods to guide our approach, this time with an eye to unsupervised and semi-supervised techniques. Implementations such as adversarial learning [31,26], disentangled latent representations [32–35], and few-shot learning [36,37] can all be used to train models that can perform harmonization without overlapping subjects. This general approach can be a significant advantage in multi-site studies and historic studies where the data collection for supervised learning can be infeasible, impractical, or impossible [7]. It is important to note, however, that without voxel-to-voxel regularization (as is directly possible only with supervised approaches), these methods can introduce artifacts into the images, if not careful [25].

11.3.1 Generative adversarial networks

Generative adversarial networks (GANs) were designed to create a sample from a specific distribution out of random noise by solving a minimax problem between a generator network that produces the sample and a discriminator network that judges if the sample fits in the distribution [38]. Conditional GANs [39] were later used to transform images from one population to appear to be from a different population without the need for an overlapping set. This type of unsupervised image-to-image translation was brought to the forefront by the CycleGAN method of Zhu et al. [31] and other similar methods [40,41] developed at nearly the same time. These methods quickly made the jump into medical image synthesis, demonstrating state-of-the-art results in cross-modality tasks such as synthesizing CT images from MRI [26]. This seems like a quick and simple solution to the problem of harmonization, as the type of domain adaptation done by these models is exactly the harmonization task, but the issue of input consistency quickly arose. CycleGANs and similar techniques rely on discriminator networks to decide whether a synthetic image is representative of the target population or not. This is an extremely powerful technique, but can produce images that suffer from artifacts or are otherwise not accurate representations of the truth [15]. To prevent this, the CycleGAN introduces a "cycle-consistency loss," where the image is translated to the target domain using a deep network and then translated back to the source domain using another deep network where a reconstruction loss (usually l_1) is calculated [31]. This ensures that the image produced in the target domain is capable of reproducing the input image and allows for a voxel-to-voxel regularization on the model.

However, this does not completely eliminate adverse effects of the adversarial training, as errors such as intensity or geometric distortions can creep into the synthetic results, since they can be "undone" by the reverse generator network. An illustrative example of this shows that CycleGAN can hallucinate brain tumors (or healthy tissue) simply by providing biased data during training [25]. This is compounded by the fact that such cycle-based methods can also perform geometric shifts when the data in the two populations are too dissimilar [42]. For this reason, we must be very careful not only to carefully balance our training sets, but to also closely inspect the results of GAN-based synthesis for possible artifacts or subtle shifts. These types of concerns led researchers to investigate other structures to stabilize synthesis. Zhang et al. [43] reduce the geometry shift by adding a supervised segmentation network to the synthesized image from the CycleGAN. Yang [15] uses extra consistency loss to constrain structural consistency in CycleGAN. Constraining the CycleGAN with additional information like segmentation labels and additional losses can greatly alleviate the geometry shift problem.

11.3.2 Learning interpretable representations

With GAN-based approaches being widely applied to medical image synthesis and computer vision in general, there was a large push to create interpretable models. This led to works such as those based on variational autoencoders (VAEs) [44] drawing more and more attention. Similar to GANs, VAEs are considered a type of generative model, which can be unsupervised but also have the capability of learning interpretable representations [45]. There are two general classes of interpretability, namely mathematical or statistical and semantic. Mathematical or statistical representations satisfy certain mathematical properties or follow well-studied distributions and can be understood using features associated with these attributes. For example, VAEs typically assume a latent space that is Gaussian distributed and whose values can be interpreted using a simple statistical framework. Semantically meaningful features, which do not have to follow well-known distributions, instead are associated with certain image attributes [46]. The idea of creating interpretable models is particularly appealing in deep learning based approaches as understanding the model behavior is usually difficult, leading to the common phrase "black box" being used to refer to deep learning models. By learning interpretable representations, researchers are able to better understand the model learning process, leading to improved model designs.

As a specific example of an interpretable representation in harmonization, we point to recent work that attempts to disentangle domain-invariant information from domain-specific information [33–35,18]. This general approach makes it possible to modify the domain-specific information while preserving the domain-invariant information. For example, in MRI the underlying physical properties of the tissues are seen as the domain-invariant information while the acquisition environment (hardware, software, imaging parameters, etc.) is seen as the domain-specific information. Then, as the physical properties (the domain-invariant pieces) do not change between domains, we can use this as a basis for harmonization. This framework was used for harmonization by Jog et al. [5], where the authors assumed knowledge of the imaging equation as well as knowledge of the underlying nuclear magnetic resonance properties of three tissue classes. Then, by carrying out tissue classification for a given image, the authors were able to estimate the specific acquisition parameters of that image. With these parameters and a set of atlas images with underlying tissue parameter maps, synthetic images could be created based on any set of MR imaging equations. Images in the atlas could therefore be harmonized to an input image by applying the acquisition parameters of the input image to the tissue parameters of the atlas images. While the framework was innovative, the specific approach was not robust enough for routine application due to the complex nature of the MR imaging equations and the broad assumptions made on the tissues.

With the development of deep learning based disentangled representation learning, image synthesis has moved toward using paired medical images that are sharing certain attributes and creating a data-driven latent space. In recent years, multiple groups [47,34,35] have used multi-contrast MRI to learn a data-driven disentangled representation where contrast-agnostic anatomy images serve as domain-invariant information and a contrast embedding captures domain-variant information. Since the anatomical and contrast representations are disentangled, cross-site harmonization can be easily achieved by combining anatomical representations from a source site with the contrast representation from a target site. We can see in Fig. 11.5 that there is a substantial effect of domain-variant contrast variable (called θ here) on the syn-

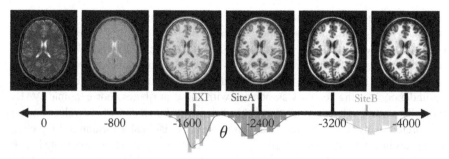

FIGURE 11.5

By manipulating the domain-varying latent variable θ, we can simulate many different contrasts of an input T1-weighted image. This can be used to create a T1-weighted image that matches any of the distributions of θ calculated from three example sites (IXI, SiteA, and SiteB) which are shown underneath the axes. We can also use this for inter-contrast synthesis by providing a θ value from a T2-weighted (left). There is also an area of undetermined contrast between T1- and T2-weighting which is not present in any training data but still shows the same anatomical features.

thetic image, even with no change to the underlying domain-invariant information. We can also see the distribution of contrast embeddings from three example sites: public data from a single site of the IXI dataset [48] and two private datasets from Johns Hopkins (SiteA and SiteB). This technique can be especially useful in harmonization as the two aspects of the disentangled representation can be manipulated separately, producing meaningful changes in contrast and matching source data to the target domain.

11.3.3 One-/few-shot harmonization

In most examples of unsupervised harmonization, large datasets are required for training, but in some cases the data from one domain or the other are limited. To overcome this we turn to one- or few-shot training techniques, where the focus is on limited training data. Cohen and Wolf [37] focused on translating images from a sparse domain A to domain B, which has abundant images. Their methodology uses one encoder network and one decoder network for each domain and trains these networks with multiple cycle consistency losses. TuiGAN [49], on the other hand, learns a translation model with only one unpaired image from each domain, then uses multi-scale conditional GANs to progressively translate images from a coarse level up to fine details. Although each method showed improvement in synthetic results given the amount of training data, the performance is much worse when compared to training with abundant data and cannot achieve the quality needed for medical image analysis.

To reach this needed quality, additional downstream tasks, such as segmentation, have been combined with the harmonization process to aid in learning. Instead of

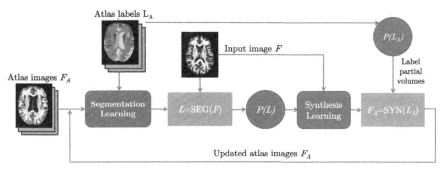

FIGURE 11.6

Using one source image and a set of atlas images with segmentations, CAMELION can perform harmonization and synthesis in an iterative fashion, each time updating the atlas images with harmonized versions synthesized from their labels.

tackling the difficult challenge of training a robust image-level harmonization model with a small amount of data, these methods focused on harmonizing those few source images such that the pre-trained downstream task can perform well. Karani et al. [50] used three convolutional layers in front of a segmentation network to harmonize the test image, training these layers using the segmentation results as a guide. This ensured that the test image would produce good segmentation results, but does not necessarily harmonize the test image to be visually similar to the images in the target domain. To take this strategy further, SDA-Net [3] introduced autoencoders to harmonize the few test images not just at the image level but also at the feature level of the task network. This allowed the network, pretrained on an existing domain, to determine if the image or specific intermediate features were different from the target. By combining both image-level and feature-level harmonization, SDA-Net showed improvement in downstream task performance, as demonstrated in the last row of Fig. 11.1.

In addition to traditional few-shot learning methods, we can also look at the process of fine-tuning an existing task network, such as a segmentation model. A potential downside of this approach is that it requires training data (manual delineations) in order to fine-tune the weights. However, harmonization does not always have to be performed on the input or testing image. By harmonizing a group of atlas images to a single testing image, we could use the existing training data to fine-tune the segmentation network. CAMELION (Contrast Adaptive Method for Label Identification) [51] does just this by alternating between training a segmentation network from known atlas images and a synthesis network that learns to synthesize images with the contrast of the testing image shown in Fig. 11.6. In this way, after each iteration the atlas images approach the appearance of the testing image and the segmentation network is steadily fine-tuned to segment the testing contrast. When testing data is scarce, including auxiliary tasks, feature-level harmonization and intermediate segmentations can boost performance by providing additional avenues for learning.

11.3.4 Conclusion

The task of harmonizing medical images has taken on increasing importance in recent years, in part because of the lack of robustness of many trained deep network models to carry out various image processing tasks on data that is different than their training data. Harmonization is also important for consistency of numerical results in both cross-sectional and longitudinal studies. Although standardization of acquisition parameters can help to some extent, harmonization using image synthesis methods are starting to emerge as a standard part of preprocessing in medical image analysis algorithms. Like registration, resampling, and shading correction, we expect that harmonization will become a very important step in most analysis of medical images in the future.

References

[1] R. Shinohara, J. Oh, G. Nair, P. Calabresi, C. Davatzikos, J. Doshi, R. Henry, G. Kim, K. Linn, N. Papinutto, D. Pelletier, D. Pham, D. Reich, W. Rooney, S. Roy, W. Stern, S. Tummala, F. Yousuf, A. Zhu, N. Sicotte, R. Bakshi, Volumetric analysis from a harmonized multisite brain MRI study of a single subject with multiple sclerosis, American Journal of Neuroradiology 38 (8) (2017) 1501, https://doi.org/10.3174/ajnr.A5254, http://www.ajnr.org/content/38/8/1501.abstract.

[2] B.E. Dewey, C. Zhao, J.C. Reinhold, A. Carass, K.C. Fitzgerald, E.S. Sotirchos, S. Saidha, J. Oh, D.L. Pham, P.A. Calabresi, P.C. van Zijl, J.L. Prince, DeepHarmony: a deep learning approach to contrast harmonization across scanner changes, Magnetic Resonance Imaging 64 (2019) 160–170, https://doi.org/10.1016/j.mri.2019.05.041, http://www.sciencedirect.com/science/article/pii/S0730725X18306490.

[3] Y. He, A. Carass, L. Zuo, B.E. Dewey, J.L. Prince, Self domain adapted network, in: International Conference on Medical Image Computing and Computer-Assisted Intervention, Springer, 2020, pp. 437–446.

[4] S. Roy, A. Carass, J. Prince, A compressed sensing approach for MR tissue contrast synthesis, in: Information Processing in Medical Imaging, Springer, Berlin, Heidelberg, 2011, pp. 371–383, https://doi.org/10.1007/978-3-642-22092-0_31.

[5] A. Jog, A. Carass, S. Roy, D. Pham, J. Prince, MR image synthesis by contrast learning on neighborhood ensembles, Medical Image Analysis 24 (1) (2015) 63–76, https://doi.org/10.1016/j.media.2015.05.002, http://www.sciencedirect.com/science/article/pii/S1361841515000699.

[6] R.T. Shinohara, E.M. Sweeney, J. Goldsmith, N. Shiee, F.J. Mateen, P.A. Calabresi, S. Jarso, D.L. Pham, D.S. Reich, C.M. Crainiceanu, Statistical normalization techniques for magnetic resonance imaging, NeuroImage: Clinical 6 (2014) 9–19, https://doi.org/10.1016/j.nicl.2014.08.008.

[7] J.P. Fortin, N. Cullen, Y.I. Sheline, W.D. Taylor, I. Aselcioglu, P.A. Cook, P. Adams, C. Cooper, M. Fava, P.J. McGrath, M. McInnis, M.L. Phillips, M.H. Trivedi, M.M. Weissman, R.T. Shinohara, Harmonization of cortical thickness measurements across scanners and sites, NeuroImage 167 (2018) 104–120, https://doi.org/10.1016/j.neuroimage.2017.11.024, https://linkinghub.elsevier.com/retrieve/pii/S105381191730931X.

[8] L.G. Nyúl, J.K. Udupa, On standardizing the MR image intensity scale, Magnetic Resonance in Medicine 42 (6) (1999) 1072–1081.

[9] R. Pomponio, G. Erus, M. Habes, J. Doshi, D. Srinivasan, E. Mamourian, V. Bashyam, I.M. Nasrallah, T.D. Satterthwaite, Y. Fan, L.J. Launer, C.L. Masters, P. Maruff, C. Zhuo, H. Völzke, S.C. Johnson, J. Fripp, N. Koutsouleris, D.H. Wolf, R. Gur, R. Gur, J. Morris, M.S. Albert, H.J. Grabe, S.M. Resnick, R.N. Bryan, D.A. Wolk, R.T. Shinohara, H. Shou, C. Davatzikos, Harmonization of large MRI datasets for the analysis of brain imaging patterns throughout the lifespan, NeuroImage 208 (2020) 116,450, https://doi.org/10.1016/j.neuroimage.2019.116450, https://www.sciencedirect.com/science/article/pii/S1053811919310419.

[10] S. Roy, W.T. Wang, A. Carass, J.L. Prince, J.A. Butman, D.L. Pham, PET attenuation correction using synthetic CT from ultrashort echo-time MR imaging, Journal of Nuclear Medicine 55 (12) (2014) 2071–2077.

[11] F. Rousseau, Brain hallucination, in: Computer Vision – ECCV 2008, Springer, Berlin, Heidelberg, 2008, pp. 497–508, https://doi.org/10.1007/978-3-540-88682-2_38.

[12] A. Jog, A. Carass, S. Roy, D.L. Pham, J.L. Prince, Random forest regression for magnetic resonance image synthesis, Medical Image Analysis 35 (2017) 475–488, https://doi.org/10.1016/j.media.2016.08.009.

[13] D. Nie, R. Trullo, J. Lian, L. Wang, C. Petitjean, S. Ruan, Q. Wang, D. Shen, Medical image synthesis with deep convolutional adversarial networks, IEEE Transactions on Biomedical Engineering 65 (12) (2018) 2720–2730.

[14] L. Zuo, B.E. Dewey, A. Carass, Y. He, M. Shao, J.C. Reinhold, J.L. Prince, Synthesizing realistic brain MR images with noise control, in: International Workshop on Simulation and Synthesis in Medical Imaging, Springer, 2020, pp. 21–31.

[15] H. Yang, J. Sun, A. Carass, C. Zhao, J. Lee, Z. Xu, J. Prince, Unpaired brain MR-to-CT synthesis using a structure-constrained cycleGAN, in: Deep Learning in Medical Image Analysis and Multimodal Learning for Clinical Decision Support, Springer, 2018, pp. 174–182.

[16] Y. Pan, M. Liu, C. Lian, T. Zhou, Y. Xia, D. Shen, Synthesizing missing PET from MRI with cycle-consistent generative adversarial networks for Alzheimer's disease diagnosis, in: International Conference on Medical Image Computing and Computer-Assisted Intervention, Springer, 2018, pp. 455–463.

[17] B.E. Dewey, C. Zhao, A. Carass, J. Oh, P.A. Calabresi, P.C.M. van Zijl, J.L. Prince, Deep harmonization of inconsistent MR data for consistent volume segmentation, in: A. Gooya, O. Goksel, I. Oguz, N. Burgos (Eds.), Simulation and Synthesis in Medical Imaging, Springer International Publishing, 2018, pp. 20–30.

[18] Y. Liu, L. Zuo, A. Carass, Y. He, A. Filippatou, S.D. Solomon, S. Saidha, P.A. Calabresi, J.L. Prince, Variational intensity cross channel encoder for unsupervised vessel segmentation on OCT angiography, in: Medical Imaging 2020: Image Processing, vol. 11313, International Society for Optics and Photonics, 2020, p. 113130Y.

[19] O. Ronneberger, P. Fischer, T. Brox, U-Net: convolutional networks for biomedical image segmentation, in: N. Navab, J. Hornegger, W.M. Wells, A.F. Frangi (Eds.), Medical Image Computing and Computer-Assisted Intervention – MICCAI 2015, Springer International Publishing, 2015, pp. 234–241.

[20] K. He, X. Zhang, S. Ren, J. Sun, Identity mappings in deep residual networks, in: European Conference on Computer Vision, Springer, 2016, pp. 630–645.

[21] T. Wang, Y. Lei, Y. Fu, J.F. Wynne, W.J. Curran, T. Liu, X. Yang, A review on medical imaging synthesis using deep learning and its clinical applications, Journal of Applied Clinical Medical Physics 22 (1) (2021) 11–36.

[22] O. Oktay, J. Schlemper, L.L. Folgoc, M. Lee, M. Heinrich, K. Misawa, K. Mori, S. Mc-Donagh, N.Y. Hammerla, B. Kainz, et al., Attention U-net: learning where to look for the pancreas, arXiv preprint, arXiv:1804.03999, 2018.

[23] H. Tang, E. Wu, Q. Ma, D. Gallagher, G. Perera, T. Zhuang, MRI brain image segmentation by multi-resolution edge detection and region selection, Computerized Medical Imaging and Graphics 24 (6) (2000) 349–357.

[24] C. Zhao, A. Carass, J. Lee, Y. He, J.L. Prince, Whole brain segmentation and labeling from CT using synthetic MR images, in: Q. Wang, Y. Shi, H.I. Suk, K. Suzuki (Eds.), Machine Learning in Medical Imaging, Springer International Publishing, 2017, pp. 291–298.

[25] J.P. Cohen, M. Luck, S. Honari, Distribution matching losses can hallucinate features in medical image translation, in: A.F. Frangi, J.A. Schnabel, C. Davatzikos, C. Alberola-López, G. Fichtinger (Eds.), Medical Image Computing and Computer Assisted Intervention – MICCAI 2018, in: Lecture Notes in Computer Science, Springer International Publishing, Cham, 2018, pp. 529–536, https://doi.org/10.1007/978-3-030-00928-1_60.

[26] J.M. Wolterink, A.M. Dinkla, M.H. Savenije, P.R. Seevinck, C.A. van den Berg, I. Išgum, Deep MR to CT synthesis using unpaired data, in: International Workshop on Simulation and Synthesis in Medical Imaging, Springer, 2017, pp. 14–23.

[27] M. Sohail, M.N. Riaz, J. Wu, C. Long, S. Li, Unpaired multi-contrast MR image synthesis using generative adversarial networks, in: International Workshop on Simulation and Synthesis in Medical Imaging, Springer, 2019, pp. 22–31.

[28] S.U. Dar, M. Yurt, L. Karacan, A. Erdem, E. Erdem, T. Çukur, Image synthesis in multi-contrast MRI with conditional generative adversarial networks, IEEE Transactions on Medical Imaging 38 (10) (Oct. 2019) 2375–2388, https://doi.org/10.1109/TMI.2019.2901750.

[29] A. Chartsias, T. Joyce, M.V. Giuffrida, S.A. Tsaftaris, Multimodal MR synthesis via modality-invariant latent representation, IEEE Transactions on Medical Imaging 37 (3) (2017) 1–814, https://doi.org/10.1109/TMI.2017.2764326.

[30] B.E. Dewey, K.C. Fitzgerald, E.S. Sotirchos, K. Nakamura, D.D. Ontaneda, P.A. Calabresi, E.M. Mowry, J. Prince, T2-weighted synthesis for accurate estimation of intracranial volume, in: ACTRIMS Forum 2019, ACTRIMS, 2019.

[31] J.Y. Zhu, T. Park, P. Isola, A.A. Efros, Unpaired image-to-image translation using cycle-consistent adversarial networks, arXiv:1703.10593, 2017, http://arxiv.org/abs/1703.10593.

[32] A. Chartsias, T. Joyce, G. Papanastasiou, S. Semple, M. Williams, D.E. Newby, R. Dharmakumar, S.A. Tsaftaris, Disentangled representation learning in cardiac image analysis, Medical Image Analysis 58 (2019) 101,535, https://doi.org/10.1016/j.media.2019.101535, http://www.sciencedirect.com/science/article/pii/S1361841519300684.

[33] B.E. Dewey, S. Suthiphosuwan, J.L. Lambe, J. Oh, P.A. Calabresi, J.L. Prince, Automated cervical spinal cord measurement from T1-MPRAGE brain imaging, in: ACTRIMS Forum 2020, vol. 26, 2020, pp. 16–89, https://doi.org/10.1177/1352458520917096, http://journals.sagepub.com/doi/10.1177/1352458520917096.

[34] L. Zuo, B.E. Dewey, A. Carass, Y. Liu, Y. He, P.A. Calabresi, J.L. Prince, Information-based disentangled representation learning for unsupervised MR harmonization, in: Information Processing in Medical Imaging, Springer, 2021.

[35] J. Ouyang, E. Adeli, K.M. Pohl, Q. Zhao, G. Zaharchuk, Representation disentanglement for multi-modal brain MR analysis, in: Information Processing in Medical Imaging, Springer, 2021.

[36] S. Valverde, M. Salem, M. Cabezas, D. Pareto, J.C. Vilanova, L. Ramió-Torrentà, Á. Rovira, J. Salvi, A. Oliver, X. Lladó, One-shot domain adaptation in multiple sclerosis lesion segmentation using convolutional neural networks, NeuroImage: Clinical 21 (2019) 101,638, https://doi.org/10.1016/j.nicl.2018.101638, https://linkinghub.elsevier.com/retrieve/pii/S2213158218303863.

[37] T. Cohen, L. Wolf, Bidirectional one-shot unsupervised domain mapping, in: 2019 IEEE/CVF International Conference on Computer Vision (ICCV), IEEE, Seoul, Korea (South), 2019, pp. 1784–1792, https://doi.org/10.1109/ICCV.2019.00187, https://ieeexplore.ieee.org/document/9009515/.

[38] I.J. Goodfellow, J. Pouget-Abadie, M. Mirza, B. Xu, D. Warde-Farley, S. Ozair, A. Courville, Y. Bengio, Generative adversarial networks, arXiv preprint, arXiv:1406.2661, 2014.

[39] M. Mirza, S. Osindero, Conditional generative adversarial nets, arXiv preprint, arXiv:1411.1784, 2014.

[40] Y. Choi, M. Choi, M. Kim, J. Ha, S. Kim, J. Choo, StarGAN: unified generative adversarial networks for multi-domain image-to-image translation, in: 2018 IEEE/CVF Conference on Computer Vision and Pattern Recognition, 2018, pp. 8789–8797, https://doi.org/10.1109/CVPR.2018.00916.

[41] Y. Pan, M. Liu, C. Lian, T. Zhou, Y. Xia, D. Shen, Synthesizing missing PET from MRI with cycle-consistent generative adversarial networks for Alzheimer's disease diagnosis, in: A.F. Frangi, J.A. Schnabel, C. Davatzikos, C. Alberola-López, G. Fichtinger (Eds.), Medical Image Computing and Computer Assisted Intervention – MICCAI 2018, vol. 11072, Springer International Publishing, Cham, 2018, pp. 455–463, https://doi.org/10.1007/978-3-030-00931-1_52, http://link.springer.com/10.1007/978-3-030-00931-1_52.

[42] H. Fu, M. Gong, C. Wang, K. Batmanghelich, K. Zhang, D. Tao, Geometry-consistent generative adversarial networks for one-sided unsupervised domain mapping, in: Proceedings of the IEEE/CVF Conference on Computer Vision and Pattern Recognition, 2019, pp. 2427–2436.

[43] Z. Zhang, L. Yang, Y. Zheng, Translating and segmenting multimodal medical volumes with cycle- and shape-consistency generative adversarial network, in: 2018 IEEE/CVF Conference on Computer Vision and Pattern Recognition, IEEE, Salt Lake City, UT, 2018, pp. 9242–9251, https://doi.org/10.1109/CVPR.2018.00963, https://ieeexplore.ieee.org/document/8579061/.

[44] D.P. Kingma, M. Welling, Auto-encoding variational Bayes, arXiv preprint, arXiv:1312.6114, 2013.

[45] A. Alemi, et al., Deep variational information bottleneck, in: International Conference on Learning Representations, 2017.

[46] I. Higgins, L. Matthey, A. Pal, C. Burgess, X. Glorot, M. Botvinick, S. Mohamed, A. Lerchner, beta-VAE: learning basic visual concepts with a constrained variational framework, in: International Conference on Learning Representations, 2017.

[47] B.E. Dewey, L. Zuo, A. Carass, Y. He, Y. Liu, E.M. Mowry, S. Newsome, J. Oh, P.A. Calabresi, J.L. Prince, A disentangled latent space for cross-site MRI harmonization, in: A.L. Martel, P. Abolmaesumi, D. Stoyanov, D. Mateus, M.A. Zuluaga, S.K. Zhou, D. Racoceanu, L. Joskowicz (Eds.), Medical Image Computing and Computer Assisted Intervention – MICCAI 2020, Springer International Publishing, Cham, 2020, pp. 720–729.

[48] IXI Brain Development Dataset, https://brain-development.org/ixi-dataset/. (Accessed 10 December 2019).

[49] J. Lin, Y. Pang, Y. Xia, Z. Chen, J. Luo, TuiGAN: learning versatile image-to-image translation with two unpaired images, in: A. Vedaldi, H. Bischof, T. Brox, J.M. Frahm

(Eds.), Computer Vision – ECCV 2020, in: Lecture Notes in Computer Science, Springer International Publishing, Cham, 2020, pp. 18–35, https://doi.org/10.1007/978-3-030-58548-8_2.

[50] N. Karani, E. Erdil, K. Chaitanya, E. Konukoglu, Test-time adaptable neural networks for robust medical image segmentation, Medical Image Analysis 68 (2020) 101,907.

[51] D.L. Pham, Y.Y. Chou, B.E. Dewey, D.S. Reich, J.A. Butman, S. Roy, Contrast adaptive tissue classification by alternating segmentation and synthesis, in: N. Burgos, D. Svoboda, J.M. Wolterink, C. Zhao (Eds.), Simulation and Synthesis in Medical Imaging, Springer International Publishing, Cham, 2020, pp. 1–10.

Medical image super-resolution with deep networks

12

Can Zhao[a,g], Samuel W. Remedios[c,g], Shuo Han[f,g], Bowen Li[c,d,e], and Jerry L. Prince[b]

[a]*NVIDIA, Santa Clara, CA, United States*
[b]*Department of Electrical and Computer Engineering, Johns Hopkins University, Baltimore, MD, United States*
[c]*Department of Computer Science, Johns Hopkins University, Baltimore, MD, United States*
[d]*PAII Inc, Bethesda, MD, United States*
[e]*Department of Health Sciences Informatics, Johns Hopkins University, Baltimore, MD, United States*
[f]*Department of Biomedical Engineering, Johns Hopkins University, Baltimore, MD, United States*

12.1 Introduction to super-resolution

In this section, we introduce basic concepts of super-resolution (SR) and give a brief history of SR methods prior to deep learning.

12.1.1 Basic concepts

Definitions of resolution. Before we discuss SR, we introduce two definitions of *resolution* commonly used in medical imaging. *Spatial resolution* refers to the ability to "resolve," or separate, small details; *digital resolution* is the voxel or pixel separation of a digital image. Fig. 12.1 shows an example of (a) a brain MR image with low spatial and digital resolutions, (b) an interpolated image with a high digital resolution but a low spatial resolution, and (c) an ideal image with high spatial and high digital resolutions. These two definitions are related: high digital resolutions are a necessary but not sufficient condition for images with high spatial resolutions. To obtain a high digital resolution, image interpolation can be used. To obtain a high spatial resolution, however, at least one improvement of the following is needed: more advanced imaging devices, a trade-off between resolutions and noise, or the application of *super-resolution* (SR) post-processing. In this chapter, we simply refer to *spatial resolution* as *resolution* and *digital resolution* as *pixel/voxel size*.

---

[g] These three authors contributed equally to this chapter.

(a) Acquired image

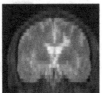

Digital resolution: 1×6 mm
Spatial resolution: 1×6 mm

Interpolate →

(b) Interpolated image

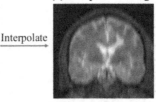

Digital resolution: 1×1 mm
Spatial resolution: 1×6 mm

(c) Ideal HR image

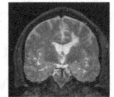

Digital resolution: 1×1 mm
Spatial resolution: 1×1 mm

FIGURE 12.1

Images with different spatial and digital resolutions: (a) a brain image with low spatial and digital resolutions; (b) an interpolated image with a high digital resolution but a low spatial resolution; (c) an ideal image with high spatial and digital resolutions.

Motivations for SR. High resolution (HR) images, as shown in Fig. 12.1(c), are desired in many applications since they provide less ambiguity and more details of objects of interest than low resolution (LR) images, as shown in Figs. 12.1(a)–(b). This is particularly true in medical imaging where a better resolution permits better discrimination of anatomical details. Additionally, image processing analyses, such as volume estimation after segmentation, depend on the digital resolution of the image. However, the acquisition of HR images is difficult for some modalities. For example, in microscopy inherent limitations of the devices can make HR images infeasible, in computed tomography (CT) there are increased radiation risks, and in magnetic resonance imaging (MRI) a longer scan time is required which increases patient discomfort and motion artifacts. To this end, signal processing and machine learning techniques have been developed to improve the resolutions of acquired images; this process is called SR.

Imaging scenarios. All SR methods add high-frequency information to a given acquired image, but there are different approaches to do so. If multiple images of the same anatomy are acquired, an SR algorithm can fuse the image content to produce a better spatial resolution than any of the acquired images. This approach is known as multi-image SR (MISR). While MISR methods can leverage data from multiple acquisitions, the need firstly to acquire multiple images and secondly to accurately register all these images might make the method difficult for routine use.

Single image SR (SISR) is an alternative to MISR that eliminates the need to acquire and register multiple images, but it has the disadvantage that it must acquire high-frequency information either from internal image statistics (the single image itself) or from an external dataset (containing both low-frequency images and their high-frequency counterparts).

Section 12.1.2.1 has more details on both MISR and SISR. Whether the high-frequency originates internally or externally from one of these scenarios determines the fundamental nature of the SR algorithm, as we discuss in Section 12.2.1.1.

12.1.2 **Brief history of SR methods prior to deep networks**

We first introduce the observation model used in SR. In general, image acquisition can be modeled as receiving an LR image I_{LR} from a degraded noisy sampling of an HR image I_{HR},

$$I_{LR} = (h * I_{HR}) \downarrow_s + n, \tag{12.1}$$

where h is the point-spread function (PSF), also called the blur kernel, the operator $(\cdot) \downarrow_s$ is downsampling with a scale factor of s, and n is noise. This observation model describes how an LR image is obtained from the true underlying HR image. The goal of SR is to recover I_{HR} from I_{LR}. This problem is ill-posed because there exists more than one input I_{HR} that can yield the observed image I_{LR}.

SR methods aim to estimate the missing high frequency information, and different methods have different sources of such information. These SR methods are discussed below, with some of them summarized in Table 12.1.

12.1.2.1 *SR through mathematical modeling*

The MISR framework combines high frequency information from multiple inputs, while SISR estimates high frequency information using prior knowledge.

MISR. When multiple images are acquired from the same scene, MISR aims to fuse high frequency content from all images. There are several types of multiple inputs. MISR can use input images of the same contrast but acquired from different orientations (multi-orientation SR) [1], the same orientation but different contrasts (multi-contrast SR) [2], or the same orientation and contrast but with different blur kernels (multi-acquisition SR) [3]. An example of multi-orientation SR approach in which a single HR tongue MR image is created from three LR MR images with different orientations is shown in Fig. 12.2. MISR depends on image registration to co-locate the corresponding information across multiple inputs. One challenge of MISR is to handle multiple inputs that are not perfectly registered [1].

Table 12.1 Different data scenarios give rise to different applicable SR methods.

Category	Method	SISR	MISR	External data Paired	Unpaired
Methods Prior to Deep Networks	Interpolation	✓	✗	✗	✗
	Deconvolution	✓	✗	✗	✗
	Iterative Back-Projection	✗	✓	✗	✗
	Projection Onto Convex Sets	✗	✓	✗	✗
	NLM (Brain hallucination)	✗	✓	✗	✗
Methods with Deep Networks	Fully-supervised learning	✓	✗	✓	✗
	Unsupervised learning	✓	✗	✗	✓
	Semi-supervised learning	✓	✗	✓	✓
	Self-supervised learning	✓	✗	✗	✗
	Multi-input supervised learning	✗	✓	✓	✗

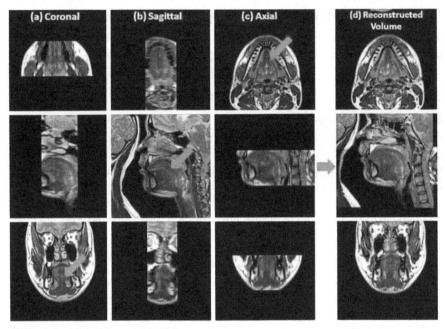

FIGURE 12.2

Multi-image super resolution (MISR) on tongue MRI in Woo et al. [1]: (a)–(c) three LR inputs from three acquisition orientations; and (d) the MISR result (no true HR image available).

Several methods are considered to be variants of MISR. Iterative back-projection [4–7], as the name implies, is an iterative method inspired by the back-projection reconstruction used in CT, aiming to reconstruct the HR image pixel-by-pixel by determining corresponding receptive fields in the set of LR images. Leveraging assumptions on the imaging (and therefore degradation) process, the initial HR estimate is iteratively improved by computing a loss between the true LR images and the simulated LR images obtained from the HR estimate. Projection onto convex sets (POCS) [8,9] takes a different approach: signals are said to have a set of properties $\pi_i, i = 1, 2, \ldots, m$ and are organized into closed convex sets C_i such that any signal with property π_i is in the set C_i. Importantly, the solution set $C_s = \bigcap_{i=1}^{m} C_i$ contains the desired signal with the correct properties and a signal in C_s can be achieved via weak convergence by the central theorem of POCS, $f^{(k+1)} = P_m P_{m-1} \cdots P_1 f^{(k)}$, with f an arbitrary signal and P_i a projector. By recursively finding a valid chain of projectors, POCS reconstructs the desired signal. For MISR, POCS makes use of multiple LR images as signals with properties and also has the ability to fold in other arbitrary priors represented in set form. Markov random fields (MRF) constitute another method of performing MISR. Under the MRF formulation, after all the images are intensity matched and registered, a maximum a posteriori MRF specifies the likelihood of an intensity in the HR image given the set of LR images. This Bayesian approach expresses the desired HR image as $\hat{I}_{HR} = \text{argmax}_{I_{HR}} \Pr(I_{LR}^1, I_{LR}^2, \ldots, I_{LR}^n | I_{HR}) \Pr(I_{HR})$ and has been applied to enhance the resolution of multiple acquisitions of tongue MRI [1].

SISR. Model-based SISR methods are sometimes called single image deconvolution. The modeling process aims to fit the following equation:

$$\hat{I}_{HR} = \arg \min_{I_{HR}} \mathcal{L}\big(I_{LR}, (h * I_{HR}) \downarrow_s \big) + \lambda \mathcal{R}(I_{HR}), \qquad (12.2)$$

where $\mathcal{L}$ denotes a loss function, usually ℓ_1- or ℓ_2-loss, and $\mathcal{R}$ denotes a λ-weighted regularizer. In Eq. (12.2), the first term comes directly from the observation model in Eq. (12.1). The second term is the regularizer $\mathcal{R}$, which comes from the prior knowledge that pixels/voxels in an image are spatially correlated and the corresponding regularizer includes MRF priors [10]. This spatial correlation could be translated into sparsity in image signals and the corresponding regularizer includes total variation [11–13].

Despite its long history in signal and image processing—as early as the Wiener filter [14] in 1949—deconvolution has had limited use in medical imaging. On its own, deconvolution does not address the ill-posed nature of the SR problem and, even with the use of regularizers, is highly susceptible to noise. Also, in practice, it is difficult to know the PSF h precisely and the deconvolution results can have severe artifacts.

To address issues with model-based SR, example-based SR methods have become dominant in recent years, especially since improved hardware capability has enabled very extensive signal modeling to be exploited through the use of deep neural networks.

12.1.2.2 Example-based SR

While model-based SR uses prior knowledge such as spatial correlation and sparsity, example-based SR obtains HR information from exemplars, which can be used in different ways. Two common types of methods are described below.

Non-local means. Non-local means (NLM) SR methods are also based on Eq. (12.2). Yet the regularizer $\mathcal{R}(I_{HR})$ is computed using exemplars, instead of using prior knowledge. The regularizer has the form of $\mathcal{R}(I_{HR}) = (I_{HR} - \hat{I}_{NLM})^2$, where the NLM estimation $\hat{I}_{NLM}$ is computed using HR exemplars. To understand NLM, first consider image interpolation. In image interpolation, to estimate the intensity of a point $\mathbf{v}$ that was not acquired, a weighted average of nearby points $\mathbf{k} \in \mathcal{N}(\mathbf{v})$ is used, i.e., $\hat{I}_{HR}(\mathbf{v}) = \sum_{\mathbf{k} \in \mathcal{N}(\mathbf{v})} w(|\mathbf{v} - \mathbf{k}|) I_{LR}(\mathbf{k})$. This is thought of abstractly as a "local mean," where the weights w are computed using only the spatial Euclidean distance $|\mathbf{v} - \mathbf{k}|$.

NLM [15], on the other hand, compute weights w from the features extracted from exemplars instead. The underline assumption in NLM is that points with similar features should have similar intensities. In NLM, the estimated intensity for point $\mathbf{v}$ is $\hat{I}_{NLM}(\mathbf{v}) = \sum_{\mathbf{k} \in \mathcal{N}(\mathbf{v})} w(\mathbf{v}, \mathbf{k}) I_{LR}(\mathbf{k})$, where the weight $w(\mathbf{v}, \mathbf{k})$ is large when the

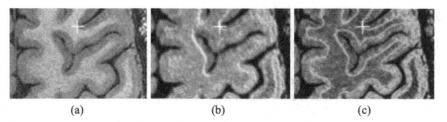

(a) (b) (c)

FIGURE 12.3

Similarity map in NLM methods [16]: (a) the exemplar image with a point of interest indicated by a cross sign; (b) the similarity map showing similarities between pixels and the point of interest computed from [2], where the bright intensities indicate high similarity with the pixel with cross sign; and (c) the similarity map computed from [16].

feature similarity between $\mathbf{v}$ and $\mathbf{k}$ is large. An example of a similarity map used to compute $w(\mathbf{v}, \mathbf{k})$ for point $\mathbf{v}$ is shown in Fig. 12.3 [16]. The similarity map and weights $w(\mathbf{v}, \mathbf{k})$ could be computed using features from an HR exemplar acquired from the same subject but with a different contrast from the LR input as in so-called "brain hallucination" [2,16,17] or computed from the input itself [18], where the features can be hand-crafted [2,16–18] or learned through sparse representation from HR exemplars [19].

NLM SR methods are based on Eq. (12.2). Thus their performance relies on the precisely known PSF h, which is often unavailable in practice.

Machine learning-based. While NLM computes the weights from examplars, learning-based methods aim to directly learn the appearance of desired HR images from the examplars. In fully-supervised SR (the most common training schema), LR/HR image pairs are presented as training data $\mathcal{D}$. From the training data and with machine learning methods, it is possible to learn the likely appearance of an HR image given the corresponding LR image. A fully-supervised SR method with a loss function $\mathcal{L}$ can be represented as learning ideal weights Θ which parameterize a mapping f_Θ using a training dataset $\mathcal{D} = (I_{\mathrm{LR},i}, I_{\mathrm{HR},i}), i \in \{1, 2, \ldots, N\}$, such that

$$\Theta = \arg\min_{\Theta} \frac{1}{N} \sum_{i=1}^{N} \mathcal{L}\big(f_\Theta(I_{\mathrm{LR},i}), I_{\mathrm{HR},i}\big), \tag{12.3}$$

where f_Θ extracts features from LR images and regresses these features into HR image intensities. In medical imaging, researchers have used machine learning tools for f_Θ such as random forests [20] and anchored neighborhood regression [21] prior to deep networks.

In the past few years, deep networks have been the most successful machine learning framework in SR. They learn what features to use from the training data, whereas most prior methods rely on handcrafted features. This shift in problem formulation has led to a vast improvement in SR qualitatively and quantitatively.

The remainder of this chapter is organized into two main parts. In Section 12.2, the broad components of contemporary deep learning approaches in SR are summarized. In Section 12.3, applications of SR techniques are shown, demonstrating the benefits of using super-resolved images on subsequent tasks.

12.2 SR methods with deep networks

SR methods with deep networks are constantly evolving but generally make use of novel permutations of basic concepts and building blocks, including different types of acquired data, network architectures, and loss functions. Here, we will enumerate these basic building blocks and describe the role that they play in SR deep network designs.

12.2.1 Data acquisition

Deep network-based SR methods with different data acquisition are introduced below and summarized in Table 12.1.

12.2.1.1 Fully-supervised, unsupervised, and self-supervised learning

Fully-supervised learning with real HR and simulated LR images. Ideally, LR and HR images that are used as training data should be both acquired from real scans; in this way, the networks can generalize better to test data which, in practice, are real scans themselves. However, paired real LR/HR are often unavailable and therefore most works choose to simulate LR images from real HR images. In this case, for better generalization, it is often preferred to model the HR-to-LR degeneration according to real acquisitions. Eq. (12.1) can often be used in these simulations. Some works combine the blur kernel h and the downsampling operator $(\cdot) \downarrow_s$ of Eq. (12.1) as a cubic interpolation [22,23], which, however, reports good performance only on simulated test LR images. A more common choice of h is a Gaussian function [24–30]. Several other works [31–33] also use a rect function. Meanwhile, in MRI, a more realistic degeneration is to discard the outer components in the frequency domain (i.e., the k-space) for the in-plane directions (and the through-plane direction if phase encoding is used in the slice direction) [29,34–37]. This is equivalent to applying h as a sinc function in the image domain.

Unsupervised learning with unpaired real LR and HR images. Some works do not simulate LR images and use unpaired real HR/LR scans instead [38,39]. Compared with paired data, unpaired data do not need the degeneration model or suffer from misalignment between LR and HR images. The CycleGAN [40] is the most commonly used framework in such cases. More details are discussed in Section 12.2.3.2.

Semi-supervised learning with paired and unpaired LR and HR images. Sometimes there are only a small amount of paired LR/HR images that are available. In this case, semi-supervised learning [39] uses not only these paired images but also a relatively large amount of unpaired images as training data. This can be regarded as a mixture of fully-supervised and unsupervised learning.

Self-supervised learning with the test LR image itself. While both fully-supervised and unsupervised learning require external HR training data, self-supervised learning extracts 2D HR/LR patches as training data from the 3D test LR image itself [29,41,42]. Specifically, this 3D image is HR along in-plane directions and LR along the through-plane direction, i.e., from an anisotropic acquisition. An example is shown in the first row of Fig. 12.4(b). Self-supervised methods then use 2D in-plane HR patches to simulate LR patches, train the network in a supervised fashion, and apply it to LR patches that are extracted along the through-plane direction. An example illustration of this framework [42] is shown in Fig. 12.4. With self-supervision, these methods are less affected by domain shift, i.e., the discrepancy between training and testing images.

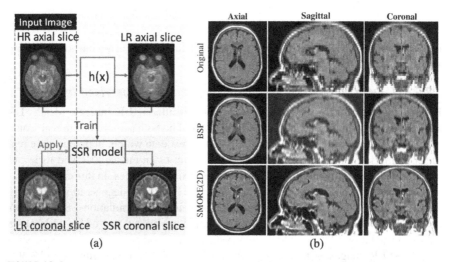

(a) (b)

FIGURE 12.4

A self-supervised MR image super-resolution algorithm, SMORE [29,42]: (a) high-level workflow of SMORE; (b) example SMORE results ($0.828 \times 0.828 \times 0.828$ mm) from the original ($0.828 \times 0.828 \times 4.4$ mm) MR image. **SSR**, self-supervised super-resolution; **BSP**, cubic B-spline interpolation.

12.2.1.2 Multiple network inputs

Some MISR algorithms take as input images with the same anatomy but different contrasts. For example, the works in [26,34] take as input LR T2-weighted (T2w) and HR T1-weighted (T1w) MRI from the same subjects to estimate the corresponding HR T2w MRI. Some MISR algorithms take as input images with different imaging orientations. For example, the work in [24] uses scans of long-axis and short-axis views in cardiac MRI. The extra inputs can often improve the accuracy of these networks. One challenge of MISR is to handle imperfect registration between multiple inputs.

12.2.2 Network architectures

12.2.2.1 General frameworks

Most of recent works are based on supervised training. These works usually train a feedforward CNN, and some of them use a conditioned generative adversarial network (GAN) [27,30,34,36,37,43] (see Section 12.2.3.2 for more details). In some cases, recurrent neural networks (RNNs) can be used. This technique can be applied to videos (cine images in MRI) to explore context along the time dimension [35]. It can also be used to formulate the problem as a step-by-step process where each step only partially improves the resolution [23,44]. For unpaired training, GANs, especially CycleGANs, are usually used; in these approaches, generators learn the degeneration from HR to LR and different generators learn SR from LR to HR [38,39].

12.2.2.2 Upsampling before or within networks

Super-resolving an LR image requires upsampling to increase its spatial size. There are two common approaches to do so: upsampling the image before or within the network. When upsampling before the network, interpolation in the spatial domain is used for most modalities such as CT and microscopy [38,41,45,46]; for MRI, however, zero-padding in the frequency domain is usually used for in-plane SR [29,36,37,47,48]. When upsampling within the network, transpose convolution can be used [23,31,39,49]. A more sophisticated operation is pixel shuffle where the channel dimension of feature maps is rearranged into their spatial dimensions [22,26,27,33,35,50]. Applying upsampling within the network means a smaller input image; in this case, the network can have a relatively large receptive field and is more memory-efficient. However, transpose convolution and pixel shuffle only work for integer upsampling factors, while non-integer upsampling factors are common in medical imaging.

12.2.2.3 Components in networks

Many networks are modifications of either the U-Net [51] or the enhanced deep super-resolution (EDSR) network [52]. Their architectures are shown in Fig. 12.5. Experiments in natural images show that U-Nets can better capture global features and thus are more robust when the registration between multiple inputs or between input and output data is not perfect [53]. EDSR networks mimic high-pass filters, are easier to train, require less training data, and perform better when the training images are paired without spatial shift.

Global residual connection. Many works use networks similar to EDSR that learn the residual between LR and HR images instead of the HR image directly [24–27,29,35,39,48,50]. This can be done by adding the input image (or the feature maps after a few convolutions) to the output (or feature maps just before the last few convolutions). In this case, the main body of the network learns the residual between the

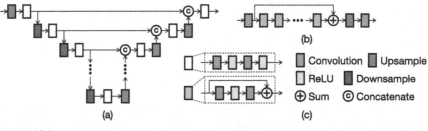

FIGURE 12.5

Example network architectures: (a) an example U-Net architecture; (b) an example EDSR architecture; and (c) the layer compositions of a white box in (a) and a gray box in (b) and names of other layers.

HR and LR images. As an analogue to residual blocks, it can be regarded as a global residual connection and is believed to make optimization easier.

Pooling layers. Some networks [30–32,41] are modified from the U-Net [51] (Fig. 12.5 (a)), which has an architecture that comprises an encoder and a decoder with concatenations across each resolution level. In each level of the encoder, a pooling operation or strided convolution is used to reduce the image spatial size; in the corresponding level of the decoder, the spatial size is restored using interpolation or transpose convolution. With pooling, the U-Net architecture yields a large receptive field that incorporates more global information. On the other hand, many other works do not rely on pooling layers [24–27,48,54] (Fig. 12.5 (b)); accordingly, their feature maps can have a fixed spatial size throughout the entire architecture.

Building blocks. Many works [22,25–27,49,54] use residual blocks where the input to a block is added to its output. Some works [36,55] use densely connected blocks where the input of a convolution is concatenated to the input of its following convolution. Spatial or channel attention [56], where a learnable probability map is multiplied to the features spatially or channel-wise, can also be used [22,30]. Networks can also have more complicated operations such as wavelet transforms [22].

Normalization layers. Due to memory constraints, SR networks are often trained or evaluated using image patches [23,26,31,33,39,47,48,55] especially for 3D images. With normalization layers, the output patches usually have inconsistent intensity levels, which causes a "checkerboard" effect when stitched up. As a result, most SR networks do not have normalization layers. On the other hand, if a network takes the whole image as the input, it can benefit from these operations [25,27,30,32,35]. In GANs, however, the discriminator network can have normalization layers regardless of whether patches or the whole image are used as input since its purpose is to distinguish the synthetic from real data.

12.2.2.4 Progressive networks

For higher upsampling factors (four times or higher, for example), multiple identical or similar networks, each of which learns partial SR (two times, for example) [27,34]—whether their weights are shared or not—can be cascaded. In such cases, the super-resolution process is done progressively. This type of architecture shares similarity with RNNs as mentioned in Section 12.2.2.1.

12.2.3 Loss functions

12.2.3.1 Paired losses

For supervised training, paired losses are used to encourage the network output to be close to the target. Common choices include mean squared error (MSE) [26,27, 30–34,37,44,48,55] and mean absolute error (MAE) [23,35,36,39,50]. In addition to MSE/MAE, some works [25,27,30,34,37] calculate a VGG loss that is named after the Visual Geometry Group (VGG) [57] at the University of Oxford. To calculate this loss, image features are extracted from some layers of a VGG network, which is pre-trained for natural image classification, then MSE/MAE is measured between these features of the network output and features of its target image. The Gram-matrix loss can also be calculated using the VGG features [30,34]. This loss converts these spatially arranged features from a VGG network to channel-wise correlations then measures their consistency between the network output and its target. Additionally, other variations of MSE/MAE can also be used, such as the smooth ℓ_1-loss [24], the triplet loss [27], a spatially weighted or filtered MSE/MAE loss [25,43], and MAE/MSE of image gradients [37,55,58].

12.2.3.2 Unpaired losses

Unpaired losses can be used in addition to paired losses in supervised learning or used alone in unsupervised learning. These losses are mainly related to GANs. The GAN generator learns SR from LR to HR, and the discriminator takes the distribution of HR images into account. Some works [25,27,43] use the entropy-based conventional GAN loss; for training stability, some works use MSE or ℓ_2-norm between the discriminator output and 1 or 0 [30,38], and others [34,36,37,39] use the loss of Wasserstein GAN with gradient penalty. If a CycleGAN is used, an additional generator network learns to degrade an HR image into LR [38,39]. In this case, an additional GAN loss is used for this second generator to learn the distribution of true LR images. Furthermore, a cycle-consistency loss is also used. This loss encourages an image to match itself after being processed by the cascade of these two generator networks.

12.3 Applications of super-resolution in medical images

In this section, we introduce the applications of SR in different medical image modalities and tasks.

12.3.1 Super-resolution in different image modalities

Here, we introduce the unique challenges and solutions for SR in each modality.

12.3.1.1 Super-resolution in CT

The first challenge for CT SR is to get paired training data. Ideally, many paired LR/HR images are required to train an SR deep network in a fully supervised manner. In practice, however, it is infeasible to ask patients to take multiple CT scans because of the additional radiation dose. Such paired LR/HR data are not available or only available in very limited amounts. In most cases, if researchers want to apply fully supervised training, they need to simulate LR images from HR images using, for example, the model in Eq. (12.1).

This leads to the second challenge—the blur kernel must be known to perform these simulations. Since CT images are reconstructed from sinograms, it is inaccurate to model the LR mechanism of CT images with simple bicubic downsampling. This leaves researchers with two choices. One is to *assume* a known blur kernel and then perform fully-supervised training. This requires the assumed blur kernel to be close enough to the true downsampling process; otherwise, the trained network can only work on simulated LR images and will not perform well on real clinical LR data. Although this type of approach is sub-optimal if blur kernel is not well modeled, it is adopted by most CT SR works. To better model the blur kernel, Tang et al. [59] performed SR on sinograms. The other approach is to perform unpaired training which does not require any knowledge of the blur kernel. You et al. [39] adopt this approach by collecting a small amount of paired LR/HR images and a large amount of unpaired LR/HR images and training a CycleGAN in a semi-supervised manner.

The third challenge is that the intensity scales vary a lot for bones and tissues [39]. If the network is trained with traditional ℓ_1- or ℓ_2-loss, the network will mainly pay attention to bones since they have high intensities. Although this is not a problem for applications like dental and abdominal CT, it will cause problems in brain CT where the soft tissues have very small contrasts and already suffer from high-level noise.

12.3.1.2 Super-resolution in MRI

The major challenge for MRI SR remains to be the difficulty of the acquisition of paired training data. Generally, to achieve HR MRI with adequate signal-to-noise ratio, the acquisition time must be very long. It is an expensive process which lowers patient throughput and raises the probability of both patient discomfort and motion artifacts. It means that HR MRI is difficult to acquire, and preparing paired LR/HR MRI data is even harder.

There are two possible solutions for this dilemma. The first is to train an SR network with a small amount of HR MRI data. It is known that deep networks do not perform well if the data distributions for training and testing data are different. It requires researchers to ensure that the LR testing MRI have similar contrast as the HR training MRI, which greatly limits its usage in clinical practice since small changes in the pulse sequences can result in different image contrasts. The second possible solution is to perform self-supervised training which extracts training data from the testing MRI itself. By doing so, training and testing data can have exactly the same contrast. This is performed in Zhao et al. [29,42].

The second challenge is to model the blur kernel. Unlike CT, the MRI blur kernel can be better modeled. Since MRI is sampled in the k-space, i.e., the frequency domain, within a limited region, it is usually equivalent to applying a sinc kernel in the image domain along the phase- and frequency-encoding directions. However, the blur kernel along the slice direction is still not known precisely.

12.3.1.3 Super-resolution in optical coherence tomography

Optical coherence tomography (OCT) SR also faces the challenge of lack of paired LR/HR training data. Similar to CT, researchers solve it by using unpaired training [60]. Another problem for OCT is the high speckle noise. Therefore, OCT SR is often performed together with speckle reduction [60,61].

12.3.1.4 Super-resolution in microscopy

Same as other modalities, microscopy SR has the challenge of lack of paired LR/HR training data. Similar to MRI, researchers solve it by self-supervised training [41, 58]. It also has the problem of an unknown blur kernel, which can be tackled by unsupervised training using CycleGANs [38].

To summarize, medical image SR generally faces the challenge of lack of training data. Acquiring paired LR/HR images is difficult or even infeasible for most modalities. This encourages different training schemes including unsupervised, semi-supervised, and self-supervised learning.

12.3.2 Super-resolution used for different tasks

Is image super-resolution helpful to other tasks? This question has been answered with a "Yes" in computer vision [71] for tasks including edge detection, segmentation, and recognition. For medical imaging, researchers have published a number of works to demonstrate the applications of SR and almost all of them show an improvement of performance. Some publications show that doctors prefer SR results [39,62] to the original LR images. Many publications show that SR improves the segmentation results [24,27,42,65–70]. Since segmentation results are often followed by tasks like pathology detection, SR has been demonstrated to be useful to more tasks. The applications of SR are summarized in Table 12.2.

12.3.2.1 Super-resolution for image quality enhancement

The most common application of SR is to improve image quality including accuracy to the ground truth HR and visual quality. Accuracy is often evaluated with the structural similarity index measure [72] and peak signal-to-noise ratio. Visual quality is evaluated with qualitative visual comparison. These two kinds of evaluation are included in almost all SR publications. Non-reference visual quality scores like the information fidelity criterion [73], "no-reference metrics"-SR [74], and spectral and spatial sharpness measure [75] are also evaluated in some literature [39,62,76].

Table 12.2 Application of Super-Resolution on Different Tasks.

Task	Modality	Publication	SR Supervision	SR Model	Comments
Diagnostic acceptability	CT	You et al., 2019 [39]	semi-supervised	2D CycleGAN	three doctors
	CT & MRI	Georgescu et al., 2020 [62]	fully supervised	2.5D CNN	six doctors
	MRI	Pham et al., 2019 [63]	fully supervised	3D CNN	multitask learning
	MRI	Delannoy et al., 2020 [64]	fully supervised	2.5D CNN	multitask learning
	MRI	Zhao et al., 2019 [42]	self-supervised	2D CNN	
	MRI	Oktay et al., 2016 [24]	fully supervised	2D CNN	
Segmentation	CT	Hatvani et al., 2018 [65]	fully supervised	2D CNN	
	OCT	Yun et al., 2020 [66]	fully supervised	3D CNN	
	Fundus	Gheshlaghi et al., 2020 [67]	fully supervised	2D CNN	
	Fundus & MRI	Mahapatra et al., 2019 [27]	fully supervised	2D CNN	
	MRI	Ozyurt et al., 2020 [68]	fully supervised	2D CNN	
	MRI	Sert et al., 2019 [69]	fully supervised	2D CNN	
	Microscopy	Kang et al., 2020 [70]	fully supervised	2D CNN	
Pathology detection	**Fundus**	Mahapatra et al., 2019 [27]	fully supervised	2D CNN	after segmentation
	MRI	Ozyurt et al., 2020 [68]	fully supervised	2D CNN	after segmentation
	MRI	Sert et al., 2019 [69]	fully supervised	2D CNN	after segmentation
Cell quantification	**Microscopy**	Kang et al., 2020 [70]	fully supervised	2D CNN	after segmentation
Motion tracking	**MRI**	Oktay et al., 2016 [24]	fully supervised	2D CNN	

12.3.2.2 Super-resolution for diagnostic acceptability

The second application of SR is to improve diagnostic acceptability for doctors. In medical imaging, it is important that doctors recognize the impact of SR on diagnosis. This application is evaluated by human observer scores from radiologists. You et al. [39] has three doctors evaluate their results which were compared with Lanczos interpolation and other SR methods on two CT datasets. Georgescu et al. [62] has six doctors evaluate their SR results which were compared with Lanczos interpolation on CT and MR images. Note that You et al. [39] is a semi-supervised method using a CycleGAN; it shows that even with only a little guidance from paired HR training data, the SR results can have better diagnostic acceptability than traditional upsampling methods, i.e., interpolation.

12.3.2.3 Super-resolution for segmentation

The third application of SR is to improve the performance of segmentation. There are two approaches. One is multitask learning, i.e., to train segmentation and SR simultaneously. This is performed in [63,64]. The other way is to treat SR and segmentation as two separate steps. This is adopted in more works [24,27,42,65–70]. These results show that SR improves the performance of segmentation in various modalities, including CT, MRI, fundus imaging, OCT, and microscopy. Especially in the self-supervised approach, such as in Zhao et al. [42], the SR result was obtained without any external training data; all the training data is extracted from the LR input image itself. This shows the potential of improving segmentation without obtaining any external HR data.

12.3.2.4 Super-resolution for clinical abnormality detection

Segmentation is not the final goal for medical image analysis. Researchers use segmentation results to perform other tasks. SR enhanced segmentation results are shown to improve segmentation-based pathology detection [27,68,69]. In Sert et al. [69] and Ozyurt et al. [68], SR results improve MRI brain tumor detection. In Mahapatra et al. [27], SR results improve retinal microaneurysm detection in fundus imaging. Both are important clinical applications.

12.3.2.5 Super-resolution for cell quantification and motion tracking

Similar to clinical abnormality detection, SR-enhanced segmentation is shown to be effective in improving segmentation-based cell quantification [70] in microscopy data and motion tracking [24] in cardiac data.

12.4 Conclusions

Enhancing image quality by improving the resolution is a practical problem which would assist both clinicians and researchers. A common question with SR is how an algorithm estimates HR information which does not exist in LR input data. Model-based SR methods use prior knowledge such as sparsity in image signals. Deep learning-based SR methods, on the other hand, obtain HR information from HR training data. With the development of deep learning, these SR algorithms have achieved the new state-of-the-art in this field. In this chapter, we first introduced some basic concepts in SR and a brief history of SR methods before deep networks, then we included a complete workflow of SR methods with deep networks from data acquisition to neural network building, and to the optimization procedure with different loss functions. Finally, we investigated the applications of SR methods in medical images, including a discussion of multiple image modalities such as CT, MRI, OCT, and microscopy; and a discussion of tasks: such as improving diagnostic acceptability, enhancing segmentation, facilitating clinical abnormality detection, cell quantification, and motion tracking.

Compared to SR for natural images, there are several challenges that are unique to medical images, including training data acquisition, blur kernel modeling or estimation for specific image modalities, application to clinical data instead of well established research data, and artifact reduction (e.g., motion artifacts and speckle noise reduction). These are important research topics in this field. Another important topic is the clinical application of SR. Although we included several examples in this chapter, they are often presented as one of the evaluation experiments in SR methodology papers. We hope to see more clinical oriented research works on SR in the future.

References

[1] J. Woo, Y. Bai, S. Roy, E.Z. Murano, M. Stone, J.L. Prince, Super-resolution reconstruction for tongue MR images, in: Medical Imaging 2012: Image Processing, vol. 8314, SPIE, 2012, pp. 113–120.

[2] F. Rousseau, Brain hallucination, in: Proceedings of the European Conference on Computer Vision (ECCV), 2008, pp. 497–508.

[3] M. Delbracio, G. Sapiro, Burst deblurring: removing camera shake through Fourier burst accumulation, in: Proceedings of the IEEE Conference on Computer Vision and Pattern Recognition (CVPR), 2015.

[4] M. Irani, S. Peleg, Super resolution from image sequences, in: [1990] Proceedings. 10th International Conference on Pattern Recognition, vol. 2, 1990, pp. 115–120.

[5] S. Peled, Y. Yeshurun, Superresolution in MRI: application to human white matter fiber tract visualization by diffusion tensor imaging, Magnetic Resonance in Medicine 45 (1) (2001) 29–35.

[6] Z. Yan, Y. Lu, Super resolution of MRI using improved IBP, in: 2009 International Conference on Computational Intelligence and Security, vol. 1, 2009, pp. 643–647.

[7] A. Souza, R. Senn, Model-based super-resolution for MRI, in: 2008 30th Annual International Conference of the IEEE Engineering in Medicine and Biology Society, 2008, pp. 430–434.

[8] H. Stark, P. Oskoui, High-resolution image recovery from image-plane arrays, using convex projections, Journal of the Optical Society of America A 6 (11) (1989) 1715–1726.

[9] R.Z. Shilling, M.E. Brummer, K. Mewes, Merging multiple stacks MRI into a single data volume, in: 3rd IEEE International Symposium on Biomedical Imaging: Nano to Macro, 2006, 2006, pp. 1012–1015.

[10] W. Wu, Z. Liu, W. Gueaieb, X. He, Single-image super-resolution based on Markov random field and contourlet transform, Journal of Electronic Imaging 20 (2) (2011) 1–18.

[11] A. Marquina, S.J. Osher, Image super-resolution by TV-regularization and Bregman iteration, Journal of Scientific Computing 37 (3) (2008) 367–382.

[12] X. Zhang, E.Y. Lam, E.X. Wu, K.K.Y. Wong, Application of Tikhonov regularization to super-resolution reconstruction of brain MRI images, in: Medical Imaging and Informatics, 2008, pp. 51–56.

[13] F. Shi, J. Cheng, L. Wang, P. Yap, D. Shen , LRTV: MR image super-resolution with low-rank and total variation regularizations, IEEE Transactions on Medical Imaging 34 (12) (2015) 2459–2466.

[14] N. Wiener, Extrapolation, Interpolation, and Smoothing of Stationary Time Series, Wiley, 1949.

[15] A. Buades, B. Coll, J.M. Morel, A review of image denoising algorithms, with a new one, Multiscale Modeling & Simulation 4 (2) (2005) 490–530.

[16] K. Jafari-Khouzani, MRI upsampling using feature-based nonlocal means approach, IEEE Transactions on Medical Imaging 33 (10) (2014).

[17] F. Rousseau, A non-local approach for image super-resolution using intermodality priors, Medical Image Analysis 14 (4) (2010) 594–605.

[18] J. Manjón, P. Coupé, A. Buades, D.L. Collins, M. Robles, MRI superresolution using self-similarity and image priors, International Journal of Biomedical Imaging 2010 (2010) 425891.

[19] D. Zhang, J. He, Y. Zhao, M. Du, MR image super-resolution reconstruction using sparse representation, nonlocal similarity and sparse derivative prior, Computers in Biology and Medicine 58 (2015) 130–145.

[20] A. Jog, A. Carass, J.L. Prince, Improving magnetic resonance resolution with supervised learning, in: 2014 IEEE 11th International Symposium on Biomedical Imaging (ISBI), 2014, pp. 987–990.

[21] A. Jog, A. Carass, J.L. Prince, Self super-resolution for magnetic resonance images, in: Medical Image Computing and Computer Assisted Intervention (MICCAI) 2016, 2016, pp. 553–560.

[22] Z. Chen, X. Guo, C. Yang, B. Ibragimov, Y. Yuan, Joint spatial-wavelet dual-stream network for super-resolution, in: Medical Image Computing and Computer-Assisted Intervention (MICCAI) 2020, 2020, pp. 184–193.

[23] L. Chen, X. Yang, G. Jeon, M. Anisetti, K. Liu, A trusted medical image super-resolution method based on feedback adaptive weighted dense network, Artificial Intelligence in Medicine 106 (2020) 101857.

[24] O. Oktay, W. Bai, M. Lee, R. Guerrero, K. Kamnitsas, J. Caballero, A. de Marvao, S. Cook, D. O'Regan, D. Rueckert, Multi-input cardiac image super-resolution using convolutional neural networks, in: Medical Image Computing and Computer-Assisted Intervention (MICCAI) 2016, 2016, pp. 246–254.

[25] D. Mahapatra, B. Bozorgtabar, S. Hewavitharanage, R. Garnavi, Image super-resolution using generative adversarial networks and local saliency maps for retinal image analysis, in: Medical Image Computing and Computer-Assisted Intervention (MICCAI) 2017, 2017, pp. 382–390.

[26] K. Zeng, H. Zheng, C. Cai, Y. Yang, K. Zhang, Z. Chen, Simultaneous single- and multi-contrast super-resolution for brain MRI images based on a convolutional neural network, Computers in Biology and Medicine 99 (2018) 133–141.

[27] D. Mahapatra, B. Bozorgtabar, R. Garnavi, Image super-resolution using progressive generative adversarial networks for medical image analysis, Computerized Medical Imaging and Graphics 71 (2019) 30–39.

[28] C. Pham, A. Ducournau, R. Fablet, F. Rousseau, Brain MRI super-resolution using deep 3D convolutional networks, in: 2017 IEEE 14th International Symposium on Biomedical Imaging (ISBI 2017), 2017, pp. 197–200.

[29] C. Zhao, B.E. Dewey, D.L. Pham, P.A. Calabresi, D.S. Reich, J.L. Prince, SMORE: a self-supervised anti-aliasing and super-resolution algorithm for MRI using deep learning, IEEE Transactions on Medical Imaging (2020).

[30] Y. Almalioglu, K.B. Ozyoruk, A. Gokce, K. Incetan, G.I.G.M.A. Simsek, K. Ararat, R.J. Chen, N.J. Durr, F. Mahmood, M. Turan, EndoL2H: deep super-resolution for capsule endoscopy, IEEE Transactions on Medical Imaging 39 (12) (2020) 4297–4309.

[31] L. Heinrich, J.A. Bogovic, S. Saalfeld, Deep learning for isotropic super-resolution from non-isotropic 3D electron microscopy, in: Medical Image Computing and Computer Assisted Intervention (MICCAI) 2017, 2017, pp. 135–143.

[32] J. Park, D. Hwang, K.Y. Kim, S.K. Kang, Y.K. Kim, J.S. Lee, Computed tomography super-resolution using deep convolutional neural network, Physics in Medicine and Biology 63 (14) (2018) 145011.

[33] C. Ye, Y. Qin, C. Liu, Y. Li, X. Zeng, Z. Liu, Super-resolved q-space deep learning, in: Medical Image Computing and Computer Assisted Intervention (MICCAI) 2019, 2019, pp. 582–589.

[34] Q. Lyu, H. Shan, C. Steber, C. Helis, C. Whitlow, M. Chan, G. Wang, Multi-contrast super-resolution MRI through a progressive network, IEEE Transactions on Medical Imaging 39 (9) (2020) 2738–2749.

[35] J. Lin, Y. Chang, W. Hsu, Efficient and phase-aware video super-resolution for cardiac MRI, in: Medical Image Computing and Computer Assisted Intervention (MICCAI) 2020, 2020, pp. 66–76.

[36] Y. Chen, F. Shi, A.G. Christodoulou, Y. Xie, Z. Zhou, D. Li, Efficient and accurate MRI super-resolution using a generative adversarial network and 3D multi-level densely connected network, in: Medical Image Computing and Computer Assisted Intervention (MICCAI) 2018, 2018, pp. 91–99.

[37] Q. Lyu, H. Shan, G. Wang, MRI super-resolution with ensemble learning and complementary priors, IEEE Transactions on Computational Imaging 6 (2020) 615–624.

[38] S. Deng, X. Fu, Z. Xiong, C. Chen, D. Liu, X. Chen, Q. Ling, F. Wu, Isotropic reconstruction of 3D EM images with unsupervised degradation learning, in: Medical Image Computing and Computer Assisted Intervention (MICCAI) 2020, 2020, pp. 163–173.

[39] C. You, G. Li, Y. Zhang, X. Zhang, H. Shan, M. Li, S. Ju, Z. Zhao, Z. Zhang, W. Cong, M.W. Vannier, P.K. Saha, E.A. Hoffman, G. Wang, CT super-resolution GAN constrained by the identical, residual, and cycle learning ensemble (GAN-CIRCLE), IEEE Transactions on Medical Imaging 39 (1) (2020) 188–203.

[40] J. Zhu, T. Park, P. Isola, A.A. Efros, Unpaired image-to-image translation using cycle-consistent adversarial networks, in: Proceedings of the IEEE International Conference on Computer Vision (ICCV), 2017, pp. 2223–2232.

[41] M. Weigert, L. Royer, F. Jug, G. Myers, Isotropic reconstruction of 3D fluorescence microscopy images using convolutional neural networks, in: Medical Image Computing and Computer Assisted Intervention (MICCAI) 2017, 2017, pp. 126–134.

[42] C. Zhao, M. Shao, A. Carass, H. Li, B.E. Dewey, L.M. Ellingsen, J. Woo, M.A. Guttman, A.M. Blitz, M. Stone, P.A. Calabresi, H. Halperin, J.L. Prince, Applications of a deep learning method for anti-aliasing and super-resolution in MRI, Magnetic Resonance Imaging 64 (2019) 132–141.

[43] L. Han, Z. Yin, A cascaded refinement GAN for phase contrast microscopy image super resolution, in: Medical Image Computing and Computer Assisted Intervention (MICCAI) 2018, 2018, pp. 347–355.

[44] L. Mukherjee, H.D. Bui, A. Keikhosravi, A. Loeffler, K.W. Eliceiri, Super-resolution recurrent convolutional neural networks for learning with multi-resolution whole slide images, Journal of Biomedical Optics 24 (12) (2019) 1–15.

[45] K. Umehara, J. Ota, T. Ishida, Application of super-resolution convolutional neural network for enhancing image resolution in chest CT, Journal of Digital Imaging 31 (4) (2018) 441–450.

[46] A. Kudo, Y. Kitamura, Y. Li, S. Iizuka, E. Simo-Serra, Virtual thin slice: 3D conditional GAN-based super-resolution for CT slice interval, in: International Workshop on Machine Learning for Medical Image Reconstruction, Springer, 2019, pp. 91–100.

[47] K. Xuan, D. Wei, D. Wu, Z. Xue, Y. Zhan, W. Yao, Q. Wang, Reconstruction of isotropic high-resolution MR image from multiple anisotropic scans using sparse fidelity loss and adversarial regularization, in: Medical Image Computing and Computer Assisted Intervention (MICCAI) 2019, 2019, pp. 65–73.

[48] A.S. Chaudhari, Z. Fang, F. Kogan, J. Wood, K.J. Stevens, E.K. Gibbons, J.H. Lee, G.E. Gold, B.A. Hargreaves, Super-resolution musculoskeletal MRI using deep learning, Magnetic Resonance in Medicine 80 (5) (2018) 2139–2154.

[49] S. McDonagh, B. Hou, A. Alansary, O. Oktay, K. Kamnitsas, M. Rutherford, J.V. Hajnal, B. Kainz, Context-sensitive super-resolution for fast fetal magnetic resonance imaging, in: Molecular Imaging, Reconstruction and Analysis of Moving Body Organs, and Stroke Imaging and Treatment, 2017, pp. 116–126.

[50] X. Zhao, Y. Zhang, T. Zhang, X. Zou, Channel splitting network for single MR image super-resolution, IEEE Transactions on Image Processing 28 (11) (2019) 5649–5662.

[51] O. Ronneberger, P. Fischer, T. Brox, U-Net: convolutional networks for biomedical image segmentation, in: Medical Image Computing and Computer Assisted Intervention (MICCAI) 2015, 2015, pp. 234–241.

[52] B. Lim, S. Son, H. Kim, S. Nah, K.M. Lee, Enhanced deep residual networks for single image super-resolution, in: Proceedings of the IEEE Conference on Computer Vision and Pattern Recognition (CVPR) Workshops, 2017, pp. 136–144.

[53] S. Nah, S. Baik, S. Hong, G. Moon, S. Son, R. Timofte, K.M. Lee, NTIRE 2019 challenge on video deblurring and super-resolution: dataset and study, in: Proceedings of the IEEE/CVF Conference on Computer Vision and Pattern Recognition (CVPR) Workshops, 2019.

[54] C. Zhao, A. Carass, B.E. Dewey, J. Woo, J. Oh, P.A. Calabresi, D.S. Reich, P. Sati, D.L. Pham, J.L. Prince, A deep learning based anti-aliasing self super-resolution algorithm for MRI, in: Medical Image Computing and Computer-Assisted Intervention (MICCAI) 2018, 2018, pp. 100–108.

[55] Z. Li, Q. Liu, Y. Li, Q. Ge, Y. Shang, D. Song, Z. Wang, J. Shi, A two-stage multi-loss super-resolution network for arterial spin labeling magnetic resonance imaging, in: Medical Image Computing and Computer Assisted Intervention (MICCAI) 2019, 2019, pp. 12–20.

[56] S. Woo, J. Park, J. Lee, I.S. Kweon, CBAM: convolutional block attention module, in: Proceedings of the European Conference on Computer Vision (ECCV), 2018, pp. 3–19.

[57] K. Simonyan, A. Zisserman, Very deep convolutional networks for large-scale image recognition, in: International Conference on Learning Representations (ICLR), 2015.

[58] C. Zhao, S. Son, Y. Kim, J.L. Prince, iSMORE: an iterative self super-resolution algorithm, in: Simulation and Synthesis in Medical Imaging, 2019, pp. 130–139.

[59] C. Tang, W. Zhang, L. Wang, A. Cai, N. Liang, L. Li, B. Yan, Generative adversarial network-based sinogram super-resolution for computed tomography imaging, Physics in Medicine and Biology 65 (23) (2020) 235006.

[60] V. Das, S. Dandapat, P.K. Bora, Unsupervised super-resolution of OCT images using generative adversarial network for improved age-related macular degeneration diagnosis, IEEE Sensors Journal 20 (15) (2020) 8746–8756.

[61] Y. Huang, Z. Lu, Z. Shao, M. Ran, J. Zhou, L. Fang, Y. Zhang, Simultaneous denoising and super-resolution of optical coherence tomography images based on generative adversarial network, Optics Express 27 (9) (2019) 12289–12307.

[62] M. Georgescu, R.T. Ionescu, N. Verga, Convolutional neural networks with intermediate loss for 3D super-resolution of CT and MRI scans, IEEE Access 8 (2020) 49112–49124.

[63] C. Pham, C. Tor-Díez, H. Meunier, N. Bednarek, R. Fablet, N. Passat, F. Rousseau, Simultaneous super-resolution and segmentation using a generative adversarial network: application to neonatal brain MRI, in: 2019 IEEE 16th International Symposium on Biomedical Imaging (ISBI 2019), 2019, pp. 991–994.

[64] Q. Delannoy, C. Pham, C. Cazorla, C. Tor-Díez, G. Dollé, H. Meunier, N. Bednarek, R. Fablet, N. Passat, F. Rousseau, SegSRGAN: super-resolution and segmentation using generative adversarial networks—application to neonatal brain MRI, Computers in Biology and Medicine 120 (2020) 103755.

[65] J. Hatvani, A. Horváth, J. Michetti, A. Basarab, D. Kouamé, M. Gyöngy, Deep learning-based super-resolution applied to dental computed tomography, IEEE Transactions on Radiation and Plasma Medical Sciences 3 (2) (2019) 120–128.

[66] H.R. Yun, M.J. Lee, H. Hong, K.W. Shim, Super-resolution image generation for improvement of orbital thin bone segmentation, in: P.Y. Lau, M. Shobri (Eds.), International Workshop on Advanced Imaging Technology (IWAIT) 2020, vol. 11515, 2020, pp. 111–114.

[67] S.H. Gheshlaghi, O. Dehzangi, A. Dabouei, A. Amireskandari, A. Rezai, N.M. Nasrabadi, Efficient OCT image segmentation using neural architecture search, in: 2020 IEEE International Conference on Image Processing (ICIP), 2020, pp. 428–432.

[68] F. Özyurt, E. Sert, D. Avcı, An expert system for brain tumor detection: fuzzy c-means with super resolution and convolutional neural network with extreme learning machine, Medical Hypotheses 134 (2020) 109433.

[69] E. Sert, F. Özyurt, A. Doğantekin, A new approach for brain tumor diagnosis system: single image super-resolution based maximum fuzzy entropy segmentation and convolutional neural network, Medical Hypotheses 133 (2019) 109413.

[70] M. Kang, E. Cha, E. Kang, J.C. Ye, N. Her, J. Oh, D. Nam, M. Kim, S. Yang, Accuracy improvement of quantification information using super-resolution with convolutional neural network for microscopy images, Biomedical Signal Processing and Control 58 (2020) 101846.

[71] D. Dai, Y. Wang, Y. Chen, L. Van Gool, Is image super-resolution helpful for other vision tasks?, in: 2016 IEEE Winter Conference on Applications of Computer Vision (WACV), 2016, pp. 1–9.

[72] Z. Wang, A.C. Bovik, H.R. Sheikh, E.P. Simoncelli, Image quality assessment: from error visibility to structural similarity, IEEE Transactions on Image Processing 13 (4) (2004) 600–612.

[73] H.R. Sheikh, A.C. Bovik, G. de Veciana, An information fidelity criterion for image quality assessment using natural scene statistics, IEEE Transactions on Image Processing 14 (12) (2005) 2117–2128.

[74] C. Ma, C. Yang, X. Yang, M. Yang, Learning a no-reference quality metric for single-image super-resolution, Computer Vision and Image Understanding 158 (2017) 1–16.

[75] C.T. Vu, D.M. Chandler, S3: a spectral and spatial sharpness measure, in: 2009 First International Conference on Advances in Multimedia, 2009, pp. 37–43.

[76] T. Song, S.R. Chowdhury, F. Yang, J. Dutta, PET image super-resolution using generative adversarial networks, Neural Networks 125 (2020) 83–91.

Medical image denoising

13

Yi Zhang, Hu Chen, and Wenchi Ke

College of Computer Science, Sichuan University, Chengdu, China

13.1 Introduction

In recent decades, medical images have been increasingly used to diagnose diseases. By observing these images, it is possible to drill down into the internal view of the human body, obtaining information about the brain, heart, blood vessels, and so on. However, due to the imaging mode and the complicated structure of the human body, noise exists ubiquitously in medical images, which becomes an obstacle for doctors to find a precise diagnosis. Therefore, it is essential to denoise medical images. Denoising has become a mandatory preprocessing stage in medical imaging systems. Medical images involve not just one type of image, but also a variety of images with signal-related noise types collected from various devices. It is difficult to completely remove this noise by utilizing the natural image denoising techniques available in the literature.

This chapter focuses on the denoising methods for medical images. It is noted that the methods mentioned in this chapter simply refer to the noise removal in the post-reconstruction image. The reconstruction methods are beyond the scope of this chapter [1].

13.2 Denoising approaches

Generally, there are four modalities of medical images: ultrasound (US), magnetic resonance (MR), computed tomography (CT), and positron emission tomography (PET). The noise in these images is different due to the different imaging principles and processes. Obviously, the images of the different modalities differ widely. Therefore, the noise removal method should properly consider the differences of noise in different modes. The post-reconstruction denoising methods can be divided into three categories: spatial domain filtering, dictionary learning, and deep learning.

13.2.1 Spatial domain filtering

Overall, spatial domain filtering approaches for image denoising are composed of two parts: one is a subregion of the image, the other is a predefined operation on this area.

The spatial filter processes the pixels in the specified area and generates a new pixel value to replace the original value of the reference pixel. According to the predefined operations, spatial filtering can be divided into linear filtering and non-linear filtering.

13.2.1.1 Linear filtering

Linear filtering is defined as a convolution. It is based on a kernel, which represents the shape and size of the neighborhood to be analyzed. The kernel slides across the whole image. In case of a $(2n + 1) \times (2m + 1)$ window, linear filtering can be defined as

$$h(i, j) = \sum_{l=-n}^{n} \sum_{k=-m}^{m} f(i - l, j - k) w(l, k), \tag{13.1}$$

where w is the kernel defined as a matrix, h is the output image, and f is the original image.

The mean filter is the easiest linear filter, which replaces the original pixel value of the image with the average value of the pixels from its neighborhood. Mean filtering, however, changes the edge pixel values and may cause edge blur. Improved results can be obtained when filtering with a Gaussian filter (see Eq. (13.2))

$$G_{\mu_x, \mu_y, \sigma}(x, y) = e^{-\frac{(x - \mu_x)^2 + (y - \mu_y)^2}{2\sigma^2}}, \tag{13.2}$$

where the weights of pixels in the inspected neighborhood are not equal and decrease with the distance from the reference pixel. Nevertheless, even Gaussian filter is not able to perfectly eliminate the noise as it still causes some blur. In medical images, edges play a rather important role in the diagnosis. Therefore, linear filtering is not widely used in medical image denoising because of the blurred edges it produces.

13.2.1.2 Non-linear filtering

The main difference between non-linear and linear filtering is that non-linear filtering considers the ordering of pixels in a $(2n + 1) \times (2m + 1)$ window and can be defined as

$$h(i, j) = [\{ f(k, l) \mid k = i - n, \dots, i + n; l = j - m, \dots, j + m \}] \tag{13.3}$$

where $[A]$ is an operation mainly to sort the set A and take one particular new value, f is the original image.

The median filter is one of the most common non-linear filters. Median filtering selects the pixel whose value is the median of the neighborhood pixel values to replace the pixel value in the original image. Median filtering can remove isolated noise in the filter area. Isolated noise generally means that there is no noise in the pixels adjacent to the noise, such as salt and pepper noise. Like linear filtering, non-linear filtering will adversely affect edges. Under normal circumstances, non-linear filtering will have better object edge retention than linear filtering.

13.2.1.3 Adaptive filtering

Of the spatial domain filtering methods, the adaptive filtering technology is an important category. It is based on the idea of assigning weighting coefficients to pixels of the filter window whose characteristics are based on statistical properties. Lee's filter, adaptive weighted median filtering, and bilateral filtering are classic adaptive filters.

Lee's filter [2] is a spatial domain filter that uses local statistics. These statistics are the local mean and variance calculated in pixel (i, j) over a $(2n + 1) \times (2m + 1)$ window. The local mean, local variance, and filtered image are defined as

$$l_{\text{mean}}(i, j) = \frac{1}{(2n + 1)(2m + 1)} \sum_{l=i-n}^{i+n} \sum_{k=j-m}^{j+m} f(l, k), \tag{13.4}$$

$$l_{\text{var}}(i, j) = \frac{1}{(2n + 1)(2m + 1)} \sum_{l=i-n}^{i+n} \sum_{k=j-m}^{j+m} [f(l, k) - l_{\text{mean}}(i, j)]^2, \tag{13.5}$$

$$h(i, j) = l_{\text{mean}}(i, j) + \sqrt{\frac{v_d}{l_{\text{var}}(i, j)}} [f(i, j) - l_{\text{mean}}(i, j)], \tag{13.6}$$

where f is the input image, l_{mean} is the local mean, l_{var} is the local variance, v_d is the global variance of the image, and h is the output image.

Adaptive weighted median filter [3] is based on the well-known median filter through the introduction of weight coefficients that are responsible for repeating the individual terms from Eq. (13.3). By adjusting the weight coefficients and consequently the smoothing characteristics of the filter according to the local statistics around each point of the image, compared with standard median filtering, the advantage of the weighted median is that it better preserves image details or edges.

In the adaptive weighted median, the ratio $l_{\text{var}}^2 / l_{\text{mean}}$ can characterize the local image content by performing space-varying weighted median filtering with the weight coefficients adjusted according to the local statistics of the image. The weights for individual positions are defined as follows:

$$w(i, j) = \mathcal{Z}^+ \left(w(K + 1, K + 1) - c\, d\, l_{\text{var}}^2 / l_{\text{mean}} \right) \tag{13.7}$$

where c is a scaling constant, l_{mean}, l_{var} are the local mean and variance, d the distance of the pixel (i, j) from the center of the $(K + 1) \times (K + 1)$ window, and $\mathcal{Z}^+(x)$ denotes the nearest integer to x if x is positive, or zero if x is negative.

13.2.1.4 Bilateral filtering

The idea underlying bilateral filtering [4] is to consider both the spatial information and the range information of the pixels to be filtered. Two pixels can be close to each other, that is, occupying nearby spatial locations, or they can be similar to each other, that is, they may have similar values in a perceptually meaningful fashion. Closeness refers to the vicinity in the spatial domain and similarity to vicinity in the intensity range. The bilateral filter is defined as follows:

$$h(i, j) = \frac{1}{w_p(i, j)} \sum_{l=i-n}^{i+n} \sum_{k=j-m}^{j+m} G_s \left[\|(l, k) - (i, j)\| \right] G_r \left[f(l, k) - f(i, j) \right] f(l, k),$$

(13.8)

where G_r is the Gaussian kernel for smoothing differences in intensities, G_s is the Gaussian kernel for smoothing differences in coordinates, and

$$w_p(i, j) = \sum_{l=i-n}^{i+n} \sum_{k=j-m}^{j+m} G_s \left[\|(l, k) - (i, j)\| \right] G_r \left[(f(l, k) - f(i, j)) \right]$$

(13.9)

is a weight derived from spatial closeness and intensity difference.

Traditional filtering is domain filtering, which enforces closeness by weighing pixel values with coefficients that fall off with distance. Similarly, this method defines range filtering, which averages image values with weights that decay with dissimilarity. Range filters are non-linear because their weights depend on image intensity or color. Computationally, they are not more complex than standard range filters. Most importantly, they preserve edges.

13.2.1.5 Non-local means filtering

Let us assume that images contain a substantial number of redundant local structures. This property can be exploited to reduce noise by performing appropriately weighted averages of pixel intensities. Non-local means filtering can be defined as follows:

$$h(s) = \frac{\sum_{t \in R_s} w(s, t) f(t)}{\sum_{t \in R_s} w(s, t)},$$

(13.10)

where R_s is a matrix (search window) centered at pixel s, $h(s)$ is the filtered pixel intensity at pixel s, $f(t)$ is the pixel intensity at pixel t in the original image, and $w(s, t)$ is the weight assigned to an individual pixel t within window R_s when filtering pixel s. In the non-local means method, this weight is representing the similarity between two patches of the same shape P centered at pixels s and t. Weights are defined as follows:

$$w(s, t) = \exp \left(-\frac{\sum_{\delta \in P} G_\sigma(\delta) [f(s + \delta) - f(t + \delta)]^2}{n^2} \right),$$

(13.11)

where G_σ is a Gaussian kernel, δ represents the relative offsets of pixels inside a patch P, and n is a smoothing parameter used to control the amount of denoising and is usually taken to be proportional to the assumed or known noise level.

The non-local means algorithm is different from the linear filtering, which only compares the gray levels of independent pixels, because it also combines the local gray value structure of the entire image for comparison. In addition, it incorporates the local gray value feature into the similarity measure between pixels and performs an overall comparison of the gray distributions in the pixel field. The size of the weight is determined according to the similarity between the two fields.

However, there are two main disadvantages of the NLM algorithm. The first is the large number of calculations. The algorithm needs to traverse all pixels in the image when calculating the current pixel value and relies on the gray value comparison between pixels to judge self-similarity. The second is that dissimilar points may be introduced, resulting in cumulative deviation and a decrease in the denoising effect.

13.2.1.6 Anisotropic diffusion filtering

Based on partial differential equations, the concepts of heterogeneous diffusion and iterative smoothing are introduced into image denoising. The basic anisotropic diffusion filter model [5] is:

$$\frac{\partial f}{\partial t} = \text{div}[c(\|\nabla f\|)], \tag{13.12}$$

$$f(t=0) = f_0, \tag{13.13}$$

$$c(\|\nabla f\|) = \exp(-(\|\nabla f\|/K))^2, \tag{13.14}$$

where div is the divergence operator, ∇ is the gradient operator, $c(\|\nabla f\|)$ is the diffusion equation, K is the constant that controls the sensitivity to edges and is usually chosen experimentally, and t is the time, which is related to the diffusion duration in the noise reduction process.

Under normal circumstances, the edge part of the image usually has a larger gradient value. By setting the diffusion equation, the model implements weaker smoothing at the edge of the image to maintain the edge information. In addition, the flat area usually has a smaller gradient value, and a larger diffusion coefficient is set to implement stronger smoothing in the flat part of the image.

At isolated noise points, the smoothing effect of the model is poor. Because this kind of noise has a large gradient, it remains an edge. The design of the diffusion coefficient makes the edge retention effect of the model unsatisfactory. The anisotropic diffusion equation itself is mathematically ill-conditioned and cannot guarantee the uniqueness of the solution. Some improved methods do not have these shortcomings, such as coherence-enhancing diffusion filtering by Weickert et al. [6].

13.2.1.7 Total variation

By observing the total variation of images with different noise levels, the total variation of images contaminated by noise is significantly larger than that of images without noise. According to this concept, Rudin [7] proposed the total variation model. The total variation model is defined as follows:

$$\min_{h} \int_{\Omega} ||\nabla h|| dxdy + \frac{\lambda}{2} \int_{\Omega} ||h - f||_2^2 dxdy, \qquad (13.15)$$

where h is the denoised image, f is the input image, Ω is the image domain, $|| \cdot ||$ is the L_1-norm operator, ∇ is the gradient operator, and λ is the Lagrange weight coefficient.

In the total variation method, the edge information of the image can be maintained well in the denoising process. However, the method may treat the noise in the non-edge area as an edge, resulting in a ladder effect.

13.2.1.8 Block matching 3D

Block matching 3D (BM3D) [8] introduces a denoising strategy based on an enhanced sparse representation. The enhancement of the sparsity is achieved by grouping similar 2D image blocks into 3D data arrays. In general, BM3D can be divided into two main parts: basic estimate and final estimate. Each part contains three consecutive steps: (1) grouping, (2) collaborative filtering, and (3) aggregation.

1. The aim of the group step is to find patches that are similar to the currently processed one and then stack them together in a 3D array (group)

$$G(P) = \{Q : d(P, Q) < r\}, \qquad (13.16)$$

where G is a 3D array (group), P is the reference patch, Q is the similar block within the search window, $d(P, Q)$ is the Euclidean distance between two blocks, and r represents the size of the search window. The order of integration of individual patches has little effect on the results.

2. In the collaborative filtering step either the threshold or Wiener filter is applied. In particular, the threshold is utilized when basic estimate is performed:

$$Q(P) = T_{3D}^{-1} (\gamma (T_{3D} (G(P)))), \qquad (13.17)$$

where $Q(P)$ is the filtered result of $G(P)$, T_{3D} is a 3D linear transform (e.g., Walsh–Hadamard, discrete cosine, or Haar transform), and γ is the threshold operator

$$\gamma(x) = \begin{cases} 0 & \text{if } |x| < \lambda, \\ x & \text{otherwise.} \end{cases} \qquad (13.18)$$

Wiener filter, on the other hand, is applied during the final estimate:

$$Q(P) = T_{3D}^{-1} (w \cdot T_{3D} (G(P))). \qquad (13.19)$$

Here, $Q(P)$ is the filtered result of $G(P)$, T_{3D} is the same 3D linear transform as above, and w are Wiener filter shrinkage coefficients,

$$w = \frac{|T_{3D} (Q_{\text{basic}} (P))|^2}{|T_{3D} (Q_{\text{basic}} (P))|^2 + \sigma^2}, \qquad (13.20)$$

where Q_{basic} is the Q derived in basic estimate and σ is the standard deviation of noise.

3. The aggregation step is responsible for computing the estimates of the true-image through weighted averages of all of the obtained blockwise estimates that are overlapping.

The complete algorithm flow is shown in Table 13.1.

Table 13.1 Block matching 3D (BM3D) algorithm.

Part I: Basic estimate
Block-wise estimates. For each block in the noisy image perform steps 1 & 2:
1	*Grouping.* Find blocks that are similar to the currently processed one and stack them together in a 3D array (group).
2	*Collaborative thresholding.* Apply a 3D transform to the formed group, attenuate the noise through thresholding of the transform coefficients, invert the 3D transform to produce estimates of all grouped blocks, and return the estimates of the blocks to their original positions.
3	*Aggregation.* Compute the basic estimate of the true-image through weighted averages of all of the obtained block-wise estimates that are overlapping.
Part II: Final estimate
Block-wise estimates. In each block, perform steps 1 & 2:
1	*Grouping.* Use block matching within the basic estimate to find the locations of the blocks similar to the currently processed one. Using these locations, form two groups (3D arrays), one from the noisy image and one from the basic estimate.
2	*Collaborative Wiener filtering.* Apply a 3D transform to both groups. Perform Wiener filtering on the noisy one using the energy spectrum of the basic estimate as the true (pilot) energy spectrum. Produce estimates of all grouped blocks by applying the inverse 3D transform to the filtered coefficients and return the estimates of the blocks to their original positions.
3	*Aggregation.* Compute a final estimate of the true-image by aggregating all of the obtained local estimates using the weighted average.

13.2.2 Dictionary learning method

In the dictionary learning method, the dictionary is an overcomplete basis. The elements in this basis are called atoms that are learned from application-specific training images. Then, an object image can be sparsely represented as a linear combination of these atoms. Usually, an object image is decomposed into small, overlapping patches. The dictionary learning method acts on these patches, and an average of the corresponding values in the overlapping patches is computed at a given location. Since the dictionary is learned from training images, it is expected to have a better sparsifying capability than any other generic sparse transform. Additionally, the redundancy of the atoms facilitates a sparser representation. More importantly, the dictionary tends to capture local image features effectively because of patch-based analysis and, most importantly, structural self-similarity in many cases. Dictionary learning-based patch processing aims at solving the following problem:

$$\min_{h,D,\alpha}\left[\|h-f\|_2^2+\mu\sum\|R_{i,j}(f)-D\alpha_{i,j}\|_2^2\right],\qquad(13.21)$$

where h and f denotes the processed and original images, respectively, $R_{i,j}$ represents the operator that extracts the $n\times n$ patch (centered at (i,j)) from image f, D is an $n\times K$ matrix, which is composed of K n-vector atoms (columns), α, denoting the coefficient set, is a $K\times n$ matrix. Finally, $h=D\alpha$. If there are only s (provided $s\ll K$) non-zero coefficients in α, then the coefficient set α is said to be sparse.

More details on the use of dictionary learning for image synthesis can be found in Chapter 5.

13.2.3 Deep learning

More recently, artificial neural networks have been rapidly developed and have achieved amazing breakthroughs in many tasks, such as speech recognition, object recognition and target detection. Convolutional neural networks (CNN) are also widely used in image denoising. In traditional denoising methods, problems such as a low acceleration factor, long iterative reconstruction time, difficult parameter selection, and high computational complexity remain. The deep learning technology applied to image denoising has many advantages, such as reducing scanning cost, improving image quality, and speeding up imaging. It needs to be pointed out that the deep learning method does not consume a lot of computing resources when it is applied, and the main computing cost is on the training of the model.

13.2.3.1 Convolutional neural networks

The basic structure of the CNN used in image denoising is the encoding–decoding structure. The encoder is mainly for patch encoding. The main function of this step is to sparsely represent the image. The goal of the decoder is reconstruction; in this step, the processed overlapping patches are merged into a final complete image. These overlapping patches must be properly weighted before the summation.

In the methods based on a CNN, the problem of image denoising is transformed into an approximate problem from low-quality image, $X\in R^{m\times n}$, to normal-quality image, $Y\in R^{m\times n}$. The problem can be formulated as follows:

$$\arg\min_f\|f(X)-Y\|^2,\qquad(13.22)$$

where f is a function regarded as the optimal approximation of the complex degradation process involving quantum noise and other factors. The function f can be approximated by a CNN.

More details on the different CNN architectures that are used for medical image synthesis are available in Chapter 6.

13.2.3.2 Generative adversarial networks

Minimizing the squared error between the reference and predicted voxel values causes the CNN to predict the mean of these values, resulting in smoothed images that lack the texture of a typical routine-dose image. This kind of smoothing may limit the quantification of small structures in denoised images.

Accordingly, the generative adversarial network (GAN) [9] was introduced to solve this problem. A typical GAN can be divided into two parts: a generator G and a discriminator D. Both D and G are trained by solving the following min–max problem:

$$\min_{G} \max_{D} L_{GAN}(D, G) = E_{x \sim P_x}[\log D(x)] + E_{z \sim P_z}[\log(1 - D(G(x)))], \quad (13.23)$$

where G is the generator, D is the discriminator, $E[\cdot]$ is the expectation operation, and P_r, P_z are the real and noisy data distributions, respectively.

The task of the generator G, which is often a CNN with an encoding–decoding structure, is to predict the noise, then subtract the prediction noise from the input and obtain the denoised image. The task of the discriminator D is to determine whether the input is a real image or not. When the performance of the generator G improves, the performance of discriminator D also improves. This helps improving the denoising ability of CNN. GANs used for medical image synthesis are reviewed in Chapter 7.

13.3 Evaluation metrics

To determine the effect of the image denoising algorithm, the denoised image needs to be quantitatively evaluated. Currently, there is no such evaluation method that convincingly evaluates denoised images. Therefore, it is necessary to combine multiple evaluation methods. Common methods include the signal-to-noise ratio, peak signal-to-noise ratio, mean square error, structural similarity index and visual quality assessment.

The signal-to-noise ratio (SNR) is the ratio of the power of the signal to the noise. The larger the value, the better the image quality. The peak signal-to-noise ratio (PSNR) is defined as the ratio between the maximum power that can be present in a signal and the power of noise affecting the signal. Similar to SNR, the greater the value of PSNR, the higher the quality of the denoised image. The mean square error (MSE) represents the second moment of the error, which is the mean value of the square of the error and the expected loss of the square of the signal at each pixel position. The closer the MSE to 0, the less noise in the image. The structural similarity index (SSIM) [10] shows how much the denoised image matches the original image. In the calculation of SSIM, three factors are included to quantify the similarity between two images: the similarity of brightness, contrast, and structure. The value of SSIM is between 0 and 1. The closer the value of SSIM to 1, the greater the similarity between the two images, that is, the better the denoising effect.

Although quantitative evaluation indicators can reflect the ability of image denoising, there is no perfect quantitative evaluation of visual quality. The final evaluation of denoised images should still rely on humans. A denoising method has excellent quantification results, but if the expected denoising result cannot be observed by humans, this algorithm still does not meet the actual goal of denoising. To measure visual quality, no mathematical or specific method is available. If visual evaluation is necessary, different people need to score the denoising results. The final average score can be used as a quantitative visual evaluation indicator.

Interested readers can find more information regarding method validation and evaluation metrics in Chapter 25.

13.4 Examples of applications

13.4.1 Ultrasound

Ultrasound travels through soft tissues and fluids, but it bounces back or echoes off denser surfaces. For diagnostic uses, ultrasound is usually between 2 and 18 MHz. The denser the object the ultrasound hits, the greater the ultrasound bounces back. Bouncing back or echo gives the ultrasound image its features. Varying shades of gray reflect different densities. Higher-frequency ultrasound can provide better-quality images because the ultrasound waves are more easily absorbed by the skin and other tissues that these ultrasound waves cannot penetrate deeply. Lower-frequency ultrasound waves can penetrate deeper, but the image quality is lower.

In ultrasound images, the noise is usually speckle noise. Speckle noise appears as a small circle on the image, which may cover up the detailed information of the soft tissue. This obstacle can significantly affect the diagnosis of diseases. Speckle noise is caused by the backscattering phenomenon that occurs when ultrasound waves propagate through a biological medium and is difficult to reduce during the process of image acquisition. Noise is generally considered to have a multiplicative Gaussian nature.

13.4.1.1 Non-local means filtering

Coupé et al. [11] apply non-local means to the denoising of US images. Fig. 13.1 shows the denoising performance of the non-local means algorithm for US images. The obviousness of liver metastasis and the appearance of liver parenchyma have improved.

13.4.1.2 Generative adversarial networks

GANs have also been applied to ultrasound image speckle removal. A method combining a residual neural network and a GAN has been proposed [12]. In the generator, the image input goes through six ResNet block chains, and then the output is obtained. In the discriminator, there are four convolution modules. Different modules have different numbers of channels. Global average pooling is used as the last layer of the network. The denoising result of the GAN is shown in Fig. 13.1.

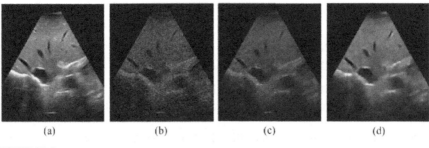

(a)   (b)   (c)   (d)

FIGURE 13.1

Denoising of ultrasound images using non-local means filtering and generative adversarial networks. From left to right: original image, noisy image, image denoised using a non-local means filtering approach [11], image denoised using a generative adversarial network [12].

13.4.2 Magnetic resonance imaging

Magnetic resonance imaging uses a magnetic field and radio waves to generate images of the body with high quality, especially parts of the body that cannot be seen well through other medical imaging modalities, to examine the internal body structures. The basis of MR imaging is the hydrogen atom. The many hydrogen atoms in a human body, when placed in a magnetic field, line up in the direction of the field. The positively charged hydrogen atoms become almost uniformly aligned. A radio frequency wave is pulsed into the body to deflect the aligned protons. When the protons return to their original position, energy is released. The intensity of the received signal is then plotted on a grayscale, and cross-sectional images are built. In MR images, the noise is usually Rician noise [13].

13.4.2.1 Unbiased non-local means filtering

Unbiased non-local means has been proposed for the denoising of MR images [14]. It is an improved algorithm based on the NLM algorithm. The MR image follows a Rician distribution leading to low contrast. In the squared magnitude image, the noise bias is no longer signal-dependent and can easily be removed. Such a bias is equal to σ^2, as shown by Nowak [15],

$$NLM(f(\boldsymbol{p})) = \sum_{\forall \boldsymbol{q} \in f} w(\boldsymbol{p}, \boldsymbol{q}) f(\boldsymbol{q}),$$

$$0 \leq w(\boldsymbol{p}, \boldsymbol{q}) \leq 1, \tag{13.24}$$

$$\sum_{\forall \boldsymbol{q} \in f} w(\boldsymbol{p}, \boldsymbol{q}) = 1,$$

where $\boldsymbol{p}$ is the point being filtered, $\boldsymbol{q}$ represents each one of the pixels in image f, and $w(\boldsymbol{p}, \boldsymbol{q})$ are weights based on the similarity between the neighborhoods of pixels

p and q. The similarity $w(p, q)$ is calculated as

$$w(p, q) = \frac{1}{Z(p)} e^{-\frac{d(p,q)}{h^2}}, \quad Z(p) = \sum_{\forall q \in f} e^{-\frac{d(p,q)}{h^2}}, \tag{13.25}$$

where $Z(p)$ is the normalizing constant, h is an exponential decay control parameter, d is a Gaussian weighted Euclidean distance of all the pixels of each neighborhood.

In the squared magnitude image, the noise bias is no longer signal-dependent and can be easily removed. Such a bias is equal to σ^2; therefore, a simple bias subtraction recovers its original value. This value can be estimated as the mean value of the background intensities of the squared noisy image where the signal should be zero:

$$UNLM = \sqrt{NLM(Y)^2 - 2\sigma^2}, \quad \sigma = \sqrt{\frac{\mu}{2}}, \tag{13.26}$$

with μ being the mean value of the background of the squared noisy image.

Unbiased NLM still requires many calculations. It takes approximately 7 min for a typical size dataset ($256 \times 256 \times 90$ pixels) to be filtered through the 2D version of the filter and the parameter settings. Improved methods based on NLM also include adaptive blockwise NLM [16], optimized blockwise NLM [17], and prefiltered rotationally invariant NLM for 3D MRI [18].

13.4.2.2 Block matching 3D & 4D

Elahi et al. [19] introduced a denoising strategy based on an enhanced sparse representation. The enhancement of the sparsity is achieved by grouping similar 2D image blocks into 3D data arrays. In this work, a new noise reduction method based on the improved BM3D algorithm is proposed.

Block matching 4D (BM4D) [20] is an extension of the BM3D algorithm to volumetric data denoising. In BM3D, the basic data patches are blocks of pixels, and BM4D utilizes cubes of voxels. The group formed by stacking mutually similar cubes is hence a four-dimensional orthogonality whose fourth dimension, along which the cubes are stacked, embodies the non-local correlation across the data. Thus, collaborative filtering simultaneously exploits the local correlations present among voxels in each cube as well as the non-local correlation between the corresponding voxels of different cubes. The denoised result is shown in Fig. 13.2.

13.4.2.3 Convolutional neural networks

The wider deep neural network (WDNN) proposed in [21] is a typical CNN method for MR images. The input of the network is the image with noise, and then the output is the predicted noise image. The output subtracted from the input is then the denoised MR image. In the network, the components are connected sequentially. In WDNN, the loss function is not the MSE but L_1-loss. Using MSE loss can produce blur artifacts. The denoised result is shown in Fig. 13.3.

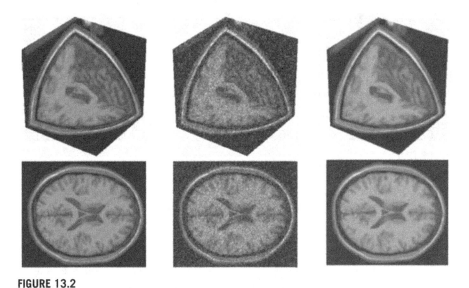

FIGURE 13.2

Denoising of MR images using block matching 4D [20]. From left to right: noise-free image, noisy image, and denoised image.

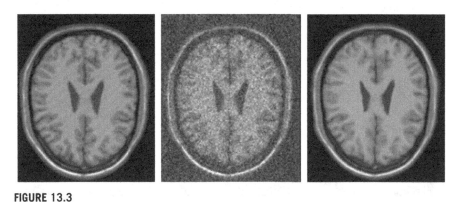

FIGURE 13.3

Denoising of MR images using the wider deep neural network proposed in [22]. From left to right: original image, noisy image, and denoised image.

The multichannel version of the denoising deep neural network (MCDnCNN) implemented in [21] is a CNN denoising method similar to WDNN. In MCDnCNN, 3D data is applied to the network. The MCDnCNN network consists of one input layer of convolution with a rectified linear unit (ReLU), eight layers of convolution with batch normalization and ReLU, and one output layer of convolution. The denoised result is shown in Fig. 13.4. Here, MCDnCNNg means a general model for Rician denoising with an unknown noise level and MCDnCNNs means a model trained on a specific noise level.

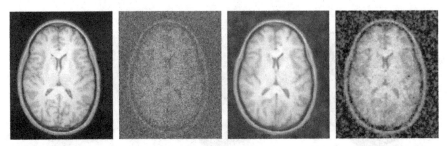

FIGURE 13.4

Denoising of MR images using the multichannel version of the denoising deep neural network (MCDnCNN) implemented in [21]. From left to right: MR image without noise, MR image with artificial noise, corresponding denoised image using (MCDnCNN) [21], and corresponding denoised image using optimized blockwise non-local means filtering [17].

The convolutional neural network for denoising of magnetic resonance images (CNN-DMRI) described in [23] utilizes the encoder–decoder structure for denoising MR images. The network takes a noisy MRI as input and outputs its clear version. It is actually a generative network that utilizes the encoder–decoder framework. The result is shown in Fig. 13.5.

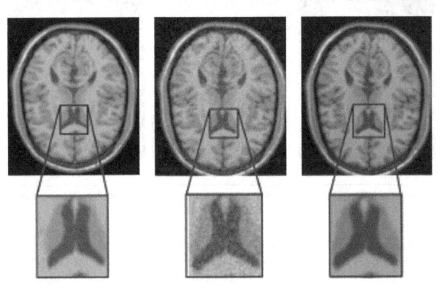

FIGURE 13.5

Denoising of MR images using the convolutional neural network for denoising of magnetic resonance images (CNN-DMRI) described in [23]. From left to right: clean MRI scan, MRI corrupted with 13% noise, and denoised MRI.

13.4.3 **Computed tomography**

For CT images, the main reason for noise is the photon starvation phenomenon due to the reduction in the radiation dose. The CT imaging technique allows visualizing the internal body structures without any overlap and hence has become widespread in medical diagnosis. However, high-dose radiation increases the risk of cancer during the whole lifetime of patients and operators. For this reason, the simplest and most effective solution is to deliver fewer X-rays to an object or directly lower the tube current (mA) as much as possible. However, the quality of the low-dose CT images produced by this method is degraded. A second approach is to maintain the same beam intensity and acquire fewer projections over the same acquisition arc. This approach, known as sparse view CT, produces images suffering from streaking artifacts due to undersampling in the projection domain, as shown in Fig. 13.6.

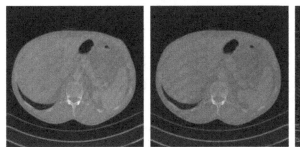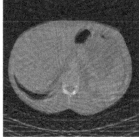

FIGURE 13.6

Comparison of CT images at normal and low doses. From left to right: normal-dose CT, low-dose CT (low beam intensity), and low-dose CT (fewer projections) [24].

13.4.3.1 *Non-local means filtering*

Non-local methods have been introduced into CT image denoising. Based on non-local methods, adaptive non-local means filtering (ANLM) has been proposed [25]. ANLM is a computationally efficient technique for local noise estimation directly from CT images. The original NLM denoising based on a single noise level may be too weak in some places, too strong in other places, or both. Therefore, the ANLM modified the NLM algorithm to adapt to the local noise level and adjusted the strength of $h = k \times SD$ locally, where SD is the estimated noise level of the pixel denoised and k is a proportionality factor that serves to tune the denoising strength. The denoising result of ANLM is shown in Fig. 13.7.

In clinical CT images, the pixels representing different organs or tissues with various levels of attenuation tend to be distributed in a large scope. Therefore, selective averaging of pixels belonging to a given image structure/texture would, by exploiting the repetitive regularity of these pixels, suppress the noise/artifact without compromising structure identification. Parallelized non-local means [26] was proposed to accelerate non-local means calculations under a computationally unified

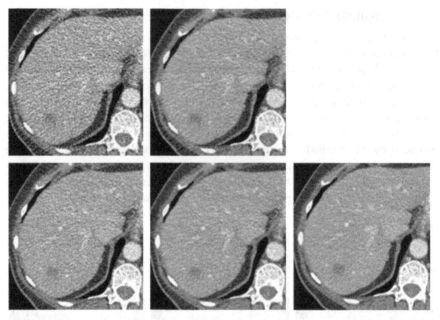

FIGURE 13.7

Effects of adaptive non-local means filtering and lower dose levels on the appearance of neuroendocrine tumor metastasis in the liver (axial view) [25]: (top row) simulated quarter-dose image (left) and simulated half-dose image (right); (bottom row) simulated quarter-dose image after adaptive non-local means filtering (left), simulated half-dose image after adaptive non-local means filtering (center), and original full dose CT image (right).

device architecture (CUDA)-based parallelization framework. Compared with the original algorithm, the speed of calculation using parallelized non-local means increased by 50 times.

13.4.3.2 Block matching 3D

Feruglio et al. [27] used the BM3D technique to denoise optical projection tomography, while Kang et al. [28] denoised low-dose coronary CT angiography.

13.4.3.3 Dictionary learning

Based on the popular idea of sparse representation, Chen et al. adapted K-SVD [29] to deal with low-dose CT images [30]. Using this method, the quality of low-dose CT can reach the image quality of a normal dose acquisition.

13.4.3.4 Convolutional neural networks

The simple CNN method has great potential in artifact reduction and structure preservation. Furthermore, a deeper CNN, residual encoder–decoder CNN (RED-CNN), has been used in CT image denoising [1]. In RED-CNN, the autoencoder-encoding and CNNs are combined, and residual structures and shortcuts are introduced. The CNN architecture of RED-CNN is shown in Fig. 13.8. In essence, the structure of RED-CNN has similarities with most CNNs, but two new concepts are introduced: including shortcuts and deconvolutional structures. The RED-CNN method can be divided into three stages: patch extraction, stack encoders (noise and artifact reduction), and stack decoders (structural detail recovery). As shown in Fig. 13.9, the difference between the low-dose image denoised by residual encoder–decoder CNN and the original normal-dose image is small. All details can be preserved, and most noise and artifacts can be suppressed.

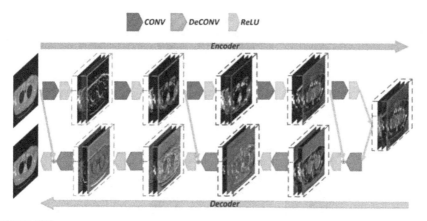

FIGURE 13.8

Architecture of the residual encoder-decoder CNN (RED-CNN) proposed in [1].

13.4.3.5 Generative adversarial networks

Noise is present not only in low-dose acquisition but also in routine-dose acquisition. Minimizing the squared error between the reference and predicted voxel values causes the CNN to predict the mean of these values, resulting in smoothed images that lack the texture of a typical routine-dose CT image. This kind of smoothing may limit the quantification of small structures in denoised images. Accordingly, the Wasserstein GAN with VGG style loss (WGAN-VGG) [9] was introduced to solve this problem. The denoising result of WGAN-VGG is shown in Fig. 13.10.

13.4.4 Positron emission tomography

Positron emission tomography is a functional imaging modality that is widely used to observe molecular-level activities inside tissues through the injection of specific radioactive tracers. Due to various physical degradation factors and the limited number of detected photons, the image resolution and SNR of PET images are poor. In

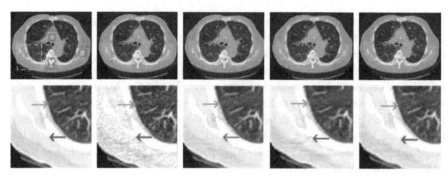

FIGURE 13.9

Comparison of three denoising approaches applied to CT images [1]. From left to right: original image, noisy image, image denoised using dictionary learning, block matching 3D, and residual encoder–decoder CNN. The red (dark gray in print version) boxes are the areas of interest that contain some important information for diagnosis. Zoomed parts over the region of interest marked by the blue (light gray in print version) box in the first row appear in the second row. The arrows indicate two regions for visual differences. The blood vessels in the lungs are highlighted by the blue (light gray in print version) arrow. Streaking artifacts near the bone are marked by the red (dark gray in print version) arrow.

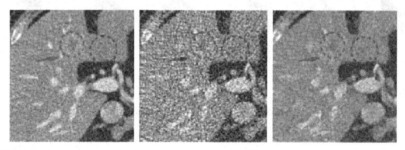

FIGURE 13.10

Denoising of CT images using a Wasserstein GAN with VGG style loss [9]. From left to right: full dose image reconstructed with filtered backprojection (FBP), quarter-dose image reconstructed with FBP, and quarter-dose image denoised with Wasserstein GAN with VGG style loss. The green (at the bottom, light gray in print version) arrow points to the vessel and the red (at the top, mid gray in print version) arrow points to a bright spot. Through these two arrows, it can be judged whether the algorithm causes over-smoothing. Within the red (on the left, mid gray in print version) and blue (on the right, dark gray in print version) circles are two attenuation liver lesions.

PET, the main denoising methods are post-reconstruction techniques. In addition, the noise is mainly Gaussian noise and Poisson noise.

PET images are characterized by a low SNR and blurred edges in comparison with other modalities, such as CT or MR imaging techniques. Therefore, postprocessing techniques to reduce the influence of noise are a mandatory step.

13.4.4.1 Spatial domain filtering

In general, the image domain denoising methods used for PET are the same as for the previous modalities. Non-local means filtering [31,32] is one of the most common methods for denoising PET images. However, although the NLM method can reduce the noise to a certain extent, it also brings local or edge blur. Therefore, the bilateral filtering technique [33] was introduced to denoise PET images. BM3D [34] can also be used to reduce noise in PET images, but it is not common.

13.4.4.2 Convolutional neural networks

Methods based on CNNs have also been applied to PET image denoising. In [35], the network consists of a cascade of five residual blocks. Each residual block contains two repetitions of a 3 × 3 convolutional layer, a batch normalization layer and an ReLU layer. The skip connection is added between the beginning and the end of each block. One thing to note is that a skip connection is added between the first and last stages of the whole network. The denoising result is shown in Fig. 13.11.

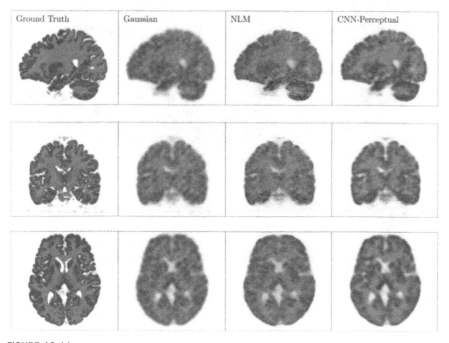

FIGURE 13.11

Comparison of two denoising approaches applied to PET images [35]. From left to right: the original image, the noisy image, the image after denoising with non-local means filtering, and the image after denoising with the CNN described in [35].

13.4.4.3 Generative adversarial networks

Generative adversarial networks have also been used in the denoising of PET images. 3D c-GAN [36], an end-to-end framework based on 3D conditional GANs, can estimate high-quality full-dose PET images from low-dose PET images. The generator in 3D c-GANs adopted a U-net-like [37] architecture as the generator network. The U-net network architecture is widely used in tasks such as detection and segmentation in the field of medical imaging. The denoising result of 3D c-GANs is shown in Fig. 13.12.

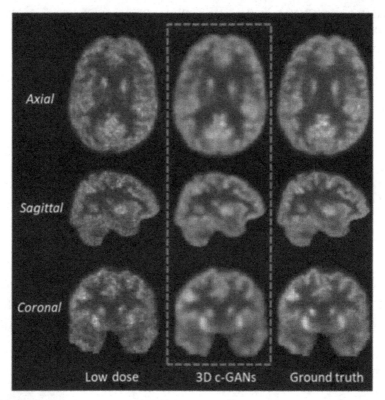

FIGURE 13.12

Denoising of PET images using 3D conditional GANs (3D c-GANs) [36]. From left to right: low dose image; 3D c-GANs denoised result; and original full-dose image.

13.5 Summary

The advancement of image processing has formed a consensus in the field of medical diagnosis. Because medical images greatly improve the reliability of the diagnosis, medical imaging is a new trend in disease diagnostics. However, in clinically acquired medical images, noise is inevitably introduced into the images due to many unavoidable interference factors. Unlike natural images, the presence of noise in medical images is always fatal. Noise makes it hard to observe lesions and eventually leads to errors in the diagnosis of diseases based on medical images.

While the denoising algorithm eliminates noise, it should not only examine the effect of noise removal but also pay attention to the ability to retain the original biological characteristics when removing noise. Therefore, the major requisites of a medical image denoising solution can be listed as (i) preservation of edges and other finer details, (ii) maintenance of structural similarity, (iii) nonappearance of artifacts, and (iv) low complexity of operations.

In the past two decades, a large number of noise reduction techniques have been introduced for the purpose of noise reduction. Broadly speaking, noise reduction techniques can be divided into spatial domain filtering and deep learning. As shown in Table 13.2, the existing techniques cannot meet all the requirements of a good noise reduction algorithm. Thus, filtering-based techniques tend to smooth the image, while other techniques may have high computational complexity. The spatial domain filter methods are more generalized and can be applied in multiple modes. But they cannot achieve the same level of effect as deep learning. Deep learning methods achieve better results, but they can only be used in specific modalities, or even in specific dataset.

Table 13.2 Summary of denoising methods applied to medical images.

		US	MRI	CT	PET
Spatial domain filtering	Linear filtering	✓	✓	✓	✓
	Adaptive filtering [16,18]	✓	✓	✓	✓
	Bilateral filtering [4]	✓	✓	✓	✓
	Non-local filtering [11,14,17,18,25]	✓	✓	✓	✓
	Anisotropic diffusion filtering [5]	✓	✓	✓	✓
	Total variation [7]			✓	
	Block matching 3D [8,19,20]				✓
Dictionary learning	K-SVD [29,30]			✓	
Deep learning	WDNN [22]		✓		
	MCDnCNN [21]		✓		
	CNN-DMRI [23]		✓		
	CNN-3/RED-CNN [1]			✓	
	CNN of Gong et al. [35]				✓
	WGAN-VGG [38]			✓	
	GAN [12]	✓	✓	✓	✓

WDNN: wider deep neural network; MCDnCNN: multichannel version of denoising deep neural network; CNN-DMRI: convolutional neural network for denoising of magnetic resonance images; RED-CNN: residual encoder-decoder CNN; WGAN-VGG: Wasserstein GAN with VGG style loss.

References

[1] H. Chen, Y. Zhang, M.K. Kalra, F. Lin, Y. Chen, P. Liao, J. Zhou, G. Wang, Low-dose CT with a residual encoder–decoder convolutional neural network, IEEE Transactions on Medical Imaging 36 (12) (2017) 2524–2535.

[2] J.-S. Lee, Digital image enhancement and noise filtering by use of local statistics, IEEE Transactions on Pattern Analysis and Machine Intelligence 2 (1980) 165–168.

[3] T. Loupas, W. McDicken, P.L. Allan, An adaptive weighted median filter for speckle suppression in medical ultrasonic images, IEEE Transactions on Circuits and Systems 36 (1) (1989) 129–135.

[4] C. Tomasi, R. Manduchi, Bilateral filtering for gray and color images, in: Sixth International Conference on Computer Vision (IEEE Cat. No. 98CH36271), IEEE, 1998, pp. 839–846.

[5] P. Perona, J. Malik, Scale-space and edge detection using anisotropic diffusion, IEEE Transactions on Pattern Analysis and Machine Intelligence 12 (7) (1990) 629–639.

[6] J. Weickert, Coherence-enhancing diffusion filtering, International Journal of Computer Vision 31 (2) (1999) 111–127.

[7] L.I. Rudin, S. Osher, Total variation based image restoration with free local constraints, in: Proceedings of 1st International Conference on Image Processing, vol. 1, IEEE, 1994, pp. 31–35.

[8] K. Dabov, A. Foi, V. Katkovnik, K. Egiazarian, Image denoising by sparse 3-d transform-domain collaborative filtering, IEEE Transactions on Image Processing 16 (8) (2007) 2080–2095.

[9] J.M. Wolterink, T. Leiner, M.A. Viergever, I. Išgum, Generative adversarial networks for noise reduction in low-dose CT, IEEE Transactions on Medical Imaging 36 (12) (2017) 2536–2545.

[10] Z. Wang, A.C. Bovik, H.R. Sheikh, E.P. Simoncelli, Image quality assessment: from error visibility to structural similarity, IEEE Transactions on Image Processing 13 (4) (2004) 600–612.

[11] P. Coupé, P. Hellier, C. Kervrann, C. Barillot, Nonlocal means-based speckle filtering for ultrasound images, IEEE Transactions on Image Processing 18 (10) (2009) 2221–2229.

[12] D. Mishra, S. Chaudhury, M. Sarkar, A.S. Soin, Ultrasound image enhancement using structure oriented adversarial network, IEEE Signal Processing Letters 25 (9) (2018) 1349–1353.

[13] J. Sijbers, A. Den Dekker, Maximum likelihood estimation of signal amplitude and noise variance from MR data, Magnetic Resonance in Medicine: An Official Journal of the International Society for Magnetic Resonance in Medicine 51 (3) (2004) 586–594.

[14] J.V. Manjón, J. Carbonell-Caballero, J.J. Lull, G. García-Martí, L. Martí-Bonmatí, M. Robles, MRI denoising using non-local means, Medical Image Analysis 12 (4) (2008) 514–523.

[15] R.D. Nowak, Wavelet-based Rician noise removal for magnetic resonance imaging, IEEE Transactions on Image Processing 8 (10) (1999) 1408–1419.

[16] J.V. Manjón, P. Coupé, L. Martí-Bonmatí, D.L. Collins, M. Robles, Adaptive non-local means denoising of MR images with spatially varying noise levels, Journal of Magnetic Resonance Imaging 31 (1) (2010) 192–203.

[17] J.V. Manjón, P. Coupé, A. Buades, D.L. Collins, M. Robles, New methods for MRI denoising based on sparseness and self-similarity, Medical Image Analysis 16 (1) (2012) 18–27.

[18] P. Coupé, J.V. Manjón, M. Robles, D.L. Collins, Adaptive multiresolution non-local means filter for three-dimensional magnetic resonance image denoising, IET Image Processing 6 (5) (2012) 558–568.

[19] P. Elahi, S. Beheshti, M. Hashemi, BM3D MRI denoising equipped with noise invalidation technique, in: 2014 IEEE International Conference on Acoustics, Speech and Signal Processing (ICASSP), IEEE, 2014, pp. 6612–6616.

[20] M. Maggioni, V. Katkovnik, K. Egiazarian, A. Foi, Nonlocal transform-domain filter for volumetric data denoising and reconstruction, IEEE Transactions on Image Processing 22 (1) (2012) 119–133.

[21] D. Jiang, W. Dou, L. Vosters, X. Xu, Y. Sun, T. Tan, Denoising of 3D magnetic resonance images with multi-channel residual learning of convolutional neural network, Japanese Journal of Radiology 36 (9) (2018) 566–574.

[22] X. You, N. Cao, H. Lu, M. Mao, W. Wanga, Denoising of MR images with Rician noise using a wider neural network and noise range division, Magnetic Resonance Imaging 64 (2019) 154–159.

[23] P.C. Tripathi, S. Bag, CNN-DMRI: a convolutional neural network for denoising of magnetic resonance images, Pattern Recognition Letters (2020).

[24] T. Humphries, D. Si, S. Coulter, M. Simms, R. Xing, Comparison of deep learning approaches to low dose CT using low intensity and sparse view data, in: Medical Imaging 2019: Physics of Medical Imaging, vol. 10948, International Society for Optics and Photonics, 2019, p. 109484A.

[25] Z. Li, L. Yu, J.D. Trzasko, D.S. Lake, D.J. Blezek, J.G. Fletcher, C.H. McCollough, A. Manduca, Adaptive nonlocal means filtering based on local noise level for CT denoising, Medical Physics 41 (1) (2014) 011908.

[26] H. Wu, W. Zhang, D. Gao, X. Yin, Y. Chen, W. Wang, Fast CT image processing using parallelized non-local means, Journal of Medical and Biological Engineering 31 (6) (2011) 437–441.

[27] P.F. Feruglio, C. Vinegoni, J. Gros, A. Sbarbati, R. Weissleder, Block matching 3D random noise filtering for absorption optical projection tomography, Physics in Medicine and Biology 55 (18) (2010) 5401.

[28] D. Kang, P. Slomka, R. Nakazato, J. Woo, D.S. Berman, C.-C.J. Kuo, D. Dey, Image denoising of low-radiation dose coronary CT angiography by an adaptive block-matching 3D algorithm, in: Medical Imaging 2013: Image Processing, vol. 8669, International Society for Optics and Photonics, 2013, p. 86692G.

[29] M. Aharon, M. Elad, A. Bruckstein, K-SVD: an algorithm for designing overcomplete dictionaries for sparse representation, IEEE Transactions on Signal Processing 54 (11) (2006) 4311–4322.

[30] Y. Chen, X. Yin, L. Shi, H. Shu, L. Luo, J.-L. Coatrieux, C. Toumoulin, Improving abdomen tumor low-dose CT images using a fast dictionary learning based processing, Physics in Medicine and Biology 58 (16) (2013) 5803.

[31] J. Dutta, R.M. Leahy, Q. Li, Non-local means denoising of dynamic pet images, PLoS ONE 8 (12) (2013) e81390.

[32] C. Chan, R. Fulton, R. Barnett, D.D. Feng, S. Meikle, Postreconstruction nonlocal means filtering of whole-body PET with an anatomical prior, IEEE Transactions on Medical Imaging 33 (3) (2013) 636–650.

[33] F. Hofheinz, J. Langner, B. Beuthien-Baumann, L. Oehme, J. Steinbach, J. Kotzerke, J. van den Hoff, Suitability of bilateral filtering for edge-preserving noise reduction in PET, EJNMMI Research 1 (1) (2011) 1–9.

[34] S. Peltonen, U. Tuna, E. Sánchez-Monge, U. Ruotsalainen, PET sinogram denoising by block-matching and 3D filtering, in: 2011 IEEE Nuclear Science Symposium Conference Record, IEEE, 2011, pp. 3125–3129.

[35] K. Gong, J. Guan, C.-C. Liu, J. Qi, PET image denoising using a deep neural network through fine tuning, IEEE Transactions on Radiation and Plasma Medical Sciences 3 (2) (2018) 153–161.

[36] Y. Wang, B. Yu, L. Wang, C. Zu, D.S. Lalush, W. Lin, X. Wu, J. Zhou, D. Shen, L. Zhou, 3D conditional generative adversarial networks for high-quality PET image estimation at low dose, NeuroImage 174 (2018) 550–562.

[37] O. Ronneberger, P. Fischer, T. Brox, U-Net: convolutional networks for biomedical image segmentation, in: International Conference on Medical Image Computing and Computer-Assisted Intervention, Springer, 2015, pp. 234–241.

[38] Q. Yang, P. Yan, Y. Zhang, H. Yu, Y. Shi, X. Mou, M.K. Kalra, Y. Zhang, L. Sun, G. Wang, Low-dose CT image denoising using a generative adversarial network with Wasserstein distance and perceptual loss, IEEE Transactions on Medical Imaging 37 (6) (2018) 1348–1357.

Data augmentation for medical image analysis

14

He Zhao[a], Huiqi Li[a], and Li Cheng[b]

[a]*Beijing Institute of Technology, Beijing, China*
[b]*ECE, University of Alberta, Edmonton, AB, Canada*

14.1 Introduction

Medical image analysis has gained a lot of attention in the clinic. With the help of modern algorithms, computer-aided diagnosis assists doctors to deal with the large variations in pathology and intra- and inter-observers. Deep learning together with the high computational ability converts the human-designed features to a learning-based feature extraction process. Even without prior knowledge about the domain, the model can learn the meaningful features directly from data [1]. Therefore, a large amount of data are required to build the deep learning algorithms for learning a hierarchical feature representation. High accuracy by using a large dataset makes convolutional neural networks (CNNs) popular in medical image analysis tasks, such as liver lesion classification [2], brain analysis [3], and retinal image analysis [4]. For example, the method proposed by Google uses 1.28 million retinal images to train their systems to diagnose diabetic retinopathy [5], while deep CNNs also achieve a desirable result on skin lesion classification [6]. Unfortunately, such a large amount of data with labels is not always accessible in practical medical applications. There are two reasons which limit labeled data access in the medical image area. Firstly, it is a time-consuming and tedious task that requires experienced experts to spend a long time annotating. Secondly, it is also hard to get a desirable amount of disease images in the applications as the diseases are not common. Based on the type of variance, the features of images can be divided into two categories which are pertinent and non-pertinent features, respectively [7]. In medical images, pertinent features contain the most useful information to determine the organs or lesions, while non-pertinent features are those which vary between images such as the intensity difference. For most medical image applications, it is hard to build a large dataset, especially due to rare diseases and patient privacy. Training small datasets is harmful to the model to capture generalized pertinent features and may cause a performance drop due to the overfitting problem. In order to avoid the problem of overfitting and improve the performance of deep learning algorithms [8], researchers try to utilize data augmentation techniques [9–12]. Data augmentation is a way that can remove non-pertinent variance by feeding the model with different sources of data and it has been studied

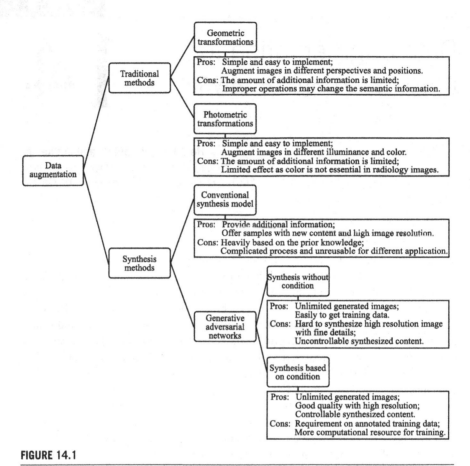

FIGURE 14.1

Summary of different data augmentation methods.

by the community to create more data for model training. In what follows, the works on data augmentation will be discussed, including the efforts on computer vision and medical image analysis. We will start from the traditional methods and end with the generative adversarial networks. The summary of methods is displayed in Fig. 14.1 which contains the pros and cons of each method.

14.2 Traditional methods for augmentation

The early works augment data by applying simple transformations on original images, where the techniques include geometric transformations and color space transformations.

14.2.1 **Geometric transformations**

Geometric transformation is one of the conventional methods to augment data, which aims to make the model invariant to the changes in position and orientation. Some typical operations include rotation with a certain angle, horizontal or vertical flipping, random patch cropping, scaling, shifting, and so on [13]. It provides a chance for the model to learn invariance without additional labeled data [14].

The rotation is done by rotating the images following a specific direction and angle between 0° and 360°. This operation changes the angles of an object in the images and helps the model to recognize the object with different angle locations. For most of the cases, rotation can improve the model performance, while sometimes it may not be a good choice when the direction of the object will influence the result, e.g., the digit numbers six and nine. Horizontal flipping is much more commonly used in retinal image analysis because usually there is a difference between right and left eyes. By using this operation, the model can learn the appearance from either left or right eyes without new data and labels. Random cropping is a technique to create a subset of images from the original image. This operation does not change the semantic information in the image but can provide a different situation of the object. It helps the model generalize better because the objects can be located in different positions and the contents are not the same in each cropping patch. Image shifting is another useful transformation to alleviate the position bias in the training data. Let us take optic disc segmentation in retinal fundus images as an example. When all the training images are centered on the optic disc, the model should recall the positions of optic discs in the center of the image. It will require the model to be tested on this kind of image to get perfect results. Unsatisfactory results may be generated for retinal images centered on the macular.

The geometric transformations are widely used in the augmentation of various kinds of images. They are easily implemented and helpful to overcome positional and angular biases. On the other hand, it is necessary when using geometric transformations to make sure the transformation has not changed the label of original images. Due to the complexity of medical data, the positional variances created by geometric transformations are not enough in some applications, which is a limitation of this method.

14.2.2 **Photometric transformations**

Another kind of data augmentation is carried on color space, which is called color space transformation or photometric transformation. This technique aims to make the model invariant to change of lighting and color. The color images have three channels, where each channel is with different pixel density. Lighting biases are the most frequent challenges for image classification or segmentation tasks, which may cause unsatisfactory results. To avoid this issue, one simple way is to edit the pixel with a constant value to increase or decrease the density. In [15], the authors not only apply geometric transformation but also change the values of RGB channels with a random scale to enlarge the variance. The work of [16] has evaluated pixel value shuffling, which can help to improve the robustness of deep learning models. Krizhevsky et al. [17] apply principal component analysis (PCA) on the training images and alter the intensities of the RGB channels. They add the principal components with the magnitudes of the corresponding eigenvalues and a random variable from the Gaussian distribution. In [18], the authors randomly manipulate the brightness, color, and contrast with an arbitrary value of [0.5, 1.5]. They add an additional lighting noise as that has been done in [17]. This strategy has also been employed in [19] to augment skin images for melanoma analysis.

Compared with geometric transformations, the photometric transformations introduce other information which is illuminance and color diversity rather than spatial information of the object. In most applications, color may not be the essential characteristic and the improvement with color augmentation will be limited. Furthermore, this kind of augmentation can be hardly useful in most medical imaging data, as the radiology images are not sensitive to color.

The work of [20] has discussed the performance of several geometric and photometric transformation methods on natural images with a CNN model structure. There are also evaluations on medical image research [21,22] to discuss which augmentation technique is better. Interested readers may refer to these papers for more details. Some researchers also use label propagation for data augmentation [23,24]. The idea is based on Gaussian random fields, which allows the labels to be propagated to unlabeled data. A weighted undirected graph is constructed by the label propagation. The weights of graph edges reflect the similarity between the two data samples. By this operation, the unlabeled data can also be used to train models, which can also be regarded as a data augmentation method. Some researchers attempt to build a data augmentation method automatically, such as [25–27], where a policy is learned to choose which operation is suitable for the target dataset.

14.2.3 Augmentation on medical images

In this section, we will focus on the augmentation strategies on medical images. Hauberg et al. [28] propose a learned data augmentation approach on a class by class basis. They learn a probabilistic transformation model in the Riemanian sub-manifold of the Lie group of diffeomorphisms. In [29], the authors utilize two non-linear transformations called Simard transformation [30] and Ronneberger transformation [31] to generate new training images and corresponding vessel ground-truths in retinal fundus images. The new structures and scenes are created, and the generated images and vessel annotations can be used as new training data by applying these operations. In [32], a patch-based augmentation method is employed on the retinal vessel segmentation task, where random patches are selected for rotation, flipping, and nosing on both image and ground-truth. They state that this kind of strategy achieves a better performance than the usual operations. To augment the magnetic resonance imaging (MRI) volumes for prostate image segmentation, Milletari et al. employ nonlinear transformations by B-spline interpolation and histogram matching to vary the intensity distribution of data [33]. Roth et al. [34] enrich 3D computed tomography (CT) data by applying spatial deformations which include random translation, rotations, and non-rigid deformations. The non-rigid deformation is computed by fitting a thin-plate-spline to a regular grid of 2D control points and a deformed image can be generated using a radial basis function.

14.3 Synthesis-based methods

Although the conventional augmentation methods increase the number of training examples and are easily implemented, these strategies are highly sensitive to the choice of parameters [35] and have the limitation of emulating real variations [36]. In medical image research, careful consideration of the application will lead to which types of transformations are appropriate. For example, only sagittal reflection and intensity augmentation are used in [37] for brain lesion segmentation. In [31], the elastic deformations lead to the largest improvement for microscopy images, while this operation may not be useful in brain images. In addition, some patient-specific variations may not be removed by geometric transformations.

Besides the conventional methods which rely on existing images and apply transforms to create new training data, some researches are carried out to explore generating new data with different content and appearance-looking combinations. We call this kind of strategy a synthesis-based method in this chapter and it can be divided into methods based on domain knowledge and data-driven mechanisms.

14.3.1 Conventional synthesis model

The conventional synthesis model is heavily based on domain knowledge. To synthesize retinal fundus images, Fiorini et al. [38] focus on reconstructing the textural background from scratch. The background is generated by a patch-based tiling algorithm which is derived from the Image Quilting technique [39], where small examples of existing images are stitched together to obtain the phantom. Then a model learning the distributions of key morphometric quantities from real images is employed to reproduce optic disc on the retinal fundus. Finally, a model-based approach [40,41] is utilized to generate the vascular structures, where the features of vessel trees are included. The work of Menti et al. [42] aims to derive vessels and textures from real data utilizing active shape contours and Kalman filter techniques. For the neuronal images, GENESIS [43], NEURON [44], and L-Neuron [45] are the most well-known efforts. GENESIS is a simulation method for constructing realistic models of neurobiological systems. It was one of the first simulation systems specifically designed for modeling nervous systems. NEURON is developed similarly for modeling individual neurons and neuron networks. L-Neuron is based on a set of recursive rules that concisely describe dendritic geometry and topology through locally interrelated morphological parameters.

14.3.2 Generative adversarial networks

Leveraging the advances in generative adversarial networks (GANs) [46], some researchers try to synthesize realistic image and label pairs from a random noise vector that is generated from a simple distribution [7,47]. A generative adversarial network provides a new potential way to augment data making it possible to create augmented data without making decisions of which type to choose. Although the variational autoencoders (VAEs) [48] allow generating images with controllable latent variables, the synthesized samples tend to be blurry compared with generative adversarial networks. Nowadays, more efforts are put on GANs to synthesize realistic-looking images. It has been suggested that GANs can have a significant benefit when used for data augmentation in some classification tasks [2,49]. It can also augment more challenging variance data such as lesion shape or size. By providing a sufficient number of training samples with different shapes and sizes, the model will gain the ability to create samples with more variance. Performing the same augmentation results by the conventional methods will lead to a very complex model considering realistic shape, size, and the surroundings around the lesion. On the other hand, the generated image quality may be one disadvantage of GAN compared with conventional augmentation methods. But this limitation has less effect on improving the performance of other analysis tasks, as it has been proven that fully realistic images are not compulsory [50,51]. Balancing the pros and cons, the strategy using GANs is still an advanced method for data augmentation.

There are many efforts to utilize GANs to create artificial instances with similar characteristics to the original dataset. In the work of [52], Antoniou et al. discuss how the generative manifold can learn better classifiers and propose a class-based generative model to learn a representation for data augmentation. A conditional GAN is trained based on class-provided images with encoder–decoder model structure. The model learns a meaningful representation of training data and encapsulates the feature with a random vector engaging the variance to create extra augmented data. A synthetic refiner network is proposed in [53] to improve the quality of simulated images by GAN, where synthetic images created by the simulator are refined by the generator which is optimized by adversarial loss and self-regularization loss. The refined images are then used to train eye gaze estimation model.

In medical image research, some researchers explore image synthesis directly from a noise vector, while others decide to generate augmented images based on conditional information. The condition-based generative model has the potential to synthesize rare pathological cases, where the conditional information could be provided by medical experts through text descriptions or the masks of anatomical structures. All the attempts have shown the potentiality of GANs working on medical image analysis as a data augmentation method. The GAN models can offer an effective way to explore the manifold of training data and increase the data variance, which is hard to augment by other methods. However, this kind of augmentation cannot extend the distribution beyond the extremes of the training data.

14.3.2.1 Synthesis without condition

Images generated without condition can also be known as unconditional synthesis, where no extra information is provided to synthesize the data and the images are generated directly from a random vector. The structure of deep convolutional GAN (DCGAN) [54] is widely employed by researchers to generate augmented data from random noise. In [2], the authors try to synthesize labeled lesions on CT scans for each class of lesion separately, including cysts, metastases, and hemangiomas. Three generators are employed for individual classes in their work. They find the generated lesions are helpful to improve the sensitivity and specificity when the augmented data are combined with real data. While this technique is also utilized for many applications such as chest X-ray [49], lung nodule CT images [55], retinal fundus images [56], and brain MR images [57,58]. In [56], the authors not only use the discriminator to distinguish the fake from real but also take it as a segmentor. The generated data together with the unlabeled data can be used to train the discriminator (segmentor) to achieve a better segmentation performance. It has been stated that the data generated from a random vector achieves a comparable quality to real ones on MR images although there is still a discrepancy in anatomic accuracy [57]. A visual Turing test has been carried out in [55] with two radiologists to evaluate the quality of generated nodules as augmented data.

Due to the limitation of DCGAN to synthesize large size images, other generative model structures have also been used for data augmentation, such as the Laplacian pyramid GAN [59], Wasserstein GAN [60], and progressive growing of GAN [61]. Bowles et al. [7] investigate the application of GAN in different modalities of medical images for the segmentation tasks as a way of data augmentation and compare the performance with rotation augmentation. Their model is based on a progressive growing of GAN, where the network can generate images with large sizes and stable training progress by a progressive growing training strategy. The same idea is also employed to create new training data for retinal fundus images with retinopathy of prematurity by [62] and dermoscopic images in [63]. In [63], a single source of noise is used instead of multiple sources for each scale and their model is trained in an end-to-end manner. As an improved version of GAN [46], the Wasserstein GAN has been used to improve the training stability and generate more plausible images. Several works have taken advantage of this variant of GAN to augment data on different image modalities, such as MR images [64], CT scans [65], histopathology images [66], or dermoscopic images [67]. Fig. 14.2 displays the examples of augmentation applications using unconditional GAN.

14.3.2.2 Synthesis based on condition

Although synthesis from a random vector needs less labeled data to train the generative model, this type of image generation is not controllable and the image quality is not satisfactory sometimes. To augment data with specific structure and position of lesions or vessels, researchers tend to introduce additional information to the generator where the conditional generative model [72] is utilized in their augmentation

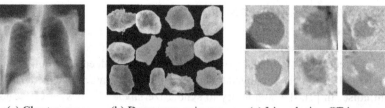

(a) Chest x-ray   (b) Dermoscopy image   (c) Liver lesion CT images

FIGURE 14.2

Examples of applications using unconditional generative adversarial networks: (a) synthesized chest X-ray image [49]; (b) dermoscopy images generated by [67]; and (c) liver lesion images from [2].

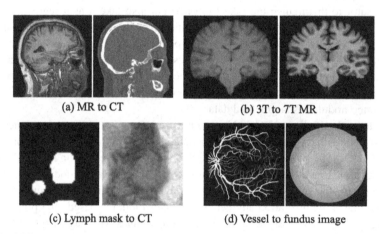

(a) MR to CT   (b) 3T to 7T MR

(c) Lymph mask to CT   (d) Vessel to fundus image

FIGURE 14.3

Examples of applications using conditional generative adversarial networks: (a) CT image generated from an MR image [68]; (b) 7T MR image and its 3T MR input [69]; (c) augmented CT image and its input lymph mask [70]; and (d) synthesized retinal fundus image and its corresponding vessel map [71].

models. In this kind of method, pix2pix [73] and CycleGAN [74] are two model structures usually used to augment data. The pix2pix-based model is used for the cases where paired or aligned data are available, while the CycleGAN-based model is used to handle the tasks where no paired data are provided or the registration is challenging. One of the most common applications for this augmentation strategy is to augment data across modality such as from MRI to CT, or transformation from 3T to 7T MR images. Another kind of application is to create new data from existing annotations, e.g., from labeled masks to images. In what follows, we will introduce the work on these two kinds of applications with different data, while Fig. 14.3 illustrates the examples of images generated by state-of-the-art methods.

It is well known that CT is a critical imaging modality for many medical applications, but it exposes patients to radiation during image acquisition. As MRI does not involve radiation and is much safer than CT, the community is motivated to augment CT data from MR images to help training segmentation or classification methods on CT images. Within MR images, images acquired at 7T have a higher signal-to-noise ratio and better tissue contrast compared to 3T MRI, which leads to a more accurate disease diagnosis. However, 7T images are less available and may take a longer time to acquire. This raised the interest of researchers to generate 7T images from 3T MRI data. Nie et al. [69] propose a fully convolutional network based generative model to augment data from different sources with an additional constraint on the gradient similarity between real and synthesized images to generate high quality results. To engage the global information into their generator, the auto-context model is applied to achieve a context-aware GAN. To overcome the slice discontinuity and blurry problem on the boundary, Yu et al. [75] propose an edge-aware GAN to capture the image structure information and voxel-wise intensity to improve the quality of generated images. Besides the generator and discriminator, they investigate an edge detector to offer more information to the generator. In [68], the authors find that training with unpaired data with CycleGAN achieves better generated results than using the aligned images, where the reason is likely because the registration could not handle local alignment well. Several works further improve the CycleGAN model with extra loss and components. Hiasa et al. [76] extend the CycleGAN approach by adding the gradient consistency loss to improve the accuracy at the boundaries. The shape consistency loss is employed in [77] to avoid the geometric distortion, where two segmentors are utilized to extract semantic labels and the shape constraints on the anatomy during translation for both modalities. Other works [78,79] follow a similar idea but apply the segmentor to only one modality. Besides the works above, many papers have published cross-modality image synthesis approaches aiming to generate CT, positron emission tomography and MR images [80–85], but also different sequences in MR images [86–90]. Interested readers may refer to them for further reading.

Synthesizing images from labeled masks is another way to avoid the problem of lack of annotated data. The synthesized images together with their corresponding labeled masks can be regarded as new annotated training data. The authors in [91] propose a method to generate synthetic image–label pairs by learning the generative models of deformation fields and intensity transformations. Two generators are used for the deformation field and intensity field respectively. The deformation field generator creates a dense pixel-wise deformation field for both image and ground-truth. The intensity field generator generates an intensity mask to change the pixel intensity of an image. Tang et al. [70] utilize pix2pix GAN [73] to synthesize a large number of CT-realistic images from customized lymph node masks, where the model can learn the structural and contextual information of lymph nodes and surroundings. They state that by using the generative model, the augmented data achieves more diverse results than the ones generated by affine transformations. The simple pix2pix model is utilized in [47] to synthesize abnormal brain MR images from tumor labels. They illustrate that the tumor segmentation model gains an improvement when leveraging the synthesized images as augmented data and achieves comparable results when trained only on the synthesized images. Mok et al. [92] use conditional GAN to augment training images for brain tumor segmentation. The generator is conditioned on a segmentation map and generates brain MR images in a coarse-to-fine manner, which also outputs tumor boundaries in the generation process to ensure the tumor is well delineated with a clear boundary in the generated image. Zhao et al. [93] generate labeled examples by using learning-based registration methods leveraging unlabeled images on brain MRI data. They employed two generators to learn spatial transformation and appearance transformation separately, where the anatomical and imaging diversities are captured in the unlabeled images. The new training examples are synthesized by sampling transformations and applying them to the existing labeled examples. A stylized GAN is proposed by [71], where the retinal fundus images and neuronal images are generated from the vascular or neuronal structures. A perceptual feature descriptor is introduced to extract content features and style features for the generator to synthesize stylized retinal images based on the input of style reference. As an improved version of [71], the authors in [94] propose a recurrent generative model to synthesize different style images within a single model, where the gated recurrent unit is engaged to control the information flow of different styles. The synthesized images have been used to train a supervised vessel segmentation model without annotated data. Instead of augmenting healthy retinal images, Zhou et al. [95] try to synthesize images with diabetic retinopathy. The proposed model is conditioned on vessel and lesion masks with adaptive grading vectors sampled from the latent grading space, which can be adopted to control the synthesized grading severity. To increase the quality of generated images, a multi-scale discriminator is designed to operate from large to small receptive fields. Finally, their model has achieved a charming result of synthesizing diabetic retinopathy images with rather high resolution and quality.

14.3.3 Pros and cons of synthesis methods

Compared with traditional augmentation methods, synthesis-based augmentation introduces a way to explore the features of existing data beyond the superficial information. It offers samples that do not appear in the training set but belong to the distribution. New contents are provided in the augmented data making the images more meaningful and powerful to improve model performance than the simple geometric and photometric transformations. However, the synthesis-based methods have their limitations. The conventional synthesis model is heavily based on prior knowledge and needs to be well designed for each component. Take the retinal fundus synthesis as an example. The conventional method needs to consider the orientation and branching of blood vessels to build a skeleton tree. The width of vessels on different locations should also be determined by a separate model with the texture appearance designed following other rules. All the processes make the conventional methods complicated and only usable for certain applications. On the other hand, the

GAN-based synthesis models are more flexible. They are constructed by data mining and learn to generate new images from either a random vector or a map. However, such models are not easy to train and require more data than the conventional synthesis method, which restrains their usage on a rather small amount of data. Compared with the conditional synthesis model, the unconditional GAN model can be easily used to synthesize additional data with only images required. It is much more convenient when it is hard to obtain images with mask annotations due to the laborious and time-consuming work in the medical imaging area. In general, the unconditional model cannot synthesize large size with fine details and it is harder to train than the conditional one. Although the BigGAN [96] provides the ability to generate high resolution images with a random vector as input, it requires a large amount of computational resources to achieve the goal. In addition, the content of generated images by the unconditional model cannot be controlled. Given a random vector, the GAN is not able to predict what the synthesized image will be like. On the other hand, the conditional model achieves higher resolution and an easy training process with the help of additional information that further guides the direction of the synthesized content. These advantages make the conditional GAN-based methods become a more and more popular data augmentation way in most applications.

14.4 Case study: data augmentation for retinal vessel segmentation

In this section, a concrete example is given on retinal vessel segmentation to show how the augmentation method works on medical imaging analysis tasks.

Retinal vessel segmentation is a fundamental step in retinal image analysis. There is only a small set of annotated retinal image datasets available, e.g., DRIVE [97] contains 40 pixel-level annotated images and STARE [98] consists of 20 images with segmentation maps. Moreover, lots of the retinal fundus image datasets do not have any vessel segmentation. This situation is also faced by clinical practice. Lacking annotated training data on retinal images limits the usage of vessel segmentation methods. In the case of missing labeled training data, the most common solution is training the model with the existing annotated dataset and testing directly on the images. However, the performance usually drops significantly due to the discrepancy between different datasets. Table 14.1 and Fig. 14.4 show the performance of a supervised segmentation method (i.e., Deep Retinal Image Understanding (DRIU) [12]) pretrained on DRIVE and tested on STARE. The quantitative results show that the model trained on the existing labeled dataset, e.g., DRIVE, seems not to perform well on a new test set, e.g., STARE. Moreover, the performance of pretrained DRIU model is even worse than an unsupervised model, i.e., Multi-Scale Line Detector (MSLD) [99]. Fig. 14.4 displays the visual segmentation results of the two methods. The pretrained DRIU method has more false negative pixels compared with MSLD, which illustrates that the pretrained model with images from other datasets may not achieve a better performance than the unsupervised method. The experimental re-

Table 14.1 The performance of a supervised (DRIU) and unsupervised (MSLD) method on the STARE test dataset with F1-score (%), sensitivity (%), and specificity (%).

	F1	Sensitivity	Specificity
DRIU trained on DRIVE	68.32	67.12	98.03
MSLD	77.74	74.15	98.63

| False Negative | False Positive | True Positive |

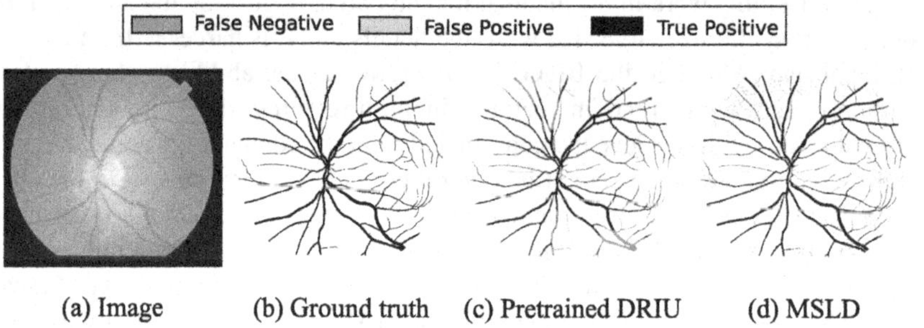

(a) Image   (b) Ground truth   (c) Pretrained DRIU   (d) MSLD

FIGURE 14.4

The visual segmentation results of the pretrained supervised segmentation method (DRIU) and the unsupervised method (MSLD).

sults have shown that the discrepancy between different datasets does not allow a pretrained supervised model to achieve a satisfactory performance on another dataset.

To solve this problem, we select a conditional GAN-based method as the data augmentation way to generate images with the appearance of given data. The synthesized images together with the existing labels are used to train the supervised model to obtain a higher performance on the test set. The process can be divided into two steps as shown in Fig. 14.5. Step 1 focuses on the construction of a synthesized dataset with the desirable style appearance, while step 2 proceeds to learn a supervised model based on the generated images. In step 1, the synthesis method is built based on recurrent generative adversarial networks (R-sGAN) [94]. It takes random vessel trees as conditional information input and outputs the generated retinal fundus images. One of the biggest advantages of this method is that it is able to generate images with different style appearances. In what follows, we will give an introduction on how to use R-sGAN to generate new data for vessel segmentation. Interested readers may also refer to [94] for detailed information.

The core component of R-sGAN is the GRU module which consists of generator gate, reset gate, and update gate. The generator G of GAN is incorporated as the generator gate and the discriminator D is utilized as a part of losses. Each time point τ is treated as a cell of GRU with the input of current vessel trees y_τ and cell state $h_{\tau-1}$ while generating different style retinal images. The style information is stored in the cell state when training the model. As shown in Fig. 14.6(b), GRU consists of three parts: generator gate, reset gate, and update gate. The reset gate and update

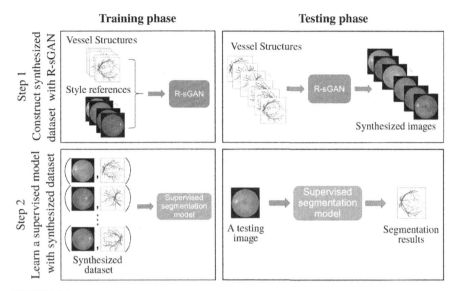

FIGURE 14.5

The flowchart of data augmentation on retinal vessel segmentation application.

gate control the information flow and the generator gate combines the current vessel structure and cell state to generate new images. By introducing different style reference images in the training stages, the model obtains the ability to synthesize multiple styles in different time states. Concretely, the reset gate and the update gate share the same fully convolutional network (FCN) structure but for different purposes, which are calculated by

$$r_\tau = \sigma\left(f_\gamma\left(y_\tau, h_{\tau-1}\right)\right), \quad u_\tau = \sigma\left(f_\mu\left(y_\tau, h_{\tau-1}\right)\right), \tag{14.1}$$

where f_γ and f_μ are the FCN modules and σ is the sigmoid activation function. The cell state after the reset gate is changed to

$$\widetilde{h}_{\tau-1} = r_\tau \otimes h_{\tau-1}, \tag{14.2}$$

where $\otimes$ indicates the element-wise multiplication. The generator gate takes the new cell state $\widetilde{h}_{\tau-1}$, vessel structure y_τ, and a noise vector z_τ as inputs and learns a mapping by a U-net-structured convolutional neural network G,

$$\widetilde{x}_\tau = G\left(y_\tau, \widetilde{h}_{\tau-1}, z_\tau\right). \tag{14.3}$$

By merging the signals from these three gates, the output becomes

$$h_\tau = (1 - u_\tau) \otimes h_{\tau-1} \oplus u_\tau \otimes \widetilde{x}_\tau, \tag{14.4}$$

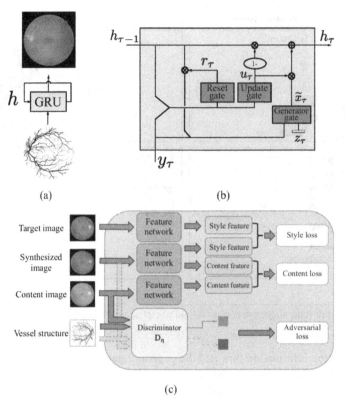

FIGURE 14.6

Model structure of R-sGAN: (a) the overall synthesis process; (b) detailed information of GRU network; and (c) the loss functions used to train the model.

where $\oplus$ refers to element-wise addition. With the help of reset gate and update gate, the GRU cell is able to capture the different styles and maintain the vessel structures over the sequence of time states.

Fig. 14.6(c) displays the main loss functions to train R-sGAN, which contain the adversarial loss, style loss, and content loss. The adversarial loss is used to guarantee the images are with a realistic appearance, which is trained by minimizing the following function:

$$\mathcal{L}_{\text{adv}} = -\sum_{\tau} \log D\left(\boldsymbol{h}_\tau, \boldsymbol{y}_\tau\right). \tag{14.5}$$

The style loss is engaged to evaluate how faithful the synthesized images is with respect to the style reference, while the content loss is used to enforce the generated images maintaining the vessel structure as the conditional information. These two losses are calculated based on the feature representation generated by feature network (e.g., VGG [100]). For the style loss, the Gram matrix $G^l = (g^l_{mn})$ is utilized to capture the textural representation, which is defined as the inner product between the mth and nth vectorized feature maps in the lth layer,

$$g_{mn} = \sum_k \phi'_{mk} \phi'_{nk}, \tag{14.6}$$

where ϕ' is the vectorized version of feature map ϕ in feature network. With the style representation G^l the style loss can be defined as

$$\mathcal{L}_{\text{sty}} = \sum_\tau \sum_l \left\| G^l(x_\tau) - G^l(h_\tau) \right\|^2, \tag{14.7}$$

where x_τ is the style reference image. Similarly, the content loss is calculated based on the difference of feature maps between the generated image and the vessel structure content, which is defined as

$$\mathcal{L}_{\text{cont}} = \sum_\tau \sum_l \left\| \phi^l(x^c_\tau) - \phi^l(h_\tau) \right\|^2, \tag{14.8}$$

where x^c_τ stands for the image providing the vessel structures. With all the components above, R-sGAN can generate realistic-looking retinal images with specific style appearance. This characteristic facilitates the segmentation method on the applications with less data or even no annotated data for training.

In Fig. 14.7, the augmented images generated by R-sGAN are displayed. The generated images maintain the vessel structures while obtaining the appearance-looking of style reference images from the test set. The segmentation performance improves with a significant margin by using the generated images as augmented inputs to train the supervised model. The quantitative results are shown in Table 14.2, while the visual results are shown in Fig. 14.8. Compared with the pretrained model, DRIU trained with augmented data generated by R-sGAN achieves superior performance with less false alarm and false positive points. To further reveal how large data augmentation benefits will be achieved in the segmentation tasks, visual comparisons on more challenging datasets will be presented. Fig. 14.9 displays the segmentation results of pretrained DRIU, DRIU trained with augmented data, and MSLD on Kaggle dataset [101] and images captured by mobile device [102]. In the Kaggle dataset, there is noticeable variability in contrast and luminance, mostly due to the presence of diabetic retinopathy. For the images captured by mobile devices, the imaging quality may differ a lot due to the less experienced user and lead to low quality and poorly illuminated fundus images. On these two datasets, the pretrained DRIU model and MSLD method cannot obtain satisfactory results, either by capturing the lesion or

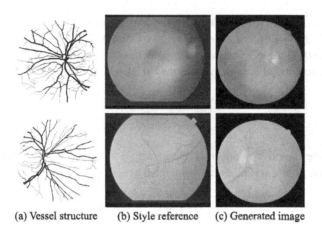

(a) Vessel structure   (b) Style reference   (c) Generated image

FIGURE 14.7

Two exemplar images generated by R-sGAN with vessel structures from the DRIVE dataset and style references from the STARE dataset.

Table 14.2 The performance of DRIU models with different training strategies on STARE dataset with F1-score (%), sensitivity (%), and specificity (%).

	F1	Sensitivity	Specificity
DRIU trained on DRIVE	68.32	67.12	98.03
DRIU trained on augmented data	79.60	79.49	98.36

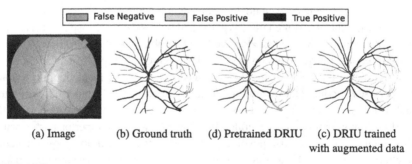

(a) Image   (b) Ground truth   (d) Pretrained DRIU   (c) DRIU trained with augmented data

FIGURE 14.8

Visual segmentation comparison of the supervised segmentation models (DRIU) with different training strategies.

missing the vessel structures. On the other hand, the model trained with augmented data achieves a better result with main vessel trunks and some detailed branches will less false alarm even on the blurry and less visible images.

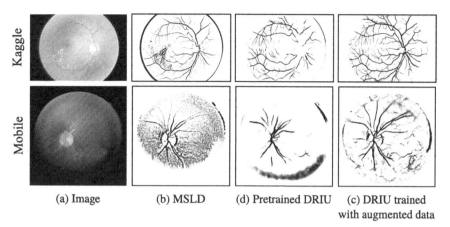

(a) Image   (b) MSLD   (d) Pretrained DRIU   (c) DRIU trained
                                                                  with augmented data

FIGURE 14.9

Visual segmentation comparison of the supervised models (DRIU) with different training strategies.

14.5 Research challenges and future work

Benefiting from the generative adversarial network, the augmentation methods have moved to a new stage. However, there are still challenges that need to be solved in medical imaging. Image quality is the most important thing in GAN-based methods to generate augmented data. Although most of the generated data have the desired appearance, the anatomic structures may not match with the clinical situation, such as the optic disc shape in the retinal fundus images or the appearance of tumor in brain MR images. The structure may be good enough from the image point of view, but the augmented image may be a failure case in the clinical sense. How to augment data with clinically meaningful structure is a future work to be explored. Most of the generative models gain good quality of augmented images by training with paired data where extensive labeling work needs to be done in order to create the training dataset. Some works utilize CycleGAN to loose the restriction where an unpaired translation is performed, while most of the recent works focus on synthesizing images from existing ground-truth. There is little work trying to augment ground-truth data. For some applications, such as retinal images or neuronal images, vascular or neuronal structures contain the most useful information. So augmenting the vascular or neuronal ground-truth is very helpful to create new data and it provides more potential for the generative models to learn the essential structures in this type of image. Another new direction is to augment data not only in the image space but also in the feature space, which works like domain adaptation. Finally, there is no effective way to measure the quality of generated images. Some of the traditional evaluation metrics such as structural similarity index measure and peak signal-to-noise ratio can be used for paired data evaluation, but the results do not always correspond to the real visual quality or match visual conception of the human. Interested readers may refer to Chapter 25 for more information. The way to validate the augmented data by clinical experts is another choice but expensive and time-consuming. Thus the validation metrics of the generated images remain to be explored.

14.6 Summary

In this chapter, we have reviewed the augmentation methods used in medical image analysis. Deep learning methods in medical image analysis achieve a significant performance in many applications. However, they rely on a large amount of data to train the model to avoid overfitting problems and improve the model performance. Data augmentation is a very useful strategy to create a large dataset with variance, which agrees with the situation that labeled data in medical imaging is very limited. Several kinds of augmentation methods have been discussed, including conventional methods such as image rotation or flipping, and methods based on synthesis. Benefiting from the development of generative adversarial networks, the quality and variance of augmented data are substantially improved. Models trained with the augmented data obtain a higher performance in medical image analysis. The augmentation in medical image analysis has a bright future but comes with challenges that need to be explored.

References

[1] I. Goodfellow, Y. Bengio, A. Courville, Y. Bengio, Deep Learning, vol. 1, MIT Press, Cambridge, 2016.

[2] M. Frid-Adar, E. Klang, M. Amitai, J. Goldberger, H. Greenspan, Synthetic data augmentation using GAN for improved liver lesion classification, in: IEEE International Symposium on Biomedical Imaging, IEEE, 2018, pp. 289–293.

[3] J.H. Cole, R.P. Poudel, D. Tsagkrasoulis, M.W. Caan, C. Steves, T.D. Spector, G. Montana, Predicting brain age with deep learning from raw imaging data results in a reliable and heritable biomarker, NeuroImage 163 (2017) 115–124.

[4] H. Zhao, H. Li, L. Cheng, Improving retinal vessel segmentation with joint local loss by matting, Pattern Recognition 98 (2020) 107068.

[5] V. Gulshan, L. Peng, M. Coram, M.C. Stumpe, D. Wu, A. Narayanaswamy, S. Venugopalan, K. Widner, T. Madams, J. Cuadros, et al., Development and validation of a deep learning algorithm for detection of diabetic retinopathy in retinal fundus photographs, JAMA 316 (22) (2016) 2402–2410.

[6] A. Esteva, B. Kuprel, R.A. Novoa, J. Ko, S.M. Swetter, H.M. Blau, S. Thrun, Dermatologist-level classification of skin cancer with deep neural networks, Nature 542 (7639) (2017) 115–118.

[7] C. Bowles, L. Chen, R. Guerrero, P. Bentley, R. Gunn, A. Hammers, D.A. Dickie, M.V. Hernández, J. Wardlaw, D. Rueckert, GAN augmentation: augmenting training data using generative adversarial networks, arXiv preprint, arXiv:1810.10863.

[8] L. Perez, J. Wang, The effectiveness of data augmentation in image classification using deep learning, arXiv preprint, arXiv:1712.04621.

[9] A.A.A. Setio, F. Ciompi, G. Litjens, P. Gerke, C. Jacobs, S.J. van Riel, M.M.W. Wille, M. Naqibullah, C.I. Sánchez, B. van Ginneken, Pulmonary nodule detection in CT images: false positive reduction using multi-view convolutional networks, IEEE Transactions on Medical Imaging 35 (5) (2016) 1160–1169.

[10] H.R. Roth, L. Lu, J. Liu, J. Yao, A. Seff, K. Cherry, L. Kim, R.M. Summers, Improving computer-aided detection using convolutional neural networks and random view aggregation, IEEE Transactions on Medical Imaging 35 (5) (2016) 1170–1181.

[11] J.-Z. Cheng, D. Ni, Y.-H. Chou, J. Qin, C.-M. Tiu, Y.-C. Chang, C.-S. Huang, D. Shen, C.-M. Chen, Computer-aided diagnosis with deep learning architecture: applications to breast lesions in US images and pulmonary nodules in CT scans, Scientific Reports 6 (1) (2016) 1–13.

[12] K.-K. Maninis, J. Pont-Tuset, P. Arbeláez, L. Van Gool, Deep retinal image understanding, in: International Conference on Medical Image Computing and Computer-Assisted Intervention, Springer, 2016, pp. 140–148.

[13] M.D. Bloice, C. Stocker, A. Holzinger, Augmentor: an image augmentation library for machine learning, arXiv preprint, arXiv:1708.04680.

[14] H. Zhang, M. Cisse, Y.N. Dauphin, D. Lopez-Paz, Mixup: beyond empirical risk minimization, arXiv preprint, arXiv:1710.09412.

[15] D. Eigen, C. Puhrsch, R. Fergus, Depth map prediction from a single image using a multi-scale deep network, in: Advances in Neural Information Processing Systems, 2014, pp. 2366–2374.

[16] F.J. Moreno-Barea, F. Strazzera, J.M. Jerez, D. Urda, L. Franco, Forward noise adjustment scheme for data augmentation, in: IEEE Symposium Series on Computational Intelligence, IEEE, 2018, pp. 728–734.

[17] A. Krizhevsky, I. Sutskever, G.E. Hinton, ImageNet classification with deep convolutional neural networks, in: Advances in Neural Information Processing Systems, 2012, pp. 1097–1105.

[18] A.G. Howard, Some improvements on deep convolutional neural network based image classification, arXiv preprint, arXiv:1312.5402.

[19] C.N. Vasconcelos, B.N. Vasconcelos, Convolutional neural network committees for melanoma classification with classical and expert knowledge based image transforms data augmentation, arXiv preprint, arXiv:1702.07025.

[20] L. Taylor, G. Nitschke, Improving deep learning using generic data augmentation, arXiv preprint, arXiv:1708.06020.

[21] F. Perez, C. Vasconcelos, S. Avila, E. Valle, Data augmentation for skin lesion analysis, in: OR 2.0 Context-Aware Operating Theaters, Computer Assisted Robotic Endoscopy, Clinical Image-Based Procedures, and Skin Image Analysis, Springer, 2018, pp. 303–311.

[22] B. Abdollahi, N. Tomita, S. Hassanpour, Data augmentation in training deep learning models for medical image analysis, in: Deep Learners and Deep Learner Descriptors for Medical Applications, Springer, 2020, pp. 167–180.

[23] X. Zhu, Z. Ghahramani, J.D. Lafferty, Semi-supervised learning using Gaussian fields and harmonic functions, in: Proceedings of the International Conference on Machine Learning (ICML-03), 2003, pp. 912–919.

[24] X. Lu, B. Zheng, A. Velivelli, C. Zhai, Enhancing text categorization with semantic-enriched representation and training data augmentation, Journal of the American Medical Informatics Association 13 (5) (2006) 526–535.

[25] J. Lemley, S. Bazrafkan, P. Corcoran, Smart augmentation learning an optimal data augmentation strategy, IEEE Access 5 (2017) 5858–5869.

[26] T. Tran, T. Pham, G. Carneiro, L. Palmer, I. Reid, A Bayesian data augmentation approach for learning deep models, in: Advances in Neural Information Processing Systems, 2017, pp. 2797–2806.

[27] E.D. Cubuk, B. Zoph, D. Mane, V. Vasudevan, Q.V. Le, AutoAugment: learning augmentation strategies from data, in: Proceedings of the IEEE Conference on Computer Vision and Pattern Recognition, 2019, pp. 113–123.

[28] S. Hauberg, O. Freifeld, A.B.L. Larsen, J. Fisher, L. Hansen, Dreaming more data: class-dependent distributions over diffeomorphisms for learned data augmentation, in: Artificial Intelligence and Statistics, 2016, pp. 342–350.

[29] A. Oliveira, S. Pereira, C.A. Silva, Augmenting data when training a CNN for retinal vessel segmentation: how to warp?, in: IEEE Portuguese Meeting on Bioengineering, IEEE, 2017, pp. 1–4.

[30] P.Y. Simard, D. Steinkraus, J.C. Platt, et al., Best practices for convolutional neural networks applied to visual document analysis, in: ICDAR, vol. 3, 2003.

[31] O. Ronneberger, P. Fischer, T. Brox, U-Net: convolutional networks for biomedical image segmentation, in: International Conference on Medical Image Computing and Computer-Assisted Intervention, Springer, 2015, pp. 234–241.

[32] Y. Jiang, H. Zhang, N. Tan, L. Chen, Automatic retinal blood vessel segmentation based on fully convolutional neural networks, Symmetry 11 (9) (2019) 1112.

[33] F. Milletari, N. Navab, S.-A. Ahmadi, V-Net: fully convolutional neural networks for volumetric medical image segmentation, in: International Conference on 3D Vision, IEEE, 2016, pp. 565–571.

[34] H.R. Roth, C.T. Lee, H.-C. Shin, A. Seff, L. Kim, J. Yao, L. Lu, R.M. Summers, Anatomy-specific classification of medical images using deep convolutional nets, in: IEEE International Symposium on Biomedical Imaging, IEEE, 2015, pp. 101–104.

[35] A. Dosovitskiy, P. Fischer, J.T. Springenberg, M. Riedmiller, T. Brox, Discriminative unsupervised feature learning with exemplar convolutional neural networks, IEEE Transactions on Pattern Analysis and Machine Intelligence 38 (9) (2015) 1734–1747.

[36] Z. Eaton-Rosen, F. Bragman, S. Ourselin, M.J. Cardoso, Improving data augmentation for medical image segmentation, in: International Conference on Medical Imaging with Deep Learning, 2018.

[37] K. Kamnitsas, C. Ledig, V.F. Newcombe, J.P. Simpson, A.D. Kane, D.K. Menon, D. Rueckert, B. Glocker, Efficient multi-scale 3D CNN with fully connected CRF for accurate brain lesion segmentation, Medical Image Analysis 36 (2017) 61–78.

[38] S. Fiorini, L. Ballerini, E. Trucco, A. Ruggeri, Automatic generation of synthetic retinal fundus images, in: STAG, 2014, pp. 41–44.

[39] A.A. Efros, W.T. Freeman, Image quilting for texture synthesis and transfer, in: Proceedings of the 28th Annual Conference on Computer Graphics and Interactive Techniques, 2001, pp. 341–346.

[40] J.A. Adam, Blood vessel branching: beyond the standard calculus problem, Mathematics Magazine 84 (3) (2011) 196–207.

[41] F. Oloumi, R.M. Rangayyan, A.L. Ells, Parabolic modeling of the major temporal arcade in retinal fundus images, IEEE Transactions on Instrumentation and Measurement 61 (7) (2012) 1825–1838.

[42] E. Menti, L. Bonaldi, L. Ballerini, A. Ruggeri, E. Trucco, Automatic generation of synthetic retinal fundus images: vascular network, in: International Workshop on Simulation and Synthesis in Medical Imaging, Springer, 2016, pp. 167–176.

[43] J.M. Bower, H. Cornelis, D. Beeman, Genesis, the general neural simulation system, 2014.

[44] N.T. Carnevale, M.L. Hines, The NEURON Book, Cambridge University Press, 2006.

[45] G.A. Ascoli, J.L. Krichmar, L-neuron: a modeling tool for the efficient generation and parsimonious description of dendritic morphology, Neurocomputing 32 (2000) 1003–1011.

[46] I. Goodfellow, J. Pouget-Abadie, M. Mirza, B. Xu, D. Warde-Farley, S. Ozair, A. Courville, Y. Bengio, Generative adversarial nets, in: Advances in Neural Information Processing Systems, 2014, pp. 2672–2680.

[47] H.-C. Shin, N.A. Tenenholtz, J.K. Rogers, C.G. Schwarz, M.L. Senjem, J.L. Gunter, K.P. Andriole, M. Michalski, Medical image synthesis for data augmentation and anonymization using generative adversarial networks, in: International Workshop on Simulation and Synthesis in Medical Imaging, Springer, 2018, pp. 1–11.

[48] D.P. Kingma, M. Welling, Auto-encoding variational Bayes, in: International Conference on Learning Representations, 2014.

[49] A. Madani, M. Moradi, A. Karargyris, T. Syeda-Mahmood, Chest X-ray generation and data augmentation for cardiovascular abnormality classification, in: Medical Imaging 2018: Image Processing, vol. 10574, International Society for Optics and Photonics, 2018, p. 105741M.

[50] A. Dosovitskiy, P. Fischer, E. Ilg, P. Hausser, C. Hazirbas, V. Golkov, P. van der Smagt, D. Cremers, T. Brox, FlowNet: learning optical flow with convolutional networks, in: Proceedings of the IEEE International Conference on Computer Vision, 2015, pp. 2758–2766.

[51] S.R. Richter, V. Vineet, S. Roth, V. Koltun, Playing for data: ground truth from computer games, in: European Conference on Computer Vision, Springer, 2016, pp. 102–118.

[52] A. Antoniou, A. Storkey, H. Edwards, Data augmentation generative adversarial networks, arXiv preprint, arXiv:1711.04340.

[53] A. Shrivastava, T. Pfister, O. Tuzel, J. Susskind, W. Wang, R. Webb, Learning from simulated and unsupervised images through adversarial training, in: Proceedings of the IEEE Conference on Computer Vision and Pattern Recognition, 2017, pp. 2107–2116.

[54] A. Radford, L. Metz, S. Chintala, Unsupervised representation learning with deep convolutional generative adversarial networks, arXiv preprint, arXiv:1511.06434.

[55] M.J. Chuquicusma, S. Hussein, J. Burt, U. Bagci, How to fool radiologists with generative adversarial networks? A visual turing test for lung cancer diagnosis, in: IEEE International Symposium on Biomedical Imaging, IEEE, 2018, pp. 240–244.

[56] A. Lahiri, V. Jain, A. Mondal, P.K. Biswas, Retinal vessel segmentation under extreme low annotation: a GAN based semi-supervised approach, in: IEEE International Conference on Image Processing, IEEE, 2020, pp. 418–422.

[57] C. Bermudez, A.J. Plassard, L.T. Davis, A.T. Newton, S.M. Resnick, B.A. Landman, Learning implicit brain MRI manifolds with deep learning, in: Medical Imaging 2018: Image Processing, vol. 10574, International Society for Optics and Photonics, 2018, p. 105741L.

[58] A.K. Mondal, J. Dolz, C. Desrosiers, Few-shot 3D multi-modal medical image segmentation using generative adversarial learning, arXiv preprint, arXiv:1810.12241.

[59] E.L. Denton, S. Chintala, R. Fergus, et al., Deep generative image models using a Laplacian pyramid of adversarial networks, in: Advances in Neural Information Processing Systems, 2015, pp. 1486–1494.

[60] M. Arjovsky, S. Chintala, L. Bottou, Wasserstein generative adversarial networks, in: Proceedings of the International Conference on Machine Learning, vol. 70, 2017, pp. 214–223.

[61] T. Karras, T. Aila, S. Laine, J. Lehtinen, Progressive growing of GANs for improved quality, stability, and variation, in: International Conference on Learning Representations, 2018.

[62] A. Beers, J. Brown, K. Chang, J.P. Campbell, S. Ostmo, M.F. Chiang, J. Kalpathy-Cramer, High-resolution medical image synthesis using progressively grown generative adversarial networks, arXiv preprint, arXiv:1805.03144.

[63] C. Baur, S. Albarqouni, N. Navab, MelanoGANs: high resolution skin lesion synthesis with GANs, arXiv preprint, arXiv:1804.04338.

[64] C. Han, H. Hayashi, L. Rundo, R. Araki, W. Shimoda, S. Muramatsu, Y. Furukawa, G. Mauri, H. Nakayama, GAN-based synthetic brain MR image generation, in: IEEE International Symposium on Biomedical Imaging, IEEE, 2018, pp. 734–738.

[65] Q. Wang, X. Zhou, C. Wang, Z. Liu, J. Huang, Y. Zhou, C. Li, H. Zhuang, J.-Z. Cheng, WGAN-based synthetic minority over-sampling technique: improving semantic fine-grained classification for lung nodules in CT images, IEEE Access 7 (2019) 18450–18463.

[66] B. Hu, Y. Tang, I. Eric, C. Chang, Y. Fan, M. Lai, Y. Xu, Unsupervised learning for cell-level visual representation in histopathology images with generative adversarial networks, IEEE Journal of Biomedical and Health Informatics 23 (3) (2018) 1316–1328.

[67] X. Yi, E. Walia, P. Babyn, Unsupervised and semi-supervised learning with categorical generative adversarial networks assisted by Wasserstein distance for dermoscopy image classification, arXiv preprint, arXiv:1804.03700.

[68] J.M. Wolterink, A.M. Dinkla, M.H. Savenije, P.R. Seevinck, C.A. van den Berg, I. Išgum, Deep MR to CT synthesis using unpaired data, in: International Workshop on Simulation and Synthesis in Medical Imaging, Springer, 2017, pp. 14–23.

[69] D. Nie, R. Trullo, J. Lian, L. Wang, C. Petitjean, S. Ruan, Q. Wang, D. Shen, Medical image synthesis with deep convolutional adversarial networks, IEEE Transactions on Biomedical Engineering 65 (12) (2018) 2720–2730.

[70] Y.-B. Tang, S. Oh, Y.-X. Tang, J. Xiao, R.M. Summers, CT-realistic data augmentation using generative adversarial network for robust lymph node segmentation, in: Medical Imaging 2019: Computer-Aided Diagnosis, vol. 10950, International Society for Optics and Photonics, 2019, p. 109503V.

[71] H. Zhao, H. Li, S. Maurer-Stroh, L. Cheng, Synthesizing retinal and neuronal images with generative adversarial nets, Medical Image Analysis 49 (2018) 14–26.

[72] M. Mirza, S. Osindero, Conditional generative adversarial nets, arXiv preprint, arXiv:1411.1784.

[73] P. Isola, J.-Y. Zhu, T. Zhou, A.A. Efros, Image-to-image translation with conditional adversarial networks, in: Proceedings of the IEEE Conference on Computer Vision and Pattern Recognition, 2017, pp. 1125–1134.

[74] J.-Y. Zhu, T. Park, P. Isola, A.A. Efros, Unpaired image-to-image translation using cycle-consistent adversarial networks, in: Proceedings of the IEEE International Conference on Computer Vision, 2017, pp. 2223–2232.

[75] B. Yu, L. Zhou, L. Wang, Y. Shi, J. Fripp, P. Bourgeat, EA-GANs: edge-aware generative adversarial networks for cross-modality MR image synthesis, IEEE Transactions on Medical Imaging 38 (7) (2019) 1750–1762.

[76] Y. Hiasa, Y. Otake, M. Takao, T. Matsuoka, K. Takashima, A. Carass, J.L. Prince, N. Sugano, Y. Sato, Cross-modality image synthesis from unpaired data using CycleGAN, in: International Workshop on Simulation and Synthesis in Medical Imaging, Springer, 2018, pp. 31–41.

[77] Z. Zhang, L. Yang, Y. Zheng, Translating and segmenting multimodal medical volumes with cycle-and shape-consistency generative adversarial network, in: Proceedings of the IEEE Conference on Computer Vision and Pattern Recognition, 2018, pp. 9242–9251.

[78] C. Chen, Q. Dou, H. Chen, P.-A. Heng, Semantic-aware generative adversarial nets for unsupervised domain adaptation in chest X-ray segmentation, in: International Workshop on Machine Learning in Medical Imaging, Springer, 2018, pp. 143–151.

[79] Y. Zhang, S. Miao, T. Mansi, R. Liao, Task driven generative modeling for unsupervised domain adaptation: application to X-ray image segmentation, in: International Conference on Medical Image Computing and Computer-Assisted Intervention, Springer, 2018, pp. 599–607.

[80] A. Chartsias, T. Joyce, R. Dharmakumar, S.A. Tsaftaris, Adversarial image synthesis for unpaired multi-modal cardiac data, in: International Workshop on Simulation and Synthesis in Medical Imaging, Springer, 2017, pp. 3–13.

[81] Y. Huo, Z. Xu, S. Bao, A. Assad, R.G. Abramson, B.A. Landman, Adversarial synthesis learning enables segmentation without target modality ground truth, in: IEEE International Symposium on Biomedical Imaging, IEEE, 2018, pp. 1217–1220.

[82] H. Yang, J. Sun, A. Carass, C. Zhao, J. Lee, Z. Xu, J. Prince, Unpaired brain MR-to-CT synthesis using a structure-constrained CycleGAN, in: Deep Learning in Medical Image Analysis and Multimodal Learning for Clinical Decision Support, Springer, 2018, pp. 174–182.

[83] W. Wei, E. Poirion, B. Bodini, S. Durrleman, N. Ayache, B. Stankoff, O. Colliot, Learning myelin content in multiple sclerosis from multimodal MRI through adversarial training, in: International Conference on Medical Image Computing and Computer-Assisted Intervention, Springer, 2018, pp. 514–522.

[84] Y. Pan, M. Liu, C. Lian, T. Zhou, Y. Xia, D. Shen, Synthesizing missing PET from MRI with cycle-consistent generative adversarial networks for Alzheimer's disease diagnosis, in: International Conference on Medical Image Computing and Computer-Assisted Intervention, Springer, 2018, pp. 455–463.

[85] V. Sandfort, K. Yan, P.J. Pickhardt, R.M. Summers, Data augmentation using generative adversarial networks (CycleGAN) to improve generalizability in CT segmentation tasks, Scientific Reports 9 (1) (2019) 1–9.

[86] B. Yu, L. Zhou, L. Wang, J. Fripp, P. Bourgeat, 3D CGAN based cross-modality MR image synthesis for brain tumor segmentation, in: IEEE International Symposium on Biomedical Imaging, IEEE, 2018, pp. 626–630.

[87] S. Olut, Y.H. Sahin, U. Demir, G. Unal, Generative adversarial training for MRA image synthesis using multi-contrast MRI, in: International Workshop on Predictive Intelligence in Medicine, Springer, 2018, pp. 147–154.

[88] Q. Yang, N. Li, Z. Zhao, X. Fan, E.-C. Chang, Y. Xu, et al., MRI image-to-image translation for cross-modality image registration and segmentation, arXiv preprint, arXiv:1801.06940.

[89] F. Liu, SUSAN: segment unannotated image structure using adversarial network, Magnetic Resonance in Medicine 81 (5) (2019) 3330–3345.

[90] S.U. Dar, M. Yurt, L. Karacan, A. Erdem, E. Erdem, T. Çukur, Image synthesis in multi-contrast MRI with conditional generative adversarial networks, IEEE Transactions on Medical Imaging 38 (10) (2019) 2375–2388.

[91] K. Chaitanya, N. Karani, C.F. Baumgartner, A. Becker, O. Donati, E. Konukoglu, Semi-supervised and task-driven data augmentation, in: International Conference on Information Processing in Medical Imaging, Springer, 2019, pp. 29–41.

[92] T.C. Mok, A.C. Chung, Learning data augmentation for brain tumor segmentation with coarse-to-fine generative adversarial networks, in: International MICCAI Brainlesion Workshop, Springer, 2018, pp. 70–80.

[93] A. Zhao, G. Balakrishnan, F. Durand, J.V. Guttag, A.V. Dalca, Data augmentation using learned transformations for one-shot medical image segmentation, in: Proceedings of the IEEE Conference on Computer Vision and Pattern Recognition, 2019, pp. 8543–8553.

[94] H. Zhao, H. Li, S. Maurer-Stroh, Y. Guo, Q. Deng, L. Cheng, Supervised segmentation of un-annotated retinal fundus images by synthesis, IEEE Transactions on Medical Imaging 38 (1) (2018) 46–56.

[95] Y. Zhou, X. He, S. Cui, F. Zhu, L. Liu, L. Shao, High-resolution diabetic retinopathy image synthesis manipulated by grading and lesions, in: International Conference on Medical Image Computing and Computer-Assisted Intervention, Springer, 2019, pp. 505–513.

[96] A. Brock, J. Donahue, K. Simonyan, Large scale GAN training for high fidelity natural image synthesis, in: International Conference on Learning Representations, 2018.

[97] J. Staal, M.D. Abràmoff, M. Niemeijer, M.A. Viergever, B. van Ginneken, Ridge-based vessel segmentation in color images of the retina, IEEE Transactions on Medical Imaging 23 (4) (2004) 501–509.

[98] A. Hoover, V. Kouznetsova, M. Goldbaum, Locating blood vessels in retinal images by piecewise threshold probing of a matched filter response, IEEE Transactions on Medical Imaging 19 (3) (2000) 203–210.

[99] U.T. Nguyen, A. Bhuiyan, L.A. Park, K. Ramamohanarao, An effective retinal blood vessel segmentation method using multi-scale line detection, Pattern Recognition 46 (3) (2013) 703–715.

[100] K. Simonyan, A. Zisserman, Very deep convolutional networks for large-scale image recognition, arXiv:1409.1556.

[101] Diabetic retinopathy detection, www.kaggle.com/c/diabetic-retinopathy-detection, 2015.

[102] X. Xu, W. Ding, X. Wang, R. Cao, M. Zhang, P. Lv, F. Xu, Smartphone-based accurate analysis of retinal vasculature towards point-of-care diagnostics, Scientific Reports 6 (1) (2016) 1–9.

Unsupervised abnormality detection in medical images with deep generative methods

15

Xiaoran Chen and Ender Konukoglu
Computer Vision Lab, ETH Zürich, Zürich, Switzerland

15.1 Overview

Detecting pathological structures in medical images is often the first step of diagnosis of diseases and plays a critical role in assessing the clinical condition and planning further treatment. Common practice requires the doctors and radiologists with clinical knowledge and years of experience to find the regions that deviate from healthy anatomy and identify the diseases based on visual alternation. Nowadays, manual detection and assessment still remains the main approach in clinical practice. Although manual detection is reliable and accurate, it is still a time-consuming process. With the recent advance in the field of machine learning, automating the detection of pathological regions has been an active research area at the intersection of medical image analysis and computer vision.

Learning-based algorithms make use of machine learning algorithms and learn to detect pathological abnormalities from large datasets through model training. Once the algorithms are well trained, they are able to perform detection on incoming images in a short time without requiring much effort from the experts. Generally, the automated detection algorithms can be learned in two ways, with supervised models or with generative models. We would like to shortly discuss the supervised methods and return to the unsupervised methods with more details.

15.1.1 Supervised detection methods

Supervised methods aim to learn a mapping from the data, in our case, images, to their corresponding annotations and then detect with the learned mapping to make predictions on test data. Earlier works in the line of supervised methods include Ayachi et al. [1], where the detection problem was formulated as a pixel-wise classification problem and applied support vector machine to distinguish between normal and abnormal pixels with features based on textures and intensities, and classification forest [2] where the model was provided with non-local spatial information along with initial probability estimates to include context information for higher detection accuracy. While the problem gains more attention in the field, public challenges have been initiated by the medical image computing community especially for lesion detection, some examples are the Multi-modal Brain Tumor Image Segmentation (BraTS) and Ischemic Stroke Lesion Segmentation (ISLES). A benchmark on BraTS was released in [3] with evaluation and comparison of the existing models and provided an overview of the research status for the topic. With the introduction of fully convolutional neural networks [4], DeepMedic [5] and U-Nets [6] have been able to extract more complicated features from images and include information within a large spatial range in each image by building deep neural networks with convolutions. Supervised methods since then have seen significant improvement in segmentation accuracy on several types of medical images.

As supervised methods learn the mapping between input data and the corresponding annotations, test images should come from similar acquisition settings to the training data to ensure the same level of accuracy of the method. As the annotations are pre-defined using the training data, a supervised model is in fact trained to detect *pre-specified* types of abnormalities in the training set. One possible limitation to the supervised methods is that the radiologists often cannot decide the type of abnormalities before localizing them in the imaging results to ensure the methods have been trained to segment them. To reduce the limitation, we turn to approaches that can detect the abnormalities in a similar way as the radiologists. This leads to the other approach for this problem which is unsupervised methods.

15.1.2 Unsupervised detection methods

Unsupervised methods aim to learn prior knowledge of healthy data and detect abnormalities that exhibit dissimilar traits and disagree with the learned prior knowledge. This only requires the collection of healthy data and does not further need additional annotations of either healthy or abnormal data. The development of automated abnormality detection using unsupervised approaches can contribute to algorithm innovation and clinical assistance. From the algorithm development perspective, a successful unsupervised abnormality detection method would contribute to both the clinical applications of learning methods and the theories for unsupervised learning models, as well as inspire further works for robust detection of unseen data samples. From the clinical perspective, the unsupervised detection method can be used for fast pre-screening of images in large volumes to help radiologists assess the imaging results of more patients in a shorter time.

One of the earlier works [7] introduced a mixture model to represent the distribution of different tissue types through the expectation-maximization (EM) algorithm while ensuring the robustness against abnormalities with typicality weights and then detected the abnormalities by the typicality weights and contextual information. Moon et al. [8] extended the EM segmentation method by adding classes to represent tumor and edema and extracting prior knowledge for them in T1 pre- and post-contrast images to obtain a more accurate segmentation of the abnormalities.

This is then improved by Prastawa et al. [9] which first detected an abnormal region with a registered brain atlas for healthy brains and then segmented the tumor and edema in the abnormal region using estimates of different tissue properties obtained from healthy brains. Later works such as Tomas et al. [10] segmented both abnormalities and healthy tissues by learning a spatially global within-the-subject intensity distribution and a spatially local intensity distribution from a healthy reference population. Due to the curse of dimensionality in modeling high-dimensional distributions, works often make use of dimensionality reduction techniques, such as patch-based mixture model [11], principal component analysis [12,13], and sparse representation [14].

With the emergence of deep-learning-based generative models, generative models have been enabled to approximate complicated distributions from large datasets. The most popular ones are generative adversarial networks (GANs) [15] which aim to estimate the data distribution from a given dataset by training a generator and a discriminator and then generate new samples that resemble the samples of the given dataset, and variational autoencoders (VAEs) [16] which are a non-linear latent variable model and approximate the data distribution by maximizing the evidence lower bound through latent projections (encoding) and reconstruction (decoding).

Both GANs and VAEs have the capability of learning a distribution for normal samples and can be adapted for unsupervised abnormality detection at the image level and pixel level. Schlegl et al. [17] proposed AnoGAN, which trained a GAN on healthy images only to obtain the distribution of healthy data and detected the abnormalities by optimizing the projection to find the healthy image closely matched to the abnormal image and calculating the difference between the two images. Fast-AnoGAN [18] extended AnoGAN by implementing an additional latent-image encoder for accelerated z-mapping of a query image during detection. Other works, such as OCGAN [19] and ALOCC [20], also adapt adversarial learning to detect abnormal samples for natural images. On the other hand, An et al. [21] proposed to train a VAE to maximize the probability of the reconstructed normal images and detect abnormal samples if the per-image probability of reconstructed test images is below a certain threshold. Several works adapt this approach to perform unsupervised abnormality detection on different types of inputs [22–24]. Within the application of medical research, Baur et al. [25] proposed to use a deep spatial autoencoding model and detected multiple sclerosis (MS) lesions in brain magnetic resonance (MR) images by the difference between input and reconstructed images. Pawlowski et al. [26] detected abnormalities in brain computed tomography images using an autoencoder with Monte-Carlo dropout. Chen et al. [27] proposed to detect abnormalities by implementing latent consistency in an adversarial autoencoder (AAE) to enhance more faithful reconstruction of healthy structures in abnormal images and reduce false detections. Zimmerer et al. [28] proposed a novel term composed of the multiplication of the derivative of the Kullback–Leibler term and the reconstruction error, and showed robust detection at both image- and pixel-level.

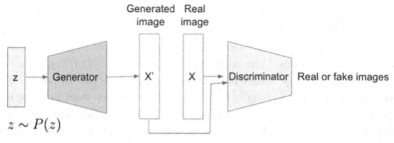

FIGURE 15.1

Structure of generative adversarial network (GAN).

15.2 Generative methods for unsupervised abnormality detection

In this section, we provide more details about deep-learning-based generative methods for our task. Before this, let us define the notations. Let's denote an image as $X \in \mathbb{R}^{m \times n}$, then a set of images can be indexed as $\{X^1, \ldots, X^N\}$, where the pixels of images can be indexed as $\{X^{(i,1)}, \ldots, X^{(i,P)}\}$. We denote a healthy image as X_H and an abnormal image as X_A. Given a healthy dataset, we aim to estimate the distribution of healthy images, P_H, and evaluate the probability of an unseen image and its pixels, $P_H(X^i)$. In the detection step, if a test image is an abnormal image X_A, the pixel $X_A{}^i$ within the brain can be either in an abnormal region I_A as $X_A^{(i \in I_A)}$ or in a normal region I_H as $X_A^{(i \in I_H)}$. Since the distribution is estimated with only healthy images and thus can only generate healthy images, the probability of the pixels in abnormal regions $P_H(X_A^{(i \in I_A)})$ are expected to be low, whereas pixels in healthy regions will have high probability $P_H(X_A^{(i \in I_H)})$.

15.2.1 GAN-based models

A GAN consists of a generator and discriminator and aims to estimate the distribution of some given data inputs and afterwards sample from this distribution, see Fig. 15.1. The generator learns a mapping where a latent variable sampled from a latent distribution is mapped to the data space. The discriminator takes the data sample as its input and is trained to predict whether this sample is generated by the generator or a real sample from the data samples. The model can be applied to different types of data, such as text, audio, and images. Let us take images as the example, and denote the latent variable as z, $z \sim P(z)$, where $z \in \mathbb{R}^d$, the image as X where $X \in \mathbb{R}^{m \times n}$ and $X \sim P(X)$. The minimax optimization of a GAN is formulated as

$$\min_G \max_D [\mathbb{E}_{X \sim P(X)} \log D(x) + \mathbb{E}_{z \sim P(z)} \log(1 - D(G(z)))], \qquad (15.1)$$

where $P(X)$ is the true distribution of data and P_z is the latent distribution of z, and the generator and discriminator are updated alternatively.

15.2.1.1 AnoGAN

Adopting the structure of a GAN to estimate the distribution of normal images, P_H, Schlegl et al. [17] proposed a novel model, AnoGAN. Given a set of healthy images X_H, the generator G learns a distribution P_G, which is also the distribution for healthy images P_H as mentioned above, by a mapping $G(z)$ from a latent distribution $P(z)$. The aim of the generator is to generate new samples that highly resemble the training data from the estimated P_G. The discriminator D is a classification network which takes in both training data and generated data generated with $G(z)$ and outputs the probability of a sample being a real data sample. At convergence, the estimated P_G should be a good approximation of P_H such that the discriminator cannot distinguish between real and generated samples.

In order to localize the abnormalities, we would like to be able to compare the difference between healthy and abnormal images, which requires a mapping from the image to the latent space. To do this, a new loss function, which is also referred to as the anomaly score, is defined as

$$L(z_\gamma) = (1 - \lambda) \sum ||x - G(z_\gamma)|| + \lambda \sum ||f(x) - f(G(z_\gamma))||, \qquad (15.2)$$

where x is the input test image during detection, z_γ is a latent variable to be optimized, and $f(\cdot)$ are the features of the input images at an intermediate layer of the trained discriminator. The loss function includes a residual loss, which measures the ℓ_1-distance between the generated image $G(z_\gamma)$ and the input image, and a discrimination loss which further enforces the feature matching using the rich learned features of D. This loss not only considers the pixel-wise similarity but requires the matched healthy image to exhibit similar features as the input image. By minimizing $L(z_\gamma)$, we obtain the inverse mapping from the image space to the latent space. For an abnormal image, the abnormalities can be detected by calculating the residual loss for each pixel, which is equivalent to the ℓ_1-loss.

15.2.2 f-AnoGAN

For real-time application, the projection optimization can take a considerable amount of time during detection as AnoGAN needs to optimize the latent-image projection in order to find the most closely-matched healthy image for a test image. To deal with this, the model is extended into f-AnoGAN [18] with an additional encoder and replacement of GAN with the more stable Wasserstein GAN (WGAN) [29]. WGAN can be trained with

$$L = \min_G \max_D [\mathbb{E}_{X \sim P(X)} D(X)] - \mathbb{E}_{z \sim P(z)}[D(G(z))]. \qquad (15.3)$$

f-AnoGAN improves the projection optimization in the detection step by introducing an encoder E and two architectures, *ziz* and *izi* architectures, as illustrated in

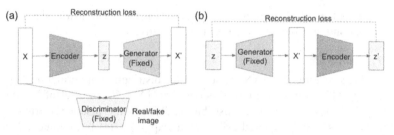

FIGURE 15.2

Detection of abnormalities on new images using an encoder: (a) *izi* architecture: an image is encoded into a latent sample by the trainable encoder and the latent sample is mapped to an image by the trained generator, the similarity between the input and generated image is enforced by the trained discriminator, this is also introduced as the discriminator guided encoder training; (b) *ziz* architecture: a random latent sample drawn from $P(z)$ is mapped to an image through the trained generator and the image is encoded back into the random latent sample.

Fig. 15.2. The training of the additional encoder E uses the generator and discriminator from the trained WGAN. Specifically, the *ziz* architecture resembles the reversed structure of an autoencoder, where the decoder is the trained generator G of WGAN. The encoder in this architecture is trainable and the training minimizes the loss in Eq. (15.4), where d is the dimension of the latent sample,

$$L_{ziz}(x) = \frac{1}{d}||z - E(G(z))||^2. \tag{15.4}$$

The *izi* architecture is a standard autoencoder structure. By fixing the parameters in the generator, it is used as a decoder and forms an autoencoder structure together with the trainable encoder. The parameters of the discriminator are also fixed and the discriminator is used to guide the training of the *izi* architecture by enforcing similarity between the input image and the generated image in the feature space. Overall, the encoder is trained by minimizing

$$L_E = \frac{1}{n}||x - G(E(x))||^2 + \frac{\kappa}{n}||f(x) - f(G(E(x)))||^2, \tag{15.5}$$

where n is the number of pixels in each image, κ is a weighting factor, and $f(\cdot)$ is the features at an intermediate layer of the discriminator. The encoder is trained on the same training data as the WGAN training, i.e., only on normal images, and both generator and discriminator are fixed during the encoder training.

To detect the abnormalities, f-AnoGAN does not perform additional optimization during detection and uses the residual loss from the test image and its reconstruction for pixel-wise abnormality detection, which is calculated as $|x - G(E(x))|$.

15.2.3 **Autoencoding-based models**

Besides GANs, autoencoding-based methods have also been applied to unsupervised detection. The basic architecture of an autoencoding model consists of two mappings, the encoder f_E and the decoder f_D. To obtain the distribution for normal data, the encoding mapping f_E takes as input a healthy image X_H and encodes it into a lower-dimensional representation z and $z \sim P_z$. The latent representation is then decoded by the mapping f_D back into an image, which is also known as the reconstruction $X'_H = f_D(z)$. The functions f_E and f_D are optimized to minimize a reconstruction loss $L(X_H, X'_H)$, which is often defined as the ℓ_1- or ℓ_2-loss. During detection, autoencoder-based methods are not capable of reconstructing the abnormal variation in the images as they are not trained to represent such patterns in the encoding and decoding mappings. In this case, we can also see the reconstruction loss as an unnormalized pixel-wise probability map of the image based on the data distribution $P_H(X) = \frac{1}{Z}L(X, X')$ where Z is an unknown normalization constant.

The basic architecture of an autoencoding model is an autoencoder, which consists of two deterministic mappings, the encoder f_E and the decoder f_D. Given an input image X, the encoder maps it to a latent representation z, $z = f_E(X)$, and the decoder decodes the latent representation to obtain a reconstructed image X'. The model is often trained to minimize a loss defined between X and X', such as ℓ_1- or ℓ_2-loss. Another widely-used autoencoding model is the denoising autoencoder (DAE) where the encoder takes a corrupted image, $X + \epsilon$, as input and aims to reconstruct a noise-free image. Autoencoders and DAE are not generative models as they do not approximate P_H and only serve as dimension-reduction models. Despite this, they provide the idea to learn data representation through the encoding–decoding scheme and lay the structure for generative models such as VAEs, adversarial autoencoders (AAEs) [30], and α-GAN [31]. We here briefly introduce each of them.

Variational autoencoders, as shown in Fig. 15.3 (left), equip autoencoders with stochastic inference to estimate P_H. A VAE first encodes X_H into a latent representation z which is sampled from an arbitrary distribution $P(z)$ and then reconstructs the input image by decoding the sampled z from the latent distribution. Unlike autoencoders which consist of deterministic mappings, the encoder and decoder of a VAE represent probabilistic mappings, modeling $Q(z|X)$ and $P(X|z)$, respectively. Formally, trained on only healthy images X_H, the underlying principle of a VAE can be written as

$$P_H(X_H) = \int P(X_H|z_H)P(z_H)dz, \qquad (15.6)$$

where training a VAE maps z_H to a structured latent space defined by $P(z)$, an arbitrarily defined distribution, such as Gaussian, by matching $Q(z|X)$ to $P(z)$ through Kullback–Leibler (KL) divergence $KL[Q(z|X)||P(z)]$. To ensure z preserves information of X_H, we maximize $\mathbb{E}_{z \sim Q(z|X)}P(X|z)$ which can also be implemented as a reconstruction loss. The optimization task of a VAE can now be solved by maximizing an evidence lower bound (ELBO) (Eq. (15.7)) as derived in [32],

$$\log P_H(X_H) \geq E_{z \sim Q(z|X)}[\log(X|z)] - KL[Q(z|X)||P(z)]. \qquad (15.7)$$

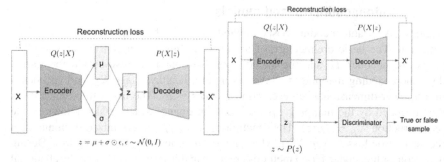

FIGURE 15.3

(left) Structure of a variational autoencoder, (right) structure of an adversarial autoencoder.

Adversarial autoencoders, as shown in Fig. 15.3 (right), have a similar architecture as VAEs but replace distribution matching through KL-divergence by adversarial learning. Earlier studies, such as [33] and [34], have found that VAEs often generate blurry reconstructions, and theoretically explained the blurriness. Bousquet et al. [34] suggest that the Wasserstein autoencoder, a generalized version of AAEs, can mitigate the blurriness using an adversarial loss to match $Q(z) = E_{X_H}[Q(z|X_H)]$ and $P(z)$. The encoder of AAEs can also be seen as the generator G of GANs and a discriminator is added to distinguish $z \sim P(z)$ from generated $z = f_E(X_H)$, which can be trained with GAN or WGAN.

α-**GAN**, as shown in Fig. 15.4, is another method to achieve sharper images with autoencoder-based methods and improve the reconstruction quality on the image level. In the original paper of α-GAN, the model matches $Q(z|X)$ and $P(z)$ similarly as AAE and yet enforces another adversarial loss with an additional discriminator D_X to distinguish between X_H and X'_H. Again, the addition of D_X introduces an adversarial loss that can be written in a similar form as

$$\min_{G} \max_{D} E_{z \sim P(z)}[\log D(z)] + E_{z \sim Q(z)}[\log(1 - D(z))]. \qquad (15.8)$$

In other words, the decoder can be seen as the image generator of a GAN. The adversarial loss is now imposed for both the latent representation and the image.

15.2.3.1 Spatial-VAEGAN

Baur et al. [25] proposed the spatial autoencoder/VAE, where the dense layer connecting the encoder to the latent representation is replaced with a convolution layer, in order to capture the global anatomical information of healthy images. The modification can be applied to both autoencoders and VAEs. The authors then combine the spatial autoencoder/VAE with a discriminator for images to form a spatial-VAEGAN. The model can be trained with

$$L_{VAE} = \lambda_1 ||X - X'|| + \lambda_2 KL(Q(z|X)||P(z)) - \lambda_3 \log D(X'), \qquad (15.9)$$

$$L_D = -\log D(X) - \log(1 - D(X')), \qquad (15.10)$$

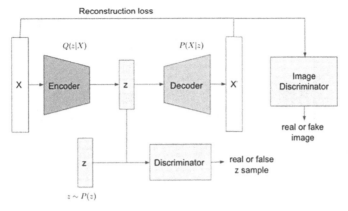

FIGURE 15.4

Structure of αGAN.

where Eq. (15.9) is used to optimize the VAE networks, Eq. (15.10) is used to optimize the discriminator, and z is modeled as a multivariate Gaussian in spatial VAE.

15.2.3.2 Constrained AAE (cAAE)

Most autoencoder-based detection methods rely on the assumption that abnormal images can be reconstructed as healthy images in the autoencoding process and the abnormalities can therefore be detected by reconstruction errors. However, the autoencoder-based models are not enforced to encode the input and reconstructed image closely in the latent space. Chen et al. [27] proposed the constrained AAE (cAAE) to deal with this limitation by introducing consistency in latent representation. cAAE is based on the architecture of an AAE with an additional ℓ_2-loss of latent representations. Given an input image X, its latent representation z can be obtained by $z = f_E(X_H)$; X can be reconstructed by the AAE as X', its latent representation can be obtained by $z' = f_E(X')$. A cAAE can be trained using

$$L_{rec} = ||X - X'||_2 + \lambda ||z - z'||, \tag{15.11}$$

$$L_{cAAE} = L_{rec} + L_{WGAN}, \tag{15.12}$$

where L_{WGAN} is the objective of Wasserstein GAN as described in Section 15.2.1.1 and λ is a weighting factor.

15.2.3.3 Context-encoding VAE (ceVAE)

Spatial-VAEGAN, cAAE, and other autoencoder-based methods mostly detect pixelwise abnormalities using reconstruction errors. Zimmerer et al. [35] argued that detecting solely based on reconstruction errors may ignore higher-level representations for the images as well as contextual information and proposed the context-encoding VAE (ceVAE) (Fig. 15.5). The ceVAE consists of two branches, a context-encoding (CE) branch and a VAE branch. In the CE branch, an encoder f_E and decoder f_D are

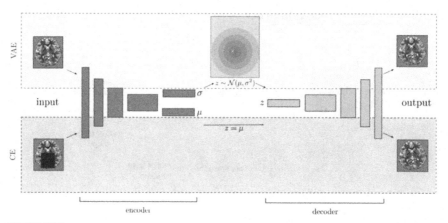

FIGURE 15.5

Structure of Context-Encoding VAE (ceVAE).

used to reconstruct noisy healthy image $\tilde{X}_H$ and are optimized using the ℓ_1-loss as

$$L_{CE} = ||X_H - \tilde{X}_H||. \tag{15.13}$$

In the VAE branch, f_E is trained normally in the formulation of VAE to obtain $Q(z|X)$ parameterized by $\mu_{z|X}$ and $\sigma_{z|X}$,

$$L_{VAE} = ||X - X'|| + KL[Q(z|X)||P(z)], \tag{15.14}$$

where X' is the reconstruction of X and $P(z)$ is a pre-defined latent distribution and defined a unit-Gaussian in ceVAE. The encoder and decoder are shared in the CE and VAE branches. Overall, the ceVAE can be trained as

$$L_{ceVAE} = L_{VAE} + L_{CE}. \tag{15.15}$$

Combining CE and VAE branches can regularize the method and prevent posterior collapse while still learning rich discriminative features using the CE branch. The abnormalities are detected using reconstruction errors and gradients of the ELBO with respect to the input image. The ELBO of a given image can be computed by $ELBO(X)$, the abnormality score is defined for each image as

$$A(X) = h\left(||X - X'||, \frac{\partial ELBO(X)}{\partial X}\right), \tag{15.16}$$

where h is an element-wise multiplication function.

15.2.4 Restoration with MAP estimation and image prior

Instead of reconstruction-based methods, Chen et al. [36] formulated the unsupervised detection problem as an image restoration and proposed a two-step detection

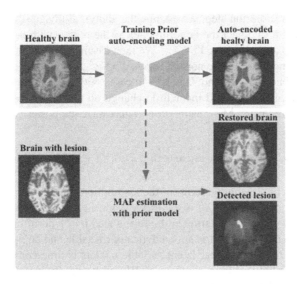

FIGURE 15.6

Illustration of the detection method using MAP-based restoration. The method includes two stages, upper for training prior distribution by an autoencoding model, and lower for iterative restoration with MAP estimation.

method (Fig. 15.6) with (1) image-prior learning using Gaussian mixture VAE (GM-VAE) [37] and (2) image restoration using maximum a posteriori (MAP) estimation.

In the image-prior learning step, the GMVAE is trained on healthy images to capture the distribution of normal data with a more expressive latent distribution, namely mixtures of Gaussians. Following the formulation in [37], the derivation of the ELBO for GMVAEs, though slightly more complicated, is similar to that for VAEs (see Eq. (15.17)),

$$
\begin{aligned}
\text{ELBO}(X) = {}& \mathbb{E}_{Q(z|X)} \big[\log P(X|z) \big] \\
& - \mathbb{E}_{Q(\omega|X)P(k|z,\omega)} \left[\text{KL} \left[Q(z|X) || P(z|\omega, k) \right] \right] \\
& - \text{KL} \left[Q(\omega|X) || P(\omega) \right] \\
& - \mathbb{E}_{Q(z|X)Q(\omega|X)} \left[\text{KL} \left[P(k|z, \omega) || P(k) \right] \right].
\end{aligned}
$$

$$(15.17)$$

Enforcing the mixtures of Gaussian in the latent space leads to two additional distributions $Q(\omega|X)$ and $P(c|z, \omega)$; $Q(\omega|X)$ is modeled as a Gaussian distribution with diagonal covariance $Q(\omega|X) = \mathcal{N}\left(\omega; \mu_\omega(X), \text{diag}\left(\sigma_\omega^2(X)\right)\right)$; $P(c|z, \omega)$ can be computed analytically for a given ω and z; $P(X|z)$ and $Q(z|X)$ are modeled in the same way as in the VAE model. For more details regarding the training of a GMVAE, we refer the interested reader to the original paper [37].

In the image restoration step, we assume the abnormal image is a normal image with noise and aim to detect the abnormalities as the region with noise. We denote an image with abnormalities as $Y \in \mathbb{R}^N$. We then assume that the noisy image Y is obtained by adding noise to the normal image $X \in \mathbb{R}^N$, namely $Y = X + D$, where D denotes the abnormalities and $D \in \mathbb{R}^N$. In cases with no abnormalities, we have $Y = X$, i.e., the method should incur little change on the input image. The image restoration is solved using MAP estimation to maximize the posterior distribution of X given Y as

$$\arg \max_X \log P(X|Y) = \arg \max_X \left[\log P(Y|X) + \log P(X) \right], \tag{15.18}$$

where $P(Y|X)$ is the likelihood term for the assumptions on D and can also be seen as a data consistency term, $P(X)$ is the image prior, i.e., the distribution of healthy images. The data consistency term can be formulated by ℓ_1-norm or total variation (TV) norm. Note that $\log P(X)$ is not analytically tractable and computing this term via sampling for most non-linear latent variable models is time-consuming and impractical for potential real-time application. We substitute $P(X)$ as ELBO to solve the approximated MAP estimation problem as

$$\arg \max_X \log P(X|Y) \approx \arg \max_X \left[\log P(Y|X) + \text{ELBO}(X) \right]. \tag{15.19}$$

We use a gradient ascent method to optimize the aforementioned objective function. Particularly, we iteratively approximate the gradients of $P(X|Y)$ by taking the gradient of Eq. (15.19) and perform gradient ascent as in

$$G_{X^i} = \frac{\partial \left[\log P(Y|X) + \text{ELBO}(X) \right]}{\partial X} \Big|_{X = X^i}, \tag{15.20}$$

$$X^{i+1} = X^i + \alpha_i \cdot G_{X^i}, \tag{15.21}$$

where α_i is the step size for each iteration, and the initial image is the input image, i.e., $X^0 = Y$. We obtain the noise-free image $\hat{X}$ as $\hat{X} = X^N$ upon the convergence of the MAP estimation. The abnormalities can be detected as the absolute difference between the input and restored image, $|Y - \hat{X}|$. In other words, by optimizing Eq. (15.19) with respect to the input image, Y is restored to fit the image prior P_H and the data consistency prevents a large deviation between the restored image and the input image such that the healthy structures remain mostly unchanged.

15.3 Application on real-world abnormalities
15.3.1 Retinal OCT dataset

The retinal optical coherence tomography (OCT) dataset used in the work of [17,18] consists of clinical high-resolution retinal spectral-domain optical coherence tomography (SD-OCT) volumes acquired by a Heidelberg Spectralis device. AnoGAN and

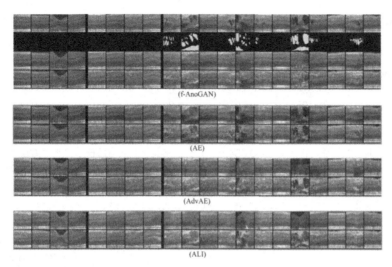

(f-AnoGAN)

(AE)

(AdvAE)

(ALI)

FIGURE 15.7

Detection on retinal OCT image patches. Rows 1–2 show real input images and ground-truth annotations. Rows 3–4 present detection results by f-AnoGAN. Rows 5–6 illustrate detection results by autoencoder (AE). Rows 7–8 provide detection results by adversarial autoencoder (AdvAE). Rows 9–10 give detection results by adversarial learned inference (ALI) [38]. Note that the detection is performed for patches extracted from both normal (columns 1–8) and abnormal (columns 9–20) images.

f-AnoGAN have been applied to anomaly detection on the retinal OCT dataset. The GAN/WGAN within the framework is trained on 2D patches of 64 × 64 pixels randomly extracted from the 3D OCT volumes of clinically-confirmed healthy subjects. The detection is performed on 10 SD-OCT volumes of healthy subjects and 10 diseased cases containing retinal fluid with binary annotations by clinical experts. The test datasets are not used for training the GAN/WGAN.

The methods are evaluated for image-level detection, in other words, to determine whether an image is anomalous, and also compared to other methods, such as autoencoder, adversarial autoencoder [30], adversarial learned inference [38], and direct use of a trained discriminator of WGAN. In Table 15.1, f-AnoGAN outperformed the other baseline methods. As shown in Fig. 15.7, the detection by f-AnoGAN also better matches with the annotated bio-markers for diseased retina than the baseline methods.

15.3.2 Brain MRI datasets

Autoencoder-based methods have been applied for anomaly detection in brain MR images. Several datasets have been used for the detection (see Table 15.2), including

Table 15.1 Detection results on OCT samples using different models: autoencoder (AE), adversarial autoencoder (AAE), adversarial learned inference (ALI), discriminator of WGAN, AnoGAN and f-AnoGAN.

Model	Precision	Sensitivity	Specificity	f-score	AUC
AE	0.6824	0.7195	0.8550	0.7005	0.8688
AAE	0.6405	0.7856	0.8092	0.7057	0.8649
ALI	0.5063	0.7434	0.6863	0.6023	0.7897
Discriminator	0.4909	0.6831	0.6931	0.5713	0.7504
AnoGAN	0.7202	0.8049	0.8645	0.7602	0.9114
f-AnoGAN	**0.7863**	**0.8091**	**0.9049**	**0.7975**	**0.9301**

Table 15.2 Summary of datasets used for unsupervised abnormality detection for brain MRI images.

Dataset	Availability	Modalities	Healthy subjects	Diseased subjects
CamCAN	public	T1, T2	652	0
BraTS-2017	public	FLAIR, T1c, T1, T2	0	285
ATLAS	public	T1	0	220
HCP	public	T1, T2	1200	0
ISLES2015 (SISS)	public	FLAIR, T2w TSE, T1w TFE/TSE, DWI	0	64
MS Lesion	inhouse	FLAIR, T1	83	49

(1) CamCAN,[1] Cambridge Centre for Ageing and Neuroscience dataset, described in [39]; (2) BraTS-2017,[2] Multimodal Brain Tumor Image Segmentation Challenge dataset, described in [40], (3) ATLAS,[3] Anatomical Tracings of Lesions After Stroke (ATLAS) dataset, described in [41], (4) HCP,[4] Human Connectome Project, as described in [42], (5) ISLES2015,[5] Ischemic Stroke Lesion Segmentation, and (6) MS Lesion, an in-house dataset used for training and evaluation by [25].

Spatial-VAEGAN [25] performs on the in-house MS Lesion, where the model is first trained on the 2D images of healthy subjects and then evaluated on the 2D images with abnormalities. The method also post-processes the reconstructed images obtained from training a $5 \times 5 \times 5$ median filter to filter out small residuals and slightly eroded brain masks to remove skull stripping artifacts. The method is evaluated using the metrics of Dice scores and area under the precision–recall curve (AUPRC). In order to calculate the Dice scores, the reconstructed images are thresholded by the value at the 98th percentile of the models reconstruction errors on the

---

[1] http://www.cam-can.org/.
[2] https://www.med.upenn.edu/sbia/brats2018.html.
[3] http://fcon_1000.projects.nitrc.org/indi/retro/atlas.html.
[4] https://www.humanconnectome.org/study/hcp-young-adult.
[5] http://www.isles-challenge.org/ISLES2015/.

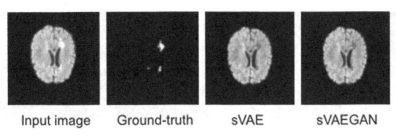

Input image   Ground-truth   sVAE   sVAEGAN

FIGURE 15.8

Detection visualization on MS Lesion obtained with spatial-VAE (sVAE) and spatial-VAEGAN (sVAEGAN) models.

Table 15.3 Detection performance on MS Lesion obtained with spatial-VAE, spatial-VAEGAN and AnoGAN models.

Model	Dice scores ($\mu \pm \sigma$)	AUPRC
Spatial-VAE	0.5922 ± 0.1958	0.6890
Spatial-VAEGAN	**0.6050 ± 0.1927**	**0.6906**
AnoGAN	0.3748 ± 0.2192	0.4178

Table 15.4 Detection performance on 32×32 T2-weighted MRI from BraTS-2017. λ is a weighting factor for the consistency term in the constrained adversarial autoencoder (cAAE).

Model	AUC	Histogram Overlap (%)
VAE	0.897	26
AAE	0.885	28
cAAE ($\lambda = 0.5$)	0.906	25
cAAE ($\lambda = 1.0$)	**0.923**	**17**

training dataset. In Table 15.3, spatial-VAEGAN has been shown to outperform the other baseline methods, such as spatial-VAE and AnoGAN. Visualized detection is shown in Fig. 15.8.

cAAE [43] is trained on down-sampled T2-weighted MR images of size 32×32 from the HCP dataset and evaluated on BraTS-2017. The model is evaluated using the area under the receiver operator characteristic curve (AUROC) and overlap between the histograms of reconstruction errors on healthy and abnormal pixels, as well as compared to baseline methods such as VAE. As indicated in Table 15.4, cAAE achieves a higher AUC than the other models and less histogram overlap, indicating that the abnormalities can be better separated with the reconstruction errors obtained from the model. Visualized detection is shown in Fig. 15.9.

ceVAE [35] uses the HCP dataset to learn healthy anatomy and performs detection on BraTS-2017 and ISLES-2015, where images are down-sampled to the size of 64×64. ceVAE is evaluated for slice- and pixel-wise detection with reconstruc-

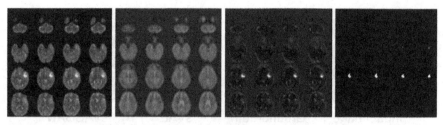

FIGURE 15.9

Tumor detection by constrained adversarial autoencoder on down-sampled T2-weighted images of BraTS-2017 dataset. From left to right, columns 1–4 show input image with brain tumors, columns 5–8 illustrate reconstructed image, columns 9–12 present reconstruction errors, while columns 13–16 provide ground-truth annotations.

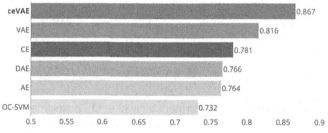

FIGURE 15.10

Slice-wise detection on BraTS-2017 by different models: context-encoding VAE (ceVAE), VAE, context encoder (CE), denoising autoencoder (DAE), autoencoder (AD) and one-class support vector machine (OC-SVM).

tion errors, gradient of KL-loss and a combination of reconstruction and KL losses. The method is compared to the baseline methods of autoencoder, context encoder, VAE, denoising autoencoder, and one-class support vector machine with the metric of AUROC and Dice scores. The results are reported as histograms in their work depicted in Fig. 15.10. Different detection outcomes are also shown for each dataset in Fig. 15.11. For the good cases, tumors are detected at the correct location and the contour aligns well with the ground truth. For the medium cases, the tumors are detected at the correct location but in a different shape from the annotated tumor. For the bad cases, the tumors appear similar to the healthy anatomy and the method can mistaken healthy tissues as a tumor or fail to detect any abnormality for the images with tumors.

The restoration method [36] is a two-stage detection, where the VAE or Gaussian mixture VAE model is trained on CamCAN datasets consisting only of healthy subjects in the first stage and the incoming images are restored by maximizing the posterior probability using the learned prior and data consistency in the second stage. The detection is applied to T2-weighted MR images of BraTS-2017 and T1-weighted

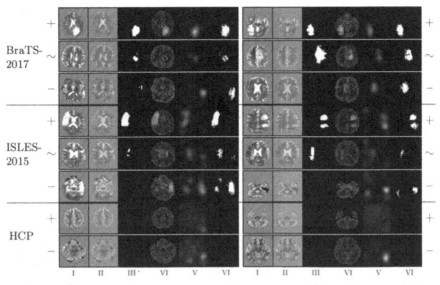

FIGURE 15.11

Detection of context-encoding VAE on the BraTS-2017, ISLES2015, and HCP datasets. The authors provided three cases of detection, where + marks a good case, ~ a medium case, and - a bad case. From left to right, the columns are: (I) the original sample, (II) the reconstruction, (III) the ground truth, (IV) the reconstruction error, (V) the gradient of the KL loss, and (VI) the resulting segmentation.

Table 15.5 Detection performance on BraTS-2017 evaluated for the restoration methods in comparison with baselines. The Gaussian mixture VAE (GMVAE) is trained with a different number of Gaussian mixtures, c, and results are shown for $c = 3$, $c = 6$, and $c = 9$.

Models	AUC	Dice (1%fpr)	Dice (5%fpr)	Dice (10%fpr)
VAE	0.69	0.09 ± 0.06	0.19 ± 0.15	0.26 ± 0.17
AAE	0.70	0.03 ± 0.03	0.18 ± 0.14	0.23 ± 0.15
AnoGAN	0.65	0.02 ± 0.02	0.10 ± 0.06	0.19 ± 0.13
VAE (restore, TV)	0.80	$\mathbf{0.34 \pm 0.20}$	0.36 ± 0.27	0.40 ± 0.24
GMVAE (restore, TV, $c = 3$)	0.82	0.21 ± 0.20	0.39 ± 0.22	0.38 ± 0.20
GMVAE (restore, TV, $c = 6$)	0.81	0.31 ± 0.14	0.40 ± 0.22	0.37 ± 0.16
GMVAE (restore, TV, $c = 9$)	**0.83**	0.32 ± 0.23	$\mathbf{0.45 \pm 0.20}$	$\mathbf{0.42 \pm 0.19}$

MR images of ATLAS as shown in Fig. 15.12 and evaluated using AUROC and Dice scores, as in Tables 15.5–15.6. Dice scores are calculated with a threshold on the reconstruction errors allowing $\tau\%$ false positives after applying the restoration on healthy images.

Table 15.6 Detection performance on the ATLAS dataset evaluated for the restoration methods in comparison with baselines. The Gaussian mixture VAE (GMVAE) is trained with a different number of Gaussian mixtures, c, and results are shown for $c = 3$, $c = 6$, and $c = 9$.

Models	AUC	Dice (1%fpr)	Dice (5%fpr)	Dice (10%fpr)
VAE	0.64	0.00 ± 0.00	0.01 ± 0.01	0.01 ± 0.01
AAE	0.63	0.00 ± 0.00	0.01 ± 0.01	0.01 ± 0.01
AnoGAN	0.64	0.00 ± 0.00	0.01 ± 0.01	0.02 ± 0.02
VAE (restore, TV)	**0.79**	0.10 ± 0.06	0.11 ± 0.05	0.11 ± 0.05
GMVAE (restore, TV, $c = 3$)	**0.79**	0.06 ± 0.06	0.09 ± 0.07	**0.08 ± 0.07**
GMVAE (restore, TV, $c = 6$)	**0.79**	**0.10 ± 0.09**	**0.12 ± 0.12**	**0.08 ± 0.07**
GMVAE (restore, TV, $c = 9$)	0.77	0.08 ± 0.07	0.10 ± 0.08	0.07 ± 0.07

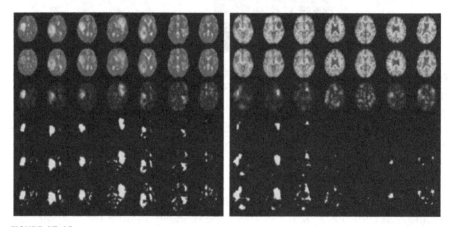

FIGURE 15.12

Detection of Gaussian mixture VAE (restore, TV) with $c = 9$ for BraTS-2017 (left) and $c = 6$ for ATLAS (right). From top to bottom, the rows are: (1) input images, (2) restored images, (3) absolute difference between the input and restored images, (4) segmentation with 1% fpr threshold, (5) segmentation with 5% fpr threshold, and (6) segmentation with 10% fpr threshold. Input images in the columns are randomly selected from the respective datasets.

15.4 Discussion

As several works have been originally trained and evaluated on different datasets, an extensive performance for most existing methods has been summarized by [43] and, more recently, [44], where models are trained and evaluated using the same datasets. The summary papers benchmark the autoencoding and GAN-based models mentioned in Sections 15.2.1–15.2.3. Baur et al. [44] evaluate the models with both public and in-house datasets.

Compared to methods with supervision, the unsupervised learning method largely relaxes the demand of annotations. With only subject-wise annotations denoting whether the individual is healthy or not, the generative models can learn data distribution from a large number of healthy scans and apply on test subjects to detect and localize the abnormalities. The unsupervised methods have the potential to detect any types of abnormalities without tedious annotations and can deal with rare and novel types of abnormalities.

Despite its advantages, we have also observed failure cases where healthy structures are mistaken as abnormalities or abnormalities are mistaken as healthy structures. In the case of reconstruction-based detection, the reconstruction errors between the healthy and abnormal pixels are not large enough to distinguish the healthy and tumor pixels. This can result from the blurry reconstruction of the autoencoding models, where details in the healthy anatomy are not well reconstructed. Although the reconstruction quality is less of an issue for the restoration-based detection, the method still depends on the approximation of healthy data distribution which cannot be directly calculated.

Other challenges also remain for the unsupervised detection methods, for example, 3D contextual information, multi-domain detection, and images from different domains. As most of the current methods are trained on 2D images and applied for 2D detection, contextual information between each slices has not been fully leveraged and captured by the generative models. Utilization of such information is likely to improve detection accuracy. Besides, the radiologists often request scans of several imaging modalities to ensure accurate diagnosis. The images from different modalities are complementary to one another and contouring of the pathological structure takes different aspects of information on each of them. The unsupervised methods can also take advantages of the multi-modality datasets to learn the healthy data distribution to further enhance the detection. On the other hand, in clinical practice, the test images can be acquired from various imaging devices and therefore exhibit domain shift. The current methods have not yet been extensively evaluated on domain shift and possible modifications may be necessary to deal with the issue.

References

[1] R. Ayachi, N. Ben Amor, Brain tumor segmentation using support vector machines, symbolic and quantitative approaches to reasoning with uncertainty, in: ECSQARU, 2009, pp. 736–747.

[2] D. Zikic, B. Glocker, E. Konukoglu, J. Shotton, A. Criminisi, D. Ye, C. Demiralp, O. Thomas, T. Das, R. Jena, et al., Context-sensitive classification forests for segmentation of brain tumor tissues, in: Proc. MICCAI-BraTS, 2012, pp. 1–9.

[3] S. Bauer, T. Fejes, J. Slotboom, R. Wiest, L.-P. Nolte, M. Reyes, Segmentation of brain tumor images based on integrated hierarchical classification and regularization, in: MICCAI BraTS Workshop, MICCAI Society, Nice, 2012.

[4] J. Long, E. Shelhamer, T. Darrell, Fully convolutional networks for semantic segmentation, in: Proceedings of the IEEE Conference on Computer Vision and Pattern Recognition, 2015, pp. 3431–3440.

[5] K. Kamnitsas, C. Ledig, V.F. Newcombe, J.P. Simpson, A.D. Kane, D.K. Menon, D. Rueckert, B. Glocker, Efficient multi-scale 3D CNN with fully connected CRF for accurate brain lesion segmentation, Medical Image Analysis 36 (2017) 61–78.

[6] O. Ronneberger, P. Fischer, T. Brox, U-Net: convolutional networks for biomedical image segmentation, in: International Conference on Medical Image Computing and Computer-Assisted Intervention, Springer, 2015, pp. 234–241.

[7] K. van Leemput, F. Maes, D. Vandermeulen, A. Colchester, P. Suetens, Automated segmentation of multiple sclerosis lesions by model outlier detection, IEEE Transactions on Medical Imaging 20 (8) (2001) 677–688.

[8] N. Moon, E. Bullitt, K. van Leemput, G. Gerig, Automatic brain and tumor segmentation, in: International Conference on Medical Image Computing and Computer-Assisted Intervention, Springer, 2002, pp. 372–379.

[9] M. Prastawa, E. Bullitt, S. Ho, G. Gerig, A brain tumor segmentation framework based on outlier detection, Medical Image Analysis 8 (3) (2004) 275–283.

[10] X. Tomas-Fernandez, S.K. Warfield, A model of population and subject (MOPS) intensities with application to multiple sclerosis lesion segmentation, IEEE Transactions on Medical Imaging 34 (6) (2015) 1349–1361.

[11] M.J. Cardoso, C.H. Sudre, M. Modat, S. Ourselin, Template-based multimodal joint generative model of brain data, in: International Conference on Information Processing in Medical Imaging, Springer, 2015, pp. 17–29.

[12] E.I. Zacharaki, A. Bezerianos, Abnormality segmentation in brain images via distributed estimation, IEEE Transactions on Information Technology in Biomedicine 16 (3) (2012) 330–338.

[13] G. Erus, E.I. Zacharaki, C. Davatzikos, Individualized statistical learning from medical image databases: application to identification of brain lesions, Medical Image Analysis 18 (3) (2014) 542–554.

[14] K. Zeng, G. Erus, A. Sotiras, R.T. Shinohara, C. Davatzikos, Abnormality detection via iterative deformable registration and basis-pursuit decomposition, IEEE Transactions on Medical Imaging 35 (8) (2016) 1937–1951.

[15] I. Goodfellow, J. Pouget-Abadie, M. Mirza, B. Xu, D. Warde-Farley, S. Ozair, A. Courville, Y. Bengio, Generative adversarial nets, in: Advances in Neural Information Processing Systems, 2014, pp. 2672–2680.

[16] D.P. Kingma, M. Welling, Auto-encoding variational Bayes, arXiv preprint, arXiv:1312.6114.

[17] T. Schlegl, P. Seeböck, S.M. Waldstein, U. Schmidt-Erfurth, G. Langs, Unsupervised anomaly detection with generative adversarial networks to guide marker discovery, in: International Conference on Information Processing in Medical Imaging, Springer, 2017, pp. 146–157.

[18] T. Schlegl, P. Seeböck, S.M. Waldstein, G. Langs, U. Schmidt-Erfurth, f-AnoGAN: fast unsupervised anomaly detection with generative adversarial networks, Medical Image Analysis 54 (2019) 30–44.

[19] P. Perera, R. Nallapati, B. Xiang, OCGAN: one-class novelty detection using GANs with constrained latent representations, in: Proceedings of the IEEE/CVF Conference on Computer Vision and Pattern Recognition, 2019, pp. 2898–2906.

[20] M. Sabokrou, M. Khalooei, M. Fathy, E. Adeli, Adversarially learned one-class classifier for novelty detection, in: Proceedings of the IEEE Conference on Computer Vision and Pattern Recognition, 2018, pp. 3379–3388.

[21] J. An, S. Cho, Variational autoencoder based anomaly detection using reconstruction probability, Special Lecture on IE 2 (1) (2015) 1–18.

[22] M. Schreyer, T. Sattarov, D. Borth, A. Dengel, B. Reimer, Detection of anomalies in large scale accounting data using deep autoencoder networks, arXiv preprint, arXiv:1709.05254.

[23] M. Lopez-Martin, B. Carro, A. Sanchez-Esguevillas, J. Lloret, Conditional variational autoencoder for prediction and feature recovery applied to intrusion detection in IoT, Sensors 17 (9) (2017) 1967.

[24] M. Yousefi-Azar, V. Varadharajan, L. Hamey, U. Tupakula, Autoencoder-based feature learning for cyber security applications, in: 2017 International Joint Conference on Neural Networks (IJCNN), IEEE, 2017, pp. 3854–3861.

[25] C. Baur, B. Wiestler, S. Albarqouni, N. Navab, Deep autoencoding models for unsupervised anomaly segmentation in brain MR images, arXiv preprint, arXiv:1804.04488.

[26] N. Pawlowski, M.C.H. Lee, M. Rajchl, S. McDonagh, E. Ferrante, K. Kamnitsas, S. Cooke, S.K. Stevenson, A.M. Khetani, T. Newman, F.A. Zeiler, R.J. Digby, J.P. Coles, D. Rueckert, D.K. Menon, V.F.J. Newcombe, B. Glocker, Unsupervised lesion detection in brain CT using Bayesian convolutional autoencoders, 2018.

[27] X. Chen, E. Konukoglu, Unsupervised detection of lesions in brain MRI using constrained adversarial auto-encoders, arXiv preprint, arXiv:1806.04972.

[28] D. Zimmerer, F. Isensee, J. Petersen, S. Kohl, K. Maier-Hein, Unsupervised anomaly localization using variational auto-encoders, in: International Conference on Medical Image Computing and Computer-Assisted Intervention, Springer, 2019, pp. 289–297.

[29] M. Arjovsky, S. Chintala, L. Bottou, G.A.N. Wasserstein, arXiv preprint, arXiv:1701.07875.

[30] A. Makhzani, J. Shlens, N. Jaitly, I. Goodfellow, B. Frey, Adversarial autoencoders, arXiv preprint, arXiv:1511.05644.

[31] S. Lutz, K. Amplianitis, A. Smolic, AlphaGAN: generative adversarial networks for natural image matting, arXiv preprint, arXiv:1807.10088.

[32] C. Doersch, Tutorial on variational autoencoders, arXiv preprint, arXiv:1606.05908.

[33] A.B.L. Larsen, S.K. Sønderby, H. Larochelle, O. Winther, Autoencoding beyond pixels using a learned similarity metric, arXiv preprint, arXiv:1512.09300.

[34] O. Bousquet, S. Gelly, I. Tolstikhin, C.-J. Simon-Gabriel, B. Schoelkopf, From optimal transport to generative modeling: the VEGAN cookbook, arXiv preprint, arXiv:1705.07642.

[35] D. Zimmerer, S.A. Kohl, J. Petersen, F. Isensee, K.H. Maier-Hein, Context-encoding variational autoencoder for unsupervised anomaly detection, arXiv preprint, arXiv:1812.05941.

[36] X. Chen, S. You, K.C. Tezcan, E. Konukoglu, Unsupervised lesion detection via image restoration with a normative prior, Medical Image Analysis 64 (2020) 101713.

[37] N. Dilokthanakul, P.A. Mediano, M. Garnelo, M.C. Lee, H. Salimbeni, K. Arulkumaran, M. Shanahan, Deep unsupervised clustering with Gaussian mixture variational autoencoders, arXiv preprint, arXiv:1611.02648.

[38] V. Dumoulin, I. Belghazi, B. Poole, O. Mastropietro, A. Lamb, M. Arjovsky, A. Courville, Adversarially learned inference, arXiv preprint, arXiv:1606.00704.

[39] J.R. Taylor, N. Williams, R. Cusack, T. Auer, M.A. Shafto, M. Dixon, L.K. Tyler, R.N. Henson, et al., The Cambridge centre for ageing and neuroscience (CAM-CAN) data repository: structural and functional MRI, MEG, and cognitive data from a cross-sectional adult lifespan sample, NeuroImage 144 (2017) 262–269.

[40] B.H. Menze, A. Jakab, S. Bauer, J. Kalpathy-Cramer, K. Farahani, J. Kirby, Y. Burren, N. Porz, J. Slotboom, R. Wiest, et al., The multimodal brain tumor image segmentation benchmark (BRATS), IEEE Transactions on Medical Imaging 34 (10) (2015) 1993.

[41] S.-L. Liew, J.M. Anglin, N.W. Banks, M. Sondag, K.L. Ito, H. Kim, J. Chan, J. Ito, C. Jung, N. Khoshab, et al., A large, open source dataset of stroke anatomical brain images and manual lesion segmentations, Scientific Data 5 (2018) 180011.

[42] D.C. Van Essen, K. Ugurbil, E. Auerbach, D. Barch, T.E. Behrens, R. Bucholz, A. Chang, L. Chen, M. Corbetta, S.W. Curtiss, et al., The human connectome project: a data acquisition perspective, NeuroImage 62 (4) (2012) 2222–2231.

[43] X. Chen, N. Pawlowski, M. Rajchl, B. Glocker, E. Konukoglu, Deep generative models in the real-world: an open challenge from medical imaging, arXiv preprint, arXiv:1806.05452.

[44] C. Baur, S. Denner, B. Wiestler, N. Navab, S. Albarqouni, Autoencoders for unsupervised anomaly segmentation in brain MR images: a comparative study, Medical Image Analysis (2020) 101952.

Regularizing disentangled representations with anatomical temporal consistency

16

Gabriele Valvano[a,b]**, Andrea Leo**[c]**, and Sotirios A. Tsaftaris**[b]

[a]*IMT School for Advanced Studies Lucca, Lucca, Italy*
[b]*School of Engineering, University of Edinburgh, Edinburgh, United Kingdom*
[c]*Department of Translational Research on New Technologies in Medicine and Surgery, University of Pisa, Pisa, Italy*

16.1 Introduction

In recent years, medical imaging has experienced a groundbreaking success of deep neural networks and supervised learning. However, the performance of machine learning algorithms largely depends on their ability to extract good high-level representations from the data [1], which is a challenging problem and usually requires large quantities of labeled data. Unfortunately, collecting large-scale fully-annotated medical datasets is expensive and requires experts.

On the other hand, semi-supervised learning (SSL) suggests that it is possible to include unlabeled data to train better models, exploiting data correlations. For example, in medical image segmentation, physicians may annotate only the end-diastolic and the end-systolic temporal instances of a cardiac cine magnetic resonance (MR) image [2]. Yet all the images in the cardiac cycle may be used to add knowledge into the model. It is common to formulate SSL as a multi-task learning problem [3–6], where one minimizes the supervised cost on the annotated images, but also other unsupervised or self-supervised objectives, which do not require labels. For example, it is possible to train a model to perform object segmentation while also minimizing the self-reconstruction cost. Sharing model parameters across tasks leads to richer and more meaningful data representations.

However, improving the supervised task in multi-task learning is only possible when the tasks do not compete, which is not always the case [7]. For example, optimizing one learning objective may require data representations, which instead hamper the convergence of another training objective. A possible workaround for the problem is constraining the representation to separate out, or *disentangle*, features useful for both tasks from those that are task-specific [8,9].

Biomedical Image Synthesis and Simulation. **https://doi.org/10.1016/B978-0-12-824349-7.00023-2**

There has been an increasing interest in learning disentangled representations for many computer vision applications, such as image-to-image translation [10–12], semantic segmentation [6], and landmark detection [13]. These methods usually decompose an image into two subsets of representations: the *content* and the *style*. The image content aims to capture spatial information required for spatially-equivariant tasks, such as object detection and segmentation. On the other hand, the style representation captures image appearance in terms of color intensity and textures. The hope of such decomposition and desired equivariances and invariances is to push semantic meaning into the different information contents. In medical imaging, we can associate the image content with the anatomical information varying across patients. Instead, the image style contains the imaging modality's information, which changes with scanner and acquisition physics. It is also possible to further factorize the representation. For example, decoupling the spatial information related to specific anatomical structures assists semantic segmentation tasks [6]. Disentangling pathology helps for pathology segmentation and pseudo-healthy image synthesis [14,15]. Disentangling artifacts helps improve the image quality and the subsequent analysis [16].

In this chapter, we focus on the task of cardiac image segmentation. We discuss whether it is possible to regularize the learning of disentangled representation in cardiac MRI by exploiting the anatomical region-specific spatio-temporal dynamics. In particular, we show that inductive biases, such as temporal coherence, are of fundamental importance to encourage the model to deal with real-world dynamics and improve generalization. Herein, we leverage the temporal evolution of the heart's contraction as captured by unlabeled cine MRIs. We use a self-supervised objective to constrain the latent representation to be predictable in time. As a result, we improve segmentation performance on unseen data.

In the following, we adopt SDNet, a framework that Chartsias et al. [6] introduced in the context of medical imaging for object segmentation via disentangled representations. SDNet decouples factors specific to the imaging modality (style) from those related to the patient anatomy (content). Compared to other frameworks for content-style disentanglement [17,18], SDNet discretizes content representation to preserve pixel-to-pixel correspondences with the image whilst encouraging the removal of continuous modality-related information from the spatial content representation. This additional discretization bottleneck encourages disentanglement but also provides a more interpretable content representation [19], which is of importance for healthcare applications.

We endow SDNet with the ability to predict anatomical temporal dynamics, inherently building a better representation that increases model robustness in a scarcity of annotations. We graphically present the method in Fig. 16.1 and summarize the key aspects as follows:

- We regularize the learning of disentangled representations in SDNet through a modality invariant transformer that, conditioned on the temporal information, transforms the anatomical factors to predict future instants in a cine MRI.

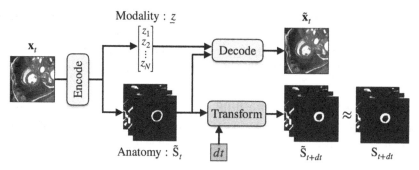

Modality : $\underline{z}$
$$\begin{bmatrix} z_1 \\ z_2 \\ \vdots \\ z_N \end{bmatrix}$$

Anatomy : $\tilde{S}_t$ dt $\tilde{S}_{t+dt}$ S_{t+dt}

FIGURE 16.1

Method overview. Given the input image $\mathbf{x}_t$ at time t, the model extracts a multi-channel binary representation S_t (anatomical factors) and a residual vector $\underline{z}$ (modality factors). In this work, we aim at regularizing S_t constraining it to be predictable: conditioned on the temporal gap dt, a neural network must be able to predict the representation at time $t + dt$.

- We show that the transformer provides a self-supervised signal which has a regularizing effect on the extracted representation, and it helps perform the cardiac segmentation task.
- We report increased performance compared to SDNet for semi-supervised learning when the amount of available annotations decreases, and we achieve comparable results to a fully supervised training using fewer labels.
- We show an example of how it is possible to employ our model for cardiac temporal synthesis.

This chapter extends our previous publication [20], including the analysis of the model on an additional cardiac dataset, metrics for each anatomical structure, and a more in-depth analysis of the model components and the learned representations. We made code for reproducing the experiments available at https://github.com/vioss/sdtnet.

16.2 Related work

Deep neural networks are excellent tools for medical image analysis [21], and the UNet [22] is a popular and effective approach for image segmentation. The UNet has an autoencoding architecture characterized by skip-connections, i.e., interconnections between the encoder and the decoder at multiple depth levels. Fundamental to the UNet success, the skip-connections limit the gradient vanishing problem and improve the segmentation of high-resolution details. Unfortunately, training a UNet in standard fully-supervised learning is expensive in terms of label collection, and the model does not perform well when annotations are scarce. For this reason, semi-supervised methods have emerged as appealing alternatives to increase model accuracy while keeping low the labeling cost.

In the following, we first discuss semi-supervised approaches, their assumptions, and limitations. Then we discuss why disentangled representations help to learn in semi-supervised settings. Finally, we discuss the importance of learning temporal transitions and how they can increase data representation quality.

16.2.1 Semi-supervised learning

Semi-supervised learning is the process of training using both annotated and unannotated data. Under specific assumptions [23], optimizing training objectives on the unlabeled data also improves the supervised task, for which annotations may be scarce. Among SSL methods, several approaches regularize the training process requiring that the model predictions remain consistent after applying realistic perturbations on the unlabeled data [24–26]. Other approaches leverage pre-trained models to predict additional labels for unannotated samples [4], which are used for co-training [27,28], self-training [29,30] and multi-view learning [31,32]. To SSL also belong generative models that learn the data distribution while also performing a supervised objective. Having learned high-quality features for the generative task, they use them to perform the supervised objective, too [5,33,34]. Finally, graph-based methods consider labeled and unlabeled data as nodes inside a graph, and they learn to propagate labels from the labeled nodes to the unlabeled ones [35,36].

Each of the above SSL categories relies on at least one of the following hypotheses: (i) the *manifold assumption*: high dimensional data lie on a low-dimensional manifold; (ii) the *smoothness assumption*: if two data points are close, the corresponding model predictions should be close; and (iii) the *clustering assumption*: two points that are in the same cluster most likely belong to the same class. In this work, we assume that the smoothness assumption holds even in disentangled features space, and we force the model to map similar images to similar representations. In particular, we regularize SDNet [6] anatomical representations using their temporal consistency as a self-supervised objective, and improve the segmentation task.

16.2.2 Disentangled representations

Disentangled representations have been used in many computer vision tasks, endowing machine learning models of the possibility to extract explanatory factors from the data. Higgins et al. [37] proposed a formal definition of disentangled representations which exploits the concept of "symmetry transformations." Symmetry transformations are transformations changing only specific aspects of the real world state while keeping other aspects unchanged (or invariant). According to this definition, a vector representation is disentangled if it can be decomposed it into several sub-spaces, each one of which is compatible with and can be transformed independently by a unique symmetry transformation [37]. As a result, we must assume that changes in the world state only sparsely affect the representation. Vice versa, localized changes in the encoded data are sparse over real-world transformations.

For these properties, disentangled representations increase the model interpretability, and improve its generalization on unseen data, thanks to the concept of equivariance. Moreover, confining single factors of variations in specific subsets of features allows interpretable latent code manipulation, which is desirable in many applications, such as modality transfer [12,11], image generation [38,39], and domain adaptation [40,17,41].

A shared definition of disentanglement is still open to debate. However, many researchers think that disentangled representations should be *factorized*, i.e., they should contain statistically independent latent variables [42]. Obtaining this type of representations would allow compact and meaningful information encoding, which is useful to increase model generalizability [9] and to increase the robustness against nuisance factors and adversarial attacks [43].

In the context of medical imaging, Chartsias et al. [6,40] explored the use of factorized representations for semi-supervised learning and multi-modal image segmentation. Qin et al. [18] exploited disentangled representations for unsupervised domain adaptation. Haochuan et al. [14] used disentanglement in the context of pathology segmentation. Here, we present an innovative method exploiting temporal information to regularize the learning of disentangled representations and improve the segmentation task.

16.2.3 Improving disentanglement with temporal transitions

Real-world transformations preserve a considerable amount of invariant structure, which profoundly influences biological vision. For example, objects have smooth temporal dynamics, and thus temporal smoothness facilitates the development of object recognition in humans [44]. More broadly, the sensorimotor contingencies theory states that human perception emerges from a sensorimotor flux of data, e.g., experiencing how sensory experience changes in time, or as a consequence of our actions [45]. This flux of data has properties and constraints that are learned by our brain to better understand the world around us.

Driven by these observations, Caselles-Dupré et al. [46] argued that the transitions from one state of the system into another are necessary for learning good disentangled representations. In particular, rather than simply training a neural network with unrelated samples $\{\underline{a}, \underline{b}, \underline{c}\}$, we can introduce temporal transitions by teaching the model to go from the state at time t, $\{\underline{a}_t, \underline{b}_t, \underline{c}_t\}$, to the state at time $t+1$, $\{\underline{a}_{t+1}, \underline{b}_{t+1}, \underline{c}_{t+1}\}$.

Even in medical imaging the use of temporal information has being explored. For example, Krebs et al. [47] used the temporal information contained in cine MRIs to detect cardiac abnormalities via a probabilistic registration model. In image segmentation, Bai et al. [48] and Qin et al. [18] used the temporal information for label propagation on unannotated images. In this chapter we show that we can use cardiac temporal dynamics to improve the quality of disentangled representations.

Outside medical imaging, Hsieh et al. [49] proposed to decompose the input images in a set of time-dependent representations (pose) and a set of fixed representations (content). Specifically, they suggest using such a decomposition for video prediction, where they keep the content fixed and make inference on the pose vector to predict future frames in a temporal sequence. With a similar idea, we decompose the image in time-dependent *anatomical* factors and fixed *imaging modality* factors. After such a decomposition, we predict future temporal frames only based on the time-dependent representation. However, we should highlight that our objective is not to obtain good temporal predictions. Rather we demonstrate that learning temporal dynamics regularizes the (learning of) disentangled representations, encouraging it to change smoothly and consistently in time. As a direct consequence, we show that this also improves the segmentation capabilities of the model. In other words, this chapter demonstrates once more what is quite known for a while that several correlated tasks in a multi-task learning setting encourage the learning of better representations [50]. We describe below two self-supervised tasks that aid the performance of a supervised task (segmentation).

16.3 Methods

16.3.1 Spatial Decomposition Network

Many medical imaging modalities contain spatial information about the patient's anatomy modulated by modality-specific characteristics. The Spatial Decomposition Network (SDNet) [6] decouples anatomical factors from their appearance, obtaining (i) improved performance with limited annotations compared to other supervised approaches, and (ii) more interpretable representations. Below, we briefly review SDNet, upon which we build our model, but first formalize the notation we adopt.

Notation. Below, we use italic lowercase letters to denote scalars s and underlined italic lowercase letters for vectors $\underline{v}$. Two-dimensional images (matrices) are defined using bold lowercase letters, as $\mathbf{x} \in \mathbb{R}^{n \times m}$, where $n, m \in \mathbb{N}$ are the matrix dimensions. We refer to tensors $T \in \mathbb{R}^{r \times s \times t}$ using uppercase letters, with $r, s, t \in \mathbb{N}$. Lastly, we denote functions $\Phi(\cdot)$ with capital Greek letters.

16.3.1.1 Model

Overall, we can interpret SDNet as an autoencoder that receives a 2-dimensional image $\mathbf{x}$ as input and decomposes it into disjoint anatomical components S and modality-dependent factors $\underline{z}$ (we present the block diagram of SDNet as the yellow boxes in Fig. 16.2). The general idea is that jointly within these two representations, all of the available information is captured, and thus it should be possible to (perfectly) reconstruct the input image. This is a self-supervised task. Moreover, using only the anatomical information should be enough to perform (supervised) tasks that only need information about image anatomy, such as semantic segmentation. With this decomposition of an image $\mathbf{x}$ in a tuple of modality and anatomical factors $(\underline{z}, S)$, we can train SDNet to minimize supervised, self-supervised, and adversarial objectives, resulting in a multi-task learning problem.

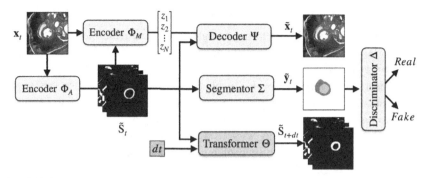

FIGURE 16.2

Block diagram of SDNet (described in Section 16.3.1) and SDTNet (Section 16.3.2). The components of SDNet are represented using yellow (light gray in print version) boxes, while SDTNet also includes the transformer network Θ, represented in light blue (mid gray in print version). In SDTNet, we train Θ to predict the future modality-independent anatomical factors conditioned on the temporal information dt. Notice that improving the quality of the anatomical representation S_t can make the segmentor job easier, facilitating the extraction of good segmentation masks $\tilde{y}_t$.

16.3.1.1.1 Supervised objective

With the goal of performing semantic segmentation, we train a segmentor $\Sigma(\cdot)$ to extract label maps $\tilde{y}$ from the anatomical representation of the image, such that the prediction $\tilde{y} = \Sigma(S)$ approximates the available ground-truth mask y.

16.3.1.1.2 Unsupervised objective

Conditioned on the anatomical representation S, a modality encoder $\Phi_M(x)$ learns to map the image x to factors z which are image modality-dependent. In particular, z is encouraged to follow a multivariate Gaussian distribution, as in the VAE framework [51]. A decoder $\Psi(\cdot)$ combines z and S to reconstruct the input image $\tilde{x} = \Psi(z, S) \approx x$, providing a loss signal to improve both modality and anatomy factors based on the reconstruction error.

16.3.1.1.3 Adversarial objective

Disentanglement is not trivial and requires inductive biases [52,53,19]. One strong bias is data, but expending annotations to provide such bias is perhaps conflicting to semi-supervised learning. One possibility is to provide shape priors that can help constrain the obtained segmentations to be close to reality. An adversarial loss [54] encourages the predicted segmentations $\tilde{y}$ to be realistic even when no manual annotation is available for the input image. Such a training signal is provided by a mask discriminator $\Delta(\cdot)$ that learns to say apart real from predicted segmentation masks.

16.3.1.1.4 Encouraging disentanglement

SDNet uses two specific biases to disentangle anatomical from modality factors of an image. In particular, SDNet models the anatomical factors S as discrete multi-channel binary maps, and the modality factors z as continuous variables which affect image appearance at a global level. S is obtained using a channel-wise softmax activation function to force each pixel in the multi-channel output of the anatomy encoder to have activations that sum up to one. During a forward pass, this multi-channel output is thresholded as $S \mapsto \lfloor S + 0.5 \rfloor$, while the training gradients are simply propagated through the thresholding operation during backpropagation, as in the straight-through operator [55]. Since S is binarized, it cannot easily encode continuous modality-dependent characteristics. As a result, SDNet must encode any modality information in z. To ensure that z does not also encode anatomical information, SDNet uses a very restrictive model to extract z, obtained through an information bottleneck [51].

16.3.1.2 Limitations and proposed approach

Compared to classical supervised approaches, SDNet obtains better segmentation performance in a scarcity of annotations. However, its ability to segment strictly relies on the extracted anatomical representations, and improving the anatomical factors makes the task easier for the segmentor. In this chapter, we introduce a spatio-temporal prior in SDNet, encouraging the model to learn the temporal dynamics of the anatomies. In particular, we use the temporal information that is intrinsically available in cardiac cine MRIs, and train SDNet to foresee future instants of the anatomical factors in a cardiac cycle. By encouraging the extraction of temporally correlated factors, we impose the association of similar images with similar representations, with beneficial effects on the subsequent segmentation task.

We aim to build upon SDNet limitations based on a simple hypothesis: small transformation in the input domain **x** should be associated with small changes in the anatomical representation. Specifically, the S factors of different cardiac phases should be similar within the same cardiac cycle, while any difference should be consistent across subjects. Moreover, anatomical components that move together in time, such as the heart, should be separated from static ones.

We introduce such regularization via an additional neural network in the SDNet framework which we term as "the transformer" $\Theta(\cdot)$, whose role is to learn the temporal dynamics of the anatomical factors during a cardiac cycle. In particular, the transformer encourages S to have smooth and consistent temporal transformations, which acts as a regularizer on the disentangled representation.

We provide the block diagram of the extended model, which we name Spatial Decomposition and Transformation Network (SDTNet), in Fig. 16.2. The anatomy and modality encoders, the decoder, the segmentor and discriminator architectures follow those proposed by Chartsias et al. [6]. We analyze the SDTNet and the transformer in more details below.

16.3.2 Spatial Decomposition and Transformation Network

As illustrated in Fig. 16.2, the transformer receives as inputs the anatomical factors S_t at the current time point t, and the information about a temporal gap dt. Assuming that the image appearance $\underline{z}$ is constant throughout the cardiac cycle – the imaging modality does not change – and that the only variations regard the patient anatomy, in SDTNet the transformer learns to deform the input S_t and predict the anatomical transformation.

In the following, we first describe the global framework and the training objectives. Then, we describe transformer architecture and optimization.

16.3.2.1 Cost function and training

We optimize SDTNet using a multi-task learning formulation, where the semi-supervised training objective is the sum

$$Loss = a_0 \cdot \mathcal{L}_S + a_1 \cdot \mathcal{L}_{US} + a_2 \cdot \mathcal{L}_{ADV} + a_3 \cdot \mathcal{L}_{TR}, \qquad (16.1)$$

where we use the scaling parameters $a_0 = 10$, $a_1 = 1$, and $a_2 = 10$ as in [6], and a_3 determined experimentally. In the specific, $\mathcal{L}_S$ is the supervised segmentation cost; $\mathcal{L}_{US}$ is an unsupervised objective containing an image reconstruction term and a regularizer on the modality representation $\underline{z}$; $\mathcal{L}_{ADV}$ is an adversarial cost obtained through a mask discriminator. And $\mathcal{L}_{TR}$ is the cost associated with the training of the temporal transformer network.

As discussed in [6], separating the anatomy into segmentation masks is challenging because the image reconstruction process encourages parts having similar color intensities to appear in the same channels. For this reason, it is crucial to give more importance to the segmentation losses and use higher values for a_0 and a_2. We chose instead $a_3 = 0.8$ to scale $\mathcal{L}_{TR}$ approximately to the same amplitude of $a_1 \cdot \mathcal{L}_{US}$ and thus obtain similar unsupervised contributions.

16.3.2.1.1 Supervised objective

In our model $\mathcal{L}_S$ is the cost associated to the segmentation task, when labels are provided. It consists in the differentiable Dice loss [56], defined as $\mathcal{L}_S = 1 - \frac{2|\tilde{\mathbf{y}} \cdot \mathbf{y}|}{|\tilde{\mathbf{y}}| + |\mathbf{y}|}$, where $\mathbf{y}$ is the ground-truth segmentation and $\tilde{\mathbf{y}}$ is that predicted by the segmentor. We evaluate $\mathcal{L}_S$ as the average Dice loss obtained on every region to segment.

16.3.2.1.2 Unsupervised objective

The cost associated to the unsupervised task $\mathcal{L}_{US}$ is the sum of contributions:

$$\mathcal{L}_{US} = |\mathbf{x} - \tilde{\mathbf{x}}| + a_{KL} \cdot D_{KL}\big[Q(\underline{z} \mid \mathbf{x}) \parallel N(\underline{0}, \underline{I})\big] - MI(\underline{z}, \tilde{\mathbf{x}}).$$

The first term in the formula is the mean absolute error between the input image $\mathbf{x}$ and its reconstruction $\tilde{\mathbf{x}}$, where $\tilde{\mathbf{x}}$ is the output of the decoder $\Psi(\cdot)$. The second term $D_{KL}[\cdot]$ is the KL divergence between the distribution of the latent representation extracted by the modality encoder, $Q(\underline{z} \mid \mathbf{x})$, and a multivariate Gaussian $N(\underline{0}, \underline{I})$

with zero mean and identity covariance matrix. As in [6], we use $a_{KL} = 0.1$ to avoid posterior collapse. Finally, the last term $MI(\cdot)$ is the mutual information between the latent code z and the reconstruction $\tilde{x}$ and it is approximated using an additional neural network, as suggested by Chen et al. [57]. Maximizing the mutual information term helps to build a meaningful latent space for z and prevent the posterior collapse, thus encouraging the decoder $\Psi(\cdot)$ to use the modality factors.

16.3.2.1.3 Adversarial objective

We use a least-squares mask discriminator [58] to introduce an adversarial term $\mathcal{L}_{ADV}$ in the loss function. We use unpaired data to train the discriminator so that it can distinguish the ground-truth segmentation masks from those that are predicted by the segmentor. The adversarial term introduces a shape prior-based contribution in the model, which encourages the segmentor to output plausible segmentation masks even for unlabeled images.

16.3.2.1.4 Self-supervised consistency objective

The term $\mathcal{L}_{TR}$ is the self-supervised cost provided by an anatomy transformer $\Theta(\cdot)$. As previously discussed, we use $\mathcal{L}_{TR}$ to regularize the anatomical factors through spatio-temporal constraints. During training, the transformer gradually learns to change the input tensor S_t such that it can match S_{t+dt}. Since the anatomical space is binary, we propose to train the transformer using the Dice loss between predicted and future binary anatomical factors:

$$\mathcal{L}_{TR} = 1 - \frac{2|\tilde{S}_{t_0+dt} \cdot S_{t_0+dt}|}{|\tilde{S}_{t_0+dt}| + |S_{t_0+dt}|}.$$

It is possible to give a distance-based interpretation to $\mathcal{L}_{TR}$. In particular, minimizing $\mathcal{L}_{TR}$ is a form of contrastive loss minimization [59], where the learned representation favors small distances between pairs of *similar* examples and large distances for *dissimilar* pairs. Analogously, we constrain the representation of temporally close cardiac phases to be encoded closer (in terms of Dice distance) through the consistency objective $\mathcal{L}_{TR}$. However, to avoid the collapse of the *attract-only* force introduced by $\mathcal{L}_{TR}$, we use the weighted sum of $\mathcal{L}_S$, $\mathcal{L}_{US}$, and $\mathcal{L}_{ADV}$ as a *repulse-only* force for modeling dissimilar points.

We describe the transformer more in detail in Section 16.3.2.2.

16.3.2.1.5 Optimization strategy

Training a neural network to perform many different tasks at the same time while using limited annotations is a challenging problem. In fact, the loss landscape can be noisy, and the training becomes unstable. On top of that, learning can be subject to additional noise whenever we must necessarily use small batch sizes, e.g., equal to 4, to cope with memory constraints. Thus, models that perform well on the training set may perform poorly on the validation and test samples.

We reduce this problem optimizing the model toward solutions residing in flat local minima of the training loss landscape, which can generalize better (a concept

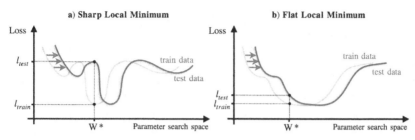

a) Sharp Local Minimum b) Flat Local Minimum

FIGURE 16.3

Effect of dataset shift on a model residing in a sharp or a flat local minimum. We plot the loss landscapes of train data in gray color and test data in red color (dark gray in print version). Given an optimized model with parameters W^*, the same dataset shift from train to test data (blue horizontal arrows) has an increased performance impact if the model resides in a sharp minimum (dashed vertical lines).

depicted in Fig. 16.3). In particular, we make this possible using two approaches: the exponential moving average (EMA) and adopting a cyclical learning rate scheduling [60].

EMA consists of maintaining a moving average of the trained parameters and in using the averaged ones for inference. During the test, this is equivalent to performing an assembly of the model in correspondence of the last iterations.

A cyclical learning rate scheduling, instead, consists of a periodic ranging of the learning rate between a minimum and a maximum values. When the learning rate has a high value, it can help the model escaping sharp local minima. On the contrary, when it has a smaller amplitude, it helps to settle in the bottom of flat loss valleys. In our case, we used a triangular wave linearly ranging between 10^{-4} and 10^{-5} within a period of 20 epochs. We chose the cycle length according to the guidelines provided in [60].

Both EMA and the learning rate scheduling considerably facilitate comparisons with the baselines, by reducing loss fluctuations at the end of the training and thus reducing the effect of the chosen early stopping criterion. We used Adam optimizer [61] and stopped training based on the segmentation loss on a validation set, as in [6].

16.3.2.2 Transformer architecture

The transformer is a modified UNet [22], adapted to work in the binary anatomical space. We also include a long residual connection between the UNet input and its output, which allows initializing the transformer to operate an identity mapping (plus noise, as we randomly initialize the network weights). To ensure that the output of the transformer $\tilde{S}_{t+dt}$ resides in the binary anatomical space, we process it with a softmax operator and then binarize it again with the thresholding operator $\tilde{S}_{t+dt} \mapsto \lfloor \tilde{S}_{t+dt} + 0.5 \rfloor$.

We introduce the temporal information in the transformer bottleneck through a conditioning mechanism which modulates the extracted features maps to operate the temporal transformation. We use a scalar value of dt to represent the time-gap between the current cardiac phase and the time frame we want to predict. The value dt is the input to a multi-layer perceptron (MLP) with three fully connected layers having 128, 128, and 7744 units, respectively. The MLP prediction is first reshaped to a dimension of $22 \times 22 \times 16$ and then concatenated with the anatomical features maps extracted by the contracting encoder of the UNet. To encourage the use of the temporal features maps we bounded both the MLP output and the anatomical features in the range [0, 1] using a sigmoid activation function, resulting in signals of comparable amplitude.

16.4 Experiments

16.4.1 Data

We introduce the datasets used for our experiments below. In all the cases, we performed the experiments using 3-fold cross-validation. We randomly divided the total number of MRI scans to use 70% of patients for training, 15% for validation and 15% for the test sets.

ACDC. We used 2-dimensional cine-MR images from the 2017 Automatic Cardiac Diagnosis Challenge [2]. Images were acquired from 100 patients with diverse pathological conditions and using different 1.5T and 3T MR scanners. The cine-MRIs also have a different temporal resolution. Manual segmentations are provided for each patient in correspondence to the end-diastolic (ED) and end-systolic (ES) cardiac phases for: right ventricle (RV), left ventricle (LV), and myocardium (MYO). ES and ED phase instants are also provided as metadata.

LVSC. We also evaluated the models on cardiac MRI from the Left Ventricular Segmentation Challenge [62] made available by the Cardiac Atlas Project. These are gated SSFP cine, acquired in short-axis and covering the whole heart in patients with coronary artery disease and myocardial infarction. The images were acquired using a heterogeneous mix of 1.5T scanner types and imaging parameters on 100 patients. Image temporal resolution ranges between 19 and 30 frames for the cardiac cycle. Manual segmentations are provided for the left ventricular myocardium.

16.4.2 Image pre-processing and temporal axis

Given a patient volume scan, we considered outliers and clipped image pixels with values outside the 5th to 95th percentiles interval. We also subtracted the median and divided the images on the patient's interquartile range. We resampled images to 176×176 pixels to deal with memory constraints. Finally, we applied data augmentation on the 2D slices at run-time, consisting of: (i) translations between ± 10 pixels on both vertical and horizontal axis, (ii) rotations between $\pm \pi/2$, and (iii) addition of small random noise sampled from $N(\mu = 0; \sigma = 0.02)$.

Since our goal was to introduce temporal smoothness in the anatomical factors rather than learning to predict the whole cardiac cycle, we split the cine sequences into two halves: frames in the ED-ES interval and frames from ES to the end of the cardiac cycle. Then, we reversed the latter frames in their temporal order, to mimic once again the cardiac contraction. As a result, we could avoid dealing with the inherent uncertainty of the temporal instants in the middle of the cardiac cycle, where predicting if the heart will contract or dilate in the next frame is not possible by relying only on the current image.

To account for a temporal resolution changing across patients, we normalized the frame indexes on the total number of frames in the sequence. Thus, temporal distances between two consecutive frames were always considered relative to the whole contraction time and $t \in [0, 1]$.

16.4.3 Baselines and evaluation

We compare SDTNet with the fully supervised training of a UNet [22] and the semi-supervised training of SDNet [6]. We analyze the performance obtained using different fractions of annotations in the training set. In these experiments, if a model can use the extra unlabeled images, we employ them for optimizing the unsupervised, adversarial, or self-supervised objectives.

We measure performance using Dice score and Hausdorff distance between predicted $\tilde{y}$ and ground-truth segmentation masks y, for each cardiac structure.

16.5 Results and discussion

In the following, we first analyze the advantages of introducing temporal consistency in the learned disentangled representations (Section 16.5.1). Then, we investigate the anatomical factors extracted by the model and how the transformer modifies them, subject to the temporal signals (Section 16.5.2).

16.5.1 Semi-supervised segmentation

We compare SDTNet with the baselines qualitatively in Fig. 16.4, and quantitatively in Tables 16.1, 16.2, and 16.3. We provide below an analysis of the results using questions before each paragraph to help guide the reader.

Does using temporal information help? As can be seen from the tables, learning temporal dynamics regularizes the training of SDTNet, especially when dealing with a limited number of annotations. The model improves the performance of SDNet for almost every percentage of available annotations both in ACDC and LVSC datasets, increasing the Dice score and decreasing the Hausdorff distance. Moreover, we observe that the fully-supervised UNet has a consistent performance deterioration when the number of annotations reduces below 25% of the training set. In LVSC, the UNet is always the worst model, while in ACDC it performs worse than both the disentanglement frameworks when using less than 100% of annotation. This behavior can be justified observing that when the number of annotated data decreases, the training

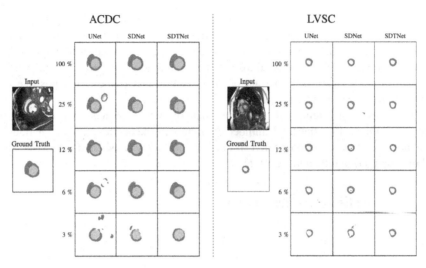

FIGURE 16.4

Segmentation masks predicted by the considered models at various levels of training annotations. As can be seen, using temporal consistency to regularize disentanglement (SDTNet) leads to the best performance, especially when annotations are scarce.

Table 16.1 Dice score average and standard deviation (subscript) for the segmentation of myocardium (MYO), left ventricle (LV), and right ventricle (RV) on ACDC dataset. We compare models at various proportions of training annotations. Results are the average of three-fold cross-validation. Best results in **bold**.

	ACDC – Dice Score											
	UNet				**SDNet**				**SDTNet**			
Labels	RV	MYO	LV	Average	RV	MYO	LV	Average	RV	MYO	LV	Average
100%	81.5_{05}	84.5_{03}	89.2_{04}	**85.0_{04}**	78.4_{06}	83.5_{03}	89.2_{04}	83.7_{04}	77.8_{06}	83.7_{03}	88.1_{04}	83.2_{04}
25%	76.3_{06}	83.5_{03}	87.2_{05}	82.3_{05}	73.6_{07}	79.7_{04}	86.4_{05}	79.9_{05}	77.3_{06}	84.5_{03}	87.5_{04}	**83.1_{04}**
12%	66.8_{07}	76.9_{04}	82.4_{06}	75.3_{06}	68.8_{07}	79.0_{04}	83.5_{05}	77.1_{05}	67.8_{08}	82.1_{03}	86.0_{04}	**78.6_{05}**
6%	46.5_{08}	61.1_{06}	73.2_{08}	60.3_{07}	54.3_{08}	66.2_{05}	75.3_{07}	65.3_{07}	52.6_{09}	70.6_{05}	76.0_{07}	**66.4_{07}**
3%	34.6_{08}	46.6_{07}	56.9_{09}	46.0_{08}	42.0_{09}	60.1_{06}	71.8_{07}	57.9_{07}	45.0_{09}	60.3_{07}	69.1_{07}	**58.1_{08}**

set is not sufficiently representative of the data distribution and methods that *only* rely on supervision fail. On the other hand, using the unlabeled data, both SDNet and SDTNet learn more robust representations and perform well even with fewer annotations. These results show the advantage of disentangled representations and temporal priors in the absence of enough labels, which is important when dealing with rare pathologies or anatomical variants.

What happens when we have lots of annotations? When using all of the available annotations, SDNet, SDTNet, and the fully supervised UNet perform similarly on LVSC data. Instead, on ACDC, the UNet performs the best. These observations are coherent with recent findings [6,19] reporting that disentanglement is most effec-

Table 16.2 Hausdorff distance average and standard deviation (subscript) for the segmentation of myocardium (MYO), left ventricle (LV), and right ventricle (RV) on ACDC dataset. We compare models at various proportions of training annotations. Results are the average of three-fold cross-validation. Best results in **bold**.

	ACDC – Hausdorff Distance											
	UNet				SDNet				SDTNet			
Labels	RV	MYO	LV	Average	RV	MYO	LV	Average	RV	MYO	LV	Average
100%	10.5_{06}	6.9_{03}	4.7_{02}	$\mathbf{7.4_{07}}$	14.5_{10}	5.0_{02}	3.3_{01}	7.6_{07}	13.6_{09}	5.4_{02}	9.8_{02}	9.6_{04}
25%	11.7_{08}	13.1_{06}	6.9_{04}	10.6_{06}	20.5_{12}	12.0_{04}	9.6_{04}	14.0_{07}	14.5_{11}	4.7_{01}	3.6_{01}	$\mathbf{7.6_{04}}$
12%	27.8_{10}	31.0_{08}	17.3_{08}	25.4_{09}	22.8_{11}	16.3_{05}	11.6_{07}	16.9_{08}	25.6_{10}	8.4_{04}	11.1_{07}	$\mathbf{15.0_{07}}$
6%	69.8_{11}	49.0_{08}	34.6_{12}	51.1_{10}	42.5_{09}	50.7_{07}	41.4_{08}	44.9_{08}	47.3_{15}	32.0_{08}	43.1_{09}	$\mathbf{40.8_{11}}$
3%	76.7_{10}	66.8_{07}	59.7_{10}	67.7_{09}	58.6_{14}	45.6_{08}	35.3_{11}	46.5_{11}	51.1_{14}	37.2_{09}	35.2_{12}	$\mathbf{41.2_{34}}$

Table 16.3 Average and standard deviation (subscript) performance for myocardium segmentation on LVSC dataset. We report Dice score in the left table and Hausdorff distance in the right table. We compare models at various proportions of training annotations, reporting the average of three-fold cross-validation. Best results in **bold**.

	LVSC – Dice Score		
Labels	UNet	SDNet	SDTNet
100%	68.3_{07}	$\mathbf{69.8_{07}}$	69.6_{07}
25%	66.1_{09}	67.0_{09}	$\mathbf{67.3_{08}}$
12%	58.8_{12}	65.0_{12}	$\mathbf{66.1_{10}}$
6%	49.0_{15}	53.1_{14}	$\mathbf{54.5_{15}}$
3%	34.7_{16}	46.1_{13}	$\mathbf{48.6_{14}}$

	LVSC – Hausdorff Distance		
Labels	UNet	SDNet	SDTNet
100%	22.7_{10}	$\mathbf{12.2_{04}}$	15.9_{08}
25%	22.9_{11}	$\mathbf{12.1_{05}}$	$\mathbf{12.1_{05}}$
12%	33.2_{09}	28.3_{13}	$\mathbf{18.8_{09}}$
6%	53.2_{09}	$\mathbf{42.9_{12}}$	51.8_{11}
3%	64.2_{12}	48.7_{08}	$\mathbf{36.3_{10}}$

tive when there are not strong supervisory signals. When the number of annotations increases, the UNet is simple to optimize because it does not require the simultaneous minimization of multiple objectives, or finding a trade-off between supervised and unsupervised/adversarial losses. This points to the need to have dynamic mechanisms to balance different costs' contribution in a disentanglement framework. It is possible to close the performance gap between UNet, SDNet, and SDTNet in ACDC, by using a higher weight on a_0 to give more importance to the supervised cost in Eq. (16.1).

Can we double up self-supervision by leveraging the cycle in the heart? Inspired by Wang et al. [63], we also experimented introducing *cycle consistency* across the cardiac cycle for learning visual correspondences. In other words, given the prediction of the transformer $\tilde{S}_{t+dt} = \Theta(S_t, dt)$, we trained the model to learn to go back in time and estimate: $\tilde{S}_t = \Theta(\tilde{S}_{t+dt}, -dt)$ where $\tilde{S}_t \approx S_t$. However, the cycle consistency did not improve segmentation, and in some cases the transformer even collapsed, predicting constant anatomical channels for any time point.

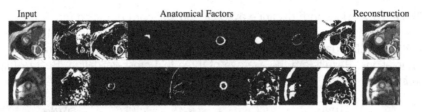

FIGURE 16.5

Example of anatomical factors extracted from an input image for ACDC (top row) and LVSC (bottom row) datasets. Anatomies are represented as multi-channel binary maps and can contain well defined anatomical components, such as left/right ventricle and myocardium, or other geometrical content needed for the image reconstruct through the image decoder (rightmost image).

16.5.2 **What does the model learn?**

How do anatomy factors look like? As in [6], we use eight anatomical channels to represent the patient anatomy. We show an example of the multi-channel anatomical factors learned by SDTNet in Fig. 16.5. Some of the binary channels contain well defined anatomical parts, such as the cardiac structures, and others the remaining spatial information, which is necessary to reconstruct the input image through the decoder.

How do predicted images look like in time? Observe that if we assume that the modality factor z remains constant throughout the whole cardiac cycle, it is possible to use SDTNet for temporal image synthesis. In fact, given an image at $t = 0$, it is possible to generate futures frames of the temporal sequence using the following steps: (i) extract S_0 and $\underline{z}_0$ from the input image $\mathbf{x}_0$; (ii) keep $\underline{z}_0$ fixed and predict the future frames with the transformer, as $\tilde{S}_{dt} = \Theta(S_0, \, dt)$ while changing dt in the range [0, 1]; and (iii) use the decoder to reconstruct the future frame $\tilde{\mathbf{x}}_{t>0} = G(\tilde{S}_{dt}, \underline{z}_0)$. We report an example of the procedure in Fig. 16.6. As can be seen from the figure, the model can predict cardiac contraction. Interestingly, the image colors appear flat, and the reason can be found in the design of the decoder $\Psi(\cdot)$. In fact, as [6], we use a decoder architecture based on FiLM [64], which reintroduces the modality-specific colors into the anatomical channels by simply scaling and multiplying the whole binary maps. Because of its design, FiLM cannot introduce texture-related information, and the image reconstruction shows flat colors. An alternative to FiLM layers is using a decoder based on SPADE [65] which is less restrictive, and it allows reproducing textures in the reconstructed image, rather than just intensity values. Contrarily to FiLM, SPADE uses the anatomical channels to modulate modality-dependent features maps, which can also contain textures, and the reconstructed images become more realistic [66]. An in-depth comparison between SPADE and FiLM-based decoders in terms of disentanglement and segmentation performance can be found in [19].

What does the transformer learn? In Fig. 16.7, we report images of features maps extracted at the transformer bottleneck. In particular, we show examples of features

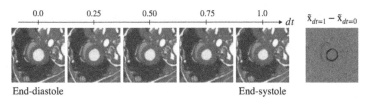

FIGURE 16.6

Example of temporal interpolation from ED to ES cardiac phases. Images were obtained by keeping fixed the anatomical factors S_t at time $t = 0$ and ranging dt in $[0, 1]$.

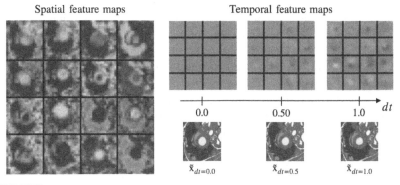

FIGURE 16.7

Features maps in the transformer bottleneck. On the left, we show 16 out of the 64 feature maps extracted by the anatomical representations S_t. On the right, we show the feature maps predicted by the MLP (top row) when ranging dt from 0 (ED cardiac phase) to 1 (ES cardiac phase). Color maps linearly range from 0 (dark blue – dark gray in print version) to 1 (yellow – light gray in print version).

extracted by the anatomical channels (left), and the 16 temporal features maps predicted by the MLP used to condition the transformer (right) when it receives as input dt in $\{0.0,\ 0.5,\ 1.0\}$. As can be seen, the MLP outputs globally larger signals in correspondence of the complete cardiac contraction, that is, when we go from ED to ES cardiac phase.

16.6 Conclusion

This chapter discussed how disentangled representations aid semi-supervised learning by decomposing a medical image into anatomical and imaging modality-specific factors. The presence of a reconstruction cost and a segmentation loss render disentangled representations suitable for semi-supervised learning by taking advantage of the semantic information residing in the image content. More broadly, disentanglement allows intuitive factorization of the image into spatial and non-spatial factors. Such a factorization increases model interpretability, which is a key advantage in healthcare. Furthermore, it allows intuitive image manipulations by combining factors across patients and modalities [6], it is well suited for multi-modal learning [17,66], and has considerable potential to automatically detect artifacts and pathologies [14–16].

In this chapter, we built on a recent disentanglement framework that produces interpretable representations [6]. We also showed how to regularize the disentangled representation based on temporal transitions of the image components. We motivated and demonstrated that by conditioning the anatomical factors to undergo smooth temporal changes, it is possible to increase model performance on a post hoc task, such as semantic segmentation. We introduced the temporal information using a self-supervised objective and a transformer neural network, reporting increased performance in a lack of annotations. Lastly, we showed that the transformer model could potentially work for video prediction tasks and cardiac temporal synthesis.

In the future, it would be interesting to explore other forms of anatomical consistency, e.g., substituting the temporal axis with the third spatial dimension and imposing spatial smoothness between adjacent slices. Moreover, it would be nice to investigate the model for spatio-temporal image synthesis rather than semantic segmentation, which could be useful for anomaly detection. Finally, it would be exciting to explore entirely unsupervised settings where no annotated images are needed to decouple the image's anatomical components.

Acknowledgments

This work was supported by the Erasmus+ Programme of the European Union, during an exchange between IMT School for Advanced Studies Lucca and the School of Engineering, University of Edinburgh. S.A. Tsaftaris acknowledges the support of the Royal Academy of Engineering and the Research Chairs and Senior Research Fellowships scheme. We thank NVIDIA Corporation for donating the Titan Xp GPU used for this research.

References

[1] Y. Bengio, A. Courville, P. Vincent, Representation learning: a review and new perspectives, IEEE Transactions on Pattern Analysis and Machine Intelligence 35 (8) (2013) 1798–1828.

[2] O. Bernard, A. Lalande, C. Zotti, F. Cervenansky, X. Yang, P.-A. Heng, I. Cetin, K. Lekadir, O. Camara, M.A.G. Ballester, et al., Deep learning techniques for automatic MRI cardiac multi-structures segmentation and diagnosis: is the problem solved?, IEEE Transactions on Medical Imaging 37 (11) (2018) 2514–2525.

[3] V. Cheplygina, M. de Bruijne, J.P. Pluim, Not-so-supervised: a survey of semi-supervised, multi-instance, and transfer learning in medical image analysis, Medical Image Analysis 54 (2019) 280–296.

[4] Y. Ouali, C. Hudelot, M. Tami, An overview of deep semi-supervised learning, arXiv preprint, arXiv:2006.05278.

[5] T. Salimans, I. Goodfellow, W. Zaremba, V. Cheung, A. Radford, X. Chen, Improved techniques for training GANs, in: Advances in Neural Information Processing Systems (NeurIPS), 2016, pp. 2234–2242.

[6] A. Chartsias, T. Joyce, G. Papanastasiou, S. Semple, M. Williams, D.E. Newby, R. Dharmakumar, S.A. Tsaftaris, Disentangled representation learning in cardiac image analysis, Medical Image Analysis 58 (2019) 101535.

[7] Y. Gong, S. Karanam, Z. Wu, K.-C. Peng, J. Ernst, P.C. Doerschuk, Learning compositional visual concepts with mutual consistency, in: Conference on Computer Vision and Pattern Recognition (CVPR), 2018, pp. 8659–8668.

[8] Y. Bengio, et al., Learning deep architectures for AI, Foundations and Trends in Machine Learning 2 (1) (2009) 1–127.

[9] S. van Steenkiste, F. Locatello, J. Schmidhuber, O. Bachem, Are disentangled representations helpful for abstract visual reasoning?, arXiv preprint, arXiv:1905.12506.

[10] M. Liu, T. Breuel, J. Kautz, Unsupervised image-to-image translation networks, in: Advances in Neural Information Processing Systems (NeurIPS), 2017, pp. 700–708.

[11] H.-Y. Lee, H.-Y. Tseng, J.-B. Huang, M. Singh, M.-H. Yang, Diverse image-to-image translation via disentangled representations, in: European Conference on Computer Vision (ICCV), 2018, pp. 36–52.

[12] X. Huang, M. Liu, S. Belongie, J. Kautz, Multimodal unsupervised image-to-image translation, in: Proc. European Conference on Computer Vision (ECCV), 2018, pp. 179–196.

[13] D. Lorenz, L. Bereska, T. Milbich, B. Ommer, Unsupervised part-based disentangling of object shape and appearance, in: Conference on Computer Vision and Pattern Recognition (CVPR), 2019, pp. 10955–10964.

[14] H. Jiang, A. Chartsias, X. Zhang, G. Papanastasiou, S. Semple, M. Dweck, D. Semple, R. Dharmakumar, S.A. Tsaftaris, Semi-supervised pathology segmentation with disentangled representations, in: Domain Adaptation and Representation Transfer, and Distributed and Collaborative Learning, Springer, 2020, pp. 62–72.

[15] T. Xia, A. Chartsias, S.A. Tsaftaris, Pseudo-healthy synthesis with pathology disentanglement and adversarial learning, Medical Image Analysis 64 (2020) 101719.

[16] H. Liao, W.-A. Lin, S.K. Zhou, J. Luo, ADN: artifact disentanglement network for unsupervised metal artifact reduction, IEEE Transactions on Medical Imaging 39 (3) (2019) 634–643.

[17] J. Yang, N.C. Dvornek, F. Zhang, J. Chapiro, M. Lin, J.S. Duncan, Unsupervised domain adaptation via disentangled representations: application to cross-modality liver segmentation, in: International Conference on Medical Image Computing and Computer Assisted Intervention (MICCAI), Springer, 2019, pp. 255–263.

[18] C. Qin, B. Shi, R. Liao, T. Mansi, D. Rueckert, A. Kamen, Unsupervised deformable registration for multi-modal images via disentangled representations, in: IPMI, Springer, 2019, pp. 249–261.

[19] X. Liu, S. Thermos, G. Valvano, A. Chartsias, A. O'Neil, S.A. Tsaftaris, Metrics for exposing the biases of content-style disentanglement, arXiv preprint, arXiv:2008.12378.

[20] G. Valvano, A. Chartsias, A. Leo, S.A. Tsaftaris, Temporal consistency objectives regularize the learning of disentangled representations, in: Domain Adaptation and Representation Transfer (DART), Springer, 2019, pp. 11–19.

[21] S.K. Zhou, H. Greenspan, C. Davatzikos, J.S. Duncan, B. van Ginneken, A. Madabhushi, J.L. Prince, D. Rueckert, R.M. Summers, A review of deep learning in medical imaging: imaging traits, technology trends, case studies with progress highlights, and future promises, Proceedings of the IEEE (2021).

[22] O. Ronneberger, P. Fischer, T. Brox, U-Net: convolutional networks for biomedical image segmentation, in: International Conference on Medical Image Computing and Computer Assisted Intervention (MICCAI), Springer, 2015, pp. 234–241.

[23] O. Chapelle, B. Schölkopf, A. Zien (Eds.), Semi-Supervised Learning, The MIT Press, 2006, pp. 4–7.

[24] Y. Taigman, M. Yang, M. Ranzato, L. Wolf, DeepFace: closing the gap to human-level performance in face verification, in: Conference on Computer Vision and Pattern Recognition (CVPR), 2014, pp. 1701–1708.

[25] H. Zhang, Z. Zhang, A. Odena, H. Lee, Consistency regularization for generative adversarial networks, in: International Conference on Learning Representations (ICLR), 2020.

[26] K. Chaitanya, E. Erdil, N. Karani, E. Konukoglu, Contrastive learning of global and local features for medical image segmentation with limited annotations, in: Advances in Neural Information Processing Systems (NeurIPS) 33, 2020.

[27] A. Blum, T. Mitchell, Combining labeled and unlabeled data with co-training, in: Annual Conference on Computational Learning Theory, 1998, pp. 92–100.

[28] S. Qiao, W. Shen, Z. Zhang, B. Wang, A. Yuille, Deep co-training for semi-supervised image recognition, in: European Conference on Computer Vision (ICCV), 2018, pp. 135–152.

[29] W. Bai, O. Oktay, M. Sinclair, H. Suzuki, M. Rajchl, G. Tarroni, B. Glocker, A. King, P.M. Matthews, D. Rueckert, Semi-supervised learning for network-based cardiac MR image segmentation, in: International Conference on Medical Image Computing and Computer Assisted Intervention (MICCAI), Springer, 2017, pp. 253–260.

[30] C. Ouyang, C. Biffi, C. Chen, T. Kart, H. Qiu, D. Rueckert, Self-supervision with superpixels: training few-shot medical image segmentation without annotation, in: European Conference on Computer Vision, Springer, 2020, pp. 762–780.

[31] J. Zhao, X. Xie, X. Xu, S. Sun, Multi-view learning overview: recent progress and new challenges, Information Fusion 38 (2017) 43–54.

[32] V. Noroozi, S. Bahaadini, L. Zheng, S. Xie, W. Shao, S.Y. Philip, Semi-supervised deep representation learning for multi-view problems, in: 2018 IEEE International Conference on Big Data, IEEE, 2018, pp. 56–64.

[33] S. Kohl, B. Romera-Paredes, C. Meyer, J. De Fauw, J.R. Ledsam, K. Maier-Hein, S.A. Eslami, D.J. Rezende, O. Ronneberger, A probabilistic U-Net for segmentation of ambiguous images, in: Advances in Neural Information Processing Systems (NeurIPS), 2018, pp. 6965–6975.

[34] X. Yi, E. Walia, P. Babyn, Generative adversarial network in medical imaging: a review, Medical Image Analysis 58 (2019) 101552.

[35] L. Grady, Random walks for image segmentation, IEEE Transactions on Pattern Analysis and Machine Intelligence 28 (11) (2006) 1768–1783.

[36] S. Zheng, S. Jayasumana, B. Romera-Paredes, V. Vineet, Z. Su, D. Du, C. Huang, P.H. Torr, Conditional random fields as recurrent neural networks, in: International Conference on Computer Vision (ICCV), 2015, pp. 1529–1537.

[37] I. Higgins, D. Amos, D. Pfau, S. Racaniere, L. Matthey, D. Rezende, A. Lerchner, Towards a definition of disentangled representations, arXiv preprint, arXiv:1812.02230.

[38] Y. Li, K.K. Singh, U. Ojha, Y.J. Lee, MixNMatch: multifactor disentanglement and encoding for conditional image generation, in: Conference on Computer Vision and Pattern Recognition (CVPR), 2020, pp. 8039–8048.

[39] W. Nie, T. Karras, A. Garg, S. Debnath, A. Patney, A. Patel, A. Anandkumar, Semi-supervised StyleGAN for disentanglement learning, in: International Conference on Machine Learning (ICML), in: PMLR, 2020, pp. 7360–7369.

[40] A. Chartsias, G. Papanastasiou, C. Wang, S. Semple, D. Newby, R. Dharmakumar, S.A. Tsaftaris, Disentangle, align and fuse for multimodal and zero-shot image segmentation, arXiv preprint, arXiv:1911.04417.

[41] Q. Meng, J. Matthew, V.A. Zimmer, A. Gomez, D.F. Lloyd, D. Rueckert, B. Kainz, Mutual information-based disentangled neural networks for classifying unseen categories in different domains: application to fetal ultrasound imaging, IEEE Transactions on Medical Imaging (2020).

[42] H. Kim, A. Mnih, Disentangling by factorising, arXiv preprint, arXiv:1802.05983.

[43] A.A. Alemi, I. Fischer, J.V. Dillon, K. Murphy, Deep variational information bottleneck, arXiv preprint, arXiv:1612.00410.

[44] J.N. Wood, A smoothness constraint on the development of object recognition, Cognition 153 (2016) 140–145.

[45] J.K. O'Regan, A. Noë, A sensorimotor account of vision and visual consciousness, Behavioral and Brain Sciences 24 (5) (2001) 939.

[46] H. Caselles-Dupré, M. Garcia-Ortiz, D. Filliat, Symmetry-based disentangled representation learning requires interaction with environments, in: Advances in Neural Information Processing Systems (NeurIPS), 2019.

[47] J. Krebs, H. Delingette, B. Mailhé, N. Ayache, T. Mansi, Learning a probabilistic model for diffeomorphic registration, IEEE Transactions on Medical Imaging 38 (9) (2019) 2165–2176.

[48] W. Bai, H. Suzuki, C. Qin, G. Tarroni, O. Oktay, P.M. Matthews, D. Rueckert, Recurrent neural networks for aortic image sequence segmentation with sparse annotations, in: International Conference on Medical Image Computing and Computer Assisted Intervention (MICCAI), Springer, 2018, pp. 586–594.

[49] J.-T. Hsieh, B. Liu, D.-A. Huang, L.F. Fei-Fei, J.C. Niebles, Learning to decompose and disentangle representations for video prediction, in: Advances in Neural Information Processing Systems (NeurIPS), 2018, pp. 517–526.

[50] R. Caruana, Multitask learning, Machine Learning 28 (1) (1997) 41–75.

[51] D.P. Kingma, M. Welling, Auto-encoding variational Bayes, in: International Conference on Learning Representations (ICLR), 2014.

[52] F. Locatello, S. Bauer, M. Lucic, G. Rätsch, S. Gelly, B. Schölkopf, O. Bachem, Challenging common assumptions in the unsupervised learning of disentangled representations, in: International Conference on Learning Representations Workshops (ICLRW), 2019, pp. 4114–4124.

[53] F. Locatello, S. Bauer, M. Lucic, G. Rätsch, S. Gelly, B. Schölkopf, O. Bachem, A commentary on the unsupervised learning of disentangled representations, in: AAAI Conference on Artificial Intelligence (AAAI), 2020, pp. 13681–13684.

[54] I. Goodfellow, J. Pouget-Abadie, M. Mirza, B. Xu, D. Warde-Farley, S. Ozair, A. Courville, Y. Bengio, Generative adversarial nets, in: Advances in Neural Information Processing Systems (NeurIPS), 2014, pp. 2672–2680.

[55] Y. Bengio, N. Léonard, A. Courville, Estimating or propagating gradients through stochastic neurons for conditional computation, arXiv preprint, arXiv:1308.3432.

[56] F. Milletari, N. Navab, S.-A. Ahmadi, V-Net: fully convolutional neural networks for volumetric medical image segmentation, in: Fourth International Conference on 3D Vision (3DV), IEEE, 2016, pp. 565–571.

[57] X. Chen, Y. Duan, R. Houthooft, J. Schulman, I. Sutskever, P. Abbeel, InfoGAN: interpretable representation learning by information maximizing generative adversarial nets, in: Advances in Neural Information Processing Systems (NeurIPS), 2016, pp. 2172–2180.

[58] X. Mao, Q. Li, H. Xie, R.Y.K. Lau, Z. Wang, S.P. Smolley, On the effectiveness of least squares generative adversarial networks, IEEE Transactions on Pattern Analysis and Machine Intelligence (2018).

[59] R. Hadsell, S. Chopra, Y. LeCun, Dimensionality reduction by learning an invariant mapping, in: Conference on Computer Vision and Pattern Recognition (CVPR), vol. 2, IEEE, 2006, pp. 1735–1742.

[60] L.N. Smith, Cyclical learning rates for training neural networks, in: Winter Conference on Applications of Computer Vision (WACV), IEEE, 2017, pp. 464–472.

[61] D.P. Kingma, J. Ba, Adam: a method for stochastic optimization, in: International Conference on Learning Representations (ICLR), 2015.

[62] A. Suinesiaputra, B.R. Cowan, A.O. Al-Agamy, M.A. Elattar, N. Ayache, A.S. Fahmy, A.M. Khalifa, P. Medrano-Gracia, M.-P. Jolly, A.H. Kadish, et al., A collaborative resource to build consensus for automated left ventricular segmentation of cardiac MR images, Medical Image Analysis 18 (1) (2014) 50–62.

[63] X. Wang, A. Jabri, A.A. Efros, Learning correspondence from the cycle-consistency of time, in: Conference on Computer Vision and Pattern Recognition (CVPR), 2019, pp. 2566–2576.

[64] E. Perez, F. Strub, H. de Vries, V. Dumoulin, A.C. Courville, FiLM: visual reasoning with a general conditioning layer, in: AAAI Conference on Artificial Intelligence (AAAI), vol. 32, 2018.

[65] T. Park, M.-Y. Liu, T.-C. Wang, J.-Y. Zhu, Semantic image synthesis with spatially-adaptive normalization, in: Proc. IEEE Conference on Computer Vision and Pattern Recognition (CVPR), 2019, pp. 2337–2346.

[66] A. Chartsias, G. Papanastasiou, C. Wang, S. Semple, D. Newby, R. Dharmakumar, S. Tsaftaris, Disentangle, align and fuse for multimodal and semi-supervised image segmentation, IEEE Transactions on Medical Imaging (2020).

Image imputation in cardiac MRI and quality assessment

17

Yan Xia[a,b], **Nishant Ravikumar**[a,b], **and Alejandro F. Frangi**[a,b]

[a]*Centre for Computational Imaging and Simulation Technologies in Biomedicine (CISTIB), School of Computing, University of Leeds, Leeds, United Kingdom* [b]*Leeds Institute for Cardiovascular and Metabolic Medicine (LICAMM), School of Medicine, University of Leeds, Leeds, United Kingdom*

17.1 Introduction

Medical imaging is an indispensable tool for medical diagnosis and imaging research, providing detailed visualization of the interior of a human body as well as visual representation of the function of organs or tissues. However, image quality can be adversely affected by numerous imaging artifacts, which could ultimately reduce diagnostic accuracy and scientific relevance. Typical artifacts involve motion artifacts due to respiration or other movement of the imaging organs, manifesting as blurring or ghosting that may smear the image, or equipment-related ones, such as spike artifacts, appearing as dark stripes overlaid on the image, or zipper artifacts, exhibiting increased noise that extends throughout the image slices. Types and manifestations of artifacts can be found in [1,2]. A common strategy to account for corrupted slices is to discard the affected samples in the cohort. However, excluding data not only reduces statistical power and causes biased results, but is also of ethical and financial concern as partially acquired subject data remains unused, and limits the application of such methods with less precision compared with the analysis of all individuals.

Also, in practice, physicians usually acquire a relatively sparse set of images to reduce acquisition and visual inspection time, leading to highly anisotropic volume images. For example, in many clinical settings, only every sixth slice is acquired in a magnetic resonance (MR) imaging scan, resulting in 83% of the anatomical data being missing. Such clinically acquired scans can be viewed as missing slices and will pose challenges to subsequent postprocessing algorithms, such as segmentation and non-rigid registration, which are important for downstream analysis.

Another scenario is multi-modal/multi-contrast imaging. For instance, combinations of various MR contrast images provide different information about pathologies. Multiple MR contrasts such as T1-weighted, T2-weighted, and T2-FLAIR (fluid-attenuated inversion recovery) are often required for accurate diagnosis and segmentation of the cancer margin and radiomic studies. Also, structural MRI and positron

Biomedical Image Synthesis and Simulation. https://doi.org/10.1016/B978-0-12-824349-7.00024-4

emission tomography (PET) contain complementary information for improving the diagnosis of Alzheimer's disease [3]. However, a complete set of different contrast or modality images is often difficult to obtain. For example, in the Alzheimer's Disease Neuroimaging Initiative (ADNI-1) database [4], approximately half of subjects lack corresponding PET scans, whereas all subjects have MRI data. Previous studies usually simply discard subjects without PET data [5].

Rather than re-acquiring all the data as a complete set, it is not uncommon to fill missing data with substituted one. This process is called missing data imputation. Thus, retrieving missing information due to image artifacts, due to large slice thickness or due to missing different contrast/modality images, can be regarded as an image imputation task.

In this chapter, we focus on cardiac MR (CMR) imaging as a use case, where the aforementioned problems are typically present. CMR imaging is generally accepted as the reference standard for several aspects in cardiovascular medicine, such as the accurate assessment of left and right ventricular (LV/RV) volume, mass, and function, and the quantification of myocardial fibrosis, providing insights into cardiac diseases in a single diagnostic session [6]. Accurate and reproducible ventricular volume assessments, and associated ejection fraction (EF) and stroke volume (SV), are important in the management of various cardiac diseases because they are strong predictors of clinical outcomes [7]. The measurements directly relate to the volume of these ventricular chambers, whose extents are defined by the basal and apical slices [8]. Most published studies addressing computation of EF and SV assume a complete data set, i.e., all imaging planes being available for all cardiac time frames. This assumption may not hold in CMR imaging as certain datasets may have missing or corrupted information due to imaging artifacts and acquisition/storage errors [9,10]. For instance, short axis (SAX) cine stacks are reconstructed from images acquired across multiple breath-holds (typically 1–3 slices/breath-hold). Consequently, cardiac and respiratory motion, together with fast flowing blood in the vicinity, may cause inter-slice motion artifacts. In addition, adjacent tissues with different characteristics or implants may cause local loss of signal in certain slices [10]. Due to insufficient radiographer experience in scan acquisition planning, natural cardiac muscle contraction, breathing motion, and imperfect triggering, CMRs may display incomplete LV coverage, posing further challenges to quantitative LV characterization and accurate diagnosis [11].

Although several automated, learning-based image quality assessment techniques have been proposed for CMR images [12,11], a common strategy is to discard incomplete samples in the cohort [13], resulting in a loss in statistical power and potentially biased inference. Thus, image imputation for these corrupted/missing slices is an important step after quality assessment in order to enable quantitative assessment of cardiac function and facilitate downstream tasks such as deformable registration and segmentation. However, large inter-slice spacing in CMR imaging and variation in the intensity distributions of anatomy across slices, pose a significant challenge to traditional data imputation and interpolation approaches, as illustrated in Fig. 17.1.

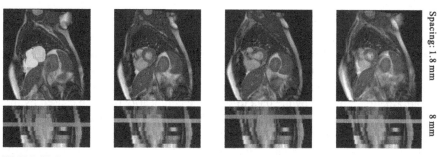

FIGURE 17.1

Typical CMR images from UK Biobank with in-plane spatial resolution 1.8 × 1.8 mm, slice thickness 8 mm. The three rows display short axis (SAX) slices and long axis (LAX) slices. Large inter-slice spacing and variation in the intensity distributions of the same anatomical regions across consecutive slice positions can be observed. The first three images in the top row show three consecutive slices and mean imputation of the middle slice is shown in the forth image. The color bars in LAX slice show the corresponding slice position for SAX slices. CMR images were reproduced with the permission of UK Biobank©.

17.2 **Image imputation strategies**
17.2.1 **Traditional methods**

Traditional interpolation methods can be adapted to this scenario to retrieve missing/corrupted slices from their adjacent slices, by using intensity/object-based interpolation. Intensity-based interpolation methods are essentially weighted average schemes of the input image, and thus yield blurring effects and unrealistic results. In object-based methods, on the other hand, the extracted information from available slices is used for guiding the interpolation process in a more accurate manner. An important object interpolation category is based on image registration, where corresponding points between consecutive slices are found and then the interpolation is applied to find the in-between slices. Such methods include the modified version of control grid interpolation [14], multi-resolution registration-based slice interpolation [15], and higher-order splines-based interpolation [16]. However, registration-based slice interpolation methods have several limitations: first, the consecutive slices must have similar anatomical features. Second, the registration method must be able to estimate the correct transformation to match these similar features. Violation of either of these aspects yields false correspondence maps, which leads to incorrect interpolation results. Additionally, such methods do not leverage statistical information concerning the anatomy and appearance that can be extracted from populations, which implies that they are sensitive to the input data, and susceptible to producing physically implausible solutions due to the presence of local minima. A comprehensive summary of common methods for slice interpolation was described in [17,18].

17.2.2 Statistical methods

State-of-the-art methods for imputation, or estimation of missing values, often use statistics learned across the entire dataset. Generally, data imputation methods have been proposed to deal with this problem, such as using the mean imputation or model-based missing data estimation [19]. Stochastic regression imputation methods can use the information provided by the data to solve the collinearity problem caused by the high correlation of predicted variables [20]. If the missing mechanism is random, the missing variable can be imputed by the marginal distribution of the observed data using maximum likelihood estimation [21]. This has been achieved previously by fitting parametric mixture models (such as Gaussian mixtures, for example) to the observed data using the EM algorithm, and sampling from the model to impute the missing data [22]. There are also other statistical imputation methods, including factor analysis, manifold learning, and principal component analysis, which often use linear subspace models to capture covariation across a dataset [23,24]. These models assume each observed data point is a noisy, sparse observation of a lower-dimensional linear subspace. However, in many settings such as imaging, such linear models are insufficient in capturing data representations [25,26].

17.2.3 Slice imputation methods

To tackle the clinically acquired sparse data, one strategy is to fill in the missing slices by identifying redundant, relevant detail in a scan and re-synthesizing high-frequency information [27,28]. However, medical images are often sparsely acquired and hence it is hard to accurately estimate functional representations without prior knowledge. To obtain enough fine-scale information to recover the missing data, [29] proposed a probabilistic generative model that captures repetitive anatomical structure across subjects in clinical image collections and derived an algorithm for filling in the middle slices in scans with large through-plane spacing. There also exist methods that attempt to exploit the temporal aspect of dynamic CMR data, to recover important image features and render a high-resolution sequence [30,31].

17.2.4 Super-resolution methods

Super-resolution methods can be viewed as imputation of higher-resolution pixel data. These methods generally fall into two main categories: reconstruction through the combination of multiple acquired low-resolution (LR) orthogonal scans to achieve the higher resolution [32,33], and example-based super-resolution, which aims to up-sample LR images to their most likely high-resolution (HR) version via knowledge of the relationship between HR and LR image features from example data [34,35]. The former not only requires additional acquisitions from multiple orthogonal views, but also depends on the quality of alignment of the images for fusion. The latter group requires correspondences between LR and HR image patches from an example database, which may not always be available or feasible to acquire in clinical applications. Alternatively, [36] used in-plane HR information to restore LR through-plane slices. They first trained a regression model to generate in-plane image patches at the original resolution acquired, from LR image patches generated by filtering the original image patches. Subsequently, they applied the trained regression model in the through-plane direction to generate self-supervised HR images.

17.2.5 Generative models

Data-driven image synthesis using generative adversarial networks (GANs) [37] has significantly improved various medical image synthesis tasks, such as data augmentation, super-resolution, denoising and cross-modality domain adaption [38–41], to name a few. GAN-based image translation techniques are closely related to image imputation, since they can estimate the missing data by modeling the intrinsic manifold of the image data [42]. GANs comprise two sub-networks that are trained simultaneously, namely, the generator and the discriminator. They are trained by optimizing a suitable adversarial loss and automatically adapting to the differences between the synthesized and real images in the target domain. In addition, GANs can be extended to a conditional model [43] if both the generator and discriminator are conditioned on some extra auxiliary information, such as class labels or data from other modalities. Recent studies on image-to-image translation have demonstrated that such conditional GANs are highly effective in learning the mapping between statistically dependent source and target domain images [44]. One successful application involves casting the image imputation problem as a cross-domain images-to-image translation task so that a GAN network can estimate the missing data using the other available datasets, for instance, generating MR images from the other contrast inputs [45,42].

17.3 Image imputation via conditional GAN

In this section, we investigate a conditional GAN to generate missing CMR slices, following manual, semi- or fully-automatic quality control. The network aims to generate missing SAX slices for CMR images across different positions. First, a 3D regression network learns features relevant to identifying the position of the missing CMR slice and predicts its corresponding position. Conditioned on these pre-trained, extracted feature representations, a generator and discriminator are subsequently trained to synthesize a realistic image in place of the missing slice. The network architecture is illustrated in Fig. 17.2. In the next section, we will present the learning algorithm and key components.

17.3.1 Image imputation conditional GAN (I2-GAN) for CMR

The conditional generative model [43] aims to transform the features from CMR volumes with full ventricular coverage into the query CMR volumes, which miss slices in certain positions. The conditional generator is defined as $G : \mathbb{R}^F \to \mathbb{R}^S$,

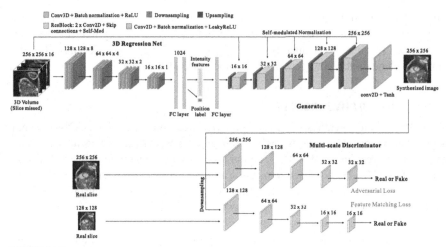

FIGURE 17.2

Structure of the investigated I2-GAN network for cardiac missing data imputation. The 3D regression network maps the input volume to a vector containing intensity features and position label. The former is the condition to feed to the generator. The generator contains several residual blocks, where all normalization layers are self-modulated with auxiliary slice information to ensure that fine details are propagated throughout the network. The multi-scale discriminative net helps capture both global and local spatial features.

where F is the dimension of the intrinsic intensity features, and S is the dimension of cardiac slice. The discriminator is denoted as $D : \mathbb{R}^S \to \mathbb{R}$. The optimization of the G and D can be reformulated as:

$$\mathcal{L}_D = \mathbb{E}_x \left[(D(x) - 1)^2 \right] + \mathbb{E}_f \left[D(G(f))^2 \right], \tag{17.1}$$

$$\mathcal{L}_G = \mathbb{E}_f \left[D(G(f))^2 \right], \tag{17.2}$$

where x denotes the image slice and f denotes the conditioning feature. The architecture of the regressor, generator, and discriminator will be discussed in the subsequent sections.

17.3.2 3D regression net

As visual perception tasks in medical image analysis benefit from leveraging inter-slice context [46], a deep 3D convolutional neural network is used to learn CMR image intensity features f relevant to predicting the position of missing slices. Note that the input cardiac volumetric image for this network is an incomplete image stack with the missing slice. As shown in Fig. 17.2, the trunk architecture of the regression net consists of four 3D convolutional layers and two fully-connected layers for feature extraction. Two layers are configured for extracting the 1024-dimensional feature vector f and regressing a single scalar y, representing the missing slice position, separately.

17.3.3 Generator with self-modulated normalization

The generator network follows a full pre-activation ResNet architecture [47] implemented in recent popular conditional GAN and pix2pix models [48,49,44,50,51]. The model consists of the residual blocks, followed by nearest neighbor upsampling layers.

For feature normalization, we are motivated by the concept of conditional batch normalization that has been adopted in multiple previous studies [52,53,51,54,55] and suggests a new conditioning mechanism to incorporate external conditioning information (such as labels, embedding, masks, or generator's own inputs) into image synthesis through batch normalization. It is typically implemented as a learning-based affine transformation over modulated features with parameters inferred from auxiliary data. For the missing slice imputation problem, we intuitively used the two adjacent slices as input to ensure the normalization is spatially dependent.

17.3.4 Multi-scale discriminator

The discriminator of I2-GAN takes the generated samples and the real images in the target CMR volume as inputs. A multi-scale discriminator is adopted [56–58] that operates at different image scales, as shown in Fig. 17.2. The benefits of applying this two-scale image pyramid structure are: the discriminator with the larger receptive field yields a global view of the image and can guide the generator to synthesize globally coherent images, whereas the other discriminator encourages the generator to capture finer details.

17.3.5 Optimization

Instead of using pixel-wise loss in image-space, which struggles with capturing high-frequency details, a feature matching loss [59,58] is employed to optimize the GAN to match the statistics of feature representations in multiple intermediate layers of D. Thus, the final joint objective combines both the adversarial loss and feature matching loss:

$$
\mathcal{L}_{I2} = \min_G \left(\max_{D_1,D_2} \sum_{k=1,2} -\left(\mathbb{E}_x \left[(D_k(x) - 1)^2 \right] + \mathbb{E}_f \left[D_k(G(f))^2 \right] \right) \right.
$$
$$
\left. + \lambda \sum_{k=1,2} \mathbb{E}_x \sum_{i=1}^{T} \frac{1}{N_i} \left\| D_k^i(x) - D_k^i(G(f)) \right\|_1 \right),
$$
(17.3)

where i means the ith layer features in D, N_i is the number of features in each layer, T is total number of layers, and λ controls the relative weighting of the feature matching loss to the adversarial loss. The conditioned G and D nets can be optimized by $\mathcal{L}_{I2}$ to infer the missing features from query input volumes.

17.4 Evaluation

17.4.1 Dataset

CMR images from the UK Biobank (UKBB) were used to train and validate the investigated I2-GAN method. CMR images were acquired using a clinical wide bore 1.5T system (MAGNETOM Aera, Syngo Platform VD13A, Siemens Healthcare, Erlangen, Germany) equipped with 18 channels anterior body surface coil (45 mT/m and 200 T/m/s gradient system). 2D cine balanced steady-state free precession (b-SSFP) SAX image stacks were acquired with the following acquisition protocol: in-plane spatial resolution 1.8×1.8 mm, slice thickness 8 mm, slice gap 2 mm, image size 198×208. Each volumetric sequence contains 50 cardiac phases. Further acquisition details can be found in [60]. We focus on the SAX b-SSFP cine CMR datasets for which the ground-truth slices are available and randomly remove one slice to generate incomplete volumes, before using the data imputation methods to synthesize the missed slices.

17.4.2 Competing methods

For missing image imputation task, we investigated the performance of a conventional intensity-based and registration-based interpolation method, a standard pix2pix network and the I2-GAN. The network training procedure for I2-GAN can be found in [61]. The registration-based slice interpolation approach [16] first uses a symmetric similarity measure to perform structure registration, to calculate displacement fields between neighboring slices. Then, along every correspondence point trajectory, the displacement fields are utilized to calculate a high-order intensity interpolating spline for structural motion. The standard pix2pix framework was also used [44], which comprises an image-conditional GAN architecture that utilizes the adversarial and pixel-wise losses, for image-to-image translation tasks. The method takes a set of pairs of corresponding images for training and aims to model the conditional distribution of real images given the input images through minimax optimization.

17.4.3 Evaluation design

We conducted several experiments to assess the accuracy and robustness of the investigated methods. The first experiment was performed by evaluating the quality of the images generated by different competing methods within a single cardiac phase. To quantitatively assess synthesis performance, the structural similarity index measurement (SSIM) [62] and the peak signal-to-noise ratio (PSNR) were used to measure the image quality of the synthesized CMR images, relative to the original images. The

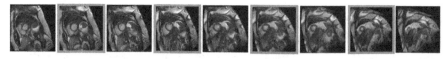

FIGURE 17.3

For clinical quantification evaluation such as LVEDV, LVSV, and LVEF, we removed the half of intermediate slices (indicated in the green boxes – mid gray boxes in print version) in each of original image stacks and then restored them using the I2-GAN model. The volumetric differences derived between the original (full) and imputed cardiac image stacks were quantified. CMR images were reproduced with the permission of UK Biobank©.

results obtained using the I2-GAN were compared with those of the other approaches investigated.

In addition, to assess the impact of MSI in real clinical applications, such as measurements of cardiac function based on blood volumes, we designed an experiment where incomplete data was simulated and volumetric differences between the original (full) and imputed cardiac image volumes were quantified. In this experiment, we considered a challenge case, where we intentionally removed the half of intermediate slices in the original image stacks and restored them using the investigated I2-GAN model, as illustrated in Fig. 17.3. Several key clinical parameters including the LV end-diastolic volume (LVEDV) and end-systolic volume (LVESV), LV stroke volume (LVSV), LV ejection fraction (LVEF), LV myocardial mass (LVM), RV end-diastolic volume (RVEDV) and end-systolic volume (RVESV), RV stroke volume (RVSV) and RV ejection fraction (RVEF) were computed from segmentation results of 900 test subjects using the automated LV/RV segmentation method proposed in [63].

17.4.4 Synthesis quality assessment

First, a qualitative comparison of the synthesized slices is depicted in Fig. 17.4, between the mean imputation, registration-based interpolation, pix2pix GAN, and I2-GAN for 2 subjects of the UKBB dataset in the ED phase. Simple mean imputation simply computes the linearly weighted average of two adjacent slices and thus yields uncertain and highly blurred edges in the interpolated slices, as expected. Results of the registration-based method are marginally better than linear interpolation. However, large dissimilarity between adjacent CMR slices yields false correspondence maps during registration, and consequently leads to incorrect interpolation results. By comparison, the slices generated with pix2pix GAN are realistic with sharp edges. As illustrated in Fig. 17.4, the method reasonably restores anatomical structures that are almost entirely blurred in the interpolation methods, such as LV/RV blood pool and LV myocardium by learning about these structures from the neighboring slice features. Further improvement can be obtained by the I2-GAN approach, which generates the most visually comparable result to the reference CMR slices and yields more plausible results in terms of preserving fine structural details. The observed dif-

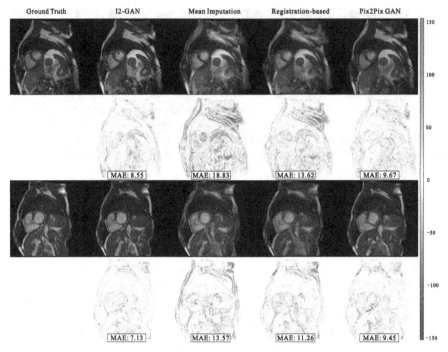

FIGURE 17.4

Qualitative comparison of the ground truth and the synthesized slices between the mean imputation, registration-based interpolation, pix2pix GAN, and the I2-GAN approach for 2 subjects from the UKBB dataset in the ED phase (intra-phase). The second and fourth rows show the error image, with the original missed slice at the same position as the ground truth. CMR images were reproduced with the permission of UK Biobank©.

ferences in appearance between the synthesized slices, using each approach, is further highlighted by the corresponding error images in Fig. 17.4.

As depicted in Fig. 17.5, similar observations are obtained upon closer investigation of synthesized slices of the cardiac structures. We chose different slice positions from apex to base, in order to assess the capability of the investigated approach to restore the missing slice at different positions within the heart. Again, the generative models such as the pix2pix model and I2-GAN model can well approximate the ground-truth CMR slices for LV/RV blood pool and LV myocardium, with the I2-GAN yielding more perceptual and plausible structural details. Note that the manual segmentation of LV endocardium (LV endo), LV myocardium (LV myo), and RV endocardium (RV endo) of the same UKBB datasets from [64] are also shown in the first column of Fig. 17.5, to help illustrate the preservation of cardiac tissue boundaries in the synthesized slices.

An overview of the quantitative comparison of different methods on 970 subjects from a single cardiac phase (ED phase) is presented in Fig. 17.6. The SSIM and PSNR

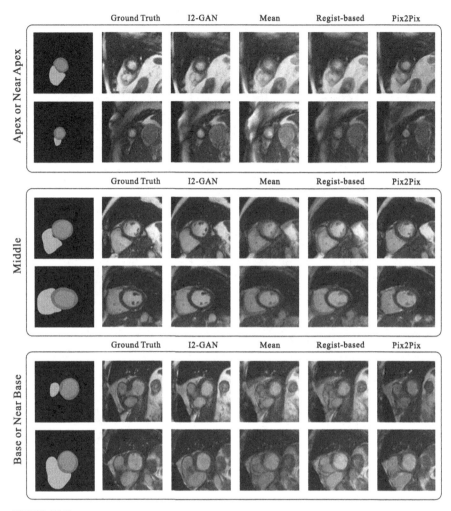

FIGURE 17.5

Close-up for visual comparison of ground truth and synthesized CMR image slices. We compared mean slice imputation, registration-based interpolation, pix2pix GAN, and I2-GAN approach, for 6 subjects from the UKBB dataset in the ED phase (intra-phase). The first column depicts the manual segmentation of LV endocardium (blue – mid gray in print version), LV myocardium (purple – dark gray in print version), and RV endocardium (green – light gray in print version) from [64]. Different slice positions from apex to base are chosen and shown. CMR images were reproduced with the permission of UK Biobank©.

metrics were computed over the entire CMR slice, and over pixels corresponding to three segmented cardiac regions of interest (ROIs) (refer to Fig. 17.5) using the manual reference masks produced in [64]. Consistent with qualitative analysis, the

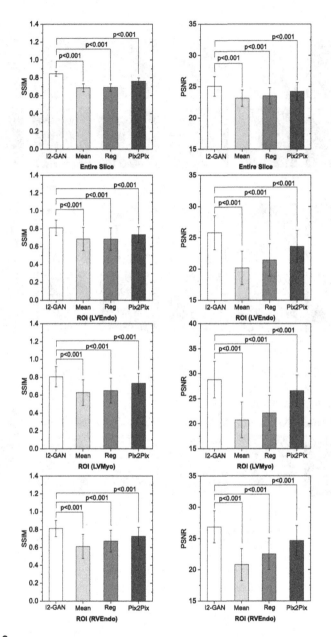

FIGURE 17.6

SSIM and PSNR measurements between the ground truth and synthesized target images from the mean imputation, registration-based interpolation, pix2pix GAN, and the I2-GAN approach on 970 subjects from a single cardiac phase (ED phase). The Wilcoxon signed rank test is used for all comparisons (i.e., I2-GAN vs. mean, I2-GAN vs. Reg, and I2-GAN vs. pix2pix) to assess the statistical significance of the results.

Table 17.1 Mean and standard deviation of the clinical measures derived from 900 automated segmentation results, between the originally-acquired images and I2-GAN imputed images. LVEDV and LVESV represent LV end-diastolic volume and end-systolic volume, LVSV and LVEF represent LV stroke volume and ejection fraction, LVM represents LV myocardial mass, RVEDV and RVESV represent RV end-diastolic volume and end-systolic volume, RVSV and LVEF represent RV stroke volume and ejection fraction.

Parameters	b-SSFP reference images (n = 900)	I2-GAN imputed images (n = 900)	p-value
LVEDV (mL)	145.0 ± 31.3	145.0 ± 31.2	0.893
LVESV (mL)	63.0 ± 19.0	63.2 ± 19.5	0.826
LVSV (mL)	82.2 ± 17.4	81.7 ± 18.3	0.638
LVEF (%)	56.9 ± 6.25	56.7 ± 7.26	0.447
LVM (g)	83.3 ± 21.6	82.9 ± 20.8	0.661
RVEDV (mL)	152.0 ± 35.4	158.7 ± 35.8	<0.001
RVESV (mL)	69.2 ± 20.8	71.6 ± 22.2	0.022
RVSV (mL)	82.7 ± 19.2	87.1 ± 21.9	<0.001
RVEF (%)	54.7 ± 6.38	55.1 ± 8.61	0.328

GAN-based methods significantly outperform the traditional methods in terms of the quality of the synthesized missing slices, which is reflected in the average SSIM values of the entire slice: 0.872 ± 0.027 for the I2-GAN method and 0.790 ± 0.037 for pix2pix GAN, compared with 0.686 ± 0.044 for mean imputation and 0.691 ± 0.041 for registration-based interpolation. The computed PSNR values are 26.88 ± 1.63 for the I2-GAN method, 23.15 ± 1.30 for mean imputation, 23.51 ± 1.32 for registration-based interpolation, and 24.72 ± 1.44 for pix2pix GAN. The nonparametric statistical Wilcoxon signed rank test, which does not assume the data to be normally distributed, was used for all comparisons (i.e., I2-GAN vs. mean, I2-GAN vs. registration-based interpolation and I2-GAN vs. pix2pix).

17.4.5 Cardiac parameters calculation

The mean and standard deviation of quantitative cardiac functional and volumetric indices are presented in Table 17.1, along with analysis of the mean absolute errors (MAE) between the reference and I2-GAN synthesized CMR images shown in Fig. 17.7. We can see that the I2-GAN imputed images yield an MAE of 2.65 mL in LVEDV when it comes to half of intermediate slices missed in the stacks. Given the mean value of 145 mL across the evaluated 900 CMR datasets, this only yields a relative error of 1.82%. LVESV has a slightly higher MAE compared to LVEDV (5.19 mL vs 2.65 mL), but this is expected as the model was trained with images only at the ED phase. In general, the clinical parameters in RV regions showed the worse results than those of LV regions due to the variations of automatically segmenting RVs. The

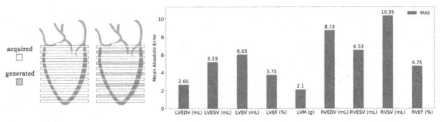

FIGURE 17.7

Mean absolute errors of the clinical measures derived from automated segmentation of 900 test subjects between originally-acquired images and sparsely-sampled images (missing half of slices) imputed by the I2-GAN, demonstrating accurate image synthesis obtained by I2-GAN.

mean and standard deviation of quantitative cardiac functional and volumetric indices in Table 17.1 showed that no significant differences were found between the reference and synthesized images concerning the indices of LVEDV, LVESV, LVSV, LVEF, LVM, RVESV, and RVEF, demonstrating the accurate image synthesis achieved by the I2-GAN.

Fig. 17.8 shows a comparison of myocardial wall thickness maps derived from automated segmentation on the original images and the imputed images by the I2-GAN method for 3 subjects of different views at the ED phase. Wall thickness was obtained by estimating the minimum distance between epicardium and endocardium in the subject space and then mapped onto a template surface mesh [65] for side-to-side visual comparison. The thickness maps derived from the imputed images are comparable to those of the original acquired data, even in the presence of this challenging case where a half of the intermediate slices was removed. We also evaluated the myocardial wall thickness at the cardiac ED and ES phases. Wall thickness was computed in each image stack and expressed as the bulls-eye plot based on the AHA 17-segment model. A comparison of the mean and standard deviation values of the regional wall thickness analysis of 900 automated segmentations between the reference and I2-GAN imputed CMR images is shown in Fig. 17.9. We observed that the I2-GAN method provided better agreement with the results derived from the original complete images, in terms of the mean and standard deviation values, thereby confirming the image synthesis quality of the I2-GAN.

17.5 Research challenges and future directions

Missing image data or presence of various artifacts due to respiratory and patient motion, blurring and signal loss in image stacks, or sparsely acquired data with low resolution in slice direction may influence the accuracy of anatomical and functional

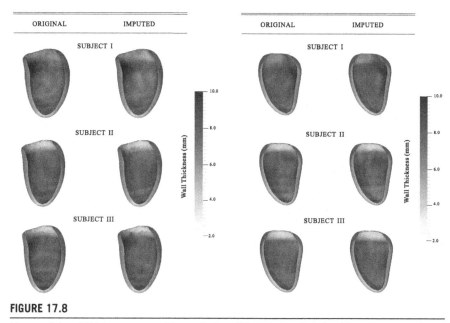

FIGURE 17.8

Myocardial wall thickness maps (shown in two different views) derived from automated segmentation on the original images and the imputed images by the I2-GAN method. Wall thickness was obtained by estimating the minimum distance between epicardium and endocardium in the subject space and then mapped onto a template surface mesh for visual comparison.

quantification, and thus often leads to the removal of the entire subject from all subsequent analyses. In this chapter, we presented CMR imaging as an example and investigated several data imputation approaches.

One challenge for the medical image imputation is that visual differences and quantitative information in medical images are more complex and non-trivial than natural images and thus the state-of-the-art data imputation methods developed in the computer vision domain may have difficulties to produce realistic and plausible synthesized medical images. For instance, the typical reconstruction pixel-wise loss will struggle to recover high-frequency details such as texture. Minimizing mean square error encourages finding pixel-wise averaging of plausible solutions in the original pixel space, which typically results in blurred images and thus yields unsatisfying perceptual quality. Similarly, maximum likelihood training does not model the properties of human visual perception and tends to output average images rather than plausible ones, which is not desired in the medical imaging. In this chapter, we investigated a GAN-like imputation model, namely I2-GAN, that can produce more visually realistic and plausible CMR images with well preserved fine details and texture information. The I2-GAN followed the concept of conditional batch normalization that incorporates external guidance information (such as labels, embedding,

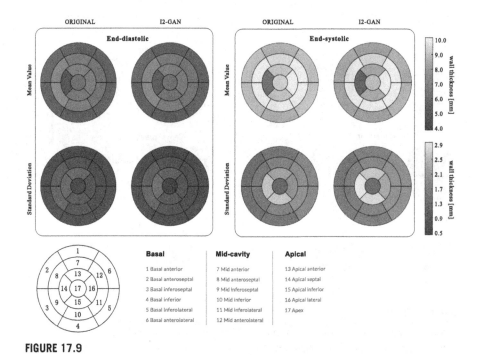

FIGURE 17.9

Bulls-eye plots of the regional wall thickness analysis (AHA 17-segment model) obtained by averaging results of 900 subjects. Image stacks reconstructed by the I2-GAN method were compared with the original images.

masks or generator's own inputs) into conditional generative model throughout batch normalization. To enhance the performance and stabilize the training, the I2-GAN exploited the feature space instead, and employed the discriminator-based feature matching loss combined with adversarial training. Feature matching changes the final objective for the generator to minimizing the statistical difference between the intermediate feature representations of the real images and the synthesized images. Herein, the L_1-distance between the means of their feature vectors is measured, and feature matching reformulates the goal from beating the opponent to matching features in real images to obtain fine details and perceptually more convincing results.

Also, most imputation methods are in a supervised manner. However, in many real-world scenarios, fully observed medical data is unavailable or difficult to acquire. Thus, imputing missing image data in an unsupervised fashion is needed. To this end, unsupervised statistical imputation methods, such as dictionary learning, factor analysis, manifold learning would be exploited. For instance, in [26], the authors proposed a probabilistic model that models high dimensional imaging data with very sparse pixel observations and derived a variational learning strategy that employs developments in deep neural networks and variational inference.

17.6 Summary

The development of robust and generic techniques for missing data imputation can have a transformative impact on medical imaging researches by preventing incomplete data from being completely disregarded, when analyzing any given cohort. In this chapter, we presented CMR imaging as an exemplar and investigated how the traditional interpolation methods and learning GAN architectures perform to impute missing slices in CMR images. Although we focused on the missing slice imputation problem here, the GAN-based models can be extended to other scenarios, such as super-resolution and incomplete multi-modal/multi-contrast imaging, where relatively sparse set of images are acquired to reduce acquisition and visual inspection time or a complete set of different images is often difficult to obtain. With the dedicated image imputation methods, the accuracy of subsequent postprocessing algorithms and downstream analyses (such as segmentation, classification, registration) can be retained.

Acknowledgments

This work was supported in part by the Royal Academy of Engineering Chair in Emerging Technologies Scheme (CiET1819/19), the MedIAN Network (EP/N026993/1), and TUSCA (EP/V04799X/1) funded by the Engineering and Physical Sciences Research Council (EPSRC).

References

[1] J. Zhuo, R.P. Gullapalli, MR artifacts, safety, and quality control, Radiographics 26 (1) (2006) 275–297.

[2] A. Stadler, W. Schima, A. Ba-Ssalamah, J. Kettenbach, E. Eisenhuber, Artifacts in body MR imaging: their appearance and how to eliminate them, European Radiology 17 (5) (2007) 1242–1255.

[3] V.D. Calhoun, J. Sui, Multimodal fusion of brain imaging data: a key to finding the missing link(s) in complex mental illness, Biological Psychiatry: Cognitive Neuroscience and Neuroimaging 1 (3) (2016) 230–244.

[4] C.R. Jack Jr, M.A. Bernstein, N.C. Fox, P. Thompson, G. Alexander, D. Harvey, B. Borowski, P.J. Britson, J.L. Whitwell, C. Ward, et al., The Alzheimer's disease neuroimaging initiative (ADNI): MRI methods, Journal of Magnetic Resonance Imaging: An Official Journal of the International Society for Magnetic Resonance in Medicine 27 (4) (2008) 685–691.

[5] D. Zhang, D. Shen, A.D.N. Initiative, et al., Multi-modal multi-task learning for joint prediction of multiple regression and classification variables in Alzheimer's disease, NeuroImage 59 (2) (2012) 895–907.

[6] D.J. Pennell, Cardiovascular magnetic resonance: twenty-first century solutions in cardiology, Clinical Medicine 3 (3) (2003) 273.

[7] A.L. Knauth, K. Gauvreau, A.J. Powell, M.J. Landzberg, E.P. Walsh, J.E. Lock, P.J. del Nido, T. Geva, Ventricular size and function assessed by cardiac MRI predict major adverse clinical outcomes late after tetralogy of Fallot repair, Heart 94 (2) (2008) 211–216.

[8] A.F. Frangi, W.J. Niessen, M.A. Viergever, Three-dimensional modeling for functional analysis of cardiac images, a review, IEEE Transactions on Medical Imaging 20 (1) (2001) 2–5.

[9] P.F. Ferreira, P.D. Gatehouse, R.H. Mohiaddin, D.N. Firmin, Cardiovascular magnetic resonance artefacts, Journal of Cardiovascular Magnetic Resonance 15 (1) (2013) 41.

[10] A. van der Graaf, P. Bhagirath, S. Ghoerbien, M. Götte, Cardiac magnetic resonance imaging: artefacts for clinicians, Netherlands Heart Journal 22 (12) (2014) 542–549.

[11] L. Zhang, A. Gooya, M. Pereanez, B. Dong, S.K. Piechnik, S. Neubauer, S.E. Petersen, A.F. Frangi, Automatic assessment of full left ventricular coverage in cardiac cine magnetic resonance imaging with Fisher-discriminative 3-D CNN, IEEE Transactions on Biomedical Engineering 66 (7) (2018) 1975–1986.

[12] G. Tarroni, O. Oktay, W. Bai, A. Schuh, H. Suzuki, J. Passerat-Palmbach, A. de Marvao, D. O'Regan, S. Cook, B. Glocker, P. Matthews, D. Rueckert, Learning-based quality control for cardiac MR images, IEEE Transactions on Medical Imaging 38 (5) (2018) 1127–1138.

[13] V. Klinke, S. Muzzarelli, N. Lauriers, D. Locca, G. Vincenti, P. Monney, C. Lu, D. Nothnagel, G. Pilz, M. Lombardi, A.C. van Rossum, A. Wagner, O. Bruder, H. Mahrholdt, J. Schwitter, Quality assessment of cardiovascular magnetic resonance in the setting of the European CMR registry: description and validation of standardized criteria, Journal of Cardiovascular Magnetic Resonance 15 (1) (2013) 55.

[14] D.H. Frakes, L.P. Dasi, K. Pekkan, H.D. Kitajima, K. Sundareswaran, A.P. Yoganathan, M.J. Smith, A new method for registration-based medical image interpolation, IEEE Transactions on Medical Imaging 27 (3) (2008) 370–377.

[15] J. Leng, G. Xu, Y. Zhang, Medical image interpolation based on multi-resolution registration, Computers & Mathematics with Applications 66 (1) (2013) 1–18.

[16] A. Horváth, S. Pezold, M. Weigel, K. Parmar, P. Cattin, High order slice interpolation for medical images, in: International Workshop on Simulation and Synthesis in Medical Imaging, Springer, 2017, pp. 69–78.

[17] G.J. Grevera, J.K. Udupa, An objective comparison of 3-D image interpolation methods, IEEE Transactions on Medical Imaging 17 (4) (1998) 642–652.

[18] G.J. Grevera, J.K. Udupa, Y. Miki, A task-specific evaluation of three-dimensional image interpolation techniques, IEEE Transactions on Medical Imaging 18 (2) (1999) 137–143.

[19] P.J. García-Laencina, J.-L. Sancho-Gómez, A.R. Figueiras-Vidal, Pattern classification with missing data: a review, Neural Computing & Applications 19 (2) (2010) 263–282.

[20] G.L. Schlomer, S. Bauman, N.A. Card, Best practices for missing data management in counseling psychology, Journal of Counseling Psychology 57 (1) (2010) 1.

[21] Y. Dong, C.-Y.J. Peng, Principled missing data methods for researchers, SpringerPlus 2 (1) (2013) 222.

[22] E. Richardson, Y. Weiss, On GANs and GMMs, in: Advances in Neural Information Processing Systems, 2018, pp. 5847–5858.

[23] C.M. Bishop, et al., Neural Networks for Pattern Recognition, Oxford University Press, 1995.

[24] R.J. Little, D.B. Rubin, Statistical Analysis with Missing Data, vol. 793, John Wiley & Sons, 2019.

[25] H. Lee, R. Grosse, R. Ranganath, A.Y. Ng, Convolutional deep belief networks for scalable unsupervised learning of hierarchical representations, in: Proceedings of the 26th Annual International Conference on Machine Learning, 2009, pp. 609–616.

[26] A.V. Dalca, J. Guttag, M.R. Sabuncu, Unsupervised data imputation via variational inference of deep subspaces, arXiv preprint, arXiv:1903.03503.

[27] J.V. Manjón, P. Coupé, A. Buades, V. Fonov, D.L. Collins, M. Robles, Non-local MRI upsampling, Medical Image Analysis 14 (6) (2010) 784–792.

[28] E. Plenge, D.H. Poot, W.J. Niessen, E. Meijering, Super-resolution reconstruction using cross-scale self-similarity in multi-slice MRI, in: International Conference on Medical Image Computing and Computer-Assisted Intervention, Springer, 2013, pp. 123–130.

[29] A.V. Dalca, K.L. Bouman, W.T. Freeman, N.S. Rost, M.R. Sabuncu, P. Golland, Medical image imputation from image collections, IEEE Transactions on Medical Imaging 38 (2) (2018) 504–514.

[30] N. Basty, V. Grau, Super resolution of cardiac cine MRI sequences using deep learning, in: Image Analysis for Moving Organ, Breast, and Thoracic Images, Springer, 2018, pp. 23–31.

[31] Y. Guo, L. Bi, E. Ahn, D. Feng, Q. Wang, J. Kim, A spatiotemporal volumetric interpolation network for 4d dynamic medical image, in: Proceedings of the IEEE/CVF Conference on Computer Vision and Pattern Recognition, 2020, pp. 4726–4735.

[32] S. ur Rahman, S. Wesarg, Upsampling of cardiac MR images: comparison of averaging and super-resolution for the combination of multiple views, in: Proceedings of the 10th IEEE International Conference on Information Technology and Applications in Biomedicine, IEEE, 2010, pp. 1–4.

[33] A. Gholipour, J.A. Estroff, S.K. Warfield, Robust super-resolution volume reconstruction from slice acquisitions: application to fetal brain MRI, IEEE Transactions on Medical Imaging 29 (10) (2010) 1739–1758.

[34] J.V. Manjón, P. Coupé, A. Buades, D.L. Collins, M. Robles, MRI superresolution using self-similarity and image priors, International Journal of Biomedical Imaging (2010).

[35] F. Rousseau, P.A. Habas, C. Studholme, A supervised patch-based approach for human brain labeling, IEEE Transactions on Medical Imaging 30 (10) (2011) 1852–1862.

[36] C. Zhao, B.E. Dewey, D.L. Pham, P.A. Calabresi, D.S. Reich, J.L. Prince, SMORE: a self-supervised anti-aliasing and super-resolution algorithm for MRI using deep learning, IEEE Transactions on Medical Imaging 40 (3) (2021) 805–817.

[37] I. Goodfellow, J. Pouget-Abadie, M. Mirza, B. Xu, D. Warde-Farley, S. Ozair, A. Courville, Y. Bengio, Generative adversarial nets, in: Advances in Neural Information Processing Systems, 2014, pp. 2672–2680.

[38] X. Zhuang, J. Shen, Multi-scale patch and multi-modality atlases for whole heart segmentation of MRI, Medical Image Analysis 31 (2016) 77–87.

[39] Z. Han, B. Wei, A. Mercado, S. Leung, S. Li, Spine-GAN: semantic segmentation of multiple spinal structures, Medical Image Analysis 50 (2018) 23–35.

[40] H. Yang, J. Sun, A. Carass, C. Zhao, J. Lee, Z. Xu, J.L. Prince, Unpaired brain MR-to-CT synthesis using a structure-constrained CycleGAN, in: Deep Learning in Medical Image Analysis and Multimodal Learning for Clinical Decision Support, Springer, 2018, pp. 174–182.

[41] I. Sánchez, V. Vilaplana Besler, Brain MRI super-resolution using generative adversarial networks, in: International Conference on Medical Imaging with Deep Learning, Amsterdam, 4–6 July 2018, 2018, pp. 1–8.

[42] D. Lee, J. Kim, W.-J. Moon, J.C. Ye, Collagan: collaborative GAN for missing image data imputation, in: Proceedings of the IEEE Conference on Computer Vision and Pattern Recognition, 2019, pp. 2487–2496.

[43] M. Mirza, S. Osindero, Conditional generative adversarial nets, arXiv preprint, arXiv: 1411.1784.

[44] P. Isola, J.-Y. Zhu, T. Zhou, A.A. Efros, Image-to-image translation with conditional adversarial networks, in: Proceedings of the IEEE Conference on Computer Vision and Pattern Recognition, 2017, pp. 1125–1134.

[45] M. Yurt, S.U.H. Dar, A. Erdem, E. Erdem, T. Çukur, mustGAN: multi-stream generative adversarial networks for MR image synthesis, arXiv preprint, arXiv:1909.11504.

[46] K. Kamnitsas, C. Ledig, V.F. Newcombe, J.P. Simpson, A.D. Kane, D.K. Menon, D. Rueckert, B. Glocker, Efficient multi-scale 3D CNN with fully connected CRF for accurate brain lesion segmentation, Medical Image Analysis 36 (2017) 61–78.

[47] K. He, X. Zhang, S. Ren, J. Sun, Deep residual learning for image recognition, in: Proceedings of the IEEE Conference on Computer Vision and Pattern Recognition, 2016, pp. 770–778.

[48] T. Karras, T. Aila, S. Laine, J. Lehtinen, Progressive growing of GANs for improved quality, stability, and variation, in: International Conference on Learning Representations (ICLR), 2017.

[49] J.-Y. Zhu, T. Park, P. Isola, A.A. Efros, Unpaired image-to-image translation using cycle-consistent adversarial networks, in: Proceedings of the IEEE International Conference on Computer Vision, 2017, pp. 2223–2232.

[50] T. Miyato, T. Kataoka, M. Koyama, Y. Yoshida, Spectral normalization for generative adversarial networks, in: International Conference on Learning Representations (ICLR), 2018.

[51] H. Zhang, I. Goodfellow, D. Metaxas, A. Odena, Self-attention generative adversarial networks, STAT 1050 (2018) 21.

[52] H. de Vries, F. Strub, J. Mary, H. Larochelle, O. Pietquin, A.C. Courville, Modulating early visual processing by language, in: Advances in Neural Information Processing Systems, 2017, pp. 6594–6604.

[53] T. Miyato, M. Koyama, cGANs with projection discriminator, in: International Conference on Learning Representations (ICLR), 2018.

[54] T. Chen, M. Lučić, N. Houlsby, S. Gelly, On self-modulation for generative adversarial networks, in: International Conference on Learning Representations (ICLR), 2019.

[55] T. Park, M.-Y. Liu, T.-C. Wang, J.-Y. Zhu, Semantic image synthesis with spatially-adaptive normalization, in: Proceedings of the IEEE Conference on Computer Vision and Pattern Recognition, 2019, pp. 2337–2346.

[56] I. Durugkar, I. Gemp, S. Mahadevan, Generative multi-adversarial networks, in: International Conference on Learning Representations (ICLR), 2017.

[57] T. Nguyen, T. Le, H. Vu, D. Phung, Dual discriminator generative adversarial nets, in: Advances in Neural Information Processing Systems, 2017, pp. 2670–2680.

[58] T.-C. Wang, M.-Y. Liu, J.-Y. Zhu, A. Tao, J. Kautz, B. Catanzaro, High-resolution image synthesis and semantic manipulation with conditional GANs, in: Proceedings of the IEEE Conference on Computer Vision and Pattern Recognition, 2018, pp. 8798–8807.

[59] T. Salimans, I. Goodfellow, W. Zaremba, V. Cheung, A. Radford, X. Chen, Improved techniques for training GANs, in: Advances in Neural Information Processing Systems, 2016, pp. 2234–2242.

[60] S.E. Petersen, P.M. Matthews, J.M. Francis, M.D. Robson, F. Zemrak, R. Boubertakh, A.A. Young, S. Hudson, P. Weale, S. Garratt, R. Collins, S. Piechnik, S. Neubauer, UK Biobank's cardiovascular magnetic resonance protocol, Journal of Cardiovascular Magnetic Resonance 18 (1) (2015) 8.

[61] Y. Xia, L. Zhang, N. Ravikumar, R. Attar, S.K. Piechnik, S. Neubauer, S.E. Petersen, A.F. Frangi, Recovering from missing data in population imaging–cardiac MR image imputation via conditional generative adversarial nets, Medical Image Analysis (2020) 101812.

[62] Z. Wang, A.C. Bovik, H.R. Sheikh, E.P. Simoncelli, Image quality assessment: from error visibility to structural similarity, IEEE Transactions on Image Processing 13 (4) (2004) 600–612.

[63] R. Attar, M. Pereañez, A. Gooya, X. Albà, L. Zhang, M.H. de Vila, A.M. Lee, N. Aung, E. Lukaschuk, M.M. Sanghvi, K. Fung, J.M. Paiva, S.K. Piechnik, S. Neubauer, S.E. Petersen, A.F. Frangi, Quantitative CMR population imaging on 20,000 subjects of the UK Biobank imaging study: LV/RV quantification pipeline and its evaluation, Medical Image Analysis 56 (2019) 26–42.

[64] S.E. Petersen, N. Aung, M.M. Sanghvi, F. Zemrak, K. Fung, J.M. Paiva, J.M. Francis, M.Y. Khanji, E. Lukaschuk, A.M. Lee, V. Carapella, Y.J. Kim, P. Leeson, S.K. Piechnik, S. Neubauer, Reference ranges for cardiac structure and function using cardiovascular magnetic resonance (CMR) in Caucasians from the UK Biobank population cohort, Journal of Cardiovascular Magnetic Resonance 19 (1) (2017) 18.

[65] W. Bai, W. Shi, A. de Marvao, T.J. Dawes, D.P. O'Regan, S.A. Cook, D. Rueckert, A biventricular cardiac atlas built from 1000+ high resolution MR images of healthy subjects and an analysis of shape and motion, Medical Image Analysis 26 (1) (2015) 133–145.

Image synthesis for low-count PET acquisitions: lower dose, shorter time

18

Kevin T. Chen[a] **and Greg Zaharchuk**[b]

[a]*Department of Biomedical Engineering, National Taiwan University, Taipei, Taiwan*
[b]*Department of Radiology, Stanford University, Stanford, CA, United States*

18.1 Introduction to low-count imaging

The strength of positron emission tomography (PET) lies in the quantification of the radioactive pharmaceutical (radiotracer) concentrations in subjects, which can interrogate specific metabolic mechanisms of interest. Applications where PET has seen widespread use include examples such as oncology [1], neurodegeneration [2], and cardiology [3]. However, there is a tradeoff between radiation exposure of the subjects and the quality of the reconstructed images. If there are fewer detector counts resulting from the radioactive decay collected by the scanner in the form of coincidence annihilation photons, there will be more noise in the reconstructed image, resulting in lower image quality (Fig. 18.1). With current reconstruction and hardware setups, reducing the radiation dose while preserving the image quality would imply lengthening the scan time [4]. However, collecting more counts, either by lengthening scan time or injecting a larger amount of dose, is often impractical: longer scan times will cause patient discomfort and provide a larger chance for patient motion to occur, which can degrade the image quality; injecting large amounts of dose will violate radiation safety principles, which dictate that radiation exposure should be as low as reasonably achievable (ALARA). The ability to limit radiation exposure is especially relevant for vulnerable populations such as pediatric patients, immunocompromised patients, and patients requiring frequent follow-up PET scans. Moreover, from an economic viewpoint, PET scanning is expensive for several reasons: machines and radiotracers (the price of many novel tracers can exceed $2000/dose) are expensive and exams are relatively long, limiting the number of scans that can be performed per day per scanner. The logistics of scheduling patients for scanning also limit the use of PET. These factors taken together impede the scalability of PET studies, such as in large-scale clinical trials.

Biomedical Image Synthesis and Simulation. https://doi.org/10.1016/B978-0-12-824349-7.00025-6

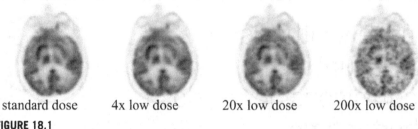

standard dose   4x low dose   20x low dose   200x low dose

FIGURE 18.1

Reconstructions based on list-mode samples demonstrating the tradeoff between image quality (image noise) and dose reduction. Modified from [5].

To collect PET counts more efficiently, hardware approaches could be taken. In current PET scanner models, the scanner typically collects less than 1% of all the coincidence events [6]. With new total-body PET scanners such as the EXPLORER, the effective count rate of the scanner could be increased 40-fold [7]. However, the cost of the scanner (~US $10M for the scanner itself [6]) could be a limiting factor to its widespread use. Hardware approaches are out of the scope of this book, and we will therefore restrict our discussion to potential software improvements.

On the other side of the equation, efforts have been made to tackle the image noise that results from PET reconstructions. As image noise contributes negatively to human visual object recognition [8], in current clinical practice, a post-reconstruction Gaussian filter is applied to smooth out the noise in PET images such that they are more interpretable by the clinicians. In addition, many applications have been devised to denoise PET images [9,10]. As one can imagine, if denoising methods are applied based on current standard dose levels, further degrees of image enhancement will be needed if the counts are further reduced. However, the clinically relevant information in the images must also be preserved without being lost to over-smoothing, which may affect the detectability of lesions. Thus, a balance between noise reduction and image detail must be considered. Irrespective of the technical improvements, there have been studies investigating whether lower-count images could be read directly [11,12]. Although these studies have shown that dose or time reduction can be achieved, perhaps not surprisingly, the uncertainty of the read increases with the amount of count decimation [11]. This shows that there is still a need for methods that further enhance low-count images such that they are interpretable by clinicians. With current software advances including deep learning methods, the lower boundary of counts needed for an interpretable image can be pushed further. These advances involve the modification of the PET imaging pipeline, from before reconstruction (processing in sinogram space), during reconstruction (modification of the reconstruction algorithm), and after reconstruction (post-processing of the reconstructed image) (Fig. 18.2).

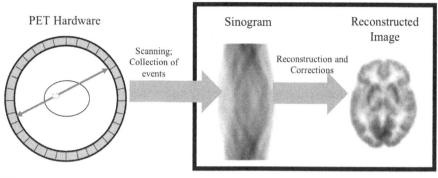

FIGURE 18.2

Schematic of the PET imaging pipeline. Software applications which modify the PET pipeline have been demonstrated in the processing of the sinogram and the reconstructed image as well as in novel reconstruction algorithms (boxed region).

18.2 Significance of low-count imaging

Low-count imaging enables new scanning protocols to be implemented in the clinic and in research studies. The benefits of low-count imaging are manifold, resulting in a "win–win–win" situation for patients, clinicians, and researchers.

18.2.1 Potential low-count imaging protocols

18.2.1.1 Low dose imaging

A lower injected dose brings about the obvious benefit of subjecting those scanned to less ionizing radiation. This also allows the clinic to split doses under current manufactured amounts among multiple subjects, though for many tracers this would reflect "off-label" use. Under current radiation safety regulations, the design of scanning protocols can be more creative and flexible. This includes enabling more frequent follow ups for longitudinal studies, where each of the follow-ups can be performed at a lower injected dose. On the other hand, low-dose imaging abilities will also allow for scanning of subjects with a standard injected dose, but who have a longer radiotracer uptake time than what is typically done, i.e., scanning patients with low effective dose at the scanner will also be possible. Some agents which require long periods of time to bind to desired targets, such as immunological PET approaches using monoclonal antibodies labeled with ^{89}Zr, would benefit from the ability to create improved quality images at lower effective doses [13–15]. Such methods may also accrue benefits at the individual patient level; if a patient arrives late, for example, the reduced counts associated with the "over-decayed" radiotracer could be enhanced to provide better diagnostic quality, rather than requiring waste of the dose and rescheduling of the patient.

18.2.1.2 Short time imaging

The ability to collect fewer counts for an interpretable image also means the ability to collect data (under current dose injection standards) over a shorter period of time. This means a higher throughput of scanned subjects per scanner, increasing the efficiency in which scanners are utilized. Moreover, with subjects spending less time in the scanner, the collected counts will also be less susceptible to cumulative motion of the subject, eliminating some of the potential image blurring effects. This also may make dynamic imaging with short time frames to follow tracer kinetics more robust and feasible. In clinical settings, not only the time on the scanner but the time in radiotracer uptake rooms must be considered, as sometimes the number of rooms for radiotracer uptake can be the limiting factor in terms of total throughput.

18.2.2 Benefits of low-count imaging

18.2.2.1 Radiation dose

It has been shown that a standard [^{18}F]-fluorodeoxyglucose (FDG) PET/computed tomography (CT) scan is associated with an effective radiation dose of around 6–32 mSv, and a 0.5–0.6% increase in lifetime cancer risk [16]. With extremely reduced dose, the equivalent radiation exposure of a subject could be reduced from the order of a couple of head CTs to that from a few trans-continental flights (0.035 mSv per flight, https://www.cdc.gov/nceh/radiation/air_travel.html).

18.2.2.2 Economics

Issues affecting the scalability of PET studies include economic factors such as the cost of the radiotracer and scan time. With low-dose PET imaging techniques, the radiotracer (under current manufacturing standards) could be split among multiple subjects (i.e., if 90% dose reduction could be achieved, one radiotracer dose could be distributed between 10 subjects, with resultant cost savings). On the other hand, tracers with shorter half-lives, such as ^{11}C agents, could also potentially be manufactured at a remote site, which under current standards would not be feasible because of the time spent delivering the tracers. Alternatively, under the short-time scanning regime, scanner throughput could be enhanced to enable more patients to be scanned per day, again reducing cost, since most PET costs (technologist, electricity, siting, etc.) are fixed. This would benefit the operation of the imaging center in cost reduction and/or flexibility in scheduling.

18.2.2.3 New study designs and related logistics

Low-count imaging also opens up the possibilities of new study designs. For example, in the imaging of neurodegenerative diseases, multiple radiotracers have been developed to image multiple different molecular markers contributing to the disease; low-dose imaging could therefore allow for more frequent scanning with multiple tracers under current radiation safety standards. More frequent follow-ups will also help scientists elucidate the spatiotemporal development of the diseases of interest. There is also the potential for more flexibility in the protocol design for dual-tracer studies during the same scanning session. While current dual-tracer scans involve tracers with short half-lives or use advanced methods to disentangle the signals from the two tracers [17–20], low-dose imaging and its enhancement through deep learning will allow the design of protocols such as a scan of a radiotracer at ultra-low-dose with a long half-life followed by a scan of another radiotracer at standard-dose while assuming that the counts collected during the latter portion will drown out those remaining from the earlier portion.

18.3 Overview of methods and examples

In this section, a survey of selected works related to low-count PET imaging will be covered. Methods related to the acquisition of low-count PET data and low-count PET data enhancement, from non-deep learning methods to deep learning methods, and in the general order of model complexity, are included. Finally, methods for evaluating these algorithms will be discussed, as the performance of these algorithms are dependent on the application and the metrics one desires to use.

18.3.1 Low-count PET data generation methods

For current commercial PET models, machine learning approaches can be considered to enhance the low-count image, though such models require training before deployment. When taking a supervised learning approach in applying machine learning-based methods to low-count PET image enhancement, a database of low-count data is required for training. With PET imaging and the ability to save its raw data in list-mode format, there is flexibility to retrospectively extract a subset of the pre-existing data to reconstruct low-count PET images. This is especially relevant in the case of low-dose PET imaging, as actual (rather than simulated) low-dose injections would be the gold standard to obtain actual training data, though few such studies have been done. Therefore, many studies employ simulations to generate low-count images for training.

18.3.1.1 Low-dose data simulation

Some methods proposed in the literature for generating low-dose simulations include list-mode decimation, where the list-mode data are binned into independent subsets of the original data [21,22]. List-mode decimation involves Poisson thinning where the collected annihilation coincidence events (a Poisson process) are randomly assigned into subsets, which also form Poisson processes. The consideration with this approach includes modeling the random events, as the random detection rate increases quadratically while the true detection rate increases linearly [22]. Low-dose simulations reconstructed with this method will show tracer activity reduced by the same factor as the decimation process. Another method used to generate low-dose data is to randomly sample the data by a certain factor in each bin of the PET sinogram, a method which was used by a study to be introduced in Section 18.3.2.2 [23].

18.3.1.2 Low-dose data acquisition

Practical considerations regarding the manufacture and recommended use of radio-tracers limit the number of actual low-dose studies currently performed. The current studies that use the injection of a low radiotracer dose were designed to examine the accuracy of these acquisitions compared to the standard-dose images [22,24], as well as to validate a previously described simulation method [22,25], which gives evidence for the validity of retrospective generation of low-dose images from the PET list-mode files. The low-dose images can then be used for further image enhancement.

18.3.1.3 Short-time data reconstruction

On the other hand, short time frames (with the reconstruction and image corrections performed over a shorter amount of time than the original long-frame image) will produce images with similar uptake as the original reconstructed image, though consideration should be taken in selecting the optimal time interval, since for example, noise properties resulting from the different number of counts collected over time of the reconstructed image would differ depending on the interval chosen for reconstruction, due to radiodecay and changes in biodistribution.

18.3.2 Low-count PET data enhancement methods

Many methods have been devised to synthesize high-quality images from low-count PET data. This section, in line with the scope of this book, will focus on software-based approaches, though as discussed previously hardware approaches such as lengthening the field of view can capture more events for better signal-to-noise ratio properties of the reconstructions. A summary of the methods surveyed in this section is provided in Table 18.1.

18.3.2.1 Non-deep learning methods

Before the popularity of deep learning, there have been studies using traditional machine learning methods as well as direct modification of the reconstruction algorithm to enhance or reconstruct low-count PET data. Kang et al. proposed a regression forest structure to first predict an initial standard-dose FDG PET image from features extracted from the short-time PET (a 3-minute acquisition obtained after the original 12-minute acquisition) and a structural magnetic resonance (MR) image. Then the initial prediction was iteratively refined to improve the quality of the prediction [26].

An et al. employed a multilevel canonical correlation analysis technique to map patches of the short-time PET (a 3-minute acquisition obtained after the original 12-minute acquisition) and the standard-dose FDG PET image to a common space. Then, a subset of the most relevant patches was used to predict the standard-dose image. MR-based patches were similarly used to predict the PET information and the results from the PET-based and the MR-based pipelines were fused [27].

Wang et al. proposed a mapping-based sparse representation where patches from the short-time PET data and multimodal MR data were derived and mapped to a fea-

Table 18.1 Selected low-count PET enhancement methods discussed in this chapter. Abbreviations used: CNN, convolutional neural network; DASB, 3-amino-4-(2-dimethylaminomethylphenylsulfanyl)-benzonitrile; FDG, fluorodeoxyglucose; GAN, generative adversarial network; NHP, non-human primates.

Paper	Method	Body part	Radio-tracer	Inputs	Equivalent dose percentage	Low-count imaging method
Non-Deep Learning Methods						
Kang et al. [26]	Regression forest	Brain	$[^{18}F]$-FDG	PET+MR	~25%	Short frames
An et al. [27]	Canonical correlation analysis	Brain	$[^{18}F]$-FDG	PET+3MR	~25%	Short frames
Wang et al. [28]	Sparse representation	Brain	$[^{18}F]$-FDG	PET+3MR	~25%	Short frames
Wang et al. [29]	Dictionary learning	Brain	$[^{18}F]$-FDG	PET+3MR	~25%	Short frames
Bland et al. [30]	Kernel reconstruction	Brain	$[^{18}F]$-FDG	PET+MR	1%-50%	Decimation
Deep Learning Methods: Processing in the Image Domain						
Xiang et al. [31]	2D CNN	Brain	$[^{18}F]$-FDG	PET+MR	~25%	Short frames
Gong et al. [32]	2D CNN	Brain/ Lung	$[^{18}F]$-FDG	PET	20% (brain)/10% (lung)	Short frames and decimation
Schaef-ferkoetter et al. [33]	3D U-Net	Torso	$[^{18}F]$-FDG	PET	various	Decimation
Spuhler et al. [34]	2D U-Net (dilated kernels)	Brain	$[^{18}F]$-FDG	PET	10%	Decimation
Yang et al. [35]	3D Pyramid network	Whole-body	$[^{18}F]$-FDG	PET+CT	~12.50%	Short frames
Xu et al. [36]	2D U-Net	Brain	$[^{18}F]$-FDG	PET+2MR	0.50%	Decimation
Chen et al. [37]	2D U-Net	Brain	$[^{18}F]$-Florbetaben	PET+3MR	1%	Decimation
Chen et al. [38]	2D U-Net	Brain	$[^{18}F]$-Florbetaben	PET+2MR	~5%	Short frames
da Costa-Luis et al. [39]	3D CNN	Brain	$[^{18}F]$-FDG	PET+MR	1%/10%	Decimation
Wang et al. [40]	3D GAN	Brain	$[^{18}F]$-FDG	PET	~25%	Short frames

continued on next page

Table 18.1 (*continued*)

Paper	Method	Body part	Radio-tracer	Inputs	Equivalent dose percentage	Low-count imaging method
Wang et al. [41]	3D GAN	Brain	[18F]-FDG	PET+3MR	~25%	Short frames
Lu et al. [42]	Convolutional autoencoder/2D and 3D U-Net/GAN	Lung	[18F]-FDG	PET	10%	Decimation
Xue et al. [43]	3D GAN	Whole-body	[18F]-FDG	PET	~50%	Short frames
Gong et al. [44]	Hybrid 2D/3D GAN	Whole-body	[18F]-FDG	PET	20%	Decimation
Ouyang et al. [45]	2D GAN	Brain	[18F]-Florbetaben	PET	1%	Decimation
Lei et al. [46]	3D CycleGAN	Whole-body	[18F]-FDG	PET	~12.50%	Short frames
Zhao et al. [47]	2D CycleGAN	Brain	[18F]-FDG	PET	10%/30%	Decimation
Zhou et al. [48]	2D CycleGAN	Lung	[18F]-FDG	PET	~1%	Decimation
Deep Learning Methods: Processing in the Sinogram Domain						
Sanaat et al. [23]	3D U-Net	Brain	[18F]-FDG	PET	5%	Decimation
Deep Learning Methods: Modified Reconstruction						
Kim et al. [49]	2D CNN	Brain	[11C]-DASB/[18F]-FDG	PET	16.70% (training)/various (testing)	Decimation
Gong et al. [50]	3D U-Net	Whole-body	[18F]-FDG	PET	10% (training)/various (testing)	Decimation
Hashimoto et al. [51]	3D U-Net	Brain (NHP)	[18F]-FDG	PET	20%/10%	Decimation
Gong et al. [52]	3D U-Net	Brain	[18F]-FDG	PET+MR	12.50%	Decimation

ture space which the standard-dose PET data were also mapped to. The underlying assumption of this method is that the short-time PET and MR data in feature space will have a similar distribution as that of the mapping of the standard-dose PET. During training, as the short-time PET and MR data were first mapped to the feature space of the standard-dose PET, the mapped training inputs were used to build the dictionary to predict the standard-dose PET. This output could be fed into subse-

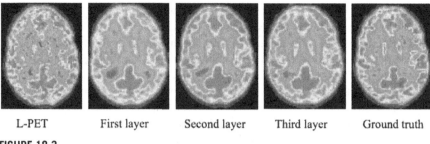

| L-PET | First layer | Second layer | Third layer | Ground truth |

FIGURE 18.3

Representative PET image showing the effect of the incremental refinement of the mapping-based sparse representation approach presented by Wang et al. [28] © Institute of Physics and Engineering in Medicine. Reproduced by permission of IOP Publishing. All rights reserved.

quent layers of the algorithm in place of the original short-time PET input for further refinement of the output (Fig. 18.3) [28].

The same authors also proposed a separate, semi-supervised tripled dictionary learning method for generating PET images from multimodal short-time frame PET and MR data. Instead of using a pre-defined dictionary, the proposed method is used to learn the dictionary atoms that map the relationship between the short-time frame PET and MR input patches with those from the standard-dose PET. Moreover, the proposed method also learns to generate patches in the case of missing certain input modalities [29].

Instead of a post-reconstruction processing algorithm in the image space, incorporating anatomical information or imposing constraints during the reconstruction process (e.g., Bowsher priors [53]) will also improve the signal-to-noise properties of the reconstructed image and thus see potential application in low-count imaging, though likely not explicitly presented as such [54]. One specific example, however, of how modifications in reconstruction could be applied in low-count imaging is the method proposed in Bland et al., where the reconstruction method was modified by incorporating MR-based anatomical information in a kernel formulation, representing the PET images as a combination of MR image-derived basis functions. Through the kernel representation the PET reconstructions are shown to achieve better noise properties and greater anatomical detail, and thus this method was applied to enhance low-dose PET images. The dose levels were varied from 50% to 1% of the original, and the authors found that for simulated images, this reconstruction method achieved comparable similar mean squared error to the ground truth at 10% dose with those reconstructed using traditional expectation maximization methods [30].

18.3.2.2 Deep learning-based methods

With the popularity of deep learning rising since the performance of the AlexNet [55] in the ImageNet challenge (2012), deep neural networks have been applied to multiple disciplines including the medical field. These networks reduce the need for specifically-designed features, instead relying on large amounts of training data and a designated ground truth (in the case of supervised learning) to train the model to perform a specific task. In medical imaging, the convolutional neural network (CNN) has become popular due to its translational equivariance and invariance, where the network is able to pick up features in the images and produce representations of those features irrespective of their position in the field of view [56]. This has allowed the CNN and related networks to be applied to tasks such as segmentation, classification, and image transformation, of which image denoising (or low-count imaging) is a specific example. A variant of the CNN, the U-Net, has also seen widespread application in this field due to its ability to extract features at multiple scales [57].

Since the advent of PET/CT scanners and the development and spread of PET/MR scanners in the past decade, multimodal data are usually present when conducting PET scans. The morphological information obtained with the other modality is often complementary to the functional information of PET, and thus can also be integrated into the low-count imaging networks to better localize the tracer uptake in the synthesized images.

One of the earlier methods, proposed by Xiang et al., was an auto-context deep 2D CNN structure which generated PET images from a short-time frame PET and a structural MR image. The CNN module was applied in succession to refine the output image (Fig. 18.4) [31]. Gong et al. proposed a CNN structure composed of five residual blocks for generating high-quality PET images. As the amount of real training data is an important factor in the performance of the network, the authors proposed a fine-tuning structure where the network was first trained on simulation data and then fine-tuned with real data [32]. Schaefferkoetter et al. used a 3D U-Net structure to capture the uptake information between slices and used a single trained network to denoise low-dose images with various dose reduction levels. They showed through clinical readings that the synthesized images had better image quality and better lesion detection, especially at the lower dose levels, than the traditional Gaussian filter post-processing method [33].

Modifications to the convolution operation are also proposed for low-count imaging. Spuhler et al. used a U-Net with dilated convolutional kernels to avoid overblurring of the resultant image and were able to produce high-quality PET images from 10%-dose PET images [34].

Yang et al. proposed using two pyramid networks, a type of modified CNN, to separately obtain features from the PET and CT information, and then combine them in an attention mechanism to enhance whole-body PET data from ultra-short PET scans [35].

Xu et al. proposed a modified U-Net structure with residual learning to generate FDG PET images from a low-dose PET image (as low as 1/200 of the original) and two simultaneously acquired MR images. Apart from qualitative metrics, the authors also conducted a reader study where radiologists rated the image quality [36]. Chen et al. used a similar structure to generate amyloid PET images from simultaneously acquired PET images and three structural MR images, where the PET images were simulated from 1% of the list-mode data. In this work, expert readers not only

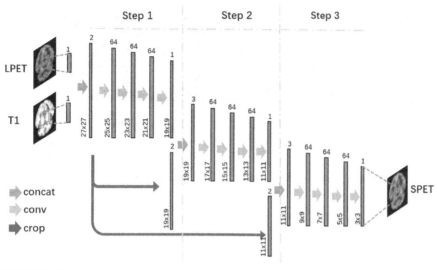

FIGURE 18.4

The deep auto-context convolutional neural network (CNN) architecture proposed by Xiang et al., using three CNN modules to progressively refine the estimation of a standard-dose PET (SPET) image from a low-dose PET (LPET) and a T1-weighted MR image. Image reproduced from [31].

rated the image quality but also read the images as they would in the clinic to assess their diagnostic value (Fig. 18.5) [37]. Building upon this method, the authors also proposed using transfer learning to generate images from short-time PET reconstructions acquired from another site that used a different scanner vendor and suggested that different transfer learning methods should be considered depending on the application [38]. To prevent overfitting on a small number of training datasets, da Costa-Luis et al. proposed using a simpler CNN structure with PET and an MRI input where denoising of the FDG PET images was possible at 1/10 and 1/100 of the original counts [39].

Another class of neural networks called generative adversarial networks (GANs), introduced in Chapter 7 of this book, have also seen their use in medical imaging rise. Devised by Goodfellow et al. [58], this setup pits two networks, the generator and the discriminator, against each other, where the generator aims to produce results close to the ground truth such that they could not be distinguished by the discriminator, which classifies the generated images as "real" or "fake." This network setup will allow the synthesis of images with detailed structure and texture more similar to that of the ground truth.

Wang et al. used a 3D GAN to enhance short-time PET images. The authors compared the proposed method with U-Net-like structures and 2D networks and showed that the 3D GAN network achieved better results. Additionally, the authors also showed the value of using pre-trained low-count imaging networks on different

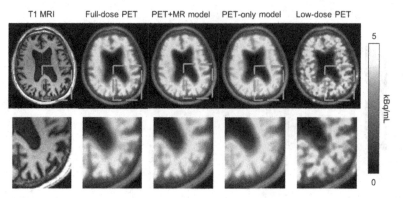

FIGURE 18.5

Representative amyloid-positive patient PET images overlaid onto the T1-weighted MR image. This demonstrated the denoising abilities of the trained models in [37] as well as the importance of the MRI-based anatomical information to more accurately portray the tracer uptake (middle column). Modified from [5].

population groups, where the amount of training data could be reduced [40]. In a related work, the authors also investigated the value of multimodal inputs [41]. Lu et al. compared the performance of different network structures (convolutional autoencoders, U-Nets, and GANs) to enhance 10%-dose lung PET images [42]. Xue et al. proposed a GAN structure where the generator portion employed residual learning and attention models [43]. Gong et al. used a Wasserstein GAN [59], which replaces the classifier discriminator portion with a "critic" neural network that evaluates the realness of the generated image, with hybrid 2D/3D elements along with transfer learning-based methods for low-dose PET enhancement [44]. Finally, Ouyang et al. combined a GAN with additional components such as feature masking and task-specific perceptual loss to generate amyloid PET images from those simulated from 1% of the list-mode data, while also evaluating the contribution of each of the components [45].

Another variant of GANs is the CycleGAN [60], which is also introduced in Chapter 7 and consists of two coupled GANs, each performing the inverse mapping of the other. Lei et al. employed such a structure to generate whole-body PET images from those reconstructed with 1/8 of the original acquisition time (Figs. 18.6, 18.7) [46]. Zhao et al. proposed a CycleGAN structure that employs the adversarial Wasserstein loss, cycle consistency loss, identity loss, and supervised learning loss to produce PET images enhanced from those reconstructed with 10% or 30% of the events. The network was trained and tested on a group of human brain images as well as simulations with artificially embedded FDG-avid lesions for additional testing. The authors also pointed out through the simulation studies that the tradeoff between dose reduction and uptake value accuracy should be considered [47]. A similar approach (CycleGAN with Wasserstein loss) was also proposed by Zhou et al. to enhance images with a fixed number of decimated counts [48].

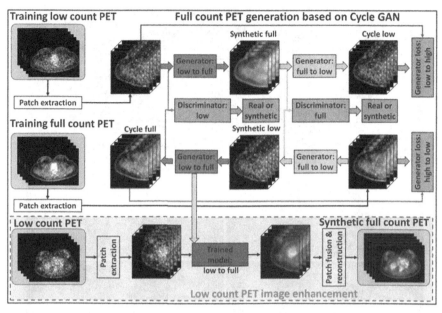

FIGURE 18.6

A schematic of low-count PET synthesis using the cycle-consistent generative adversarial network (CycleGAN). During the training phase, a convolutional neural network was used to generate synthetic full-count patches from the low-count patches, and a discriminator was trained to distinguish between the synthetic and ground-truth full-count patches. The inverse of this process was then performed to generate cycle low-count patches from the synthetic full-count patches. Simultaneously, another network was also trained to synthesize the cycle full-count PET patches from the ground truth full-count PET. During testing, the low-to-full-count portion of the network was used to synthesize a full-count PET image from its low-count counterpart. [46] © Institute of Physics and Engineering in Medicine. Reproduced by permission of IOP Publishing. All rights reserved.

Instead of treating low-count PET image enhancement as an image post-processing problem, studies have also been carried out focusing on image processing in the sinogram space. Sanaat et al. proposed to use a 3D U-Net structure to produce a sinogram that resembles a standard-dose one from low-dose simulations. The low-dose sinograms were produced by randomly extracting 5% of the events from the original. The authors pointed out that this method allows the selection of reconstruction algorithms and post-reconstruction processing methods to be independent of the network training, and also showed the proposed method performed better than an image space-based method (Fig. 18.8) [23].

Similar to what was discussed in the previous section, another approach to low-count PET imaging involves modifying the reconstruction algorithm itself. Kim et al. used a CNN structure along with a local linear fitting function to output images

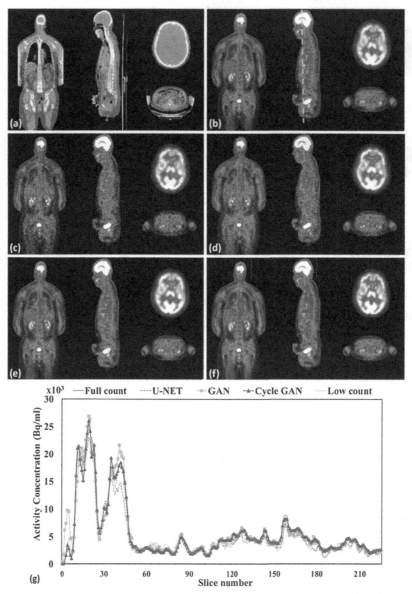

FIGURE 18.7

Sagittal, coronal, and two transverse slices of a whole-body PET image, showing the (a) CT, (b) full-count PET, (c) low-count PET, and low-count PET image processed with the (d) U-Net, (e) generative adversarial network (GAN), and (f) CycleGAN. (g) The PET image profiles following the yellow dashed line on (b) are shown for the full-count, low-count, and the low-count PET images processed with the U-Net, GAN, and CycleGAN. [46] © Institute of Physics and Engineering in Medicine. Reproduced by permission of IOP Publishing. All rights reserved.

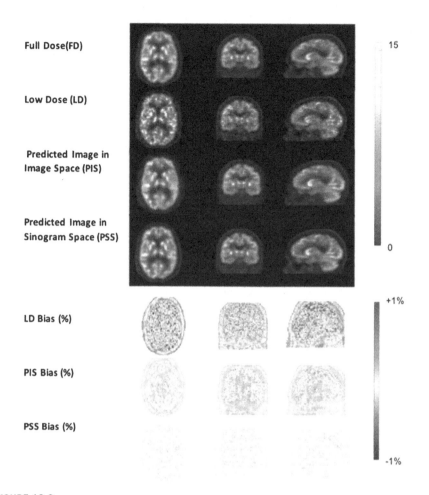

FIGURE 18.8

FDG PET image of a 65-year-old male patient with cognitive symptoms of possible neu-rodegenerative etiology, with the low-dose PET image (second row) and standard-dose image (first row) as reference. The predicted standard-dose PET image enhanced from the decimated low-dose reconstruction (PIS, third row) shows significantly reduced noise compared with low dose PET image, while the image reconstructed from the enhanced decimated sinogram (PSS, fourth row) is superior in reflecting the anatomical features [23]. The bias map for the low-dose, PIS, and PSS images is shown in rows five, six, and seven, respectively. Figure and caption courtesy of Amirhossein Sanaat.

for use as priors in the iterative reconstruction algorithm [49]. Gong et al. proposed using the 3D U-Net-derived image to inform the reconstruction algorithm, similar to the setup where the image to be solved is represented by a combination of kernels [61]. This method allowed reconstruction to be robust to images from various noise

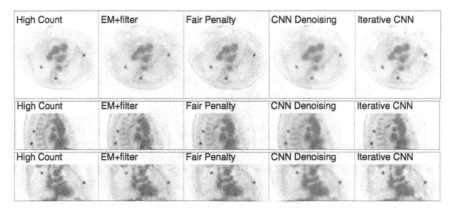

FIGURE 18.9

Transverse, sagittal, and coronal slices of a lung PET image, showing from left to right the high count ground truth, and four low-count image processing methods: Gaussian post-expectation-maximization (EM) reconstruction filtering (standard reconstruction), fair penalty-based penalized reconstruction, convolutional neural network (CNN) denoising based on the method in Chen et al. [63], and the proposed iterative reconstruction method with an embedded CNN [50]. Image courtesy of Kuang Gong.

and dose levels (Fig. 18.9) [50]. On the other hand, images from the deep learning network can be used as priors within the iterative reconstruction algorithm, and both the network and the resulting image can be updated during each iteration. One such example is the deep image prior, which has been shown to be promising in applications regarding inverse problems. With this method, instead of adding a penalty term to the optimization equation and searching for the optimal denoised image in image space, the image is formulated as the output of a deep network and the search is performed in the network's parameter space [62]. Hashimoto et al. used this framework to filter dynamic PET images, demonstrating its use in denoising low-dose data [51], while Gong et al. applied this method and incorporated a 3D U-Net into the maximum likelihood expectation maximization method to high-quality PET images [52].

18.3.3 Method evaluation and application

To evaluate the efficacy of the image enhancement methods, the generated images are compared against the ground-truth image, which is usually the image reconstructed with the data collected under a standard-dose scan. From a quantitative point of view, the performance of the method depends on the similarity (in tracer uptake and image quality) between the images. Examples include using the metrics peak signal-to-noise ratio, structural similarity [64], and root mean square error. The values in each voxel, whether represented as counts, standard uptake values, or normalized ratios to a certain reference region can also be compared across image types to determine the performance of the method. For example, the denoising performance of the network or algorithm can also be measured by the voxel-wise coefficient of variation (mean over standard deviation) in regions of interest [26]. The ratio between different areas of the image (e.g., gray vs. white matter or a tracer-avid lesion vs. background) can also be calculated to assess whether the proposed method is able to recover the contrast between these regions [52].

On the other hand, the PET images are normally used in the clinic through visual assessment of the clinicians. Therefore, a visual inspection of the image quality as well as determining whether the generated images provide the same diagnostic information is equally important in the evaluation of these low-count imaging methods. Examples include rating each image with a five-point Likert scale based on categories such as general image quality, image sharpness, and image noise [33], or evaluating the accuracy of the readings (e.g., lesion detection, amyloid positivity) done on the synthesized images as compared to those done on the standard-dose images. These latter tasks are most relevant to the use of lower count PET but incur high costs in terms of reviewer's time and the known variability between and within individual readers. Also, it is difficult to test all possible "edge" cases for performance, given the long tail of rare diseases in many clinical applications.

To apply these methods, one must keep in mind the application and endpoint metrics of the study. For example, image texture might be more important for studies involving visual reads, since the readers will have bias based on the images they are accustomed to reading. How the images are read will also be a factor in determining efficacy of the algorithms: what the clinicians look for in images that are read as only positive vs. negative (as in amyloid PET) would be different than an FDG image, where uptake in a specific region is often assessed. If metrics such as the standard uptake value ratios or other kinetic parameters are of concern, image texture might not be as big an issue compared with those that rely on visual reads. Regional-based or voxel-based analyses will also have different requirements in terms of image quality, as image noise will be averaged out in region-based studies. In approaching these issues, the authors have started with the basic networks, given the extremely good performance of the U-Net [65], and gradually added complexity as the clinical or analytical needs arise.

18.4 Future directions and research challenges

18.4.1 Practical considerations

Translating the low-count PET imaging technique to the clinic is not a trivial task, as the added flexibility in the imaging protocol compared to current standards requires adjustments to the current setup. First of all, more actual low-count (especially low-dose) imaging studies need to be carried out to validate the use of these radiotracers in a low-dose regime and to compare with simulated studies. This use of the radiotracers (considered off-label if not used at the dose on their label, except for FDG) may face additional FDA scrutiny before seeing routine use. On the other hand, with shorter duration scans potentially increasing the throughput of subjects scanned per day, adjustments such as increasing the number of radiotracer uptake rooms needs to be considered to account for the increased volume of subjects.

18.4.2 Hardware considerations

Using the current PET scanners in an ultra-low dose setting also warrants other additional considerations. One such example is the intrinsic radiation stemming from the scintillating crystals which detect the incoming annihilation photons. Many current PET scanners utilize lutetium-based scintillators, such as cerium-doped lutetium oxyorthosilicate (LSO), due to its high light output, relatively higher density, and short decay time. However, the radioactive isotope, lutetium-176, has a natural abundance of 2.6% and will decay to hafnium-176 predominantly through a beta decay and three gamma emissions, contributing to a background radiation of approximately 300 counts per second per cubic centimeter [66]. In actual low-dose studies, this intrinsic radiation might not be negligible and needs to be taken into consideration for an accurate quantification of the radiotracer of interest. On the other hand, hardware advances outside the scope of this chapter, such as building advanced PET scanners that allow the collection of more coincidence events or transitioning to PET/MRI machines that remove the CT component and thus a large portion of the subject's received dose, are also active areas of research.

18.4.3 Software considerations

Efforts to reduce the injected radiotracer dose further brings about the interesting topic of whether the dose could be eliminated entirely. In this "zero-dose" setup, the issue becomes modality translation, or synthesizing an image of one modality from that of another. While controversial, as PET imaging shows specific functional information, it is possible that such information would be subtly embedded in other imaging modalities and could be teased out through advanced deep learning techniques [5,67]. Current works in the literature have shown the challenges of this method, especially in predicting functional images from structural ones. For example, in predicting an FDG image from a T2-weighted MR image, Rajagopal et al. were able to synthesize an FDG-like image in areas where the organs have consistent uptake, but were unable to do so in organs where the uptake is variable [68]. On the other hand, more promising results were shown when the different imaging modalities measure the same physiological mechanism, such as predicting ^{15}O-water based PET cerebral blood flow images from multiple MRI images, including arterial spin labeling [69].

Bias is another issue that is becoming recognized in the field of artificial intelligence, as the way data are collected and processed can produce results that overfit on or encode characteristics specific to the original training data [70], and is not generalizable to the greater population of interest [71]. The quantitative nature of PET imaging also means that the accuracy of the synthesized PET images and their associated values must be carefully assessed with the application of these methods [72]. To establish utility of these machine learning-based methods, we need to show that the methods generalize to images acquired on other scanners and with other tracers. Previous studies have demonstrated this in smaller datasets where data bias occurs across PET/MRI scanner models, something that needs to be accounted for when applying a CNN trained at one site to data acquired at another [38]; as well as showing that the performance of the CNN improves when the training and testing data are derived from the same patient population [69]. With various PET radiotracers currently being used for imaging, we must also assess the performance of our methods, before applying them to new data acquired with injections from a different radiotracer. Moreover, privacy issues such as sharing patient information as well as data ownership issues limit the ability to collect a large centralized database of medical images from multiple institutions for network training [73–75]; these factors taken together will pose challenges to the generalizability of the low-count imaging methods.

Attenuation correction methods that do not require the CT component will also provide another way to remove potential radiation exposure to the subject and are discussed in Chapter 19.

18.5 Summary

The issues of reducing image noise, lowering radiotracer dose, and shortening acquisition time in PET imaging are deeply intertwined. With advances in image processing, especially with the use of deep learning-based methods, numerous methods have been proposed to overcome the tradeoff between image noise and PET counts. These methods have the potential to significantly impact the radiation risk to subjects, economics, and logistics of both research and clinical PET studies. While promising, further studies (using both simulations and actual low-count acquisitions) are needed to assess their effect on more radiotracers and their actual diagnostic value. Combining these advances with even more sophisticated hardware will enable researchers and clinicians to push the dose reduction to extreme levels, further diminishing one of the most consequential risks of this imaging modality, and thus greatly expanding the modality's utility.

References

[1] S.S. Gambhir, Molecular imaging of cancer with positron emission tomography, Nat. Rev. Cancer 2 (9) (2002) 683–693.

[2] K. Ishii, PET approaches for diagnosis of dementia, Am. J. Neuroradiol. 35 (11) (2014) 2030–2038.

[3] N. Ghosh, et al., Assessment of myocardial ischaemia and viability: role of positron emission tomography, Eur. Heart J. 31 (24) (2010) 2984–2995.

[4] M. Oehmigen, et al., Radiotracer dose reduction in integrated PET/MR: implications from national electrical manufacturers association phantom studies, J. Nucl. Med. 55 (8) (2014) 1361–1367.

[5] G. Zaharchuk, Next generation research applications for hybrid PET/MR and PET/CT imaging using deep learning, Eur. J. Nucl. Med. Mol. Imaging 46 (13) (2019) 2700–2707.

[6] S.R. Cherry, et al., Total-body PET: maximizing sensitivity to create new opportunities for clinical research and patient care, J. Nucl. Med. 59 (1) (2018) 3–12.

[7] R.D. Badawi, et al., First human imaging studies with the EXPLORER total-body PET scanner, J. Nucl. Med. 60 (3) (2019) 299–303.

[8] E.M. Banko, et al., How the visual cortex handles stimulus noise: insights from amblyopia, PLoS ONE 8 (6) (2013).

[9] J. Dutta, R.M. Leahy, Q. Li, Non-local means denoising of dynamic PET images, PLoS ONE 8 (12) (2013) e81390.

[10] A. Le Pogam, et al., Denoising of PET images by combining wavelets and curvelets for improved preservation of resolution and quantitation, Med. Image Anal. 17 (8) (2013) 877–891.

[11] F. Schiller, et al., Limits for reduction of acquisition time and administered activity in (18)F-FDG PET studies of Alzheimer dementia and frontotemporal dementia, J. Nucl. Med. 60 (12) (2019) 1764–1770.

[12] S. Tiepolt, et al., Influence of scan duration on the accuracy of beta-amyloid PET with florbetaben in patients with Alzheimer's disease and healthy volunteers, Eur. J. Nucl. Med. Mol. Imaging 40 (2) (2013) 238–244.

[13] E.C. Dijkers, et al., Development and characterization of clinical-grade ^{89}Zr-trastuzumab for HER2/neu immunoPET imaging, J. Nucl. Med. 50 (6) (2009) 974–981.

[14] O.F. Ikotun, et al., Imaging the L-type amino acid transporter-1 (LAT1) with Zr-89 immunoPET, PLoS ONE 8 (10) (2013) e77476.

[15] W. Wei, et al., ImmunoPET: concept, design, and applications, Chem. Rev. 120 (8) (2020) 3787–3851.

[16] B. Huang, M.W. Law, P.L. Khong, Whole-body PET/CT scanning: estimation of radiation dose and cancer risk, Radiology 251 (1) (2009) 166–174.

[17] C. Bell, et al., Design and utilisation of protocols to characterise dynamic PET uptake of two tracers using basis pursuit, Phys. Med. Biol. 62 (12) (2017) 4897–4916.

[18] G. El Fakhri, et al., Dual-tracer PET using generalized factor analysis of dynamic sequences, Mol. Imaging Biol. 15 (6) (2013) 666–674.

[19] A.D. Joshi, et al., Signal separation and parameter estimation in noninvasive dual-tracer PET scans using reference-region approaches, J. Cereb. Blood Flow Metab. 29 (7) (2009) 1346–1357.

[20] R.A. Koeppe, et al., Dual-[11C]tracer single-acquisition positron emission tomography studies, J. Cereb. Blood Flow Metab. 21 (12) (2001) 1480–1492.

[21] S. Gatidis, et al., Towards tracer dose reduction in PET studies: simulation of dose reduction by retrospective randomized undersampling of list-mode data, Hell. J. Nucl. Med. 19 (1) (2016) 15–18.

[22] J. Schaefferkoetter, et al., Low dose positron emission tomography emulation from decimated high statistics: a clinical validation study, Med. Phys. 46 (6) (2019) 2638–2645.

[23] A. Sanaat, et al., Projection-space implementation of deep learning-guided low-dose brain PET imaging improves performance over implementation in image-space, J. Nucl. Med. (2020).

[24] D. Fallmar, et al., Validation of true low-dose (18)F-FDG PET of the brain, Eur. J. Nucl. Med. Mol. Imaging 6 (5) (2016) 269–276.

[25] K.T. Chen, et al., True ultra-low-dose amyloid PET/MRI enhanced with deep learning for clinical interpretation, Eur. J. Nucl. Med. Mol. Imaging (2021).

[26] J. Kang, et al., Prediction of standard-dose brain PET image by using MRI and low-dose brain [18F]FDG PET images, Med. Phys. 42 (9) (2015) 5301–5309.

[27] L. An, et al., Multi-level canonical correlation analysis for standard-dose PET image estimation, IEEE Trans. Image Process. 25 (7) (2016) 3303–3315.

[28] Y. Wang, et al., Predicting standard-dose PET image from low-dose PET and multimodal MR images using mapping-based sparse representation, Phys. Med. Biol. 61 (2) (2016) 791–812.

[29] Y. Wang, et al., Semisupervised tripled dictionary learning for standard-dose PET image prediction using low-dose PET and multimodal MRI, IEEE Trans. Biomed. Eng. 64 (3) (2017) 569–579.

[30] J. Bland, et al., MR-guided kernel EM reconstruction for reduced dose PET imaging, IEEE Trans. Radiat. Plasma Med. Sci. 2 (3) (2018) 235–243.

[31] L. Xiang, et al., Deep auto-context convolutional neural networks for standard-dose PET image estimation from low-dose PET/MRI, Neurocomputing 267 (2017) 406–416.

[32] K. Gong, et al., PET image denoising using a deep neural network through fine tuning, IEEE Trans. Radiat. Plasma Med. Sci. 3 (2) (2019) 153–161.

[33] J. Schaefferkoetter, et al., Convolutional neural networks for improving image quality with noisy PET data, EJNMMI Res. 10 (1) (2020) 105.

[34] K. Spuhler, et al., Full-count PET recovery from low-count image using a dilated convolutional neural network, Med. Phys. (2020).

[35] X. Yang, et al., CT-aided low-count whole-body PET imaging using cross-modality attention pyramid network, J. Nucl. Med. 61 (Supplement 1) (2020) 1416.

[36] J. Xu, et al., Ultra-low-dose 18F-FDG brain PET/MR denoising using deep learning and multi-contrast information, in: SPIE Medical Imaging, 2020, Houston, TX.

[37] K.T. Chen, et al., Ultra-low-dose (18)F-florbetaben amyloid PET imaging using deep learning with multi-contrast MRI inputs, Radiology 290 (3) (2019) 649–656.

[38] K.T. Chen, et al., Generalization of deep learning models for ultra-low-count amyloid PET/MRI using transfer learning, Eur. J. Nucl. Med. Mol. Imaging (2020).

[39] C.O. da Costa-Luis, A.J. Reader, Micro-networks for robust MR-guided low count PET imaging, IEEE Trans. Radiat. Plasma Med. Sci. (2020).

[40] Y. Wang, et al., 3D conditional generative adversarial networks for high-quality PET image estimation at low dose, NeuroImage 174 (2018) 550–562.

[41] Y. Wang, et al., 3D auto-context-based locality adaptive multi-modality GANs for PET synthesis, IEEE Trans. Med. Imaging 38 (6) (2019) 1328–1339.

[42] W. Lu, et al., An investigation of quantitative accuracy for deep learning based denoising in oncological PET, Phys. Med. Biol. 64 (16) (2019) 165019.

[43] H. Xue, et al., A 3D attention residual encoder–decoder least-square GAN for low-count PET denoising, Nucl. Instrum. Methods Phys. Res., Sect. A, Accel. Spectrom. Detect. Assoc. Equip. 983 (2020) 164638.

[44] Y. Gong, et al., Parameter-transferred Wasserstein generative adversarial network (PT-WGAN) for low-dose PET image denoising, arXiv:1910.06749, 2020.

[45] J. Ouyang, et al., Ultra-low-dose PET reconstruction using generative adversarial network with feature matching and task-specific perceptual loss, Med. Phys. 46 (8) (2019) 3555–3564.

[46] Y. Lei, et al., Whole-body PET estimation from low count statistics using cycle-consistent generative adversarial networks, Phys. Med. Biol. 64 (21) (2019) 215017.

[47] K. Zhao, et al., Study of low-dose PET image recovery using supervised learning with CycleGAN, PLoS ONE 15 (9) (2020) e0238455.

[48] L. Zhou, et al., Supervised learning with cyclegan for low-dose FDG PET image denoising, Med. Image Anal. 65 (2020) 101770.

[49] K. Kim, et al., Penalized PET reconstruction using deep learning prior and local linear fitting, IEEE Trans. Med. Imaging 37 (6) (2018) 1478–1487.

[50] K. Gong, et al., Iterative PET image reconstruction using convolutional neural network representation, IEEE Trans. Med. Imaging 38 (3) (2019) 675–685.

[51] F. Hashimoto, et al., Dynamic PET image denoising using deep convolutional neural networks without prior training datasets, IEEE Access 7 (2019) 96594–96603.

[52] K. Gong, et al., PET image reconstruction using deep image prior, IEEE Trans. Med. Imaging 38 (7) (2019) 1655–1665.

[53] J.E. Bowsher, et al., Utilizing MRI information to estimate F18-FDG distributions in rat flank tumors, in: IEEE Nuclear Science Symp. Cpnf. Record, 2004, pp. 2488–2492.

[54] K.T. Chen, et al., An efficient approach to perform MR-assisted PET data optimization in simultaneous PET/MR neuroimaging studies, J. Nucl. Med. (2018).

[55] A. Krizhevsky, I. Sutskever, G.E. Hinton, ImageNet classification with deep convolutional neural networks, in: Neural Information Processing Systems, 2012, Lake Tahoe, Nevada.

[56] A.S. Lundervold, A. Lundervold, An overview of deep learning in medical imaging focusing on MRI, Z. Med. Phys. 29 (2) (2019) 102–127.

[57] O. Ronneberger, P. Fischer, T. Brox, U-Net: Convolutional Networks for Biomedical Image Segmentation, 2015.

[58] I.J. Goodfellow, et al., Generative adversarial nets, in: Advances in Neural Information Processing Systems 27 (Nips 2014), 2014.

[59] M. Arjovsky, S. Chintala, L. Bottou, Wasserstein GAN, arXiv:1701.07875, 2017.

[60] J.-Y. Zhu, et al., Unpaired image-to-image translation using cycle-consistent adversarial networks, arXiv:1703.10593, 2017.

[61] G. Wang, J. Qi, PET image reconstruction using kernel method, IEEE Trans. Med. Imaging 34 (1) (2015) 61–71.

[62] D. Ulyanov, A. Vedaldi, V. Lempitsky, Deep image prior, arXiv:1711.10925, 2017.

[63] H. Chen, et al., Low-dose CT via convolutional neural network, Biomed. Opt. Express 8 (2) (2017) 679–694.

[64] Z. Wang, et al., Image quality assessment: from error visibility to structural similarity, IEEE Trans. Image Process. 13 (4) (2004) 600–612.

[65] A. Hauptmann, J. Adler, On the unreasonable effectiveness of CNNs, arXiv:2007. 14745v1, 2020.

[66] F. Wilkinson III, Scintillators, in: M.N. Wernick, J.N. Aarsvold (Eds.), Emission Tomography: The Fundamentals of PET and SPECT, Academic Press, 2004, pp. 229–254.

[67] G. Zaharchuk, G. Davidzon, AI for optimization and interpretation of PET/CT and PET/MR images, Semin. Nucl. Med. (2020).

[68] A. Rajagopal, et al., Deep learning-based MR-derived PET prediction for patient-conforming PET phantoms, J. Nucl. Med. 61 (Supplement 1) (2020) 1417.

[69] J. Guo, et al., Predicting (15)O-Water PET cerebral blood flow maps from multi-contrast MRI using a deep convolutional neural network with evaluation of training cohort bias, J. Cereb. Blood Flow Metab. (2019) 271678X19888123.

[70] R. Steed, A. Caliskan, Image representations learned with unsupervised pre-training contain human-like biases, arXiv:2010.15052, 2020.

[71] J. Zou, L. Schiebinger, AI can be sexist and racist — it's time to make it fair, Nature 559 (2018) 324–326.

[72] L.K. Shiyam Sundar, et al., Potentials and caveats of AI in hybrid imaging, Methods (2020).

[73] K. Chang, et al., Distributed deep learning networks among institutions for medical imaging, J. Am. Med. Inform. Assoc. 25 (8) (2018) 945–954.

[74] M.J. Sheller, et al., Multi-institutional deep learning modeling without sharing patient data: a feasibility study on brain tumor segmentation, Brainlesion 11383 (2019) 92–104.

[75] P. McClure, et al., Distributed weight consolidation: a brain segmentation case study, in: Advances in Neural Information Processing Systems 31 (NeurIPS 2018), 2018.

PET/MRI attenuation correction

Claes N. Ladefoged and Anders B. Olin

Department of Clinical Physiology and Nuclear Medicine, Rigshospitalet, Copenhagen, Denmark

19.1 Correction of photon attenuation

Detailed insight into a patient's anatomy and physiology by non-invasive medical imaging is an important tool in modern medicine to detect, diagnose, and monitor diseases, as well as plan treatment. Positron emission tomography (PET) is a unique imaging technique for identifying normal and abnormal functional processes in the body in a quantifiable manner. PET is an essential non-invasive clinical tool for obtaining correct diagnosis in especially oncology, cardiology, and neurology [1–3].

PET imaging visualizes the distribution of a radioisotope-labeled substance (radiotracer), which is injected into a patient prior to or during PET examination. How the substance distributes depends on its characteristics, making PET a versatile technique as different radiotracers offer visualization of different physiological processes. An example is the primary workhorse of PET examinations, [18F] fluorodeoxyglucose ([18F]FDG), a glucose-analog which is taken up by high-glucose-using cells, often used in oncology and neurology. Within the body, the decay of a radioisotope emits a positron that travels a short distance before colliding with an electron resulting in an annihilation—an event that produces a pair of gamma photons propagating in approximately opposite directions, each with the energy of 511 keV. The scanner can detect these photons using a ring of detectors outside the scanned volume; two photons are assumed to originate from the same source if they arrive at a pair of detectors within a defined timing window. The annihilation event is then considered to have occurred somewhere along a line of response (LOR), which connects these two detectors. In PET systems with so-called time-of-flight (TOF), the time difference between arrival of the two photons can be used to narrow down the event location on the LOR. The collection of LORs gathered over an acquisition period can be used to reconstruct PET images.

Meanwhile, to obtain accurate PET images, it is important perform several corrections [4] – an essential one being correction of photon attenuation. It is very likely that the photons will interact with matter as they travel through the body, either preventing them from reaching the detector (attenuation) or resulting in false LORs not passing through the true site of annihilation (scattered events). See Fig. 19.1A for illustrations of these effects. The probability of photon attenuation increases with tis-

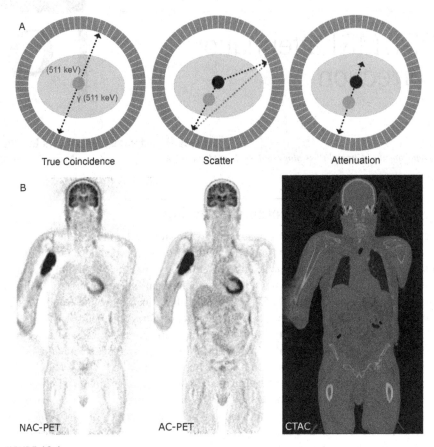

FIGURE 19.1

(A) Diagram of a PET detector ring with annihilation event (red stars – mid gray in print version) producing photons (γ) that are either detected as a true coincidence or undergo interaction with matter (black stars) resulting in scatter or attenuation. (B) Example of a PET image before and after correction for attenuation and scatter (NAC-PET and AC-PET) using CT-based AC (CTAC). Notice differences in background noise and redistribution of activity within the scanned volume.

sue density and path length through the tissue. As a result, the reconstructed PET images will be more affected in the center of a volume and near high-density tissue, compared to areas near the surface and in low-density tissue.

Attenuation correction (AC) restores the true tissue activity but requires a mapping of the attenuating properties or linear attenuation coefficient (LAC) values of the patient's body—called an attenuation map. Traditionally in stand-alone PET scanners, the attenuation factor is measured as the ratio between a transmission scan, where a radioactive source is rotated around the patient prior to radiotracer injection, and a baseline scan without the patient (blank scan). Unfortunately, these scans produce noisy images and are time consuming.

PET is rarely performed alone today, as it exclusively provides functional information and therefore relies on other imaging modalities, such as computed tomography (CT) and magnetic resonance imaging (MRI), to provide complementary structural information. Dual modality scanners, e.g., combining PET and CT (PET/CT), allow for sequential acquisition of anatomical and functional information without the need to reposition patients. As a secondary benefit, CT provides images that can be rescaled to an estimate of an attenuation map to perform CT-based AC (CTAC) of PET [5]. An example of a PET image before and after correction for scatter and attenuation using CTAC is shown in Fig. 19.1B. However, CT images have an inherently low soft-tissue contrast, which for many applications makes an additional MRI scan a necessity at the expense of extra costs, logistics management, patient comfort, but also potential spatial misalignment between scan sessions.

MRI excels over CT in that it provides superior soft tissue contrast and spares the patient from ionizing radiation, while also being able to obtain functional information such as perfusion and diffusion imaging for functional tissue characterization. Therefore, the desire to combine functional PET with the strengths of MRI into a "one-stop-shop" solution has – despite many technical challenges [6] – led to the creation of four commercially available PET/MRI systems. Phillips Healthcare first introduced their sequential PET/MRI system with TOF support (Ingenuity TF) in January 2010. This was soon after in November 2010 followed by Siemens Healthineers who installed a fully-integrated PET/MRI system (Biograph mMR), and later in 2011 by General Electric (GE) Healthcare who introduced a TOF capable PET/MRI system (SIGNA). Recently, in 2018, United Imaging Healthcare released their fully-integrated TOF PET/MRI (uPMR 790). The fully-integrated design, employed by three of the vendors, allows for simultaneous data acquisition from both modalities, which ensures better image alignment, reduced scan time, and offers more accurate methods for data correction (e.g., motion and partial volume effect [7,8]) and image reconstruction (e.g., joint reconstruction [9]), as well as advanced tissue characterization by combined data analysis of multiple functional parameters [10].

A concern for PET/MRI is the challenge of performing attenuation correction without a readily available transmission scan. One strategy is to perform MRI-based attenuation correction (MRAC), but this is nontrivial, since the MRI signal is related to proton density and holds no clear relationship to photon attenuation, preventing a straightforward rescaling of intensities as done in CTAC. This is evident when considering bone and air (Fig. 19.2), which both result in almost no MRI signal despite having some of the highest and lowest attenuating densities, respectively. Especially this ambiguity between the bone and air makes it difficult to utilize MRI intensities for deriving attenuation maps, and is further complicated by several other artifacts. An example is presence of metal objects (e.g., hip and dental implants) that can corrupt the MRI to a degree where there is a complete lack of signal in an area exceeding the metal object itself [11]. Thus, attenuation correction has proven to be one of the most challenging issues with PET/MRI, and even a decade after the introduction of the first clinical PET/MRI system it is still an active research area.

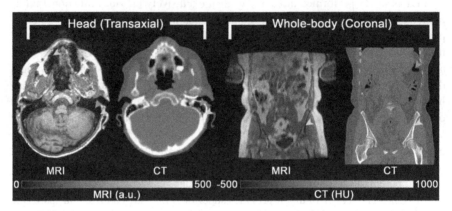

FIGURE 19.2

No direct relationship between MRI intensities and CT Hounsfield Units (HU). Arrows indicate areas of bone (yellow – light gray in print version) and air (red – mid gray in print version). Notice that the areas represent opposite extremes on the CT image, whereas on the MRI, both areas result in lack of signal.

19.2 Implications of inaccurate attenuation correction

Inaccurate attenuation correction not only affects quantitative properties of PET (i.e., the measured activity at a given location), but also locally distorts the visual representation of the tracer distribution. An example of inaccurate MRAC that could potentially obscure correct diagnosis is demonstrated in Fig. 19.3. Initial vendor-provided solutions for attenuation correction in the PET/MRI systems, some of which are still in use today, are based on a segmentation of dedicated MR images into classes of fat, lung, soft tissue, and air/background, where each class is assigned a predefined fixed LAC value [12,13]. Most of these methods rely on the Dixon MRI sequence, which provides water and fat images well-suited for soft tissue segmentation—but without the ability to represent the bone class. An example of the Dixon MRI, the 4-class attenuation map and an aligned reference CT is shown in Fig. 19.4.

Studies comparing PET with MRAC to the same PET with CTAC as reference have shown a general underestimation and a spatially varying error of PET values, which primarily can be attributed to the lack of bone in the attenuation maps [14,15]. The quantitative error is highest in the brain, because the relative amount of bone is high, and the skull furthermore surrounds the brain, thus affecting all LORs. Consequently, not accounting for bone affects the quantification with underestimations reaching 25% in the cortical structures closest to bone areas, and radially decreasing to 5% underestimation in the center of the brain [15]. When imaging regions outside

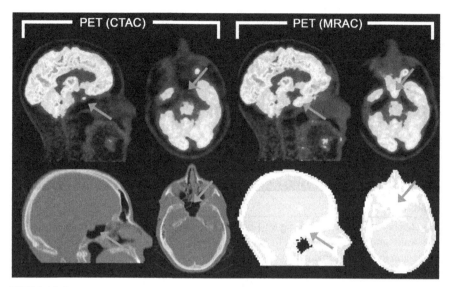

FIGURE 19.3

Inaccurate attenuation correction jeopardizes correct clinical reading of PET. PET image re-construction with CTAC or MRAC respectively result in different estimates of the PET-tracer distribution due to erroneous classification of air as tissue (arrows) in the MRAC map. The errors leads to a wrongfully increased PET uptake, which can be misinterpreted as tumor tissue.

the head, which we will refer to as whole-body, the error of neglecting bone is limited to areas in or near the bone. Samarin et al. reported an 11% average underestimation of PET uptake in bone lesions when failing to account for bone tissue [14], and Aznar et al. confirmed this finding, reporting underestimation exceeding 20% in some cases [16].

The impact of these errors in a clinical setting depends on the use case. When the PET images are used qualitatively, e.g., for detection, staging, or diagnosis of a disease, absolute quantification might be less important, and with a knowledge of the systematic bias, confident diagnosis can often still be reached in the majority of the clinical patients [17]. In neurology, it was shown that the cortical underes-timation in amyloid PET uptake did not alter the clinical diagnosis compared to CTAC [18]. In oncology, the underestimation could potentially affect small lesion or node detectability [16]. Nevertheless, several authors have reported identical de-tection rates of bone and pulmonary lesions when reading PET based on CTAC and MRAC [19,20], and recently, use of MRAC methods without bone was deemed ade-quate to assess pediatric sarcoma and prostate cancer patients [21,22].

The impact of MRAC related errors are larger when the PET images are assumed to be quantitative and thereby used directly as a prognostic factor or for diagnosis.

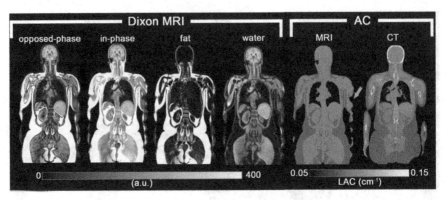

FIGURE 19.4

Dixon MRI is an option for deriving MRI-based attenuation map. The Dixon sequence provides water and fat images arising from in-phase and opposed-phase images. MRI-based attenuation map is a segmentation of the images into of air, lung, fat, and soft tissue, but ignores bone as seen on the aligned CT. The arrow points to areas with truncation due to a narrow transaxial MRI field-of-view.

In oncology, absolute tumor uptake level is important to distinguish between benign and malignant processes, estimate prognosis, decide treatment strategy, and get an insight into tumor grade and cell differentiation [23–26]. The non-uniformity of the error associated with the brain influences use of reference regions for normalization of activity and kinetic modeling [27–30]. This was demonstrated by Ladefoged et al., who showed that differentiating brain tumor tissue from reactive changes due to radiation therapy can be obscured by inaccurate attenuation correction [31]. The shape of the biological tumor volume was distorted in more than 1/3 of the 68 evaluated examinations, e.g., illustrated for one patient with overestimated volume due to incorrect tissue segmentation in the nasal cavities (Fig. 19.5).

The greatest sources of error other than neglecting bone in whole-body MRAC are related to metal implant-induced artifacts, involuntary and non-rigid motion (e.g., cardiac and breathing), coil-related signal variations, and truncation artifacts (Fig. 19.4) due to the MRI scanner bore having a smaller transaxial field-of-view (FOV) than the PET (approx. 45 vs 60 cm) [11,17,32,33]. Metal artifacts can obscure or completely obliterate the PET signal, challenging a clinical reading [34,35], and truncation have been shown to lead to a significant reduction in lesion activity [36]. The size and shape of the artifacts can often vary between scans, which complicates use of PET/MRI. This is especially important for treatment monitoring or treatment response evaluation (e.g., using PERCIST criteria [37]) where patients are followed over time. A study of non-small cell lung cancer patients showed how the lack of reproducible MRAC, primarily caused by motion-induced artifacts, resulted in inconsistent PET values with errors exceeding 20% potentially impacting the treatment planning [38].

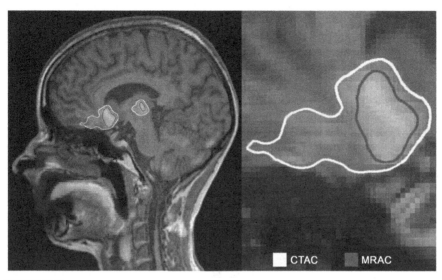

FIGURE 19.5

Inaccurate attenuation correction biases quantitative evaluation of the O-(2-(18)F-fluoroethyl)-L-tyrosine (FET) PET uptake. MRAC using 4-class Dixon resulted in over-estimated tumor volume compared to PET with CTAC. Figure adapted from Frontiers in Neuroscience [31].

Absolute quantification becomes extremely important when the PET/MRI system is used as a research tool (e.g., for pre-clinical and drug development studies). True quantification requires that all of the above shortcomings of MRAC must be addressed. The challenges of the initial vendor-provided solutions have hampered the usability and dissemination of PET/MRI, both for clinical and research applications, especially in neurology and neuro-oncology where the modality otherwise has been considered a game changer [39].

19.3 History of PET/MRI attenuation correction

The topic of attenuation correction for PET/MRI has been an active field of research since before the first commercially available system arrived in 2010. Having to infer the attenuation map rather than estimating it, as is the case with PET/CT, has proven to be difficult even a decade later. The present section focuses on the various approaches to synthesize attenuation maps grouped into four major categories: segmentation, atlas, emission, and deep learning. The highlighted methods do not make for a comprehensive list, but were chosen because they provide an overview of the research development throughout the years in the field. Due to the apparent application of PET/MRI in neurology and the associated challenges by neglecting bone, most of the described methods have been developed for head MRAC.

19.3.1 Segmentation-based

In segmentation-based MRAC, an acquired predefined MRI sequence is post-processed by dividing the image into a number of classes, each representing an underlying tissue type with associated attenuation coefficients. We refer to Chapter 4 for an explanation of image-based segmentation. This category of methods requires a priori knowledge about the number of expected classes (e.g., air, lung, fat, soft tissue, and bone). The first segmentation-based methods, mainly based on the Dixon MRI sequence, ignored the bone class due to the limited or non-existing MRI signal in bone caused by its short relaxation time. Nevertheless, all four manufacturers of clinical PET/MRI systems opted for this approach as their initial head and/or whole-body MRAC method [12,13,40,41].

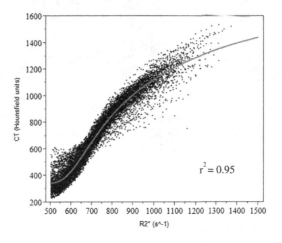

FIGURE 19.6

Continuous bone information extracted using a sigmoid mapping function between MRI (measured with UTE-derived R2 signal) and CT bone voxels. Figure originally published in NeuroImage [42].

The severe PET quantification bias due to the lack of bone (see Section 19.2) gave rise to a second generation of segmentation-based methods capable of segmenting bone by utilizing specialized MRI sequences with short echo time. The two most used sequences, ultrashort echo time (UTE) and zero echo time (ZTE), are able to display a signal in cortical bone (i.e., dense bone) that can be separated from soft tissue, and thereafter scaled to attenuation coefficients. One of the first methods utilizing UTE to represent the bone class by a single constant value was implemented on the Siemens Biograph mMR as a product for head MRAC in 2013 [43,44]. The addition of bone reduced the overall bias, but a significant cortical PET underestimation as high as 15% remained, which was attributed to inaccurate bone segmentation and a lack of intra-subject bone density variation [45,46]. Thus, several authors proposed to map the bone signal of UTE to continuous CT values (Fig. 19.6) [46,42,47]. This removed the radial bias and lowered the average PET error to $< 5\%$. A similar approach for

ZTE-based segmentation with continuous bone representation was implemented for head MRAC on the GE SIGNA [48].

Unfortunately, utilizing bone signal from UTE or ZTE are associated with a high amount of noise at the interface between air and tissue. For the head this typically materializes at the sinuses and skull base [45,49]. The noise translates into wrongfully assigned bone areas and results in overestimated PET activity of up to 25%. Spatial awareness achieved by aligning the UTE to an anatomical template was suggested to limit tissue misclassification in areas with known air/tissue interface-related errors, reducing regional PET errors to 1% in any region of the brain in a study with 154 patients [46]. The same spatial awareness approach was later suggested for the ZTE sequence, yielding statistically significant bias reduction [50]. To avoid co-registering anatomical templates, it was suggested to automatically identify noisy regions by morphological processing and edge detection [51].

The use of UTE and ZTE outside the head is limited due to the low FOV of the sequences (approximately 34 cm). Attempts to increase the FOV are associated with progressively increasing artifacts, increased sensitivity towards motion due to longer acquisition times, or lower image resolution, all of which impede the image quality and identification of bone [52,53]. Thus, at the expense of increasing scan time, it was proposed to combine the short echo time sequence (UTE/ZTE) with the traditional Dixon sequence into a hybrid segmentation approach both for thorax and pelvis [54,55]. Adding bone to the pelvis reduced the underestimation from 11% to 3% in bone lesions and from 8% to 4% in soft tissue lesions.

19.3.2 Atlas-based

The atlas-based category covers a range of methods, which usually rely on co-registration of an atlas database of one or more CT images (often with paired MRI) to the incoming patient MRI. The aligned CT(s) can then be used to synthesize the final attenuation map. The atlas either consists of a single patient (single-atlas), a single template obtained by anatomically aligning and averaging several patients (template), or multiple patients (multi-atlas). We refer to Chapter 4 for explanation of the techniques behind the registration-based MRAC methods introduced below. A variation of the multi-atlas methods is the patch-based methods for which an atlas of patches are used rather than full volumes (see also Chapter 5).

The first atlas-based methods were proposed before the first commercial scanner [56,57], and it was demonstrated how warping a single atlas CT to the MRI of a patient through deformable registration resulted in an effective method for head MRAC [58]. The single-atlas approach depends on the general representativeness of the subject used in the atlas and the accuracy of the registration between the incoming MRI and the atlas.

Template-based methods reflect a wider patient population as the atlas is an average of multiple patients. For head MRAC, it was proposed to align a CT template to a patient MRI by specifically matching the bone in the CT template to a bone-enhanced version of the patient MRI [59]. The method removed the 5% average PET underestimation in 13 patients when neglecting bone, and was later implemented for head MRAC in the GE SIGNA system. To enhance the local registration accuracy, it was suggested to utilize a segmentation-tool to derive six tissue classes from the patient MRI, which was then non-rigidly registered to a template of average tissue classes with an aligned template CT [60]. However, similar to single-atlas methods, template-methods accuracy are determined by the precision of the single registration.

Multi-atlas approaches partially compensate for the mis-registration issue by relying on multiple registrations between atlas MR images and patient MRI. It was suggested to use a local morphological similarity measure to identify the best matching atlas MR images, and fuse the corresponding atlas CT images at voxel-level weighted by the MRI similarity to provide the final patient CT (Fig. 19.7) [61]. The approach significantly improved the accuracy compared to selecting only the single best matching atlas despite having a lower sharpness. To enhance the sharpness, it was suggested to only base the fusion step on atlas CTs belonging to the modal tissue class for each voxel [62], or alternatively to iteratively co-register the deformed CTs to their joint mean [63].

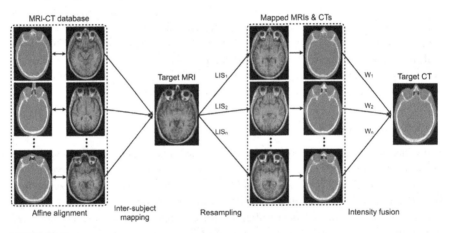

FIGURE 19.7

CT synthesis diagram for a given MRI image. All the MRIs in the atlas set are registered to the target MRI. The CTs in the atlas set are then mapped using the same transformation to the target MRI. A local similarity measure (LIS) between the mapped and target MRIs is converted to weights (W) to reconstruct the target CT. Figure originally published in Transactions on Medical Imaging [61].

Multi-atlas approaches are often limited by slow processing time (30–120 minutes) from the many registrations [64]. An alternative approach is to extract patches from the patient MRI and match against MRI/CT atlas patches based on their similarity. The search space for patch candidates can be restricted by the anatomical distance between the patches (e.g., within $11 \times 11 \times 11$ voxels) when the patient MRI is registered to atlas space using a single registration. This approach, denoted patch-based, assumes that similar intensity normalized patches represent similar composition of tissue densities. The identified CT patches can be weighted and combined based on the non-linear similarity of the MRI patches, e.g., by computing the similarity index using the L^2-norm for each candidate patch [65] or using a local diffeomorphic mapping [66]. A Bayesian framework for identifying and combining the most relevant atlas patches was proposed for UTE-based head MRAC, which was shown to be more accurate than a multi-atlas approach in cases with abnormal anatomy [67]. Contrary to the other atlas-based methods that will always insert a CT value even in areas with no MRI signal due to, e.g., metal artifacts, the patch based approach might not find a candidate patch with sufficiently high similarity score. It was suggested to regularize these cases by assigning such voxels by the median of the neighborhood, mimicking the behavior of the atlas-based methods [68].

Atlas approaches for whole-body MRAC is challenging due to large inter-patient variation and intra-patient non-rigid motion between MRI and CT relevant for generation of the atlases. It was proposed to overcome the inter-patient variation by identifying the single most relevant CT from a multi-atlas database based on patient demographics (such as sex, height, and age), and only superimposing CT bone into a pre-segmented Dixon MRAC map, which decreased the PET bias from -15% to 1% across 12 patients [69]. Similarly, it was proposed to represent the major bones in the body (i.e., femur, hip, spine, and skull) by a database of 200 regional MRI with supplementary bone models extracted from CT images. The regional database MR images are non-linearly aligned to local areas in the patient MRI identified as likely containing a major bone, and the subsequently warped bone model is used to superimpose continuous bone information to a Dixon MRAC map. The approach demonstrated a reduction in bone tissue bias from -25% to -5% across 20 patients, and was implemented for both head and whole-body MRAC on the Siemens Biograph mMR in 2017 [70,71].

19.3.3 Emission-based

The emission-based methods, first proposed in 1979 [72], use the assumption that information about tissue composition is present in the emission data due to the photon attenuation, and an attenuation map can therefore be derived from the PET emission data alone. It was proposed to formulate the problem as an optimization task where attenuation and emission are reconstructed simultaneously in a maximum a posteriori setting by imposing prior knowledge about the attenuation coefficients present in the image to help guide the algorithm to a meaningful solution [73]. The method, referred to as maximum-likelihood reconstruction of attenuation and activity (MLAA), was proposed before the introduction of PET/CT to replace the transmission scans acquired alongside a standalone PET or SPECT acquisition to limit the scan time. With the introduction of PET/MRI systems, MRI information can be used as anatomical prior to guide reconstruction [74], which reduced the PET bias in lung lesions across 19 patients from -6% to -3% and from -13% to -3% in the brain averaged across 8 patients [75,76]. The anatomical MRI prior can be weighted according to signal strength, reducing the impact of, e.g., metal implant-induced signal voids [77].

MLAA is challenged by cross-talk between the estimated activity and attenuation images, but can be limited by the presence of TOF information [78,79] or MRI priors in non-TOF systems [80].

Emission-based methods can furthermore be used in synergy with other MRAC methods to improve their shortcomings, e.g., to recover signal lost due to truncation (Fig. 19.8) and metal implant-induced artifacts [81,82], or to account for flexible hardware components outside the patient volume (e.g., flex-coils, headphones) [83].

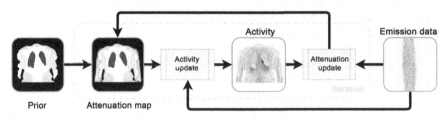

FIGURE 19.8

Use of MLAA to recover signal outside MRI field-of-view. A prior image, here the 4-class Dixon attenuation map, and the PET emission data are input to an iterative algorithm that reconstructs both activity and attenuation.

19.3.4 Deep learning-based

Machine learning-based methods typically involve training a model to convert input image intensities, or features derived from the images, to attenuation coefficients. Although several machine learning-based methods have been proposed since before or at the time of the first commercially available PET/MRI system [84,85], we will in this section focus on the subcategory of machine learning methods known as deep learning-based. We refer to Chapters 6 and 7 for an explanation of the deep learning-based MRAC methods introduced below.

The first generation of deep learning-based MRAC methods used a convolutional neural network (CNN) organized as an encoder–decoder for converting 2D MRI slices into synthetic CT slices. Two pioneer studies were initially proposed, both using T1-weighted MRI as input to their models. The first predicted continuous CT values after adding skip connections between encoder and decoder inspired by the U-net architecture [86,87], whereas the second suggested to classify each voxel into multi-class tissue labels (air, soft tissue, and bone) each assigned discrete LAC values [88].

A wave of methods followed, aimed at refining the initial methods. The first generative adversarial network (GAN) used for MRAC purposes was proposed to help guide the image generation towards more realistic synthetic CTs in both head and pelvis [89]. Other refinements utilized multiple MRI sequences for enhanced accuracy in the interface between the tissues, e.g., by combining Dixon and ZTE, applied to both head and pelvis MRAC [90,91]. In the head, the combination provided more accurate bone representation than using Dixon alone, and the pelvic method out-performed the hybrid segmentation-based method proposed by the same group [54], lowering the bias in bone lesions from 3% to only 1% across 16 patients. Unsupervised learning using cyclic GAN (cycleGAN) was proposed for use of unpaired MRI and CT data, with performance comparable to using paired data [92,93].

A recent study showed a direct correlation between size of training database and robustness of a head MRAC method, and concluded that a robust method requires hundreds of paired datasets when training a deep learning method from scratch [94]. The authors further showed that when transfer learning from the large cohort, only a few subjects were needed to adapt the model to new MRI sequences with different resolution and noise patterns. Transfer learning the model for head/neck MRAC was possible using only ten subjects [95]. Examples from both the head and head/neck application are shown Section 19.5. A similar finding was demonstrated for pelvic MRAC trained using a model pre-trained with head MR images [96].

Since the MRI can be corrupted, e.g., by motion and other artifacts, a category of methods base CT synthesis on PET images before any correction for attenuation or scatter has been performed (NAC-PET). Since these methods do not rely on any anatomical information, they can be applied across systems, e.g., also for PET examination without CT to avoid the added radiation dose when the CT is only acquired for attenuation correction purposes. Training data are available in large quantities since the methods are based on NAC-PET and CT that are readily available from pre-aligned PET/CT examinations. The first proposed method trained an U-net using 100 subjects, which demonstrated low regional PET bias within 1% of the reference CT in all regions of the brain [97]. A GAN-based method was suggested for both head and whole-body attenuation correction [98,99]. The authors performed a clinical assessment of 20 patients with brain diseases and found no difference in diagnostic image information compared to the reference CT. Average PET bias in the whole-body datasets was low (0.9%) but a wide range of errors up to 30% for individual patients was observed. The errors were mainly attributed to motion between the PET and CT data most pronounced in the thorax area and the loss of spatial context by being trained with only 2D information. A supervised cycleGAN trained with 3D patches was suggested for enhanced spatial resolution, but similarly reported high average PET errors of 10% in 39 lung patients [100]. Several authors proposed to help the network during training, e.g., by adding the emission-based MLAA derived attenuation map as input [101], or to predict CT images from synthetic PET images predicted from a preceding network for NAC-PET to AC-PET conversion [102]. The latter demonstrated a mean ($\pm$standard deviation) PET error of $3.3\% \pm 5.4\%$ in lymphoma lesions from 20 patients, but local mean absolute errors exceeded 13%.

Recently, a final collection of methods proposed to bypass the attenuation map generation completely, and directly synthesize attenuation, scatter, and TOF corrected PET images from the NAC-PET images [103,104]. The models were demonstrated to be stable and acceptable across tracers, but outliers were observed that warrants careful use of this type of methodology [105], and abnormal NAC-PET noise levels could challenge the ability to differentiate organ/lesion boundaries, even when the model was trained on 900 whole-body datasets [106]. The latter method was evaluated on 150 independent validation patients and showed similar PET accuracy as the NAC-PET to CT methods, with low average bias but regional absolute relative differences exceeding 10% in the thorax.

19.4 Comparison of attenuation correction methods

A multitude of reviews have been proposed during the years, assessing the status and advantages of the state-of-the-art methods for attenuation correction (see, e.g., [32,107–109]). Nonetheless, choosing a single method, or even a single category of methods, that fits all the needs both in the clinic and in research is challenging, since each of the categories has their own set of advantages and drawbacks (Table 19.1). For implementation into clinical routine, the most important factors are accuracy, robustness, and clinical feasibility (i.e., acquisition time and method processing time). The following comparison of the categories serves as general remarks, and do not necessarily apply to all methods within that category.

Table 19.1 Comparison of attenuation correction method categories.

Category	Processing	Requires		Can overcome		
		Specialized sequences	Training data	Rare anatomy	MRI artifacts	Changes to the input sequence
Segmentation	Seconds	✓		✓		
Atlas	Minutes-hours		✓		(✓)	(✓)
Emission	Minutes			✓	(✓)	
Deep learning	Seconds		✓		(✓)	

The fastest processing time is achieved by segmentation- and deep learning-based methods, which can synthesize an attenuation map in less than one minute, allowing for evaluation of the image before the patient leaves the scanner. Atlas-based methods are usually computation intensive, which might not fit into a clinical routine setting where time is critical. The requirement to use specialized sequences with longer acquisition time for bone representation (e.g., UTE and ZTE) further hampers the clinical feasibility of methods utilizing these.

The segmentation- and emission-based methods are both able to handle rare anatomy and challenging cohorts (e.g., pediatrics and anatomical changes due to surgery) as long as there is a signal present [31]. Methods of the other categories require special training data for each cohort [110,111], and cases of rare anatomy and post-surgery patients might not be possible to obtain a database for at all.

MRI artifacts affect the segmentation-based methods the most. The loss of signal due to metal implants can only partly be corrected for using specialized sequences [112], but these are rarely part of clinical protocols due to their long acquisition time.

The atlas-based methods are less sensitive to metal, as the global registration allows for placement of CT information over the signal voids albeit with limited local registration accuracy, and deep learning-based methods have recently shown promising results for, e.g., dental artifact correction (see, e.g., [94,112] and Section 19.5.1). Emission-based methods are only partially exempt from MRI artifacts as many of these use MRI priors. Motion-related artifacts affect methods across all categories, but are most pronounced in methods relying on input images with long acquisition time (specialized MRI sequences, emission-, and NAC-PET-based methods). Truncation artifacts in whole-body affect all MRI-based methods, but can be alleviated by specialized sequences to extend the FOV at the cost of increased acquisition time [113,36].

Most methods are vulnerable to larger changes to the underlying MRI sequence, as this often result in major intensity shifts or changes to the tissue intensity relationship, which prompts a recalibration or retraining of the method [64]. Atlas-based methods are to a large degree the exception, since most registration algorithms are able to handle changes in signal-to-noise ratio or a shift in intensity. Methods based on PET data (both emission and deep learning) are similarly affected by change in radiotracer or scanner resolution.

Comparison of methods based on accuracy and robustness is challenging. Most published methods limit their evaluation to their own proposed method and a vendor-provided solution; moreover, the methods do not follow a standard protocol for how to perform the evaluation. To this date, no large scale comparison of whole-body attenuation correction methods has ever been performed. A single multi-center study has compared several state-of-the-art head MRAC methods applied to the same patients and evaluated using the same scheme. More specifically, the authors evaluated 11 methods from the segmentation-, atlas-, and emission-based categories, on a cohort of 359 subjects from 3 radiotracers, and found that the best performing segmentation and atlas methods were all within a few percents of the CT-based reference in any region of the brain [64].

When translating the quantitative accuracy improvements into clinical impact, it was demonstrated that state-of-the-art research methods reproduce the CTAC clinical metrics used to evaluate treatment response in both adult and pediatric neurooncology patients, which was not previously possible with clinical vendor-provided MRAC solutions [31,114]. A recent study evaluated the impact of MRAC on dementia diagnosis accuracy, and found that while quantitative metrics used for diagnosis were most accurately calculated by state-of-the-art research methods, visual evaluation with PET and MRI showed agreement between the Siemens Biograph mMR atlas-based method and CTAC [115]. However, atlas registration failed for 22% of the patients, which had to be rescanned or excluded from analysis. Similar findings were reported for the GE SIGNA atlas-based method, in a study where the errors associated with the method did not alter Alzheimer's disease diagnosis, albeit a minor reduction in sensitivity was observed [116].

19.5 State-of-the-art attenuation correction methods

The largest multi-center study to date compared state-of-the-art head MRAC methods from segmentation-, atlas-, and emission-based categories. Eleven methods applicable to Siemens Biograph mMR data were selected and evaluated against a reference CT on a large cohort of Alzheimer's disease subjects. A visual comparison of the methods are provided in Fig. 19.9. Several methods based on deep learning have been proposed since the study was performed. The following examples illustrate state-of-the-art performances of head, head/neck, and pelvis MRAC using deep learning.

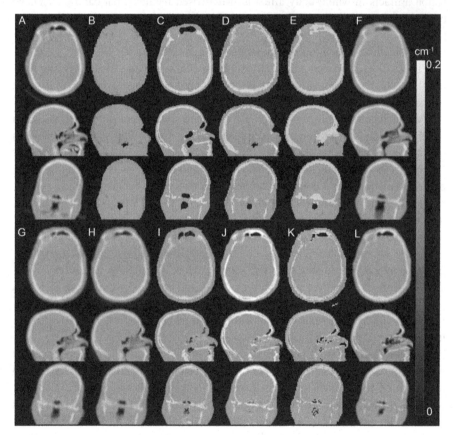

FIGURE 19.9

Attenuation correction maps for a sample patient that minimizes the difference of the overall brain error to the median error compared to CT (A) across all methods: (B) vendor-provided Dixon-based without bone [12] and (C) UTE-based with bone [43], (D) [71], (E) [117], (F) [60], (G) [61], (H) [62], (I) [80], (J) [47], (K) [42], and (L) [46]. Subfigures B, C, J, K, and L are segmentation-based; D, E, F, G, and H are atlas-based; and I is emission-based. Figure originally published in NeuroImage [64].

19.5.1 **Head MRAC**

The inaccuracy of initial vendor-provided solutions for head MRAC pushed many users to acquire a secondary low-dose CT image to be used as attenuation map for brain PET/MRI examinations. One of the largest cohorts with paired PET/MRI and CT data has been acquired since November 2013 at Rigshospitalet, Copenhagen, Denmark. The cohort consists of more than 1000 subjects, and was recently used to train a deep learning model for head MRAC [94]. The network architecture is a 3D U-net trained with Dixon MR images as input and provides the corresponding synthetic CT. The method demonstrated high visual resemblance to the reference CT, and resulted in PET errors within 1% in any region of the brain across more than 300 patients. An example of the method performance is shown in Fig. 19.10. Statistical surface projections (SSP), a tool routinely used to assess reduced PET uptake indicative of cognitive brain disease, showed no clinically relevant differences of using the deep learning method compared to CTAC in a blinded evaluation; thus, the method was implemented for clinical routine use at Rigshospitalet.

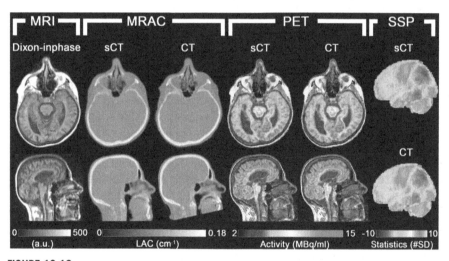

FIGURE 19.10

Performance of deep learning-based method for deriving synthetic CT (sCT) from Dixon in-phase MRI applied for attenuation correction of [18F]FDG-PET brain scan—compared to the reference CTAC. PET images (visualized on top of T1-weighted MPRAGE) shows near identical tracer uptake, confirmed by the statistical surface projection (SSP) shown for the left lateral region.

The most obvious benefit of the large training cohort was observed when investigating the model's ability to overcome outlier patients; increased training cohort size directly impacted the robustness of the method. As an example, the model was able to recover the dental region despite for a metal artifact-induced signal void (Fig. 19.11).

The ability to transfer learn to a small cohort without loss of robustness was demonstrated following a large system upgrade that involved changes to the under-

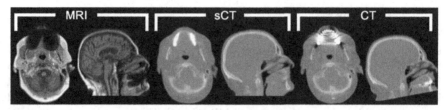

FIGURE 19.11

Example case showing robustness towards metallic dental implants for the deep learning model (sCT). Metal implants caused significant streak artifacts in CT and signal large signal voids in the input MRI.

lying MRI sequence prompting a recalibration of the model. When applying transfer learning from the large model, as little as 5 subjects were needed to retrain. The resulting model outperformed a model trained with higher number of subjects ($n = 91$) but without any transfer learning.

19.5.2 Whole-body MRAC

Whole-body MRAC is challenging due to the complex anatomy, motion, and difficulties in obtaining aligned MRI/CT pairs. A strategy to obtain excellent image alignment is to scan patients using fixation devices both during CT and PET/MRI, as is standard procedure in radiotherapy CT acquisitions. This setup was utilized to train a model with Dixon MRI input using only ten head/neck cancer patients, after applying transfer learning from the head MRAC model [95]. The synthesized CTs were evaluated both for radiotherapy and PET applications, with the latter showing a mean uptake in the tumor differing from CTAC by an average ($\pm$ standard deviation) of 0.4% $\pm$ 1.2%. An example of the method performance is shown in Fig. 19.12A. The same group has in another ongoing (unpublished) study investigated the use of PET/MRI for radiotherapy of the pelvic region. Here, fine-tuning using transfer learning from the head model has demonstrated promising preliminary results when using 26 patients (Fig. 19.12B), despite the similarity between the head and pelvis being less apparent.

19.6 Future directions and remaining challenges

Attenuation correction for PET/MRI has come a long way since the introduction of the first clinical system. Researchers have repeatedly proposed increasingly accurate MRAC methods, but only few of these are available through the vendors, which often prevents their use in clinical routine, and thus has been hampering dissemination of PET/MRI as a clinical tool despite initial excitement [39,118,119]. Several research methods have been made available open source (see, e.g., Table 19.2), but local implementation of these methods in a workflow where they can be imported back to

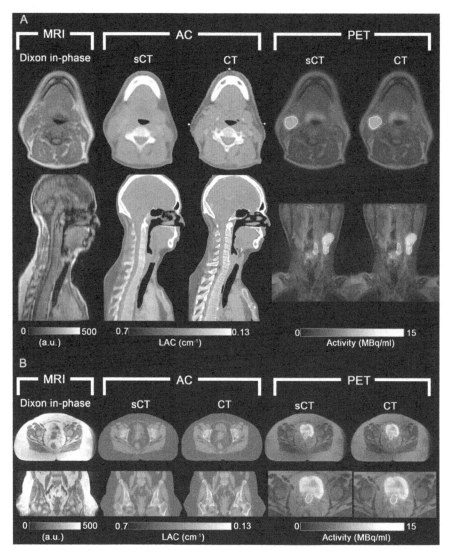

FIGURE 19.12

Performance of deep learning-based method for deriving synthetic CT (sCT) from Dixon in-phase MRI applied for attenuation correction of (A) [^{18}F]FDG-PET head/neck scan and (B) a [^{68}Ga]NODAGA-E[c(RGDyK)]2) (RGD)-PET pelvis scan. PET with sCT shows near identical tracer uptake to the PET with reference CT. The PET images are visualized on top of an anatomical MRI, and the tumor tissue is delineated for visualization purposes in green (light gray in print version).

the system and used for the PET reconstruction still requires a significant amount of work. Therefore, to facilitate the translation from research to clinical practice, selected methods should ideally be made available through the vendors as work-in-progress packages, which would accelerate large-scale use and evaluation.

Table 19.2 Examples of methods with open source access to code.

Author	Area	Method type	Link
Ladefoged et al. [46]	Head	Segmentation-based	https://github.com/claesnl/RESOLUTE_AC and https://github.com/UCL/petmr-RESOLUTE
Burgos et al. [61]	Head	Atlas-based	http://niftyweb.cs.ucl.ac.uk/program.php?p=PCT
Han et al. [87]	Head	Deep Learning-based	https://github.com/ChengBinJin/MRI-to-CT-DCNN-TensorFlow
Nie et al. [89]	Head & Pelvis	Deep Learning-based	https://github.com/ginobilinie/medSynthesisV1
Ladefoged et al. [94]	Head	Deep Learning-based	https://github.com/CAAI/DeepMRAC
Olin et al. [95]	Head\Neck	Deep Learning-based	https://github.com/andersolin/DeepMRAC_headneck

Fair identification of the best methods raises the need for reference datasets and standardized quantitative evaluation protocols. Reference datasets should include cross-site data for determining the robustness of a method, since methods trained and evaluated on single site data do not capture the variation due to differences in scanner manufacturer, MRI sequences, software versions, or hardware (e.g., differences in applied coils and coil arrangements) across sites. Today, most PET/MRI systems have incorporated methods accounting for bone in head MRAC, but for whole-body, the GE SIGNA system does not account for bone and the Siemens Biograph mMR only accounts for the major bones. The implemented methods are, however, most likely sufficient to accurately determine a diagnosis for the vast majority of the patients seen in clinical routine, but no solution currently exists for the final group of patients comprising pediatrics, abnormal anatomy (e.g., post-surgery cases), and patients with metal implant-induced artifacts. Reference datasets should be made available to accelerate development of methods for these patients as well.

The largest comparative multi-center study to date was initiated by Siemens in 2014, and involved two workshops in Denmark and United Kingdom organized by Rigshospitalet and University College London, respectively, bringing together worldwide experts within the field. The study concluded that attenuation correction for brain imaging of patients with normal anatomy is a solved topic since the remaining errors were within the variation known from PET/CT [64]. An updated comparison study should however be performed, including the new generation of deep learning-based methods to fully understand their performance and limitations in comparison with the established methods. Similarly, a large-scale comparison should be performed for whole-body methods with reference datasets and metrics important for accurate clinical diagnosis. This evaluation should not only focus on pelvis, where the highest amount of whole-body AC methods are targeted, but focus on all regions of the body, to show performance for, e.g., head/neck, lung, and bone lesion applications.

Finally, while attenuation correction with the current vendor-provided methods may be deemed "sufficient," fulfilling the entire potential of PET/MRI demands a truly quantitative modality, which allows for new and improved ways of performing diagnosis, staging, follow-up, treatment response assessment, and radiation treatment planning [120,109]. The quantitative potential has been delayed by a lack of adaptation of robust MRAC methods into the clinical routine, which must be the overarching goal for the community going forward.

19.7 Summary

Accurate attenuation correction of PET data, usually performed using CT, is a prerequisite to achieve quantitative images. For attenuation corrections in PET/MRI, initial vendor-provided MRI-based solutions neglected the bone class, which resulted in spatially varying PET errors that had implications for clinical use and was detrimental to research purposes. An active research community has for over a decade proposed methods for synthesizing CT from MRI or PET data to bring the quantitative errors down to a likely acceptable level for both head and whole-body applications. Identification of the best methods is challenged by the lack of reference datasets and evaluation protocols. Only few proposed methods are available on the scanners, often limiting the use of state-of-the-art methods for internal research purposes. Other remaining challenges for attenuation correction methods mainly revolve around their ability to handle abnormal anatomy, special cohorts (e.g., pediatrics), and image artifacts (e.g., metal- or motion-induced).

References

[1] B.E. Hillner, B.A. Siegel, D. Liu, A.F. Shields, I.F. Gareen, L. Hanna, S.H. Stine, R.E. Coleman, Impact of positron emission tomography/computed tomography and positron emission tomography (PET) alone on expected management of patients with cancer: initial results from the National Oncologic PET Registry, Journal of Clinical Oncology 26 (13) (2008) 2155–2161.

[2] Y.F. Tai, P. Piccini, Applications of positron emission tomography (PET) in neurology, Journal of Neurology, Neurosurgery and Psychiatry 75 (5) (2004) 669–676.

[3] S.L. Kitson, V. Cuccurullo, A. Ciarmiello, D. Salvo, L. Mansi, Clinical applications of positron emission tomography (PET) imaging in medicine: oncology, brain diseases and cardiology, Current Radiopharmaceuticals 2 (4) (2009) 224–253.

[4] R. Boellaard, Standards for PET image acquisition and quantitative data analysis, Journal of Nuclear Medicine 50 (1) (2009) 11S–20S.

[5] J.P. Carney, D.W. Townsend, V. Rappoport, B. Bendriem, Method for transforming CT images for attenuation correction in PET/CT imaging, Medical Physics 33 (4) (2006) 976–983.

[6] G. Delso, S. Ziegler, PET/MRI system design, European Journal of Nuclear Medicine and Molecular Imaging 36 (1) (2009) 86–92.

[7] C. Catana, T. Benner, A. Kouwe, L. Byars, M. Hamm, D.B. Chonde, C.J. Michel, G. El Fakhri, M. Schmand, A.G. Sorensen, MRI-assisted PET motion correction for neurologic studies in an integrated MR-PET scanner, Journal of Nuclear Medicine 52 (1) (2011) 154–161.

[8] B.F. Hutton, B.A. Thomas, K. Erlandsson, A. Bousse, A. Reilhac-Laborde, D. Kazantsev, S. Pedemonte, K. Vunckx, S. Arridge, S. Ourselin, What approach to brain partial volume correction is best for PET/MRI?, Nuclear Instruments & Methods in Physics Research. Section A, Accelerators, Spectrometers, Detectors and Associated Equipment 702 (2013) 29–33.

[9] M.J. Ehrhardt, K. Thielemans, L. Pizarro, D. Atkinson, S. Ourselin, B.F. Hutton, S.R. Arridge, Joint reconstruction of PET-MRI by exploiting structural similarity, Inverse Problems 31 (1) (2014) 015001.

[10] J. Ferda, E. Ferdová, O. Hes, J. Mraček, B. Kreuzberg, J. Baxa, PET/MRI: multiparametric imaging of brain tumors, European Journal of Radiology 94 (2017) A14–A25.

[11] S.H. Keller, S. Holm, A.E. Hansen, B. Sattler, F. Andersen, T.L. Klausen, L. Hojgaard, A. Kjaer, T. Beyer, L. Højgaard, A. Kjær, T. Beyer, Image artifacts from MR-based attenuation correction in clinical, whole-body PET/MRI, Magnetic Resonance Materials in Physics, Biology and Medicine 26 (1) (2013) 173–181.

[12] A. Martinez-Möller, M. Souvatzoglou, G. Delso, R.A. Bundschuh, C. Chefd'hotel, S.I. Ziegler, N. Navab, M. Schwaiger, S.G. Nekolla, Tissue classification as a potential approach for attenuation correction in whole-body PET/MRI: evaluation with PET/CT data, Journal of Nuclear Medicine 50 (4) (2009) 520–526.

[13] V. Schulz, I. Torres-Espallardo, S. Renisch, Z. Hu, N. Ojha, P. Bornert, M. Perkuhn, T. Niendorf, W.M. Schafer, H. Brockmann, T. Krohn, A. Buhl, R.W. Gunther, F.M. Mottaghy, G.A. Krombach, Automatic, three-segment, MR-based attenuation correction for whole-body PET/MR data, European Journal of Nuclear Medicine and Molecular Imaging 38 (1) (2011) 138–152.

[14] A. Samarin, C. Burger, S.D. Wollenweber, D.W. Crook, I.A. Burger, D.T. Schmid, G.K. Schulthess, F.P. Kuhn, PET/MR imaging of bone lesions–implications for PET quantification from imperfect attenuation correction, European Journal of Nuclear Medicine and Molecular Imaging 39 (7) (2012) 1154–1160.

[15] F.L. Andersen, C.N. Ladefoged, T. Beyer, S.H. Keller, A.E. Hansen, L. Højgaard, A. Kjær, I. Law, S. Holm, Combined PET/MR imaging in neurology: MR-based attenuation correction implies a strong spatial bias when ignoring bone, NeuroImage 84 (2013) 206–216.

[16] M.C. Aznar, R. Sersar, J. Saabye, C.N. Ladefoged, F.L. Andersen, J.H. Rasmussen, J. Løfgren, T. Beyer, Whole-body PET/MRI: the effect of bone attenuation during MR-based attenuation correction in oncology imaging, European Journal of Radiology 83 (7) (2014) 1177–1183.

[17] C. Brendle, H. Schmidt, A. Oergel, I. Bezrukov, M. Mueller, C. Schraml, C. Pfannenberg, C. Fougère, K. Nikolaou, N. Schwenzer, Segmentation-based attenuation correction in positron emission tomography/magnetic resonance, Investigative Radiology 50 (5) (2015) 339–346.

[18] Y. Su, B.B. Rubin, J. McConathy, R. Laforest, J. Qi, A. Sharma, A. Priatna, T.L. Benzinger, Impact of MR-based attenuation correction on neurologic PET studies, Journal of Nuclear Medicine 57 (6) (2016) 913–917.

[19] L.M. Sawicki, J. Grueneisen, C. Buchbender, B.M. Schaarschmidt, B. Gomez, V. Ruhlmann, A. Wetter, L. Umutlu, G. Antoch, P. Heusch, Comparative performance of 18F-FDG PET/MRI and 18F-FDG PET/CT in detection and characterization of pulmonary lesions in 121 oncologic patients, Journal of Nuclear Medicine 57 (4) (2016) 582–586.

[20] M. Wiesmüller, H.H. Quick, B. Navalpakkam, M.M. Lell, M. Uder, P. Ritt, D. Schmidt, M. Beck, T. Kuwert, C.C. Gall, Comparison of lesion detection and quantitation of tracer uptake between PET from a simultaneously acquiring whole-body PET/MR hybrid scanner and PET from PET/CT, European Journal of Nuclear Medicine and Molecular Imaging 40 (1) (2013) 12–21.

[21] J. Qi, P.D. Thakrar, M.B. Browning, N. Vo, S.S. Kumbhar, Clinical utilization of whole-body PET/MRI in childhood sarcoma, Pediatric Radiology (2020).

[22] B. Bogdanovic, A. Gafita, S. Schachoff, M. Eiber, J. Cabello, W.A. Weber, S.G. Nekolla, Almost 10 years of PET/MR attenuation correction: the effect on lesion quantification with PSMA: clinical evaluation on 200 prostate cancer patients, European Journal of Nuclear Medicine and Molecular Imaging (2020).

[23] W.A. Weber, H. Wieder, Monitoring chemotherapy and radiotherapy of solid tumors, European Journal of Nuclear Medicine and Molecular Imaging 33 (1) (2006) 27–37.

[24] H. Jadvar, A. Alavi, S.S. Gambhir, 18F-FDG uptake in lung, breast, and colon cancers: molecular biology correlates and disease characterization, Journal of Nuclear Medicine 50 (11) (2009) 1820–1827.

[25] J.F. Eary, F. O'Sullivan, Y. Powitan, K. Chandhury, C. Vernon, J.D. Bruckner, E.U. Conrad, Sarcoma tumor FDG uptake measured by PET and patient outcome: a retrospective analysis, European Journal of Nuclear Medicine and Molecular Imaging 29 (9) (2002) 1149–1154.

[26] S.F. Barrington, N.G. Mikhaeel, L. Kostakoglu, M. Meignan, M. Hutchings, S.P. Müeller, L.H. Schwartz, E. Zucca, R.I. Fisher, J. Trotman, Role of imaging in the staging and response assessment of lymphoma: consensus of the International Conference on Malignant Lymphomas Imaging Working Group, Journal of Clinical Oncology 32 (27) (2014) 3048.

[27] K. Ishii, F. Willoch, S. Minoshima, A. Drzezga, E.P. Ficaro, D.J. Cross, D.E. Kuhl, M. Schwaiger, Statistical brain mapping of ^{18}F-FDG PET in Alzheimer's disease: validation of anatomic standardization for atrophied brains, Journal of Nuclear Medicine 42 (4) (2001) 548–557.

[28] I. Yakushev, C. Landvogt, H.G. Buchholz, A. Fellgiebel, A. Hammers, A. Scheurich, I. Schmidtmann, A. Gerhard, M. Schreckenberger, P. Bartenstein, Choice of reference area in studies of Alzheimer's disease using positron emission tomography with fluorodeoxyglucose-F18, Psychiatry Research 164 (2) (2008) 143–153.

[29] P. Borghammer, M. Chakravarty, K.Y. Jonsdottir, N. Sato, H. Matsuda, K. Ito, Y. Arahata, T. Kato, A. Gjedde, Cortical hypometabolism and hypoperfusion in Parkinson's disease is extensive: probably even at early disease stages, Brain Structure and Function 214 (4) (2010) 303–317.

[30] L. Rischka, G. Gryglewski, N. Berroterán-Infante, I. Rausch, G.M. James, M. Klöbl, H. Sigurdardottir, M. Hartenbach, A. Hahn, W. Wadsak, M. Mitterhauser, T. Beyer, S. Kasper, D. Prayer, M. Hacker, R. Lanzenberger, Attenuation correction approaches for

serotonin transporter quantification with PET/MRI, Frontiers in Physiology 10 (2019) 1422.

[31] C.N. Ladefoged, F.L. Andersen, A. Kjær, L. Højgaard, I. Law, RESOLUTE PET/MRI attenuation correction for O-(2-^{18}F-fluoroethyl)-L-tyrosine (FET) in brain tumor patients with metal implants, Frontiers in Neuroscience 11 (2017) 453.

[32] D. Izquierdo-Garcia, C. Catana, MR imaging-guided attenuation correction of PET data in PET/MR imaging, PET Clinics 11 (2) (2016) 129–149.

[33] U. Attenberger, C. Catana, H. Chandarana, O.A. Catalano, K. Friedman, S.A. Schonberg, J. Thrall, M. Salvatore, B.R. Rosen, A.R. Guimaraes, Whole-body FDG PET-MR oncologic imaging: pitfalls in clinical interpretation related to inaccurate MR-based attenuation correction, Abdominal Imaging 40 (6) (2015) 1374–1386.

[34] C.N. Ladefoged, F.L. Andersen, S.H. Keller, J. Löfgren, A.E. Hansen, S. Holm, L. Højgaard, T. Beyer, PET/MR imaging of the pelvis in the presence of endoprostheses: reducing image artifacts and increasing accuracy through inpainting, European Journal of Nuclear Medicine and Molecular Imaging 40 (4) (2013) 594–601.

[35] M.L. Lassen, S. Rasul, D. Beitzke, M.E. Stelzmüller, J. Cal-Gonzalez, M. Hacker, T. Beyer, Assessment of attenuation correction for myocardial PET imaging using combined PET/MRI, Journal of Nuclear Cardiology 26 (4) (2019) 1107–1118.

[36] M.E. Lindemann, M. Oehmigen, J.O. Blumhagen, M. Gratz, H.H. Quick, MR-based truncation and attenuation correction in integrated PET/MR hybrid imaging using HUGE with continuous table motion, Medical Physics 44 (9) (2017) 4559–4572.

[37] R.L. Wahl, H. Jacene, Y. Kasamon, M.A. Lodge, From RECIST to PERCIST: evolving considerations for PET response criteria in solid tumors, Journal of Nuclear Medicine 50 (1) (2009) 122S–150S.

[38] A. Olin, C.N.C. Ladefoged, N.H.N. Langer, S.H.S.S.H. Keller, L. Johan, A.E.A. Hansen, A. Kjær, S.S.W. Langer, B.M.B. Fischer, F.F.L. Andersen, J.O. Löfgren, A.E.A. Hansen, A. Kjær, S.S.W. Langer, B.M.B. Fischer, F.F.L. Andersen, Reproducibility of MR-based attenuation maps in PET/MRI and the impact on PET quantification in lung cancer, Journal of Nuclear Medicine 59 (6) (2017) 999–1004.

[39] D.L. Bailey, H. Barthel, T. Beyer, R. Boellaard, B. Gückel, D. Hellwig, H. Herzog, B.J. Pichler, H.H. Quick, O. Sabri, K. Scheffler, H.P. Schlemmer, N.F. Schwenzer, H.F. Wehrl, Summary report of the first international workshop on PET/MR imaging, March 19–23, 2012, Tübingen, Germany, Molecular Imaging and Biology 15 (4) (2013) 361–371.

[40] S.D. Wollenweber, S. Ambwani, A.H.R. Lonn, D.D. Shanbhag, S. Thiruvenkadam, S. Kaushik, R. Mullick, H. Qian, G. Delso, F. Wiesinger, Comparison of 4-class and continuous fat/water methods for whole-body, MR-based pet attenuation correction, IEEE Transactions on Nuclear Science 60 (5) (2013) 3391–3398.

[41] G. Liu, T. Cao, L. Hu, J. Zheng, L. Pang, P. Hu, Y. Gu, H. Shi, Validation of MR-based attenuation correction of a newly released whole-body simultaneous PET/MR system, BioMed Research International 2019 (2019) 8213215.

[42] M.R. Juttukonda, B.G. Mersereau, Y. Chen, Y. Su, B.G. Rubin, T.L.S. Benzinger, D.S. Lalush, H. An, MR-based attenuation correction for PET/MRI neurological studies with continuous-valued attenuation coefficients for bone through a conversion from R2* to CT-Hounsfield units, NeuroImage 112 (2015) 160–168.

[43] C. Catana, A. Kouwe, T. Benner, C.J. Michel, M. Hamm, M. Fenchel, B. Fischl, B. Rosen, M. Schmand, A.G. Sorensen, Toward implementing an MRI-based PET attenuation-correction method for neurologic studies on the MR-PET brain prototype, Journal of Nuclear Medicine 51 (9) (2010) 1431–1438.

[44] V. Keereman, Y. Fierens, T. Broux, Y. De Deene, M. Lonneux, S. Vandenberghe, MRI-based attenuation correction for PET/MRI using ultrashort echo time sequences, Journal of Nuclear Medicine 51 (5) (2010) 812–818.

[45] J.C. Dickson, C. O'Meara, A. Barnes, A comparison of CT- and MR-based attenuation correction in neurological PET, European Journal of Nuclear Medicine and Molecular Imaging 41 (6) (2014) 1176–1189.

[46] C.N. Ladefoged, D. Benoit, I. Law, S. Holm, A. Kjær, L. Højgaard, A.E. Hansen, F.L. Andersen, Region specific optimization of continuous linear attenuation coefficients based on UTE (RESOLUTE): application to PET/MR brain imaging, Physics in Medicine and Biology 60 (20) (2015) 8047–8065.

[47] J. Cabello, M. Lukas, S. Förster, T. Pyka, S.G. Nekolla, S.I. Ziegler, S. Forster, T. Pyka, S.G. Nekolla, S.I. Ziegler, MR-based attenuation correction using ultrashort-echo-time pulse sequences in dementia patients, Journal of Nuclear Medicine 56 (3) (2015) 423–429.

[48] F. Wiesinger, L.I. Sacolick, A. Menini, S.S. Kaushik, S. Ahn, P. Veit-Haibach, G. Delso, D.D. Shanbhag, Zero TE MR bone imaging in the head, Magnetic Resonance in Medicine 75 (1) (2016) 107–114.

[49] G. Delso, K. Zeimpekis, M. Carl, F. Wiesinger, M. Hullner, P. Veit-Haibach, Cluster-based segmentation of dual-echo ultra-short echo time images for PET/MR bone localization, EJNMMI Physics 1 (1) (2014) 7.

[50] G. Delso, B. Kemp, S. Kaushik, F. Wiesinger, T. Sekine, Improving PET/MR brain quantitation with template-enhanced ZTE, NeuroImage 181 (June) (2018) 403–413.

[51] J. Yang, F. Wiesinger, S. Kaushik, D. Shanbhag, T.A. Hope, P.E. Larson, Y. Seo, Evaluation of sinus/edge-corrected zero-echo-time-based attenuation correction in brain PET/MRI, Journal of Nuclear Medicine 58 (11) (2017) 1873–1879.

[52] R. Boellaard, H.H. Quick, Current image acquisition options in PET/MR, Seminars in Nuclear Medicine 45 (3) (2015) 192–200.

[53] A. Boss, M. Weiger, F. Wiesinger, Future image acquisition trends for PET/MRI, Seminars in Nuclear Medicine 45 (3) (2015) 201–211.

[54] A.P. Leynes, J. Yang, D.D. Shanbhag, S.S. Kaushik, Y. Seo, T.A. Hope, F. Wiesinger, P.E. Larson, Hybrid ZTE/Dixon MR-based attenuation correction for quantitative uptake estimation of pelvic lesions in PET/MRI, Medical Physics 44 (3) (2017) 902–913.

[55] K.H. Su, H.T. Friel, J.W. Kuo, R. Al Helo, A. Baydoun, C. Stehning, A.N. Crisan, M.S. Traughber, A. Devaraj, D.W. Jordan, P. Qian, A. Leisser, R.J. Ellis, K.A. Herrmann, N. Avril, B.J. Traughber, R.F. Muzic, UTE-mDixon-based thorax synthetic CT generation, Medical Physics 46 (8) (2019) 3520–3531.

[56] E.R. Kops, H. Herzog, Template based attenuation correction for PET in MR-PET scanners, in: IEEE Nuclear Science Symposium and Medical Imaging Conference, IEEE, 2008, pp. 3786–3789.

[57] M.L. Montandon, H. Zaidi, Atlas-guided non-uniform attenuation correction in cerebral 3D PET imaging, NeuroImage 25 (1) (2005) 278–286.

[58] E. Schreibmann, J.A. Nye, D.M. Schuster, D.R. Martin, J. Votaw, T. Fox, MR-based attenuation correction for hybrid PET-MR brain imaging systems using deformable image registration, Medical Physics 37 (5) (2010) 2101–2109.

[59] S.D. Wollenweber, S. Ambwani, G. Delso, A.H.R. Lonn, R. Mullick, F. Wiesinger, Z. Piti, A. Tari, G. Novak, M. Fidrich, Evaluation of an atlas-based PET head attenuation correction using PET/CT & MR patient data, IEEE Transactions on Nuclear Science 60 (5) (2013) 3383–3390.

[60] D. Izquierdo-Garcia, A.E. Hansen, S. Forster, D. Benoit, S. Schachoff, S. Furst, K.T. Chen, D.B. Chonde, C. Catana, An SPM8-based approach for attenuation correction combining segmentation and nonrigid template formation: application to simultaneous PET/MR brain imaging, Journal of Nuclear Medicine 55 (11) (2014) 1825–1830.

[61] N. Burgos, M.J. Cardoso, K. Thielemans, M. Modat, S. Pedemonte, J. Dickson, A. Barnes, R. Ahmed, C.J. Mahoney, J.M. Schott, J.S. Duncan, D. Atkinson, S.R. Arridge, B.F. Hutton, S. Ourselin, Attenuation correction synthesis for hybrid PET-MR scanners: application to brain studies, IEEE Transactions on Medical Imaging 33 (12) (2014) 2332–2341.

[62] I. Merida, N. Costes, R.A. Heckemann, A. Hammers, Pseudo-CT generation in brain MR-PET attenuation correction: comparison of several multi-atlas methods, EJNMMI Physics 2 (1) (2015) A29.

[63] J. Sjölund, D. Forsberg, M. Andersson, H. Knutsson, Generating patient specific pseudo-CT of the head from MR using atlas-based regression, Physics in Medicine and Biology 60 (2) (2015) 825.

[64] C.N. Ladefoged, I. Law, U. Anazodo, K.S. Lawrence, D. Izquierdo-Garcia, C. Catana, N. Burgos, M.J. Cardoso, S. Ourselin, B. Hutton, I. Mérida, N. Costes, A. Hammers, D. Benoit, S. Holm, M. Juttukonda, H. An, J. Cabello, M. Lukas, S. Nekolla, S. Ziegler, M. Fenchel, B. Jakoby, M.E. Casey, T. Benzinger, L. Højgaard, A.E. Hansen, F.L. Andersen, A multi-centre evaluation of eleven clinically feasible brain PET/MRI attenuation correction techniques using a large cohort of patients, NeuroImage 147 (2017) 346–359.

[65] D. Andreasen, K. van Leemput, R.H. Hansen, J.A. Andersen, J.M. Edmund, Patch-based generation of a pseudo CT from conventional MRI sequences for MRI-only radiotherapy of the brain, Medical Physics 42 (4) (2015) 1596–1605.

[66] Y. Wu, W. Yang, L. Lu, Z. Lu, L. Zhong, M. Huang, Y. Feng, Q. Feng, W. Chen, Prediction of CT substitutes from MR images based on local diffeomorphic mapping for brain PET attenuation correction, Journal of Nuclear Medicine 57 (10) (2016) 1635–1641.

[67] S. Roy, W.T. Wang, A. Carass, J.L. Prince, J.A. Butman, D.L. Pham, PET attenuation correction using synthetic CT from ultrashort echo-time MR imaging, Journal of Nuclear Medicine 55 (12) (2014) 2071–2077.

[68] A. Torrado-Carvajal, J.L. Herraiz, E. Alcain, A.S. Montemayor, L. Garcia-Canamaque, J.A. Hernandez-Tamames, Y. Rozenholc, N. Malpica, Fast patch-based pseudo-CT synthesis from T1-weighted MR images for PET/MR attenuation correction in brain studies, Journal of Nuclear Medicine 57 (1) (2015) 136–144.

[69] H.R. Marshall, J. Patrick, D. Laidley, F.S. Prato, J. Butler, J. Théberge, R.T. Thompson, R.Z. Stodilka, Description and assessment of a registration-based approach to include bones for attenuation correction of whole-body PET/MRI, Medical Physics 40 (8) (2013) 082509.

[70] D.H. Paulus, H.H. Quick, C. Geppert, M. Fenchel, G. Hermosillo, D. Faul, F. Boada, K.P. Friedman, T. Koesters, Y. Zhan, G. Hermosillo, D. Faul, F. Boada, K.P. Friedman, T. Koesters, Whole-body PET/MR imaging: quantitative evaluation of a novel model-based MR attenuation correction method including bone, Journal of Nuclear Medicine 56 (7) (2015) 1061–1066.

[71] T. Koesters, K.P. Friedman, M. Fenchel, Y. Zhan, G. Hermosillo, J. Babb, I.O. Jelescu, D. Faul, F.E. Boada, T.M. Shepherd, Dixon sequence with superimposed model-based bone compartment provides highly accurate PET/MR attenuation correction of the brain, Journal of Nuclear Medicine 57 (6) (2016) 918–924.

[72] Y. Censor, D.E. Gustafson, A. Lent, H. Tuy, A new approach to the emission computerized tomography problem: simultaneous calculation of attenuation and activity coefficients, IEEE Transactions on Nuclear Science 26 (2) (1979) 2775–2779.

[73] J. Nuyts, P. Dupont, S. Stroobants, R. Benninck, L. Mortelmans, P. Suetens, Simultaneous maximum a posteriori reconstruction of attenuation and activity distributions from emission sinograms, IEEE Transactions on Medical Imaging 18 (5) (1999) 393–403.

[74] A. Mehranian, H. Zaidi, Joint estimation of activity and attenuation in whole-body TOF PET/MRI using constrained gaussian mixture models, IEEE Transactions on Medical Imaging 34 (9) (2015) 1808–1821.

[75] A. Mehranian, H. Zaidi, A.J. Reader, MR-guided joint reconstruction of activity and attenuation in brain PET-MR, NeuroImage 162 (2017) 276–288.

[76] A. Mehranian, H. Zaidi, Emission-based estimation of lung attenuation coefficients for attenuation correction in time-of-flight PET/MR, Physics in Medicine and Biology 60 (12) (2015) 4813–4833.

[77] S. Ahn, L. Cheng, D.D. Shanbhag, H. Qian, S.S. Kaushik, F.P. Jansen, F. Wiesinger, Joint estimation of activity and attenuation for PET using pragmatic MR-based prior: application to clinical TOF PET/MR whole-body data for FDG and non-FDG tracers, Physics in Medicine and Biology 63 (4) (2018) 045006.

[78] M. Defrise, A. Rezaei, J. Nuyts, Time-of-flight PET data determine the attenuation sinogram up to a constant, Physics in Medicine and Biology 57 (4) (2012) 885–899.

[79] A. Rezaei, M. Defrise, G. Bal, C. Michel, M. Conti, C. Watson, J. Nuyts, Simultaneous reconstruction of activity and attenuation in time-of-flight PET, IEEE Transactions on Medical Imaging 31 (12) (2012) 2224–2233.

[80] D. Benoit, C.N. Ladefoged, A. Rezaei, S.H. Keller, F.L. Andersen, L. Højgaard, A.E. Hansen, S. Holm, J. Nuyts, Optimized MLAA for quantitative non-TOF PET/MR of the brain, Physics in Medicine and Biology 61 (24) (2016) 8854–8874.

[81] J. Nuyts, C. Michel, M. Fenchel, G. Bal, C. Watson, Completion of a truncated attenuation image from the attenuated pet emission data, in: IEEE Nuclear Science Symposium and Medical Imaging Conference, IEEE, 2010, pp. 2123–2127.

[82] N. Fuin, S. Pedemonte, O.A. Catalano, D. Izquierdo-Garcia, A. Soricelli, M. Salvatore, K. Heberlein, J.M. Hooker, K. Van, C. Catana, PET/MR imaging in the presence of metal implants: completion of the attenuation map from PET emission data, Journal of Nuclear Medicine 58 (5) (2017) 840–845.

[83] T. Heußer, C.M. Rank, Y. Berker, M.T. Freitag, M. Kachelrieß, MLAA-based attenuation correction of flexible hardware components in hybrid PET/MR imaging, EJNMMI Physics 4 (1) (2017) 1–23.

[84] M. Hofmann, F. Steinke, V. Scheel, G. Charpiat, J. Farquhar, P. Aschoff, M. Brady, B. Scholkopf, B.J. Pichler, MRI-based attenuation correction for PET/MRI: a novel approach combining pattern recognition and atlas registration, Journal of Nuclear Medicine 49 (11) (2008) 1875–1883.

[85] A. Johansson, M. Karlsson, T. Nyholm, CT substitute derived from MRI sequences with ultrashort echo time, Medical Physics 38 (5) (2011) 2708–2714.

[86] O. Ronneberger, P. Fischer, T. Brox, U-Net: convolutional networks for biomedical image segmentation, in: International Conference on Medical Image Computing and Computer-Assisted Intervention, Springer, 2015, pp. 234–241.

[87] X. Han, MR-based synthetic CT generation using a deep convolutional neural network method, Medical Physics 44 (4) (2017) 1408–1419.

[88] F. Liu, H. Jang, R. Kijowski, T. Bradshaw, A.B. McMillan, Deep learning MR imaging-based attenuation correction for PET/MR imaging, Radiology 286 (2) (2017) 676–684.

[89] D. Nie, R. Trullo, J. Lian, C. Petitjean, S. Ruan, Q. Wang, D. Shen, Medical image synthesis with context-aware generative adversarial networks, in: International Conference on Medical Image Computing and Computer-Assisted Intervention, vol. 10435, Springer, 2017, pp. 417–425.

[90] K. Gong, J. Yang, K. Kim, G.E. Fakhri, Y. Seo, Q. Li, Attenuation correction for brain PET imaging using deep neural network based on Dixon and ZTE MR images, Physics in Medicine and Biology 63 (12) (2018) 125011.

[91] A.P. Leynes, J. Yang, F. Wiesinger, S.S. Kaushik, D.D. Shanbhag, Y. Seo, T.A. Hope, P.E.Z. Larson, Direct pseudoCT generation for pelvis PET/MRI attenuation correction using deep convolutional neural networks with multi-parametric MRI: zero echo-time and Dixon deep pseudoCT (ZeDD-CT), Journal of Nuclear Medicine 59 (5) (2018) 852–858.

[92] J.M. Wolterink, A.M. Dinkla, M.H. Savenije, P.R. Seevinck, C.A. van den Berg, I. Išgum, Deep MR to CT synthesis using unpaired data, in: International Workshop on Simulation and Synthesis in Medical Imaging, Springer, 2017, pp. 14–23.

[93] H. Yang, J. Sun, A. Carass, C. Zhao, J. Lee, Z. Xu, J. Prince, Unpaired brain MR-to-CT synthesis using a structure-constrained CycleGAN, in: Deep Learning in Medical Image Analysis and Multimodal Learning for Clinical Decision Support, Springer, 2018, pp. 174–182.

[94] C.N. Ladefoged, A.E. Hansen, O.M. Henriksen, F.J. Bruun, L. Eikenes, S.K. Øen, A. Karlberg, L. Højgaard, I. Law, F.L. Andersen, AI-driven attenuation correction for brain PET/MRI: clinical evaluation of a dementia cohort and importance of the training group size, NeuroImage 222 (2020) 117221.

[95] A.B. Olin, A.E. Hansen, J.H. Rasmussen, C.N. Ladefoged, A.K. Berthelsen, K. Håkansson, I.R. Vogelius, L. Specht, A.B. Gothelf, A. Kjaer, B.M. Fischer, F.L. Andersen, Feasibility of multiparametric positron emission tomography/magnetic resonance imaging as a one-stop shop for radiation therapy planning for patients with head and neck cancer, International Journal of Radiation Oncology, Biology, Physics 108 (5) (2020) 1–10.

[96] A. Torrado-Carvajal, J. Vera-Olmos, D. Izquierdo-Garcia, O.A. Catalano, M.A. Morales, J. Margolin, A. Soricelli, M. Salvatore, N. Malpica, C. Catana, Dixon-VIBE deep learning (DIVIDE) pseudo-CT synthesis for pelvis PET/MR attenuation correction, Journal of Nuclear Medicine 60 (3) (2019) 429–435.

[97] F. Liu, H. Jang, R. Kijowski, G. Zhao, T. Bradshaw, A.B. McMillan, A deep learning approach for ^{18}F-FDG PET attenuation correction, EJNMMI Physics 5 (1) (2018) 24.

[98] K. Armanious, T. Küstner, M. Reimold, K. Nikolaou, C. Fougère, B. Yang, S. Gatidis, Independent brain ^{18}F-FDG PET attenuation correction using a deep learning approach with Generative Adversarial Networks, Hellenic Journal of Nuclear Medicine 22 (3) (2019) 179–186.

[99] K. Armanious, T. Hepp, T. Küstner, H. Dittmann, K. Nikolaou, C. La Fougère, B. Yang, S. Gatidis, Independent attenuation correction of whole body [^{18}F]FDG-PET using a deep learning approach with Generative Adversarial Networks, EJNMMI Research 10 (1) (2020) 1–9.

[100] X. Dong, T. Wang, Y. Lei, K. Higgins, T. Liu, W.J. Curran, H. Mao, J.A. Nye, X. Yang, Synthetic CT generation from non-attenuation corrected PET images for whole-body PET imaging, Physics in Medicine and Biology 64 (21) (2019) 215016.

[101] D. Hwang, S.K. Kang, K.Y. Kim, S. Seo, J.C. Paeng, D.S. Lee, J.S. Lee, Generation of PET attenuation map for whole-body time-of-flight ^{18}F-FDG PET/MRI using a deep

neural network trained with simultaneously reconstructed activity and attenuation maps, Journal of Nuclear Medicine 60 (8) (2019) 1183–1189.

[102] Z. Hu, Y. Li, S. Zou, H. Xue, Z. Sang, X. Liu, Y. Yang, X. Zhu, D. Liang, H. Zheng, Obtaining PET/CT images from non-attenuation corrected PET images in a single PET system using Wasserstein generative adversarial networks, Physics in Medicine and Biology (2020).

[103] X. Dong, Y. Lei, T. Wang, K. Higgins, T. Liu, W.J. Curran, H. Mao, J.A. Nye, X. Yang, I. Sciences, Deep learning-based attenuation correction in the absence of structural information for whole-body PET imaging, Physics in Medicine and Biology 65 (5) (2020) 055011.

[104] H. Van, H. Massa, S. Hurley, S. Cho, T. Bradshaw, A. McMillan, A deep learning-based approach for direct whole-body PET attenuation correction, Journal of Nuclear Medicine 60 (1) (2019) 569.

[105] H. Arabi, K. Bortolin, N. Ginovart, V. Garibotto, H. Zaidi, Deep learning-guided joint attenuation and scatter correction in multitracer neuroimaging studies, Human Brain Mapping 41 (13) (2020).

[106] I. Shiri, H. Arabi, P. Geramifar, G. Hajianfar, P. Ghafarian, A. Rahmim, M.R. Ay, H. Zaidi, Deep-JASC: joint attenuation and scatter correction in whole-body ^{18}F-FDG PET using a deep residual network, European Journal of Nuclear Medicine and Molecular Imaging 47 (11) (2020) 2533–2548.

[107] M. Hofmann, B. Pichler, B. Schölkopf, T. Beyer, Towards quantitative PET/MRI: a review of MR-based attenuation correction techniques, European Journal of Nuclear Medicine and Molecular Imaging 36 (1) (2009) 93–104.

[108] A. Mehranian, H. Arabi, H. Zaidi, Vision 20/20: magnetic resonance imaging-guided attenuation correction in PET/MRI: challenges, solutions, and opportunities, Medical Physics 43 (3) (2016) 1130–1155.

[109] C. Catana, Attenuation correction for human PET/MRI studies, Physics in Medicine and Biology (2020).

[110] E. Vogelius, S. Shah, Pediatric PET/MRI: a review, Journal of the American Osteopathic College of Radiology 6 (1) (2017) 15–27.

[111] I. Bezrukov, H. Schmidt, S. Gatidis, N. Schwenzer, B.J. Pichler, Quantitative evaluation of segmentation- and atlas-based attenuation correction for PET/MR on pediatric patients, Journal of Nuclear Medicine 56 (7) (2015) 1067–1075.

[112] G. Schramm, C.N. Ladefoged, Metal artifact correction strategies in MRI-based attenuation correction in PET/MRI, BJR Open 1 (1) (2019) 20190033.

[113] J.O. Blumhagen, H. Braun, R. Ladebeck, M. Fenchel, D. Faul, K. Scheffler, H.H. Quick, Field of view extension and truncation correction for MR-based human attenuation correction in simultaneous MR/PET imaging, Medical Physics 41 (2) (2014) 022303.

[114] C.N. Ladefoged, L. Marner, A. Hindsholm, I. Law, L. Højgaard, F.L. Andersen, Deep learning based attenuation correction of PET/MRI in pediatric brain tumor patients: evaluation in a clinical setting, Frontiers in Neuroscience 12 (2019) 1005.

[115] S.K. Øen, T.M. Keil, E.M. Berntsen, J.F. Aanerud, T. Schwarzlmüller, C.N. Ladefoged, A.M. Karlberg, L. Eikenes, Quantitative and clinical impact of MRI-based attenuation correction methods in [^{18}F] FDG evaluation of dementia, EJNMMI Research 9 (1) (2019) 83.

[116] T. Sekine, A. Buck, G. Delso, B. Kemp, E.E. Ter Voert, M. Huellner, P. Veit-Haibach, S. Kaushik, F. Wiesinger, G. Warnock, The impact of atlas-based MR attenuation correction on the diagnosis of FDG-PET/MR for Alzheimer's diseases – a simulation study combining multi-center data and ADNI-data, PLoS ONE 15 (6) (2020) 1–14.

[117] U.C. Anazodo, J.D. Thiessen, T. Ssali, J. Mandel, M. Günther, J. Butler, W. Pavlosky, F.S. Prato, R.T. Thompson, K.S. St. Lawrence, Feasibility of simultaneous whole-brain imaging on an integrated PET-MRI system using an enhanced 2-point Dixon attenuation correction method, Frontiers in Neuroscience 9 (2015) 1–11.

[118] D.L. Bailey, H. Barthel, B. Beuthin-baumann, T. Beyer, S. Bisdas, R. Boellaard, J. Czernin, A. Drzezga, U. Ernemann, C. Franzius, B. Gückel, R. Handgretinger, M. Hartenbach, D. Hellwig, H. Nadel, S.G. Nekolla, T. Pfluger, B.J. Pichler, H.H. Quick, O. Sabri, B. Sattler, J. Schäfer, F. Schick, B.A. Siegel, H.P. Schlemmer, N.F. Schwenzer, J.V.D. Hoff, P. Veit-Haibach, H.F. Wehrl, Combined PET/MR: where are we now? Summary report of the second international workshop on PET/MR imaging April 8–12, 2013, Tübingen, Germany, Molecular Imaging and Biology 16 (3) (2014) 295–310.

[119] D.L. Bailey, G. Antoch, P. Bartenstein, H. Barthel, A.J. Beer, S. Bisdas, D.A. Bluemke, R. Boellaard, C.D. Claussen, C. Franzius, M. Hacker, H. Hricak, C. Fougère, B. Gückel, S.G. Nekolla, B.J. Pichler, S. Purz, H.H. Quick, W. Weber, H.F. Wehrl, T. Beyer, Combined PET/MR: the real work has just started. Summary report of the third international workshop on PET/MR imaging; February 17–21, 2014, Tübingen, Germany, Molecular Imaging and Biology 17 (3) (2015) 297–312.

[120] C. Catana, H.H. Quick, H. Zaidi, Current commercial techniques for MRI-guided attenuation correction are insufficient and will limit the wider acceptance of PET/MRI technology in the clinic, Medical Physics 45 (9) (2018) 4007–4010.

Image synthesis for MRI-only radiotherapy treatment planning

20

Jason Dowling[a], Laura O'Connor[b,c], Oscar Acosta[d], Parnesh Raniga[a],
Renaud de Crevoisier[d], Jean-Claude Nunes[d], Anais Barateau[d], Hilda Chourak[d],
Jae Hyuk Choi[b], and Peter Greer[b,c]

[a]*CSIRO Health and Biosecurity, Herston, Queensland, Australia*
[b]*University of Newcastle, Callaghan, New South Wales, Australia*
[c]*Calvary Mater Newcastle Hospital, Waratah, New South Wales, Australia*
[d]*Univ Rennes, CLCC Eugène Marquis, INSERM, LTSI - UMR 1099, Rennes, France*

20.1 Introduction

The aim of radiation therapy is to direct a sufficient amount of ionizing radiation to induce cancer cell death while avoiding damage to healthy tissue within the patient. Modern image-guided external beam radiation therapy relies on computed tomography (CT) scans. These 3D scans are geometrically accurate and provide patient electron density information which is needed to predict radiation absorption and scattering during treatment delivery. However, CT scanning is poor at identifying the boundaries and location of soft tissue organs. Magnetic resonance imaging (MRI) is exceptionally good at identifying soft tissues and this information can be critical in delivering accurate treatment and reducing treatment related toxicity. MRI-only radiation therapy has received considerable recent research and commercial interest as it enables the integration of structural and functional imaging information available from MRI with both traditional treatment workflows, or with the increasing deployment of combined MRI-linear accelerator systems.

This chapter aims to provide an end-to-end overview of the main issues involved in generating synthetic CT (sCT, also known as pseudo or substitute CT) from MRI scans for MRI-only radiation therapy treatment planning. The chapter will provide a practical overview of MR image acquisition for treatment planning and common methods used to generate sCT. This chapter also provides an overview of methods for the clinical validation of sCT (both with and without patient CT ground truth) in addition to a summary of issues related to deployment of this software into a radiation oncology environment. An example MRI and generated sCT are shown in Fig. 20.1.

Biomedical Image Synthesis and Simulation. https://doi.org/10.1016/B978-0-12-824349-7.00027-X

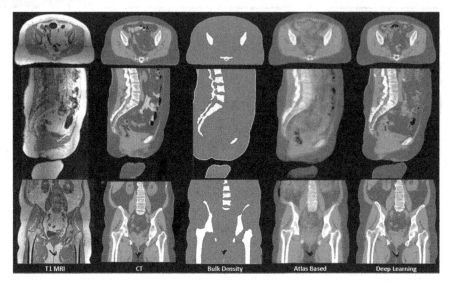

FIGURE 20.1

Example sCT comparison between various methods from a T1-weighted MRI of a female pelvis. The columns show: the original MRI, the actual planning CT, a bulk density sCT, a multi-atlas based conversion, and a conditional generative adversarial network (cGAN) based sCT. The rows show the axial, sagittal, and coronal views from the 3D volumes. The mean (standard deviation) absolute error in Hounsfield Units (HU) between the CT and the bulk density volume is 101.3 (111); atlas based is 52.5 (95.4); cGAN is 52.5 (122.9).

20.2 External beam radiation therapy summary

The first step in the standard radiation therapy planning process is to acquire a planning (usually called a simulation) CT scan. This acquisition is shown in Fig. 20.2. The purpose of the planning CT scan is to provide the computer based treatment planning system with an anatomically correct and geometrically accurate data set, as well as providing electron density information of the tissues in the body. The image is imported into a treatment planning system which provides tools to outline the treatment regions and their prescribed radiation dose. The system also enables contouring of at risk organs to which dose is to be limited. An example treatment plan for prostate cancer is shown in Fig. 20.4, which shows the prescribed dose distribution to the prostate, and also outlines at-risk anatomy (such as the femoral heads) where the dose must be constrained. This data set is used to plan the radiation beam delivery and to accurately track and model how the treatment dose will be distributed within the patient's body using specific calculation algorithms. Fig. 20.5 shows a linear accelerator (LINAC) which delivers this prescribed dose to the patient. Once a patient is set up on the treatment couch, the radiation therapists will leave the room and check that the patient anatomy aligns with the plan. This is usually done by capturing orthogonal X-rays of the patient using the LINAC, and then comparing these with digitally reconstructed radiographs (simulated X-rays generated from the planning CT). A cone beam CT may also be used for this purpose. Automated adjustments to the patient position are made from the image comparison, and finally the treatment dose is delivered. A typical console set up used to control the LINAC is shown in Fig. 20.6.

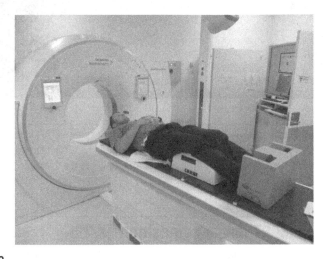

FIGURE 20.2

Patient positioning for standard CT based planning for prostate cancer radiation therapy.

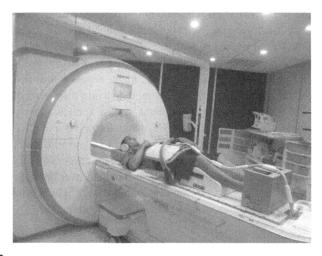

FIGURE 20.3

Patient positioning and equipment required for MRI based planning for prostate cancer radiation therapy (compare with Fig. 20.2).

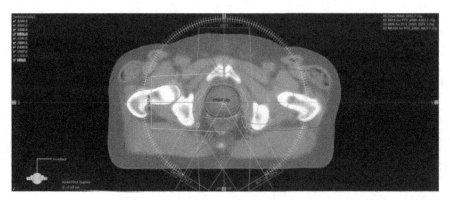

FIGURE 20.4

Sample external beam radiation therapy treatment planning screen. This figure shows the prescribed dose which will be delivered to the patient's prostate. This plan requires electron density information (usually acquired from a CT scan). Only the axial image is shown here however the plan will be generated in 3D.

20.3 Planning CT image acquisition

Traditionally a CT scan would be acquired as a planning scan. The aim of the CT planning session is to replicate the conditions for treatment, to ensure the radiation beam placement and dose planning are delivered with the highest accuracy. Therefore, the role of patient positioning in radiation therapy differs from diagnostic scanning and immobilization, reproducibility, and accessibility for the radiation beams to the treatment region take priority. A flat couch top is used. Ancillary equipment is commonly used to ensure patient comfort, to minimize patient movement during treatment, increase reproducibility for treatment delivery, and to increase accessibility to the treatment region (to gain as many access points for the radiation beams to deliver the dose to the treatment region, while minimizing body regions in the path of the beam). Ancillary equipment used in radiation therapy commonly includes: indexable knee cushions and ankle stocks for pelvis and lower body region immobilization; vacuum bags filled with beans, which conform to the shape of the body used for pelvic/abdominal regions, extremities, and chest; and thermoplastic casts which, when heated, can be stretched and moulded over the region of interest, then cool and set as a custom rigid immobilization device. The thermoplastic casts are commonly used for brain/face and head and neck treatments.

20.4 Planning MRI acquisition

In the case of MRI-only planning, the CT scan is replaced with a planning MRI scan. An example patient setup is shown in Fig. 20.3. The shift from CT to MRI introduces

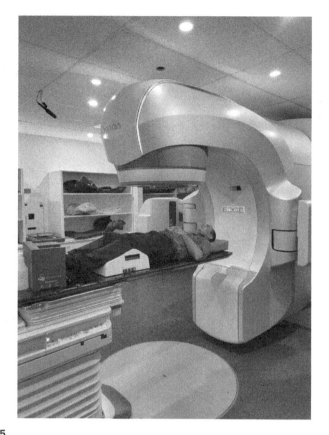

FIGURE 20.5

This figure shows a medical linear accelerator (LINAC) which guides high energy X-rays to a target location within a patient's body. This guidance requires a treatment plan, such as the one shown in Fig. 20.4. The treatment couch can move in different directions and the gantry, which delivers the radiation beam, rotates around the patient enabling radiation to be delivered at many different angles.

some complexities, as MRI scanning conditions need to meet the CT scanning and planning system requirements. MRI adaptations include the requirement for slightly larger bore sizes in MRI, of at least 60 cm to accommodate radiation therapy positioning and ancillary devices. To acquire an MRI scan for planning purposes, a flat couch top, similar to the treatment couches, is required to be positioned over the spine array coils. The flat couch top is required to have indexable locking, similar to the treatment couches for indexing on immobilization devices. Patient immobilization and positioning equipment needs to be constructed from MRI-safe plastics. Additionally, the majority of specially designed MRI coils are not compatible with radiation therapy positioning and ancillary equipment, therefore large body coils or

FIGURE 20.6

Console setup for the LINAC shown in Fig. 20.5.

flex coils are mainly utilized. Coil bridges or holders are used to allow for the positioning of coils over the imaging region, without compressing the external contour. Coil holders allow for positioning of flex coils under and around ancillary equipment to ensure best possible coverage of the imaging regions.

The MRI scanner is ideally equipped with an external laser bridge, to align patients and to place reference marks. Traditionally, the external marks will be indicated on the CT scan with small high density CT opaque markers. These markers are rarely compatible with MRI, and there is a need for additional liquid or oil filled markers.

As the focus of radiation therapy planning is to specifically locate the treatment region, high geometrical accuracy is of upmost importance. As such, distortion minimizing protocols are utilized in MRI. This includes the use of high bandwidth to reduce patient-induced susceptibility distortions; no slice gaps; vendor supplied or 3rd party gradient non-linearity 3D distortion correction software; and scanning at isocenter to reduce distortion effects away from isocenter.

Additionally, radiation therapy planning software is designed to be used for conventional CT scans. As such, there are certain imaging conditions which must be met for radiation therapy planning. This may include isotropic voxels, so that the scan can be viewed in three planes in the planning software, and the use of only true axial slices.

It is also important to include the entire body contour, including skin edge if the scan is to be used for MRI planning, to ensure the entire body volume is being accounted for in the planning process. Traditionally, radiation therapy calculations require at least 2 cm above and below the treatment regions to account for radiation scatter effects for the dose calculations. As some treatment fields can routinely be large, such as head and neck treatments or pelvic treatments which include nodal regions, this requires a planning MRI scan that may extend up to almost 40 cm from superior to inferior. Therefore MRI scanning techniques such as Tim CT or stitched MRI sequences may be required for these large field of view techniques, to minimize the effect of gradient non-linearity distortion outside of the geometrically accurate region around the isocenter.

The synthetic CT generation process for MRI planning is usually designed around specific MRI sequences and parameters. It is important to standardize the sequence parameters used for sCT generation. Deviations from protocol can lead to inaccuracies in the sCT generation process, which can introduce errors in the treatment planning and delivery process. MRI sequences adapted for sCT generation include standard T1-weighted and T2-weighted sequences for anatomical imaging, DIXON MRI sequences to aid in tissue classification, ultra-short echo time sequences for bone visualization and time of flight sequences for vessel classification. Bony anatomy is commonly used as an image guidance structure for localization of radiation treatment regions, for treatment delivery. Bone regions such as cortical bone can be indistinguishable at air/bone interfaces such as around the sinuses in the skull region. As such, cortical bone imaging techniques such as ultra-short echo time sequences may be required to differentiate bony anatomy from air cavities for radiation treatment image guidance accuracy.

Additional image guidance structures, such as fiducial markers, may be used in radiation therapy surgically implanted into the treatment region to help locate and guide the radiation treatments. The markers are usually around 4 mm in size and made of biologically inert metals such as gold. The markers are required to be visualized on the planning scans. As such, MRI scanning techniques, which are particularly sensitive to the magnetic susceptibility of these materials, are usually utilized to locate the fiducial markers, with the degree of artefact controlled to not degrade the image quality.

20.5 Methods used for sCT generation

20.5.1 Bulk density

A simple approach to generate sCT is to assume that the patient is water-equivalent and assign the same Hounsfield Unit (HU) value to all voxels within the patient's body contour [1–6]. The advantage of this approach, which is frequently used in MRI planning for brachytherapy, is that it is simple and fast (assuming the body contour is available). An additional advantage is that no image registration is needed. However, the bulk density method lacks accuracy as tissue heterogeneity is ignored and it is not possible to generate realistic digitally reconstructed radiographs (DRRs). Manual or automated contouring of the bone is required for DRR generation. A thorough review of bulk density methods for MRI-only radiation therapy is provided in [7]. The bulk-density approach shows promise as a method for sCT quality assurance of sCT's generated through more advanced methods [8].

20.5.2 Atlas and patch based methods

Another approach to sCT generation is to utilize image registration (see also Chapter 4). Rigid and affine registration methods typically generate two output files: a resampled moving image aligned to the target image, along with a transformation matrix (representing global translation, rotation, shearing, and scaling). Non-rigid (or deformable) image registration typically takes the result of rigid or affine registration and maps each voxel from this moving image to a target, resulting in a deformation field (containing the 3D change in position for each voxel), along with a resampled moving image. Atlas based methods involve propagation of the transformation matrix (and usually the deformation field). In this context an atlas (or training) set consists of previously co-registered CT-MR images from one or more patients (often with corresponding labels representing patient anatomy of interest). The accuracy between the co-registered MR and CT is critical, and often involves structure guided registration (for example, to account for large differences in the bladder for pelvis sCT generation). For sCT generation, one or more atlas MR images are registered to a target MR image, and the corresponding CT-MR image can then be propagated to the MR image target. For tissue segmentation of the target image the atlas labels can also be propagated to the target image. After the atlas MR image is registered to a target MR image this CT-MR image can then be propagated to the MR image target. In a multi-atlas approach, the propagated CT-MR images will be fused (for example, using local weightings obtained from intensity similarities from the registered MR images) [9–12].

Patch based methods involve feature extraction and patch partitioning from interpatient group-wise affine registration [6,13]. The target feature patches are selected using the approximate nearest neighbor search from the training cohort and sCT patches are generated using the multipoint-wise aggregation scheme.

Atlas and patch based methods have been successfully validated and used in multi-center clinical trials and commercial applications. They may be more robust across different MRI models and vendors than other methods as they include a priori geometric information [14]. The main problem with these approaches is that many image registrations are usually required, which can take considerable time. An additional concern is that registration error, particularly if the target anatomy is outside the range of atlas training volumes, can lead to errors in generated sCT volumes.

20.5.3 **Tissue class methods**

Tissue-classification methods have been developed, and commercially deployed. These involve the identification of different tissue classes in an MR image, followed by the assignment of a single HU value to each tissue class [15] (see also Chapter 4). An alternate approach is regression based methods which use mapping of the MRI signal to HU, however, these require the initial identification of bone and surrounding tissue regions, and the application of separate mapping functions [16].

The advantages of these approaches are robustness to abnormal anatomy and conversion speed (as there are no image registrations required). Disadvantages are that multiple MR sequences may be required (increasing the potential for patient discomfort and movement during MR scanning) and that calibration may be required for different MRI scanners.

20.5.4 **Deep learning methods**

Deep learning (DL) approaches to sCT generation show great promise, particularly with regards to execution speed. Recent comparative papers have supported the development of DL based methods [17,18] and most sCT generation research is now focused in this area. The DL networks for sCT generation from MRI can be roughly divided into two classes: generator-only models based on a convolutional neural network (CNN) and its variants (such as the well-known U-Net), and the generative adversarial network (GAN) and its variants. A description of these methods are provided in Chapters 6 and 7.

20.5.4.1 CNN approaches for sCT generation

A CNN often consists of multiple layers of non-linear functions with large numbers of trainable parameters. Generator-only models based on CNN architectures are usually divided into encoding and decoding parts: a convolutional encoder–decoder (CED) network architecture. In the encoding part, low-level feature maps are downsampled to high-level feature maps. In the decoding part, the high-level feature maps are upsampled to low-level feature maps using the transposed convolutional layer to construct the prediction image. The encoder network uses a set of combined convolution filtering for detecting image features, batch normalization [19] for accelerating network convergence, and rectified linear unit activation [20] as activation functions, followed by max-pooling to reduce the data dimensions. The decoder network takes the output of the encoder network and combines extracted image features in multiple resolution scales to generate a targeted image output through an image upsampling process. Generator-only models learn to minimize an objective function called loss function which is an intensity based similarity measurement between the generated image (sCT) and the corresponding ground truth image (real CT).

In sCT generation from MRI, variants of CNN based generators have been proposed, including CNN based on dilated convolutions, deep embedding CNN (DECNN), and convolutional encoder–decoder (CED) networks. The most well-known CED network is the U-shaped CNN (U-Net) architecture. This network has a CED structure with direct skip connections between the encoder and decoder. The encoding path consists of a set of convolutions (no dilated convolutions), followed by instance normalization or batch normalization, a non-linear activation function (ReLU, LeakyRELU, or PreLU), and max-pooling. In 2017, Han was the first to publish a sCT generation study from MRI with a U-Net architecture [21]. The DECNN model proposed by Xiang et al. [22] is derived by inserting multiple embedding blocks into the CNN architecture. The deep CED network [23], and ResNet [24] consists of a combined encoder network (the popular VGG 16-layer net model) and a decoder network (reversed VGG16) with multiple symmetrical skip connections between layers. The ResNet architecture [24] has three convolutional layers (containing convolution operations, a batch normalization layer, a ReLU) activation function, followed by nine residual blocks (containing convolutional layers, batch normalization layers, and ReLU activation function) with fully connected layers.

One limitation of sCT models based on CNNs is that they may lead to blurry results due to general misalignment between MR and CT [25].

20.5.4.2 GAN approaches for sCT generation
20.5.4.2.1 Classical GAN

The adversarial learning strategy was proposed by Goodfellow et al. [26] and can be applied to generate sCT with higher quality than generator-only models. The original method trains simultaneously two separate neural networks, the generator G and the discriminator D. These two neural networks form a two-player min–max game where G tries to produce realistic images to fool D while D tries to distinguish between real and synthetic data. In the original version [26], the discriminator and generator are implemented as multilayer perceptrons and more recently implemented as CNNs.

GANs have a number of advantages for sCT generation. The adversarial network prevents the generated images from blurring and preserves details, especially edge features. In addition, the accuracy of sCT within the bone region is enhanced. And finally, the discriminator detects patch features in both real and fake images, mitigating misregistration problems caused by an imperfect alignment between MRI and CT in training.

Most GANs use the binary cross-entropy [26] or the least-squares loss function [27,28] as the discriminator loss function. However, this sigmoid cross-entropy loss function leads to the saturation problem in GAN learning (the well-known problem of vanishing gradients [29]). Mao et al. [27] adopted the least-squares loss function for the discriminator and showed that minimizing the objective function of LS-GAN minimizes the Pearson χ^2 divergence [30]. Emami et al. [28] replaced the negative log-likelihood objective with a least square loss, which was more stable during training and generated better sCT quality.

The loss function of the generator and discriminator comparing the generated sCT and real CTs used in these GANs is the least-squares loss function (l_2-loss) [28].

To tackle the training instability of GANs, a plethora of extensions and subclasses have been proposed (as follows).

20.5.4.2.2 Conditional-GAN (cGAN)

Since the original GAN allows no explicit control on the actual data generation, Goodfellow et al. [26] proposed the conditional GAN (cGAN) to incorporate additional information such as class labels in the synthesis process. cGAN is an extension of the GAN model in which both the generator and the discriminator are conditioned on some additional information (the sCT image output is conditioned on the MR image input).

Different generator architectures in a cGAN have been proposed, including SE-ResNet, DenseNet, U-Net, Embedded Net, and the atrous spatial pyramid pooling method. Pix2pix proposed by Isola et al. [31] is a successful cGAN variant for high-resolution image-to-image translation. A l_1-norm loss has been added to the standard GAN losses consisting of generator loss (such as least-square error or binary cross entropy) and discriminator loss. The use of a loss function based on l_1 alone leads to reasonable but blurred results; while cGAN alone leads to sharp results but introduces image artifacts [31].

One of the main advantages of cGANs is that the networks learn reasonable image-to-image translations even if the training dataset size is small.

20.5.4.2.3 CycleGAN

For image-to-image translations between two modalities, the principles of the cycleGAN are to extract characteristic features of both modalities and discover the underlying relationship between them [32]. Of note, the cycleGAN based framework does not require paired MRI/CT images [25,33]. The cycleGAN involves two GANs: one to generate sCT from MRI and a second to generate MRI from sCT (the output of the first GAN). These dual GANs learn simultaneously and a cyclic loss function minimizes the discrepancy between the original CT and the sCT obtained from the chained generators.

20.6 **Validation (with matching CT)**

Methods and algorithms derived to produce synthetic CT scans require validation against the existing gold standard CT. This is important not only for the development phase of new methods of sCT generation but also for clinical validation of a sCT system implementation in a radiotherapy center before routine use. The derived sCT is compared to the CT scan of the same patient using a variety of different metrics. As the two scans are acquired at different time points they do not represent exactly the same anatomical state and therefore this introduces uncertainty into the comparison in addition to any difference in the underlying scan values. Validation should ultimately answer the question "is the sCT fit for purpose?" In terms of radiation therapy the sCT must provide accurate dose calculation and it may also be required in some cases for image guidance purposes particularly using bony anatomy. The scope of the clinical application of the sCT must be carefully defined, for example, in general the sCT would not be suitable for soft-tissue image guidance. In most cases the MRI anatomy or anatomical contours generated from the MRI would be used [34,35]. However, if the sCT generation algorithm is designed to produce soft tissue anatomy from the MRI scan with sufficient accuracy for image guidance then this must form part of the validation process.

Another consideration, for validation of methods which require training, is the use of a separate test-set and the number of validation datasets. Validation of a model should never be performed with data used to generate the model. A separate (set-aside) data set of patient scans not used in training the model must be used for validation to ensure model generalization. Leave-one-out approaches can be used where this is feasible. The test set should be large enough to encompass the range of anatomical variation expected in the population. Wherever possible the model should also be evaluated on data from different institutions/scanners. Whether the sCT generation is to be used for patients with prosthetic implants then this must be clearly stated in the clinical scope of use [36]. A difficulty encountered in all validation is the accuracy required and the criteria that should be applied. There is also generally a trade-off involved. While the use of sCT will slightly degrade dose calculation accuracy, if its use improves targeting accuracy of the treatment then this can be a worthwhile trade, given the use of reduced margins and high dose gradients in modern treatments.

20.6.1 Image registration for validation

It not possible to acquire CT and MRI simultaneously and even with careful patient positioning and immobilization, there may be internal differences (such as bladder and rectum filling). Before comparisons of sCT and CT are performed the scans must be registered. Authors have used both rigid and non-rigid registration for this purpose. The advantage of non-rigid registration is that differences in anatomy between the two scan sessions can be minimized to isolate the HU differences between the scans. A particular problem is the body contour where anatomy can be present in some regions in one scan but not in the other due to normal pose differences resulting in large errors in some quantitative comparison metrics. However, there is also potential to mask out systematic differences in the anatomy from the two scanners or the effect of geometric distortions from MRI on the sCT. Validation methods should ensure that these effects are considered. Some approaches have utilized "filling" in the missing body contour of one scan so that the contour matches the other scan or only quantifying the differences to within a certain distance of the skin surface, e.g., minus 1 cm.

20.6.2 Image quality metrics
20.6.2.1 Mean absolute error

Voxel-wise comparisons of the HU values in the sCT and CT is commonly used for validation and is particularly useful in sCT model generation as discussed in previous sections. The MAE is the mean of the absolute value differences between all voxels in the two scans (sCT and CT). This metric is sensitive to the image registration of the two scans and is particularly prone to large differences at high gradients in HU, for example, at bone/tissue or tissue/air interfaces. Here, partial voluming effects also introduce large differences in the HU values. Comparisons that calculate MAE for different anatomical regions or as a function of HU have also been employed (such as [10]). Histograms of MAE vs HU can be developed. An advantage of MAE is that it is easy to calculate and allows comparison of methods developed for non-radiation therapy applications, for example for attenuation correction for MRI-PET scanners. However, for radiation therapy it is not sufficient to assess an sCT generation method on MAE alone.

20.6.2.2 Peak signal-to-noise ratio

As a voxel-wise evaluation is not enough to determine a sCT generation method efficiency, other metrics evaluating the overall sCT quality are increasingly used in image synthesis for MRI-only radiotherapy. The peak signal-to-noise ratio (PSNR) is a measure of the noise induced in the sCT. It is based on a distortion metric, the MSE. Thus, the higher the PSNR, the closer the sCT to the original CT. PSNR and MSE are respectively defined as

$$PSNR = 10 \log_{10} \left(\frac{Q^2}{MSE} \right), \tag{20.1}$$

$$MSE = \frac{1}{N} \sum_{i=1}^{N} (sCT_i - CT_i)^2, \tag{20.2}$$

with N being the number of voxels, sCT_i and CT_i the intensities in HU of the ith voxel, and Q the range of intensity values.

20.6.2.3 Dice similarity coefficient

The geometric accuracy of the derived sCT can be evaluated by computing the Dice similarity coefficient (DSC) between automatically generated and manual contours for specific anatomical structures. This is important for structures that will be used for image guidance or are critical for dose calculation accuracy. For pelvic sites, the DSC of the bony anatomy has been evaluated. The DSC measures the similarity between two sets, X (manual contours) and Y (generated contours), $D(X, Y) = 2|X \cap Y|/|X| + |Y|$, where $|X|$ denotes the cardinality of the set X, $D(X, Y) \in [0, 1]$, with $D(X, Y) = 0$ if and only if the sets are disjoint and $D(X, Y) = 1$ if and only if the sets are identical.

20.6.2.4 Structural similarity index measure

This index is based on the human visual system, exploiting the light and the structural information contained in both images. The structural similarity index measure (SSIM) assesses the perceptual difference between the reference and the synthetic CTs. It quantifies the similarity between the ground truth and the generated image regardless of the distortion type (random noise, blur effect, etc.). To do so, luminance, contrast, and structure of both images are compared. The structural comparison is made after luminance subtraction and variance normalization

$$SSIM = \frac{(\mu_{CT}\mu_{sCT} + C_1)(2\sigma_{CTsCT} + C_2)}{(\mu_{CT}^2 + \mu_{sCT}^2 + C_1)(\sigma_{CT}^2 + \sigma_{sCT}^2 + C_2)},\tag{20.3}$$

$$C_1 = (k_1 Q^2), \quad k_1 = 0.01,\tag{20.4}$$

$$C_2 = (k_2 Q^2), \quad k_2 = 0.03,\tag{20.5}$$

with μ_{CT} being the mean CT intensity, μ_{sCT} the mean sCT intensity; σ_{CT}, σ_{sCT}, and σ_{CTsCT} are the standard deviations of the CT, the sCT and the covariance; Q corresponds with the dynamic range of intensity values.

As image distortion may be space-variant, and only a local area can be simultaneously perceived with high resolution by a human observer [37], the SSIM can be also locally computed. Thus, spatially dependent quality maps can be obtained, giving precise indications on the localization of the sCT depreciated quality.

20.6.3 Dosimetric evaluations

The primary method for comparing sCT and CT quality for radiation therapy applications needs to be a comparison of the dose delivered to a target volume. There are two main types of dosimetric evaluations, dose difference metrics and dose-volume histogram (DVH) comparisons. In order to evaluate the sCT scans in terms of the accuracy of dose calculation, an identical radiation therapy plan is calculated on both CT and sCT. Transferring the plan from one scan to the other requires image registration. The contours used for planning on the reference (usually CT) scan can also be transferred for DVH evaluation. The planned fields or arcs are tied to the isocenter coordinate within the patient CT. The isocenter will be transferred to the sCT based on the registration of the two scans. Care should be taken that the isocenter location on the sCT is representative of the location on CT relative to the main anatomical structures that will influence dose, for example, bony anatomy. Once a dose is calculated, different dose metrics can be evaluated. Point dose comparisons and the more comprehensive gamma evaluation [38] have been used. The gamma evaluations have been both two-dimensional on axial slices and three-dimensional over the entire volume [16,10]. A range of gamma criteria have been employed from 1%, 1 mm to 3%, 3 mm without any consensus on the required criteria or pass-rates. Given that DVHs can be compared between the two plans then agreement of DVH values at certain clinically relevant cut-points can be compared. For target coverage, these would normally include target dose coverage metrics as well as maximum and minimum dose metrics such as the highest dose received by 2% of the target volume (D2%) and the lowest dose received by 98% of the target volume (D98%) [39]. For organs at risk, the most clinically relevant DVH parameters should be chosen. It would be greatly beneficial if consensus dose evaluation criteria and accuracy were established for this field with the increasing clinical utilization of synthetic CT scans in treatment planning.

20.7 **Quality control (without matching CT)**

The accuracy of dose calculation will impact directly on the dose delivery to the patient and the quality of the patient's treatment. Currently, for CT scan based patient dose calculations, the consistency of the HU and subsequently derived electron densities (EDs) are not checked on a patient-by-patient basis. The constancy of the CT scanner HU for a particular set or sets of scan parameters are verified experimentally usually on a monthly basis or after scanner modifications or updates. This is based on the high level of consistency and reliability of CT scanner produced HU values and these quality control practices are present in major international quality assurance guidelines for radiation therapy. Transfer of the CT data to the treatment planning system is also validated periodically.

For clinical implementation of synthetic CT the initial phase of commissioning would include comparison with gold-standard CT scans. This phase would establish that the MRI scans are sufficiently similar to those used to generate the MRI to sCT model and that the conversion software is operating to specification. However, following implementation of MRI-only planning, these CT scans are no longer available for quality control purposes. For synthetic CT scans derived from MRI scans via computer methods, there are currently no accepted practices and standards for ongoing quality assurance. These scans can be thought of as CT from a virtual scanner and the HU-to-ED calibration must correspond to this virtual scanner. As above it should be verified regularly that the output of the synthetic CT algorithm is consistent for a standard MRI scan input, especially after software upgrades. The consistency of the scanner MRI data should also be checked regularly with appropriate phantom measurements and quality assurance procedures including image distortion.

Since the commissioning phase is unlikely to involve a large number of patients, and experience with clinical synthetic CT scans is still limited, a period of patient-specific synthetic CT quality control is advisable. These quality assurance checks should encompass the clinical use of the sCT including image-guidance and will include verification that the acquired MRI scan is suitable for sCT generation and image guidance. This will include for prostate treatment visibility of gold fiducial markers. Tyagi et al. implemented an MRI-only workflow for prostate patients [15]. They implemented a simple questionnaire at MRI to assess whether MRI scans should be repeated and utilized orthogonal scout X-ray images from a CT room setup of the patient to validate fiducial marker locations on MRI. The use of cone-beam CT scans acquired at the first fraction to verify the sCT was investigated by Palmér et al [40]. Another approach is the use of an independent calculation. Choi et al. developed a bulk-anatomical density scan method for prostate where the densities used were optimized to give close to zero mean isocenter difference to CT scan calculations [8]. This method uses the MRI defined body and bone contours to derive a bulk density calculation that is independent of the sCT scan and of sufficient accuracy to validate the sCT dose calculation. Another challenge is the quality control of multi-center studies or clinical trials involving MRI-only planning. An example of quality assurance checks used in the HIPSTER [41] and NINJA [42] clinical trials is shown below

(Tables 20.1 and 20.2). These encompass a series of checklists used to assure MRI image acquisition, the integrity and utility of the sCT and MRI scans; and dosimetric and spatial accuracy of the sCT scan.

Table 20.1 Quality assurance checks of MRI and sCT integrity for the MRI-only workflow substudy of the NINJA trial. Note that LFOV is a large field of view scan (where the whole pelvis, including external skin, is captured).

Item	Details	
Distortion correction	Confirm that 3D distortion correction was activated for the LFOV scan. Check distortion corrections for other scans.	☐
Image transfer	Confirm that sCT corresponds to the LFOV MRI scan to verify that correct sCT has been assigned to the patient. Confirm that sCT is correctly oriented.	☐
Image alignment	Confirm the sCT aligns to the LFOV MRI scan and that offsets from DICOM origin have been applied if applicable	☐
Image integrity	Visually inspect the entire sCT volume for any missing tissue or major artefacts. These differences may not affect dose calculation but should be noted.	☐
Field of view	Ensure that the sCT has sufficient field-of-view to cover all external contours and sufficient extension superiorly and inferiorly for dose calculations.	☐
HU to electron density conversion	Check that the correct calibration curve has been applied to the sCT.	☐
Scan alignment / patient motion	Ensure that the prostate and/or gold seeds are aligned in each MRI scan sequence. Ensure that patient or prostate motion has not occurred between scans.	☐
Fiducial marker visibility	Verify that the fiducial markers are clearly visible on MRI and distinguishable from calcifications.	☐

Table 20.2 Quality assurance checks of sCT dose calculation for the MRI-only workflow substudy of the NINJA trial. Note that DVH = dose volume histogram, BADBT = bulk-anatomical density bone and entire tissue scan [8].

Item	Details	
DVH	Confirm that DVH parameters on sCT are within 2% of BADBT map plan.	☐
Dose at isocenter	Verify that isocenter dose on sCT is within 2% of BADBT map plan.	☐
Dose distribution	Verify that 3D Gamma comparison at 2%, 2 mm criteria > 95% pass-rate for the entire body volume (−1.5 cm to avoid skin region where dose is uncertain). [Use BADBT map.]	☐

20.8 **Deployment**

In order to utilize any computed aided systems in a clinical environment, they need to be integrated into the clinical workflow in a manner that is efficient and does not impart any extra overheads. Ideally, the system should adhere as much as possible to agreed upon standards for interoperability and upgradability. In the case of MRI alone radiotherapy, the Digital Imaging and Communications in Medicine (DICOM)[1] and its extension the DICOM Radiation Therapy (DICOM-RT) are the main standards with which data are exported out of and imported into the imaging and radiation-therapy modalities. For the installation of MRI-alone software as part of an Australian multi-center clinical trial [42], the incoming MR images are in DICOM format and the output of the system is a DICOM-RT structure set file representing the organs in the pelvis and a DICOM dataset for the sCT image.

The DICOM standard also specifies a way of managing and running work-flows, namely the Unified Procedure Step. This extension allows for the definition and execution of workflows (typically post-processing) either automatically, semi-automatically, or manually. For the Australian trial, there was consideration for a deployment algorithm as part of a system that implemented the Unified Procedure Step standard; however, there were no easily available implementations of these parts of the standard. Moreover, there do not appear to be any vendor systems that can ef-fectively communicate with a Unified Procedure Step system.

Therefore, a much simpler system was developed that runs jobs on data that is pushed to the DICOM node of the system. This can be thought of as a very much simplified push workflow. The disadvantage is that any required parameters have to be incorporated into the DICOM tags of the dataset rather than being passed onto the system as would be when utilizing a Unified Procedure Step. The main components of the implemented system are the DICOM node, a job queue, and an implementation of the sCT generation algorithm. The DICOM node was implemented in Python using the PyDICOM library.[2] It was setup to listen for incoming data on a particular port and would match the series description of the incoming data to what was expected. DICOM data that were matched would be written to disk and a job queued to process these. Once the job manager dispatches the job (the Python rq library[3] was used as the job manager), the algorithm is run on this data. The resultant DICOM-RT and DICOM datasets are then pushed into a DICOM node for the treatment planning system from which they can be imported for treatment planning.

Another consideration was how to provide a platform that can be easily updated if required that can host specialized versions of the workflow for different institutions. This need was due to the differences in DICOM compliance and the use of differ-ent vendor tags. The platform for the Australian trial was developed with a DICOM listener component with plugins that perform the actual processing. When data is

---

[1] https://www.dicomstandard.org.

[2] https://pydicom.github.io/.

[3] https://python-rq.org/.

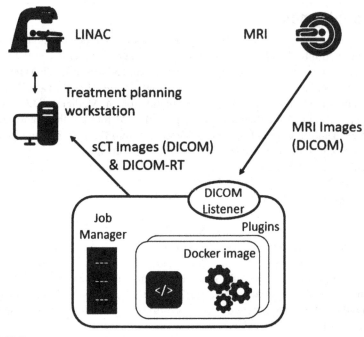

FIGURE 20.7

Overview of the system and flow of data between the modalities. Data flows between the MRI machine and the platform and between the platform and the treatment planning workstation are basic DICOM (DIMSE) C-STORE operations (otherwise known as DICOM push).

received by the listener, each series is passed onto a match function of the plugin. If the data matches, the plugin is put on the job queue and is later executed with the series as input. A plugin contains a software container (docker[4] in our case) that houses the algorithm and data to be utilized by the algorithm. The use of the software container allows us to have site specific versions of the system in place and have them easily updatable. Once the data is processed, the resultant sCT DICOM dataset and DICOM-RT dataset are pushed to a site specific, picture archiving system. The system is illustrated in Fig. 20.7.

Future work will involve investigating the development of a prototype based on the DICOM and IHE Radiology AI Workflow for imaging which adopts the Unified Procedure Step for deploying algorithms. In addition, methods for integrating MRI-only algorithms into more universal workflow systems, especially those utilizing the Fast Healthcare Interoperability Resources standard will be explored. There is also a

[4] https://www.docker.com.

second generation of the DICOM-RT standard currently under development[5] which will need to considered for future systems.

20.9 Summary

This chapter has provided a high level overview of sCT generation from MRI, including image acquisition, sCT generation, quality assurance, and deployment. Challenges include acquisition, quality assurance, speed of sCT generation, robustness of methods across different MRI models and magnet strengths, outlier anatomy, metal artifacts, and fiducial marker imaging [43,7]. The use of MRI based sCT has promise in improving patient outcomes, reduced healthcare costs, enabling the fusion of MRI functional and structural information, and real-time imaging during treatment through combined MRI-linear accelerators.

Recent review papers on sCT generation for radiation therapy can be found in [43–49]. Vandewinckele et al. [50] also include a review of sCT in the context of artificial intelligence applications. In addition, recently published guidance on the use of MRI for radiation therapy has been provided by the Institute of Physics and Engineering in Medicine [51]. Note that the sCT methods described can also be applied to attenuation correction in PET-MRI (Chapter 19) and recent reviews are provided in [52,53].

References

[1] Y.K. Lee, M. Bollet, G. Charles-Edwards, M.A. Flower, M.O. Leach, H. McNair, E. Moore, C. Rowbottom, S. Webb, Radiotherapy treatment planning of prostate cancer using magnetic resonance imaging alone, Radiotherapy and Oncology 66 (2) (2003) 203–216, https://doi.org/10.1016/S0167-8140(02)00440-1, ISSN 0167-8140, https://www.sciencedirect.com/science/article/pii/S0167814002004401.

[2] L. Chen, R.A. Price Jr., L. Wang, J. Li, L. Qin, S. McNeeley, C.M. Ma, G.M. Freedman, A. Pollack, MRI-based treatment planning for radiotherapy: dosimetric verification for prostate IMRT, International Journal of Radiation Oncology, Biology, Physics 60 (2) (2004) 636–647, https://doi.org/10.1016/j.ijrobp.2004.05.068, ISSN 0360-3016 (Print) 0360-3016.

[3] K. Eilertsen, L.N. Vestad, O. Geier, A. Skretting, A simulation of MRI based dose calculations on the basis of radiotherapy planning CT images, Acta Oncologica 47 (7) (2008) 1294–1302, https://doi.org/10.1080/02841860802256426, ISSN 0284-186x.

[4] J. Lambert, P.B. Greer, F. Menk, J. Patterson, J. Parker, K. Dahl, S. Gupta, A. Capp, C. Wratten, C. Tang, M. Kumar, J. Dowling, S. Hauville, C. Hughes, K. Fisher, P. Lau, J.W. Denham, O. Salvado, MRI-guided prostate radiation therapy planning: investigation of dosimetric accuracy of MRI-based dose planning, Radiotherapy and Oncology 98 (3) (2011) 330–334, https://doi.org/10.1016/j.radonc.2011.01.012, ISSN 0167-8140.

---

[5] https://www.dicomstandard.org/News-dir/ftsup/docs/sups/sup147.pdf.

[5] J. Kim, K. Garbarino, L. Schultz, K. Levin, B. Movsas, M.S. Siddiqui, I.J. Chetty, C. Glide-Hurst, Dosimetric evaluation of synthetic CT relative to bulk density assignment-based magnetic resonance-only approaches for prostate radiotherapy, Radiation Oncology 10 (1) (2015) 239, https://doi.org/10.1186/s13014-015-0549-7, ISSN 1748-717X.

[6] A. Largent, A. Barateau, J.C. Nunes, C. Lafond, P.B. Greer, J.A. Dowling, H. Saint-Jalmes, O. Acosta, R. de Crevoisier, Pseudo-CT generation for MRI-only radiation therapy treatment planning: comparison among patch-based, atlas-based, and bulk density methods, International Journal of Radiation Oncology, Biology, Physics 103 (2) (2019) 479–490, https://doi.org/10.1016/j.ijrobp.2018.10.002, ISSN 0360-3016.

[7] N. Tyagi, Challenges and Requirements, Springer International Publishing, 2019, pp. 119–129.

[8] J.H. Choi, D. Lee, L. O'Connor, S. Chalup, J.S. Welsh, J. Dowling, P.B. Greer, Bulk anatomical density based dose calculation for patient-specific quality assurance of MRI-only prostate radiotherapy, Frontiers in Oncology 9 (2019) 997, https://doi.org/10.3389/fonc.2019.00997, ISSN 2234-943X (Print) 2234-943x.

[9] J.A. Dowling, J. Lambert, J. Parker, O. Salvado, J. Fripp, A. Capp, C. Wratten, J.W. Denham, P.B. Greer, An atlas-based electron density mapping method for magnetic resonance imaging (MRI)-alone treatment planning and adaptive MRI-based prostate radiation therapy, International Journal of Radiation Oncology, Biology, Physics 83 (1) (2012) e5–e11, https://doi.org/10.1016/j.ijrobp.2011.11.056, ISSN 1879-355X.

[10] J.A. Dowling, J. Sun, P. Pichler, D. Rivest-Hénault, S. Ghose, H. Richardson, C. Wratten, J. Martin, J. Arm, L. Best, S.S. Chandra, J. Fripp, F.W. Menk, P.B. Greer, Automatic substitute computed tomography generation and contouring for magnetic resonance imaging (MRI)-alone external beam radiation therapy from standard MRI sequences, International Journal of Radiation Oncology, Biology, Physics 93 (5) (2015) 1144–1153, https://doi.org/10.1016/j.ijrobp.2015.08.045, ISSN 0360-3016.

[11] C. Siversson, F. Nordström, T. Nilsson, T. Nyholm, J. Jonsson, A. Gunnlaugsson, L.E. Olsson, Technical note: MRI only prostate radiotherapy planning using the statistical decomposition algorithm, Medical Physics 42 (10) (2015) 6090–6097, https://doi.org/10.1118/1.4931417, ISSN 0094-2405.

[12] E. Persson, C. Gustafsson, F. Nordström, M. Sohlin, A. Gunnlaugsson, K. Petruson, N. Rintelä, K. Hed, L. Blomqvist, B. Zackrisson, T. Nyholm, L.E. Olsson, C. Siversson, J. Jonsson, MR-OPERA: a multicenter/multivendor validation of magnetic resonance imaging-only prostate treatment planning using synthetic computed tomography images, International Journal of Radiation Oncology, Biology, Physics 99 (3) (2017) 692–700, https://doi.org/10.1016/j.ijrobp.2017.06.006, ISSN 0360-3016.

[13] D. Andreasen, K. van Leemput, J.M. Edmund, A patch-based pseudo-CT approach for MRI-only radiotherapy in the pelvis, Medical Physics 43 (8 Part 1) (2016) 4742–4752, https://doi.org/10.1118/1.4958676, ISSN 0094-2405.

[14] J.J. Wyatt, J.A. Dowling, C.G. Kelly, J. McKenna, E. Johnstone, R. Speight, A. Henry, P.B. Greer, H.M. McCallum, Investigating the generalisation of an atlas-based synthetic-CT algorithm to another centre and MR scanner for prostate MR-only radiotherapy, Physics in Medicine and Biology 62 (24) (2017) N548–N560, https://doi.org/10.1088/1361-6560/aa9676.

[15] N. Tyagi, S. Fontenla, J. Zhang, M. Cloutier, M. Kadbi, J. Mechalakos, M. Zelefsky, J. Deasy, M. Hunt, Dosimetric and workflow evaluation of first commercial synthetic CT software for clinical use in pelvis, Physics in Medicine and Biology 62 (8) (2017) 2961–2975, https://doi.org/10.1088/1361-6560/aa5452, ISSN 0031-9155 (Print) 0031-9155.

[16] J. Korhonen, M. Kapanen, J. Keyriläinen, T. Seppälä, M. Tenhunen, A dual model HU conversion from MRI intensity values within and outside of bone segment for MRI-based of prostate cancer, Medical Physics 41 (1) (2014) 011704, https://doi.org/10.1118/1.4842575, ISSN 0094-2405.

[17] A. Largent, A. Barateau, J.C. Nunes, E. Mylona, J. Castelli, C. Lafond, P.B. Greer, J.A. Dowling, J. Baxter, H. Saint-Jalmes, O. Acosta, R. de Crevoisier, Comparison of deep learning-based and patch-based methods for pseudo-CT generation in MRI-based prostate dose planning, International Journal of Radiation Oncology, Biology, Physics 105 (5) (2019) 1137–1150, https://doi.org/10.1016/j.ijrobp.2019.08.049, ISSN 0360-3016.

[18] H. Arabi, J.A. Dowling, N. Burgos, X. Han, P.B. Greer, N. Koutsouvelis, H. Zaidi, Comparative study of algorithms for synthetic CT generation from MRI: consequences for MRI-guided radiation planning in the pelvic region, Medical Physics 45 (11) (Nov. 2018) 5218–5233, https://doi.org/10.1002/mp.13187, ISSN 2473-4209.

[19] S. Ioffe, C. Szegedy, Batch normalization: accelerating deep network training by reducing internal covariate shift, arXiv:1502.03167 [cs], Mar. 2015.

[20] V. Nair, G.E. Hinton, Rectified linear units improve restricted Boltzmann machines, in: Proceedings of the 27th International Conference on International Conference on Machine Learning, ICML'10, Madison, WI, USA, ISBN 9781605589077, Omnipress, 2010, pp. 807–814.

[21] X. Han, MR-based synthetic CT generation using a deep convolutional neural network method, Medical Physics 44 (4) (Apr. 2017) 1408–1419, https://doi.org/10.1002/mp.12155, ISSN 2473-4209.

[22] L. Xiang, Q. Wang, D. Nie, L. Zhang, X. Jin, Y. Qiao, D. Shen, Deep embedding convolutional neural network for synthesizing CT image from T1-weighted MR image, Medical Image Analysis 47 (July 2018) 31–44, https://doi.org/10.1016/j.media.2018.03.011, ISSN 13618415.

[23] F. Liu, P. Yadav, A.M. Baschnagel, A.B. McMillan, MR-based treatment planning in radiation therapy using a deep learning approach, Journal of Applied Clinical Medical Physics 20 (3) (2019) 105–114, ISSN 1526-9914.

[24] K. He, X. Zhang, S. Ren, J. Sun, Deep residual learning for image recognition, in: 2016 IEEE Conference on Computer Vision and Pattern Recognition (CVPR), Las Vegas, NV, USA, June, ISBN 978-1-4673-8851-1, IEEE, 2016, pp. 770–778, https://doi.org/10.1109/CVPR.2016.90.

[25] J.M. Wolterink, A.M. Dinkla, M.H.F. Savenije, P.R. Seevinck, C.A.T. van den Berg, I. Išgum, Deep MR to CT synthesis using unpaired data, in: Simulation and Synthesis in Medical Imaging, in: Lecture Notes in Computer Science, Springer, Cham, Sept. 2017, pp. 14–23, ISBN 978-3-319-68126-9 978-3-319-68127-6.

[26] I.J. Goodfellow, J. Pouget-Abadie, M. Mirza, B. Xu, D. Warde-Farley, S. Ozair, A. Courville, Y. Bengio, Generative adversarial networks, arXiv:1406.2661 [cs, stat], June 2014.

[27] X. Mao, Q. Li, H. Xie, R.Y.K. Lau, Z. Wang, S.P. Smolley, Least squares generative adversarial networks, in: 2017 IEEE International Conference on Computer Vision (ICCV), 2017, pp. 2813–2821, https://doi.org/10.1109/ICCV.2017.304.

[28] H. Emami, M. Dong, S.P. Nejad-Davarani, C. Glide-Hurst, Generating synthetic CTs from magnetic resonance images using generative adversarial networks, Medical Physics 45 (8) (2018) 3627–3636, https://doi.org/10.1002/mp.13047, ISSN 2473-4209, aapm.onlinelibrary.wiley.com/doi/abs/10.1002/mp.13047.

[29] Y. Bengio, P. Simard, P. Frasconi, Learning long-term dependencies with gradient descent is difficult, IEEE Transactions on Neural Networks 5 (2) (1994) 157–166, https://doi.org/10.1109/72.279181.

[30] K.N.D. Brou Boni, J. Klein, L. Vanquin, A. Wagner, T. Lacornerie, D. Pasquier, N. Reynaert, MR to CT synthesis with multicenter data in the pelvic era using a conditional generative adversarial network, Physics in Medicine and Biology (Feb. 2020) 1361–6560, https://doi.org/10.1088/1361-6560/ab7633, ISSN 0031-9155.

[31] P. Isola, J.-Y. Zhu, T. Zhou, A.A. Efros, Image-to-image translation with conditional adversarial networks, in: 2017 IEEE Conference on Computer Vision and Pattern Recognition (CVPR), Honolulu, HI, July, ISBN 978-1-5386-0457-1, IEEE, 2017, pp. 5967–5976, https://doi.org/10.1109/CVPR.2017.632, http://ieeexplore.ieee.org/document/8100115/.

[32] J.-Y. Zhu, T. Park, P. Isola, A.A. Efros, Unpaired image-to-image translation using cycle-consistent adversarial networks, IEEE International Conference on Computer Vision (Oct. 2017).

[33] H. Yang, J. Sun, A. Carass, C. Zhao, J. Lee, Z. Xu, J. Prince, Unpaired brain MR-to-CT synthesis using a structure-constrained CycleGAN, arXiv:1809.04536 [cs], Sept. 2018.

[34] J. Korhonen, M. Kapanen, J.J. Sonke, L. Wee, E. Salli, J. Keyriläinen, T. Seppälä, M. Tenhunen, Feasibility of MRI-based reference images for image-guided radiotherapy of the pelvis with either cone-beam computed tomography or planar localization images, Acta Oncologica 54 (6) (2015) 889–895, https://doi.org/10.3109/0284186x.2014.958197, ISSN 0284-186x.

[35] J. Wyatt, H. McCallum, Applying a commercial atlas-based synthetic computed tomography algorithm to patients with hip prostheses for prostate magnetic resonance-only radiotherapy, Radiotherapy and Oncology 133 (2019) 100–105, https://doi.org/10.1016/j.radonc.2018.12.029, ISSN 0167-8140.

[36] J.J. Wyatt, R.L. Brooks, D. Ainslie, E. Wilkins, E. Raven, K. Pilling, R.A. Pearson, H.M. McCallum, The accuracy of magnetic resonance – cone beam computed tomography soft-tissue matching for prostate radiotherapy, Physics and Imaging in Radiation Oncology 12 (2019) 49–55, https://doi.org/10.1016/j.phro.2019.11.005, ISSN 2405-6316.

[37] Z. Wang, A.C. Bovik, H.R. Sheikh, E.P. Simoncelli, Image quality assessment: from error visibility to structural similarity, IEEE Transactions on Image Processing 13 (2004) 600, https://doi.org/10.1109/TIP.2003.819861, ISSN 10577149.

[38] D.A. Low, W.B. Harms, S. Mutic, J.A. Purdy, A technique for the quantitative evaluation of dose distributions, Medical Physics 25 (5) (1998) 656–661, https://doi.org/10.1118/1.598248, ISSN 0094-2405 (Print) 0094-2405.

[39] N. Hodapp, The ICRU report 83: prescribing, recording and reporting photon-beam intensity-modulated radiation therapy (IMRT), Strahlentherapie und Onkologie 188 (1) (2012) 97–99, https://doi.org/10.1007/s00066-011-0015-x, ISSN 0179-7158.

[40] E. Palmér, E. Persson, P. Ambolt, C. Gustafsson, A. Gunnlaugsson, L.E. Olsson, Cone beam CT for QA of synthetic CT in MRI only for prostate patients, Journal of Applied Clinical Medical Physics 19 (6) (2018) 44–52, https://doi.org/10.1002/acm2.12429, ISSN 1526-9914.

[41] P. Greer, J. Martin, M. Sidhom, P. Hunter, P. Pichler, J.H. Choi, L. Best, J. Smart, T. Young, M. Jameson, T. Afinidad, C. Wratten, J. Denham, L. Holloway, S. Sridharan, R. Rai, G. Liney, P. Raniga, J. Dowling, A multi-center prospective study for implementation of an MRI-only prostate treatment planning workflow, Frontiers in Oncology 9 (2019) 826, https://doi.org/10.3389/fonc.2019.00826, ISSN 2234-943X (Print) 2234-943x.

[42] J. Martin, P. Keall, S. Siva, P. Greer, D. Christie, K. Moore, J. Dowling, D. Pryor, P. Chong, N. McLeod, A. Raman, J. Lynam, J. Smart, C. Oldmeadow, C.I. Tang, D.G. Murphy, J. Millar, K.H. Tai, L. Holloway, P. Reeves, A. Hayden, T. Lim, T. Holt, M. Sidhom, TROG 18.01 phase III randomised clinical trial of the Novel Integration of New prostate radiation schedules with adJuvant Androgen deprivation: NINJA study protocol, BMJ Open 9 (8) (2019) e030731, https://doi.org/10.1136/bmjopen-2019-030731, ISSN 2044-6055.

[43] J.A. Dowling, J. Korhonen, MR-Only Methodology, Springer International Publishing, 2019, pp. 131–151.

[44] M.F. Spadea, M. Maspero, P. Zaffino, J. Seco, Deep learning-based synthetic-CT generation in radiotherapy and PET: a review, 2021.

[45] T. Wang, Y. Lei, Y. Fu, J.F. Wynne, W.J. Curran, T. Liu, X. Yang, A review on medical imaging synthesis using deep learning and its clinical applications, Journal of Applied Clinical Medical Physics 22 (1) (2021) 11–36, https://doi.org/10.1002/acm2.13121.

[46] J.M. Edmund, T. Nyholm, A review of substitute CT generation for MRI-only radiation therapy, Radiation Oncology 12 (1) (Dec. 2017), https://doi.org/10.1186/s13014-016-0747-y, ISSN 1748-717X.

[47] E. Johnstone, J.J. Wyatt, A.M. Henry, S.C. Short, D. Sebag-Montefiore, L. Murray, C.G. Kelly, H.M. McCallum, R. Speight, Systematic review of synthetic computed tomography generation methodologies for use in magnetic resonance imaging–only radiation therapy, International Journal of Radiation Oncology, Biology, Physics 100 (1) (Jan. 2018) 199–217, https://doi.org/10.1016/j.ijrobp.2017.08.043, ISSN 03603016.

[48] L.G.W. Kerkmeijer, M. Maspero, G.J. Meijer, J.R.N. van der Voort van Zyp, H.C.J. de Boer, C.A.T. van den Berg, Magnetic resonance imaging only workflow for radiotherapy simulation and planning in prostate cancer, Clinical Oncology (The Royal College of Radiologists) 30 (11) (2018) 692–701, https://doi.org/10.1016/j.clon.2018.08.009, ISSN 0936-6555.

[49] A.M. Owrangi, P.B. Greer, C.K. Glide-Hurst, MRI-only treatment planning: benefits and challenges, Physics in Medicine and Biology 63 (5) (2018) 05tr01, https://doi.org/10.1088/1361-6560/aaaca4, ISSN 0031-9155 (Print) 0031-9155.

[50] L. Vandewinckele, M. Claessens, A. Dinkla, C. Brouwer, W. Crijns, D. Verellen, W. van Elmpt, Overview of artificial intelligence-based applications in radiotherapy: recommendations for implementation and quality assurance, Radiotherapy and Oncology 153 (2020) 55–66, https://doi.org/10.1016/j.radonc.2020.09.008, ISSN 0167-8140.

[51] R. Speight, M. Dubec, C.L. Eccles, B. George, A. Henry, T. Herbert, R.I. Johnstone, G.P. Liney, H. McCallum, M.A. Schmidt, IPEM topical report: guidance on the use of MRI for external beam radiotherapy treatment planning, Physics in Medicine and Biology 66 (5) (Feb 2021) 055025, https://doi.org/10.1088/1361-6560/abdc30.

[52] C.N. Ladefoged, I. Law, U. Anazodo, K. St Lawrence, D. Izquierdo-Garcia, C. Catana, N. Burgos, M.J. Cardoso, S. Ourselin, B. Hutton, I. Mérida, N. Costes, A. Hammers, D. Benoit, S. Holm, M. Juttukonda, H. An, J. Cabello, M. Lukas, S. Nekolla, S. Ziegler, M. Fenchel, B. Jakoby, M.E. Casey, T. Benzinger, L. Højgaard, A.E. Hansen, F.L. Andersen, A multi-centre evaluation of eleven clinically feasible brain PET/MRI attenuation correction techniques using a large cohort of patients, NeuroImage 147 (2017) 346–359, https://doi.org/10.1016/j.neuroimage.2016.12.010, ISSN 1053-8119 (Print) 1053-8119.

[53] A. Mehranian, H. Arabi, H. Zaidi, Vision 20/20: magnetic resonance imaging-guided attenuation correction in PET/MRI: challenges, solutions, and opportunities, Medical Physics 43 (3) (2016) 1130–1155, https://doi.org/10.1118/1.4941014, ISSN 0094-2405.

Review of cell image synthesis for image processing

Vladimír Ulman[a] **and David Wiesner**[b]

[a]*IT4Innovations, VSB – Technical University of Ostrava, Ostrava, Czech Republic*
[b]*Centre for Biomedical Image Analysis, Masaryk University, Brno, Czech Republic*

21.1 Introduction

The purpose of this chapter is to review *what*, *why* and *how* images with fake content are created and used for the benefit of biomedical image processing. We will illustrate it on applications that are emerging in the recent literature.

Starting with *why* synthetic biomedical images are created, the most frequent incentive is certainly the ability to obtain an additional auxiliary information that usually characterizes the content of the created image in an agreed way. The most prominent example of such auxiliary data in this field are segmentation masks that are showing true geometry of fake cells displayed in the associated synthetic images. In other words, it is the reference, expected, and correct result. In this example, one can directly compare the correct masks against masks created by some segmentation algorithm in order to estimate its segmentation performance, which is again *why* the fake images with the reference results are created and used. The principle is visually reviewed in Fig. 21.1.

Indeed, synthetic images together with associated auxiliary reference data is *what* is being created in this context. This chapter focuses specifically on artificial microscopy images showing biomedical targets of interest, and its reference, which often comes in the form of images as well. The focus here is on cell-relevant and cell-level content. It is ranging from subcellular structures, such as membranes, through ensembles of actin filaments, mitochondria, or chromatin that can outline whole nuclei, all the way up to populations of loosely connected cells such as independently developing cells on a microscopy slide. In contrast, tightly packed, large scale ensembles of globally orchestrated cells, a typical sign of embryonic development and tissue formation, are out of scope of this chapter. The reference data most often convey class-type information, geometries, that is, shape and position of the targets, or tracking data, but also, for example, a noise level or population density number.

Curious reader is immediately asking *how* such data can be obtained or *how* it could be employed to improve certain image processing pipeline. The more one starts to think about it, the more *how*-questions arise. Since we do not have room to treat

Biomedical Image Synthesis and Simulation. https://doi.org/10.1016/B978-0-12-824349-7.00028-1

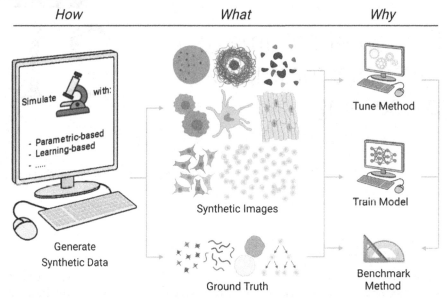

FIGURE 21.1

Illustration of the three major topics of this chapter, which are *how* and *what* synthetic data can be generated and *why* one would want to use it. A generator (left column) produces fake raw microscopy images (middle column, top) together with ground truth data (middle column, bottom). Here, the raw images can be anything from particles to cell populations as illustrated. The ground truth data is typically cell detections, sub-cellular, nuclei, or full cell segmentations and cell tracking. The two types of data can be involved in the tuning of an existing image processing method or in the training of a learning-based one (right column, top, and middle). Finally, an examined image processing method can be benchmarked by applying the method on raw synthetic images and by comparing the method's result against the associated ground truth. Data flows are visualized with the gray arrows.

every aspect of this matter, we will be only briefly describing *how* the data is created, and ask the reader to refer for the rest to the cited original literature. This way, the chapter surveys the field across published application cases of the synthetic data as well as across contemporary generative techniques that produce it.

21.1.1 Terminology

Literature recognizes multiple terms for technically the same data: annotations, training data, testing data, ground truth, or reference. We argue that, despite the context and motivation to deal with particular term varies, we are always considering here a raw microscopy image and a piece of extra information coupled to it. The raw image need not necessarily be a real one, that is, originating from some real experiment.

The raw images can be synthetic ones, fake, yet realistically looking, images created by a computer program. Such programs are often called simulators, or also generators. Literature seems to have no clear preference to any of the two terms. We, however, refer to the techniques employed in simulators as generative models, since they are capable of generating new, previously unseen data, while retaining characteristics and certain features of the modeled data class. Also notice that one of the most popular deep learning models for data synthesis in this field is called generative and adversarial network (GAN).

Even though the simulators are in the context of this field primarily image generators, they are naturally expected to include a certain degree of a true simulation of real-world processes. Indeed, we will review approaches where true simulation was (partly) involved, e.g., simulating time-lapse development of some (displayed) content [1], or simulating the image formation in a virtual microscope [2]. However, since the primary purpose is to generate images, not necessarily from the first principles, the degree of simulation typically does not match the expectation associated with this word. Consequently, the accurate simulation of biological processes is often omitted, as long as the output looks sufficiently close to real data. Thus, even when the programs generating data stick to the name simulators, such created images are often neutrally, and correctly, denoted as synthetic images, rather than simulated images.

Along a similar line, the terms simulated, fake, artificial, pseudo-real, and synthetic images are used interchangeably for the not-real raw images. Furthermore, we will also interchangeably use the terms neural networks and deep learning.

21.1.2 Applications overview

The purpose of this section is to overview the applications of annotated data in biomedical imaging. In particular, we will break it down into categories according to the following questions. What is the activity we want to achieve and on which image processing task? What is the context, that is, on what images we wish to conduct that activity? Last but not least, where did we get these images from? Apparently, the answer for the last question is trivial in this context, but in reality one could use publicly available or one's own annotated datasets instead of synthetic ones.

21.1.2.1 Subject of the application

First of all, let us briefly review what image processing methods are more or less popularly used in conjunction with synthetic images. In general, the motivation for creating synthetic images is to also create the corresponding ground truth, which is often referred to as absolute truth (owing to the principle of its construction), or as the expected result (owing to its purpose). That predetermines it for applications where similarity between result of image processing and expected result is to be assessed, or where the expected results are augmenting or extending training sets.

Training data augmentation produces for every instance in the training data a number of additional plausibly looking training instances. This often adopted trick to blow up the size of the training set, enables the trainee to observe and learn a multitude of possible appearances of the same cells. In contrast, training data synthesis creates new (independent) cells of the same kind. It is tempting to say that one without the other is less powerful, and thus both are jointly referred to as augmentation.

The prevailing subjects of application are data augmentation and image segmentation, usually with ground truth in the form of labeled masks. In this case, the augmentation often indirectly works in favor of the segmentation (this is an instance of a general principle). Detection of cells, nuclei, or smaller structures, with ground truth in the form of coordinates, is occasionally reported, e.g., in [3]. Cell classification is reported even less often, probably because it calls for multiple cell models in the synthetic images generator, which was traditionally very time consuming.

Another group consists of methods such as image restoration, denoising or deconvolution [4]. Here the form of ground truth is essentially another raw image of the same content but of higher visual quality. Using synthetic data is a must here because principally one cannot create adequate ground truth from the original real data (an excellent example is [5]), which is in contrast to the previous group of methods where using synthetic data could be seen as a matter of convenience and comfort.

A new application that emerged recently is the use of neural networks to produce another, biologically relevant, channel to complement already existing one(s). The extra channel offers a view on the same specimen as if it were prepared and acquired differently, typically it simulates another fluorescence channel, e.g., in [6,7]. This approach exploits the natural redundancy in the informational content present in many images and thus the synthesized images match reliably with the given image source(s). The transfer from transmitted light to fluorescence microscopy [6], but also image denoising or restoration, are the best examples. This idea is often used in the medical field.

Applications of methods on synthetic data with temporal dimension are also not rare. Examples are image registration [8,9], optic flow [10,11], cell tracking [12], or identification of cell's developmental stage [13].

21.1.2.2 Goal of the application

What activities one would want to conduct on a particular image processing method when having annotated, and possibly synthetic, images at hand? In fact, it ranges from the algorithm development to its deployment and quality assurance. To denote non-specifically any of such activities, the general terms of algorithm evaluation, or algorithm's performance evaluation are often used.

Algorithm developers can use such data during the research of new image processing algorithms, to see where they are good and where they are failing. They may want to tune a developed algorithm to find its best performing setting, possibly over multiple different images. In reality, the lack of adequate annotated data, here referred to as training data, was prohibiting developers to attend to this. On the other hand, in the neural networks-based image processing, due to its design, obtaining reasonable annotated data has become the first step. Also note that the process of training networks could be seen as simultaneous developing and tuning.

Users can benchmark algorithms to find the best performing one among multiple. Users should validate it, at least to have an indicative understanding of how accurate the particular algorithm is, and ideally should find its limits. This especially calls for very adequate annotated data, and is understandable that none of that is part of everyday practice. Even with GANs, the synthetic imaging is still lacking behind in offering off-the-shell solutions to produce annotated adequate data, here called as testing data.

21.1.2.3 Imaging domain

We have to ask next for what data is an evaluation relevant. Considering only the scale set out for this chapter, the literature in which synthetic data is used deals with the usual domains of image processing research. The most often occurring synthetic images are showing populations of fluorescence labeled nuclei and H&E stained tissues. Here, the motivation to use generated data is clear—it is the well known observation that manually extracted, yet unbiased, reliable, consistent, and even not-controversial annotation of real data is very hard to prepare in this field.

Fluorescence microscopy is frequently mimicked in most of its flavors. On the other hand, transmitted light or electron microscopy is rather rare. In the transmitted light microscopy, the full content of cell needs to be simulated or anyhow reproduced, which is relatively more difficult but not impossible [14–17]. Additionally, auxiliary images of refractive indices should be devised too [17], example is given later (in Fig. 21.11, Section 21.3.5). If refractive indices are used in the realm of fluorescence microscopy, they need to be defined even in regions where otherwise no fake stained content is visible [2] because the simulated light rays pass through them as well. For quantitative phase imaging, for example, we have not encountered any application so far.

Specialized simulators exist that are dedicated only to a virtual, highly realistic transfer of an image of artificial specimen through certain microscope hardware. In [18], a precise simulator was described that computes the transmission of a mathematical specimen described in a continuous domain through a 3D confocal microscope. However, digital images of high spatial resolution are used predominantly, e.g., for laser scanning confocal microscopy [19], total internal reflection fluorescence microscopy [20,19], confocal microscopy [21], single plane illumination microscopy [2], or transmitted light microscopies [17,22]. Note that in some simulators, an auxiliary image with refractive indices is among required inputs.

21.1.2.4 Modeling paradigm

The selection of the appropriate modeling paradigm naturally depends on the chosen biomedical targets, i.e., on *what* we want to generate. With that in mind, the finest sensible categorization of *how* we can approach the image generation task consists of three classes. The classes depend on the chosen computational model, generated data dimensionality and, if required, on the form of ground-truth (GT) annotation that supplements the generated images.

Computational models

In the contemporary literature, we can observe two principal computational approaches, where the employed models are either explicit or implicit. On the one hand, the explicit models, sometimes also referred to as procedural or parametric models, emerged as the first approaches to cell synthesis, e.g., in [1]. The images of cells are generated by computer programs that require no input data, involve typically a great deal of internal randomness, and offer a limited amount of modeling parameters (which usually exists only to manage the randomness). On the other hand, the implicit models essentially "only" sample from observed distributions, having little to no grasp of what exactly they are producing. We can further separate the implicit models into parametric learning models and deep learning models.

There are applications where cells are synthesized by combining and/or transforming existing, real-world examples. Here an outstanding thread of excellent work is attributed to R. F. Murphy [23,15,24], whose group pioneered generative, parametric learning of cell shapes as well as distributions of cellular content with respect to the cell shape.

Finally, the neural network-based approaches to cell synthesis are currently very popular and have a steadily growing body of applications. The respective methods are usually based on the GANs [25], but we can also observe approaches utilizing the variational autoencoders (VAE) [26]. We can only speculate, but the wide spread is probably owing to the capability of the networks to generate pretty much anything they are trained on.

Data dimensionality

Considering the broad variety of synthetic data that one may want to generate, we can define two primary aspects that affect the overall dimensionality,[1] spatial and temporal. On the one hand, the spatial dimensionality often varies from simple 2D images, e.g., in [27], to 3D images with multiple 2D-stacks, e.g., in [28]. On the other hand, the temporal dimensionality often varies from static images, e.g., in [29], to (time-lapse) sequences of images, e.g., in [30]. The spatial dimensionality is further affected by the number of image channels, where we can have either single-channel or multi-channel images.

Many of the applications of synthetic single-channel images are showing truly one fluorescence channel, displaying exactly one "face" of a cell. A classical example of a suite of end-to-end, single-channel simulators can be found in [31] and its later extensions [21]. In contrast, there are applications, e.g., in [14], from bright-field, phase-contrast, and similar microscopy fields where everything in the simulated scene is represented in one channel.

The multi-channel category can be further divided into cases where one semantic channel is described using multiple image channels, e.g., in [16], and into cases where

---

[1] Note that the dimensionality of the output is affected not only by the generated images, but also by the generated ground truth, if present.

multiple semantic channels are described each in its own separate image channel,[2] e.g., in [32–34]. The first case is similar to taking a photo with a cell phone, where the color information of the same photographed scene is represented by separate R, G, B (red, green, blue) channels, whereas the second case may apply for an acquisition of multiple fluorescent stains representing different proteins in a cell.

Ground-truth forms

Annotating images by hand is usually time consuming, error-prone, and in the case of high dimensional data (e.g., 3D time-lapse sequences) often infeasible. Hence, generating accompanying annotation along with the synthetic data is generally of great interest. The form of ground truth depends on the desired application, contemporary methods are able to produce reference annotation for cell segmentation, classification, detection or tracking. There seems to be only a handful of forms, but they can support a plethora of applications, as many tasks can actually utilize the same annotation. For example, geometric centers or morphological skeletons of segmentation masks can often serve well for the purpose of detection. Masks' labels can be easily mapped to cell classes and serve in per-cell classifications tasks. In general, the requested form of ground truth and *what* is to be simulated determines the choice of the computational model, where the latter usually dominates the decision making and the former follows.

21.2 **History**

The idea of using synthetic images is of course not new. In spite of it, not many reviews were published about this topic. The most recent we know about is from Ulman et al. [35]. According to that review, we can even say that this field has more than 20 years of somewhat active research. Indeed, that review from 2016 covered 61 papers and only 5 of them were published before the year 2000, with one or more papers published in every year. We will, of course, not repeat that review here. Instead, we will summarize in this section the pre-2016 publications that we believe were influential to the field.

The most resonating paper regarding the generation of fake testing data is still the paper by Lehmussola et al. [32] from 2007. It introduces the SIMCEP tool, a suite of Matlab® scripts to generate 2D RGB images with segmentation ground truth. The images display small populations of cells, arranged according to user-controllable clustering and overlap levels. The cell shapes are given as spline-connected, randomly displaced points arranged originally on a circle. Perlin texture is used, then Gaussian blurring and noise is added to produce the final outcome. Interestingly enough, the authors claim that the tool came into being "to allow a hands-on experience on the simulation methods presented in this paper" [32] – quite unusual application of syn-

---

[2] The ground truth can be multi-dimensional too, e.g., a segmentation mask per image channel.

thetic images. They also state that it "will provide a modular tool for future research" that could not be more true as history is still showing. Synthetic data created with this tool are available in public benchmark collections [36,37].

A fairly popular extension of the above was published five years later, a tool called SimuCell [38]. It is again a collection of Matlab scripts, it uses and extends the original work of Lehmussola et al. Nevertheless, software modularity was at the heart of this contribution allowing users to provide their own cell models. Owing to this, heterogeneous cellular populations composed of diverse cell types can be generated taking into account numerous forms of interdependencies. For example, cellular distribution can be affected by the localization pattern of some marker. Generic as it seems, still if there is any limitation in their approach, it is the focus on two-dimensional modeling.

In the meantime, Svoboda et al. [31] in 2009 formulated their universal 3-stage approach to generation of biomedical images. Inspired by various simulators mostly from medical imaging, where simulators were maturer at that time, they observed that a digital phantom (a digital image of a raw cell) should be generated at first, then submitted to a simulator of optical system (body of a microscope) and finally submitted to a simulator of a detector (digital camera) that forms the final generated realistic looking image. The idea was that one could interchange one's own module into any of the three stages. They demonstrated their approach across scales by generating images of fluorescence beads, isolated HL60 cells, and later of colon tissue [39]. All was in 3D. The generators are preferably available via the CytoPacq web interface, which is still being extended [21].

Notice the emphasis on the modularity in the latter two examples, which was one way to incorporate generality into the generators (not only) back then. Most of the modules were actual algorithms that were controlling whatever was necessary that had direct influence on the appearance—content of the generated images. This approach is slowly becoming obsolete today with the deep learning paradigm, in which appearance is learnt, instead of being programmed, and then created with inference. This appears to be a lot easier and more flexible approach.

The idea of learning from images is also not a recent one. The best-known tool for this is CellOrganizer [23,15] by Murphy et al. This group has been pioneering learnable representations of cell shapes for more than a decade. They started with learning of 2D shapes [40] already in 2007, later of 3D shapes [41], and recently re-evaluated and improved their concept [24]. Their approach also entails more dimensions. First of all, they are traditionally (also already in [40]) looking into learning and reproducing spatial arrangements of, e.g., selected proteins or full nucleus with respect to the geometry of cell membrane. While the modeling was intended primarily for biologists, from our stand point it is a modeling capable of producing multi-channel fake images with ground truth. Some channels, e.g., with proteins, aspire to generate texture, while others, e.g., that with nucleus or with cell, are useful for segmentation ground truth. Their research in shape dynamics is yet another strong point of the group.

Speaking of dynamics, an extension of the 3-stage approach towards temporal dimension [42] materialized into MitoGen [1] in 2016, an end-to-end generator of 3D time-lapse images with ground truth for segmentation and tracking. It can simulate chromatin stained populations of HL60-like cells that move on a virtual flat surface and develop throughout a full cell cycle, including mitotic divisions. The Achilles' heel of the tool is its incapability of cell-to-cell interactions—the simulation often stops whenever a very dense cell cluster is formed. Synthetic data created with this tool are available in public benchmark [43], or can be generated on-demand from a web service [21].

In the same year, Stegmaier et al. published their outstanding simulator for synthetic embryomics [44]. Unlike MitoGen, their simulator builds upon a biophysical predecessor of [45], an agent-based model that in the first place plausibly handles cell-to-cell interactions. One agent represents spatial location of one cell. Their tool similarly features dividing cells with cell cycle. Additionally, they added a feedback-loop to control local population densities (by shortening or prolonging cell cycle lengths in regions where density differs) and overall cell flow to follow closely the gross appearance of a user-provided, preprocessed real embryo. The simulation is here supervised by the user data, zebrafish embryo in their case, and it is why the authors declare their approach as "only" semi-synthetic. Finally, every simulation agent is replaced at its position with a pre-rendered image of a cell (and its mask in ground truth image) respecting also its current phase within the cell cycle. A pool of cell cycle phase-resolved images was supplied here by MitoGen [1].

Apparently, most of the generators were focused to aid cell segmentation or tracking, predominantly in images from fluorescence microscopy. This is true even today. In an attempt to highlight also other domains and applications, we remind of the following.

The group of K. Rohr has a significant trace in non-rigid registration of fluorescence labeled nuclei. With every new method of their, they evaluate its accuracy on synthetic images, recently in [8,9]. They established a procedure in which a 2D or 3D real image is deformed with a known transformation which is taken from a similar experiment. A time-lapse image sequence is created by repeating this principle. The real image and real transform warrant a high degree of realism. To study robustness of their method in [8], they were adding layers of noise of varying magnitudes.

Using generated data is de facto standard in the field of optical flow because the proper ground truth must provide one displacement vector to *every* pixel in an input image. While synthetic datasets for optical flow are common in computer vision, there is only a few examples of application of synthetic, ground-truth-enabled optical flow datasets in biomedical imaging [46,10,47,11], and of only one generator [48].

Last but not least, heroic deeds in the realm of procedural modeling were achieved to routinely generate realistic images of pap-smear specimen in bright-field microscopy [14] and colorectal adenocarcinoma tissue in H&E imaging [16]. Note that everything from the cell is visible(!) in these applications, and thus has to be generated, and modeled. From the opposite scale, we wish to remind of generators used for

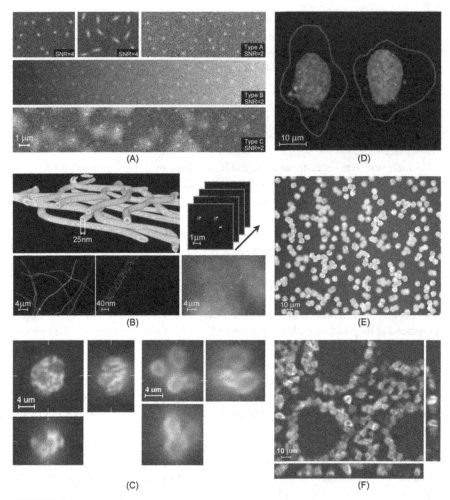

FIGURE 21.2

Examples of synthetic data obtained with well-established simulators. In particular, fluorescent particles of varying sizes [51] (A), tubular network of microtubules [49] (B), 3D cell nucleus of HL60 and four granulocytes [31] (C), multi-channel solid nuclei and membrane outlines [40] (D), 2D cell population from the influential SIMCEP [32] (E), and 3D cells from human colon tissue [39] (F). *Source: Ulman et al., 2016 [35].*

three well-known challenges. Two were focused on sub-pixel localization and deconvolution of synthetic tubular networks that were modeled in the continuous spatial domain [49], and one was utilizing a generator of synthetic images of particles for the purpose of their detection and tracking [50]. Finally, a representative digest of this school of approaches is summarized in Fig. 21.2.

21.3 **Contemporary applications**

Let us now turn our attention to discussing *what*, *why*, and *how* synthetic biomedical images have been created and used in the literature recently. This section is structured into sub-sections according to the scale and type of simulated data, i.e., *what* cellular content is displayed in the fake images. Each sub-section begins with selected examples of procedural generators followed by state-of-the-art deep learning ones, i.e., it reviews *how* are the fake images created. Motivation, context, and obtained ground truth are reported with every generator to illustrate *why* it was developed. The focus is mostly on the works published between 2017 and 2021.

Structured overview of contemporary deep learning methods and the corresponding papers is available in Table 21.1, the papers that also have the respective source code publicly available are listed in Table 21.2 along with the URLs to download it. The actual applications of end-to-end cell synthesis techniques are listed in Table 21.3 including the type of generated ground truth.

21.3.1 **Sub-cellular structures**

In the recently published literature [5,75], synthetic sub-cellular structures generated with parametric-based models were applied in the training of learning-based models. In one case [5], a resolution enhancing network was trained on semi-synthetic training data to produce a high spatial resolution image from a low resolution one. The later was created by taking a real 2D fluorescence microscopy image, degrading it with a special point spread function (PSF) and down-sampling afterwards; and the network was trained to essentially undo this. Since the reference high resolution image need not be accessible in every application, the authors were generating also purely synthetic images, here of filamentous microtubule-networks and insulin secretory granules. The ground truth was an intermediate image as it was found before the artificial microscopy degradation step. Note that the generative process was supplemented with a proper geometry simulation.

In another application [75], a true, physics-based simulator of artificial 3D fluorescence microscopy images of mitochondria was employed as well, and also because of the impossibility to create ground truth otherwise. Here, the texture was modeled with artificial fluorescent molecules that are displaced on the mitochondrion surface and whose light emission was governed with a particular photokinetics model. Finally, the outcome image was degraded with PSF and noise, and a ground-truth segmentation mask was extracted. Owing to its design, the physics-based model can evolve and simulate mitochondria over a course of time, enabling to generate a time-lapse data with associated tracking ground truth.

To answer how a distribution of coordinates can be best represented and consequently two distributions compared, images showing fake fluorescent particles were generated recently [3]. Varying PSF and noise was applied to finish the generation of the raw images, and to find limits of the considered representations.

First deep learning works aimed at simulating sub-cellular structures emerged in 2019. Yuan et al. [7] proposed a method for synthesis of 2D cellular structures uti-

Table 21.1 An overview of deep learning works in cell synthesis. The table describes year of publication, first author, reference identifier of the paper, type of cells that were synthesized, employed deep learning (DL) models, dimensionality of the generated data, and resolution of image tiles outputted by the respective DL model in pixels. Generated image tiles are often stitched together to form a bigger frame containing multiple cells [52]. Among the less-known models are Wasserstein GAN (WGAN), least squares GAN (LSGAN), spatially constrained CycleGAN (SpCycleGAN), and autoregressive networks (AR).

Year	Authors	Ref.	Cell type	DL Models	Dim.	Tile res. [pix]
2017	Goldsborough et al.	[27]	cancer	WGAN, LSGAN, VAE	2D	96×96
2017	Osokin et al.	[53]	yeast	GAN, WGAN	2D	48×80
2018	Arbelle et al.	[54]	human	Conditional GAN	2D	512×640
2018	Fu et al.	[55]	rat kidney	SpCycleGAN	3D	$512 \times 512 \times 512$
2018	Pandhe et al.	[52]	human	DCGAN, WGAN, AR	2D+t	64×64
2019	Bailo et al.	[29]	red blood	pix2pixHD	2D	1920×1200
2019	Baniukiewicz et al.	[56]	Dictyostelium	DCGAN, 3D GAN	2D, 3D	256×256
2019	Baydilli et al.	[57]	white blood	Conditional GAN	2D	128×128
2019	Böhland et al.	[58]	human	CycleGAN, U-Net	2D	520×696
2019	Dirvanauskas et al.	[59]	human	GAN	2D	600×600
2019	Dunn et al.	[28]	rat kidney, liver	SpCycleGAN, U-Net	2D, 3D	256×256
2019	Eschweiler et al.	[60]	Arabidopsis	CycleGAN, PatchGAN	2D	256×256
2019	Han et al.	[61]	rat kidney	SpCycleGAN, 3D GAN	3D	$128 \times 128 \times 128$
2019	Lafarge et al.	[62]	human	SpCycleGAN, VAE	2D	68×68
2019	Lu et al.	[63]	yeast, human	AlexNet	2D	64×64
2019	Majurski et al.	[64]	human	GAN, U-Net	2D	256×256
2019	Scalbert et al.	[65]	cancer	CNN	2D	110×104
2019	Yuan et al.	[7]	–	DCGAN, U-Net	2D	256×256
2019	Wiesner et al.	[66]	cancer	3D GAN	3D	$64 \times 64 \times 64$
2020	Aida et al.	[67]	cancer	Conditional GAN	2D	256×256
2020	Almezhghwi et al.	[68]	white blood	GAN, CNN	2D	32×32
2020	Chen et al.	[69]	cancer	Residual conditional GAN	2D	382×382
2020	Comes et al.	[70]	cancer	Social GAN	2D+t	–
2020	Comes et al.	[71]	white blood	Multi-scale GAN	2D+t	64×64
2020	Pasupa et al.	[72]	red blood	Semi-supervised GAN	2D	224×224
2020	Verma et al.	[73]	human	GAN, CNN	2D	512×512
2021	Bähr et al.	[30]	cancer	CellCycleGAN	2D+t	96×96

lizing a conditional DCGAN. The authors used three image channels to represent different structures within a cell, cell membrane, proteins and nucleus. The GAN architecture utilized an encoder–decoder generator with a U-Net-like shape, taking advantage of skip-connections to preserve important spatial features. Unlike standard "copy" connections in U-Net, the authors' GAN used three different types of skip-connections, self-gated connection, encoder-gated connection, and label-gated connection, incorporating the information in different ways. The training data were obtained from 3D microscopy images by maximum-intensity projection, producing

Table 21.2 A list of links to publicly available source codes for learning-based methods in cell synthesis. The table details year of publication, first author, reference identifier of the paper, and web address at which the source code can be obtained.

Year	Authors	Ref.	Source code link
2017	Goldsborough et al.	[27]	github.com/carpenterlab/2017_goldsborough_mlcb
2017	Osokin et al.	[53]	github.com/aosokin/biogans
2018	Arbelle et al.	[54]	github.com/arbellea/DeepCellSeg
2019	Baniukiewicz et al.	[56]	pilip.lnx.warwick.ac.uk/Frontiers_2019
2019	Böhland et al.	[58]	github.com/junyanz/pytorch-CycleGAN-and-pix2pix
2019	Dunn et al.	[28]	github.com/tbenst/DeepSynth_Software
2019	Lafarge et al.	[62]	github.com/tueimage/cytoVAE
2019	Lu et al.	[63]	github.com/alexxijielu/paired_cell_inpainting
2019	Scalbert et al.	[65]	gitlab.com/vitadx/articles/generic_isolated_cell_images_generator
2019	Ruan et al.	[24]	murphylab.cbd.cmu.edu/software
2019	Yuan et al.	[7]	github.com/divelab/cgan
2019	Wiesner et al.	[66]	cbia.fi.muni.cz/research/simulations/gan.html
2020	Aida et al.	[67]	github.com/affinelayer/pix2pix-tensorflow
2020	Comes et al.	[70]	github.com/agrimgupta92/sgan
2020	Hollandi et al.	[74]	github.com/spreka/biomagdsb
2021	Bähr et al.	[30]	github.com/stegmaierj/CellCycleGAN

more than 6000 2D multi-channel images of size 256×256 pixels. The presented evaluation showed that the approach produced better results for generating cell structures than the previous approach utilizing adversarial autoencoders published in 2017 by Johnson et al. [76].

In 2019 Lu et al. [63] used an encoder–decoder convolutional neural network (CNN) based on the architecture of AlexNet [77] to predict markers of cell proteins in fluorescence microscopy. The authors used multi-channel image patches of size 64×64 pixels containing single yeast or human cell. The authors' qualitative evaluation showed that the trained model was able to synthesize markers with realistic protein localization corresponding to given cells. Moreover, the authors demonstrated that the feature representations extracted by the model can be used for exploratory biological analysis of cells in multi-channel microscopy.

A year later, Verma et al. [73] published a study focused on improving the multi-label cell protein classification by data augmentation using various image processing techniques, including GANs. The authors evaluated the results of these methods with contemporary CNNs, e.g., DenseNet, InceptionV3, Resnet, and others, on multi-channel images of resolutions 512×512 and 256×256 pixels.

21.3.2 Shapes of cellular structures

Sometimes, the image processing method at hand works only with cell masks, and does not consider texture at all. Consider, for example, the task of restoring full segmentation masks when cells are overlapping in the images, or various spheres-fitting

Table 21.3 An overview of deep learning works in cell synthesis based on the actual applications and the corresponding ground truth. The table contains a checkmark "✓" for intended applications of listed works and also includes an information about available ground truth (GT) annotation accompanying the synthetic data. Numerous methods do not provide image GT, like a segmentation mask. Examples of non-image GT may be time-lapse series of positions [70], or known content class [57]. *Note that only methods that are applicable for end-to-end cell image synthesis are listed (e.g., no shape-only or image-formation methods).*

Year	Authors	Ref.	Nucleus detection	Cell detection	Nucleus segmentation	Cell segmentation	Cell classification	Cell tracking	Data augmentation	Binary mask	Labeled mask	Non-image GT	No GT
2017	Goldsborough et al.	[27]	–	–	–	–	–	–	✓	–	–	–	✓
2017	Osokin et al.	[53]	–	–	–	–	–	–	✓	–	–	–	✓
2018	Arbelle et al.	[54]	–	–	–	✓	–	–	–	–	✓	–	–
2018	Fu et al.	[55]	–	–	✓	–	–	–	–	✓	✓	–	–
2018	Pandhe et al.	[52]	–	–	–	–	–	–	✓	–	–	–	✓
2019	Bailo et al.	[29]	–	✓	–	✓	–	–	–	–	✓	–	–
2019	Baniukiewicz et al.	[56]	–	–	–	–	✓	–	–	✓	–	–	–
2019	Baydilli et al.	[57]	–	–	–	–	✓	–	–	–	–	✓	–
2019	Böhland et al.	[58]	✓	–	✓	–	–	–	–	✓	✓	–	–
2019	Dirvanauskas et al.	[59]	–	✓	–	–	✓	–	–	–	–	✓	–
2019	Dunn et al.	[28]	–	–	✓	–	–	–	–	✓	✓	–	–
2019	Eschweiler et al.	[60]	–	–	–	✓	–	–	–	–	✓	–	–
2019	Han et al.	[61]	✓	–	–	–	–	–	–	✓	✓	–	–
2019	Lafarge et al.	[62]	–	–	–	–	✓	–	–	–	–	✓	–
2019	Lu et al.	[63]	–	–	–	–	✓	–	–	–	✓	–	–
2019	Majurski et al.	[64]	–	–	–	✓	–	–	–	✓	–	–	–
2019	Scalbert et al.	[65]	–	✓	–	✓	–	–	–	–	✓	–	–
2019	Yuan et al.	[7]	–	–	–	–	–	–	✓	–	–	–	✓
2020	Aida et al.	[67]	–	–	–	✓	–	–	–	–	–	–	✓
2020	Almezhghwi et al.	[68]	–	–	–	–	✓	–	–	–	✓	–	–
2020	Comes et al.	[70]	–	✓	–	–	–	✓	–	–	–	✓	–
2020	Comes et al.	[71]	–	–	–	–	–	✓	✓	–	–	–	✓
2020	Hollandi et al.	[74]	–	✓	–	✓	–	–	–	✓	✓	–	–
2020	Chen et al.	[69]	–	–	–	–	✓	–	–	–	–	✓	–
2020	Pasupa et al.	[72]	–	–	–	–	✓	–	–	–	–	✓	–
2020	Verma et al.	[73]	–	–	–	–	✓	–	–	–	–	✓	–
2021	Bähr et al.	[30]	–	–	–	✓	–	✓	–	–	✓	–	–

or ellipsoids-fitting tasks to represent shapes more conveniently. Recently also, generated masks have become a vital input for GAN-based image synthesis [29]. Using simulators that produce fake cells with no texture is, therefore, an interesting option in such and similar applications.

21.3.2.1 Intentionally simple geometries

Validation of a method that restores original shapes of overlapping cells was carried out [78] using simulated binary 2D masks of rather simple clusters made of three overlapping ellipses. A similar study with 3D shapes, also without any texture, is available too [79]. To study cell separation in membrane data, 2D hexagons were used [80].

Ellipsoidal shapes are fairly popular. In [81,55], synthetic binary volumes (3D) were generated with nuclei taking ellipsoidal shapes as well. Multiple nuclei are randomly generated in different orientations and locations. Perlin texture [81] or GAN-generated texture [55] was used to finalize the process. Despite fairly simple shapes, the authors claim that training sets consisting of only these generated images were found sufficient to train a good performing segmentation network. It remains to emphasize that care was taken here to position the ellipsoids well, which will be explained below.

21.3.2.2 Shapes of single cells

It has been demonstrated [65] recently that significant improvement in generating training data for segmentation networks can be obtained when shapes and textures are processed separately. This necessitates, in particular, a dedicated shape generator and a dedicated texture generator.

A comprehensive review of models to represent nucleus and cell shapes in 2D and 3D, and learn them from image masks, was published recently [24]. Attention was put on the generative aspect of the modeling, i.e., the ability to restore faithfully the original geometry (shape) from its model's instance, and on the ability to deliver smooth transition from one geometry to another when traversing in the model's latent space from one instance to another. Further examples, where shapes are learnt and then detailed and realistic new instances of cells are generated, can be found in [14, 66,65]. However, the problem of distributing the generated cells within images was not addressed.

21.3.2.3 Placement of cells in an image

The following applications are showing that mimicking realistic, yet adjustable distributions, or layouts, of fake cells or nuclei within generated images should be taken seriously.

In [82], 2D images of neuron nuclei are created for the evaluation of segmentation methods. To generate a shape of one nucleus, the authors use spline interpolation of random points on elliptical shapes. When placing the nuclei into the image, they allow for controlled degree of overlap, and orient nuclei using the Perlin noise. The latter is interesting because it assures a certain coherency in the orientation of neighboring nuclei.

Ellipsoid-shaped cells were also used in [81,55] as part of a process to generate synthetic training data for segmentation networks. Here, however, the distribution of cells was copied from real images. It could be seen as an augmentation technique that provides new instances of individual cells while preserving their global distribution within an image.

If only a gross layout of cells in the generated images is desired, spatially-resolved weight maps are often used. In general, the randomly sampled cell position is checked against the map, and against already inserted cells, to accept or reject this position. The process iterates until the requested number of positions is obtained. The map can be pre-determined (from some real image, or completely made up) and fixed [14], or re-generated after every established position [83].

A pragmatical conclusion that can be drawn from the paragraphs above is that matching the global distribution level of the simulated objects is beneficial for creating faithfully looking fake images, but far more importantly for the training of contemporary learning-based analysis methods [81,55,6]. In an attempt to answer the follow-up question if, besides the layout, also the number of generated objects should match exactly, a generator of masks of sub-cellular microvilli has been designed [6]. It procedurally produces masks of short rods at loci given either by particular coordinates (fixed number) extracted from a real image, or given by a distribution (any number of rods) obtained from real images. The masks are afterwards texturized with pre-trained GAN. The outcome of the study was that the analysis performance was not changed even when the number of placed masks was reasonably different.

21.3.2.4 Membranes as ground truth

When tightly adjacent cells are of interest, modeling positions of cell membranes and mitochondria allowed for 2D synthetic images of tissues from electron microscopy in [84]. They used one GAN to generate the spatial layout, and then another GAN to add texture, quite similar to [65]. This approach is learning from images that, however, needed to be annotated beforehand.

Alternatively, the de facto standard approach to generate 2D images with cell membranes is to establish a population of cell centers, and compute Voronoi tessellation on it. The art is often in how the point distribution is created such that it is randomized, yet somewhat equally displaced.

A number of tools from the field of cell-centered computational biology could provide biologically justifiable individual cell shapes, population geometries, or both. In particular, the cellular Potts model [85,86] (CPM) is especially well-suited, among other benefits, also for producing "membrane-stained" images. Being a lattice-based model, in which every cell is modeled as a set of connected pixels, two touching cells typically leave no background pixels between them, see Fig. 21.3. In other words, if the boundary of a cell would be a hypothetical outer outline around all cell pixels

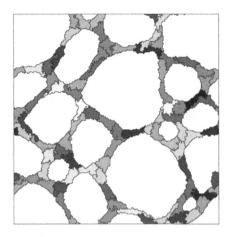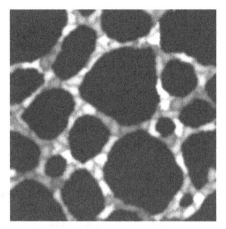

FIGURE 21.3

Example of images generated with cellular Potts model (CPM). In the 2D image with segmentation masks (left) is every mask outlined with a thin black contour that itself could be treated as a representation of cell membranes. This particular CPM-based simulator, however, was producing images (right) of fluorescence labeled full cells. *Source: new images generated using a code from [87].*

then the outline of two adjacent cells would be overlapping along the full length of the common contact.

21.3.2.5 Developing geometries

As already hinted, the computational biology field offers tools to model developing cell populations. One could take the representations of cells from the tools and complement them with (ideally also developing) textures to create annotated fake images with high-degree of realism. This has already been done in some works, e.g., in [12,44,88].

The tools can essentially provide time-resolved representations of even very large numbers of cells in loose or tight contact, at various scales, justifiably modeling various biological phenomena, and using various modeling paradigms. Examples of particularly relevant tools to the image synthesis field are the Tissue Simulation Toolkit [86], CompuCell3D [89], or Morpheus [90], all of which including the lattice-based CPM model, which has inspired the CPM-branch of image synthesis [17,88]. The apparent advantage of CPM is that it explicitly models the shape of every cell.

From the realm of off-lattice modeling, we wish to name the Chaste [91] and PhysiCell [45] tools, both offering center-based representation of cells. The cell population is governed by a balance of attractive and repulsive forces acting on pairs of nearby cells. These tools typically handle larger cell populations, compared to CPM, but at the expense of using simplified cell shapes. This is also reflected in the generators, e.g., in [12,44], that build upon this paradigm, but use only the population layout from it and otherwise provide their own cell shapes. This exciting field, together with more open-source tools available for the modelers, is being regularly surveyed, for example not long ago in [92].

Recently, [13] showed an application of synthetic data in which cell shape or texture was not important at all. In their work, time-resolved artificial point clouds were used to evaluate methods for automatic stage detection during embryonic development. Without any explicit shape or texture, point coordinate alone represents a cell in 3D space, and a particular distribution of the cells represents known developmental stage of an embryo, which is to be determined. Clearly, to maximize the correspondence between evaluation results on fake and real data, realistic cell positioning becomes (again) crucially important. Here, it was modeled from semi-accurate tracks from real embryos.

Specifically for the development and evaluation of cell tracking algorithms in 2D, but again targeting trackers that consider only the constellation of coordinates—just like in the above example, an image generator platform has been designed [93]. An interesting fact about this platform is that it comes with its own GUI and commands to control temporal behavior of the simulated cells, e.g., shape change rapidity, motility magnitude, "follow the leader" mode to offer cell clustering, or whether cells can enter/exit the image. With these commands, various time-resolved populations exhibiting different tracking phenomena could be created.

21.3.3 Static images of a single cell

For the task of visually augmenting a pipette during its operation on a cell in a video from differential interference contrast microscopy, a method for accurate online cell (and pipette) boundary tracking was developed and evaluated in [94]. The authors, therefore, developed a parametric-based simulator that produces videos showing one moving cell (but no pipette). Nevertheless, they did not provide a description of their approach, but provided its source code from which we were able to generate some example images, see Fig. 21.4.

In [95], a validation set of synthetic lens-free microscopy holograms, see Fig. 21.5, was created to evaluate performance of their novel reconstruction algorithm. Their simulator computed a hologram image from an image showing (circularly shaped) cells at some given cell density and from an absorption map image. In fact, the two images were the ground truth and also the desired outcome from the reconstruction.

In 2020 Medyukhina et al. [4] used procedural techniques to render a single 2D cell of ellipsoidal shape at very high resolution. The output image was blurred with accurate PSF, downsampled and overlaid with noise. Such image, whose original uncorrupted shape serves as ground truth, was deconvolved and the result was used to assess the quality of an examined deconvolution algorithm. In fact, the paper proposes an environment DeconvTest to execute such tests more systematically, e.g., with varying degradation parameters and evaluating multiple deconvolution algorithms.

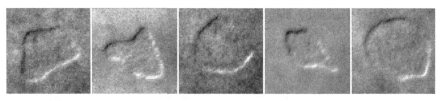

FIGURE 21.4

Example from differential interference contrast microscopy. Five 2D images with different single cells were procedurally generated to evaluate segmentation accuracy in the presence of heavy noise and interference. *Source: new images generated using a code from [94].*

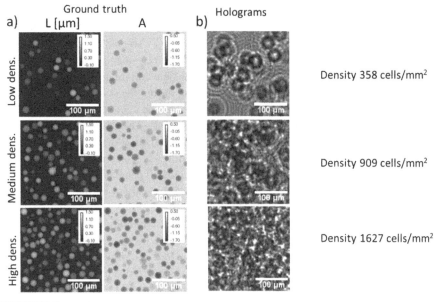

FIGURE 21.5

Example of artificial holograms from lens-free microscopy. The desired image of cells (denoted as L in a) subfigure) and possibly its absorption map image (denoted as A) is what should be ideally restored from simulated holograms (in b) subfigure). All images are artificially created for the purpose of testing an restoration algorithm. *Source: Hervé et al., 2020 [95].*

Another interesting application was the evaluation of detectors of ribonucleic acid (RNA) molecules (bright spots) considering various localization patterns and expression regimes [34]. The ground truth data was the particular RNA localization class plus the actual molecules coordinates. The coordinates were generated from extracted distributions of distances, having different distributions per localization class. The

RNA spots were placed into their own (raw) image, next to images with nucleus and cell masks.

Year 2017 saw the inception of first approaches to utilize deep learning for synthesis of microscopic cell images. Goldsborough et al. [27] proposed a study comparing results of several GAN models (i.e., DCGAN, WGAN, and LSGAN) and VAE in synthesizing realistic 2D images of breast cancer cells in fluorescence microscopy, with the training dataset containing 1.3 million images. The authors showed that GAN models were superior to VAE in learning representations for morphological profiling of cells and concluded that GANs look promising for future applications in the domain of microscopy images.

Among the first studies was also a work by Osokin et al. [53] investigating the application of GANs for synthesis of fluorescence microscopy data. The authors used a dataset of more than 25,000 2D images of single fission yeast cells to train then-contemporary GAN models (i.e., DCGAN and WGAN-GP). The study evaluated the ability of GANs to synthesize multi-channel images of size 48×80 pixels, where each channel corresponds to a specific protein. The conducted evaluation showed that the GANs are not only able to synthesize plausible cell images, but are also able to mimic changes in protein localization occurring during the cell cycle.

In 2019 Lafarge et al. [62] proposed a method for the synthesis of multi-channel human cells in fluorescence microscopy utilizing VAE. The authors' approach improved upon the original VAE by including an adversarial-driven similarity constraint, producing results that are comparable with GAN-based models. The trained model was able to synthesize realistic-looking single cell patches of size 68×68 pixels. The authors claim that the feature representations learned by the VAE are also suitable for the image-based cell profiling.

The same year Baniukiewicz et al. [56] utilized conditional GANs for multi-channel synthesis of cells in fluorescence microscopy based on an arbitrary shape mask (see Fig. 21.6). The proposed method considered 2D, pseudo-3D and fully-3D synthesis, where the 2D and pseudo-3D approaches utilized standard 2D GAN, and the fully-3D approach utilized 3D GAN [96] employing 3D convolutional layers. The models were trained on Dictyostelium cell images with resolution of 512×512 rescaled to 256×256 with 66 z-slices. The authors showed that the trained models were able to generate realistic cells based on given binary masks and that these approaches are suitable for augmenting existing datasets with new data of similar distribution. However, they concluded that the fully-3D approach is overly computationally intensive and that the pseudo-3D approach, generating individual slices separately, is much faster and still produces good results.

Baydilli et al. [57] followed with a similar method for the synthesis of white blood cells via conditional GAN conditioned on labels representing several cell classes. The authors trained the model on 266 images of 128×128 pixels and concluded that the model had improved cell classification using CNNs and is suitable for augmenting existing datasets. Iterating further on the data augmentation problem, Scalbert et al. [65] proposed a generic framework employing interesting combination of Fourier shape

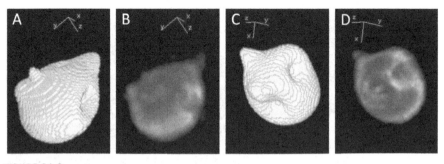

FIGURE 21.6

Example of 3D volumetric images of a single cell produced using deep learning. The figure shows synthetic cell volumes in fluorescence microscopy (B, D) produced using a learning-based method conditioned on the given cell shape (A, C). The blue color (dark gray in print version) represents low intensities and green color (light gray in print version) high intensities. *Source: Baniukiewicz et al., 2019 [56].*

descriptors and CNN feature maps to synthesize new cells with corresponding annotation.

In 2020 Pasupa et al. [72] introduced a method for augmentation of red blood cell images using semi-supervised GAN. The GAN can be trained on sparsely-annotated data and thus facilitate the generation of training datasets when the full annotation is not available. The authors showed that the augmented datasets increased the classification accuracy when used for training CNNs. A method with similar focus aimed at augmentation of cervical cancer cells using residual conditional GAN was introduced the same year by Chen et al. [69].

21.3.4 Static images of cell populations

In [82], 2D randomized elliptical shapes and background, are filled with random Perlin noise. The average texture intensity of every cell is, however, individually shifted according to a Gaussian mixture model extracted from real data. The overall realism of the synthetic image owes a lot exactly to this last step. Neuron nucleus images with segmentation ground truth were created this way.

In another similar application, careful positioning of cells was emphasized (see the first mention in Section 21.3.2.1). Here, fluorescene microscopy images of cells also of ellipsoidal shapes, and texturized once with Perlin [81] and once with GAN [55], were generated along with segmentation ground truth for the training of segmentation networks.

In [97] and in its recent extension [33], the authors present a procedural simulation system to generate 2D testing data with four types of cells, from segmentation-simple protoplasts, over cell nuclei and cytoskeleton, to difficult cytomembrane of macrophages. The cell simulation produces two channel images, for nuclei and for cytoskeleton. They create such synthetic cells with a controlled amount of overlap to evaluate performance of segmentation algorithms, see Fig. 21.7.

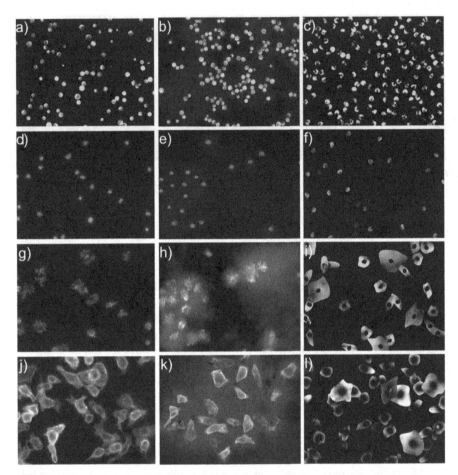

FIGURE 21.7

Example of procedurally generated 2D cells. Comparison between real and simulated images: (a)–(c) protoplast; (d)–(f) DAPI stained nuclei; (g)–(i) F-Actin channel of B cells; (j)–(l) macrophages; (a), (d), (g), and (j) are real images, (b), (e), (h), and (k) have been simulated with the approach described in [33] while (c), (f), (i), and (l) have been simulated with SimuCell. *Source: Wiesmann et al., 2017 [33].*

Multi-channel 2D images of cell populations as if displayed in the luminescence microscopy were generated to benchmark their segmentation [98]. Rather dense populations of simple-shaped cells are generated with specific synthetic labeling of nucleus and cytoplasm in the blue and green image channel, respectively. Their system offers a control of the degree of cell overlaps and clustering. In the end, PSF and noise is applied to arrive to annotated data for the benchmark.

In fluorescence microscopy, the original procedural simulator of 3D chromatin stained nuclei [1] is continuously being developed. It can produce time-lapse videos

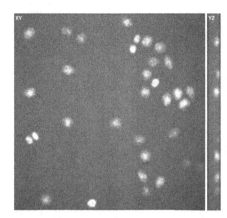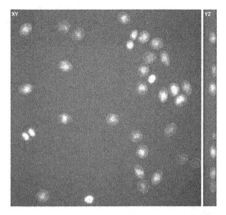

FIGURE 21.8

Example from fluorescence confocal microscopy. A single XY and YZ slices from a procedurally generated 3D raw image (left) and the same data overlaid with ground truth segmentation outline (right). Additionally, cells during interphase (most cells), shortly before (e.g., the pair at the left border) and after division (the pair of small bright cells near the center of the top border) are indicated with the segmentation outline of green, red, and cyan color (mid gray, dark gray, and light gray in print version). *Source: new images generated using the most recent code from [1].*

of small- to mid-size ensembles of developing nuclei. A frame from the time-lapse is thus showing nuclei during various stages of cell cycle, which is exemplified in Fig. 21.8.

Continuing their previous work [81] on segmentation of cell volumes, in 2018 Fu et al. [55] proposed a method utilizing synthetic data generated by GANs for improving segmentation of 3D nucleus volumes with CNNs (i.e., U-Net), addressing the scarcity of annotated (ground truth) training data. The authors introduced a new model, spatially constrained CycleGAN (SpCycleGAN), utilizing a custom loss function to reduce spatial shifting of the nuclei exhibited by the original CycleGAN. The GAN was trained to augment datasets of annotated grayscale rat kidney cell volumes in fluorescence microscopy that were subsequently used to train the CNN for segmentation. The authors synthesized two CNN training datasets of resolutions $512 \times 512 \times 512$ and $512 \times 512 \times 64$ voxels, consisting of 1600 pairs of grayscale volumes and reference binary annotations per resolution. They concluded that the segmentation results improved after augmenting the CNN training data, however, they also stated that the trained CNN had difficulties separating nuclei when they were closely touching each other.

The successive work by Dunn et al. [28] was published a year later and iterated further on the existing method, integrating combination of SpCycleGAN and 3D U-Net into an automated 3D nucleus segmentation tool, DeepSynth (see Fig. 21.9). The

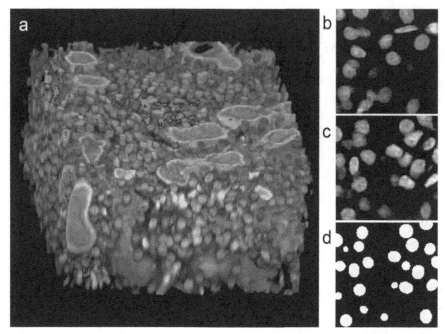

FIGURE 21.9

Example of a static cell population produced using deep learning. The figure shows: (a) 3D rendering of an image volume acquired from a real rat kidney tissue sample, where the red, green, and blue colors (light gray, dark gray, and mid gray in print version) represent different fluorescent stains; (b) single z-plane that was used to derive the synthetic image volume; (c) single z-plane from the simulated synthetic volume; and (d) binary segmentation of the z-plane shown in (c). *Source: Dunn et al., 2019 [28].*

main goal of DeepSynth was to enable accurate segmentation without the need of manually annotated data. Thus, the authors utilized a GAN to synthesize 3D nucleus textures from synthetic binary volumes representing the cell nuclei, which were obtained by translating and rotating ellipsoids of various sizes. The trained GAN was subsequently utilized to synthesize 200 pairs of 3D annotated synthetic microscopy images that were tiled into 1600 training samples for the U-Net CNN. The authors' quantitative analysis realized on volumes of rat kidney and liver cells showed that DeepSynth nucleus segmentation results are equivalent or better than the results obtained with common biomedical image processing toolkits (i.e., CellProfiler, FAR-SIGHT, and Squassh). Furthermore, the authors claim that trained DeepSynth is able to generalize and produce good results even when used on types of cells that differ from the training data, provided that the dimensions and texture of the nuclei is sufficiently similar.

In 2018 Arbelle et al. [54] proposed a method for generating cell nucleus segmentations from fluorescence microscopy images with conditional GAN. The model was based on the pix2pix architecture [99] for image-to-image translation, where grayscale images of lung cancer cells were taken as the input and segmentation masks with labeled cells were the output. The training dataset was created using 72 images of resolution 512×640 pixels with each image containing approximately 50 cells. Since only 15 images of 72 were manually annotated, the authors utilized data augmentation to increase the number of training examples. They concluded that the trained model is able to produce good segmentation results even if trained with a small number of training images.

A work with similar focus was published in 2019 by Bailo et al. [29]. The authors proposed a method for the synthesis of red blood cell populations using GANs conditioned on the cell shape masks. The model was trained on 100 multi-channel images with resolution of 1920×1200 pixels. The trained model was able to synthesize new populations utilizing synthetic masks created by randomly placing individual cell shapes from an existing shape database. The authors concluded that this method is suitable for augmenting existing datasets and showed that the augmentation had improved cell segmentation and detection results of CNNs. Augmentation was also evaluated by Böhland et al. [58], where the authors concluded that a segmentation network trained with a synthetic dataset generated by GAN can perform as well as a network trained with real-world manually annotated data.

Another method for segmentation was proposed by Majurski et al. [64]. The authors focused on improving the segmentation of cell contours with CNN (i.e., U-Net) by transfer learning of features learned by GAN. The GAN was used to extract an abstract representation from microscopy images of human stem cells (iRPE), which were partitioned into 1000 grayscale tiles of 256×256 pixels. This representation was subsequently transferred to the segmentation CNN. The authors showed that the method was able to work successfully on sparsely-annotated datasets and concluded that this approach improved the cell boundary detection and accuracy of the CNN.

An unconventional method for 3D rat kidney cell nucleus counting in fluorescence microscopy was introduced by Han et al. [61]. The work utilizes a combination of Sp-CycleGAN and 3D GAN, where the SpCycleGAN is used for generating synthetic microscopy images with annotations, and the 3D GAN is trained entirely on the respective synthetic data to perform nucleus counting by predicting the distance map volume for the input. The authors' evaluation showed that the trained 3D GAN is able to successfully locate and count the cell nuclei in 3D microscopy volumes.

In 2019 Dirvanauskas et al. [59] published a method to utilize GAN to synthesize human embryo cells called HEMIGEN. The authors used 5000 grayscale training images with resolution of 600×600 pixels containing from one to four cells. Trained HEMIGEN allows controlling the size, position and number of cells in the synthetic images, facilitating the creation of datasets suitable for classification, analysis, or training of ML models.

A year later, Almezhghwi et al. [68] introduced a study focused on improving segmentation performance of contemporary CNNs (i.e., VGG-16, ResNet and DenseNet) utilizing data augmentation via GANs. The authors' quantitative evaluation confirmed that the trained GAN outperformed other manual image processing methods for data augmentation and that the respective augmented datasets considerably improved segmentation by CNNs.

Utilizing automatically generated augmented training samples, Hollandi et al. [74] introduced nucleAIzer, a learning-based framework for cell nuclei segmentation. The authors' framework utilizes style transfer and adaptive learning to produce state-of-the-art results on diverse range of cells. The style transfer model is provided with synthetic masks that mimic the number, shape, and size of the unseen nuclei, which allows for better segmentation results.

An interesting approach to classification of cancer stem cells was presented in the same year by Aida et al. [67]. The authors proposed a modality translation from existing phase contrast images to fluorescence microscopy images using conditional GAN, specifically pix2pix. The GAN was trained to map grayscale bright-field cell images into multi-channel dark-field fluorescence images. The training dataset was created using 96 pairs of phase contrast and corresponding florescence images with resolution of 1920×1440 pixels that were subsequently divided into tiles of 256×256 pixels. The conducted evaluation showed that this approach improves the classification results. The authors concluded that the GAN had the capability to define structures that could not be described clearly by the human experts. Another approach transforming bright-field microscopy cell images into fluorescence images was introduced by Lee et al. [100] in 2021.

21.3.4.1 Membranes

A brief intermezzo about synthetic images showing small numbers of adjacent and membrane-stained cells is given here. Three-dimensional images of synthetic membranes were generated in [101–103] in order to inspect quality of segmentation methods (using Dice and other metrics). Additionally, in [101,103] the authors produced the same images with varying levels of noise to discover usability limits of their method, see Fig. 21.10.

Quite recently, images with membrane stained cells (with their centroid markers in a separate image channel acting as ground truth) were generated to train deep learning segmentation methods [60]. The training data were generated with varying quality to facilitate comprehensive evaluation of the methods. Membranes showing images from synthetic electron microscopy were devised too in [84]. Both works are based on GANs, and both are focused only on synthesis of 2D images.

21.3.5 Time-lapse sequences of cell populations

In this section we shall focus on synthetic data with temporal dimension. Mostly, we will be discussing works where a population of cells is somehow developing, and often even (virtually) proliferating, which is to say cell divisions are modeled and displayed. Speaking of divisions, simulators with explicit apoptosis (cell death) are, on the other hand, markedly rare.

Interestingly enough, apoptosis can be understood as one form of cells "vanishing" from the data. In contrast to [12], where apoptosis was recognized in the

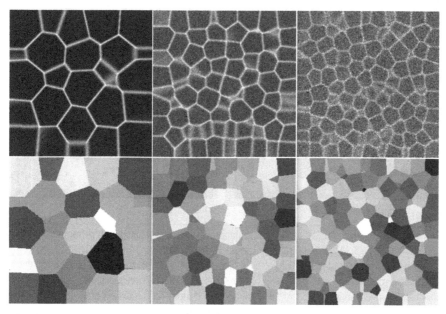

FIGURE 21.10

Example of small scale tissues shown as fluorescently labeled membranes, with full-cell segmentation ground truth. Columns from left to right show tissues generated with progressively higher noise parameters and increasing cell number, using a procedural approach. *Source: Mosaliganti et al., 2012 [101].*

simulation but dead cell was immediately after removed from the generated images, the apoptosis in [88] is modeled explicitly and allows leaving visual traces of a dead cell (in a form of a debris) in the generated images, see Fig. 21.11. This obviously should deliver a more faithful appearance of apoptosis.

Other forms of vanishing cells are less rare, still not very frequent. For example, to mimic cells leaving (and entering) the field of view, the synthetic data providers for the Cell Tracking Challenge [43] were cropping (in spatial domain only) the image data after the simulation was over. This way, simulated cells could move outside the final view because they simulate cells traveling laterally on a microscopy slide in 2D or 3D time-lapse data, or because they simulate cells displacing axially, e.g., during mitosis, in coarsely z-sampled (fake) confocal setup.

In general, however, generating synthetic data becomes substantially harder with the time dimension. The addition of this extra dimension essentially affects every parameter of any underlying generative model, opening up a lot of room for the modeler to fill. This requires to add dynamics into the generated images yet preserve their realistic look. In other words, it requires to define new steering of parameters yet preserving the often carefully tuned interplay among them in the explicit models, or just requires a lot more to learn (and memorize) inside the implicit models. The (in)abili-

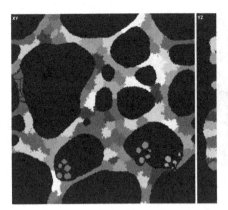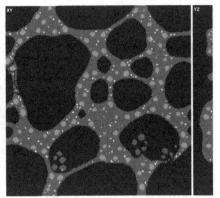

FIGURE 21.11

Example of synthetic images showing population with apoptosis and with refractive indices. A single XY and YZ slices from 3D segmentation masks (left) are showing CPM-based simulated healthy and dead cells. The latter is displayed as a cell that has just started to fall apart (blue mask in the left-hand side of the XY slice), and as three cells later after their apoptosis (round multi-compartment masks in the bottom half). Corresponding slices (right) are showing refractive indices in false colors. *Source: new images generated using a code from [88].*

ties of the modelers, learners and computing capacities together is our explanation to why we seem to observe a certain maximum capacity in terms of what our systems can practically generate.

To illustrate it, let us briefly review the following parametric-based generators of segmentation and tracking benchmark datasets. In the FiloGen project [104], thorough biophysical models, backed-up in their choice and parameters by literature, were utilized to create a realistically looking video of a single cell with several filopodia in (fake) fluorescence confocal microscopy. Their system could scale to only a handful of cells [105]. Another system, MitoGen [1], was essentially implementing the same ideas. However, to be able to scale to a few hundreds of cells, it was employing rather naive cell shape and motion models instead of the biophysically accurate ones. TRAgen [12] scaled easily to thousands of cells by using a simplified force-based motion model but trading its own texture representation module for simple in-painting of (real) images. In around the same time, suggesting the same compute capacity, a zebrafish generator [44] of semi-synthetic data was reported that could create a truly large cell populations using also a force-based model with in-painted cells, and additionally with cells movements and divisions being guided (not generating really) from an annotated template (real) image sequence. So, adding more cells into the simulation required more complex control (more parameters) which was out-weighted by relaxing (less controls) the simulation somewhere else.

Clearly, there are more parametric-based simulators than those above. Similar in the appearance to [106], time-lapse evolving populations of bacterial colonies were

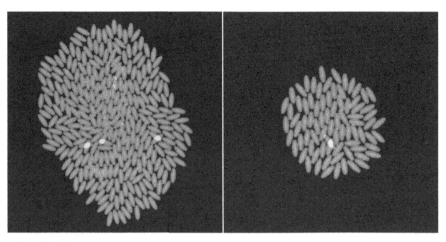

FIGURE 21.12

Examples of two frames from a simulated video of developing colony of fluorescent bacteria. The generated images are technically RGB images, and should also show a small color gradient in the background to mimic uneven illumination. *Source: Hattab et al., 2018 [107].*

simulated [107] to evaluate a novel method to detect, track and characterize cell subpopulations. Actually, the synthetic videos are supposed to be an outcome of an extension of their earlier system [97,33]. The simulation starts with one cell in the image center and cells eventually divide in the course of the simulation. The movement of cells is driven by minimizing an energy function that considers overlapping pixels, yet it is pushing the cells towards the image center, see Fig. 21.12. This is a quite different approach compared to the utilization of repulsive functions in similar agent-based systems, e.g., as in [12,44,45], but similar, on the other hand, to that based on the Cellular Pott model, e.g., as in [86,88–90].

Translation and morphological contraction and dilation experiencing single cell has been generated to create time-lapse differential inference contrast videos [94]. Essentially similar type of cell movements, plus cell rotation and small-scale local shape deformation, have been programmed into a generator of time-lapse confocal fluorescence microscopy images of 3D nuclei [1].

In 2018 Pandhe et al. [52] introduced a method to synthesize spatio-temporal data of cells in human neutrophils in differential interference contrast microscopy using combination of GANs (i.e., DCGAN and WGAN) and autoregressive models. The GAN was used for spatial synthesis of grayscale tiles of single cells, whereas the autoregressive model was utilized for temporal synthesis of cell trajectories. The spatial training dataset for GAN contained more than 17,000 single cell images of 64×64 pixels and the temporal dataset for autoregressive network contained more than 600 frames of living cell populations with resolution of 1024×1024 pixels. The synthesized trajectories and individual cell tiles generated by GAN were subsequently joined to form time-lapse sequences of moving cell populations.

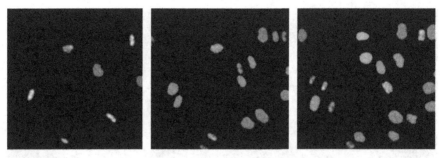

FIGURE 21.13

Example of a time-lapse sequence of living cell population produced using deep learning. The figure shows selected frames of a 2D time-lapse sequence of living cell population, where the number of cells increases with time due to simulated mitotic division. Intensity values of cell textures are based on the mean intensity and standard deviation observed in real fluorescence microscopy images. *Source: new images generated using a code from [30].*

Comes et al. [71] proposed in 2020 an utilization of Multi-scale GAN to increase temporal resolution of sequences in time-lapse microscopy. The GAN was trained to predict interleaved video frames in image sequences divided into patches with spatial resolution of 64×64 pixels. The authors showed that the model is able to increase temporal resolution and accurately reconstruct cell-interaction dynamics, which benefits the analysis of multi-cell-type migration and cell–cell interactions, and impacts the achieved quantitative results. They also added that artificial frame rate increase can be beneficial in situations where it is not feasible to speed up the acquisition rate, either due to increasing photobleaching and phototoxicity, or due to the increasing data volume.

Continuing their work on synthesis of time-lapse microscopy data, Comes et al. [70] utilized Social GAN [108] for cell motility prediction. The model was trained on video sequences of prostate cancer cells and fibrosarcoma cells ranging from 240 to 360 frames. The method was evaluated by comparing movement in second half of the sequences to the predictions based on the first half. The authors' quantitative evaluation showed that the trained model is able to successfully match the distributions of the cell motility in the data, creating plausible cell trajectories. The authors claim that the method is able to analyze trajectories of any length and that the resulting predictions can be utilized to increase robustness and accuracy of single and multi-object tracking tasks.

In 2021 Bähr et al. [30] introduced CellCycleGAN, a framework to generate 2D synthetic time-lapse microscopy sequences of living cell populations including the specific phenomena occurring during the cell-cycle (see Fig. 21.13). The method utilized a combination of parametric-based and learning-based models. Synthetic cells were obtained using statistical models of shape during a particular mitotic phase, with corresponding texture generated using GAN conditioned on the shape and cycle of a cell. The synthetic textures were subsequently combined into a frame containing the cell population, with cell movement approximated by Brownian motion across multiple frames. The framework also approximated the optical PSF using Gaussian smoothing and the acquisition sensor by including Poisson and Gaussian noise. The models were trained and adjusted to approximate human cancer cells HeLa with fluorescently stained nuclei, based on manually annotated time-lapse dataset with 40 single-channel frames containing 304 cells. For GAN training, the individual cells were separated into image patches of 96 × 96 pixels. The authors concluded that the framework was able to generate realistic looking 2D+t microscopy images, however, they also admitted that very short cell cycle phases were not yet realistic enough due to the lack of available annotated training data.

21.4 Summary

21.4.1 Modeling capabilities and paradigms

Reviewing what has been done in the field of biomedical image synthesis at cellular level, we are seeing an evolution from very naive models (judged with the optics of today) of a limited number of appearance cases to the learning of generic implicit models as we have it today. The transition was mostly smooth, with incrementally increasing modeling capabilities. The field used to be largely dominated by parametric, explicit models. The year 2017 saw the beginning of a visible shift towards implicitly learnt, deep learning-based models. It is no surprise that the pix2pix [99] and CycleGAN [109] were published in the same year.

The models are increasingly complex but the number of their parameters, meaning user-controllable nobs, became saturated rather soon. It is a question how much the limit was due to the desire to keep a decent user comfort as in [38,93,21], the use of highly specialized models that hard-coded already a great deal of domain knowledge leaving little to adjust as in [1], or the fact that generic explicit models were mostly built around features crafted by humans as it was seen in Section 21.3.2. The observation is, however, true even for generic implicit models. In GANs, for example, the networks are technically having millions of parameters depending on the specific architecture. But the network is essentially operated with only a handful of parameters, e.g., with the choice of the network architecture itself, training strategy, loss function(s), and with the choice of a training dataset in the first place.

The models are giving increasingly realistic appearances which itself is owing predominantly to the increasing performance of the contemporary hardware, and little to new theoretical discoveries. Indeed, the models are more profound, which translates into the use of more intrinsic parameters and, consequently, into an increased demand in computational resources. In the networks example, it is clearly the number (and architecture) of the parameters that makes them so incredibly sensitive, flexible, and hardware demanding at the same time. Also their rise was fueled not so much by new discoveries in theoretical computer science, but rather by the wide-spread of powerful dedicated accelerators, notably the GPUs.

The outlook in high-performance computing [110] suggests that the accelerators-based computing will dominate (at least) the full next decade. If the hardware performance was really the main limiting factor, we should be looking forward to seeing more deep learning based generators in the future.

21.4.2 Annotated datasets

Devising a new data generator or adopting an existing one for a particular application is not always easy. When modeling falls short and one cannot synthesize adequate fake data, one can resort to using some of the available annotated public datasets.

There are generally three options to choose from. One can consider fully synthetic datasets (also termed as datasets with *absolute ground truth*) [37,43,12,111–113], datasets[3] with computer generated [114] reference annotations of real images (*silver ground truth*), or datasets with manually created reference annotations of real images (*gold ground truth*) [37,43,113,115–121].

If the circumstances allow it, it was proposed [122] that the specimen is acquired using both bright-field and fluorescence imaging. And if the fluorescence image can be reliably segmented, it can "provide" cheap annotation to the bright-field image.

21.4.3 Established application domains

Originally, generators of synthetic images of cells were developed for the purpose of the evaluation of image processing, most prominently of image segmentation. The authors wanted to quantitatively evaluate the performance of their processing methods. Public datasets, many of which are featuring synthetic images, started to appear shortly after in a hope to establish reference annotated data. This good trend continues even today. To objectively compare between methods, challenges became particularly popular recently. Some challenges were benchmarking even solely on synthetic datasets [49,50], others relied on it in large [43] or in small part [123].

Training data augmentation using GANs can be already regarded as a standard approach (see also [124]), despite that it is used exclusively with the modern neural networks that became widespread only very recently. It is worth noting that the GANs are often "only" adding textures over cell masks that are still obtained otherwise, usually directly from the original real training data.

Another well established application where images of artificial cells are created are the true simulations that attempt to explain certain biological phenomena. Such simulations often generate images that are showing schematically how cells attain their geometries and form populations [125,126,90,45]. Distant as it seems, it does not take much to add texture and virtual microscopy to obtain annotated synthetic data for image processing. This path was taken, for example, in [87] that was extending a particular computational biology method [86].

---

[3] Results are available at http://celltrackingchallenge.net/ as *-denoted training datasets.

21.4.4 **Emerging application domains**

The emerging field in our view is represented with the reports where (usually) segmentation networks were successfully trained on datasets that were including synthetic images partly [127,65] or entirely [81,55,28]. It is worth noting that the vast majority of the explicit models were found unable[4] to provide useful training data. We seem to be seeking complete synthesizing networks (that would feed image analysis networks) such as in [65], or at least seeking combinations of models such as applying networks from [55,28] on results of a network from [66].

Sometimes, it is useful to complement the existing views of original data with yet another view. This can mean obtaining another fluorescence channel to avoid staining or imaging limits [53,7], labeling *in silico* [128,129,6], enhancing certain features for better man-made scoring, or transferring images into a domain of trained segmenter [67]. The ideas here may not be new but the current, predominantly network-based, implementations show impressive advancements. Since such generators are not designed for ground truth segmentation data but rather for ground truth raw microscopy images, they are opening a field of realistic generators for all image denoising, image restoration, domain transferring or visual features enhancing networks.

21.5 **Future work**

The prevailing motif why researchers have always been reaching out to synthetic data is their general reluctance to annotate real data manually, and especially in the needed quantities. Indeed, preparation of suitable datasets for training or for quantitative evaluations of image processing methods inevitably requires obtaining relevant raw images with adequate ground truth. However, there is more to it than just having large quantities of data with ground truth.

21.5.1 **Towards rich synthetic images**

The synthetic data must come with sufficient inherent variability in order to be truly useful. Considering the evaluation example, it can be only as much robust and reliable as large and solid is the underlying test data. Famously data hungry, deep learning methods can similarly become truly powerful only when supported with amounts of rich training data. We are, therefore, in a need of synthetic data that are of high variability, quality and fidelity. That is, we need comprehensive, informative and representative (*high variability*) images of nicely looking cells (*high quality*) of the wanted look and feel (*high spatial fidelity*) and behavior (*high temporal fidelity*).

Generators that routinely produce synthetic images of a very good quality and fidelity are a reality of today. Despite that, it is difficult to assess and to prove that

---

[4] Authors' own experience and absence of such literature.

generated samples are similar to the real ones, however, such certification should be carried out. Its absence weakens evaluations in down-stream reports that are based on this synthetic data. Fortunately, statistical assessments of the realism of generated data are appearing in the literature, e.g., in [31,104,130,131,65,6], or, at least, studies of visual evaluation by experts are provided, e.g., in [14,65].

Adding more variability to the fake data is not only about using permissive, potent models. There are other flavors of image data that increase the overall level of its realism and bring in its own kind of every-day image processing difficulties. Examples are various technical imaging artifacts such as spatially variable PSF, uneven illumination, malfunctions as incompletely recorded or missing images, (global) stage or specimen drifts, (global) sudden intensity change, cells only partially inside the field of view; and also various biological artifacts such as both intra- and inter-cells uneven staining, unspecific background staining, debris, leftovers after dead cells, or outstandingly different cell shapes. Simulators that generate time-lapse image series could additionally consider behavioral variances such as motility, rate of development implemented as how many and how often do cells divide, rate of failures leading to cell deaths, all that both locally and globally. Most of the works reported over here include only small subset from the above.

However, current reality of explicit models is still that rather uniformly looking cells are placed over simple background. Our take is that the current models are not generic enough to cover all known realistic instances, and especially do not offer extrapolation capacity to generate instances previously unseen by the models' designers. But the explicit modeling enables (re-)generating the same images at varying levels of noise, for example. This is something implicit models cannot do today. On the other hand, the implicit models, as we are experiencing them with GANs nowadays, do include (implicitly) a lot more from the above mentioned artifacts and allow for a greater level of generality. They deliver, therefore, usually more realistic and more varying (richer) images. Needless to say, we are after an approach that offers the best from the both worlds: reproducibility, controllability and generalizability.

21.5.2 Towards rich annotations

It would also be worthwhile to design future systems to produce, next to the image and ground truth data, also associated images of refractive indices, e.g., as in [17,88]. It would enable usage of advanced models of image formation, such as BioBeam [2]. Not only it paves a way to study properties of various optical setups when imaging certain cell populations, it especially allows for creating synthetic images of cells from non-fluorescence microscopy. Mainly, however, it calls for simulators of cells with explicit full content. All of that broadens the applications potential of synthetic data.

We are lacking time-resolved simulators—generators of time-lapse data. There are a few ones, e.g., in [1,44], but they are very complex to adopt for a new type of cells, including their appearance and behavior. Furthermore, the simulators are functioning optimistically. For example, they simulate cell populations of only well developing cells, leaving no room for occasional development failures such as apoptosis. They do not report auxiliary data, most notably the phase of cell cycle per cell. But real cells often change their appearance during their cell cycle, something that could have been exploited in next-generation robust segmentation methods but is not because ground truth is unavailable.

Be it with the networks or not, the challenge now is to figure out how to make full 3D+t learning and generation tractable not only for textures and shapes of individual cells but also for their random initial positions and movements. Reiterating that wide range of applications in the end requires only a small number of forms of ground truth (see the end of Section 21.1.2.4), most applications could become well supported with a wealth of synthetic data if we aim towards generating rich time-lapse image sequences with rich annotations.

Acknowledgments

We thank Dr. David Svoboda and Dr. Johannes Stegmaier for kindly generating new synthetic data for this chapter, and to everyone from our community who is making their source codes and data available both open source and open access. We especially thank Dr. Ninon Burgos for her patient editorship. We thank Ninon and David for their great feedback to the content of this chapter.

Fig. 21.1 was created with BioRender.com. Fig. 21.2 was reprinted with permission from John Wiley and Sons. Figs. 21.3, 21.4 and 21.8 were generated together by V.U. and D.W. Figs. 21.11 and 21.13 were kindly generated for us by David and Johannes, respectively. Figs. 21.5, 21.6, 21.7, 21.9, 21.10, 21.12 are licensed under the Creative Commons Attribution 4.0 International License,[5] the authors and the original source are referenced in the respective captions. Figs. 21.5, 21.6, and 21.9 were cropped from the original.

V.U. had been supported during the writing of this chapter by the European Regional Development Fund in the IT4Innovations National Supercomputing Center project "path to exascale" [CZ.02.1.01/0.0/0.0/16_013/0001791] within the Operational Programme Research, Development and Education.

References

[1] D. Svoboda, V. Ulman, MitoGen: a framework for generating 3D synthetic time-lapse sequences of cell populations in fluorescence microscopy, IEEE Transactions on Medical Imaging 36 (1) (2016) 310–321.

---

[5] http://creativecommons.org/licenses/by/4.0/.

[2] M. Weigert, K. Subramanian, et al., Biobeam—multiplexed wave-optical simulations of light-sheet microscopy, PLoS Computational Biology 14 (4) (2018) e1006079.

[3] A. Ahmad, C. Frindel, D. Rousseau, Detecting differences of fluorescent markers distribution in single cell microscopy: textural or pointillist feature space?, Frontiers in Robotics and AI 7 (2020) 39.

[4] A. Medyukhina, M.T. Figge, DeconvTest: simulation framework for quantifying errors and selecting optimal parameters of image deconvolution, Journal of Biophotonics 13 (4) (2020) e201960079.

[5] M. Weigert, U. Schmidt, et al., Content-aware image restoration: pushing the limits of fluorescence microscopy, Nature Methods 15 (12) (2018) 1090–1097.

[6] Y. Liu, H. Yuan, et al., Global pixel transformers for virtual staining of microscopy images, IEEE Transactions on Medical Imaging 39 (6) (2020) 2256–2266.

[7] H. Yuan, L. Cai, et al., Computational modeling of cellular structures using conditional deep generative networks, Bioinformatics 35 (12) (2019) 2141–2149.

[8] M. Tektonidis, K. Rohr, Diffeomorphic multi-frame non-rigid registration of cell nuclei in 2D and 3D live cell images, IEEE Transactions on Image Processing 26 (3) (2017) 1405–1417.

[9] Q. Gao, K. Rohr, A global method for non-rigid registration of cell nuclei in live cell time-lapse images, IEEE Transactions on Medical Imaging 38 (10) (2019) 2259–2270.

[10] J. Delpiano, J. Jara, et al., Performance of optical flow techniques for motion analysis of fluorescent point signals in confocal microscopy, Machine Vision and Applications 23 (4) (2012) 675–689.

[11] S. Manandhar, P. Bouthemy, et al., A sparse-to-dense method for 3D optical flow estimation in 3D light-microscopy image sequences, in: 2018 IEEE 15th International Symposium on Biomedical Imaging (ISBI 2018), IEEE, 2018, pp. 952–956.

[12] V. Ulman, Z. Orémuš, D. Svoboda, TRAgen: a tool for generation of synthetic time-lapse image sequences of living cells, in: International Conference on Image Analysis and Processing, Springer, 2015, pp. 623–634.

[13] M. Traub, J. Stegmaier, Towards automatic embryo staging in 3D+t microscopy images using convolutional neural networks and PointNets, in: International Workshop on Simulation and Synthesis in Medical Imaging, Springer, 2020, pp. 153–163.

[14] P. Malm, A. Brun, E. Bengtsson, Simulation of bright-field microscopy images depicting pap-smear specimen, Cytometry. Part A 87 (3) (2015) 212–226.

[15] R.F. Murphy, Building cell models and simulations from microscope images, Methods 96 (2016) 33–39.

[16] V.N. Kovacheva, D. Snead, N.M. Rajpoot, A model of the spatial tumour heterogeneity in colorectal adenocarcinoma tissue, BMC Bioinformatics 17 (1) (2016) 255.

[17] D. Svoboda, M. Kozubek, Multimodal simulations in live cell imaging, in: International Workshop on Simulation and Synthesis in Medical Imaging, Springer, 2017, pp. 89–98.

[18] D.K. Samuylov, L.A. Widmer, et al., Mapping complex spatio-temporal models to image space: the virtual microscope, in: 2015 IEEE 12th International Symposium on Biomedical Imaging (ISBI), IEEE, 2015, pp. 707–711.

[19] M. Watabe, S.N.V. Arjunan, et al., A computational framework for bioimaging simulation, PLoS ONE 10 (7) (2015) e0130089.

[20] S.H. Rezatofighi, W.T.E. Pitkeathly, et al., A framework for generating realistic synthetic sequences of total internal reflection fluorescence microscopy images, in: 2013 IEEE 10th International Symposium on Biomedical Imaging, IEEE, 2013, pp. 157–160.

[21] D. Wiesner, D. Svoboda, et al., CytoPacq: a web-interface for simulating multi-dimensional cell imaging, Bioinformatics 35 (21) (2019) 4531–4533.

[22] Z. Yin, H. Su, Microscopy image formation, restoration, and segmentation, Computer Vision for Microscopy Image Analysis (2020) 13.

[23] R.F. Murphy, CellOrganizer: image-derived models of subcellular organization and protein distribution, Methods in Cell Biology 110 (2012) 179–193, Elsevier.

[24] X. Ruan, R.F. Murphy, Evaluation of methods for generative modeling of cell and nuclear shape, Bioinformatics 35 (14) (2019) 2475–2485.

[25] I. Goodfellow, J. Pouget-Abadie, et al., Generative adversarial nets, Advances in Neural Information Processing Systems 27 (2014) 2672–2680.

[26] D.P. Kingma, M. Welling, Auto-encoding variational Bayes, in: 2nd International Conference on Learning Representations, ICLR 2014, Banff, AB, Canada, April 14–16, 2014, Conference Track Proceedings, 2014.

[27] P. Goldsborough, N. Pawlowski, et al., CytoGAN: generative modeling of cell images, bioRxiv (2017) 227645.

[28] K.W. Dunn, C. Fu, et al., DeepSynth: three-dimensional nuclear segmentation of biological images using neural networks trained with synthetic data, Scientific Reports 9 (1) (2019) 1–15.

[29] O. Bailo, D.S. Ham, Y.M. Shin, Red blood cell image generation for data augmentation using conditional generative adversarial networks, in: Proceedings of the IEEE Conference on Computer Vision and Pattern Recognition Workshops, 2019, pp. 1039–1048.

[30] D. Bähr, D. Eschweiler, et al., CellCycleGAN: spatiotemporal microscopy image synthesis of cell populations using statistical shape models and conditional GANs, in: 2021 IEEE 18th International Symposium on Biomedical Imaging (ISBI), IEEE, 2021, pp. 15–19.

[31] D. Svoboda, M. Kozubek, S. Stejskal, Generation of digital phantoms of cell nuclei and simulation of image formation in 3D image cytometry, Cytometry. Part A 75 (6) (2009) 494–509.

[32] A. Lehmussola, P. Ruusuvuori, et al., Computational framework for simulating fluorescence microscope images with cell populations, IEEE Transactions on Medical Imaging 26 (7) (2007) 1010–1016.

[33] V. Wiesmann, M. Bergler, et al., Using simulated fluorescence cell micrographs for the evaluation of cell image segmentation algorithms, BMC Bioinformatics 18 (1) (2017) 176.

[34] A. Samacoits, R. Chouaib, et al., A computational framework to study sub-cellular RNA localization, Nature Communications 9 (1) (2018) 1–10.

[35] V. Ulman, D. Svoboda, et al., Virtual cell imaging: a review on simulation methods employed in image cytometry, Cytometry. Part A 89 (12) (2016) 1057–1072.

[36] P. Ruusuvuori, T. Äijö, et al., Evaluation of methods for detection of fluorescence labeled subcellular objects in microscope images, BMC Bioinformatics 11 (1) (2010) 1–17.

[37] V. Ljosa, K.L. Sokolnicki, A.E. Carpenter, Annotated high-throughput microscopy image sets for validation, Nature Methods 9 (7) (2012) 637.

[38] S. Rajaram, B. Pavie, et al., SimuCell: a flexible framework for creating synthetic microscopy images, Nature Methods 9 (7) (2012) 634.

[39] D. Svoboda, O. Homola, S. Stejskal, Generation of 3D digital phantoms of colon tissue, in: International Conference Image Analysis and Recognition, Springer, 2011, pp. 31–39.

[40] T. Zhao, R.F. Murphy, Automated learning of generative models for subcellular location: building blocks for systems biology, Cytometry. Part A 71 (12) (2007) 978–990.

[41] T. Peng, R.F. Murphy, Image-derived, three-dimensional generative models of cellular organization, Cytometry. Part A 79 (5) (2011) 383–391.

[42] D. Svoboda, V. Ulman, Generation of synthetic image datasets for time-lapse fluorescence microscopy, in: International Conference Image Analysis and Recognition, Springer, 2012, pp. 473–482.

[43] M. Maška, V. Ulman, et al., A benchmark for comparison of cell tracking algorithms, Bioinformatics 30 (11) (2014) 1609–1617.

[44] J. Stegmaier, J. Arz, et al., Generating semi-synthetic validation benchmarks for embryomics, in: 2016 IEEE 13th International Symposium on Biomedical Imaging (ISBI), IEEE, 2016, pp. 684–688.

[45] A. Ghaffarizadeh, R. Heiland, et al., PhysiCell: an open source physics-based cell simulator for 3-D multicellular systems, PLoS Computational Biology 14 (2) (2018) e1005991.

[46] J. Hubený, V. Ulman, P. Matula, Estimating large local motion in live-cell imaging using variational optical flow, in: VISAPP: Proc. of the Second International Conference on Computer Vision Theory and Applications, 2007, pp. 542–548.

[47] E. Lihavainen, J. Mäkelä, et al., Mytoe: automatic analysis of mitochondrial dynamics, Bioinformatics 28 (7) (2012) 1050–1051.

[48] V. Ulman, J. Hubený, Pseudo-real image sequence generator for optical flow computations, in: Scandinavian Conference on Image Analysis, Springer, 2007, pp. 976–985.

[49] D. Sage, H. Kirshner, et al., Benchmarking image-processing algorithms for biomicroscopy: reference datasets and perspectives, in: 21st European Signal Processing Conference (EUSIPCO 2013), IEEE, 2013, pp. 1–4.

[50] N. Chenouard, I. Smal, et al., Objective comparison of particle tracking methods, Nature Methods 11 (3) (2014) 281–289.

[51] I. Smal, M. Loog, et al., Quantitative comparison of spot detection methods in fluorescence microscopy, IEEE Transactions on Medical Imaging 29 (2) (2009) 282–301.

[52] N. Pandhe, B. Rada, S. Quinn, Generative spatiotemporal modeling of neutrophil behavior, in: 2018 IEEE 15th International Symposium on Biomedical Imaging (ISBI 2018), IEEE, 2018, pp. 969–972.

[53] A. Osokin, A. Chessel, et al., Gans for biological image synthesis, in: Proceedings of the IEEE International Conference on Computer Vision, 2017, pp. 2233–2242.

[54] A. Arbelle, T.R. Raviv, Microscopy cell segmentation via adversarial neural networks, in: 2018 IEEE 15th International Symposium on Biomedical Imaging (ISBI 2018), IEEE, 2018, pp. 645–648.

[55] C. Fu, S. Lee, et al., Three dimensional fluorescence microscopy image synthesis and segmentation, in: Proceedings of the IEEE Conference on Computer Vision and Pattern Recognition Workshops, 2018, pp. 2221–2229.

[56] P. Baniukiewicz, J.E. Lutton, et al., Generative adversarial networks for augmenting training data of microscopic cell images, Frontiers of Computer Science 1 (2019) 10.

[57] Y.Y. Baydilli, U. Atila, K. Akyol, Improving classification performance on microscopic images using Generative Adversarial Networks (GAN), 2019.

[58] M. Böhland, T. Scherr, et al., Influence of synthetic label image object properties on GAN supported segmentation pipelines, in: Proceedings 29th Workshop Computational Intelligence, 2019, pp. 289–305.

[59] D. Dirvanauskas, R. Maskeliūnas, et al., Hemigen: human embryo image generator based on generative adversarial networks, Sensors 19 (16) (2019) 3578.

[60] D. Eschweiler, T. Klose, et al., Towards annotation-free segmentation of fluorescently labeled cell membranes in confocal microscopy images, in: International Workshop on Simulation and Synthesis in Medical Imaging, Springer, 2019, pp. 81–89.

[61] S. Han, S. Lee, et al., Nuclei counting in microscopy images with three dimensional generative adversarial networks, in: Medical Imaging 2019: Image Processing, vol. 10949, International Society for Optics and Photonics, 2019, 109492Y.

[62] M.W. Lafarge, J.C. Caicedo, et al., Capturing single-cell phenotypic variation via unsupervised representation learning, in: International Conference on Medical Imaging with Deep Learning, in: PMLR, 2019, pp. 315–325.

[63] A.X. Lu, O.Z. Kraus, et al., Learning unsupervised feature representations for single cell microscopy images with paired cell inpainting, PLoS Computational Biology 15 (9) (2019) e1007348.

[64] M. Majurski, P. Manescu, et al., Cell image segmentation using generative adversarial networks, transfer learning, and augmentations, in: Proceedings of the IEEE Conference on Computer Vision and Pattern Recognition Workshops, 2019, pp. 1114–1122.

[65] M. Scalbert, F. Couzinie-Devy, R. Fezzani, Generic isolated cell image generator, Cytometry. Part A 95 (11) (2019) 1198–1206.

[66] D. Wiesner, T. Nečasová, D. Svoboda, On generative modeling of cell shape using 3D GANs, in: International Conference on Image Analysis and Processing, Springer, 2019, pp. 672–682.

[67] S. Aida, J. Okugawa, et al., Deep learning of cancer stem cell morphology using conditional generative adversarial networks, Biomolecules 10 (6) (2020) 931.

[68] K. Almezhghwi, S. Serte, Improved classification of white blood cells with the generative adversarial network and deep convolutional neural network, Computational Intelligence and Neuroscience 2020 (2020).

[69] S. Chen, D. Gao, et al., Cervical cancer single cell image data augmentation using residual condition generative adversarial networks, in: 2020 3rd International Conference on Artificial Intelligence and Big Data (ICAIBD), IEEE, 2020, pp. 237–241.

[70] M.C. Comes, J. Filippi, et al., Accelerating the experimental responses on cell behaviors: a long-term prediction of cell trajectories using Social Generative Adversarial Network, Scientific Reports 10 (1) (2020) 1–17.

[71] M.C. Comes, J. Filippi, et al., Multi-scale generative adversarial network for improved evaluation of cell–cell interactions observed in organ-on-chip experiments, Neural Computing & Applications (2020) 1–19.

[72] K. Pasupa, S. Tungjitnob, S. Vatathanavaro, Semi-supervised learning with deep convolutional generative adversarial networks for canine red blood cells morphology classification, Multimedia Tools and Applications (2020) 1–18.

[73] R. Verma, R. Mehrotra, et al., Synthetic image augmentation with generative adversarial network for enhanced performance in protein classification, Biomedical Engineering Letters 10 (3) (2020) 443–452.

[74] R. Hollandi, A. Szkalisity, et al., nucleAIzer: a parameter-free deep learning framework for nucleus segmentation using image style transfer, Cell Systems 10 (5) (2020) 453–458.

[75] A.A. Sekh, I.S. Opstad, et al., Simulation-supervised deep learning for analysing organelles states and behaviour in living cells, arXiv preprint, arXiv:2008.12617, 2020.

[76] G.R. Johnson, R.M. Donovan-Maiye, M.M. Maleckar, Building a 3D integrated cell, bioRxiv (2017) 238378.

[77] A. Krizhevsky, I. Sutskever, G.E. Hinton, Imagenet classification with deep convolutional neural networks, Communications of the ACM 60 (6) (2017) 84–90.

[78] M. Miró-Nicolau, B. Moyà-Alcover, et al., Segmenting overlapped objects in images. A study to support the diagnosis of sickle cell disease, arXiv preprint, arXiv:2008.00997, 2020.

[79] M. Winter, W. Mankowski, et al., Separating touching cells using pixel replicated elliptical shape models, IEEE Transactions on Medical Imaging 38 (4) (2018) 883–893.

[80] J. Jara-Wilde, I. Castro, et al., Optimising adjacent membrane segmentation and parameterisation in multicellular aggregates by piecewise active contours, Journal of Microscopy 278 (2) (2020) 59–75.

[81] D.J. Ho, C. Fu, et al., Nuclei segmentation of fluorescence microscopy images using three dimensional convolutional neural networks, in: Proceedings of the IEEE Conference on Computer Vision and Pattern Recognition Workshops, 2017, pp. 82–90.

[82] M. Abdolhoseini, M.G. Kluge, et al., Neuron image synthesizer via Gaussian mixture model and Perlin noise, in: 2019 IEEE 16th International Symposium on Biomedical Imaging (ISBI 2019), IEEE, 2019, pp. 530–533.

[83] D. Svoboda, V. Ulman, Towards a realistic distribution of cells in synthetically generated 3D cell populations, in: International Conference on Image Analysis and Processing, Springer, 2013, pp. 429–438.

[84] L. Han, R.F. Murphy, D. Ramanan, Learning generative models of tissue organization with supervised gans, in: 2018 IEEE Winter Conference on Applications of Computer Vision (WACV), IEEE, 2018, pp. 682–690.

[85] J.A. Glazier, F. Graner, Simulation of the differential adhesion driven rearrangement of biological cells, Physical Review E 47 (3) (1993) 2128.

[86] R.M.H. Merks, J.A. Glazier, A cell-centered approach to developmental biology, Physica A: Statistical Mechanics and Its Applications 352 (1) (2005) 113–130.

[87] D. Svoboda, V. Ulman, et al., Vascular network formation in silico using the extended cellular Potts model, in: 2016 IEEE International Conference on Image Processing (ICIP), IEEE, 2016, pp. 3180–3183.

[88] D. Svoboda, T. Nečasová, Image-based simulations of tubular network formation, in: 2020 IEEE 17th International Symposium on Biomedical Imaging (ISBI), IEEE, 2020, pp. 1608–1612.

[89] M.H. Swat, G.L. Thomas, et al., Multi-scale modeling of tissues using CompuCell3D, Methods in Cell Biology 110 (2012) 325–366.

[90] J. Starruß, W. de Back, et al., Morpheus: a user-friendly modeling environment for multiscale and multicellular systems biology, Bioinformatics 30 (9) (2014) 1331–1332.

[91] G.R. Mirams, C.J. Arthurs, et al., Chaste: an open source C++ library for computational physiology and biology, PLoS Computational Biology 9 (3) (2013) e1002970.

[92] J. Metzcar, Y. Wang, et al., A review of cell-based computational modeling in cancer biology, JCO Clinical Cancer Informatics 2 (2019) 1–13.

[93] P. Canelas, L. Martins, et al., An image generator platform to improve cell tracking algorithms: simulation of objects of various morphologies, kinetics and clustering, in: 2016 6th International Conference on Simulation and Modeling Methodologies, Technologies and Applications (SIMULTECH), IEEE, 2016, pp. 1–12.

[94] J. Lee, C.J. Rozell, Precision cell boundary tracking on DIC microscopy video for patch clamping, in: 2017 IEEE International Conference on Acoustics, Speech and Signal Processing (ICASSP), IEEE, 2017, pp. 1048–1052.

[95] L. Hervé, D.C.A. Kraemer, et al., Alternation of inverse problem approach and deep learning for lens-free microscopy image reconstruction, Scientific Reports 10 (1) (2020) 1–12.

[96] J. Wu, C. Zhang, et al., Learning a probabilistic latent space of object shapes via 3d generative-adversarial modeling, Advances in Neural Information Processing Systems 29 (2016) 82–90.

[97] V. Wiesmann, T. Sauer, et al., Cell simulation for validation of cell micrograph evaluation algorithms, Biomedical Engineering (Biomedizinische Technik) 58 (SI-1-Track-L) (2013).

[98] E.V. Lisitsa, M.M. Yatskou, et al., Simulation model for three-channel luminescent images of cancer cell populations, Journal of Applied Spectroscopy 81 (6) (2015) 996–1003.

[99] P. Isola, J.-Y. Zhu, et al., Image-to-image translation with conditional adversarial networks, in: Proceedings of the IEEE Conference on Computer Vision and Pattern Recognition, 2017, pp. 1125–1134.

[100] G. Lee, J.-W. Oh, et al., DeepHCS++: bright-field to fluorescence microscopy image conversion using multi-task learning with adversarial losses for label-free high-content screening, Medical Image Analysis 70 (2021) 101995.

[101] K.R. Mosaliganti, R.R. Noche, et al., ACME: automated cell morphology extractor for comprehensive reconstruction of cell membranes, PLoS Computational Biology 8 (12) (2012) e1002780.

[102] S. Pop, A.C. Dufour, et al., Extracting 3D cell parameters from dense tissue environments: application to the development of the mouse heart, Bioinformatics 29 (6) (2013) 772–779.

[103] A. Badoual, A. Galan, et al., Deforming tessellations for the segmentation of cell aggregates, in: 2019 IEEE 16th International Symposium on Biomedical Imaging (ISBI 2019), IEEE, 2019, pp. 1013–1017.

[104] D.V. Sorokin, I. Peterlik, et al., FiloGen: a model-based generator of synthetic 3-D time-lapse sequences of single motile cells with growing and branching filopodia, IEEE Transactions on Medical Imaging 37 (12) (2018) 2630–2641.

[105] I. Peterlík, D. Svoboda, et al., Model-based generation of synthetic 3d time-lapse sequences of multiple mutually interacting motile cells with Filopodia, in: International Workshop on Simulation and Synthesis in Medical Imaging, Springer, 2018, pp. 71–79.

[106] L. Martins, J. Fonseca, A. Ribeiro, 'miSimBa'—a simulator of synthetic time-lapsed microscopy images of bacterial cells, in: 2015 IEEE 4th Portuguese Meeting on Bioengineering (ENBENG), IEEE, 2015, pp. 1–6.

[107] G. Hattab, V. Wiesmann, et al., A novel methodology for characterizing cell subpopulations in automated time-lapse microscopy, Frontiers in Bioengineering and Biotechnology 6 (2018) 17.

[108] A. Gupta, J. Johnson, et al., Social gan: socially acceptable trajectories with generative adversarial networks, in: Proceedings of the IEEE Conference on Computer Vision and Pattern Recognition, 2018, pp. 2255–2264.

[109] J.-Y. Zhu, T. Park, et al., Unpaired image-to-image translation using cycle-consistent adversarial networks, in: Proceedings of the IEEE International Conference on Computer Vision, 2017, pp. 2223–2232.

[110] A. Mann, Core concept: nascent exascale supercomputers offer promise, present challenges, Proceedings of the National Academy of Sciences 117 (37) (2020) 22623–22625.

[111] P. Ruusuvuori, A. Lehmussola, et al., Benchmark set of synthetic images for validating cell image analysis algorithms, in: 2008 16th European Signal Processing Conference, IEEE, 2008, pp. 1–5.

[112] M. Maška, T. Nečasová, et al., Toward robust fully 3d filopodium segmentation and tracking in time-lapse fluorescence microscopy, in: 2019 IEEE International Conference on Image Processing (ICIP), IEEE, 2019, pp. 819–823.

[113] U. Rubens, R. Mormont, et al., BIAFLOWS: a collaborative framework to reproducibly deploy and benchmark bioimage analysis workflows, Patterns (2020) 100040.

[114] C.E. Akbaş, V. Ulman, et al., Automatic fusion of segmentation and tracking labels, in: Proceedings of the European Conference on Computer Vision (ECCV), 2018, pp. 446–454.

[115] E.D. Gelasca, B. Obara, et al., A biosegmentation benchmark for evaluation of bioimage analysis methods, BMC Bioinformatics 10 (1) (2009) 368.

[116] L.P. Coelho, A. Shariff, R.F. Murphy, Nuclear segmentation in microscope cell images: a hand-segmented dataset and comparison of algorithms, in: 2009 IEEE International Symposium on Biomedical Imaging: From Nano to Macro, IEEE, 2009, pp. 518–521.

[117] L. Willis, Y. Refahi, et al., Cell size and growth regulation in the Arabidopsis thaliana apical stem cell niche, Proceedings of the National Academy of Sciences 113 (51) (2016) E8238–E8246.

[118] R. Etournay, M. Merkel, et al., TissueMiner: a multiscale analysis toolkit to quantify how cellular processes create tissue dynamics, eLife 5 (2016) e14334.

[119] G. Blin, D. Sadurska, et al., Nessys: a new set of tools for the automated detection of nuclei within intact tissues and dense 3D cultures, PLoS Biology 17 (8) (2019) e3000388.

[120] J.C. Caicedo, A. Goodman, et al., Nucleus segmentation across imaging experiments: the 2018 Data Science Bowl, Nature Methods 16 (12) (2019) 1247–1253.

[121] F. Kromp, E. Bozsaky, et al., An annotated fluorescence image dataset for training nuclear segmentation methods, Scientific Data 7 (1) (2020) 1–8.

[122] S.K. Sadanandan, P. Ranefall, et al., Automated training of deep convolutional neural networks for cell segmentation, Scientific Reports 7 (1) (2017) 1–7.

[123] V. Ulman, M. Maška, et al., An objective comparison of cell-tracking algorithms, Nature Methods 14 (12) (2017) 1141–1152.

[124] M. Kozubek, et al., When deep learning meets cell image synthesis, Cytometry. Part A 97 (2020) 222–225.

[125] S. Hoehme, M. Brulport, et al., Prediction and validation of cell alignment along microvessels as order principle to restore tissue architecture in liver regeneration, Proceedings of the National Academy of Sciences 107 (23) (2010) 10371–10376.

[126] J. Löber, F. Ziebert, I.S. Aranson, Collisions of deformable cells lead to collective migration, Scientific Reports 5 (2015) 9172.

[127] C. Castilla, M. Maška, et al., 3-D quantification of filopodia in motile cancer cells, IEEE Transactions on Medical Imaging 38 (3) (2018) 862–872.

[128] C. Ounkomol, S. Seshamani, et al., Label-free prediction of three-dimensional fluorescence images from transmitted-light microscopy, Nature Methods 15 (11) (2018) 917–920.

[129] E.M. Christiansen, S.J. Yang, et al., In silico labeling: predicting fluorescent labels in unlabeled images, Cell 173 (3) (2018) 792–803.

[130] T. Nečasová, D. Svoboda, Visual and quantitative comparison of real and simulated biomedical image data, in: Proceedings of the European Conference on Computer Vision (ECCV), 2018, pp. 385–394.

[131] Y. Feng, X. Chai, et al., Quality assessment of synthetic fluorescence microscopy images for image segmentation, in: 2019 IEEE International Conference on Image Processing (ICIP), IEEE, 2019, pp. 814–818.

Generative models for synthesis of colorectal cancer histology images

22

Srijay Deshpande[a], **Violeta Kovacheva**[b,c], **Fayyaz Minhas**[a], **and Nasir Rajpoot**[a]

[a]*Tissue Image Analytics Centre, Department of Computer Science, University of Warwick, Coventry, United Kingdom*
[b]*Grid Edge, Birmingham, United Kingdom*

22.1 Introduction

Colorectal cancer, also known as colon cancer, originates in epithelial cells lining the colon or rectum of the gastrointestinal tract, due to abnormal growth pattern of cells. Colorectal cancer is the third most diagnosed cancer and is the fourth leading cause of death worldwide [1]. In 2020, more than 1.9 million new colorectal cancer cases were diagnosed and 935,000 deaths were estimated [2]. The grade of colorectal cancer is determined by pathologists by analyzing individual cancer cells' differentiation, and other features of the tumor such as the size and shape of the cells and their spatial organization. In a routine diagnosis, a pathologist examines tissue sections on glass slides under the microscope to observe the variability of nuclear morphology. The visual analysis of colorectal tissue slides is time consuming and costly job when workloads are high.

Over the last few years, digital pathology data of whole slide images has been collected on a large scale owing to the widespread use of digital slide scanners. Generally, these whole slide images are multi-gigapixel in nature and store rich information about the tissue microenvironment, including glands, cells, nuclei, lumen, and stroma. With the rise of machine learning, automated analysis of histopathology images has become very popular, developing the domain of computational pathology. Several techniques such as nuclei detection and classification [3–7], tumor segmentation [8–11], and cancer grading [12–14] have been developed to assist the cancer diagnosis and treatment.

With the advent of deep learning, great advancements have been made in the field of computer vision, leading to the progress in several computational histopathology algorithms. These deep learning techniques are *data hungry* in nature, and require a large amount of labeled data for training and validation of models. However, the pro-

---

[c] The second author performed this work while she was affiliated with the University of Warwick.

Biomedical Image Synthesis and Simulation. https://doi.org/10.1016/B978-0-12-824349-7.00029-3

cess of acquisition of multi-gigapixel whole slide images along with their accurate annotations by expert pathologists is a very time-consuming, costly and error-prone task. Moreover, the development of efficient network designs for processing these images with huge sizes is also challenging due to limitations of memory and processing power. As a result, there is an increasing need for benchmark synthetic datasets of high-quality tissue images to validate and compare different processing algorithms. Various methods have been proposed for this purpose of generating synthetic tissue images using classical machine learning [15–22] and deep learning methods [23–28]. We shed light on them in the next literature review section.

In this chapter, we discuss two different approaches to generative modeling of colorectal cancer synthetic tissue images. First, we present a classical machine learning approach that uses a parameterized generative model [22] named TheCOT, to simulate synthetic histology image data, mimicking the tumor microenvironment. This model allows the user to have control over the input parameters like cancer grade and cellularity. It aims to generate virtual digital pathology imaging data whose spatial features and tumor microenvironment closely match the real histology data. The other method adopts a deep learning approach, specifically a conditional generative adversarial network based framework [24] to generate large tissue images by training the network on images having relatively small sizes. It illustrates the concept of methodical and seamless stitching of smaller generated tissue regions to form the high-dimensional tissue image, maintaining the local appearance and global coherence across the tissue regions. Though the TheCOT model successfully models the tumor microenvironment for colorectal adenocarcinoma, the generated images do not appear realistic. On the other hand, the deep learning based framework, which uses adversarial training, generates high-dimensional realistic tissue images, preserving their morphological characteristics.

In the subsequent section, we review the existing literature on the available methods for synthetic image generation of tissues. The next section describes the structure and components of the colorectal cancer tissue. Later, we study and compare the two methods for generating colorectal cancer tissue images. Finally, we conclude by exploring future directions of this research and mention the potential challenges.

22.2 Literature review

Initially, classical machine learning methods were applied for tissue image synthesis in the medical domain. There was an emphasis on modeling various tissue components separately and simulating the tissue microenvironment consisting of glands, stromal regions and nuclei. One of the earliest methods attempted to simulate tissue architecture using graph-based approaches [15]. In order to present realistic simulations, Lehmussola et al. proposed a simulator named SIMCEP [16], which could simulate synthetic images of fluorescence-stained cell populations with realistic cytoplasm and nuclei. Svoboda et al. [17] presented a model to simulate 3D image data of nuclei of cell populations, with realistic distribution [19], and later with healthy colon tissue [18]. SimuCell [20] toolbox managed to simulate heterogeneous cell populations expressing various protein markers. Zhao et al. [21] came up with a machine learning based approach to generate realistic cells with labeled nuclei, membranes, and a protein expressed in a cell organelle.

Deep learning solutions provided a breakthrough to the field of computational histopathology as they showed significant improvement over the previous state-of-the-art results in regards to visual understanding. The ability of generative adversarial networks (GANs) [29] to use adversarial training to generate realistic natural images with high perceptual quality motivated the researchers to adopt them for synthesizing histology images. Zhang et al. presented an adversarial learning-based approach [28] to generate medical images for the task of medical image tissue recognition. Quiros et al. proposed Pathology-GAN [23] to generate high quality cancer tissue images. They showed the model's ability to capture clinically or pathologically meaningful representations within cancer tissue images. They also demonstrated the induction of ordered latent space based on tissue characteristics, which allowed performing linear arithmetic operations to change the high-level tissue image. Hou et al. delivered an unsupervised pipeline [27] to construct both histopathology tissue images and their corresponding nuclei masks to train the nuclei segmentation supervised algorithm. The framework also computed the importance weights of training samples using output from its discriminator network to train the task-specific segmentation/classification algorithm.

The property of conditional GANs [30] to synthesize high fidelity realistic images conditioned on a fixed input inspired researchers to use them to generate tissue images from the known ground truth [25,26]. Senaras et al. [26] attempted to generate breast cancer tissue images, controlled by nuclei segmentation masks. Similar to the conditional GAN (cGAN) based framework "Pix2Pix" [31], they adapted U-net [32] for the generator neural network, and CNN based classifier "PatchGAN" [31] as the discriminator. The cGAN was widely adopted for generative image modeling in other parts of the medical imaging domain too. To synthesize multi-contrast MRI, Dar et al. provided cGAN based networks [33]. Along with the perceptual loss used in the adversarial frameworks, they utilized a pixel-wise loss for spatially registered multi-contrast images, and a cycle-consistency loss inspired by [34] for unregistered images. Recently, Halicek et al. developed a conditional generative adversarial network [35] for artificially synthesizing hyperspectral images of breast cancer cells from the standard RGB images of the normal and cancerous cells. In the field of cross-modality image generation, the cGAN based frameworks were developed for both magnetic resonance (MR) to computed tomography (CT) [36] and CT-to-MR [37] synthesis.

Although these models can successfully generate high-quality realistic images, they can only create images of limited size due to the constraints of memory and processing power. The high-resolution (large) image tiles (e.g., 8000 × 8000 pixels) provide richer context, which is important for diagnosis in computational pathology [13,38]. Thorough research has been conducted to construct high-resolution images in various domains, including medical. Uzunova et al. proposed a multi-scale GAN framework to construct high resolution CT/MR images. They adopted the approach of initially generating a low-resolution image, followed by increasing its resolution in subsequent layers using GANs applied on the portions of the image generated in the last layer. Hamghalam et al. designed a novel multi-stage attention-GAN framework [39] to generate high contrast MRI with the help of an attention mechanism. They proposed a multi-stage structure to enhance the resolution of high tissue contrast images. Other GAN based frameworks such as ProGAN [40] and SR-GAN [41] also showed the generation of high-resolution natural images. The former adopted the approach of growing GANs, i.e., gradually increasing the resolution of the generated image by adding layers in the network, one at a time. The latter employs the deep residual network (ResNet) and super-resolves the photo-realistic images with a $4\times$ up-scaling factor.

22.3 Colorectal cancer tissue structure

In this section, let us look at the colorectal cancer tissue structure and its microenvironment in detail. The healthy colorectal tissue microenvironment consists of a layer of epithelium forming glandular structures called crypts. The crypts consist mainly of three types of cells: epithelial, goblet, and stem [22]. Epithelial cells form an oval structure that surrounds the glandular lumen. The stem cells at the base of the crypts, continuously restore the epithelium. Stroma fills the space between crypts and includes several other types of cells such as lymphocytes, plasma cells and fibroblasts. The overall structure can be seen in Fig. 22.1. As colorectal adenocarcinoma starts developing from the normal tissue, the epithelium shows pre-malignant change with disordered growth and mutation, and increased dysplasia. Its aggressiveness is indicated by the histopathological grade. The traditional system of grading colorectal tissues, used by the International Union Against Cancer, identifies four differentiation grades: (1) G1, well-differentiated; (2) G2, moderately-differentiated; (3) G3, poorly-differentiated; and (4) G4, undifferentiated.

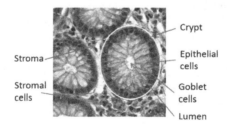

FIGURE 22.1

A hematoxilyn and eosin (H&E) image (from the GlaS dataset [42,43]) showing the structure of healthy colon cancer tissue.

The colorectal cancer grade can be identified by calculating the percentage of tumors showing the formation of gland-like structures. Well-differentiated grade, or grade 1, exhibits > 95% glands, moderately differentiated adenocarcinoma (grade 2) exhibits over 50%, poorly differentiated adenocarcinoma (grade 3) has 5–50%, and undifferentiated (grade 4) has < 5% glands. We can notice that the irregularity in the glandular formation increases with the grade of colon cancer. High grade cancer is associated with a poor rate of patient survival. Different grades of cancer can be visualized in Fig. 22.2 (top row). Grade 3 and 4 are often combined, and they are considered together for the generation of these colorectal cancer tissue images, which we discuss in the next section.

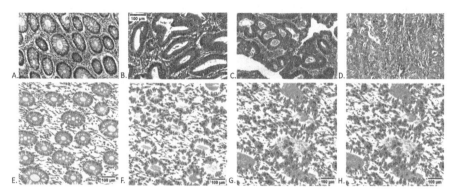

FIGURE 22.2

Samples of real (top row) and synthetic (bottom row) images for various grades: (A, E) healthy tissue, (B, F) well differentiated, (C, G) moderately differentiated, and (D, H) poorly differentiated cancerous tissue. Images are at 20× magnification. Adopted from [22].

22.4 **Model of spatial tumor heterogeneity**

Kovacheva et al. [22] proposed a model named TheCOT, to simulate colorectal cancer histology images at a sub-cellular level for healthy and cancerous tissues. It allows controlling the tissue appearance based on several user-defined parameters. The model aims to mimic the microenvironment of cells and tissues *in situ* rather than dispersed cells. It is the first model to simulate the tumor micro-environment considering different stages of cancer development. The model outputs the synthetic images given user parameters such as cancer grade, cellularity of epithelial and stromal cells, cell-overlap ratio, objective level, and image resolution. Examples of synthesized images of various grades can be seen in Fig. 22.2. These synthetic images can be used in applications where human-labeled data is crucial. Even if the model may not completely replace real images, the generated images can still be useful to validate image analysis algorithms.

In this section, we first look at the process of data acquisition. Next, we go through details of modeling of various components in the tissue microenvironment. That include epithelial and stromal cells, crypts, stromal region, goblet, and lumen cells. Lastly, we discuss results and specify the limitations of the method.

22.4.1 Data acquisition

Haemotoxylin and eosin (H&E) stained slides were collected from colon cancer patients were digitally scanned at 40× magnification by Zeiss MIRAX MIDI Slide Scanner. For cell level analysis, 42 visual fields were considered, categorized as 7 healthy, 4 well-differentiated, 26 moderately differentiated, and 5 poorly differentiated samples. These visual fields including context at 4× were graded by three pathologists and the majority vote was taken. Each nucleus in the images was hand-marked as epithelial or stromal, with 5826 nuclei marked. To analyze the crypt structures additional 31 visual fields at 20× were selected and categorized as 9 healthy and 22 cancerous samples; 480 healthy and 396 cancerous crypts were hand marked from these visual fields.

22.4.2 Modeling tissue microenvironment in colorectal adenocarcinoma

In this part, we first describe in detail the construction of individual cells (epithelial and stromal cells). Later we go through the overall organization of the crypts, stromal region, lumen, and goblet cells.

Construction of a single cell

The cell to be constructed was first assigned to one of the cell phenotypes found in real data with probability equal to the probability of phenotypes in real images of the same grade. The process of generation of shape and texture of nucleus as well as cell cytoplasm is given below.

(i) Shape

The cytoplasm for stromal cells and cell nuclei were constructed using a parametric model proposed in [45]. In this method, shapes were initialized as a circle parametrized by $(x(\theta), y(\theta))$, where $\theta \in [0, 2\pi]$ is the polar angle. The angle θ was sampled at $k = 10$ equidistant locations to generate a regular polygon (shapes are shown in Fig. 22.3, (A) and (C)). Later a polygon was constructed by randomizing spatial locations of vertices as follows:

$$x_i(\theta_i) = [U(-\alpha, \alpha) + \cos(\theta_i + U(-\beta, \beta))],$$
$$y_i(\theta_i) = [U(-\alpha, \alpha) + \sin(\theta_i + U(-\beta, \beta))],$$

(22.1)

where $U(x_1, x_2)$ is a number drawn from the uniform distribution on range $[x_1, x_2]$, $i = 1, \ldots, k$, while α and β control the randomness of the circle radius and angle of sampling, respectively. The value of α is dependent on the cancer grade S as $\alpha = 0.1(S + 1)$, $\beta = 0.05$. The cancerous grade S can take values 0 (healthy), 1 (well-differentiated), 2 (moderately differentiated), and 3 (poorly differentiated). The

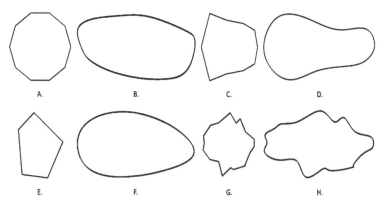

FIGURE 22.3

Examples of cell nuclei and cytoplasm shapes. Figures (A, C) show polygons constructed for $k = 10$ for (A) stromal cells, and (C) epithelial cells. Figures (B, D) show their corresponding shapes after spline interpolation [44]. Figures (E) and (G) show polygons generated for $k = 5$ and $k = 20$, respectively, and (F) and (H) show corresponding shapes after spline interpolation [44]. Adopted from [22].

$k = 10$ was chosen in a trade-off of taking too few points ($k = 5$) and not allowing enough control over the shape (Fig. 22.3(E)), and taking too many points ($k = 20$) and obtaining complicated shapes which look unrealistic (Fig. 22.3(G)).

To model sizes of nuclei, means μ_l and μ_w, and standard deviations, σ_l and σ_w, for nuclei major and minor axes were collected from the real dataset and normalized for magnification and pixel size of simulation. The size of the nucleus was computed as

$$
\begin{aligned}
\mu_l^n &= N(\mu_l, \sigma_l), \\
\mu_w^n &= N(\mu_w, \sigma_w),
\end{aligned}
$$

(22.2)

where $N(\mu, \sigma)$ is the normal distribution with mean μ and standard deviation σ. The size of the cell cytoplasm was calculated as

$$
\begin{aligned}
\mu_l^c &= U(1.5, 2.2)\mu_l^n, \\
\mu_w^c &= U(1.5, 2.2)\mu_w^n.
\end{aligned}
$$

(22.3)

Before construction, normal stromal cells were either assigned to fibroblasts or lymphocytes with equal probability. In case of the cancer tissue, stromal cells were assigned to be cancerous with probability $1 - 0.2S$. They represented tumor cells infiltrating into the stromal region. To ensure the realistic appearance of stromal cells, the fibroblast cells were re-scaled as

$$
\begin{aligned}
\hat{\mu}_w^n &= 0.8\mu_w^n, \\
\hat{\mu}_l^c &= 1.8\mu_l^c, \\
\hat{\mu}_w^c &= 0.5\mu_w^c,
\end{aligned}
$$

(22.4)

and lymphocytes as

$$
\begin{aligned}
\hat{\mu}_l^n &= 0.8\mu_l^n, \\
\hat{\mu}_w^n &= 0.8\mu_w^n, \\
\hat{\mu}_l^c &= 0.7\mu_l^c, \\
\hat{\mu}_w^c &= 0.7\mu_w^c.
\end{aligned}
\tag{22.5}
$$

This ensured fibroblast cells have thin nuclei, long and thin cytoplasm, and smaller lymphocytes than epithelial cells. The cytoplasm of epithelial cells was constructed initializing from the polygon shown in Fig. 22.3(C). The set of coordinates (x_i, y_i), $i = 1, \ldots, k$ was then scaled as follows:

$$
\begin{aligned}
\hat{x}_i(\theta_i) &= x_i(\theta_i)\,\mu_l^{n/c}, \\
\hat{y}_i(\theta_i) &= y_i(\theta_i)\,\mu_w^{n/c},
\end{aligned}
\tag{22.6}
$$

where $\mu_l^{n/c}$ can be both μ^n and μ^c. Finally, vertices in the cells were interpolated using spline interpolation method [44].

(ii) Texture

Nuclear chromatin texture is a vital factor in grading colon cancer, and hence a sophisticated method [46] was adopted to generate the texture of cytoplasm. The model was applied to the gray-scale texture of all nuclei found to belong to the real phenotypes to generate larger texture images (see Figures 9 and 11 in [22]). When a nucleus of a particular phenotype was getting synthesized, a random portion from the corresponding texture image was selected as a nucleus texture. As a sampling of nuclear texture images was done with replacement, two nuclei could have the same texture.

Crypts

The suitable radius of crypts, μ_b, was calculated as the mean length on the minor axis found from H&E images and normalized as per magnification and resolution of the image. Total number of crypts, N_c, in the generated image of size $i_h \times i_w$ was computed as follows:

$$
N_c = f_c \lfloor i_h/(2\mu_b) \rfloor \lfloor i_w/(2\mu_b) \rfloor,
\tag{22.7}
$$

where f_c is the fraction of samples taken by crypts and is given by

$$
f_c = \begin{cases}
1, & \text{if } S = 0, 1, \\
U(0.5, 0.95), & \text{if } S = 2, \\
U(0, 0.5), & \text{if } S = 3.
\end{cases}
\tag{22.8}
$$

The value ranges of f_c were derived from pathology guidelines [47] and discussions with pathologists. Crypts were simulated as elliptical structures to create colon tissue structures. The minor axis b was sampled from the gamma distribution $\Gamma(\alpha_b, \beta_b)$; α_b and β_b are the parameters of the distribution for the minor axis estimated from the set of real H&E histology images, and normalized as per magnification and pixel size of simulation. The ratio (e) between the major and minor axes was used to determine the length of the major axis (a) of elliptical crypt, $e = b/a$. The parameter e was given by $\Gamma(\alpha_e, \beta_e)$, where α_e and β_e are parameters for the distribution of e. The rotation angle of the major axis of crypt was chosen at random ϕ. The outline was computed as follows:

$$R(\theta) = \frac{ab\sqrt{2}}{\sqrt{\left(b^2 - a^2\right)\cos(2\theta - 2\phi) + a^2 + b^2}} + u, \qquad (22.9)$$

where $R(\theta)$ is the polar radius, $\theta \in [0, 2\pi]$ is the polar angle, and $u = (S^2 + 1)U(-0.06, 0.1)$ is a degree of deformation of the crypts, a function of the grade S. To avoid significant reductions in the size of the crypts and twisting of the crypt outline, a small asymmetric range was chosen for u.

Crypt centers were selected so that they do not overlap for healthy or well-differentiated samples. For higher grades, at most two crypts were allowed to overlap to a certain extent. The centers of crypts were positioned at random with a distance between vertices of $0.6b$. The positions of epithelial cells along or close to the crypt edge were selected as follows:

$$x = x_0 + rSu_x, \quad y = y_0 + rSu_y, \qquad (22.10)$$

where x_0 and y_0 were randomly selected points along the crypt, u_x and u_y are random scaling factors taken from $U(-0.25, 0.08)$, and r is the appropriate radius; r was assumed to be 6 μm from the given resolution and magnification level. The scaling factor distribution was chosen to maximize the visual similarity between real and generated images. Therefore epithelial cells became increasingly distorted with an increase in the cancer grade of the colon tissue. After placement of cells, they were rotated so they point towards the crypt center. Supposing $S < 2$, their nuclei were displaced closer to the crypt edge. All stromal cells were placed uniformly outside the crypts and rotated in the direction given by $\phi + U(-\pi/6, \pi/6)$. See Table 1 in [22] for a detailed list of parameters and their typical values.

Number of cells

The L_{max} parameter controls the maximum cell overlap: $L_{max} = 0$ means there is no overlap allowed, whereas $L_{max} = 1$ means there is no restriction for overlap. The number of cells N was calculated after number and size of crypts were determined. In the first step, the area of stromal cell was calculated as follows:

$$A = \pi[(1.7 - 0.7L_{max})r]^2. \qquad (22.11)$$

Here the multiplication factor (r) does not go below 1 and accounts for the overlap. The area covered by stroma A_s was found by counting pixels outside the crypts.

The total number of stromal cells N_s was computed as follows:

$$N_s = v_s A_s / A, \quad v_s \in [0, 1], \tag{22.12}$$

where v_s denotes the cellularity or density of stromal cells. The number of epithelial cells, N_e, was determined by

$$N_e = \frac{v_e P}{2(1.25 - L_{max})r}, \tag{22.13}$$

where P is the sum of perimeters of the crypts in the tissue images, and v_e denotes the cellularity or density of epithelial cells. The final number of cells, N, was given by

$$N = N_e + N_s. \tag{22.14}$$

Lumen and goblet cells

A non-parametric texture synthesis framework [46] was incorporated to generate the lumen texture inside the constructed crypts. In this model, the pixel value is computed by finding all patches from the texture source image that resemble the neighborhood of the pixel under consideration. One of those patches is selected at random and the value of its center pixel is assigned to the pixel in question. In order to generate texture images, the gray-scaled texture of hand-annotated lumen portion from the real H&E images was utilized. Seven cancerous crypt textures and one normal lumen texture were generated for this work. While generating crypts, a random part of the available texture images was selected and used for texture. The normal lumen texture was used to generate healthy samples. For cancer samples, a cancerous texture image was selected at random.

After placing the lumen texture, goblet cells structure was outlined using Voronoi diagrams [48]. The observed structure of the goblet cells depends upon the structure of the corresponding crypt. It was fixed using the angle at which the crypt was sliced and the length of its major and minor axes. When the crypt was round, the number of goblet cells was given by $\frac{a}{r}$, where a is the length of the major axis and r is the radius of the crypt. If the crypt was elliptical, they added additional $2k(k-1)$ goblet cells around each end of the major axis of the crypt, where $k \approx \frac{1}{e}$, e is the ratio between major and minor axes of the crypt. To determine their locations, angular increments from a center of the crypts were taken and points were placed on the outer ring keeping distance from the crypt boundary equal to cell radius r. The additional points were placed along the $2k$ angles closest to the major axis at a distance $2i$, $i = 2, \ldots, k$ from the boundary, as shown in Fig. 22.4. The center of the crypt was also considered as the center of gravity. A small variation was allowed for the location of each point, and the Voronoi diagram was constructed. Boundaries were dilated and corners at each Voronoi vertex were rounded using dilation to make boundaries more realistic. Some other texture [49] was added to the boundaries and they were convolved with a Gaussian and added to the final tissue image.

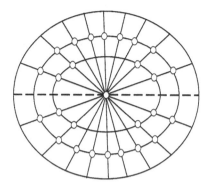

FIGURE 22.4

Initial locations for the centers of gravity (denoted by circles) for Voronoi diagram in a crypt with $k = 2$. Dashed line gives the major axis.

22.4.3 Measurement error

The measurement error induced in final generated images was fixed using a convolution of 2D Gaussian G. Zero mean Gaussian noise N_G was added with variance σ_G to approximate charge-coupled device detector noise. The degraded simulated image $\hat{I}$ was obtained as ($*$ is a convolution operator),

$$\hat{I} = I * G + N_G. \tag{22.15}$$

22.4.4 Histology simulation

The constructed cytoplasm and nuclei images were H&E stained using a user-defined color deconvolution matrix. For this work, they used the color deconvolution matrix suggested by Ruifrok and Johnston [50]. A matrix obtained from an image using the stain separation method proposed by Trahearn et al. [51] is given by

$$M = \begin{bmatrix} 0.6402 & 0.6479 & 0.4128 \\ 0.3906 & 0.7662 & 0.5102 \end{bmatrix}. \tag{22.16}$$

By simulating IHC (immunohistochemistry) stains, the applicability of the model expanded to validation of various H&E slides. The flexibility of choosing stain vector gives the researcher an opportunity to validate various stain normalization methods on images synthesized by this model. Fig. 22.5 shows some examples of simulated images with different parameters.

22.4.5 Results

The synthesized images can be seen in Figs. 22.2 and 22.5. The appearance of tissue images can be controlled by user parameters. Figs. 22.5(A) and 22.5(B) show

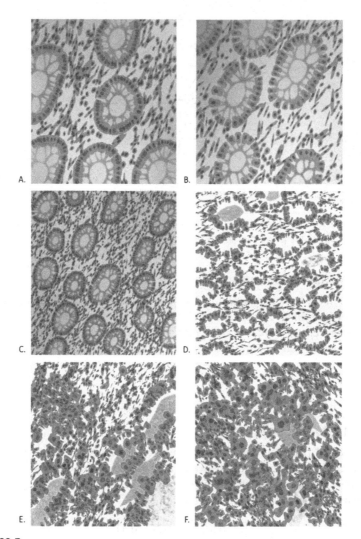

FIGURE 22.5

Examples of synthesized images demonstrating the effects of different parameter values. Figures (A), (B), and (C) show the simulated images of healthy colon tissue. The remaining figures show (D) well differentiated, (E) moderately differentiated, and (F) poorly differentiated cancer tissues. In figure (B), the cell overlap is 0.2, and all other figures have the cell overlap of 0.6. Figures (A) and (B) were generated using the stain vector proposed in [50], whereas other figures were generated using the stain matrix given in Eq. (22.16). Adopted from [22].

how changing parameters for overlap and cellularity changes the structure of synthesized images. Figs. 22.5(C) and 22.5(D) shows how tissue appearance changes after

Table 22.1 Mean score of different components of the synthetic images, by their appearance (1 = Not realistic, 5 = Very realistic, "-" means the feature is not relevant). Images of grades healthy (H), well differentiated (WD), moderately differentiated (MD), and poorly differentiated (PD) were evaluated by three pathologists at magnifications 20× and 40×. Adopted from [22].

Grade	H	H	WD	WD	MD	MD	PD	PD
Magnification	40×	20×	40×	20×	40×	20×	40×	20×
Architecture	5	5	5	4	4	4	5	5
Crypt shape	5	5	5	5	5	5	4.5	4.5
Lumen	5	5	5	5	5	5	-	-
Goblet cells	4	4	-	-	-	-	-	-
Epithelial cells	4	4	4	4	4	4	4	4
Stromal cells	3	3	3	3	3	3	3	4

varying the differentiation grade. Some parameters like size, shape, and appearance of the crypts, whether or not the nuclei are basally orientated, and the frequency of cell phenotypes change as per the cancer grade. Users can study and analyze the morphological structure variation in synthesized colorectal tissue images by altering user parameters. The model takes around 108 seconds to simulate a 40× image and around 345 seconds for a 20× image.

Evaluation by pathologists

The synthesized colorectal tissue images were evaluated by three pathologists and they were asked to score the appearance between 1 to 5. Sixteen tissue images with all cancerous grade tissues at the magnification of 20× and 40× and with cell overlap of 0.2 and 0.6, respectively, were considered for the evaluation. Different tissue components, such as crypts and stromal cells, were graded separately to test their realistic appearances. The grades for synthesized tissue appearances can be seen in Table 22.1. The overall grade was found to be 4.28 though stromal cells were found to be moderately realistic.

22.5 Deep learning based colorectal pathology image generation

Deshpande et al. presented a framework [24] based on conditional generative adversarial networks [30] to generate annotated synthetic tissue images. The key novelty of the framework is that it can generate tissue images of arbitrarily large sizes even after training on smaller images. Using small images for model training reduces the computational cost and avoids limitations in processing power and memory. Generating large tissue images can provide a broader context for designing image analysis algorithms, which can be crucial as pathologists usually inspect the contextual area around the region of interest in the tissue images. As far as we are aware, it is the first framework to generate such tissue images of large arbitrary sizes. The framework shows the ability to generate tissue regions and methodologically stitch them to achieve seamless, realistic and globally coherent tiles. These synthetic whole slide images can be beneficial to train and evaluate tissue image analysis algorithms where the data availability is limited.

22.5.1 Dataset

The Colorectal Adenocarcinoma Gland (CRAG) Dataset [52,53][1] was used for experiments on the framework. It contains colon histopathology tissue images with variable glandular morphology and has been widely used for training and performance evaluation of histology image segmentation and glandular morphology analysis methods. Each image belongs to one of three classes based on its glandular morphology: well-differentiated (no deformation of glands), moderately-differentiated (slightly deformed glands), and poorly-differentiated (highly deformed glands). Each image in the dataset has a corresponding gland segmentation mask which specifies different tissue components such as glands, stroma and background in the image (see Fig. 22.6). The tissue images with well-differentiated grades were considered for generation from the input tissue component mask in this work. The dataset contains 173 training tiles and 40 test tiles, with an average image size of 1512×1516, out of which, there are 39 tiles for training and 9 tiles for testing of well-differentiated grade.

22.5.2 Conditional generative adversarial network based framework

The framework attempted to generate high-resolution (large) tiles of colorectal cancer histology images. In conventional GAN, its two components, a generator and a discriminator are trained in a competitive manner. The generator aims to produce realistic images visually similar to the underlying distribution, whereas the discriminator tries to discriminate between real and fake images.

Similar to existing methods for tissue image generation [26], the framework also learned to produce realistic tissue images from the known ground-truth tissue component mask. The generator was effectively trained to generate smaller patches of the large tissue tile from corresponding areas of the component mask. These patches were spatially stitched to form a large tile. The discriminator consumed the entire tile as an input to predict its realism and thus enforced seamless appearance and global coherence across the tile. Since the trained generator is only responsible for generating the tissue patches, and the stitching operation of spatially adjacent patches is independent of the tile size, the framework can be used to construct arbitrarily large

---

[1] https://warwick.ac.uk/TIAlab/data/mildnet/.

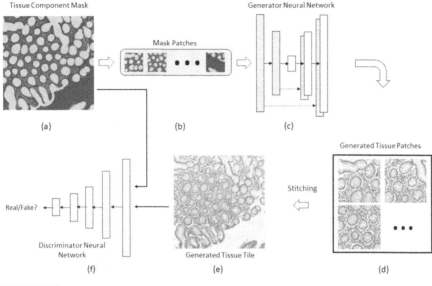

FIGURE 22.6

An overview of the framework for training phase of high resolution tissue image generation. Tissue component mask (a) is first divided into set of patches (b). Each patch is then passed through the generator neural network (c), creating corresponding tissue image patch. Generated tissue patches (d) are then stitched constructing the final tile (e) which is then passed entirely through the discriminator neural network (f) which predicts its realism.

tissue tiles even after training on relatively smaller ones with minimal computational overhead. The framework overview can be seen in Fig. 22.6. In the next part, we discuss the modeling of various components of the framework.

Patch level generation

A set of training histology images (denoted as Y) and their associated tissue masks (denoted as X) were used for training the framework. Images in the given dataset were modeled as a set of overlapping patches of fixed size, i.e., $X = \{x_{r,c}\}$ and $Y = \{y_{r,c}\}$ with each patch parameterized by its center grid coordinates in the corresponding tile. A generator network was used to generate an image patch y' given an input mask x, i.e., $y' = G(x; \theta_G)$, where θ_G represents the trainable weights of the generator. In order to train the generator in a context-aware manner, it was presented with a larger $M_{patch} \times M_{patch}$ context patch of the input mask to generate a smaller patch of size $I_{patch} \times I_{patch}$ corresponding to the center of the input mask as shown in Fig. 22.7. Input mask is zero padded from all four sides to ensure size of the generated tissue tile same as the component mask.

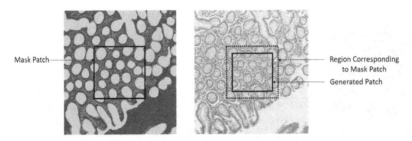

FIGURE 22.7

Mapping from input segmentation patch to target tissue image patch.

Patch stitching and discriminator modeling

The stride $s = 236$ while dividing a tile into a set of image patches was chosen so that the adjacent patches have non-zero overlap. This helped to reduce tile boundary artifacts across the patches while stitching to make a single tile $Y' = \{y'_{r,c}\}$. The pixel values of overlapped regions were computed by spatially averaging the overlapping pixel values. The values $I_{tile} = 728$, $M_{patch} = 296$, $I_{patch} = 256$, $S = 236$ were in the framework for training of the network. The generated tile was then passed through the tile-level discriminator network $D(Y, Y'; \theta_D)$ with trainable weight parameters θ_D in order to preserve the seamless appearance and global coherence across the entire tile.

Generator and discriminator

The generator and discriminator architectures were adapted from [31]. The generator used was an encoder–decoder U-shaped structure similar to the U-net [32]. It takes a segmentation mask patch as input and compresses it to a high-level representation of data with lower dimensionality via the encoder part, and decompresses it via the decoder part to a tissue image patch. The generator is the series of "ENCODE" blocks (see Fig. 22.8) where each block comprises a convolution layer followed by batch normalization layer and lastly a leaky-ReLu activation unit, and the decoder is the chain of "DECODE" blocks. The task of the "DECODE" block is to do the exact opposite job of the "ENCODE" block, it has a deconvolution layer that up-samples the input to higher dimensionality followed by a similar batch normalization layer and then leaky-ReLu activation unit. The version of the generator with skip-connections given in [31] was used in the framework, which gives the flexibility to bypass the encoding part if it does not need it.

The sizes of the input and output images for the generator used in pix2pix conditional GAN network [31] are the same, unlike in this case, where the input image size is comparatively larger. In this experiment, the generator input size is 296×296 and the output size is 256×256, as an additional encoding block was assembled for the encoder part in the generator. The first encoder block reduces the size of the image from 296 to 256, as shown in Fig. 22.8. After this step, the rest of the architecture is symmetric and having skip connections connecting encoder layers to decoder layers.

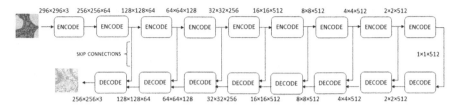

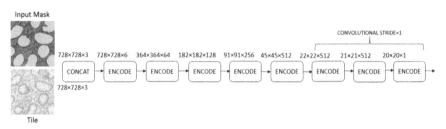

FIGURE 22.8

Architectures of the generator (top) and the discriminator (bottom).

The discriminator used was the PatchGAN discriminator [31] which accepts the input image and an unknown image (either real or fake) and decides whether the second image is generated by generator or not. The architecture of the discriminator is comprised of series of "ENCODE" blocks (see Fig. 22.8) where the output is 30×30 image in which each pixel value represents how believable the corresponding section or patch of the unknown image is.

22.5.3 Training and inference

The two neural networks (generator G and discriminator D) were trained simultaneously to learn their trainable weight parameters $\{\theta_G, \theta_D\}$ from the given dataset. The objective or loss function has two components:

1. Reconstruction Loss. In order to model regeneration errors, a tile level reconstruction loss was incorporated based on the output of the generator model after stitching. Specifically, the reconstruction loss is the expected error between generated and actual tile level images in the training data as given below:

$$\min_{\theta_G} L_R = E_{X,Y} \| Y - G(X; \theta_G) \|. \tag{22.17}$$

2. Adversarial Loss. An adversarial loss was employed to make sure that the generated image was perceptually sound and looked realistic:

$$\min_{\theta_G} \max_{\theta_D} L_{adv} = E_{X,Y \sim p_{data}(X,Y)}[log D(X, Y; \theta_D)]$$
$$+ E_{X \sim p_X(X)}[log(1 - D(X, G(X, \theta_G); \theta_D))]. \tag{22.18}$$

A weighted linear combination of the two losses ($\min_{\theta_G} \max_{\theta_D} \lambda_R L_R + \lambda_{adv} L_{adv}$) is used as a joint loss function with the weights as hyper-parameters which are tuned through cross-validation to $\lambda_R = 100.0$ and $\lambda_{adv} = 1.0$. For training, images from CRAG dataset [52,53] were cropped into tiles of 728×728 size, resulting in total of 918 samples. The network was trained for 100 epochs (Adam optimizer with initial learning rate 0.0002 and batch size 1).

It is important to note that the framework was trained to generate globally consistent patches given an input tissue component mask. Consequently, at inference time, it can be used to generate large images of arbitrary size as the stitching mechanism is independent of the tile size. It can also be noticed that this framework can be used to generate an exhaustive annotated synthetic dataset with the help of existing and methodically/randomly generated tissue component masks.

22.5.4 Experiments and results

In order to validate the performance of the framework, three types of assessments were conducted: (1) visual assessment, (2) quantitative assessment, and (3) assessment through gland segmentation, in which the concordance between gland segmentation accuracy of original and synthetic images was compared.

Visual assessment

Tiles of size 964×964 pixels and 1436×1436 pixels constructed after training the framework on images of size 728×728 pixels can be seen in Fig. 22.9. It can be observed that the shapes of the glands are preserved in the constructed images. Empirically, it was found that those shapes are maintained due to skip connections used in the generator neural network architecture. Images were coming out highly deformed if skip connections were not used. The generated tiles appear seamless and homogeneous. They show good preservation of morphological characteristics, including epithelial cells, glandular regions, and stroma along with moderate deformities in the glandular lumen.

Quantitative assessment

To assess the model quantitatively for the image construction, the Fréchet inception distance (FID) score [54] was computed, which is generally used as an evaluation metric of generative image networks [23]. To compute the FID, feature space was collected from the last pooling layer of the Inception V3 network [55] trained on the "ImageNet" dataset [56]. A set of random noise images of the same dimensionality was generated for the purpose of comparison. The lower the FID, the higher the similarity between actual and generated images, i.e., the better the quality of images.

Fig. 22.10 shows the FID scores of the generated images of different sizes. It reveals significantly lower FID between the real tiles and synthetic tiles constructed using our framework, compared to random images. This conveys that the convolution

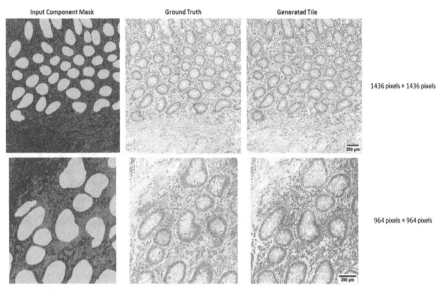

FIGURE 22.9

Construction of large image tiles from input component masks. Top row shows images of size 1436 × 1436 pixels whereas bottom row shows that of size 964 × 964 pixels. The leftmost images are tissue component masks, images at the center are ground-truth images while those at the rightmost are constructed images.

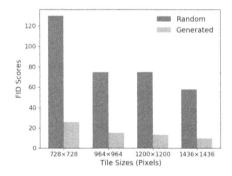

FIGURE 22.10

FID scores of the constructed tissue images of sizes 728 and 1436 using random model and our framework.

feature maps computed from these two sets of tiles (real and generated) lie close to each other in the feature space. This, therefore, indicates that the framework is reliable for generating synthetic set for experiments in the domain of computational histopathology.

Assessment through gland segmentation

The binary segmentation masks were computed using U-net based gland segmentation algorithm [32], on patches of both original and generated tiles taken from the test dataset. Sample gland segmentation masks from both set of images are shown in Fig. 22.11. The Dice index score [57] was calculated among those two sets of images.

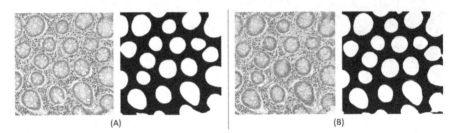

(A)   (B)

FIGURE 22.11

Patches of original tiles (A) and generated tiles (B) along with their gland segmentation mask. Average Dice index score among them is 0.93.

Dice index scores of 0.93 (with standard deviation of 0.058) and 0.88 (with standard deviation 0.17) were obtained on 471 patches of dimensionality 512×512 and on 452 patches of size 256×256, respectively. This high score indicates that both real and synthetic images share similar morphological characteristics, and it is dependable to use synthetic images constructed by our framework for evaluation of the gland segmentation algorithm.

22.5.5 Discussion

The framework demonstrated its capacity to produce large tiles even after getting trained on relatively small tiles. The constructed tiles from patch based framework do not exhibit any seams between the consecutive patches. After performing experiments on the CRAG dataset, results suggest that the generated tissue image tiles maintain morphological characteristics in the tissue regions. It was found that the constructed images are appearing realistic and maintaining consistently low FID scores.

It can be noticed that the generator neural network from the above framework is working on the patches of tiles from the training set synthesizing the corresponding portion, and the stitching operation of the generated parts generating the final tissue tile is independent of the image size. This property makes the framework computationally feasible to generate tiles of huge size. Since generating patches of the final tissue tile using a single generator can be performed in parallel, the time required to construct big images can be significantly reduced.

22.6 **Comparison**

We discussed two methods for generating colorectal cancer tissue images. The first method, TheCOT (Section 22.4), adopts the classical generative modeling approach to model the tumor microenvironment for colorectal adenocarcinoma. This approach allows us to better understand the tissue microenvironment and some underlying laws, such as the distributions of cell phenotypes and diversity in the tissue architecture. The framework offers the flexibility to control the tissue appearance by several parameters. However, these colorectal cancer tissue images generated based on input parameters do not appear realistic in nature. Moreover, the size of the generated image is constrained due to restrictions in the computational capacity.

The second method (Section 22.5) is a deep learning based model, which presents a realistic tissue image producing framework based on generative adversarial networks. The framework has the ability to generate high resolution tiles of arbitrary sizes after training on relatively lower resolution images. The model exhibits realistic morphological tissue features including appearance of glands, nuclear structure, and stromal architecture. The generated synthetic tissue tiles can be used in the assessment of digital pathology image analysis algorithms due to their realistic nature. The model has the ability to generate an unlimited amount of annotated synthetic data. The experimental results also show that the framework can be effectively used for training and evaluation of gland segmentation algorithms. Due to the ability of this framework to construct high-resolution tiles of large dimensions, and realistic nature of the generated tiles, the deep learning based model can be preferred over the TheCOT model in generating colorectal tissue images.

22.7 **Research challenges & future directions**

One of the key goals of image synthesis is to create benchmark datasets for evaluating algorithms in digital pathology, and specifically modeling the morphological and microenvironmental characteristics in cancerous tissues. Synthetic images can also be used for the purpose of data augmentation and for pre-training deep learning models. Whole slide image synthesis would lead to the generation of rich, informative images, required to model context aware neural models for nuclei detection, tumor segmentation, and survival prediction. Current research focuses on synthesizing tissue images by modeling various tissue components using state-of-the-art deep learning design techniques. The challenge of generative algorithms for modeling whole slide image is the multi-gigapixel nature of the images. State-of-the-art architectures of image synthesis fail to construct such huge images due to limitations of computing power and memory requirements. Tissue image synthesis also has the inherent challenge of modeling high fidelity images with a variety of tissue types. For instance, modeling colorectal cancer tissue images containing regions of all grades, is difficult.

In the future, these two approaches for synthetic whole slide image generation can be combined to obtain a framework, enabled with user-defined parameters, to generate arbitrary sized colorectal cancer histology images. The synthetic tissue images generated by the former framework contain crypts with reliable shapes and orientations. With the help of crypt segmentation algorithm similar to the one discussed in [58], the gland segmentation masks can be synthesized. After obtaining the masks of the tissue components such as glands and stromal region, the realistic arbitrary sized tissue image can be synthesized using the latter algorithm. A further direction of this research is to provide a user enabled controlled interface while synthesizing whole slide images. This would provide flexibility to alter the generated image as per requirements and help in the acquisition of unlimited heterogeneous data.

To conclude, we have discussed two approaches for the synthesis of colorectal cancer tissue images, including modeling their internal components with high fidelity. We saw that the constructed tiles using [24] patch based framework neither exhibit any seams nor deformities between adjacent patches. The study has several practical applications, since synthetic datasets with known ground truth allow researchers to develop state-of-the-art evaluations of various algorithms for nuclei segmentation and cancer grading. These methods can be extended in the future to generate whole slide images with various cancer grades.

References

[1] B. Stewart, C. Wild, World Cancer Report 2014, International Agency for Research on Cancer, 2014, https://books.google.co.in/books?id=OQHbngEACAAJ.

[2] H. Sung, J. Ferlay, R. Siegel, M. Laversanne, I. Soerjomataram, A. Jemal, F. Bray, Global cancer statistics 2020: GLOBOCAN estimates of incidence and mortality worldwide for 36 cancers in 185 countries, CA: A Cancer Journal for Clinicians (2021), https://doi.org/10.3322/caac.21660.

[3] Q. Vu, S. Graham, T. Kurc, M. To, M. Shaban, T. Qaiser, N. Koohbanani, S.A. Khurram, J. Kalpathy-Cramer, T. Zhao, R. Gupta, J.T. Kwak, N. Rajpoot, J. Saltz, K. Farahani, Methods for segmentation and classification of digital microscopy tissue images, Frontiers in Bioengineering and Biotechnology 7 (2019), https://doi.org/10.3389/fbioe.2019.00053.

[4] S. Graham, N.M. Rajpoot, Sams-Net: stain-aware multi-scale network for instance-based nuclei segmentation in histology images, in: 2018 IEEE 15th International Symposium on Biomedical Imaging (ISBI 2018), 2018, pp. 590–594, https://doi.org/10.1109/ISBI.2018.8363645.

[5] S. Graham, Q. Vu, S.E.A. Raza, A. Azam, Y. Tsang, J.T. Kwak, N. Rajpoot, Hover-Net: simultaneous segmentation and classification of nuclei in multi-tissue histology images, Medical Image Analysis 58 (2019) 101563, https://doi.org/10.1016/j.media.2019.101563.

[6] K. Sirinukunwattana, S.E.A. Raza, Y.-W. Tsang, D.R.J. Snead, I.A. Cree, N.M. Rajpoot, Locality sensitive deep learning for detection and classification of nuclei in routine colon cancer histology images, IEEE Transactions on Medical Imaging 35 (5) (2016) 1196–1206, https://doi.org/10.1109/TMI.2016.2525803.

[7] S. Tripathi, S. Singh, Cell nuclei classification in histopathological images using hybrid O L ConvNet, ACM Transactions on Multimedia Computing Communications and Applications 16 (2020) 1–22, https://doi.org/10.1145/3345318.

[8] S. Akbar, L. Jordan, A.M. Thompson, S.J. McKenna, Tumor localization in tissue microarrays using rotation invariant superpixel pyramids, in: 2015 IEEE 12th International Symposium on Biomedical Imaging (ISBI), 2015, pp. 1292–1295, https://doi.org/10.1109/ISBI.2015.7164111.

[9] Y. Xu, J.-Y. Zhu, E. Chang, M. Lai, Z. Tu, Weakly supervised histopathology cancer image segmentation and classification, Medical Image Analysis 18 (2014) 591–604, https://doi.org/10.1016/j.media.2014.01.010.

[10] B. Ehteshami Bejnordi, M. Veta, P.J. van Diest, B. van Ginneken, N. Karssemeijer, et al., Diagnostic assessment of deep learning algorithms for detection of lymph node metastases in women with breast cancer, JAMA 318 (2017) 2199–2210, https://doi.org/10.1001/jama.2017.14585.

[11] T. Qaiser, Y. Tsang, D. Taniyama, N. Sakamoto, K. Nakane, D. Epstein, N. Rajpoot, Fast and accurate tumor segmentation of histology images using persistent homology and deep convolutional features, Medical Image Analysis 55 (2019) 1–14, https://doi.org/10.1016/j.media.2019.03.014.

[12] P. Gupta, S.-F. Chiang, P. Sahoo, S. Mohapatra, J.-F. You, D. Onthoni, H.-Y. Hung, J.-M. Chiang, Y. Huang, W.-S. Tsai, Prediction of colon cancer stages and survival period with machine learning approach, Cancers 11 (2019), https://doi.org/10.3390/cancers11122007.

[13] M. Shaban, R. Awan, M.M. Fraz, A. Azam, Y.-W. Tsang, D. Snead, N.M. Rajpoot, Context-aware convolutional neural network for grading of colorectal cancer histology images, IEEE Transactions on Medical Imaging 39 (7) (2020) 2395–2405, https://doi.org/10.1109/TMI.2020.2971006.

[14] Y. Zhou, S. Graham, N. Alemi Koohbanani, M. Shaban, P.-A. Heng, N. Rajpoot, CGC-Net: cell graph convolutional network for grading of colorectal cancer histology images, in: 2019 IEEE/CVF International Conference on Computer Vision Workshop (ICCVW), 2019, pp. 388–398, https://doi.org/10.1109/ICCVW.2019.00050.

[15] J.M.S. Prewitt, Graphs and grammars for histology: an introduction, in: Proceedings of the Annual Symposium on Computer Application in Medical Care, 1979, pp. 18–25, https://www.ncbi.nlm.nih.gov/pmc/articles/PMC2231975/.

[16] A. Lehmussola, P. Ruusuvuori, J. Selinummi, H. Huttunen, O. Yli-Harja, Computational framework for simulating fluorescence microscope images with cell populations, IEEE Transactions on Medical Imaging 26 (7) (2007) 1010–1016, https://doi.org/10.1109/TMI.2007.896925.

[17] D. Svoboda, M. Kozubek, S. Stejskal, Generation of digital phantoms of cell nuclei and simulation of image formation in 3D image cytometry, Cytometry. Part A: The journal of the International Society for Analytical Cytology 75 (2009) 494–509, https://doi.org/10.1002/cyto.a.20714.

[18] D. Svoboda, O. Homola, S. Stejskal, Generation of 3D digital phantoms of colon tissue, in: International Conference Image Analysis and Recognition, vol. 6754, Springer, 2011, pp. 31–39, https://doi.org/10.1007/978-3-642-21596-4_4.

[19] D. Svoboda, V. Ulman, Towards a realistic distribution of cells in synthetically generated 3D cell populations, in: A. Petrosino (Ed.), Image Analysis and Processing – ICIAP 2013, Springer, Berlin, Heidelberg, 2013, pp. 429–438, https://doi.org/10.1007/978-3-642-41184-7_44.

[20] S. Rajaram, B. Pavie, N. Hac, S. Altschuler, L. Wu, SimuCell: a flexible framework for creating synthetic microscopy images, Nature Methods 9 (2012) 634–635, https://doi.org/10.1038/nmeth.2096.

[21] T. Zhao, R.F. Murphy, Automated learning of generative models for subcellular location: building blocks for systems biology, Cytometry. Part A: The journal of the International Society for Analytical Cytology 71 (2007) 978–990, https://doi.org/10.1002/cyto.a.20487.

[22] V.N. Kovacheva, D. Snead, N.M. Rajpoot, A model of the spatial tumour heterogeneity in colorectal adenocarcinoma tissue, BMC Bioinformatics 17 (1) (2016) 255, https://doi.org/10.1186/s12859-016-1126-2.

[23] A.C. Quiros, R. Murray-Smith, K. Yuan, PathologyGAN: learning deep representations of cancer tissue, in: T. Arbel, I. Ben Ayed, M. de Bruijne, M. Descoteaux, H. Lombaert, C. Pal (Eds.), Proceedings of the Third Conference on Medical Imaging with Deep Learning, in: Proceedings of Machine Learning Research, vol. 121, PMLR, 2020, pp. 669–695, http://proceedings.mlr.press/v121/quiros20a.html.

[24] S. Deshpande, F. Minhas, N. Rajpoot, Train small, generate big: synthesis of colorectal cancer histology images, in: N. Burgos, D. Svoboda, J.M. Wolterink, C. Zhao (Eds.), Simulation and Synthesis in Medical Imaging, Springer International Publishing, Cham, 2020, pp. 164–173, https://doi.org/10.1007/978-3-030-59520-3_17.

[25] C. Senaras, B. Sahiner, G. Tozbikian, G. Lozanski, M.N. Gurcan, Creating synthetic digital slides using conditional generative adversarial networks: application to Ki67 staining, in: Medical Imaging 2018: Digital Pathology, vol. 10581, International Society for Optics and Photonics, 2018, p. 1058103, https://doi.org/10.1117/12.2294999.

[26] C. Senaras, M.K.K. Niazi, B. Sahiner, M.P. Pennell, G. Tozbikian, G. Lozanski, M.N. Gurcan, Optimized generation of high-resolution phantom images using CGAN: application to quantification of Ki67 breast cancer images, PLoS ONE 13 (5) (2018) e0196846, https://doi.org/10.1371/journal.pone.0196846.

[27] L. Hou, A. Agarwal, D. Samaras, T.M. Kurc, R.R. Gupta, J.H. Saltz, Robust histopathology image analysis: to label or to synthesize?, in: 2019 IEEE/CVF Conference on Computer Vision and Pattern Recognition (CVPR), 2019, pp. 8525–8534, https://doi.org/10.1109/CVPR.2019.00873.

[28] Q. Zhang, H. Wang, H. Lu, D. Won, S.W. Yoon, Medical image synthesis with generative adversarial networks for tissue recognition, in: 2018 IEEE International Conference on Healthcare Informatics (ICHI), 2018, pp. 199–207, https://doi.org/10.1109/ICHI.2018.00030.

[29] I.J. Goodfellow, J. Pouget-Abadie, M. Mirza, B. Xu, D. Warde-Farley, S. Ozair, A. Courville, Y. Bengio, Generative adversarial nets, in: Proceedings of the 27th International Conference on Neural Information Processing Systems, vol. 2, NIPS'14, MIT Press, Cambridge, MA, USA, 2014, pp. 2672–2680.

[30] M. Mirza, S. Osindero, Conditional generative adversarial nets, arXiv preprint, arXiv:1411.1784.

[31] P. Isola, J.-Y. Zhu, T. Zhou, A.A. Efros, Image-to-image translation with conditional adversarial networks, in: 2017 IEEE Conference on Computer Vision and Pattern Recognition (CVPR), 2017, pp. 5967–5976, https://doi.org/10.1109/CVPR.2017.632.

[32] O. Ronneberger, P. Fischer, T. Brox, U-Net: convolutional networks for biomedical image segmentation, in: International Conference on Medical Image Computing and Computer-Assisted Intervention, vol. 9351, Springer, 2015, pp. 234–241, https://doi.org/10.1007/978-3-319-24574-4_28.

[33] S.U. Dar, M. Yurt, L. Karacan, A. Erdem, E. Erdem, T. Çukur, Image synthesis in multi-contrast MRI with conditional generative adversarial networks, IEEE Transactions on Medical Imaging 38 (10) (2019) 2375–2388, https://doi.org/10.1109/TMI.2019.2901750.

[34] J.-Y. Zhu, T. Park, P. Isola, A.A. Efros, Unpaired image-to-image translation using cycle-consistent adversarial networks, in: 2017 IEEE International Conference on Computer Vision (ICCV), 2017, pp. 2242–2251, https://doi.org/10.1109/ICCV.2017.244.

[35] M. Halicek, S. Ortega, H. Fabelo, C. Lopez, M. Lejeune, G.M. Callico, B. Fei, Conditional generative adversarial network for synthesizing hyperspectral images of breast cancer cells from digitized histology, in: J.E. Tomaszewski, A.D. Ward (Eds.), Medical Imaging 2020: Digital Pathology, vol. 11320, International Society for Optics and Photonics, SPIE, 2020, pp. 198–205, https://doi.org/10.1117/12.2549994.

[36] K. Boni, J. Klein, L. Vanquin, A. Wagner, T. Lacornerie, D. Pasquier, N. Reynaert, MR to CT synthesis with multicenter data in the pelvic era using a conditional generative adversarial network, Physics in Medicine and Biology 65 (2020), https://doi.org/10.1088/1361-6560/ab7633.

[37] J. Rubin, S. Abulnaga, CT-to-MR conditional generative adversarial networks for ischemic stroke lesion segmentation, in: 2019 IEEE International Conference on Healthcare Informatics (ICHI), 2019, pp. 1–7, https://doi.org/10.1109/ICHI.2019.8904574.

[38] B.E. Bejnordi, G. Zuidhof, M. Balkenhol, M. Hermsen, P. Bult, B. van Ginneken, N. Karssemeijer, G. Litjens, J. van der Laak, Context-aware stacked convolutional neural networks for classification of breast carcinomas in whole-slide histopathology images, Journal of Medical Imaging 4 (4) (2017) 044504, https://doi.org/10.1117/1.JMI.4.4.044504.

[39] M. Hamghalam, B. Lei, T. Wang, High tissue contrast MRI synthesis using multi-stage attention-GAN for segmentation, in: Proceedings of the AAAI Conference on Artificial Intelligence, vol. 34, 2020, pp. 4067–4074, https://doi.org/10.1609/aaai.v34i04.5825.

[40] H. Gao, J. Pei, H. Huang, ProGAN: network embedding via proximity generative adversarial network, in: Proceedings of the 25th ACM SIGKDD International Conference on Knowledge Discovery & Data Mining, KDD'19, Association for Computing Machinery, New York, NY, USA, 2019, pp. 1308–1316, https://doi.org/10.1145/3292500.3330866.

[41] C. Ledig, L. Theis, F. Huszár, J. Caballero, A. Cunningham, A. Acosta, A. Aitken, A. Tejani, J. Totz, Z. Wang, W. Shi, Photo-realistic single image super-resolution using a generative adversarial network, in: 2017 IEEE Conference on Computer Vision and Pattern Recognition (CVPR), 2017, pp. 105–114, https://doi.org/10.1109/CVPR.2017.19.

[42] K. Sirinukunwattana, J.P. Pluim, H. Chen, X. Qi, P.-A. Heng, Y.B. Guo, L.Y. Wang, B.J. Matuszewski, E. Bruni, U. Sanchez, A. Böhm, O. Ronneberger, B.B. Cheikh, D. Racoceanu, P. Kainz, M. Pfeiffer, M. Urschler, D.R. Snead, N.M. Rajpoot, Gland segmentation in colon histology images: the GlaS challenge contest, Medical Image Analysis 35 (2017) 489–502, https://doi.org/10.1016/j.media.2016.08.008.

[43] K. Sirinukunwattana, D.R.J. Snead, N.M. Rajpoot, A stochastic polygons model for glandular structures in colon histology images, IEEE Transactions on Medical Imaging 34 (11) (2015) 2366–2378, https://doi.org/10.1109/TMI.2015.2433900.

[44] V.N. Kovacheva, D. Snead, N.M. Rajpoot, A model of the spatial microenvironment of the colonic crypt, in: 2015 IEEE 12th International Symposium on Biomedical Imaging (ISBI), 2015, pp. 172–176, https://doi.org/10.1109/ISBI.2015.7163843.

[45] A. Lehmussola, P. Ruusuvuori, J. Selinummi, H. Huttunen, O. Yli-Harja, Computational framework for simulating fluorescence microscope images with cell populations, IEEE

Transactions on Medical Imaging 26 (7) (2007) 1010–1016, https://doi.org/10.1109/TMI. 2007.896925.

[46] A. Efros, T. Leung, Texture synthesis by non-parametric sampling, in: Proceedings of the Seventh IEEE International Conference on Computer Vision, vol. 2, 1999, pp. 1033–1038, https://doi.org/10.1109/ICCV.1999.790383.

[47] L.H. Sobin, I.D. Fleming, TNM classification of malignant tumors, fifth edition (1997), Cancer: Interdisciplinary International Journal of the American Cancer Society 80 (9) (1997) 1803–1804, https://doi.org/10.1002/(SICI)1097-0142(19971101)80: 9<1803::AID-CNCR16>3.0.CO;2-9.

[48] F. Aurenhammer, Voronoi diagrams—a survey of a fundamental geometric data structure, ACM Computing Surveys 23 (3) (1991) 345–405, https://doi.org/10.1145/116873. 116880.

[49] K. Perlin, An image synthesizer, in: Proceedings of the 12th Annual Conference on Computer Graphics and Interactive Techniques, SIGGRAPH'85, Association for Computing Machinery, New York, NY, USA, 1985, pp. 287–296, https://doi.org/10.1145/325334. 325247.

[50] A. Ruifrok, D. Johnston, Quantification of histochemical staining by color deconvolution, Analytical and Quantitative Cytology and Histology 23 (4) (2001) 291–299, http:// europepmc.org/abstract/MED/11531144.

[51] N. Trahearn, D. Snead, I. Cree, N. Rajpoot, Multi-class stain separation using independent component analysis, in: M.N. Gurcan, A. Madabhushi (Eds.), Medical Imaging 2015: Digital Pathology, vol. 9420, International Society for Optics and Photonics, SPIE, 2015, pp. 113–123, https://doi.org/10.3389/fbioe.2019.00053.

[52] S. Graham, H. Chen, J. Gamper, Q. Dou, P.-A. Heng, D. Snead, Y.W. Tsang, N. Rajpoot, Mild-Net: minimal information loss dilated network for gland instance segmentation in colon histology images, Medical Image Analysis 52 (2019) 199–211, https://doi.org/10. 1016/j.media.2018.12.001.

[53] R. Awan, K. Sirinukunwattana, D. Epstein, S. Jefferyes, U. Qidwai, Z. Aftab, I. Mujeeb, D. Snead, N. Rajpoot, Glandular morphometrics for objective grading of colorectal adenocarcinoma histology images, Scientific Reports 7 (1) (2017) 1–12, https:// doi.org/10.1038/s41598-017-16516-w.

[54] M. Heusel, H. Ramsauer, T. Unterthiner, B. Nessler, S. Hochreiter, GANs trained by a two time-scale update rule converge to a local Nash equilibrium, in: Proceedings of the 31st International Conference on Neural Information Processing Systems, NIPS'17, Curran Associates Inc., Red Hook, NY, USA, 2017, pp. 6629–6640.

[55] C. Szegedy, V. Vanhoucke, S. Ioffe, J. Shlens, Z. Wojna, Rethinking the inception architecture for computer vision, in: 2016 IEEE Conference on Computer Vision and Pattern Recognition (CVPR), 2016, pp. 2818–2826, https://doi.org/10.1109/CVPR.2016.308.

[56] J. Deng, W. Dong, R. Socher, L.-J. Li, K. Li, L. Fei-Fei, ImageNet: a large-scale hierarchical image database, in: 2009 IEEE Conference on Computer Vision and Pattern Recognition, 2009, pp. 248–255, https://doi.org/10.1109/CVPR.2009.5206848.

[57] K.H. Zou, S.K. Warfield, A. Bharatha, C.M. Tempany, M.R. Kaus, S.J. Haker, W.M. Wells III, F.A. Jolesz, R. Kikinis, Statistical validation of image segmentation quality based on a spatial overlap index, Academic Radiology 11 (2) (2004) 178–189, https:// doi.org/10.1016/S1076-6332(03)00671-8.

[58] K. Sirinukunwattana, S.E.A. Raza, Y. Tsang, D.R.J. Snead, I.A. Cree, N.M. Rajpoot, Locality sensitive deep learning for detection and classification of nuclei in routine colon cancer histology images, IEEE Transactions on Medical Imaging 35 (5) (2016) 1196–1206, https://doi.org/10.1109/TMI.2016.2525803.

Spatiotemporal image generation for embryomics applications

23

Dennis Eschweiler[a,c]**, Ina Laube**[a,c]**, and Johannes Stegmaier**[a,b]

[a]*Institute of Imaging and Computer Vision, RWTH Aachen University, Aachen, Germany*
[b]*Institute for Automation and Applied Informatics, Karlsruhe Institute of Technology, Karlsruhe, Germany*

23.1 Introduction

How does a single cell develop into a complex multicellular organism? This is a fundamental question in the field of developmental biology since the days of the Greek philosopher Aristotle in the 4th century BC [1]. The development of fluorescent proteins in the late 20th century gave a hope to biologists to visually understand the whole process of embryonic development under a microscope. These genetically encoded tags allow resolving not only the cell populations into individual lineages but also subcellular structures, for example, cell nuclei and plasma membranes [2]. Recent developments in high resolution 3D+t fluorescence imaging using vertebrate, invertebrate, and plant model organisms have been driven by the desire of biologists to reconstruct the embryonic development *in silico* [3,4]. To provide a quantitative readout of such potentially terabyte-scale data sets, the extensive use of automation and dedicated algorithms is inevitable. Required operations comprise image denoising, deconvolution, multiview fusion, registration, object detection, instance segmentation, and tracking [5–8]. While the 2D pendants of such algorithms can usually be tested on a plethora of manually annotated benchmark images, there are hardly data sets available that can be used to systematically validate the functionality of algorithms on 3D+t images and to (pre)train machine learning models on synthetic data similar to the target domain. To fill this gap, realistic simulations of 3D+t microscopy experiments of *in vitro* cultured tissue explants, organoids, and even developing embryos are important for algorithmic development. Notably, there are several attempts to create manually annotated data sets such as the Cell Tracking Challenge [9]. However, despite the usefulness of these approaches for an objective comparison of image analysis methods, the amount of manual labels for the most challenging 3D+t image data is still way below the amount needed, e.g., for reasonable training of deep neu-

---

[c] Authors contributed equally.

ral network approaches that have shown to be a game-changer in almost any field of computer vision. Creating synthetic data sets with sufficient realism with respect to object distribution, object appearance, object density, and movement dynamics is thus an important problem. Such data sets can be used to quantitatively compare the performance of image analysis algorithms and to train deep neural networks for the above-mentioned applications on synthetic data with the potential to generalize well to real data.

In this chapter, we start off by reviewing recent history on simulating embryogenesis and then summarize our previous attempts on generating realistic spatiotemporal image data for embryomics applications. The first approach is entirely synthetic and uses repulsive and adhesive forces acting between a set of virtual cell objects for a dynamically changing cell mass, including a simple geometric model to constrain the shape of the synthetic embryo [10,11]. Moreover, we describe a semi-synthetic data generation approach that relies on potentially flawed results of cell detection, segmentation, and tracking approaches obtained from real microscopy experiments [12,13]. An overview of the real microscopy data, the extracted cell centroids and the identified cell movement trajectories that served as a basis for the semi-synthetic approaches is provided in Fig. 23.1. To translate the database of (semi-)synthetic cell trajectories to artificial microscopy images, we review two conceptually different approaches based on video object databases obtained from classical simulations or extracted from real microscopy images [10,12,11] and an approach based on generative adversarial networks (GANs) that automatically learns the transfer function from a simulated mask image to the microscopy image domain in an unpaired setting [14].

23.1.1 Related work

Hypothesis-driven mathematical modeling plays a major role in explaining experimentally observed phenomena like cell-cell interactions, large-scale tissue rearrangements, tissue patterning, and organ formation occurring during embryogenesis [16]. In this brief review of related work, we shall focus on mathematical modeling of tissue formation processes in developmental biology and data-driven reconstruction of embryonic development that represent important steps towards a virtual embryo.

Even way before the development of computers, there were attempts to build mathematical models of embryonic development. From the application of physical and mathematical models on cell movement and the development of tissues [17] to physical wax models of embryos [18] there were many attempts to explain and visualize embryonic development. With the rapidly increasing capabilities of computational modeling and improved experimental possibilities, this field of research is still a highly relevant topic [19].

One of the first computer simulations of embryonic processes was performed by Goel et al. [20]. They implemented a self-sorting process of mixed cells with the goal to test different hypotheses on cell motility to see if simulated results are capable of explaining cell movements they observed during the development of real organisms

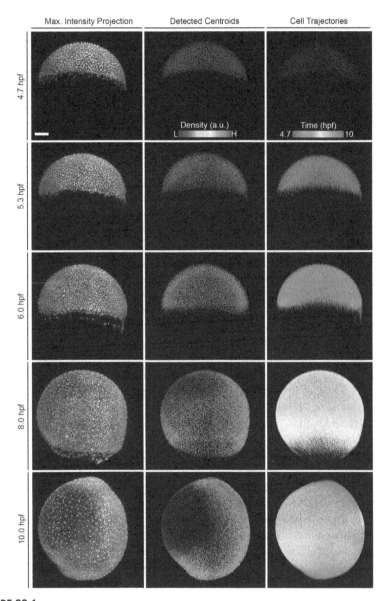

FIGURE 23.1

Example data of a developing zebrafish embryo with fluorescently labeled cell nuclei that was imaged using time-resolved 3D light-sheet microscopy [15]. The first column shows maximum intensity projections of different developmental stages in the range of 4.7–10 hpf (hours post fertilization). The second and third columns show cell centroids and cell trajectories, respectively, that were automatically extracted from the large-scale 3D+t image data and were used for the semi-synthetic data generation approaches presented in this work. Scale bar: 100 μm. Adapted from [13].

[21,22]. However, these simulations were very limited and contained only the first 14 cells of the developing embryo. In 1992, Glazier et al. adapted the Potts model, formerly known from statistical mechanics, for the behavior of cells in a cell sorting processes and simulated this now called Cellular Potts Model (CPM) on a computer [23,24]. The basic idea of this model is to represent a tissue as a lattice where each cell is characterized as a subgroup of lattice fields and each configuration of cells on the lattice has a calculable energy cost. Cells adhere to one another and volume changes of cells increase the total energy. During the simulation steps, the system is updated with the target to minimize the energy. Hogeweg et al. simulated evolutionary processes in embryo development with a virtual critter embryo based on this model [25] and CPMs were also used to model processes in embryo development like the primitive streak formation during gastrulation of chick embryos [26].

Another popular alternative to CPM are so-called vertex model approaches that represent cells via polygons (vertices connected with edges and being shared between neighboring cells) or polyhedra for 3D simulations where cell movements obey equations of motion and rearrange based on minimizing the total free energy [27]. Such vertex models can, e.g., be used to simulate dynamics of densely packed tissues like cross-sections or surfaces of epithelial sheets [28,29]. However, due to the tight attachment of the cells, the approach is unsuitable for modeling processes in which cells move freely in the extracellular space [29].

A more flexible approach is the centroid model where cells are represented by their centroid location with interaction of neighboring objects. Such models are very dynamic and due to a missing lattice or mesh structure they are well suited for simulating 3D tissues [19]. Macklin et al. propose such an agent-based cell model where no fixed lattice is required for a 2D simulation of tumor growth. Virtual agents (cells) are considered as physically interacting objects, where the object motion is determined by adhesive and repulsive forces [30]. Similar centroid model-based simulation attempts were successfully used in combination with biomechanical modeling of epithelia and the extracellular matrix to create a generic animal embryo that undergoes gastrulation [29] and for reproducing zebrafish epiboly in 3D+t including a simulation of molecular signaling [31].

With the improvements in microscopy techniques and the availability of more powerful computers, the first data-driven reconstructions have become possible towards the end of the 20th century. For instance, A. Verwey developed and analyzed several methods to align and normalize 2D microscopy frames from serial sections of mouse embryos with the purpose of reconstructing a 3D representation of the embryo [32] and similar techniques were later used to perform 3D reconstructions of mouse embryos from 2D images to build one of the first digital mouse embryo atlasses [33–35]. With the advent of 3D confocal and light-sheet microscopy [36] and the targeted labeling of structures of interest via fluorescent proteins [2], the digital reconstruction of whole embryos on a single-cell level became feasible. Single 3D frames of fixed embryos were analyzed, e.g., to compare gene expression patterns of different embryos in a common reference frame [37]. Moreover, multiple studies used 3D+t confocal or light-sheet microscopy images to detect, segment and track structures like fluorescently labeled nuclei or cell membranes in entire embryos [38,4,39,7,40,41]. Digital embryos were reconstructed for many common model organisms like *C. elegans* [38], *Drosophila* [42,43], zebrafish [4], and mouse embryos [44], as well as for plants like *A. thaliana* [45,46]. As imaging speed and protocols are steadily improved, performing multiple repeats of the same experiment became possible. After precise spatiotemporal alignment of extracted cell centroids, movement trajectories or gene expression patterns, multisample averaging can be used to create atlases, for instance, to obtain a digital average model of zebrafish embryogenesis [15] or to create a spatiotemporal digital atlas of early mouse development [44]. Aside from hypothesis-driven modeling approaches, extracting quantitative data from 3D+t microscopy experiments allows for data-driven modeling approaches. For instance, Villoutreix et al. created a data-driven multi-level digital model of a sea urchin embryo using extracted statistical properties like cell counts, cell cycle lengths, cell volumes, and surface areas to model artificial cell lineages of early developmental stages [47]. Similarly, Wang et al. used a data-driven approach to model embryogenesis of *C. elegans* based on 4D confocal microscopy images [48].

Even though remarkable results were already achieved in the past few years, comprehensive modeling of the detailed biomechanical processes that give rise to a live multicellular organism is not possible yet and automatic analyses of 3D+t microscopy images still require substantial human intervention to obtain trustworthy biological results. The dynamics simulation of the fully-synthetic simulation approaches presented in the remainder of this chapter are primarily a 3D extension of the agent-based simulation approach by Macklin et al. [30] with an additional synthetic image generation. Moreover, our semi-synthetic simulation approach presented in Section 23.2 follows a data-driven modeling approach and we used automatically identified detection, segmentation, and tracking data obtained from 3D+t light-sheet microscopy images from [15] to create synthetic cell movement trajectories of early zebrafish development [12,13]. We note that the primary focus in the present chapter is the generation of realistic synthetic image data to benchmark and train large-scale image analysis algorithms and not a physically accurate model of morphogenesis.

23.2 Spatiotemporal simulation of virtual agents with realistic movement behavior

In this section, we present our approaches for synthetic and semi-synthetic generation of realistic data sets that mimic the development of real embryos and also allow to generate realistic artificial image data of cell nuclei and cell membranes. Over the coarse of the last years, we successively improved the complexity and realism of the simulations and the original papers describing the developments are [12,10,11,13,14]. For our semi-synthetic approach, we make use of cell detections and tracking information obtained from real microscopy images [49,15,50,41] as depicted in Fig. 23.1 and thus do not only rely on an underlying physical model to simulate object behavior but rather use original cell distributions and cell movements. An overview of the proposed pipeline is depicted in Fig. 23.2.

23.2.1 Generation of the spatiotemporal database

23.2.1.1 Initialization

The first step of our pipeline is the creation of an initial 3D point cloud that represents the virtual cells of the embryo. Depending on the temporal direction of the simulation, one can either initialize the simulation at an early time point and perform the simulation in the forward direction or start with the final number of desired objects that will then be simulated in a time-reversed manner.

There are multiple options to accomplish the initial cell locations depending on the desired complexity and realism. In the simplest and fully-synthetic case a geometric model of the embryo can be assumed. For instance, early zebrafish development can be modeled as a cell mass positioned at one side of a sphere (the so called animal pole) and as cells divide and cell mass increases, the cells successively cover the sphere towards the other pole of the sphere, namely the vegetal pole [15]. Similarly, early *Drosophila* development could be imitated by evenly distributing cells on an ellipsoid and plant parts like the shoot apical meristem of *A. thaliana* could be modeled by densely filled dome-shaped structures.

In order to obtain more realistic distribution of the virtual cells, positions can also be sampled from cell positions of real embryos. From previous experiments [15], we had extracted cell positions with the TWANG segmentation algorithm [49] and followed the movement of individual cells over the course of the experiment using nearest neighbor linking of objects between adjoining frames. As these data sets are directly the output of an automatic processing pipeline without further manual corrections, it is not advisable to directly use these data sets for quantitative comparison of image analysis algorithms or for training of deep learning algorithms due to an inevitable bias towards the used method and the risk of letting the models learn to reproduce the errors. However, based on the assumption that the majority of the extracted information is correct, we place a selected number of virtual agents (the synthetic cells) at locations that follow the object distribution in the real embryo. To avoid sampling objects that actually correspond to a false positive detection in the background, it is advisable to perform a noise suppression in the selected frame used for sampling the initial positions, e.g., using a density-based outlier suppression.

The initialization of the simulation requires either a fixed number of cells N_k^{sim} to start with or a fraction $N_k^{\text{sim}} = p \cdot N_k^{\text{embryo}}$, $p \in [0, 1]$ of the N_k^{embryo} real cells at time point k. Depending on the temporal direction that is used for the synthetic data generation, k will be either the first or the last frame of the simulation, i.e., the minimum or the maximum number of cells, respectively. Each initially drawn object obtains a unique ID i, an object radius $r_i \in [r_{\text{min}}, r_{\text{max}}]$, a randomized cell cycle length $l_i \in [l_{\text{min}}, l_{\text{max}}]$, a random initialization of the current cell cycle stage the object is in $s_i \in [1, l_i]$ and a randomly drawn object video ID $o_i \in [1, N_{\text{ov}}]$ out of N_{ov} single cell video snippets [12]. The parameters should ideally reflect the properties

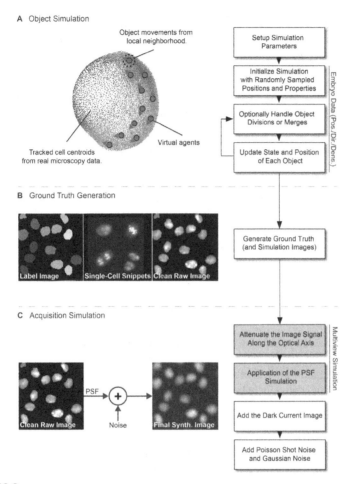

FIGURE 23.2

Overview of the proposed simulation framework. (A) A set of tracked cell centroids extracted from real microscopy images forms the basis for the object simulation. Randomly sampled virtual agents are moved over time according to the movement of nearby objects in the real embryo. Cell division/merge events (depending on the temporal direction of the simulation) are introduced for realistic object distribution and density. The object simulation results in a database of simulated object positions for each frame. (B) Simulated object locations from (A) are used to generate ground-truth images with unique integer labels per cell. In the case of a classical simulation approach a clean raw image with simulated cells is assembled from single-cell video snippets [51]. (C) To mimic the image formation process of a microscope, clean raw images from (B) undergo an acquisition simulation comprising signal attenuation, convolution with a point spread function (PSF), addition of a dark current image, as well as Poisson shot noise and additive Gaussian noise. As an alternative to a classical acquisition simulation, generative adversarial networks can be used for an unpaired image to image translation to map a ground truth mask image to an artificial microscopy image as detailed in Section 23.2.2.3. Adapted from [12].

of real biological specimens and can be derived from literature or by analyzing a few representative frames as done in [47]. As further detailed in the next sections, these additional parameters are required for the subsequent dynamic simulation with radius-dependent forces between the objects, to introduce cell division events and to generate artificial image data.

23.2.1.2 Simulating a variably changing cell mass

Over the course of development an embryo develops from the fertilized egg to a multicellular organism with thousands of cells. To incorporate this growth of cell mass to the simulation we inevitably have to incorporate cell division events that split existing objects in defined time intervals. As an initial option, the current cell cycle stage s_i and the respective cell cycle lengths l_i can be used to introduce a split event as soon as an object exceeds this maximum duration as done in [11]. To prevent generating too many cells at once, the number of objects present at a point in time can either be constrained to a maximum number of cells in the case of a completely synthetic simulation or estimated from real data by comparing the number of objects at a corresponding time point k of the simulation and the real embryo,

$$N_k^{\text{div}} = \max\left(0, \, p \cdot N_k^{\text{embryo}} - N_k^{\text{sim}}\right). \tag{23.1}$$

To match the relative amount of objects present in the real embryo, N_k^{div} division events have to be introduced. In the case of a time-reversed data synthesis, objects need to be merged rather than split, i.e., the number of merges N_k^{merge} required at a time point k can analogously be computed by the following expression:

$$N_k^{\text{merge}} = \max\left(0, \, N_k^{\text{sim}} - p \cdot N_k^{\text{embryo}}\right). \tag{23.2}$$

However, due to the random nature of these split or merge events, the resulting tissue that is formed does not necessarily develop to a realistic shape observed in real experiments. Thus, a second option is to use the internal cell cycle stage simply as an auxiliary measure that a cell is ready to divide. Instead of directly splitting the cells upon reaching the maximum stage, however, a local density difference between the real embryo and the simulation is used to identify locations where changes of the cell counts are required to obtain density accumulations of cell mass similar to those observed in a real embryo. The following local density measure ρ_{ik}^{diff} for object i at time point k can be used to identify which of the cells exhibit the strongest relative density difference compared to the real embryo:

$$\rho_{ik}^{\text{diff}} = \frac{\rho_{ik}^{\text{sim}}}{N_k^{\text{sim}}} - \frac{\rho_{ik}^{\text{embryo}}}{N_k^{\text{embryo}}}. \tag{23.3}$$

The cell density values ρ_{ik}^{sim} and $\rho_{ik}^{\text{embryo}}$ are estimated as the number of cells in the neighborhood of cell i within a fixed radius of r_ρ (e.g., we used an empirically determined radius of $r_\rho = 40$ μm and $l_{\min} = 28$ in [12]). Both quantities are scaled by the respective total number of cells present in frame k, as the simulation can also be performed using only a fraction of the real cells. Negative values of this measure indicate that the density of the simulation in a particular area is below the density of the real embryo and, vice versa, positive numbers indicate that the local density is higher in the simulated embryo. Depending on the temporal direction of the simulation, one can either introduce cell divisions in areas with maximally negative density differences during forward synthesis or introduce merges in a time-reversed simulation at locations with the maximally positive density differences. The selected cell is then either split into two daughter cells with new IDs (forward synthesis) or merged with its spatially nearest neighbor (time-reversed simulation). This procedure ensures a balanced adjustment of the cell numbers in the synthetic data set and the incorporation of the minimum cell cycle duration l_{min} prevents picking the same cell for division or merges too frequently.

23.2.1.3 Object movement and physical interaction between objects

In addition to the realistic distribution of cells in the virtual arena, a temporal simulation of the object movements is important as well. In the purely synthetic case as described in [10,11], we use the adhesive and repulsive forces proposed in [30] to mimic a densely connected tissue with objects that are attached to one another but exert a push force if neighboring objects intersect. For two interacting objects i, j with a centroid difference vector $\mathbf{d} = \mathbf{x}_j - \mathbf{x}_i$, the adhesive force is defined as

$$\Delta\mathbf{x}^{adh}(\mathbf{d}, R_M) = \begin{cases} \left(1 - \frac{\|\mathbf{d}\|}{R_M}\right)^2 \cdot \frac{\mathbf{d}}{\|\mathbf{d}\|}, & 0 \leq \|\mathbf{d}\| < R_M, \\ \mathbf{0}, & \text{else}. \end{cases} \tag{23.4}$$

Similarly, the repulsive force to push apart nearby objects is defined as

$$\Delta\mathbf{x}^{rep}(\mathbf{d}, R_N, R_M) = \begin{cases} -\left(\left(\left(1 - \frac{R_N}{R_M}\right)^2 - 1\right) \cdot \frac{\|\mathbf{d}\|}{R_N} + 1\right) \cdot \frac{\mathbf{d}}{\|\mathbf{d}\|}, & 0 \leq \|\mathbf{d}\| < R_N, \\ -\left(1 - \frac{\|\mathbf{d}\|}{R_M}\right)^2 \cdot \frac{\mathbf{d}}{\|\mathbf{d}\|}, & R_N < \|\mathbf{d}\| < R_M, \\ \mathbf{0}, & \text{else}. \end{cases} \tag{23.5}$$

The parameters R_N and R_M are approximations of the radii of the cell nuclei and the plasma membranes, respectively, and can be estimated from real data (e.g., based on statistics obtained from a 3D segmentation or using average centroid distances of neighboring objects). When an object divides a force is exerted such that the surrounding tissue expands to make room for the new cell. As the push force can yield unnatural constellations of cells in the completely synthetic scenario, an additional force was introduced to constrain the objects to a band between an inner and an outer sphere, respectively, that mimic the yolk cell and the outer surface of a zebrafish embryo [11],

$$\Delta\mathbf{x}^{\mathrm{bdr}}(\mathbf{x}, \mathbf{c}, r_i, r_o, a) = \begin{cases} \frac{\mathbf{x}-\mathbf{c}}{\|\mathbf{x}-\mathbf{c}\|} \cdot \left(1 - \frac{1}{e^{-a(\|\mathbf{x}-\mathbf{c}\|-r_i)}}\right), & \|\mathbf{x}-\mathbf{c}\| < r_i, \\ -\frac{\mathbf{x}-\mathbf{c}}{\|\mathbf{x}-\mathbf{c}\|} \cdot \left(1 - \frac{1}{e^{-a(\|\mathbf{x}-\mathbf{c}\|-r_o)}}\right), & \|\mathbf{x}-\mathbf{c}\| > r_o, \\ 0, & \text{else.} \end{cases} \quad (23.6)$$

In Eq. (23.6), the centroid of the current object is denoted as $\mathbf{x}$, $\mathbf{c}$ is the center of the spherical region of interest with the radii r_i and r_o of the inner and outer shell, respectively, and the parameter a that controls the steepness of the transition regions of the boundary potential. Due to the boundary constraint, cells progressively cover the sphere similar to epiboly movements that happen during zebrafish gastrulation. If real cell locations are available, a nearest neighbor attraction force can be added to slightly pull each of the simulated objects toward its spatially nearest neighbor $\mathcal{N}_{\mathrm{knn}}^1(\mathbf{x})$ in the real embryo,

$$\Delta\mathbf{x}^{\mathrm{nna}}(\mathbf{x}) = \mathcal{N}_{\mathrm{knn}}^1(\mathbf{x}) - \mathbf{x}. \quad (23.7)$$

Finally, the object movement of real cells obtained from the cell tracking step can be used to move the synthetic objects in a realistic manner rather than solely relying on passive tissue movements. Depending on the desired level of smoothness, a set of neighbors K surrounding a current position $\mathbf{x}$ can be used to obtain an average displacement vector of cells located at this position in the real embryo,

$$\Delta\mathbf{x}^{\mathrm{dir}}(\mathbf{x}) = \frac{1}{K} \sum_{j \in \mathcal{N}_{\mathrm{knn}}^K(\mathbf{x})} \mathbf{d}_j, \quad (23.8)$$

with $\mathbf{d}_j$ being the movement direction of neighboring cell j and the neighborhood operator $\mathcal{N}_{\mathrm{knn}}^K(\mathbf{x})$ that yields the set of indices of the K closest objects of the real embryo. In the special case of $K = 1$, the displacement vector of the closest real cell is used to move the synthetic cell. To obtain smoother trajectories, e.g., in cases of poor tracking quality one can also average the movement of the simulated objects among multiple neighbors. The large-scale movements of the tissue are still faithfully modeled by this regularization technique but single-cell movement behavior might vanish due to the averaging. In our previous work, we used $K = 10$ in the forward simulation [12] and $K = 1$ in the time-reversed scenario [13]. The total displacement of a cell in each frame can thus be expressed as the weighted sum of the individual forces,

$$
\begin{aligned}
\Delta \mathbf{x}_i^{\text{tot}} = w_{\text{adh}} \cdot & \sum_{j \in \{1,\dots,N_k^{\text{sim}}\}} \Delta \mathbf{x}^{\text{adh}}(\|\mathbf{x}_i - \mathbf{x}_j\|) \\
+ w_{\text{rep}} \cdot & \sum_{j \in \{1,\dots,N_k^{\text{sim}}\}} \Delta \mathbf{x}^{\text{rep}}(\|\mathbf{x}_i - \mathbf{x}_j\|) \\
+ w_{\text{bdr}} \cdot & \Delta \mathbf{x}^{\text{bdr}}(\mathbf{x}_i) \\
+ \min \left(w_{\text{nna}}, \frac{\|\Delta \mathbf{x}^{\text{dir}}(\mathbf{x}_i)\|}{\|\Delta \mathbf{x}^{\text{nna}}(\mathbf{x}_i)\|} \right) & \cdot \Delta \mathbf{x}^{\text{nna}}(\mathbf{x}_i) \\
+ w_{\text{dir}} \cdot & \Delta \mathbf{x}^{\text{dir}}(\mathbf{x}_i),
\end{aligned}
\tag{23.9}
$$

with weights w_{adh}, w_{rep}, w_{bdr}, w_{nna}, w_{dir} to control the contribution of the respective terms. The nearest neighbor attraction is additionally clamped by the magnitude of displacement vector $\Delta \mathbf{x}^{\text{dir}}(\mathbf{x}_i)$ to avoid large jumps in cases where a detection of the real embryo temporarily disappears [12]. Different weight settings for the three different simulation scenarios are listed in Table 23.1. Notably, the time-reversed approach yields the most realistic, yet simplest scenario for the synthesis of artificial cell locations and only involves the inverted movement directions of the real cells.

Table 23.1 Weight parameter settings for different simulation scenarios.

Simulation Scenario	w_{adh}	w_{rep}	w_{bdr}	w_{nna}	w_{dir}
Fully-Synthetic (Forward)	0.52	1.0	3.0	0.0	0.0
Semi-Synthetic (Forward)	0.0	1.0	0.0	0.1	1.0
Semi-Synthetic (Backward)	0.0	0.0	0.0	0.0	-1.0

23.2.1.4 Conclusions

While several approaches and components were tested to increase the realism of the generated data sets, the most promising approach for realistic generation of synthetic data is actually the simplest one that is initialized at the last time point, performs object simulation in a time-reversed manner and mainly relies on the underlying real data without additional constraints [13]. Starting at the latest time point already determines the maximum number of objects in the simulation and objects already reside at sufficiently distant locations, making both the adhesive and the repulsive forces dispensable. As the synthetic cells only go with the flow of the real cells backwards in time without repulsion, the nearest neighbor attraction force can also be omitted. Finally, it is possible to use a single nearest neighbor for the direction estimate as the synthetic cell only moves in this direction but is not attracted towards the actual real cell, i.e., cells can also float between the locations of two real cells and thus enlarge the number of possible synthetic cell locations. Introducing cell division or merge events (depending on the temporal direction of the simulation) based on the relative density difference compared to the real data set allows to increase or decrease the cell mass at the physiologically correct locations, respectively. Nevertheless, the fully-synthetic approach can still be useful in scenarios where no real data is available or if the automatic results are too erroneous. In some cases, a realistic movement behavior of the objects might actually not be required, e.g., to benchmark or train segmentation algorithms where single independent frames would suffice. In the next section, classical methods and an approach based on generative adversarial networks are used to synthesize artificial image data based on the simulated 3D+t object locations.

23.2.2 Generation of artificial image data

The procedures presented in the previous section yield 3D+t point clouds of moving objects including the entire lineages of all cells and the next step is to convert these spatiotemporal object databases to realistically looking synthetic microscopy images. This involves the generation of label images and synthetic microscopy images including an acquisition simulation that mimics the path through the optical system. For the latter, we present two conceptually different approaches for the creation of artificial image data from the simulated mask images. The first approach uses classical image processing techniques to imitate the image formation process of a microscope. The second approach uses unpaired image to image translation with an adapted GAN architecture to train an image generator that can translate binary masks of simulated frames to realistic images.

23.2.2.1 Mask image generation

The image generation process for each of the frames is initialized with two empty images filled with zeros. One of the images serves as the ground truth, namely a label image where pixels of the same object obtain a unique integer ID. The second image represents the synthetic raw image that is filled with synthetic objects and then undergoes an acquisition simulation. Artificial binary objects are sequentially placed at locations determined by the spatiotemporal database (Section 23.2.1) and multiplied with the unique object ID. We experimented with multiple ways to model the binary objects, e.g., using statistical shape models extracted from real segmentations [52], using a randomly parameterized spherical harmonics representation [53], or using single-cell video snippets either extracted from real microscopy images or from artificially generated cells [51]. The placed objects can be scaled according to the randomly drawn radii r_i of each object and, if information about the respective cell cycle stages is available for the video snippets, the randomly drawn cell cycle stage s_i of each object can be used to select the appropriate frame from the single-cell video snippets. In cases where real images and the associated masks are available, the raw pixel intensities are directly transferred to the synthetic raw image for all non-zero pixels of the mask. In [12,11], we used synthetic single-cell snippets extracted from a small set of synthetic 3D cell nuclei that included both segmentation masks as well as synthetic raw images for multiple cell cycles [51] (Fig. 23.5D).

To create synthetic cell plasma membranes, we rely on the frequently used Voronoi tessellation approach and additionally specify the outer surface of the embryo, e.g., using simple spherical masks or the outer surfaces obtained from available previous segmentations [14]. Based on a 3D point cloud of object centroids, the space is partitioned such that each pixel is assigned the spatially closest cell centroid. For the ground truth, we save both the instance segmentation with a unique integer label per cell and a boundary map where boundary pixels (i.e., the transitions between two cell shapes) are encoded by the maximum intensity value surrounded by the background value (Fig. 23.3A). If a cell shape segmentation is already available, it can directly serve as the segmentation ground truth and can be transformed to a realistic synthetic image with different randomized deterioration effects. Even if the used segmentation contains errors like over- or under-segmentation of cells, the transformation of the binary mask faithfully preserves the topology of the cells and thus generates a realistic microscopy image that matches the flawed segmentation.

23.2.2.2 Classical modeling of the acquisition process

Once the simulated images are assembled they still look unrealistic due to the missing acquisition simulation. As depicted in Fig. 23.2C, the acquisition simulation comprises several steps that represent the path of the fluorescent signal through the detection objective onto the image sensor. A simple approximation of the image formation process to obtain the final synthetic image $\mathbf{I}^{\text{final}}$ can be summarized with the following formula:

$$\mathbf{I}^{\text{final}} = P_\lambda \left(\mathbf{I}^{\text{raw}} * \mathbf{I}^{\text{psf}} + \mathbf{I}^{\text{dark}} \right) + \mathcal{N}(0, \sigma_{\text{agn}}). \tag{23.10}$$

In Eq. (23.10), $\mathbf{I}^{\text{raw}}$ is the undistorted synthetic input image, $\mathbf{I}^{\text{psf}}$ is a point spread function (PSF) and $\mathbf{I}^{\text{dark}}$ is a dark current image; P_λ adds Poisson shot-noise to the image, and $\mathcal{N}(0, \sigma_{\text{agn}})$ is an additive Gaussian noise component with zero mean and standard deviation σ_{agn}. Moreover, it is possible to include additional corruptions to mimic a multiview imaging setup. Multiview imaging allows imaging even large specimens either by using multiple illumination and detection pathways or by rotating the specimen and by imaging different orientations [42]. The well-resolved parts of the complementary views are then assembled to a final image with high quality. To mimic such an acquisition scenario with the presented approach, it is possible to add attenuation and additional blur along the optical axis, to mimic limited penetration depth, i.e., increased light scattering and lower signal intensities in deeper tissue regions and to use view-dependent PSFs. An empirically determined intensity offset was added to all pixels to imitate the dark current signal of the detector and we used a set of measured PSFs of a multiview light-sheet microscope [5]. Moreover, noise was added using Poisson noise to simulate the discrete nature of photon capture events of the detector and Gaussian noise to simulate temperature-dependent noise of the sensor. The acquisition simulation was implemented in XPIWIT and can be parameterized with different levels of noise, image-based PSFs and optionally intensity gradients in a selected image direction (e.g., decreasing the image intensity along the axial direction) [54].

As an alternative to using simulated object snippets, it would also be possible to extract short single-cell videos of a cell from real microscopy images. While the generated raw image would be assembled from real microscopy snippets, a ground truth would have to be generated manually for each of the 3D frames. Moreover, as the objects were already imaged through a microscope, they exhibit the typical disruptions like convolution with the real PSF and the real noise of the microscope used for acquisition. Thus, a subsequent acquisition simulation as described before would cause additional disruptions that could appear unrealistic. Changing the disruptions to imitate a different type of microscope, however, would be impossible. A solution to tackle this problem would be to apply denoising, deconvolution, and isotropic reconstruction operations to the video snippet database of extracted from real microscopy images beforehand, to preserve the possibility to add artificial and varying acquisition simulations. A conceptually different approach is the use of 3D binary segmentation masks and to learn a domain transfer to a realistic microscopy image using generative adversarial networks as detailed in the next section.

23.2.2.3 GAN-based data synthesis

With recent technological advances, deep learning-based approaches started to become capable of solving more and more complex problems. Since these approaches are by design good at replicating distributions, they are also well qualified for finding the parameter distributions of the image formation and degradation process of a microscope. As presented in the previous section, classical approaches approximate the image formation process by manually selecting a set of degradations and by determining parameters for each degradation step separately. In contrast, generative adversarial networks [55] offer the advantage of finding these parameter distributions automatically in an unsupervised manner and are capable of representing the whole image formation process of a real microscope in a single model as demonstrated in [14,56]. GANs are not only applicable in microscopy image synthesis, but they also demonstrate the ability to generate data from various medical imaging domains [57–59]. In brief, generative adversarial networks comprise a generator network that tries to generate realistic image data from a given input (e.g., a noise vector or a binary mask image) and a discriminator network that tries to identify generated images among a set of real and fake images. By optimizing the networks in an alternating fashion using competing training objectives, the generator successively produces more realistic images and the discriminator gets better at identifying those fake images. Upon convergence, the discriminator is not able to distinguish fake images from real ones and the generator is thus able to generate images that match the target distribution (e.g., real microscopy images). See Chapter 7 for a more detailed introduction to GANs.

Since large training data sets containing raw images with their associated segmentation masks are rarely available for 3D microscopy applications, an unsupervised approach like generative adversarial networks is beneficial, as only a set of unpaired binary masks and raw images of the target microscopy domain are required for training. The GAN should be able to synthesize realistic image distortions while maintaining the morphology of cells present in the binary mask and a schematic of the whole GAN-based synthesis pipeline is shown in Fig. 23.3.

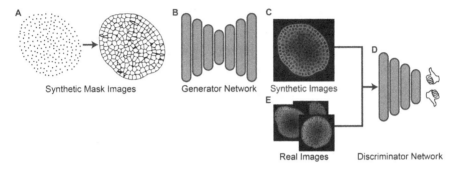

FIGURE 23.3

Schematic of the GAN-based synthesis pipeline. Synthetic mask images of cell shapes derived from point cloud data (A) are transformed to synthetic microscopy images using a trained generator network (B, C). The discriminator network assesses the generated image data in comparison to real microscopy images (D, E). Raw images extracted from the public data set [46].

The GAN-based synthesis approach requires a set of synthetic cell mask images (Fig. 23.3A, e.g., obtained by the simulation strategies described in Section 23.2.2.1) that are provided to the generator network (Fig. 23.3B) in order to create realistic fake microscopy images (Fig. 23.3C). Additionally, a set of real microscopy images are required to train the discriminator network (Fig. 23.3D) to be able to distinguish generated from real images (Fig. 23.3E). Using an encoder-decoder-like U-Net architecture [60,61] as the generator network is perfectly suited for such an image-to-image translation task, as it preserves low-level information of the masks and combines them with more abstract feature representations using skip-connections. The discriminator network for assessment of the generated images was realized using the common PatchGAN architecture [62]. In order to properly train GANs and allow them to accurately learn distributions presented in the image data, a large amount of real microscopy images are required. Since these images are acquired during the biological experiments anyway, the collection of the image data set usually comes at no additional cost. As presented in [14], realistic cell shapes in the masks are a crucial factor to achieve realistic microscopy images including accurate correspondences between structures in the masks and the synthetic images, i.e., the GAN needs to observe similar cell morphology in both mask and real microscopy images in order to find suitable synthesis parameters. If those correspondences between images and masks are not maintained, the synthetic image-mask pairs would be useless for subsequent training of supervised segmentation approaches. Applications of the GAN-based image generation are presented in the next section.

23.3 Example applications

The classical and the GAN-based synthesis approaches described in the previous sections were successfully used to generate time-resolved 3D image data of early zebrafish development [12,13] and to simulate a set of 3D confocal microscopy stacks of the shoot apical meristem of the plant model organism *A. thaliana* [14].

23.3.1 Semi-synthetic cell trajectory synthesis for zebrafish embryogenesis

Based on automatic cell tracking data that were extracted from 3D+t light-sheet microscopy images of zebrafish embryos with ubiquitously labeled fluorescent nuclei [15], we created several semi-synthetic data sets using the previously described methods [12,13]. Fig. 23.4 shows real microscopy images, automatically extracted cell detections and the identified movement trajectories in comparison to the data obtained with a semi-synthetic data generation approach. The synthetic data set comprises 75% of the objects observed in the real data set and the simulation was performed in a time-reversed manner. Both the density distributions of cell centroids and the obtained movement trajectories nicely resemble the shape of the real data at different developmental time points.

Similar results were obtained in a forward simulation setting that was based on the same real data set [12]. Exemplary result images are depicted in Fig. 23.5. The generated data comprises a variety of different data representations. On the one hand, the ground truth consists of 3D+t object locations, cell trajectories including the complete lineages and label images that contain an instance segmentation of each frame (Fig. 23.5A–C). Moreover, a set of undistorted synthetic raw images assembled from single-cell snippets is available that can be fed through an acquisition simulation (Fig. 23.5D–F). As the uncorrupted images are preserved, different complexity levels of the synthetic microscopy images can be generated, e.g., involving multiview acquisition simulation, different noise levels, or depth-dependent blur and light attenuation. Thus, the synthetic data can be adjusted to mimic the particular difficulties observed in the real application and can be flexibly used for multiple benchmark and training scenarios.

23.3.2 GAN-based simulation of the imaging system

For demonstration of the GAN-based image synthesis, we chose a publicly available data set, comprising confocal microscopy images of fluorescently labeled cell membranes of the shoot apical meristem in *A. thaliana* [46]. Parameters for organism size and cell spacing were obtained from the real data and they were used for the cell simulation concepts presented in Section 23.2.1. A collection of simulated mask images and a collection of real microscopy image slices were used for training of the synthesis pipeline presented in Section 23.2.2.3. Results are shown in Fig. 23.6, qualitatively comparing the simulated mask images and synthetic microscopy images to real data. The results clearly indicate that the topology of the cells is preserved after the domain

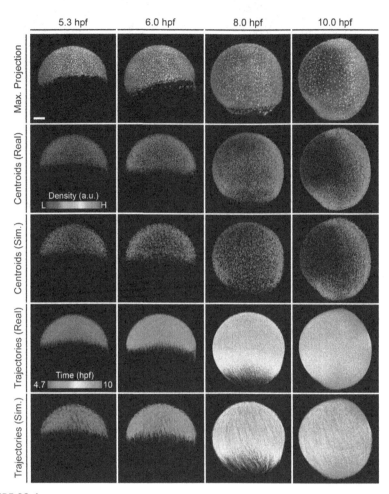

FIGURE 23.4

Comparison of real microscopy images, detected centroids and the derived simulations. The first row shows maximum intensity projections of different time points in the range of 5.3–10.0 hpf of a zebrafish embryo with fluorescently labeled cell nuclei that was imaged with light-sheet microscopy. Rows two and three show centroids that were automatically detected from the image data of a real embryo and the simulated centroids, respectively (color-code represents cell density). The last two rows show trajectories of the real and simulated data sets (color-code represents time in hpf). The simulations were done in a time-reversed fashion using 75% of the nuclei for the simulation. Scale bar: 100 μm. Adapted from [13].

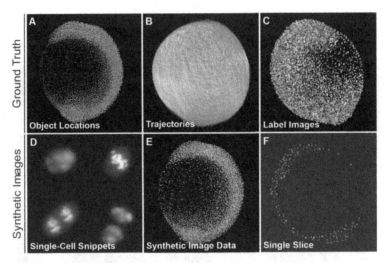

FIGURE 23.5

The synthetic ground truth generated with the approach described in [12] comprises 3D point clouds of object locations (A), movement trajectories and lineages of each contained object (B) and label images with a unique integer code for each instance (C). The synthetic microscopy images are made up of single-cell snippets that were extracted from [51] (D) and assembled to synthetic 3D+t image data (E) including an acquisition simulation with varying quality levels (F). Adapted from [12].

translation from a mask image to a synthetic microscopy image. Moreover, the signal appearance and global intensity patterns like the signal attenuation towards the center are nicely created by the generator network. The generated images can thus readily be used to benchmark image segmentation algorithms or to train supervised segmentation approaches. As demonstrated in [14], training supervised networks solely with synthetic data performs similarly well as a training with real ground-truth data.

23.4 Future directions and research challenges

Even though state-of-the-art 3D+t imaging techniques provide astonishing insights into development, there are still limitations with respect to the achievable optical and temporal resolution, penetration depth, signal intensity, homogeneity of fluorescent reporters, and the like that complicate automatic analyses. Continuously improving imaging techniques for maximum image quality thus remains an important ongoing research challenge. The current simulation attempt still requires to perform real microscopy experiments in the first place, i.e., there is no actual model of development obtained after the approach. Although cell interactions are derived from a real data set, we note that the presented approaches do not represent a physically correct sim-

Mask Images   Microscopy Images

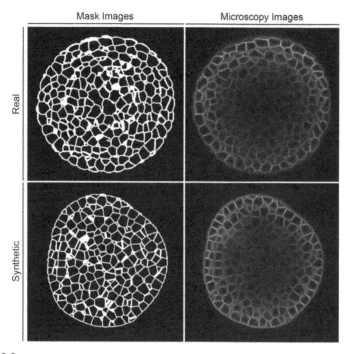

Real

Synthetic

FIGURE 23.6

Qualitative comparison of a real mask and a real image slice (upper row, data taken from [46]) and a simulated mask with the corresponding synthesized image slice (bottom row).

ulation and only qualitatively mimic the development of real embryos with respect to cell movements, cell density, and the overall distribution of cells. Biological conclusions made from the synthetic data set should thus be treated with caution. In a future work, it would be interesting to couple physically correct simulation models with data measured from real microscopy images, e.g., to initialize physical simulations with parameters measured on real specimens. This could eventually allow to test and confirm biological hypotheses *in silico*, before actually moving to *in vivo* experiments in the lab. An attempt towards this direction was recently presented, e.g., for modeling Wnt-mediated tissue patterning in zebrafish [63].

In our semi-synthetic simulation approach, the positions are still sampled from real locations of a single individual. A more general approach would be, e.g., to use ensemble average models like the ones proposed by Kobitski et al. [15], to sample locations from a mean embryo. However, due to the natural variability and an imperfect spatiotemporal alignment of the embryos, this would currently still lead to unrealistic simulations. In addition to the simple classical acquisition simulation presented in this work, there are also recent attempts to realistically model the image formation process of light-sheet microscopes [64], that could further enhance the realism of the acquisition simulation. Despite their promising ability to create realistic microscopy image data, the applications of GANs to synthesize realistic time-resolved image data remains an open problem. While the approaches work well for 2D images as demonstrated in this work, implementations for 3D images still remain a challenge due to the large memory consumption and the missing spatial context when performing tile-based processing. In order to synthesize time series with our current pipeline, each frame would have to be processed individually, leading to potential intensity or texture mismatches between consecutive frames. Recently, conditional GANs became popular and would potentially allow to condition the GAN-based frame generation on the previous generated frame, such that smooth transitions between successive frames could be obtained. Finally, the synthesis approach is currently dedicated to a single microscopy domain and would have to be retrained for all variations of the experimental conditions. Methods like BicycleGAN or StarGAN-v2 [65,66] could be adapted for microscopy image synthesis, to mimic different acquisition scenarios with a single GAN.

23.5 Summary

In this chapter, we review approaches to simulate embryonic development and present our fully- and semi-synthetic simulation approaches for realistic microscopy image generation. In the fully-synthetic simulation scenario, we place virtual cells on a prototype shape, simulate cell division events for a successively increasing cell mass and use adhesive and repulsive object interactions to perform a dynamic simulation. To obtain more realistic cell distributions and object movements, our semi-synthetic approach samples artificial object locations from detections obtained on real microscopy images and then uses interpolated single cell movements of real tracked cells to alter the positions of the virtual agents. Finally, we show how the synthetic object locations can be transformed to realistically looking microscopy image data using both classical and GAN-based image synthesis methods. Comparing the synthetic 3D+t data generation of light-sheet microscopy images of zebrafish embryos as well as synthetic confocal microscopy images of A. thaliana to real microscopy images qualitatively demonstrates the capabilities of the presented approaches. The realistic microscopy images combined with a variety of different ground truth representations offer many possibilities for quantitative algorithm benchmarks and for training supervised deep learning models with realistic synthetic data.

Acknowledgments

We thank the German Research Foundation DFG for funding (IL, Grant No STE2802/1-1; DE, Grant No STE2802/2-1) and the colleagues J. C. Otte, M. Takamiya, A. Kobitski, G. U. Nienhaus, U. Strähle, and R. Mikut at Karlsruhe Institute of Technology for providing microscopy data, for collaborating on previous analyses that are the basis of the present work and for helpful comments on the manuscript (MT, US).

References

[1] L. Wolpert, C. Tickle, A.M. Arias, Principles of Development, Oxford University Press, USA, 2015.

[2] R.Y. Tsien, The green fluorescent protein, Annual Review of Biochemistry 67 (1) (1998) 509–544.

[3] J. Huisken, D. Stainier, Selective plane illumination microscopy techniques in developmental biology, Development 136 (12) (2009) 1963–1975.

[4] P.J. Keller, A.D. Schmidt, J. Wittbrodt, E.H.K. Stelzer, Reconstruction of zebrafish early embryonic development by scanned light sheet microscopy, Science 322 (5904) (2008) 1065–1069.

[5] S. Preibisch, F. Amat, E. Stamataki, M. Sarov, R.H. Singer, E. Myers, P. Tomancak, Efficient Bayesian-based multiview deconvolution, Nature Methods 11 (6) (2014) 645–648.

[6] G. Balakrishnan, A. Zhao, M.R. Sabuncu, J. Guttag, A.V. Dalca, VoxelMorph: a learning framework for deformable medical image registration, IEEE Transactions on Medical Imaging 38 (8) (2019) 1788–1800.

[7] F. Amat, W. Lemon, D.P. Mossing, K. McDole, Y. Wan, K. Branson, E.W. Myers, P.J. Keller Fast, Accurate reconstruction of cell lineages from large-scale fluorescence microscopy data, Nature Methods 11 (9) (2014) 951–958.

[8] J. Stegmaier, F. Amat, W.B. Lemon, K. McDole, Y. Wan, G. Teodoro, R. Mikut, P.J. Keller, Real-time three-dimensional cell segmentation in large-scale microscopy data of developing embryos, Developmental Cell 36 (2) (2016) 225–240.

[9] V. Ulman, M. Maška, K.E. Magnusson, O. Ronneberger, C. Haubold, N. Harder, P. Matula, P. Matula, D. Svoboda, M. Radojevic, et al., An objective comparison of cell-tracking algorithms, Nature Methods 14 (12) (2017) 1141–1152.

[10] J. Stegmaier, New Methods to Improve Large-Scale Microscopy Image Analysis with Prior Knowledge and Uncertainty, KIT Scientific Publishing, 2016.

[11] J. Stegmaier, R. Mikut, Fuzzy-based propagation of prior knowledge to improve largescale image analysis pipelines, PLoS ONE 12 (11) (2017) e0187535.

[12] J. Stegmaier, J. Arz, B. Schott, J.C. Otte, A. Kobitski, G.U. Nienhaus, U. Strähle, P. Sanders, R. Mikut, Generating semi-synthetic validation benchmarks for embryomics, in: Proc., IEEE International Symposium on Biomedical Imaging: From Nano to Macro, 2016, pp. 684–688.

[13] M. Traub, J. Stegmaier, Towards automatic embryo staging in 3D+t microscopy images using convolutional neural networks and PointNets, in: Proc., International Workshop on Simulation and Synthesis in Medical Imaging, Springer, 2020, pp. 153–163.

[14] D. Eschweiler, T. Klose, F.N. Müller-Fouarge, M. Kopaczka, J. Stegmaier, Towards annotation-free segmentation of fluorescently labeled cell membranes in confocal microscopy images, in: Proc., International Workshop on Simulation and Synthesis in Medical Imaging, Springer, 2019, pp. 81–89.

[15] A.Y. Kobitski, J.C. Otte, M. Takamiya, B. Schäfer, J. Mertes, J. Stegmaier, S. Rastegar, F. Rindone, V. Hartmann, R. Stotzka, A. García, J. van Wezel, R. Mikut, U. Strähle, G.U. Nienhaus, An ensemble-averaged, cell density-based digital model of zebrafish embryo development derived from light-sheet microscopy data with single-cell resolution, Scientific Reports 5 (1) (2015) 8601.

[16] C.J. Tomlin, J.D. Axelrod, Biology by numbers: mathematical modelling in developmental biology, Nature Reviews. Genetics 8 (5) (2007) 331–340.

[17] D.W. Thompson, On Growth and Form, Cambridge University Press, 1942.

[18] N. Hopwood, Plastic publishing in embryology, in: Models: The Third Dimension of Science, Stanford University Press, Stanford, California, 2004, pp. 170–206.

[19] J. Sharpe, Computer modeling in developmental biology: growing today, essential tomorrow, Development 144 (23) (2017) 4214–4225.

[20] N. Goel, R.D. Campbell, R. Gordon, R. Rosen, H. Martinez, M. Yčas, Self-sorting of isotropic cells, Journal of Theoretical Biology 28 (3) (1970) 423–468.

[21] A.G. Leith, N.S. Goel, Simulation of movement of cells during self-sorting, Journal of Theoretical Biology 33 (1) (1971) 171–188.

[22] N.S. Goel, C.F. Doggenweiler, R.L. Thompson, Simulation of cellular compaction and internalization in mammalian embryo development as driven by minimization of surface energy, Bulletin of Mathematical Biology 48 (2) (1986) 167–187.

[23] J.A. Glazier, F. Graner, Simulation of biological cell sorting using a 2-dimensional extended Potts-model, Physical Review Letters 69 (13) (1992) 2013–2016.

[24] R.M. Merks, J.A. Glazier, A cell-centered approach to developmental biology, Physica A: Statistical Mechanics and Its Applications 352 (1) (2005) 113–130.

[25] P. Hogeweg, Computing an organism: on the interface between informatic and dynamic processes, Biosystems 64 (1–3) (2002) 97–109.

[26] B. Vasiev, A. Balter, M. Chaplain, J.A. Glazier, C.J. Weijer, Modeling gastrulation in the chick embryo: formation of the primitive streak, PLoS ONE 5 (5) (2010) e10571.

[27] H. Honda, M. Tanemura, T. Nagai, A three-dimensional vertex dynamics cell model of space-filling polyhedra simulating cell behavior in a cell aggregate, Journal of Theoretical Biology 226 (4) (2004) 439–453.

[28] A.G. Fletcher, M. Osterfield, R.E. Baker, S.Y. Shvartsman, Vertex models of epithelial morphogenesis, Biophysical Journal 106 (11) (2014) 2291–2304.

[29] M. Marin-Riera, M. Brun-Usan, R. Zimm, T. Välikangas, I. Salazar-Ciudad, Computational modeling of development by epithelia, mesenchyme and their interactions: a unified model, Bioinformatics 32 (2) (2016) 219–225.

[30] P. Macklin, M.E. Edgerton, A.M. Thompson, V. Cristini, Patient-calibrated agent-based modelling of ductal carcinoma in situ (DCIS): from microscopic measurements to macroscopic predictions of clinical progression, Journal of Theoretical Biology 301 (2012) 122–140.

[31] J. Delile, M. Herrmann, N. Peyriéras, R. Doursat, A cell-based computational model of early embryogenesis coupling mechanical behaviour and gene regulation, Nature Communications 8 (1) (2017) 1–10.

[32] A. Verwey, Three-Dimensional Analysis of Light Microscope Images: A Method for Studying Cell Fate in the Mouse Embryo, PhD Thesis, Applied Sciences, TU Delft, 1993.

[33] M. Kaufman, R. Brune, R. Baldock, J. Bard, D. Davidson, Computer-aided 3-d reconstruction of serially-sectioned mouse embryos: its use in integrating anatomical organisation, The International Journal of Developmental Biology 41 (2) (2002) 223–233.

[34] F.J. Verbeek, K.A. Lawson, J.B.L. Bard, Developmental bioinformatics: linking genetic data to virtual embryos, The International Journal of Developmental Biology 43 (7) (1999) 761–771.

[35] R. Brune, J. Bard, C. Dubreuil, E. Guest, W. Hill, M. Kaufman, M. Stark, D. Davidson, R. Baldock, A three-dimensional model of the mouse at embryonic day 9, Developmental Biology 216 (2) (1999) 457–468.

[36] J. Huisken, J. Swoger, F. Del Bene, J. Wittbrodt, E.H. Stelzer, Optical sectioning deep inside live embryos by selective plane illumination microscopy, Science 305 (5686) (2004) 1007–1009.

[37] C.C. Fowlkes, C.L. Luengo Hendriks, S.V.E. Keränen, G.H. Weber, O. Rübel, M.Y. Huang, S. Chatoor, A.H. DePace, L. Simirenko, C. Henriquez, A. Beaton, R. Weiszmann, S. Celniker, B. Hamann, D.W. Knowles, M.D. Biggin, M.B. Eisen, J. Malik, A quantitative spatiotemporal atlas of gene expression in the drosophila blastoderm, Cell 133 (2) (2008) 364–374.

[38] Z. Bao, J. Murray, T. Boyle, S. Ooi, M. Sandel, R. Waterston, Automated cell lineage tracing in caenorhabditis elegans, Proceedings of the National Academy of Sciences of the United States of America 103 (8) (2006) 2707–2712.

[39] N. Olivier, M.A. Luengo-Oroz, L. Duloquin, E. Faure, T. Savy, I. Veilleux, X. Solinas, D. Débarre, P. Bourgine, A. Santos, N. Peyriéras, E. Beaurepaire, Cell lineage reconstruction of early zebrafish embryos using label-free nonlinear microscopy, Science 329 (5994) (2010) 967–971.

[40] E. Faure, T. Savy, B. Rizzi, C. Melani, O. Stašová, D. Fabrèges, R. Špir, M. Hammons, R. Čúnderlík, G. Recher, et al., A workflow to process 3D+time microscopy images of developing organisms and reconstruct their cell lineage, Nature Communications 7 (8674) (2016) 1–10.

[41] M. Takamiya, J. Stegmaier, A.Y. Kobitski, B. Schott, B.D. Weger, D. Margariti, A.R.C. Delgado, V. Gourain, T. Scherr, L. Yang, et al., Pax6 organizes the anterior eye segment by guiding two distinct neural crest waves, PLoS Genetics 16 (6) (2020) e1008774.

[42] U. Krzic, S. Gunther, T. Saunders, S. Streichan, L. Hufnagel, Multiview light-sheet microscope for rapid in toto imaging, Nature Methods 9 (7) (2012) 730–733.

[43] R. Tomer, K. Khairy, F. Amat, P.J. Keller, Quantitative high-speed imaging of entire developing embryos with simultaneous multiview light-sheet microscopy, Nature Methods 9 (7) (2012) 755–763.

[44] K. McDole, L. Guignard, F. Amat, A. Berger, G. Malandain, L.A. Royer, S.C. Turaga, K. Branson, P.J. Keller, In toto imaging and reconstruction of post-implantation mouse development at the single-cell level, Cell 175 (3) (2018) 859–876.

[45] R. Fernandez, P. Das, V. Mirabet, E. Moscardi, J. Traas, J.-L. Verdeil, G. Malandain, C. Godin, Imaging plant growth in 4D: robust tissue reconstruction and lineaging at cell resolution, Nature Methods 7 (7) (2010) 547–553.

[46] L. Willis, Y. Refahi, R. Wightman, B. Landrein, J. Teles, K.C. Huang, E.M. Meyerowitz, H. Jönsson, Cell size and growth regulation in the arabidopsis thaliana apical stem cell niche, Proceedings of the National Academy of Sciences 113 (51) (2016) E8238–E8246.

[47] P. Villoutreix, J. Delile, B. Rizzi, L. Duloquin, T. Savy, P. Bourgine, R. Doursat, N. Peyriéras, An integrated modelling framework from cells to organism based on a cohort of digital embryos, Scientific Reports 6 (2016) 1–11.

[48] D. Wang, Z. Wang, X. Zhao, Y. Xu, Z. Bao, et al., An observation data driven simulation and analysis framework for early stage C. elegans embryogenesis, Journal of Biomedical Science and Engineering 11 (08) (2018) 225–234.

[49] J. Stegmaier, J.C. Otte, A. Kobitski, A. Bartschat, A. Garcia, G.U. Nienhaus, U. Strähle, R. Mikut, Fast segmentation of stained nuclei in terabyte-scale, time resolved 3D microscopy image stacks, PLoS ONE 9 (2) (2014) 1–11.

[50] B. Schott, M. Traub, C. Schlagenhauf, M. Takamiya, T. Antritter, A. Bartschat, K. Löffler, D. Blessing, J.C. Otte, A.Y. Kobitski, G.U. Nienhaus, U. Strähle, R. Mikut, J. Stegmaier, EmbryoMiner: a new framework for interactive knowledge discovery in large-scale cell tracking data of developing embryos, PLoS Computational Biology 14 (4) (2018) 1–18.

[51] D. Svoboda, V. Ulman, Generation of synthetic image datasets for time-lapse fluorescence microscopy, in: International Conference Image Analysis and Recognition, Springer, 2012, pp. 473–482.

[52] D. Bähr, D. Eschweiler, A. Bhattacharyya, D. Moreno-Andrés, W. Antonin, J. Stegmaier, CellCycleGAN: spatiotemporal microscopy image synthesis of cell populations using statistical shape models and conditional GANs, in: Proc., IEEE International Symposium on Biomedical Imaging: From Nano to Macro, IEEE, 2021, pp. 15–19.

[53] D. Eschweiler, M. Rethwisch, S. Koppers, J. Stegmaier, Spherical harmonics for shape-constrained 3D cell segmentation, in: Proc., IEEE International Symposium on Biomedical Imaging: From Nano to Macro, IEEE, 2021, pp. 792–796.

[54] A. Bartschat, E. Hübner, M. Reischl, R. Mikut, J. Stegmaier, XPIWIT – an XML pipeline wrapper for the insight toolkit, Bioinformatics 32 (2) (2016) 315–317.

[55] I.J. Goodfellow, J. Pouget-Abadie, M. Mirza, B. Xu, D. Warde-Farley, S. Ozair, A. Courville, Y. Bengio, Generative adversarial networks, in: Advances in Neural Information Processing Systems, 2014, pp. 2672–2680.

[56] D. Wiesner, T. Nečasová, D. Svoboda, On generative modeling of cell shape using 3D GANs, in: Proc., International Conference on Image Analysis and Processing, Springer, 2019, pp. 672–682.

[57] M. Gadermayr, L. Gupta, B.M. Klinkhammer, P. Boor, D. Merhof, Unsupervisedly training GANs for segmenting digital pathology with automatically generated annotations, arXiv preprint, arXiv:1805.10059.

[58] L. Gupta, B.M. Klinkhammer, P. Boor, D. Merhof, M. Gadermayr, Stain independent segmentation of whole slide images: a case study in renal histology, in: Proc., IEEE International Symposium on Biomedical Imaging: From Nano to Macro, 2018, pp. 1360–1364.

[59] K. Armanious, C. Jiang, M. Fischer, T. Küstner, T. Hepp, K. Nikolaou, S. Gatidis, B. Yang, MedGAN: medical image translation using GANs, Computerized Medical Imaging and Graphics 79 (2020) 101684.

[60] O. Ronneberger, P. Fischer, T. Brox, U-Net: convolutional networks for biomedical image segmentation, in: Proc., International Conference on Medical Image Computing and Computer-Assisted Intervention, Springer, 2015, pp. 234–241.

[61] Ö. Çiçek, A. Abdulkadir, S.S. Lienkamp, T. Brox, O. Ronneberger, 3D U-Net: learning dense volumetric segmentation from sparse annotation, in: Proc. International Conference on Medical Image Computing and Computer-Assisted Intervention, Springer, 2016, pp. 424–432.

[62] P. Isola, J.Y. Zhu, T. Zhou, A.A. Efros, Image-to-image translation with conditional adversarial networks, in: Proc., IEEE Conference on Computer Vision and Pattern Recognition, 2017, pp. 5967–5976.

[63] J. Rosenbauer, C. Zhang, B. Mattes, I. Reinartz, K. Wedgwood, S. Schindler, C. Sinner, S. Scholpp, A. Schug, Modeling of Wnt-mediated tissue patterning in vertebrate embryogenesis, PLoS Computational Biology 16 (6) (2020) e1007417.

[64] M. Weigert, K. Subramanian, S.T. Bundschuh, E.W. Myers, M. Kreysing, Biobeam – multiplexed wave-optical simulations of light-sheet microscopy, PLoS Computational Biology 14 (4) (2018) e1006079.

[65] J.-Y. Zhu, R. Zhang, D. Pathak, T. Darrell, A.A. Efros, O. Wang, E. Shechtman, Toward multimodal image-to-image translation, in: Advances in Neural Information Processing Systems, 2017, pp. 465–476.

[66] Y. Choi, Y. Uh, J. Yoo, J.-W. Ha, StarGAN v2: diverse image synthesis for multiple domains, in: Proc. IEEE/CVF Conference on Computer Vision and Pattern Recognition, 2020, pp. 8188–8197.

Further reading

[67] L. Wolpert, C. Tickle, A.M. Arias, et al., Principles of Development, Oxford University Press, USA, 2015.

[68] J. Sharpe, Computer modeling in developmental biology: growing today, essential tomorrow, Development 144 (23) (2017) 4214–4225.

[69] J. Stegmaier, New Methods to Improve Large-Scale Microscopy Image Analysis with Prior Knowledge and Uncertainty, KIT Scientific Publishing, 2016.

Biomolecule trafficking and network tomography-based simulations

24

Charles Kervrann

EPC Serpico, Inria Rennes, CNRS-UMR144, Institut Curie, PSL Research, Rennes Cedex, France

24.1 Motivation

The discovery of fluorescent labeling probes (Green Fluorescence Protein, Nobel Prize in Chemistry 2008) and recent advances in optics and digital sensors (e.g., PALM (Photo Activated Localization Microscopy), STED (Stimulated Emission Depletion Microscopy) and SIM (Structure Illumination Microscopy)) have been key developments which have served to overcome the theoretical optical diffraction limit (200 nm) established in the 19th century. Because of these technological breakthroughs and their impacts in life sciences, contemporary microscopy has been praised through prestigious awards, such as the Nobel Prizes awarded to inventors of the concepts of super-resolution microscopy (2014) and cryo-electron microscopy (2017). Fluorescent microscopy imaging has become the spearhead of modern biology as it is able to generate videos comprising dozens of gigabytes of data within an hour, and can depict long-term 4D nanoscale cell behaviors with low photo-toxicity. The ability to follow nanoscale cellular events is also proving to be of immense clinical relevance, especially for the study of cancer progression and viral infections. All these technological advances in microscopy have created new challenges for researchers in signal-image processing, and have even modified conventional paradigms once digital processing became a key component in the surmounting of the diffraction barrier (e.g., PALM, SIM).

In fluorescence microscopy, systems record signals emitted by molecules tagged with genetically engineered proteins within cells. In a conventional setup, photons are collected and registered at a given pixel (or voxel in 3D imaging). The measured fluorescence intensity is a scalar value, generally proportional to the density of tagged-molecules representing a few dozens of nanometers within a pixel/voxel (see Fig. 24.1). Fluorescence includes intensity (biomolecule density), wavelength (absorption and emission spectrum), time (fluorescence decay lifetime) and polarization (which arises from the dipole orientation). As the image data are 3D+Time signals, which could potentially depict several fluorescently tagged molecular species

Biomedical Image Synthesis and Simulation. https://doi.org/10.1016/B978-0-12-824349-7.00031-1

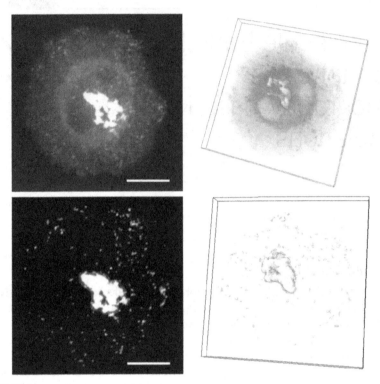

FIGURE 24.1

Acquisition of temporal series of 3D stacks in fluorescence spinning-disk confocal microscopy. (Left) One 2D image (top) extracted from a 3D stack depicting biomolecules (GFP-Rab6 proteins, see Section 24.3) in a single micro-patterned (disk-shaped) cell, and 2D image corresponding to the maximum projection of the 3D stack along the depth axis (bottom). (Right) Volume rendering of the fluorescent stack (top) and segmentation of transport vesicles and Golgi (bottom). The scale bars correspond to 5 μm.

(multi-channel images), the interpretation of these signals represents a challenge in signal-image processing, and one for which several scientific barriers must be overcome. These barriers translate into un-solved challenges in image analysis, modeling, and simulation which need to be surmounted in order for this technology to be adopted in large-scale biological studies.

24.1.1 Traffic flows of biomolecules

Eukaryotic cells are characterized by membrane bound organelles. Their abilities to divide and fulfill their various functions within integrated tissues rely on the tight regulation of membrane composition, on the generation of ubiquitous and specialized organelles and on their capability to communicate with each other. Current research efforts in cell biology have already contributed to identify hundreds of components defining key machineries of essential functions. It is well known now that, to preserve the structure, cohesion, and functions of the organism, the eukaryotic cell exchanges biomolecules between its compartments and organelles: endosomes, Golgi apparatus, endoplasmic reticulum, etc., these intracellular exchanges require physical supports such as intermediate and actin filaments, and microtubules. Microtubules are polymers of tubulin that play an important role in a number of vital cell processes such as cell division, intracellular transport, and cell architecture. Furthermore, the transport pathways of biomolecules, mediated by vesicles propelled by molecular motors of the dynein and kinesin families along the cytoskeleton, provide the routes of communication between the organelles and the extra-cellular medium. The molecular motors transform chemical energy with the mediation of adenosine tri-phosphate to mechanical work and driving energy for propelling the vesicles. It has also been established that transport from one compartment to the next one follows similar mechanistic principles, that is, formation of coated vesicles, which bud from a donor compartment and then fuse with the recipient compartment. They involve similar protein networks controlling soluble and membrane protein sorting and vesicle formation, transport vesicle movement along cytoskeleton elements (actin nucleation machineries and molecular motors) and membrane fusion.

Nevertheless, it is still difficult to understand how these different machineries using multiple protein–protein and protein–lipid interactions are interconnected and coordinated in time and space during a given reaction like for intracellular transport, for instance. A long-term goal in fundamental biology is to decipher the dynamic coordination and organization of interacting molecules within molecular complexes at the single cell level and to explore the role of transport intermediates (e.g., vesicles) to higher levels of complexity, as during remodeling of the plasma membrane, differentiation, and cell migration in contexts in forced two dimensions (micro-patterns), or in reconstituted three-dimensional environments. In that context, the mathematical and biophysical models, as well as estimation and simulation methods and algorithms, are particularly helpful to decode the traffic flows of biomolecules. Here, we focus on traffic simulation to describe the interactions between different cell compartments, membrane domains and organelles.

24.1.2 Biomolecule tracking and dynamics estimation

In fluorescence microscopy, a first important challenge is to track and analyze the motion of biomolecules, with high precision, in 3D movies. This task is challenging because of the complexity of the dynamic processes being observed, such as association, dissociation, and recomposition of proteins, all of which are driven by interactions between several molecular species and further complicated by the particular phenomena of spatial coalescence related to image resolution. To that end a number of stochastic models have been proposed to describe the individual and collective motion of biomolecules [1,2], including the jerky motions corresponding to switches between free diffusion (or Brownian motion), subdiffusion, and motor-mediated motion [3,4].

It turns out that most existing methods are tracking techniques [5] requiring optimization or simulation in order to manage several thousands of tracks. The most commonly-used tracking approach is the so-called "connexionist" (or "detect-before-track") approach [6–8] which consists in detecting particles independently in each frame in a first step [9,10], and then linking the detected particles over time. The related *data association* task is a critical step in this approach, especially if the number of particles is very high and if the trajectories interact. Multiple hypotheses tracking methods have then become popular [11,12], where a set of data association hypotheses are generated to account for all possible associations of tracking (or a suitable subset of those), identifying the most likely hypothesis according to some criterion. The aim of most Bayesian approaches for multiple object tracking [13] is to take into account the fact that the trajectories can cross each other, particles can move in and out of the frame, in and out of the depth of field, merge either by fusion to form a single particle, split into two or more particles, temporarily disappear due to mis-detection, and so on. A very popular method is the U-track method [14] which robustly tracks spots and estimates heterogeneous motion in high density scenes whilst also exploiting recursive tracking in forward and backward temporal directions. U-track enables the prediction and the recovery of abrupt transitions, from freely (or confined) diffusive to directed motion, as well as the handling of spot disappearance. Thereafter several probabilistic methods have been designed to cope with different types of sub-cellular motion [15,16]. All these methods were carefully evaluated a few years ago on the particle tracking challenge dataset [5], including robustness to noise and particle densities. It results that all trackers were very competitive, each performing at their best once on a target scenario.

Then, the tracks are exploited to infer molecular dynamics or mobility in cells. For instance, the mean-square displacement method, which is widely used in biophysics and cell imaging, allows one to interpret biomolecule tracks and discriminate free, confined diffusion and directed flow since they represent the primary modes of mobility of molecules in living cells (see [10,4]).

24.1.3 Network tomography for biomolecule trafficking modeling

The aforementioned tracking methods assume that the motion of individual particle car be represented by some known mathematical models, including Brownian motion or Markov models. Nevertheless, there is few satisfying modeling approaches able to represent the collective motion of particles and global biomolecule trafficking. In the specific case of vesicle trafficking within cells, collective motion can be inferred from the transport pathways that link "origin" regions to "destination" regions. The modeling is inspired from the network tomography (NT) concept, introduced to estimate vehicle traffic flows [17,18], and further re-popularized to determine origin-destination traffic flows in computer networks [19].

In this general modeling, we consider a network defined as a graph $G(E, V)$ which consists of $|V|$ (cardinal of V) vertices and $|E|$ (cardinal of E) edges, where E and V denote the set of edges and vertices, respectively. Each pair of neighbor

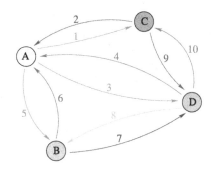

OD pair	edge number									
	1	2	3	4	5	6	7	8	9	10
$B \to A$	0	0	0	0	0	1	0	0	0	0
$B \to C$	1	0	0	0	0	1	0	0	0	0
$B \to D$	0	0	0	0	0	0	1	0	0	0
⋮					⋮					

FIGURE 24.2

4-nodes graph and routing matrix for network tomography. (Top) The vertices of the graph are labeled by letters and the edges by numbers. (Bottom) Several rows of the routing matrix **A** corresponding to the "toy" graph. The routing for the OD pairs is defined as the shortest paths using the Euclidean distance between vertices.

vertices is connected by two edges in order to enable traffic in both directions. A "toy" graph involving only four vertices is shown in Fig. 24.2 (top) for illustration. The particles are assumed to move from one vertex to another vertex by crossing edges. They follow a path defined by an origin vertex (or node), a destination vertex, and possible intermediate(s) vertex(ices). The set of paths can be then characterized by the origin and destination vertices, that is the Origin–Destination pairs (OD pairs). Given $|V|$ vertices in the graph, the number K of possible OD pairs is $K = |V|(|V| - 1)$.

In NT, given the temporal measurements corresponding to the number of particles detected as going from one vertex to a neighbor vertex in the graph, the goal is to estimate the proportions of particles for each OD pair. More formally, let $x_{k,t}$ be the number of particles belonging to the path k that joins the "Origin" node to the "Destination" node (OD pair k) at time t. The measurements $z_{e,t}$ correspond to the number of particles that pass through edge e at time t. In the traffic flow problem, we then assume the following model:

$$Z = AX, \tag{24.1}$$

where $Z = \{z_{e,t}\}_{e \in \{1,...,|E|\}, t \in \{1,...,T\}}$ and $X = \{x_{k,t}\}_{k \in \{1,...,K\}, t \in \{1,...,T\}}$ are matrices and denote the set of measurements and the unknown OD flows, respectively, and T is the number of images in the sequence. Here, **A** denotes the $|E| \times K$ routing matrix with binary elements: $a_{e,k} = 1$ if edge e belongs to the path for the OD pair k, and 0 otherwise. Usually, it is assumed that there exists a single path for one OD pair defined as the shortest path in the graph. Furthermore, a cost is associated to each edge and the Dijkstra algorithm [20] is applied to the whole graph for computing the shortest path for each OD pair. In Fig. 24.2 (bottom), we show a few rows of the binary routing matrix $\mathbf{A}$ corresponding to the graph shown in Fig. 24.2 (top) when the Euclidean distance between the vertices is considered.

In NT, the traffic flow problem (24.1) aims at estimating the matrix X given the routing matrix $\mathbf{A}$ and the counting measurements Z. This problem is an *under-constrained* problem since K is greater than $|E|$ (see (24.1)). If we are only interested in the proportions of particles on each OD pair, we need to solve the following optimization problem:

$$\min_{\bar{x}} \|\bar{z} - \mathbf{A}\bar{x}\|^2 \text{ subject to } \bar{x}_k \geq 0, \ k \in \{1, \ldots, K\}, \tag{24.2}$$

where $\bar{x} = (\bar{x}_1, \ldots, \bar{x}_K)^T$ contains the positive proportions of particles for each OD pair and $\bar{z} = (\bar{z}_1, \ldots, \bar{z}_{|E|})^T$ corresponds to temporal averages. Additional constraints can be considered. For instance, Vardi proposed a Poisson distribution for $\bar{x}$ because the data are counts [19]; as there is a lot of possible OD pairs but at the same time the traffic is observed only on a few of them, one can prefer to impose a sparsity constraint as follows:

$$\min_{\bar{x}} \|\bar{z} - \mathbf{A}\bar{x}\|^2 + \lambda\|\bar{x}\|_0 \text{ subject to } \bar{x}_k \geq 0, \ k \in \{1, \ldots, K\}, \tag{24.3}$$

where $\lambda > 0$ is weighting parameter and $\|\bar{x}\|_0 = \#\{\bar{x}_k \neq 0\}, \ k \in \{1, \ldots, K\}$.

24.2 Simulation for biomolecule trafficking analysis

In this section, we describe a network tomography-based simulation framework able to generate complex motions and interactions between moving particles with variable velocities within the cell. We design graphical representations and dynamical models built from representative fluorescence microscopy image sequences. These representations are exploited to generate artificial image sequences that mimic biomolecules trafficking observed in real image sequences.

24.2.1 History and state-of-the-art

In biomedical imaging, simulations are required for validating physical models, understanding recorded data, evaluating the performance of image analysis algorithms [5], or training complex models from large-scale synthetic datasets as recently investigated with supervised deep learning methods [21,22]. Nevertheless, the proposed simulation methods used to build benchmarking data sets are limited yet since they are not able to represent the whole complexity of interacting biomolecules as observed in real image sequences.

In past years, random walks combined with parametric drift models (e.g., [23]) and diffusion models in sub-regions in the cell [21] were considered for simulating images depicting biomolecule motions. A more realistic approach consists in simulating particles undergoing stochastic motions depending on interactions with the cytoskeleton and the cytosol within the cell as described in [24]. The intracellular particles move along the microtubule network via molecular motors, or diffuse in the cytosol. Formally, a transport vesicle is generally represented by a particle $p(t) \in \mathbb{R}^d \times \{1, \ldots, T\}, d = 2, 3$ whose dynamics follows a stochastic rule [24]:

$$dp(t) = \begin{cases} \sqrt{2K_d}\,dw(t) & \text{if } p(t) \text{ is free within the cytosol,} \\ V_m & \text{if } p(t) \text{ is bound to a microtubule,} \end{cases} \tag{24.4}$$

where w is Brownian motion, $K_d \in \mathbb{R}$ is the diffusion constant in the cytosol, and V_m is the constant drift motion along the microtubules. Thus, a given transport vesicle switches between diffusion in the cytosol (Brownian motion) and active motion along microtubule (directed motion). The molecular motor allows the vesicle to be propelled at a given speed V_m. In [24], the cells are assumed to be flat and the cytosol is represented by a two-dimensional ($d = 2$) ring of maximum radius (outer membrane of the cell) and minimum radius (nuclear envelope). The microtubules are uniformly and radially distributed, coming from the nucleus towards the outer membrane. In this line of modeling work, Klann et al. proposed an alternative mechanistic agent-based simulation able to combine signal transduction and membrane trafficking, to study the effect of receptor-mediated endocytosis on signaling [25].

More generally, two modeling approaches have been investigated for simulation at the scale of single cell in past years: *data-driven modeling* and *physics-based modeling*. The physics-based approach relies on the physical properties of the components in the cell. The main advantage is that the model parameters are easily interpreted as they are well grounded in biophysics. This approach is generally considered to investigate complex spatiotemporal biological events, for instance, to study the dynamics of microtubule networks [26–28], or to characterize diffusion of biomolecules in nano-domains [21]. By tuning the control parameters, an expert can artificially generate dynamics which are visually similar to those observed in real data, provided that the underlying dynamical models are well designed. The data-driven modeling aims at describing image sequences through statistical models learned from real images. This approach can only "imitate" dynamical processes but is not able to fully transcribe the physical properties of dynamical processes. However, unlike physics-based modeling, the data-driven approach can capture the features of complex multi-scale systems as a whole. The data-driven and physics-based approaches can also be gently combined to model the main components of the image sequence, as recently investigated in [22] to mimic calcium dynamics in astrocytes observed in lattice light sheet microscopy.

Finally, by minimizing the discrepancy between a set of descriptors computed from a real image sequence and the same set of descriptors computed from a simulated sequence, the parameters of the simulation method can be tuned to obtain an artificial sequence that reveals apparently the same dynamical characteristics as the observed sequence. This line of research is related to data assimilation, developed on a controlled trade-off between observations of a phenomena and a model accounting for its likely dynamics.

24.2.2 Network tomography-inspired simulation

The simulation approach falls in the category of data-driven methods and exploits real image sequences as inputs. In the simulation scenario, the fluorescence-tagged biomolecules are assumed to be transported via transport vesicles propelled by molecular motors along the cytoskeleton composed of actin filaments, intermediate filaments, as well as microtubules. Here, we focus on microtubules which are polymers with a diameter of about 25 nm. They have an exceptional bending stiffness and form a dense network (see the illustration in Fig. 24.3(b)). The dynein and kinesin proteins are two classes of molecular motors associated with microtubules. In stable conditions, the speed and polarization of these motors is assumed to be constant. This explains partially why the observed velocity of vesicles is constant if they move along the same microtubule. In the simulation framework, we assume that the microtubule network is static when compared to moving biomolecules.

Modeling of transport vesicle appearance

In video-microscopy, the vesicles appear as small bright spots against a dark background (Figs. 24.3(a) and 24.4). The vesicle diameter theoretically ranges from 60 to 150 nm, that is below the spatial resolution of the microscope which is about 200 nm. However, the point spread function of the microscope makes them appear as larger structures in acquired images. As illustrated in Fig. 24.4, the stretching is more significant as the vesicle moves rapidly. Furthermore, when the density of objects increases, the vesicles gather together and constitute small rods. Consequently, large vesicles or sets of nearby vesicles can be satisfyingly represented by anisotropic Gaussian spots as proposed in [30,23] with variances related to the spot dimensions ranging from 60 to 150 nm, which is very close to the pixel size. In the simulation framework, the covariance matrix of the anisotropic Gaussian spot is a function of the displacement direction. The ellipticity also depends on the velocity, induced by molecular motors bound to the microtubules. Fig. 24.5 schematically illustrates how the covariance matrix of the anisotropic Gaussian function allows one to modify the orientation of spots according to the direction of the microtubule axis. As we wish to simulate image sequences close to those acquired with a spinning disk microscope, we first measure the maximum intensity of a large number of vesicles on real sequences, which approximately follows a Gaussian distribution.

Modeling of microtubule network

In order to generate a synthetic but realistic microtubule network, we exploit real image sequences as input for the modeling. A real network can be tagged with

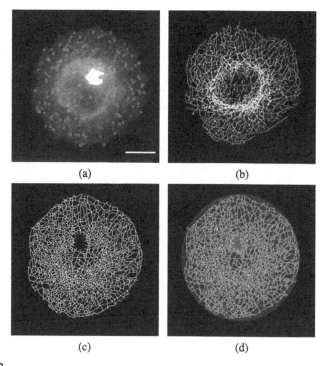

FIGURE 24.3

Biomolecule trafficking in cells. (a) GFP-Rab6 vesicles in micro-patterned (disk-shaped) cell where the Golgi and the vesicles are delineated with green and red curves (dark gray and mid gray in print version), respectively. (b) Fluorescently tagged microtubule network. (c) Extraction of a microtubules network from (b) by applying a dedicated algorithm [29] and manual correction. (d) Labeling of nodes (blue – mid gray in print version) and edges (white) of the network. The origin and destination nodes are depicted in green and red (light gray and dark gray in print version), respectively. The scale bar corresponds to 5 μm.

green fluorescence protein (GFP) as illustrated in Fig. 24.3(b) but this network is generally very complex and individual microtubules cannot be easily extracted (see Fig. 24.3(c)). Alternatively, the microtubule network can be coarsely obtained from the maximum intensity projection (MIP) map with respect to time, that is, from the paths followed by the tagged vesicles. The bright paths in the MIP map enlighten the main routes used by the vesicles, assumed to be the traffic motorways of the microtubule network. Fig. 24.6(a) shows the MIP image of a real 2D sequence of 300 images acquired with a spinning disk confocal microscope, defined as

$$\text{MIP}(I)(s) = \max_{t \in \{1,\dots,T\}} I(s,t), \quad \forall s \in \Omega, \tag{24.5}$$

where T denotes the number of images in the sequence, and $I(s,t)$ is the fluorescence intensity observed at time t and at pixel s in the image domain Ω. This simple

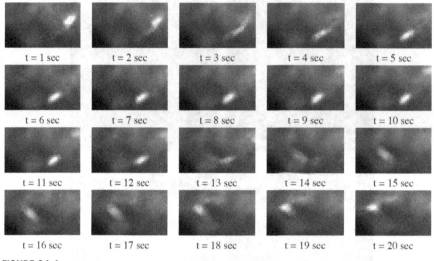

FIGURE 24.4

Appearance of vesicles in cells. Twenty regions of interest extracted from a real spinning disk confocal microscopy image sequence in which a vesicle (bright spots) moves from right to left.

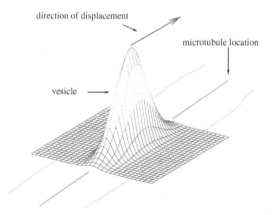

FIGURE 24.5

Gaussian model of the spot oriented in the direction of the microtubule axis. The covariance matrix of the Gaussian function depends on the velocity of the vesicle. The simulated vesicles are then elongated along with the displacement direction. The anisotropic Gaussian spots have an average length of 180 nm and a standard deviation of 90 nm.

projection allows one to select the main routes used for the intracellular trafficking, leading to a network with lower complexity. In practical imaging, the routes are extracted by applying an appropriate line detection algorithm [29] and by manually

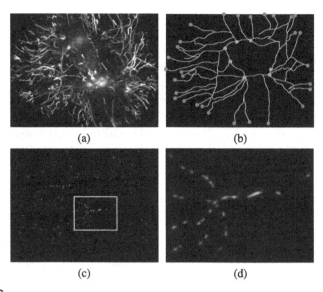

FIGURE 24.6

Design of traffic network for GFP-Rab6 proteins in a single cell. (a) Maximum intensity projection (MIP) map built from 300 images. (b) Extraction of microtubules network (white curves) and graph made of 159 nodes and 398 directed edges. The expert manually selected origin nodes (green balls – light gray balls in print version) in the central part of the network (small ring) while the destination nodes (red balls – mid gray balls in print version) are located at the periphery. (c) Simulated image at time $t = 250$. Vesicles are only going from the Golgi (central region) to the "end-points" located at the periphery of the cell. Thus, the retrograde transport from "end-points" to Golgi is prohibited and assumed to be inhibited by bio-chemical alterations. Among the 25,122 possible origin–destination pairs, 252 origin–destination pairs were observed in this simulated image sequence. (d) Zoom-in view of the region of interest delineated by a yellow (light gray in print version) rectangle in (c).

adding segments to complete the discontinued paths (see Fig. 24.6(b)). The fluorescent background is preliminary removed by applying dedicated algorithms (e.g., [31]). Each route is defined by a list of points, and each point of this list is parameterized by the width of the road, and its orientation. Finally, the crossing between routes serve to detect nodes which are further labeled as "origin" nodes and "destination" nodes, according to NT (see Fig. 24.6(b)).

Modeling of particle trafficking

According to the NT concept, the vesicles are transported along the microtubule network from origin nodes to destination nodes. The network microtubule is represented by a graph and trafficking is driven by the routing matrix. The first step of the modeling consists in building a graph from the microtubule network automatically extracted from real images as explained above. Each intersection and each end-point is labeled as a vertex of the graph G. The $|V|$ vertices form the set $V = \{v_1, \ldots, v_{|V|}\}$ and each connection between two vertices is associated with two edges allowing to establish the transport of particles in both directions. The $|E|$ edges constitute the set $E = \{e_1, \ldots, e_{|E|}\}$.

In the next step, an Origin–Destination (OD) pair is characterized by an origin vertex and a destination vertex in the graph. The user specifies a certain number of OD pairs among the $K = |V|(|V| - 1)$ possible OD pairs, and assigns to each of them a proportion of traffic. The routing is used to complete the description and aims at establishing a list of successive edges in the graph to derive an OD pair, corresponding to one or more paths, to connect an origin node to a destination node. The basic approach consists in assigning one path to only one OD pair. The resulting routing matrix is generally a binary matrix, as considered in telecommunication networks (see Fig. 24.2). Nevertheless, as all vesicles do not necessarily take the same routes for a unique origin node to reach a destination node, we identify, instead, all possible paths in the graph for each OD pair. The shortest paths are especially used to transport the vesicles and are identified with appropriate algorithms such as the Yen's algorithm [32]. A cost $C(\Gamma)$ is assigned to each path Γ and defined as the sum of costs $\{c(e_j)\}$ attached to edges $\{e_1, \ldots, e_{|E|}\}$, $C(\Gamma) = \sum_{j=1}^{N(\Gamma)} c(e_j)$, where $N(\Gamma)$ denotes the number of edges in the path Γ. In what follows, the cost $C(\Gamma)$ is proportional to the path length and is translated into a probability as follows:

$$P(\Gamma) \propto \exp\left(-\frac{C(\Gamma)}{\kappa}\right), \tag{24.6}$$

where $\kappa > 0$ is a parameter used to encourage "short" paths (if κ is small); if κ is very large, the probabilities are the same for all paths. All the probabilities are then used to establish the routing matrix $\mathbf{A}$ of dimension $|E| \times K$ and to determine the prior distribution of paths. Let $\{\Gamma^{\ell}_{e,k}\}$, $\ell = \{1, \ldots, L\}$, be the set of paths for a given OD pair k, that use the edge e, and $P(\Gamma^{\ell}_{e,k})$ denotes the associated probabilities. For a given OD pair k, we compute the elements of matrix $\mathbf{A} = \{a_{e,k}\}$ as follows:

$$a_{e,k} = \frac{\sum_{\ell=1}^{L} P(\Gamma_{e,k})}{\sum_{e'=1}^{|E|} \sum_{\ell=1}^{L} P(\Gamma_{e',k})}. \tag{24.7}$$

In summary, the strategy for simulation consists then in assigning a vesicle to an OD pair and drawing path depending on prior probabilities (24.6). The dynamics of particles is fully established from the routing matrix $\mathbf{A}$. Here, at each time step Δt, the vesicle is moved along the microtubule with a displacement step which is a proportional to the velocity. To display the vesicles in each image of the sequence as illustrated in Figs. 24.6(c)–(d), the appearance model presented earlier and illustrated in Fig. 24.5 is used.

Modeling of dynamical events

Let p be a particle assigned to an OD pair and Γ_p be a path among the shortest paths that join the origin and destination nodes of the OD pair. Let γ_p be the curve in the image domain associated to the path Γ_p. At the initialization, the vesicle is positioned at the origin of the curve γ_p. Then, it moves with variable velocities depending on curvature until it reaches its destination node, and then disappears. Nevertheless, in real image sequences, we observed additional events corresponding to "stop-and-go" [33], which may be induced by traffic congestion. These events are taken into account in the simulation framework as follows.

Let $E(p, t) = \{S, M, PS\}$ be the state of the vesicle p at time t, where "S", "M" and "PS" denote the "Stop," "Motion," and "Pseudo-Stable" states, respectively. A proportion of particles located in the neighborhood of the destination node are in the "Pseudo-Stable" state just before reaching the destination node. Formally, it means that the vesicle p stops during a time interval T_{PS}. Hence, at the initialization, a binary variable $b_p \in \{0, 1\}$ is drawn according to a Bernoulli distribution (with probability P_{PS}); if $b_p = 1$, the particle p will stop transiently before reaching the destination node. The position $r_p(t + \Delta t)$ of the particle p at time $t + \Delta t$ along the curve γ_p is then defined as follows:

$$r_p(t + \Delta t) = \begin{cases} r_p(t) + V_p(t)\Delta t & \text{if } E(p, t + \Delta t) = M, \\ r_p(t) & \text{if } E(p, t + \Delta t) = S, \\ r_p(t) & \text{if } E(p, t + \Delta t) = PS, \end{cases} \qquad (24.8)$$

where $V_p(t)$ denotes the velocity of the particle along the curve γ_p. Furthermore, we define the transition probabilities to switch from one state to another as follows:

- Probability to stop at time $t + \Delta t$ ($M \rightarrow S$),

$$P(E(p, t + \Delta t) = S \mid E(p, t) = M) = P_{M \rightarrow S};$$

- Probability to re-start at time $t + \Delta t$ ($S \rightarrow M$),

$$P(E(p, t + \Delta t) = M \mid E(p, t) = S) = P_{S \rightarrow M};$$

- Probability to stop transiently at time $t + \Delta t$ such as $0 \leq t \leq T_D$ ($M \rightarrow PS$),

$$P\left(E(p, t + \Delta t) = PS \mid E(p, t) = M, \ b_p = 1, \ |t - T_D| < \alpha T_D\right) = P_{M \rightarrow PS},$$

where $0 \leq \alpha \leq 1$ and T_D is the time necessary to reach the destination node;
- Probability to re-start at time $t + \Delta t$ in the neighborhood of the destination node ($PS \rightarrow M$),

$$P(E(p, t + \Delta t) = M \mid E(p, t) = PS, \ E(p, t - T_{PS}(p))) = P_{PS \rightarrow M}.$$

The particle p is "Pseudo-Stable" during the time interval $T_{PS}(p)$, uniformly drawn in the interval $[T_{PS}^{\min}, T_{PS}^{\max}]$. The probability to switch to the "Pseudo-Stable" state is determined by b_p and the spatial position of the particle $r_p(t)$ along the curve γ_p with respect to the position of the destination node.

Finally, we have to consider additional events such as "fusion" events when two particles p_1 and p_2 are located on the same pixel in the image domain at time t. The "fusion" event is an unlikely event and the corresponding probability is denoted P_F. If the particles are fused, the new particle p is assigned to one of the two OD pairs with the same probability. Finally we consider "turn-around" events suggesting that the particle moves back and takes another path with probability $P_T = P(\Gamma_p \to \Gamma'_p)$ to reach the destination node.

As all these probabilities cannot be set *a priori*, they are determined from the analysis of particle trajectories estimated given real image sequences.

24.3 Applications

In this section, we give a few examples of simulation, including experiments with real images depicting GFP-Rab6 vesicle trafficking. Rab6 is a member of the Rab family of small GTPases, which is involved in the vesicle budding, docking, tethering, and fusion steps during transport. It was well established that it regulates retrograde transport from the Golgi complex to the Endoplasmic Reticulum [34]. In real experiments, we used HeLa cells stably transfected with GFP-tagged proteins. The HeLa cell line is a human cancer continuous cell line. The most attractive properties of HeLa cells is the ability to proliferate indefinitely and to multiply rapidly (< 24 hours). These properties make them the perfect cell line to study molecular mechanisms of carcinogenesis. Temporal series of $380 \times 380 \times 8$ stacks were acquired with a confocal microscope equipped with spinning disk system (voxel resolution, 64.5 nm $\times 64.5$ nm $\times 300$ nm; frame rate, one stack per second).

24.3.1 Simulation of toy examples

First, we consider a very simple network which is manually defined inside a square domain of 128×128 pixels. The network is composed of five nodes and sixteen edges corresponding to eight routes (see Fig. 24.7). We selected two origin nodes (1 and 3) and two destination nodes (2 and 4). We then generated the movements of 20 spots started from the two origin nodes. In Fig. 24.7, each moving spot is assigned a particular color. At the initialization ($t = 0$), all the vesicles are located inside the vicinity of two origin nodes. Therefore, the fluorescence concentration is relatively high. Later on, the collective movements of individual vesicles form trains after a few seconds. Because of the different paths taken by them and the variance of their velocities, the packets diffuse, and eventually the vesicles are distributed over the whole network.

In the second example, we apply the simulation framework to generate a synthetic image sequence based on the network shown in Fig. 24.8(b)–(c). An image extracted from this sequence is shown in Fig. 24.8(d). The simulated image sequence is com-

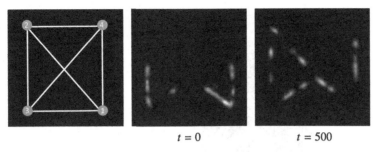

$$t = 0 \qquad t = 500$$

FIGURE 24.7

Simulation of a sequence from a 4-node network. (Left) Network composed of routes, two origin nodes (1 and 3) and two destination nodes (2, 4). (Right) Movements of 20 artificial vesicles at time $t = 0$ and $t = 500$, respectively. Each moving spot is assigned a particular color.

posed of 121 images containing 1000 moving vesicles in the whole sequence. The vesicles are moving from the center region (green – dark gray in print version) in the network to "end-points" (red – mid gray in print version) located at the periphery of the image (see Fig. 24.8(c)). For each generated vesicle, a destination among all the possible "end-points" is selected to ensure that the distribution of vesicles is uniform on all OD pairs.

A last example is shown in Fig. 24.9 and depicts a hand-crafted network (a) composed of 25 nodes and 70 edges corresponding to 35 routes. The origin nodes (green – light gray in print version) are the nodes located at the top right of the image while the destination nodes (red – mid gray in print version) are the nodes located at the bottom left. Twenty vesicles are superimposed on a dynamical background modeled as linear function of time, to mimic real fluorescence image sequences. The background intensity $I_B(s, t)$ at pixel $s \in \Omega$ and time t is represented as follows: $I_B(s, t) = a_0(s) + a_1(s)t$. The coefficients $a_0(s)$ and $a_1(s)$ varies with the spatial image position and are shown in (b) and (c), respectively. Two typical images extracted from a $128 \times 128 \times 150$ image sequence are shown in (d)–(e). The intensity of the 20 moving vesicles is assumed to follow a Gaussian law with mean 30 and standard deviation 3.

24.3.2 Simulation of GFP-Rab6 vesicle trafficking

In this section, we demonstrate the interest of the simulation methods to study the GFP-Rab6 vesicular trafficking in single micro-patterned cells. It has been established that Rab6 proteins are transiently anchored to moving transport carriers from the Golgi apparatus located at the cell center to endoplasmic reticulum entry sites or to plasma membrane [34–39], both assumed to be located at the cell periphery, where they should dissociate from membranes and recycle back to the cytosol.

In this study, shapes of the cells are constrained with micro-fabricated patterns [40] (see Figs. 24.10, 24.13, and 24.14). Micro-patterning is a well-established strat-

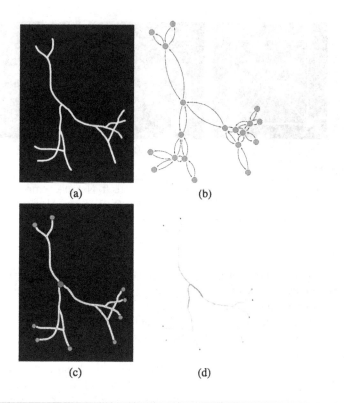

(a)   (b)

(c)   (d)

FIGURE 24.8

Simulation of a sequence from a simple microtubule network. (a) Simplistic microtubule network. (b) Associated graph. (c) Network for traffic. The origin vertex is labeled in green (dark gray in print version) while the destination vertices are labeled in red (mid gray in print version). (d) One image extracted from the whole simulated image sequence.

egy to reduce morphological variability by imposing constraints on adhesion sites, which has been shown to influence the cytoskeleton geometry and transport vesicle localization [40–42] and cellular endomembranes at the steady state within fixed cells [43].

Preliminary experiments about GFP-Rab6 vesicle traffic orientation

In this preliminary experiment, we demonstrate the dynamical orientation of Rab6 positive membranes in disk-shaped cells. According to the expert-biologists, the vesicles mostly move from the Golgi Apparatus to "end-points" located at the periphery of the cell. Accordingly, we analyzed the Rab6 vesicles fluxes with a suitable image partition composed a central region, a crown, and additional peripheral regions (see Fig. 24.11 (right)). The vesicles and Golgi are detected and segmented by applying dedicated algorithms (e.g., C-CRAFT [31], ATLAS [44] (see Fig. 24.10). The particle centers are defined as the mass centers of the connected components extracted

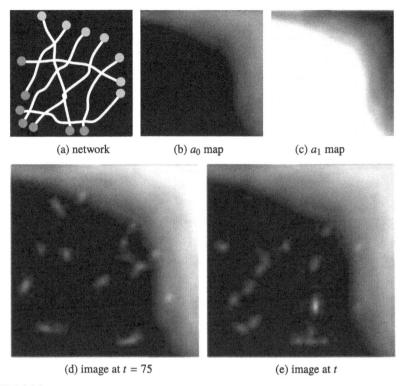

(a) network   (b) a_0 map   (c) a_1 map

(d) image at $t = 75$ (e) image at t

FIGURE 24.9

Simulation of an image sequence with background. (Top) Network (a) composed of 7 origin (red balls – mid gray balls in print version) and 7 destination nodes (green balls – light gray balls in print version), and background components a_0 and a_1 in (b) and (c), respectively. (d)–(f) Movement of 20 vesicles at time $t = 75$ and 100, respectively, with superimposed background I_B.

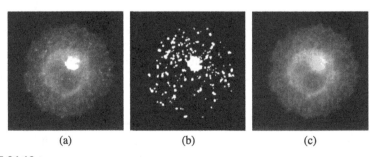

(a)   (b)   (c)

FIGURE 24.10

Background estimation and vesicle detection. Application of C-CRAFT algorithm [31] to a disk-shaped cell image sequence (a) for vesicle detection (b) background estimation (c).

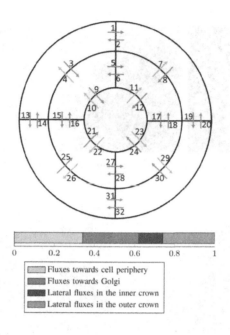

FIGURE 24.11

Cell partition of a disk-shaped cell and GFP-Rab6 vesicle flux estimation. (Top) The edge identification numbers are written next to each edge. Green (light gray in print version) edges are oriented towards the cell periphery, red (mid gray in print version) edges are oriented towards the Golgi, purple (dark gray in print version) edges correspond to lateral fluxes in the inner crown and blue (semi mid gray in print version) edges to lateral fluxes in the outer crown. (Bottom) Fluxes estimated over all registered sequences and grouped according to four different categories.

from the segmentation mask. From these coordinates, the temporally-varying number of particles in every region of the image partition has been computed, while discarding the Golgi region (central region) as trafficking is not occurring in this particular region. By applying a dedicated algorithm [45], we estimated the vesicle fluxes are furthermore grouped according to four different categories related to direction (see Fig. 24.11): (i) fluxes towards the cell periphery (green arrows in cell partitions – light gray arrows in print version); (ii) fluxes towards the Golgi (red arrows – mid gray arrows in print version); (iii) lateral fluxes in the inner crown (purple arrows – dark gray arrows in print version); and (iv) lateral fluxes in the outer crown (blue arrows – semi mid gray arrows in print version).

This study confirmed that the Rab6 positive membranes predominantly move to the cell periphery (as lateral directions are divided into two opposite directions, corresponding to $2 \times 20\%$). Here, we divided the lateral directions into two different categories to evaluate if the vesicles have the same behavior when they are close to the Golgi or close to the cell periphery. The results are reported in Fig. 24.11 (bottom). These results demonstrate that for micro-patterned cells, Rab6 positive membranes

Table 24.1 Default parameters used for GFP-Rab6 vesicle trafficking simulation.

RS = 64.5 × 64.5 nm^2	Spatial resolution of the 2D simulated image
$\Delta t = 1$ s	Time interval between two consecutive simulated images
$D_v \sim \mathcal{N}(180, 900)$	Size of Gaussian spots (vesicle)
$I_v \sim \mathcal{N}(25, 100)$	Intensity model of Gaussian spots
$V_v \sim \mathcal{N}(650, 2502)$	Velocity of vesicles
$P_{M \to S} = 0.7$	Probability for a vesicle to stop
$P_{S \to M} = 0.1$	Probability for a vesicle to re-start
$P_{PS} = 0.5$	Probability for vesicle to be in a "Pseudo-Stable" state
$P_{M \to PS} = 0.0004$	Probability for a vesicle to stop transiently
$P_F = 0.4$	Probability that a particle p_1 fuses with another particle p_2
$P_T = 0.001$	Probability that a vesicle moves back and takes another path
$T_P^{\min} S = 30$ s	Lower bound of T_{PS}
$T_{PS}^{\max} = 100$ s	Upper bound of T_{PS}

are predominantly trafficking towards the cell periphery. The lateral fluxes in the outer crown are more important than lateral fluxes in the inner crown. This indicates that GFP-Rab6 vesicles trafficking is more directed in regions close to the Golgi than in regions located at the cell periphery. This behavior is related to the vesicle docking step that is happening before vesicle reach their end-point.

Simulation of GFP-Rab6 dynamics

We applied the simulation framework described in Section 24.2.2 to mimic GFP-Rab6 vesicle dynamics as observed in spinning disk microscope images. A first simulated image sequence is shown in Fig. 24.12(b)–(d). The traffic is here uniformly distributed over each OD pair. The microtubule network, estimated from temporal series of volumes (64.5 × 64.5 × 300 nm^3) is composed of 157 vertices (Fig. 24.12(a)), involving 24,492 OD pairs. Three typical images extracted are shown in Fig. 24.12(b)–(d). In Table 24.1, we reported the typical values used to simulate this image sequence.

Meanwhile, we investigated two different cell geometries, the crossbow-shaped pattern and the circular-shaped pattern. The speed of the vesicles ranges from 1 to 10 pixels and the number of objects can be large (about a few hundreds). Several consecutive images (1 frame/s) extracted from both the real and simulated sequences are shown in Figs. 24.13 and 24.14. To assess the quality of simulated images sequences, we compare the images at time t and intensity projections along the temporal, including the Maximum Intensity Projection (MIP) and the Standard Deviation Intensity Projection (SDIP) maps defined as

$$SDIP(I))(s) = \left(\frac{1}{T} \sum_{t=1}^{T} (I(s,t) - \bar{I}(s)) \right)^{1/2}, \qquad (24.9)$$

where T denotes the number of images in the sequence, and $\bar{I}(s)$ represents the average intensity measured at pixel s. The MIP and SDIP maps computed from real

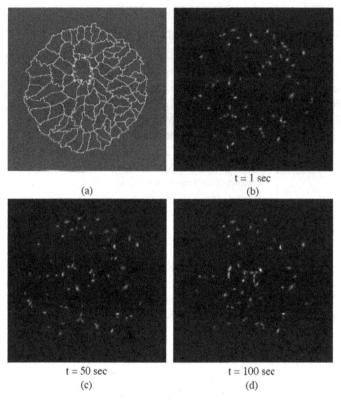

(a)

t = 1 sec
(b)

t = 50 sec
(c)

t = 100 sec
(d)

FIGURE 24.12

Simulation of GFP-Rab6 vesicles in a circular-shaped cell. (a) Microtubule network (white) and origin (green – light gray in print version) and destination (red – dark gray in print version) nodes. (b)–(d) Three images extracted from the simulated sequence.

and simulated image sequences are consistent as illustrated in Figs. 24.13 and 24.14 (bottom). The Golgi apparatus is characterized by a very bright spot on the projection maps, while vesicle trafficking is represented by a number of segments corresponding to fractions of vesicle trajectories.

Traffic estimation from simulated image sequences

In the last experiment, we applied the NT-based analysis method [46] to simulate image sequences from the network and the image partition shown in Fig. 24.15. The simulated sequence consisting of about 300 2D frames, has been obtained as before. For each generated vesicle, a destination among all the possible "end-points" is selected to ensure that the distribution of vesicles is uniform on all OD pairs. The segmentation of the OD regions has been achieved by manually partitioning the disk-shaped cell domain into five regions as illustrated with colors in Fig. 24.15 (right). In Fig. 24.16, we display the estimated OD flows (average proportions). In this ex-

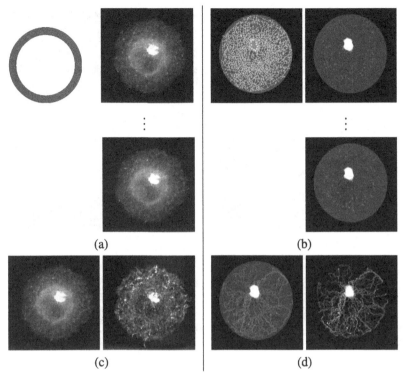

(a)   (b)

(c)   (d)

FIGURE 24.13

Comparison between real and simulated images depicting GFP-Rab6 vesicles in circular-shaped cells. (a) Circular micro-pattern (red – dark gray in print version) [40] and images extracted from a real image sequence. (b) Simulated images obtained from the network estimated by applying the algorithm [29] to the real image sequence shown in (a). The origin (green – light gray in print version) and destination (red – dark gray in print version) nodes are superimposed on the microtubule network, at the center and the periphery of the cell, respectively. (c) MIP map and SDIP maps computed from 300 real images. (d) MIP and SDIP maps computed from 300 simulated images.

periment (5 image sequences), the algorithm [46] estimated the three OD pairs that were manually selected for simulation (ground truth). The algorithm which amounts to solving the optimization problem (24.3) presented in Section 24.1.3, was able to identify the main traffic directions.

24.4 Conclusion, future directions, and new challenges

We have described a general framework for traffic flow simulation in video-microscopy at the scale of a single cell. The method, based on the concept of network

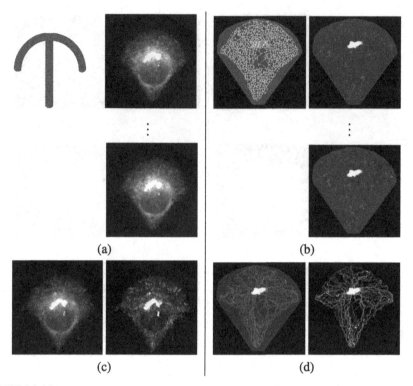

FIGURE 24.14

Comparison between real and simulated images depicting GFP-Rab6 vesicles in crossbow-shaped cells. (a) Crossbow micro-pattern (red – dark gray in print version) [40] and images extracted from a real image sequence. (b) Simulated images obtained from the network estimated by applying the algorithm [29] to the real image sequence shown in (a). The origin (green – light gray in print version) and destination (red – dark gray in print version) nodes are superimposed on the microtubule network, at the center and the periphery of the cell, respectively. (c) MIP map and SDIP maps computed from the real image sequence (a). (d) MIP and SDIP maps computed from 300 simulated images.

tomography mainly used in network communications, has been adapted to cell imaging and microscopy. It requires the extraction of origin-destination nodes automatically estimated or manually labeled by the user, as well as the setting of probabilities related "stop-and-go" events induced by traffic congestion. Background, noise and blur can be potentially added to produce more realistic images. We demonstrated the interest of the method for the modeling of GFP-Rab6 vesicle trafficking and the evaluation of image analysis algorithms. This approach is very flexible and can be adapted to many intracellular traffic simulations.

The limit of this simulation approach is related to the memory size needed to store the routing matrix and very large graphs with several thousands of nodes. In

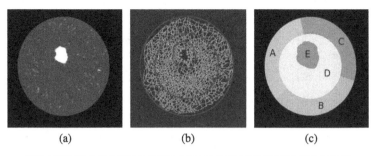

OD pair number	OD pair	OD pair number	OD pair
0	$A \rightarrow B$	10	$C \rightarrow E$
1	$A \rightarrow C$	11	$C \rightarrow D$
2	$A \rightarrow D$	12	$D \rightarrow A$
3	$A \rightarrow E$	13	$D \rightarrow B$
4	$B \rightarrow A$	14	$D \rightarrow C$
5	$B \rightarrow C$	15	$D \rightarrow E$
6	$B \rightarrow D$	16	$E \rightarrow A$
7	$B \rightarrow E$	17	$E \rightarrow B$
8	$C \rightarrow A$	18	$E \rightarrow C$
9	$C \rightarrow B$	19	$E \rightarrow D$

FIGURE 24.15

Simulated image sequences for NT estimation. (Top) Simulated image (a) extracted from a sequence obtained from the network shown in (b). The nodes and edges are labeled in blue – mid gray in print version and white, respectively. The origin (green – light gray in print version) and destination (red – dark gray in print version) are located at the center and at the periphery of the circular-shaped cell, respectively. (c) Manual partition of the cell domain into 5 regions. The central region is compelled to be an origin region. (Bottom) List of 20 possible OD pairs.

addition, additional efforts are required to extend the method dedicated to 2D+time image synthesis, to simulate temporal series of volumes for several minutes or hours as routinely acquired with microscopy set-ups. Finally, deep learning methods, including generative adversarial networks [47], combined to network tomography open new opportunities for data augmentation and data-driven simulation of biomolecule trafficking.

24.5 **Summary**

The characterization of biomolecule dynamics is essential in cell biology since it offers a better understanding of fundamental mechanisms including membrane transport, cell signaling, cell division, and motility. In that context, modeling and simulating trafficking of biomolecules has become helpful for prediction, data assimilation, learning, as well as for bioimage analysis algorithm evaluation. As the biomolecule

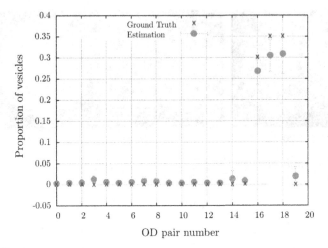

FIGURE 24.16

OD pair estimation on simulated sequences. Averaged proportions of OD pairs (with variance) from five simulated image sequences (see Fig. 24.15).

transport in a cell can be interpreted as a vesicle trafficking depending on the organization of cytoskeleton components and regulated by specific proteins, we explored the potential of network tomography for image sequence simulation. As the network may be very complex, it is estimated from real microscopy images. The user then specifies the origin and destination nodes by labeling few nodes in the graph, and adds event features, depending on prior knowledge in cell biology. The resulting simulation algorithm is data-driven and is able to generate artificial 2D image sequences depicting fluorescently tagged proteins in video-microscopy.

Acknowledgment

The author thanks very warmly Jean Salamero, Thierry Pécot, and Jérôme Boulanger, as well as the members of the Serpico and STED teams, and of the PiCT IBiSA facility, who participated to this project started a few years ago.

This work was supported by Inria Rennes computing grid facilities partly funded by France-BioImaging infrastructure (French National Research Agency - ANR-10-INBS-04-07, "Investments for the future").

References

[1] P. Bressloff, J. Newby, Stochastic models of intracellular transport, Rev. Mod. Phys. 85 (135) (2013) 135–196.

[2] N. Hozé, D. Holcman, Statistical methods for large ensembles of super-resolution stochastic single particle trajectories in cell biology, Annu. Rev. 4 (2017) 189–223.

[3] V. Briane, C. Kervrann, M. Vimond, Statistical analysis of particle trajectories in living cells, Phys. Rev. E 97 (6–1) (2018) 062121.

[4] V. Briane, M. Vimond, C. Kervrann, An overview of diffusion models for intracellular dynamics analysis, Brief. Bioinform. 21 (4) (2020) 1136–1150.

[5] N. Chenouard, I. Smal, F. de Chaumont, M. Maška, I. Sbalzarini, Y. Gong, J. Cardinale, C. Carthel, S. Coraluppi, M. Winter, A. Cohen, W. Godinez, K. Rohr, Y. Kalaidzidis, L. Liang, J. Duncan, H. Shen, Y. Xu, K. Magnusson, J. Jaldén, H. Blau, P. Paul-Gilloteaux, P. Roudot, C. Kervrann, F. Waharte, J. Tinevez, S. Shorte, J. Willemse, K. Celler, G. van Wezel, H. Dan, Y. Tsai, C. Ortiz de Solórzano, J.-C. Olivo-Marin, E. Meijering, Objective comparison of particle tracking methods, Nat. Methods 11 (3) (2014) 281–289.

[6] C. Anderson, G. Georgiou, I. Morrison, G. Stevenson, R. Cherry, Tracking of cell surface receptors by fluorescence digital imaging microscopy using a charged-coupled device camera. Low-density lipoprotein and influenza virus receptor mobility at 4 degrees C, J. Cell Sci. 101 (1992) 415–425.

[7] I. Sbalzarini, P. Koumoutsakos, Feature point tracking and trajectory analysis for video imaging in cell biology, J. Struct. Biol. 151 (2) (2005) 182–195.

[8] V. Racine, A. Hertzog, J. Jouaneau, J. Salamero, C. Kervrann, J. Sibarita, Multiple target tracking of 3D fluorescent objects based on simulated annealing, in: Proc. Int. Symp. Biomedical Imaging (ISBI), Washington, USA, 2006, pp. 1020–1023.

[9] I. Smal, M. Loog, W. Niessen, E. Meijering, Quantitative comparison of spot detection methods in fluorescence microscopy, IEEE Trans. Med. Imaging 29 (2) (2010) 282–301.

[10] C. Kervrann, C. Sorzano, S. Acton, J.-C. Olivo-Marin, M. Unser, A guided tour of selected image processing and analysis methods for fluorescence and electron microscopy, IEEE J. Sel. Top. Signal Process. 10 (1) (2016) 6–30.

[11] N. Chenouard, I. Bloch, J.-C. Olivo-Marin, Multiple hypothesis tracking for cluttered biological image sequences, IEEE Trans. Pattern Anal. Mach. Intell. 35 (11) (2013) 2736–2750.

[12] L. Liang, H. Shen, P. De Camilli, J. Duncan, A novel multiple hypothesis based particle tracking method for clathrin mediated endocytosis analysis using fluorescence microscopy, IEEE Trans. Image Process. 23 (4) (2014) 1844–1857.

[13] I. Smal, E. Meijering, K. Draegestein, N. Galjart, I. Grigoriev, A. Akhmanova, M. van Royen, A. Houtsmuller, W. Niessen, Multiple object tracking in molecular bioimaging by Rao–Blackwellized marginal particle filtering, Med. Image Anal. 12 (6) (2008) 764–777.

[14] K. Jaqaman, D. Loerke, M. Mettlen, H. Kuwata, S. Grinstein, S. Schmid, G. Danuser, Robust single-particle tracking in live-cell time-lapse sequences, Nat. Methods 5 (2008) 695–702.

[15] P. Roudot, L. Ding, K. Jaqaman, C. Kervrann, G. Danuser, Piecewise-stationary motion modeling and iterative smoothing to track heterogeneous motion in dense intracellular environments, IEEE Trans. Image Process. 26 (11) (2017) 5395–5410.

[16] R. Spilger, A. Imle, J. Lee, B. Muller, O. Fackler, R. Bartenschlager Rohr, A recurrent neural network for particle tracking in microscopy images using future information, track hypotheses, and multiple detection, IEEE Trans. Image Process. 29 (2020) 3681–3694.

[17] E. Cascetta, S. Nguyen, A unified framework for estimating or updating origin/destination matrices from traffic counts, Transp. Res. 22 (6) (1988) 437–455.

[18] H. Spiess, A maximum likelihood model for estimating origin–destination matrices, Transp. Res. 21 (5) (1987) 395–412.

[19] Y. Vardi, Network tomography: estimation source-destination traffic intensities from link data, J. Am. Stat. Assoc. 91 (433) (1996) 365–377.

[20] E. Dijkstra, A note on two problems in connexion with graphs, Numer. Math. 1 (1) (1959) 269–271.

[21] M. Lagardère, I. Chamma, E. Bouilhol, M. Nikolski, O. Thoumine, Fluosim: simulator of single molecule dynamics for fluorescence live-cell and super-resolution imaging of membrane proteins, Sci. Rep. 10 (1995) 1–14.

[22] A. Badoual, M. Arizono, A. Denizot, M. Ducros, H. Berry, V. Nägerl, C. Kervrann, Simulation of astrocytic calcium dynamics in lattice light sheet microscopy images, in: Proc. Int. Symp. Biomedical Imaging (ISBI), Nice, France, 2021.

[23] A. Genovesio, T. Liedl, V. Emiliani, W. Parak, M. Coppey-Moisan, J.-C. Olivo-Marin, Multiple particle tracking in 3D+t microscopy: method and application to the tracking of endocytosed quantum dots, IEEE Trans. Image Process. 15 (5) (2006) 1062–1070.

[24] T. Lagache, E. Dauty, D. Holcman, Quantitative analysis of virus and plasmid trafficking in cells, Phys. Rev. E 79 (1) (2009) 011921.

[25] M. Klann, H. Koeppl, M. Reuss, Spatial modeling of vesicle transport and the cytoskeleton: the challenge of hitting the right road, PLoS ONE 7 (1) (2012) e29645.

[26] F. Gibbons, J. Chauwin, M. Despósito, J. José, A dynamical model of kinesin-microtubule motility assays, Biophys. J. 80 (6) (2001) 2515–2526.

[27] F. Nédélec, Computer simulations reveal motor properties generating stable antiparallel microtubule interactions, J. Cell Biol. 158 (6) (2001) 1005–1015.

[28] P. Allain, C. Kervrann, Physical modeling of microtubules network, in: Proc. Int. Workshop New Computational Methods for Inverse Problems, NMCIP, Paris, France, 2014.

[29] C. Steger, An unbiased detector of curvilinear structures, IEEE Trans. Pattern Anal. Mach. Intell. 20 (2) (1998) 113–125.

[30] C. Bergsma, G. Streekstra, A. Smeulders, E. Manders, Velocity estimation of spots in 3D confocal image sequences of living cells, Cytometry 53 (4) (2001) 261–272.

[31] T. Pécot, P. Bouthemy, J. Boulanger, A. Chessel, S. Bardin, J. Salamero, C. Kervrann, Background fluorescence estimation and vesicle segmentation in live cell imaging with conditional random fields, IEEE Trans. Image Process. 24 (2) (2015) 667–680.

[32] J. Yen, Finding the k shortest loopless paths in a network, Manag. Sci. 17 (1971) 712–716.

[33] A. Brown, L. Wang, P. Jung, Stochastic simulation of neurofilament transport in axons: the "stop-and-go" hypothesis, Mol. Biol. Cell 16 (9) (2005) 4243–4255.

[34] J. White, L. Johannes, F. Mallar, A. Girod, G. Stephan, S. Reinsh, P. Keller, B. Tzschaschel, A. Echard, B. Goud, E. Stelzer, Rab6 coordinates a novel Golgi to ER retrograde transport pathway in live cells, J. Cell Biol. 147 (4) (1999) 743–760.

[35] P. Chavrier, B. Goud, The role of ARF and Rab GTPases in membrane transport, Curr. Opin. Cell Biol. 11 (4) (1999) 466–475.

[36] F.J. Opdam, A. Echard, H.J. Croes, J.A. van den Hurk, R.A. van de Vorstenbosch, L.A. Ginsel, B. Goud, J.À. Fransen, The small GTPase Rab6B, a novel Rab6 subfamily member, is cell-type specifically expressed and localised to the Golgi apparatus, J. Cell Sci. 113 (15) (2000) 2725–2735.

[37] A. Echard, F. Opdam, H. de Leeuw, F. Jollivet, P. Savelkoul, W. Hendriks, J. Voorberg, B. Goud, J. Fransen, Alternative splicing of the human Rab6A gene generates two close but functionally different isoforms, Mol. Biol. Cell 11 (2000) 3819–3833.

[38] I. Grigoriev, D. Splinter, N. Keijzer, P. Wulf, J. Demmers, T. Ohtsuka, M. Modesti, I. Maly, F. Grosveld, C. Hoogenraad, A. Akhmanova, Rab6 regulates transport and targeting of exocytotic carriers, Dev. Cell 13 (2) (2007) 305–314.

[39] S. Bardin, S. Miserey-Lenkei, I. Hurbain, D. Garcia-Castillo, G. Raposo, B. Goud, Phenotypic characterisation of RAB6A knockout mouse embryonic fibroblasts, Biol. Cell 107 (12) (2015) 427–439.

[40] M. Théry, V. Racine, A. Pépin, M. Piel, Y. Chen, J.-B. Sibarita, M. Bornens, The extracellular matrix guides the orientation of the cell division axis, Nat. Cell Biol. 7 (10) (2005) 947–953.

[41] K. Schauer, T. Duong, K. Bleakley, S. Bardin, M. Bornens, B. Goud, Probabilistic density maps to study global endomembrane organization, Nat. Methods 7 (7) (2010) 560–566.

[42] K. Schauer, T. Duong, C. Gomes-Santos, B. Goud, Studying intracellular trafficking pathways with probabilistic density maps, Methods Cell Biol. 118 (2013) 325–343.

[43] T. Pécot, L. Zengzhen, J. Boulanger, F. Waharte, J. Salamero, C. Kervrann, A quantitative approach for analyzing the spatio-temporal distribution of 3d intracellular events in fluorescence microscopy, eLife 7 (2018) e32311.

[44] A. Basset, J. Boulanger, J. Salamero, P. Bouthemy, C. Kervrann, Adaptive spot detection with optimal scale selection in fluorescence microscopy images, IEEE Trans. Image Process. 24 (11) (2015) 4512–4527.

[45] T. Pécot, C. Kervrann, J. Salamero, J. Boulanger, Counting-based particle flux estimation for traffic analysis in live cell imaging, IEEE J. Sel. Top. Signal Process. 10 (1) (2016) 203–216.

[46] T. Pécot, C. Kervrann, P. Bouthemy, Minimal paths and probabilistic models for origin-destination traffic estimation in live cell imaging, in: Proc. Int. Symp. Biomedical Imaging (ISBI), Paris, France, 2008, pp. 843–846.

[47] I. Goodfellow, J. Pouget-Abadie, M. Mirza, B. Xu, D. Warde-Farley, S. Ozair, A. Courville, Y. Bengio, Generative adversarial networks, in: Proc. of Int. Conf. Neural Information Processing Systems (NIPS), Montreal, Canada, 2014, pp. 2672–2680.

Further reading

[48] Serpico Website, https://team.inria.fr/serpico/publications/.

[49] J. Boulanger, Estimation non-paramétrique et contributions à l'analyse de séquences d'images. Modélisation, simulation et estimation du trafic intra-cellulaire dans des séquences de vidéo-microscopie, Thèse de l'université de Rennes 1, Mention Traitement du Signal et des Télécommunications, 2007 (in French).

[50] T. Pécot, Modélisation et estimation du trafic intracellulaire par tomographie de réseaux et microscopie de fluorescence, Thèse de l'université de Rennes 1, Mention Traitement du Signal et des Télécommunications, 2010 (in French).

Perspectives

Validation and evaluation metrics for medical and biomedical image synthesis

25

Tereza Nečasová[a], **Ninon Burgos**[b], **and David Svoboda**[a]

[a]*CBIA, Faculty of Informatics, Masaryk University, Brno, Czech Republic*
[b]*Sorbonne Université, Institut du Cerveau - Paris Brain Institute - ICM, CNRS, Inria, Inserm, AP-HP, Hôpital de la Pitié-Salpêtrière, Paris, France*

25.1 Introduction

Regardless of the application domain, each newly introduced method requires a proper validation procedure. When designing a segmentation algorithm, for example, one is excepted to provide some tests showing how the algorithm performs and whether the results are better compared with state of the art methods. In the field of image synthesis, one can legitimately ask about the explained variability in the synthetic data, whether the generated data look realistic, and whether they are sufficiently similar to their real counterpart. However, no standard pipeline currently exists for synthetic image quality assessment (see Fig. 25.1). Some authors evaluate their computer-generated data with the statement of having visually similar results, some attempt to measure the similarity using expert's assessment or various techniques. Without any broader comparison of synthesized data, there is no warranty regarding their quality. The quality assessment of the synthesized images should be an integral part of the image synthesis process. The user of the proposed synthetic image data should be assured about their plausibility before using them in further steps.

This chapter includes an overview of the validation methods applied in the field of biomedical and medical image synthesis. Three strategies can be considered, and possibly combined, when evaluating the quality of generators producing synthetic images. In the first case, the data are validated using the strength of **expert knowledge** to support the plausibility of the generated images. The second class is focused on synthetic images **paired** with their real counterparts. The third class of evaluation is done by comparing the characteristics of the **whole dataset** of real images against the characteristics in the whole dataset of synthetic images. Although the assessment in the first class can be further evaluated, it is rather more qualitative than quantitative compared with the two other classes. The main approaches of each strategy will be described in the following subsections.

Biomedical Image Synthesis and Simulation. https://doi.org/10.1016/B978-0-12-824349-7.00032-3

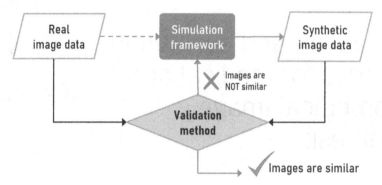

FIGURE 25.1

Processes connected with the validation of synthetic data. Synthetic images obtained from the simulation framework should be compared with real images with a clear conclusion given by a validation method (see the yellow box – light gray box in print version) whether they are sufficiently similar or not.

25.2 Expert knowledge

When developing a new framework responsible for image synthesis where the outputs are expected to resemble the real images, the most expected approach is to report the visual inspection of the synthetic data.

25.2.1 Rating based on the visual plausibility of synthetic data

A first task given to the experts can be to rate the plausibility of the synthetic data. For example, the sensitivity and specificity of a classification task is utilized when validating a framework for simulation of bright-field microscopy images depicting pap smear specimens [1]. The sensitivity relates to the ability of accurate detection of real images as being real and the specificity to the ability of accurate detection of synthetic images as synthetic. These measures are computed from the number of true positives/real images (TP), true negatives/synthetic images (TN), false positives (FP), and false negative cases (FN) as:

$$\text{sensitivity} = \frac{TP}{TP + FN}, \tag{25.1}$$

$$\text{specificity} = \frac{TN}{FP + TN}. \tag{25.2}$$

Both values range from 0 to 1 (= *ideal*). In this work, six experts from different research fields were asked to recognize the origin of a set of real and synthetic images. The experts were showed a tightly cropped, randomly selected, view of the real and synthetic scenes projected through lightly frosted glass, to account for limitations of existing display devices. They were showed only for two seconds to imitate the real conditions for assessment. The results of the experts' classification is reviewed and compared to a random classification in Table 25.1.

Table 25.1 Results of the experts' evaluation in [1]. The classifiers considered included six experts and a random classifier; TP is the number of correctly classified real images – true positives, TN is true negatives – correctly classified synthetic images, FP is false positives, and FN is false negative cases.

Classifier	TP	FP	TN	FN	Sensitivity	Specificity
Expert 1	35	29	37	17	0.67	0.56
Expert 2	39	29	29	21	0.65	0.50
Expert 3	50	16	38	14	0.78	0.70
Expert 4	49	20	36	13	0.79	0.64
Expert 5	51	17	39	11	0.82	0.70
Expert 6	58	32	21	7	0.89	0.40
Random	37	31	24	26	0.54	0.48

A similar validation approach can be found in [2], where the experts were also asked to recognize real or synthetic images resulting from a generator of magnetic resonance imaging (MRI) brain slices. They also compute TP, TN, FP, FN to derive accuracy, precision, sensitivity, and F1-score.

In [3], the synthetic whole slide histological images accompanied by the reference images are evaluated by observing the image data at different levels of magnification. The goal is to discover in which level of detail (magnification) the synthetic image is not looking realistic anymore. The measurement of realism of synthetic images is evaluated as follows:

1. open a synthetic image in a software slide viewer on a standard computer screen;
2. decrease the magnification until it "feels realistic";
3. slowly increase the magnification until it "feels wrong";
4. the current magnification is then written down as the highest realistic magnification for the current image.

The highest realistic magnification is regarded as the score that evaluates the quality of the image simulation. In order the keep some biological correctness, only experts were asked to assess the data plausibility.

The five-point Likert scale (*very poor / poor / satisfactory / good / very good*) has been used to assess the quality of synthetic tissue microscopy images generated from pre-segmented haematoxylin and eosin images of brain tumors [4]. Here, the expert histopathologists were asked to classify the images according to the following three criteria:

1. similarity to real-world tissue microscopy images,
2. reproducibility of nuclei morphometry, and
3. reproducibility in nuclei texture.

However, the particular results of the expert have not been reported.

The Likert scale has also been applied in [5], where 21 experts in ultrasound were asked to rank (*fake, rather fake, cannot decide, rather real, real*) the realism of the simulated ultrasound scans. The scans were randomly presented to the experts without giving them any hint whether observing the real or simulated one. The time spent during the analysis of each particular image was also taken into account when assessing the experts' reliability.

The objective of the work of Gong et al. [6] was to reduce gadolinium dose in contrast-enhanced brain MRI. Two neuro-radiologists were asked to assess the quality of the post-contrast MR images (low-dose, synthesized full-dose and true full-dose). They rated the general image quality, suppression of aliasing/motion artifacts and degree of enhancement compared against pre-contrast MR images using a five-point Likert scale ranging from 1 (poor) to 5 (excellent).

In [7], a model of healthy and cancerous colonic crypt micro-environment was proposed and successfully implemented to show the ability to control cancer grade, cellularity, cell overlap ratio, and image resolution. Here, the histopathologists were asked to grade the quality of synthesis on a scale from 1 to 5 (5 = *very realistic*). The averages of the grades for a combination of four types of cell objects, architecture and number of crypts, two different magnifications, and four differentiation levels are reported in Table 25.2.

Table 25.2 Results of the experts' evaluation in [7]. The values report the average evaluation of the appearance of synthetic images by three pathologists. Healthy (H), well differentiated (WD), moderately differentiated (MD), and poorly differentiated (PD) images were evaluated at magnifications 20× and 40×. (*1 = not realistic at all, 5 = very realistic, "–" means feature is not relevant.*)

	H 40×	H 20×	WD 40×	WD 20×	MD 40×	MD 20×	PD 40×	PD 20×
Architecture	5	5	5	4	4	4	5	5
Crypt shape	5	5	5	5	5	5	4.5	4.5
Lumen	5	5	5	5	5	5	–	–
Goblet cells	4	4	–	–	–	–	–	–
Epithelial cells	4	4	4	4	4	4	4	4
Stromal cells	3	3	3	3	3	3	3	4

When comparing the real and synthetic (also called as *fake*) images, one can also use a Visual Turing Test (VTT) [8]. This test is a procedure during which a stochastic sequence of binary questions is generated and given to some respondents. When applied in the field of medical image analysis, the experts are asked to distinguish between the real and synthetic images in a sequence.

VTT was applied for example in [9] for the validation of generated brain MR images. In another work [10], the authors tested the quality of synthesized lung nodules for X-ray computed tomography (CT) image augmentation potentially used for object detection. Chuquicusma et al. [11] performed VTT on images of malignant and benign lung nodules for a computer-aided diagnosis system generated by a deep convolutional generative adversarial network (DC-GAN). In the context of anomaly detection, Schlegl et al. [12] used the VTT to quantify the quality of the generated normal images.

25.2.2 Rating based on the usability of synthetic data

Experts have been asked to not only rate the plausibility of synthetic data but also their usability.

A simulation framework called SIMCEP [13] forms a cornerstone in image synthesis dedicated to fluorescence microscopy. To validate the generated images, mediated experts were asked to use four different image processing tools developed for automated image cytometry (specifically for cell enumeration). Five sets of ten images, each containing 1000 cells and different levels of overlap were analyzed with each out of four tools developed by independent research groups and the results were compared in a plot. The tools gave similar results supporting the expectation that for worse conditions such as overlapping cells, the number of enumerated cells will be lower.

In order to perform a clinical assessment of a method using a generative adversarial network (GAN) to synthesize standard-dose PET images from low-dose ones [14], the experts were asked to perform two tasks. First, they assigned a score (1–5) for each synthesized image, where range 1–3 was considered to be low quality and 4–5 high quality. Second, the experts gave the amyloid status (positive vs. negative) for each image, the amyloid status being a biomarker used in the differential diagnosis of dementia. The status defined on the standard-dose ground truths and the synthesized images were compared. The consistency between the amyloid status showed whether the method was able to maintain the pathological features.

As stated in [15], several works try to convince the readers about correlation of proposed metrics with human evaluation [16,17]. However, they also state that expert evaluation can be biased towards the visual quality of synthesized images and neglect the overall distributional characteristics, which are important for unsupervised learning.

25.3 Pairwise comparison

In medical image synthesis, a majority of approaches require paired images in their training process, for example when learning to synthesize CT from MR images [18–22], generate MR images of a certain sequence from MR images of another sequence [23–25], denoise low-dose CT images [26,27], or perform super-resolution [28]. Cross-modality synthesis is also present in microscopy imaging, where the attempt to reduce time-consuming and laborious tissue preparation results in synthesizing fluorescence images from the bright-field pairs [29]. A consequence of the need for paired images during training is that both reference and synthetic images are also often available for evaluation. The quality of the pairwise estimates is typically controlled by measuring the difference to the so called *reference image* (also known as *ground truth* or *annotation*) in the pair. The term reference image is also a reason why the pairwise comparison is sometimes called a *full reference* image quality assessment.

25.3.1 Generic pairwise performance measures

The measures the most frequently used to evaluate the synthesis accuracy by comparing real and synthetic images in a pairwise manner are listed below.

25.3.1.1 Mean absolute error

One of the most common measures is the mean absolute error (MAE) [18–22,30]. It is defined as the absolute difference between intensities in pixels of the simulated and ground-truth image,

$$MAE = \frac{\sum_{i=1}^{n} |y_i - x_i|}{n}, \tag{25.3}$$

where x_i and y_i are the intensity values of the ith pixel/voxel of the real and synthesized image, respectively, and n is the number of pixel/voxel pairs.

In the context of PET attenuation correction [18] or MR-only radiotherapy treatment planning [19], the MAE is often chosen as error metric as it is well suited when comparing CT images due to their quantitative nature.

25.3.1.2 Peak signal-to-noise ratio

The peak signal-to-noise ratio (PSNR) is a measure derived from the mean squared error (MSE),

$$MSE = \frac{\sum_{i=1}^{n} (y_i - x_i)^2}{n}, \tag{25.4}$$

with the same notations as for the MAE: x_i and y_i are the intensity values of the ith pixel/voxel of the real and synthesized image, respectively, and n is the number of pixel/voxel pairs.

PSNR compares the maximum of the intensity in the image with the error between the estimated and the ground-truth image given by the MSE,

$$PSNR = 10 \log_{10} \left(\frac{MAX^2}{MSE} \right), \tag{25.5}$$

where MAX is the maximum possible intensity of the image. Higher values of PSNR relate to better simulation. The application of PSNR to validate the plausibility of synthetic images is apparent in many papers [21,22,24–30].

25.3.1.3 Structural similarity

Even though they are simple to compute, the ability of the MAE, MSE, and PSNR measures to perceive visual quality is limited [31]. Exploiting known characteristics of the human visual system, Wang et al. [31] proposed the structural similarity (SSIM), which compares local patterns of pixel intensities that have been normalized for luminance and contrast. SSIM has been widely adopted by the image synthesis community [24,25,27–29].

SSIM is computed as a function of three components, luminance, contrast and structure, as follows:

$$SSIM(x, y) = \frac{(2\mu_x\mu_y + C_1)(2\sigma_{xy} + C_2)}{(\mu_x^2 + \mu_y^2 + C_1)(\sigma_x^2 + \sigma_y^2 + C_2)}, \tag{25.6}$$

where x is the simulated image, y is the ground-truth image, μ_i is the mean value of image i, σ_i is the variance of image i, σ_{xy} is the covariance of images x and y. The constants C_j are included to avoid instability when $\mu_x^2 + \mu_y^2$, respectively $\sigma_x^2 + \sigma_y^2$, is very close to zero. Therefore, they are set to $C_j = (K_j \cdot L)^2$, where L is the dynamic range of the pixel values (e.g., 255 for 8-bit grayscale images), and $K \ll 1$ is a small constant. The original values of K_j were set to $K_1 = 0.01$ and $K_2 = 0.03$ [31]. The higher the value of SSIM, the better the quality of the synthesized image.

In [32], the relationship between SSIM and PSNR was investigated with the conclusion that the values of the PSNR can be predicted from the SSIM and vice versa. Additionally, the PSNR and SSIM mainly differ in the sensitivity to image degradations. Similar conclusions can be found in [33], where the association between SSIM and MSE was shown.

In their work, Mason et al. [34] measured the correlations between ten pairwise metrics and the subjective score of five radiologists when assessing the quality of MR images. They showed that metrics such as SSIM and PSNR are potentially not ideal surrogate measures of MR image quality as determined by radiologist evaluation.

At this point, the reader can seriously wonder whether it is manageable to perform a proper data validation with all the previously-described metrics, together with all those that will be introduced in the following text. Fortunately, it is not needed. The above mentioned metrics (MAE, PSNR, SSIM) are the most common distance metrics and are accepted as a de facto standard among the pair-wise metrics. Therefore, if you plan to generate some dataset that form pairs (e.g., MRI–CT), you will likely be expected to evaluate at least one of these. All the metrics that come in the following paragraphs are not less important but rather mostly proposed/derived for specific purposes, so their usage is somewhat limited.

25.3.2 Application-specific pairwise performance measures

25.3.2.1 Pseudo-healthy image synthesis

To detect anomalies and better understand changes induced by diseases, Xia et al. [35] proposed to create subject-specific pseudo-healthy images from pathological ones using a CycleGAN. They assessed the quality of the image synthesis process using generic metrics, but they also designed new metrics tailored to their application: the so called *healthiness*, *identity*, and *deformation correction* metrics.

25.3.2.1.1 Healthiness

The healthiness (h) expresses a fraction of (unwanted) pathology areas present in pseudo-healthy images and can be computed as

$$h = 1 - \frac{\mathbb{E}_{x_p \sim \mathcal{P}}[N(f_p(G(x_p)))]}{\mathbb{E}_{m_p \sim \mathcal{P}_m}[N(f_p(x_p))]}, \tag{25.7}$$

where x_p is the pathological image, f_p the function providing a segmentation of pathological regions, $G(\cdot)$ the CycleGAN deriving the pseudo-healthy image from the pathological image, m_p the ground-truth mask of pathological regions, and $N(\cdot)$ the number of pixels labeled as pathological by f_p. One should pay attention that the *healthiness* can be strongly influenced by the quality of segmentation function f_p.

25.3.2.1.2 Identity

To measure the CycleGAN ability to preserve the subject identity (iD), one can measure the structural similarity of the original real pathology image and the derived pseudo-healthy image outside the pathological regions as

$$iD = \text{MS-SSIM}[(1 - m_p) \odot G(x_p), (1 - m_p) \odot x_p], \tag{25.8}$$

where MS-SSIM stands for multiscale structural similarity [36], x_p is a pathological image, m_p is its corresponding pathology mask, $G(\cdot)$ is the generator of pseudo-healthy images, and $\odot$ is the pixel-wise multiplication.

25.3.2.1.3 Deformation correction

In the case where brain tissue has recovered after some surgery or noninvasive therapy, there may be apparent structural changes. The deformation correction measure aims to assess whether such deformations have taken place. To avoid brightness influence, the images are first converted into edge maps. The classifier, that was trained over the set of edge maps of healthy images, is used to judge whether the image of treated brain contains some deformations. The output of such classifier is a continuous number between 0 and 1 [35].

In this section, the validation methods used for pairs of images were reported. Note that the frameworks for synthesis of paired data are often based on algorithms using a loss function. The loss function should differ from the validation method since we want to avoid overfitting.

25.4 **Dataset comparison**

Some synthetic data are the result of frameworks generating a whole set of images according to the given input parameters. A set of generated images resulting from these tools should be comparable with the set of real images corresponding to the particular application of the synthesized data.

If we want to compare the images not only in the corresponding pixels but also in some quantitative characteristics, the use of image descriptors is suggested. Those image descriptors can represent characteristics such as color, shape, texture or some features from the frequency domain. A survey of image feature descriptors was published in [37]. The values of a particular hidden layer of a neural network can also be considered as a descriptor (e.g., for the computation of the Fréchet Inception Distance – discussed further in Section 25.4.1.7). The most commonly derived descriptors used in validation methods of synthetic images are:

- **Haralick texture descriptors**
  Haralick descriptors [38] represent a set of texture descriptors derived from so called gray level co-occurrence matrix. In [39], contrast, correlation, homogeneity, and maximal correlation coefficient are reported to show the similarity between the real and synthetic image data. Haralick descriptors are an input parameter to affinity propagation in [7].
- **Central moments**
  A number of central moments, e.g., variance, skewness, and kurtosis, can be calculated over pixel intensities. They were used, for instance, in [40,41,1].
- **Subcellular location features**
  This respectably extensive pack of descriptors (see [42]) includes various types of patterns, such as texture features, Zernike moment features, object skeleton features and many others. In [43], the contribution of features on the classification of multiple cell objects was compared.
- **Local binary pattern**
  Local binary pattern (LBP) [44] is a texture operator which assigns to each pixel of an image a binary 8-bit number by thresholding its eight neighbors. LBP has been applied to ultrasound images to validate the method described in [45].
- **Mean square displacement**
  The mean square displacement (MSD) [46] descriptor is used for the validation of tracking objects. Svoboda et al. [39] compared MSD using a histogram, displacement profiles and ensemble-average MSD curves.
- **Spectral and spatial sharpness**
  In [47], the spectral and spatial sharpness (see [48]) accompanied the standard SSIM and PSNR metrics to validate the quality of super-resolved MR images.

The above-mentioned list of descriptors is not limited. One can easily derive a data-specific descriptor that fits particular needs. For example, in the field of live cell analysis, the derived features such as the number of tracks, the average number of time points in tracks, or the average speed of particles may help effectively compare the time-lapse image sequences [49].

One should keep in mind that image descriptors need not be necessarily used for the comparison of synthetic and real datasets. In case one is missing the real data, it is common to analyze solely the synthetic data and study the behavior of the measured characteristics. This approach is also known as *no reference* image quality assessment.

The image descriptors are commonly used as input parameters to the simulation frameworks (number of elements/objects, shape, speed of motion, etc.) or are an integral part of loss functions in GANs or variational autoencoders. One should pay attention that the use of image descriptors as the inputs for the simulation together with the subsequent validation of the same features over the generated data is not only meaningful but may be even misleading. The results would be biased and therefore worthless.

Below, the reader can find the detailed explanation of the most prominent methods that utilize image descriptors and that are relevant to the comparison of sets of biomedical images.

25.4.1 Measures based on a comparison of probability distributions
25.4.1.1 Kolmogorov–Smirnov test

The Kolmogorov–Smirnov test (K–S test) [50] is used when comparing the empirical distribution of a quantitative variable with a particular theoretical distribution (e.g., the normal distribution). The K–S test can be used as well when comparing two samples and their empirical distributions (not necessarily lying under certain model distributions) [51,39].

The tested null hypothesis is that the cumulative distribution functions are the same for both samples $A = \{a_i | i = 1, \ldots, n_A; a_i \in \mathbb{R}\}$ and $B = \{b_i | i = 1, \ldots, n_B; b_i \in \mathbb{R}\}$. The empirical cumulative distribution for sample A is defined as $F_A(x) = \frac{\#\{a \in A | a \le x\}}{n_A}$ and in the same manner for sample B. In our case, A can stand for a sample of real data and B for a sample of synthetic data. The test statistic for the two samples is based on the largest distance (see Fig. 25.2) between the two empirical distribution functions, which is

$$KS(A, B) = \sup_{x \in \mathbb{R}} |F_A(x) - F_B(x)|. \qquad (25.9)$$

The value of the Kolmogorov–Smirnov statistic is then compared to the critical value and the null hypothesis is rejected if $KS(A, B) > \sqrt{\frac{1}{n_A} + \frac{1}{n_B}} \kappa_\alpha$, where κ_α is chosen according to the level of significance α. Note that the Kolmogorov–Smirnov test is a non-parametric technique, which means it has no assumption put on the given data.

25.4.1.2 Kullback–Leibler divergence

The Kullback–Leibler (K–L) divergence, sometimes called *relative entropy* [52], belongs to the family of probability measures. It is a measure of the dissimilarity

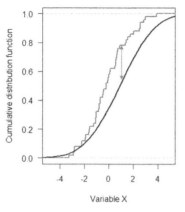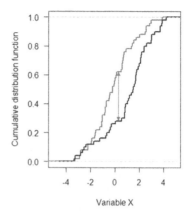

FIGURE 25.2

The distance between two distribution functions for an equation of Kolmogorov–Smirnov test. In the one-sample case (left) the distance is measured between the specific theoretical cumulative distribution (black) and the empirical distribution (red – dark gray in print version). For the two-sample case (right) the distance is computed between the two empirical distribution functions.

between two random quantities, in particular between two probability measures, as the Kolmogorov–Smirnov distance [53].

The K–L divergence measures the inefficiency of assuming that a given distribution is $P_B(x)$ when the true distribution is $P_A(x)$. It is a kind of Bregman divergence and it is defined for discrete samples as

$$D_{KL}(A \parallel B) = \sum_{x \in X} P_A(x) \log \frac{P_A(x)}{P_B(x)}, \qquad (25.10)$$

where $P_A(x)$ and $P_B(x)$ are two probability distributions [54].

Compared with statistical distances, the statistical divergence is not symmetric, i.e., it is not a metric. The K–L divergence returns the value of divergence of two probability distributions. It reveals 0 if and only if $P_A(x) = P_B(x)$ otherwise it is non-negative.

This measure was applied and visualized using boxplots for comparison of synthetic and real data of microscopy nuclei images in [4].

25.4.1.3 Kernel maximum mean discrepancy

Maximum mean discrepancy (MMD) [55] is another statistic measuring the difference between two probability distributions on the basis of samples drawn from each of them. More specifically, the aim is to find smooth functions resembling the sample values.

The test statistic is the difference between the mean function values in terms of kernel functions,

$$MMD^2(\mathbb{P}_r, \mathbb{P}_q) = \mathbb{E}_{\substack{x_r, x_r' \sim \mathbb{P}_r \\ x_q, x_q' \sim \mathbb{P}_q}} \left[k(x_r, x_r') - 2k(x_r, x_q) + k(x_q, x_q') \right], \qquad (25.11)$$

where $\mathbb{P}_r$ and $\mathbb{P}_q$ are the probability distributions for some fixed kernel function k, where r and r' are independent variables with distribution $\mathbb{P}_r$; q and q' are independent variables with distribution $\mathbb{P}_q$. The biased empirical estimate of MMD is given by substitution of empirical estimates for expected values,

$$MMD[R, S] = \left[\frac{1}{m^2} \sum_{i,j=1}^{m} k(x_i, x_j) - \frac{2}{mn} \sum_{i,j=1}^{m,n} k(x_i, y_j) + \frac{1}{n^2} \sum_{i,j=1}^{n} k(y_i, y_j) \right]^{\frac{1}{2}},$$
$$(25.12)$$

where R and S ($|R| = m$, $|S| = n$) are two samples to be compared.

Large differences indicate that samples are from different distributions, whereas small MMD suggests that the distributions are identical. In their empirical study, Xu et al. [15] showed that MMD satisfies most of the desirable properties, provided that the distances between samples are computed in a suitable feature space. To reach this conclusion, they designed a score that includes dropping and collapsing modes and is able to detect overfitting.

MMD was applied for quality assessment of generated data, for example, in [56] and [57].

25.4.1.4 Mutual information

Mutual information (MI) is related to joint entropy as introduced simultaneously by Viola [58] and Maes [59].

Given the images I and J, the joint entropy is defined as

$$H(I, J) = -\sum_{a,b} p_{IJ}(a, b) \log p_{IJ}(a, b), \qquad (25.13)$$

where p_{IJ} is the joint probability distribution of pixel intensities associated with images I and J. The joint entropy is minimized when the images I and J are similar. The individual (marginal) entropy for I is

$$H(I) = -\sum_{a} p_I(a) \log p_I(a), \qquad (25.14)$$

and for J in the same manner. MI is then given by

$$MI = H(I) + H(J) - H(I, J). \qquad (25.15)$$

In [30], mutual information was utilized to measure the similarity between original MR image and synthesized CT image resulting from a CycleGAN [60], when the paired reference image was not available.

25.4.1.5 Regional mutual information

Regional mutual information (RMI) was introduced by [61]. Compared with mutual information, the RMI takes into account information from the neighborhood of each pixel.

RMI is computed for two images I and J (each with corresponding pixels $[I_{ij}, J_{ij}]$) in the following manner:

1. For each of the pixels $[i, j]$, a vector $\boldsymbol{v}_{ij}$ is created with the values coming from the two co-occurrence matrices [38] from a neighborhood of radius r. The vector $\boldsymbol{v}_{ij}$ is then considered as a point p_k in a d-dimensional space where $d = (2r+1)^2$. Given the radius r and $m \times n$ images, there is a distribution of $N = (m - 2r)(n - 2r)$ points represented by a $d \times N$ matrix $P = [p_1, \ldots, p_N]$.
2. The points are consequently centered by the mean: $P_0 = P - \frac{1}{N} \sum_k^N p_k$.
3. The covariance of the points is then computed as $C = \frac{1}{N} P_0 P_0^T$.
4. The joint entropy $H_g(C)$ is estimated.
5. The marginal entropies $H_g(C_I)$ and $H_g(C_J)$ are estimated where C_I is a matrix in the top left of C and C_J in the bottom right, both of size $\frac{d}{2} \times \frac{d}{2}$.
6. Finally, the RMI is calculated as

$$RMI = H_g(C_I) + H_g(C_J) + H_g(C). \tag{25.16}$$

As it is also mentioned in [61], the corresponding pixels in the edges of the image can be handled in a number of ways.

In [4], the authors used RMI pair-wise, not only for the real and synthetic counterparts, but also for each pair of real-synthetic images, and also for pairs of real images to express the measure of "alikeness." For the visualization of the results, the boxplots were used for RMI values between real images next to boxplot of RMI between real and synthetic images.

25.4.1.6 Inception score

The inception score (IS) [16] is a measure for objective evaluation of trained GANs which was designed to correlate very well with subjective human judgment.

A deep convolutional network model (Google Inception v3 network [62]), pretrained on the large scale ImageNet dataset [63], is used to classify the generated images from the proposed trained model G. The probabilities of images belonging to particular classes are computed and used for the evaluation of IS. The IS for a trained model G is computed as

$$IS(G) = \exp\left(\mathbb{E}_{X \sim p_g} KL(p(y|X) \parallel p(y))\right), \tag{25.17}$$

where $X \sim p_g$ means that an image X is sampled from p_g, $p(y|X)$ is the conditional label distribution (class label y conditional on image X), and $p(y) = \int_X p(y|X) p_g(X)$ is the marginal class distribution. KL is the K–L divergence (as defined in Section 25.4.1.2), $\mathbb{E}$ is an expected value, which is further exponentiated for an easier comparison.

Two main properties are covered in IS: image quality (similarity of an image to a specific object) and image diversity (whether the dataset contains a wide range of generated objects). The distribution should have a low entropy for meaningful objects. Also, the marginal integral $\int p(y|X = G(z))dz$ should have high entropy to provide varied images by the generator. The lowest value of IS is 1, the highest value is the number of classes defined in the pre-trained model. The calculation of IS assumes a large enough number of samples (i.e., 50000 images) to be able measure the diversity.

As a validation method, IS was applied in [64] for two proposed models designed to generate multi-parameter MRI data. IS was also evaluated in [2] to show the quality of synthesized MRI brain slices using GAN.

25.4.1.7 Fréchet distance and Fréchet inception distance

The Fréchet distance [65] is a measure of distance between curves that takes into account the location and ordering of the points along the curves. It is well known for its simile to walking a dog on a leash, who is crossing the curved path. A discrete variant of this measure, which can be evaluated over any feature vectors, exists [66]. However, the most popular application in the field of image synthesis is the use of Inception feature vectors from Inception v3 model (called as the Fréchet inception distance (FID)), performed for example in [56,67]. It was applied also on SonoNet in [68] as Fréchet SonoNet distance.

FID summarizes the distance between the Inception feature vectors for real and generated images in the same domain. More specifically, the pre-trained classification model is applied to both the real and generated images and the Inception feature vectors from the hidden layer are extracted, thus the final classification probabilities are not used. It was proposed in [69] as an improvement over the existing IS (described in Section 25.4.1.6), which also uses the Inception feature vectors v3 for evaluating the quality of generated images by GAN models. They showed in the paper that FID is more consistent with the noise level than IS. FID is a distance while IS is a score with a maximum value.

The definition of FID is given by

$$d^2 = ||\mu_1 - \mu_2||^2 + Tr(C_1 + C_2 - 2 * \sqrt{C_1 * C_2}), \qquad (25.18)$$

where μ_1 and μ_2 refer to the feature-wise mean of the real and generated images, where each element is the mean feature observed across the images; C_1 and C_2 are the covariance matrices for the real and generated feature vectors; Tr is a trace – a linear algebra operation – the sum of the elements on a diagonal of the square matrix.

The best value of FID is 0 indicating that the two groups of images are identical, thus low FID values mean that the two groups of images are similar (or they have similar statistics).

25.4.2 Measures based on clustering and classification

25.4.2.1 Affinity propagation

Affinity propagation (AP) [70] is a method of clustering data. The data points create a network of nodes, where each data point is a potential exemplar. The data points given to the input of this procedure are iteratively examined according to the measure of similarity (e.g., squared error in Euclidean distance) until a good set of exemplars and corresponding clusters emerges.

Initially, the input matrix s is computed over all combinations and each "similarity" is set to some optimization criterion, for example, a negative squared error

$$s(i, k) = -\|x_i - x_k\|^2 \tag{25.19}$$

for points x_i and x_k. The values of elements belonging to the diagonal ($s(i, i)$) are able to prefer some of the points to be an exemplar.

Two types of "messages" are evaluated in each step for two points: the "responsibility" message $r(i, k)$ sent from point i to point k and the "availability" $a(i, k)$ sent from point k to point i. The first message, "responsibility,"

$$r(i, k) \leftarrow s(i, k) - \max_{k' \neq k}\{a(i, k') + s(i, k')\} \tag{25.20}$$

reflects the actual evidence for how well-suited point k is to serve as the exemplar for point i (regarding the potential exemplars of point i). The second message, "availability,"

$$a(i, k) \leftarrow \min\left\{0, r(k, k) + \sum_{i' \notin \{i,k\}} \max\{0, r(i', k)\}\right\} \tag{25.21}$$

reflects the accumulated evidence for how appropriate it would be for point i to choose point k as its exemplar (regarding the support from other points that point k should be an exemplar). These are initially set to zeros.

The "self-availability" $a(k, k)$ is updated in each step as

$$a(k, k) \leftarrow \sum_{i' \neq k} \max\{0, r(i', k)\}. \tag{25.22}$$

The messages are sent until either the cluster boundaries remain unchanged over a number of iterations, or after some predetermined number of iterations. The advantages of AP are that no specific number of clusters has to be predefined.

In [7], affinity propagation was applied to 13 Haralick texture features of 20 images of real nuclei to get different phenotypes of images. These were compared to the phenotypes clustered on synthetic images. The frequencies of phenotypes in both groups were compared using histograms.

25.4.2.2 Classification

We should keep in mind that the aim of validation methods is not to find the differences between the synthetic and real data, but to explore the similarity of the synthetic data compared with the real data. One could suggest that a classification task distinguishing real and synthetic data is a suitable solution. However, the bad result of any classifier does not prove that the data are not similar. For example, in Fig. 25.3, it is not possible to distinguish the two classes of points (blue and yellow) with any discrimination function, but at first sight one can see that the groups are not homogeneous. Furthermore, the result of a classification could be confused with a bad choice of classifier.

Some works employed classification not for differentiation of real versus synthetic dataset, but for verification that the synthetic images will be classified to the appropriate subcategories as well as real data. For instance, in [43] the synthetic images for ten classes of organelles were generated. The support vector machine classification was applied to both real and synthetic data, and results (such as confusion matrix) were reported for comparison. Similarly, in [71] the k-nearest neighbor to classify bacteria classes based on their shape was performed.

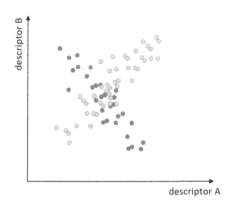

FIGURE 25.3

A classification problem. It is not possible to distinguish the two groups of points (blue and yellow – dark gray and light gray in print version) with any discriminator without transformation. However, at first sight, one can see that the groups are not homogeneous.

25.4.3 Measures based on a visualization of transformed data

25.4.3.1 Histogram

A histogram is a widely used plot for visualization of absolute or relative frequencies of a categorized quantitative variable. The quantitative variable (e.g., an image descriptor) determines the axis x with a specific binning (categorization), and the axis

y counts the frequency – relative (f) or absolute ($f*$) – in the bins,

$$f(j) = \frac{n_j/n}{d_j}, \quad f^*(j) = \frac{n_j}{d_j}, \tag{25.23}$$

where n is the total number of observations, n_j is the number of observations for a particular category j, and d_j is the width of this category. The shape of the histogram should approximate the probability density function. However, the approximation is very sensitive to the choice of the number of bins.

A quality assessment of the synthesized images at the image descriptor level was used in [39], where the distributions of five Haralick texture descriptors [38] were compared using histograms and the Kolmogorov–Smirnov test. In [7], histograms were used to compare the length of minor axis and ratio between minor and major axes of healthy crypts in colon tissue in real and synthetic images. The Gamma distribution of these two measures was fitted to the real data and subsequently plotted into both histograms.

25.4.3.2 Quantile–quantile plot

The quantile–quantile (Q–Q) plot [72] is designed for the visualization of distribution comparisons. The quantiles of two quantitative variables are plotted in the x–y figure against each other (see Fig. 25.4). The quantile matches (and therefore identical distribution) reveals if the points lie along the straight line with the slope of 1. Distant points from this line indicate deviation from the same distribution. The method is non-parametric with no assumption put on the input data. In case of image descriptors, the Q–Q plot can help compare the distribution of both groups of data in each descriptor separately, i.e., univariately [51,1,73,43].

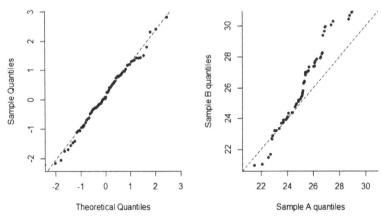

FIGURE 25.4

Example of a Q–Q plot in case of one-sample comparison (left) and two-sample comparison (right). The optimal match of distributions is achieved when the points lie on the dashed line.

25.4.3.3 Fourier ring correlation

The Fourier ring correlation (FRC) [74] is a spatial frequency correlation function that measures the degree of correlation of two images at different spatial frequencies. The images are initially transformed to the frequency domain. Afterwards, the normalized average correlation is computed for N_r concentric rings of increasing radius, which corresponds to increasing spatial frequencies centered around the $(0, 0)$ spatial frequency.

FRC for images I and J (which are transformed to the frequency domain) is computed as

$$FRC(R) = \frac{\sum_{i \in R} I(\mathbf{r}_i) \cdot J(\mathbf{r}_i)^*}{\sqrt{(\sum_{i \in R} |I(\mathbf{r}_i)|^2)(\sum_{i \in R} |J(\mathbf{r}_i)|^2)}}, \tag{25.24}$$

where R is the ring number and $\mathbf{r}_i$ are the spatial coordinates. The values of the FRC draw a curve in a plot, which can be further investigated (see Fig. 25.5).

This approach is found to be useful in electron and fluorescence microscopy [75, 76] for determining the resolution at which both images are consistent. Here, the 2σ criterion is specified as

$$F_{2\sigma}(R) = \frac{2}{\sqrt{N_p(R)/2}}, \tag{25.25}$$

where $N_p(R)$ is the number of pixels in the ring R. The optimal resolution is then found as the crossing of FRC and $F_{2\sigma}$ curves.

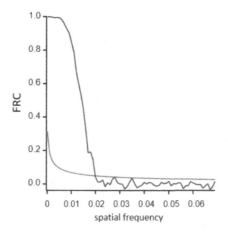

FIGURE 25.5

Fourier ring correlation. The values of FRC for each ring are plotted as a curve (blue – dark gray in print version). The red curve (mid gray in print version) depicts the $F_{2\sigma}$. Adopted from [76].

25.4.3.4 Overlapping subspaces

In [77], the validation method is based on the comparison of explained variability of both real and synthetic data in the same feature space. The descriptors (Haralick descriptors in this case) are initially preprocessed by principal component analysis to reduce the original number of dimensions into only three easy-to-visualize dimensions. The real and synthetic images are represented as data points in this feature subspace. Finally, the overlap of the clusters created around real and synthetic data (Fig. 25.6) is evaluated via Jaccard index as a quantitative measure of this technique. However, this validation method assumes that the three principal components are able to explain the majority of the original feature space given by the descriptors.

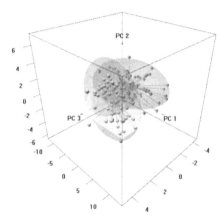

FIGURE 25.6

Interactive visualizer showing real images (yellow – light gray in print version) and synthetic images (blue – mid gray in print version) in the reduced feature space. The axes are the three main components given by principal component analysis. Each point corresponds to a particular image [77].

25.4.3.5 t-distributed stochastic neighbor embedding

The t-distributed stochastic neighbor embedding (t-SNE) [78] is also a reduction (nonlinear in this case) from a multidimensional feature space into two or three dimensions designed for visualization. The method is an improved variation of stochastic neighbor embedding (SNE) [79] with easier optimization and better results in terms of spread of the points in the 2D or 3D map.

The images are represented as high-dimensional data points in a feature space. Like SNE, the Euclidean distances between data points are converted into conditional probabilities representing similarities between the images. The similarity of data point x_j to data point x_i in SNE is expressed as

$$p_{j|i} = \frac{\exp(-\|x_i - x_j\|^2/2\sigma_i^2)}{\sum_{k \neq i} \exp(-\|x_i - x_k\|^2/2\sigma_i^2)}, \tag{25.26}$$

where σ_i is the variance of the Gaussian that is centered on data point x_i. The probability corresponds to the probability that x_j would be in a neighborhood of x_i in proportion to their probability density under the Gaussian centered at x_i. The values of $p_{i|i}$ are set to zero. The low-dimensional counterparts for data points x_i, x_j in a high-dimensional space are labeled as y_i, y_j. The conditional probability $q_{j|i}$ for the low-dimensional counterparts is evaluated in a similar way as in Eq. (25.26), but the variance of the Gaussian is set to $\frac{1}{\sqrt{2}}$. With the use of symmetric SNE, the joint probabilities are employed instead of conditional probabilities for a faster computation. They are set to $p_{ij} = \frac{p_{j|i} + p_{i|j}}{2n}$.

Compared with SNE, t-SNE employs a heavy-tailed distribution – a Student t-distribution with one degree of freedom – instead of Gaussian in the low-dimensional map. The final joint probabilities q_{ij} are defined as

$$q_{ij} = \frac{(1 + \|y_i - y_j\|^2)^{-1}}{\sum_{k \neq l}(1 + \|y_k - y_l\|^2)^{-1}}. \tag{25.27}$$

The particular locations of the data points in the map are determined by minimizing the K–L divergence over all data points using gradient descent.

A validation of synthetic data using t-SNE was applied as a qualitative method in amyloid brain PET image synthesis by [56]. Qualitative visual assessment of the real and synthetic distribution in the 2D plot via t-SNE was also applied in [10]. They compared two settings of training GAN and real images in the map. t-SNE was used in [80] to show the homogeneity of generated and real images with (or without) lesions. In this work, the aim was to generate normal-looking counterpart for the abnormal images with lesions. Similarly, in [81] t-SNE of the original and augmented cervical histopathology was a part of the qualitative validation of the training set. In [82], the authors used t-SNE in a different way – for a comparison among generated methods, not real images.

25.4.4 Measures applied to time-lapse sequences

25.4.4.1 Linear mixed models

Linear mixed models (LMM) also known as *hierarchical linear models* or *linear models with mixed effects* are an extension of linear models for dependent measurements. The extension is needed to overcome two important assumptions put on basic linear models, which are violated in data with dependent measurements. One of them is that the residuals have to be of homogeneous variance and the other that the residuals should not be correlated. The dependency can result from longitudinal data, repeated measurements or clustered data, because one observation is related to another. This method is one of the possibilities for statistical comparison of time-lapse sequenced image data as well as other dependent datasets of images.

The linear mixed model [83] is considered to be of the form

$$Y_i = X_i \beta + Z_i b_i + \varepsilon_i, \tag{25.28}$$

where $Y_i = (Y_{i1}, \ldots, Y_{in_i})'$ is the vector of repeated quantitative outcome measurements for object i, $\boldsymbol{\beta}$ is treated as a vector of fixed effects, i.e., population-average regression coefficients, and X_i is a known design matrix linking $\boldsymbol{\beta}$ to Y_i. The effect of $\boldsymbol{\beta}$ is the same for all the objects. In the case of validation of synthetic data, we are interested in the statistical significance of β_j, which is one element of vector $\boldsymbol{\beta}$. Coefficient β_j is the estimated effect of X_j, a binary variable holding the information about being a synthetic or a real image. Naturally, β_j can be the only element of $\boldsymbol{\beta}$ if X_j is the only explanatory variable in the design matrix X_i. Random effects are held by b_i, a vector of q object-specific regression coefficients. The columns in the Z_i matrix represent observed values for the q predictor variables for the ith subject, which have effects on the continuous response variable that vary randomly across subjects. In many cases, predictors with effects that vary randomly across subjects are represented in both the X_i matrix and the Z_i matrix.

The residuals $\boldsymbol{\varepsilon}_i$ are distributed as $\boldsymbol{\varepsilon}_i \sim N(\mathbf{0}, R_i)$, where R_i is a covariance matrix and depends on i only through its dimension n_i. The b_i are distributed as $b_i \sim N(\mathbf{0}, D)$, independently of each other and of the $\boldsymbol{\varepsilon}_i$, where D is a covariance matrix of the random effects [83–85].

LMM were applied in [86] to images of tubular network of endothelial cells. For the assessment of the effect of being an image from a group of real or synthetic dataset, two standard measures were chosen, the box counting fractal dimension and lacunarity [87,88], both describing the complexity of the structures depicted in the analyzed images.

25.4.4.2 Dynamic time-warping

Dynamic time warping (DTW) is an algorithm for measuring similarity between two time series which may vary in timing. In another words, one can differ from another only in being slower or faster in any part of the series ("warped"). The aim of the algorithm is to find an optimal alignment. The algorithm was originally applied for comparing speech patterns in automatic speech recognition [89].

In [90], the DTW for two time series $X := (x_1, x_2, \ldots, x_N)$ of length $N \in \mathbb{N}$ and $Y := (y_1, y_2, \ldots, y_M)$ of length $M \in \mathbb{N}$ is defined using a *local cost measure*. The local cost measure is a function

$$c : F \times F \to \mathbb{R}_{\geq 0}, \tag{25.29}$$

comparing two features x, y from a fixed feature space F. Local cost measures for each pair of elements X and Y are composed into *cost matrix* $C \in \mathbb{R}^{N \times M}$ defined by

$$C(n, m) := c(x_n, y_m). \tag{25.30}$$

The goal is to find an alignment between X and Y with the minimal overall cost. A warping path is a sequence $p = (p_1, \ldots, p_L)$ with $p_l = (n_l, m_l) \in [1 : N] \times [1 : M]$ for $l \in [1 : L]$ that corresponds to the possibility to align X and Y with a particular total cost $c_p(X, Y)$ with respect to the local cost measure c,

$$c_p(X, Y) := \sum_{l=1}^{L} c(x_{n_l}, y_{m_l}). \tag{25.31}$$

Finally, the optimal warping path is the one having minimal total cost among all possible warping paths. This task is a standard optimization problem which can be solved, e.g., by using dynamic programming.

DTW as a validation method was applied in [91]. On a dataset of tubular networks of epithelial cells, the descriptor computing the number of lagoons in the network was evaluated for each frame of the sequence. The curves resulted from real and synthetic image sequences showing the development of the networks were compared against each other.

25.5 Conclusion

A wide range of methods for the validation of generated data were described in this chapter. Even though the mathematical models offer a powerful tool in the inspection of synthetic data, they should be accompanied by a human-driven qualitative assessment. However, the human eye can be deceived by many factors, e.g., the level of details and number of dimensions, thus it is not sufficient as such. The qualitative and quantitative assessment should go hand-in-hand together and the method should be carefully chosen with regard to suitability for a particular application.

Acknowledgment

We thank Yang Song from University of New South Wales for her invaluable feedback to this chapter.

N. Burgos received funding from the French government under management of Agence Nationale de la Recherche as part of the "Investissements d'avenir" programme reference ANR-10-IAIHU-06 (Agence Nationale de la Recherche-10-IA Institut Hospitalo-Universitaire-6).

References

[1] P. Malm, A. Brun, E. Bengtsson, Simulation of bright-field microscopy images depicting Pap-smear specimen, Cytometry. Part A 87 (2015) 212–226.

[2] F. Calimeri, A. Marzullo, C. Stamile, G. Terracina, Biomedical data augmentation using generative adversarial neural networks, in: A. Lintas, S. Rovetta, P.F. Verschure, A.E. Villa (Eds.), Artificial Neural Networks and Machine Learning – ICANN 2017, Springer International Publishing, Cham, 2017, pp. 626–634.

[3] G. Apou, F. Feuerhake, G. Forestier, B. Naegel, C. Wemmert, Synthesizing whole slide images, in: 2015 9th International Symposium on Image and Signal Processing and Analysis (ISPA), 2015, pp. 154–159.

[4] D. Glotsos, S. Kostopoulos, P. Ravazoula, D. Cavouras, Image quilting and wavelet fusion for creation of synthetic microscopy nuclei images, Computer Methods and Programs in Biomedicine 162 (2018) 177–186, https://doi.org/10.1016/j.cmpb.2018.05.023.

[5] S. Vitale, J.I. Orlando, E. Iarussi, I. Larrabide, Improving realism in patient-specific abdominal ultrasound simulation using cyclegans, International Journal of Computer Assisted Radiology and Surgery 15 (2) (2020) 183–192.

[6] E. Gong, J.M. Pauly, M. Wintermark, G. Zaharchuk, Deep learning enables reduced gadolinium dose for contrast-enhanced brain MRI, Journal of Magnetic Resonance Imaging 48 (2) (2018) 330–340, https://doi.org/10.1002/jmri.25970.

[7] V.N. Kovacheva, D. Snead, N.M. Rajpoot, A model of the spatial tumour heterogeneity in colorectal adenocarcinoma tissue, BMC Bioinformatics 17 (1) (2016) 255.

[8] D. Geman, S. Geman, N. Hallonquist, L. Younes, Visual Turing test for computer vision systems, Proceedings of the National Academy of Sciences 112 (12) (2015) 3618–3623, https://doi.org/10.1073/pnas.1422953112.

[9] C. Han, H. Hayashi, L. Rundo, R. Araki, W. Shimoda, S. Muramatsu, Y. Furukawa, G. Mauri, H. Nakayama, GAN-based synthetic brain MR image generation, in: 2018 IEEE 15th International Symposium on Biomedical Imaging (ISBI 2018), 2018, pp. 734–738, https://doi.org/10.1109/ISBI.2018.8363678.

[10] C. Han, Y. Kitamura, A. Kudo, A. Ichinose, L. Rundo, Y. Furukawa, K. Umemoto, Y. Li, H. Nakayama, Synthesizing diverse lung nodules wherever massively: 3D multi-conditional GAN-based CT image augmentation for object detection, arXiv:1906.04962, 2019.

[11] M.J.M. Chuquicusma, S. Hussein, J. Burt, U. Bagci, How to fool radiologists with generative adversarial networks? A visual Turing test for lung cancer diagnosis, arXiv: 1710.09762, 2018.

[12] T. Schlegl, P. Seeböck, S.M. Waldstein, G. Langs, U. Schmidt-Erfurth, F-AnoGAN: fast unsupervised anomaly detection with generative adversarial networks, Medical Image Analysis 54 (2019) 30–44, https://doi.org/10.1016/j.media.2019.01.010.

[13] A. Lehmussola, P. Ruusuvuori, J. Selinummi, H. Huttunen, O. Yli-Harja, Computational framework for simulating fluorescence microscope images with cell populations, IEEE Transactions on Medical Imaging 26 (7) (2007) 1010–1016, https://doi.org/10.1109/tmi.2007.896925.

[14] J. Ouyang, T.K. Chen, E. Gong, J. Pauly, G. Zaharchuk, Ultra-low-dose PET reconstruction using generative adversarial network with feature matching and task-specific perceptual loss, Medical Physics (2019) 3555–3564.

[15] Q. Xu, G. Huang, Y. Yuan, C. Guo, Y. Sun, F. Wu, K. Weinberger, An empirical study on evaluation metrics of generative adversarial networks, arXiv:1806.07755, 2018.

[16] T. Salimans, I. Goodfellow, W. Zaremba, V. Cheung, A. Radford, X. Chen, X. Chen, Improved techniques for training GANs, in: D. Lee, M. Sugiyama, U. Luxburg, I. Guyon, R. Garnett (Eds.), Advances in Neural Information Processing Systems, vol. 29, Curran Associates, Inc., 2016, pp. 2234–2242.

[17] D. Lopez-Paz, M. Oquab, Revisiting classifier two-sample tests, arXiv:1610.06545, 2018.

[18] N. Burgos, M.J. Cardoso, K. Thielemans, M. Modat, S. Pedemonte, J. Dickson, A. Barnes, R. Ahmed, C.J. Mahoney, J.M. Schott, J.S. Duncan, D. Atkinson, S.R. Arridge,

B.F. Hutton, S. Ourselin, Attenuation correction synthesis for hybrid PET-MR scanners: application to brain studies, IEEE Transactions on Medical Imaging 33 (12) (2014) 2332–2341, https://doi.org/10.1109/TMI.2014.2340135.

[19] J.A. Dowling, J. Sun, P. Pichler, D. Rivest-Hénault, S. Ghose, H. Richardson, C. Wratten, J. Martin, J. Arm, L. Best, S.S. Chandra, J. Fripp, F.W. Menk, P.B. Greer, Automatic substitute computed tomography generation and contouring for magnetic resonance imaging (MRI)-alone external beam radiation therapy from standard MRI sequences, International Journal of Radiation Oncology, Biology, Physics 93 (5) (2015) 1144–1153, https://doi.org/10.1016/j.ijrobp.2015.08.045.

[20] X. Han, MR-based synthetic CT generation using a deep convolutional neural network method, Medical Physics 44 (4) (2017) 1408–1419, https://doi.org/10.1002/mp.12155.

[21] J.M. Wolterink, A.M. Dinkla, M.H.F. Savenije, P.R. Seevinck, C.A.T. van den Berg, I. Isgum, Deep MR to CT synthesis using unpaired data, CoRR, arXiv:1708.01155 [abs], 2017.

[22] D. Nie, R. Trullo, J. Lian, C. Petitjean, S. Ruan, Q. Wang, D. Shen, Medical image synthesis with context-aware generative adversarial networks, in: Medical Image Computing and Computer-Assisted Intervention – MICCAI 2017, in: Lecture Notes in Computer Science, Springer, Cham, 2017, pp. 417–425, https://doi.org/10.1007/978-3-319-66179-7_48.

[23] S. Roy, A. Carass, J.L. Prince, Magnetic resonance image example-based contrast synthesis, IEEE Transactions on Medical Imaging 32 (12) (2013) 2348–2363, https://doi.org/10.1109/TMI.2013.2282126.

[24] A. Jog, A. Carass, S. Roy, D.L. Pham, J.L. Prince, Random forest regression for magnetic resonance image synthesis, Medical Image Analysis 35 (2017) 475–488, https://doi.org/10.1016/j.media.2016.08.009.

[25] S.U. Dar, M. Yurt, L. Karacan, A. Erdem, E. Erdem, T. Çukur, Image synthesis in multi-contrast MRI with conditional generative adversarial networks, IEEE Transactions on Medical Imaging 38 (10) (2019) 2375–2388, https://doi.org/10.1109/TMI.2019.2901750.

[26] J.M. Wolterink, T. Leiner, M.A. Viergever, I. Išgum, Generative adversarial networks for noise reduction in low-dose CT, IEEE Transactions on Medical Imaging 36 (12) (2017) 2536–2545, https://doi.org/10.1109/TMI.2017.2708987.

[27] Q. Yang, P. Yan, Y. Zhang, H. Yu, Y. Shi, X. Mou, M.K. Kalra, Y. Zhang, L. Sun, G. Wang, Low-dose CT image denoising using a generative adversarial network with Wasserstein distance and perceptual loss, IEEE Transactions on Medical Imaging 37 (6) (2018) 1348–1357, https://doi.org/10.1109/TMI.2018.2827462.

[28] Y. Chen, F. Shi, A.G. Christodoulou, Y. Xie, Z. Zhou, D. Li, Efficient and accurate MRI super-resolution using a generative adversarial network and 3D multi-level densely connected network, in: A.F. Frangi, J.A. Schnabel, C. Davatzikos, C. Alberola-López, G. Fichtinger (Eds.), Medical Image Computing and Computer Assisted Intervention – MICCAI 2018, in: Lecture Notes in Computer Science, Springer International Publishing, Cham, 2018, pp. 91–99, https://doi.org/10.1007/978-3-030-00928-1_11.

[29] G. Lee, J. Oh, M. Kang, N. Her, M. Kim, W. Jeong, DeepHCS: bright-field to fluorescence microscopy image conversion using deep learning for label-free high-content screening, in: Medical Image Computing and Computer Assisted Intervention – MICCAI 2018 – 21st International Conference, Granada, Spain, September 16–20, 2018, Proceedings, Part II, 2018, pp. 335–343, https://doi.org/10.1007/978-3-030-00934-2_38.

[30] Y. Hiasa, Y. Otake, M. Takao, T. Matsuoka, K. Takashima, A. Carass, J.L. Prince, N. Sugano, Y. Sato, Cross-modality image synthesis from unpaired data using CycleGAN –

effects of gradient consistency loss and training data size, in: Simulation and Synthesis in Medical Imaging – Third International Workshop, SASHIMI 2018, Held in Conjunction with MICCAI 2018, Granada, Spain, September 16, 2018, Proceedings, in: LNCS, vol. 11037, Springer, 2018, pp. 31–41, https://doi.org/10.1007/978-3-030-00536-8_4.

[31] Z. Wang, A.C. Bovik, H.R. Sheikh, E.P. Simoncelli, Image quality assessment: from error visibility to structural similarity, IEEE Transactions on Image Processing 13 (4) (2004) 600–612, https://doi.org/10.1109/TIP.2003.819861.

[32] A. Hore, D. Ziou, Image quality metrics: PSNR vs. SSIM, in: 2010 20th International Conference on Pattern Recognition, 2010, pp. 2366–2369, https://doi.org/10.1109/ICPR.2010.579.

[33] R. Dosselmann, X.D. Yang, A comprehensive assessment of the structural similarity index, Signal, Image and Video Processing 5 (1) (2011) 81–91.

[34] A. Mason, J. Rioux, S.E. Clarke, A. Costa, M. Schmidt, V. Keough, T. Huynh, S. Beyea, Comparison of objective image quality metrics to expert radiologists' scoring of diagnostic quality of MR images, IEEE Transactions on Medical Imaging 39 (4) (2020) 1064–1072, https://doi.org/10.1109/TMI.2019.2930338.

[35] T. Xia, A. Chartsias, S.A. Tsaftaris, Pseudo-healthy synthesis with pathology disentanglement and adversarial learning, Medical Image Analysis 64 (2020) 101719.

[36] Z. Wang, E.P. Simoncelli, A.C. Bovik, Multi-scale structural similarity for image quality assessment, in: Proc. IEEE Asilomar Conf. on Signals, Systems, and Computers, 2003, pp. 1398–1402.

[37] T. Majtner, Texture-based image description in fluorescence microscopy, Doctoral thesis, Masaryk University, Faculty of Informatics, Brno, 2015.

[38] R.M. Haralick, K. Shanmugam, I. Dinstein, Textural features for image classification, IEEE Transactions on Systems, Man and Cybernetics SMC-3 (6) (1973) 610–621.

[39] D. Svoboda, V. Ulman, MitoGen: a framework for generating 3D synthetic time-lapse sequences of cell populations in fluorescence microscopy, IEEE Transactions on Medical Imaging 36 (1) (2017) 310–321.

[40] D. Svoboda, M. Kašík, M. Maška, J. Hubený, S. Stejskal, M. Zimmermann, On simulating 3D fluorescent microscope images, in: CAIP, in: Lecture Notes in Computer Science, vol. 4673, Springer, 2007, pp. 309–316.

[41] D. Svoboda, O. Homola, S. Stejskal, Generation of 3D digital phantoms of colon tissue, in: Proceedings of 8th International Conference on Image Analysis and Recognition, in: LNCS, vol. 6754, part II, Springer, Berlin, Heidelberg, 2011, pp. 31–39, https://doi.org/10.1007/978-3-642-21596-4_4.

[42] M.V. Boland, R.F. Murphy, A neural network classifier capable of recognizing the patterns of all major subcellular structures in fluorescence microscope images of HeLa cells, Bioinformatics 17 (12) (2001) 1213–1223, https://doi.org/10.1093/bioinformatics/17.12.1213.

[43] T. Zhao, R.F. Murphy, Automated learning of generative models for subcellular location: building blocks for systems biology, Cytometry. Part A 71A (12) (2007) 978–990, https://doi.org/10.1002/cyto.a.20487.

[44] T. Ojala, M. Pietikainen, D. Harwood, Performance evaluation of texture measures with classification based on Kullback discrimination of distributions, in: Proceedings of 12th International Conference on Pattern Recognition, vol. 1, 1994, pp. 582–585, https://doi.org/10.1109/ICPR.1994.576366.

[45] P. Singh, R. Mukundan, R.D. Ryke, Texture based quality analysis of simulated synthetic ultrasound images using local binary patterns, Journal of Imaging 4 (1) (2017) 3, https://doi.org/10.3390/jimaging4010003.

[46] X. Michalet, Mean square displacement analysis of single-particle trajectories with localization error: Brownian motion in an isotropic medium, Physical Review E 83 (4) (2010), https://doi.org/10.1103/physreve.82.041914.

[47] C. Zhao, B.E. Dewey, D.L. Pham, P.A. Calabresi, D.S. Reich, J.L. Prince, SMORE: a self-supervised anti-aliasing and super-resolution algorithm for MRI using deep learning, IEEE Transactions on Medical Imaging 40 (3) (2021) 805–817, https://doi.org/10.1109/TMI.2020.3037187.

[48] C.T. Vu, D.M. Chandler, S3: a spectral and spatial sharpness measure, in: 2009 First International Conference on Advances in Multimedia, 2009, pp. 37–43, https://doi.org/10.1109/MMEDIA.2009.15.

[49] L. Paavolainen, P. Kankaanpää, P. Ruusuvuori, G. McNerney, M. Karjalainen, V. Marjomäki, Application independent greedy particle tracking method for 3D fluorescence microscopy image series, in: 2012 9th IEEE International Symposium on Biomedical Imaging (ISBI), 2012, pp. 672–675, https://doi.org/10.1109/ISBI.2012.6235637.

[50] F.J. Massey, The Kolmogorov–Smirnov test for goodness of fit, Journal of the American Statistical Association 46 (253) (1951) 68–78.

[51] D.V. Sorokin, I. Peterlík, V. Ulman, D. Svoboda, T. Nečasová, K. Morgaenko, L. Eiselleová, L. Tesařová, M. Maška, FiloGen: a model-based generator of synthetic 3D time-lapse sequences of single motile cells with growing and branching filopodia, IEEE Transactions on Medical Imaging 37 (12) (2018) 2630–2641, https://doi.org/10.1109/TMI.2018.2845884.

[52] M.N. Do, M. Vetterli, Texture similarity measurement using Kullback–Leibler distance on wavelet subbands, in: Proceedings 2000 International Conference on Image Processing, vol. 3, 2000, pp. 730–733, https://doi.org/10.1109/ICIP.2000.899558.

[53] G.A.M. Venturini, Statistical distances and probability metrics for multivariate data, ensembles and probability distributions [online], Doctoral thesis, Universidad Carlos III de Madrid, Departamento de Estadística, 2015.

[54] D.J.C. MacKay, Information Theory, Inference and Learning Algorithms, Cambridge University Press, 2003.

[55] A. Gretton, K. Borgwardt, M. Rasch, B. Schölkopf, A. Smola, A kernel method for the two-sample-problem, in: B. Schölkopf, J. Platt, T. Hoffman (Eds.), Advances in Neural Information Processing Systems, vol. 19, MIT Press, 2007, pp. 513–520.

[56] H. Kang, J.-S. Park, K. Cho, D.-Y. Kang, Visual and quantitative evaluation of amyloid brain pet image synthesis with generative adversarial network, Applied Sciences 10 (7) (2020), https://doi.org/10.3390/app10072628.

[57] G. Kwon, C. Han, D. shik Kim, Generation of 3D brain MRI using auto-encoding generative adversarial networks, arXiv:1908.02498, 2019.

[58] P. Viola, W.M. Wells III, Alignment by maximization of mutual information, International Journal of Computer Vision 24 (2) (1997) 137–154, https://doi.org/10.1023/A:1007958904918.

[59] F. Maes, A. Collignon, D. Vandermeulen, G. Marchal, P. Suetens, Multimodality image registration by maximization of mutual information, IEEE Transactions on Medical Imaging 16 (1997) 187–198.

[60] J. Zhu, T. Park, P. Isola, A.A. Efros, Unpaired image-to-image translation using cycle-consistent adversarial networks, in: 2017 IEEE International Conference on Computer Vision (ICCV), 2017, pp. 2242–2251, https://doi.org/10.1109/ICCV.2017.244.

[61] D.B. Russakoff, C. Tomasi, T. Rohlfing, C.R. Maurer, Image similarity using mutual information of regions, in: Computer Vision – ECCV 2004, Springer, Berlin, Heidelberg, 2004, pp. 596–607.

[62] C. Szegedy, V. Vanhoucke, S. Ioffe, J. Shlens, Z. Wojna, Rethinking the inception architecture for computer vision, arXiv:1512.00567, 2015.

[63] J. Deng, W. Dong, R. Socher, L.-J. Li, K. Li, L. Fei-Fei, Imagenet: a large-scale hierarchical image database, in: 2009 IEEE Conference on Computer Vision and Pattern Recognition, 2009, pp. 248–255, https://doi.org/10.1109/CVPR.2009.5206848.

[64] Z. Wang, Y. Lin, K.-T. Cheng, X. Yang, Semi-supervised MP-MRI data synthesis with stitchlayer and auxiliary distance maximization, Medical Image Analysis 59 (2020) 101565, https://doi.org/10.1016/j.media.2019.101565.

[65] M.M. Fréchet, Sur quelques points du calcul fonctionnel, https://doi.org/10.1007/bf03018603, 1906.

[66] T. Eiter, H. Mannila, Computing discrete Fréchet distance, Tech. Rep., Technische Universität Wien, 1994.

[67] L. Xu, X. Zeng, H. Zhang, W. Li, J. Lei, Z. Huang, BPGAN: bidirectional CT-to-MRI prediction using multi-generative multi-adversarial nets with spectral normalization and localization, Neural Networks 128 (2020) 82–96, https://doi.org/10.1016/j.neunet.2020.05.001.

[68] L.H. Lee, J.A. Noble, Generating controllable ultrasound images of the fetal head, in: 2020 IEEE 17th International Symposium on Biomedical Imaging (ISBI), 2020, pp. 1761–1764, https://doi.org/10.1109/ISBI45749.2020.9098578.

[69] M. Heusel, H. Ramsauer, T. Unterthiner, B. Nessler, S. Hochreiter, GANs trained by a two time-scale update rule converge to a local Nash equilibrium, in: Proceedings of the 31st International Conference on Neural Information Processing Systems, NIPS'17, Curran Associates Inc., Red Hook, NY, USA, 2017, pp. 6629–6640.

[70] B.J. Frey, D. Dueck, Clustering by passing messages between data points, Science 315 (5814) (2007) 972–976, https://doi.org/10.1126/science.1136800.

[71] A. Lehmussola, P. Ruusuvuori, J. Selinummi, T. Rajala, O. Yli-Harja, Synthetic images of high-throughput microscopy for validation of image analysis methods, Proceedings of the IEEE 96 (8) (2008) 1348–1360.

[72] M.B. Wilk, R. Gnanadesikan, Probability plotting methods for the analysis for the analysis of data, Biometrika 55 (1) (1968) 1–17.

[73] D. Svoboda, M. Kozubek, S. Stejskal, Generation of digital phantoms of cell nuclei and simulation of image formation in 3D image cytometry, Cytometry. Part A 75A (6) (2009) 494–509, https://doi.org/10.1002/cyto.a.20714.

[74] R.P.J. Nieuwenhuizen, K.A. Lidke, M. Bates, D.L. Puig, D. Grünwald, S. Stallinga, B. Rieger, Measuring image resolution in optical nanoscopy, Nature Methods 10 (6) (2013) 557–562, https://doi.org/10.1038/nmeth.2448.

[75] V. Venkataramani, F. Herrmannsdörfer, M. Heilemann, T. Kuner, SuReSim: simulating localization microscopy experiments from ground truth models, Nature Methods 13 (4) (2016) 319–321, https://doi.org/10.1038/nmeth.3775.

[76] N. Banterle, K.H. Bui, E.A. Lemke, M. Beck, Fourier ring correlation as a resolution criterion for super-resolution microscopy, Journal of Structural Biology 183 (3) (2013) 363–367, https://doi.org/10.1016/j.jsb.2013.05.004.

[77] T. Nečasová, D. Svoboda, Visual and quantitative comparison of real and simulated biomedical image data, in: S.R. Laura Leal-Taixé (Ed.), Computer Vision – ECCV 2018 – Bioimage Computing Workshop, in: LNCS, vol. 11134, Springer, Munich, Germany, 2019, pp. 385–394, https://doi.org/10.1007/978-3-030-11024-6.

[78] L. van der Maaten, G. Hinton, Visualizing high-dimensional data using t-SNE, Journal of Machine Learning Research 9 (Nov) (2008) 2579–2605.

[79] G. Hinton, S. Roweis, Stochastic neighbor embedding, in: Proceedings of the 15th International Conference on Neural Information Processing Systems, NIPS'02, MIT Press, Cambridge, MA, USA, 2002, pp. 857–864.

[80] L. Sun, J. Wang, Y. Huang, X. Ding, H. Greenspan, J. Paisley, An adversarial learning approach to medical image synthesis for lesion detection, IEEE Journal of Biomedical and Health Informatics 24 (8) (2020) 2303–2314, https://doi.org/10.1109/JBHI.2020.2964016.

[81] Y. Xue, J. Ye, Q. Zhou, L.R. Long, S. Antani, Z. Xue, C. Cornwell, R. Zaino, K.C. Cheng, X. Huang, Selective synthetic augmentation with HistoGAN for improved histopathology image classification, Medical Image Analysis 67 (2021) 101816, https://doi.org/10.1016/j.media.2020.101816.

[82] A. Diaz-Pinto, A. Colomer, V. Naranjo, S. Morales, Y. Xu, A.F. Frangi, Retinal image synthesis and semi-supervised learning for glaucoma assessment, IEEE Transactions on Medical Imaging 38 (9) (2019) 2211–2218.

[83] B.T. West, Linear Mixed Models, Chapman and Hall/CRC, 2006, https://doi.org/10.1201/9781420010435.

[84] N.M. Laird, J.H. Ware, Random-effects models for longitudinal data, Biometrics 38 (4) (1982) 963, https://doi.org/10.2307/2529876.

[85] G. Molenberghs, G. Verbeke, A review on linear mixed models for longitudinal data, possibly subject to dropout, Statistical Modelling 1 (4) (2001) 235–269, https://doi.org/10.1177/1471082X0100100402.

[86] D. Svoboda, T. Nečasová, L. Tesařová, P. Šimara, Tubular network formation process using 3D cellular Potts model, in: A. Gooya, O. Goksel, I. Oguz, N. Burgos (Eds.), Simulation and Synthesis in Medical Imaging – Third International Workshop, SASHIMI 2018, Held in Conjunction with MICCAI 2018, Granada, Spain, September 16, 2018, Proceedings, in: LNCS, vol. 11037, Springer, 2018, pp. 90–99, https://doi.org/10.1007/978-3-030-00536-8_10.

[87] D.J. Gould, T.J. Vadakkan, R.A. Poché, M.E. Dickinson, Multifractal and lacunarity analysis of microvascular morphology and remodeling, Microcirculation 18 (2) (2011) 136–151, https://doi.org/10.1111/j.1549-8719.2010.00075.x.

[88] T. Smith, G. Lange, W. Marks, Fractal methods and results in cellular morphology – dimensions, lacunarity and multifractals, Journal of Neuroscience Methods 69 (2) (1996) 123–136, https://doi.org/10.1016/S0165-0270(96)00080-5.

[89] L. Rabiner, B.-H. Juang, Fundamentals of Speech Recognition, Prentice-Hall, Inc., USA, 1993.

[90] M. Müller, Dynamic time warping, in: Information Retrieval for Music and Motion, Springer, Berlin, Heidelberg, 2007, pp. 69–84, Ch. 4, https://doi.org/10.1007/978-3-540-74048-3_4.

[91] D. Svoboda, T. Nečasová, Image-based simulations of tubular network formation, in: 2020 IEEE 17th International Symposium on Biomedical Imaging (ISBI), 2020, pp. 1608–1612, https://doi.org/10.1109/ISBI45749.2020.9098736.

Uncertainty quantification in medical image synthesis

26

Riccardo Barbano[a,b], Simon Arridge[b,c], Bangti Jin[c], and Ryutaro Tanno[b,d]

[a]*Department of Medical Physics, UCL, London, United Kingdom*
[b]*Centre for Medical Image Computing, UCL, London, United Kingdom*
[c]*Department of Computer Science, UCL, London, United Kingdom*
[d]*Healthcare Intelligence, Microsoft Research Cambridge, Cambridge, United Kingdom*

26.1 Introduction

Machine learning has had a pivotal impact on medical image synthesis, which describes the task of synthesizing an image of a target modality. In this chapter, we adopt a generic definition of the task in order to encompass both traditional synthesis problems of generating images from available ones of different modalities [1–5], and reconstruction problems in which the creation of images is performed from raw acquisition data.[1] Fig. 26.1 illustrates this categorization and the far-reaching impact of machine learning methods in a number of synthesis applications.

As machine learning applications in image synthesis progress towards clinical translation, the question of their safety at the "bedside" becomes paramount [34,35]. In particular, deep learning methods [36], which have recently demonstrated great promise in image synthesis, often produce unexpectedly erroneous results in deployment domains when they deviate from the training one. Cohen et al. [34] provide several examples of such catastrophic failures in which the deep learning synthesis model overfits to biases in the training data and, as a result, either removes an existing focal pathology (e.g., lesions, tumors, etc.) or hallucinates spurious ones (see Fig. 26.2), rendering the outputs unusable for subsequent clinical decisions. More recently, Antun et al. [35] have shown that well-established deep learning approaches to under-sampled MR reconstruction are unstable under small perturbations to the input data (see Fig. 26.3). To make matters worse, such unreliable predictions are often perceptually realistic, thus increasing the risks of letting such failures go undetected and slip into the hands of clinicians. So long as the instability of machine learning models remains a challenge in image synthesis, we will be in need of an effective means to quantify the risks of failures and to ultimately prevent failures from arising.

---

[1] This class of problems are usually referred to as *inverse problems* in imaging. From a statistical standpoint, an inverse problem can also be interpreted as a generating process [6,7].

Biomedical Image Synthesis and Simulation. https://doi.org/10.1016/B978-0-12-824349-7.00033-5

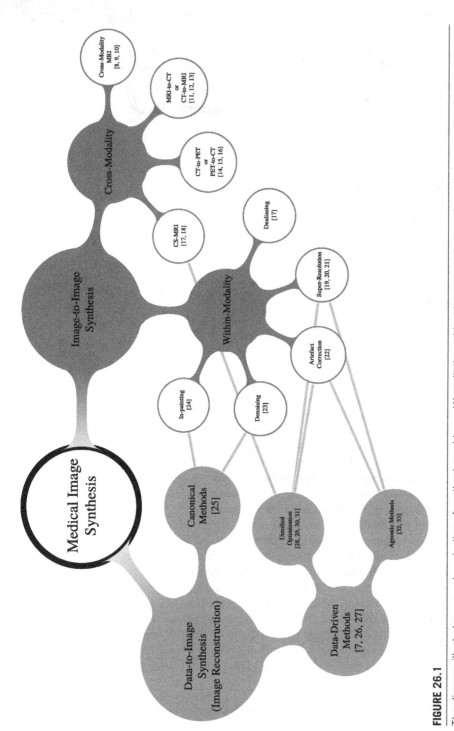

FIGURE 26.1

The diagram illustrates our categorization of synthesis problems. We split the subject into two main branches. While operating in the image domain (i.e. image-to-image synthesis), we identify two sub-categories: (i) within-modality image synthesis (e.g. denoising, super-resolution, dealiasing, artifact correction); (ii) cross-modality image synthesis, focusing on knowledge transfer across medical image modalities. For example, one may want to learn a mapping to translate image intensities between either two MRI contrasts or two image modalities: cross-modality MRI (e.g. T1, T2, FLAIR, and MRA), MRI-to-CT or CT-to-MRI, Compressed Sensing (CS)-MRI, CT-to-PET or PET-to-CT. While operating in the data acquisition domain (and data denotes the measurements collected from a given imaging modality), we identify a wide category of data-to-image synthesis. This is also referred to as inverse problems in medical imaging, or image reconstruction. We then identify two sub-groups: (i) canonical model-based regularization methods (e.g. variational and iterative) and (ii) data-driven methods, including unrolled optimization methods (physics-guided) and agnostic domain-transform methods (purely data-driven). For each sub-category, we highlight a few exemplary applications as small white circles. Some applications overlap between the two groups, and this is illustrated by linking them to the relevant sub-categories in the respective groups.

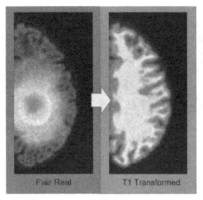

(a) A translation removing tumours

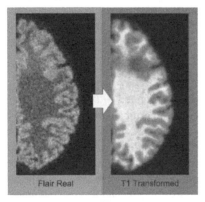

(b) A translation adding tumours

FIGURE 26.2

Examples of failures under data shifts in deep learning based FLAIR-T1 MR synthesis. Images of healthy subjects and those with tumors are shown in green and red (light gray and dark gray in print version). In (a), the model is only trained on images of healthy subjects and as a result ends up removing a tumor in the test domain. In (b), the model is trained only on images of tumor patients and tested on healthy cases, leading to the creation of a synthetic tumor, which is not present in the original image. Source: [34].

It has been argued that uncertainty quantification provides a powerful framework to address this challenge [41]. So far, the overwhelming majority of methods in synthesis (mainly, machine learning based ones but also others) deliver a single prediction, but leave users with no measure of its reliability. The ramifications and the forms of synthesis failures depend on the specifics of the downstream processing and the decision-making that consumes the synthesized images. This necessitates quantifying the risks of using synthesized images in a way that is tailored to its clinical end use. Furthermore, the users may desire to understand the sources from which the risks

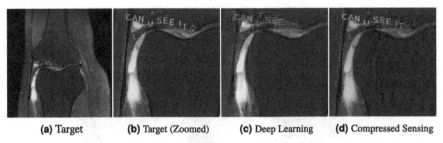

| (a) Target | (b) Target (Zoomed) | (c) Deep Learning | (d) Compressed Sensing |

FIGURE 26.3

Examples of instabilities produced by neural networks for under-sampled MRI reconstruction. In (a), small structured perturbations (in the form of text and symbols) are introduced (e.g., "CAN YOU SEE IT ♠"). In (c) and (d), the reconstructions from MRI Variational Network (MRI-VN) [37] and state-of-the-art classical methods (i.e., compressed sensing [38–40]) are shown, respectively. MRI-VN is moderately unstable with respect to structural changes; such instability coincides with the inability to reconstruct details. Note that MRI-VN has not been trained with images containing any of the letters or symbols used in the perturbation. Source: [35].

originate (e.g., the test case is under-represented in the training data vs. inherently ambiguous), so they can act accordingly to mitigate them. Uncertainty quantification allows us to formalize these practical challenges in the language of probability theory and to design potential solutions [42,43]. While the wider machine learning community has begun to realize the importance of quantifying uncertainty information [44], this topic has yet to receive the attention it deserves in image synthesis.

The scope of this chapter is to identify current and future challenges in uncertainty quantification for medical image synthesis along with possible uses in clinical practice. Throughout the chapter, although primarily focusing on uncertainty quantification in deep learning methods, we survey "classical" approaches (i.e., approaches developed prior to the advent of deep learning), because many of the concepts we cover are generally applicable to machine learning approaches. We also discuss modeling challenges from the standpoint of machine learning developers. We discuss whether uncertainty information should be directly communicated to clinicians or used as a part of the background safety mechanism within the system. Furthermore, we query to what extent risk management should depend on the specific synthesis task of interest and its downstream usage in practice. For example, the diagnosis of different conditions and different deployment environments (e.g., A&E vs standard practice) may require synthesized images of different quality and hence different degrees of reliability.

In this chapter, we provide the first comprehensive review of uncertainty quantification in medical image synthesis. Moreover, we highlight the main research gaps and foreseeable challenges. The rest of the chapter is structured as follows. In Section 26.2 we provide background on uncertainty quantification. In Section 26.3 we discuss traditional and deep learning approaches for handling uncertainty. Lastly, in

Section 26.4 we discuss the technical (and practical) challenges associated with quantifying uncertainty, and the obstacles in translating uncertainty-aware methods into clinical practice.

26.2 Troublesome uncertainty landscape

Uncertainty quantification has recently begun to attract attention in the medical imaging community [45–49].[2] To date, however, the subject remains severely underexplored for image synthesis applications.[3]

This section is structured as follows. In Section 26.2.1 we attempt to answer the question "What is uncertainty quantification?", and we present a taxonomy of uncertainty with an emphasis on the distinction between aleatoric and epistemic uncertainty. In Section 26.2.2 we motivate why we should care about quantifying uncertainty. Lastly in Section 26.2.3 we propose a case study where we exemplify how an existing synthesis framework may benefit from uncertainty quantification.

26.2.1 What is uncertainty quantification?

Imagine you were given a machine learning model $F(\cdot; \theta)$ that takes a query instance x_q (e.g., an input magnetic resonance (MR) image) and makes a prediction $\hat{y}_q = F(x_q; \theta)$ about a target image of interest y_q (e.g., a computed tomography (CT) image), where y_q and $\hat{y}_q$ denote the target output variable and its estimate from the model $F(\cdot; \theta)$, respectively. The model $F(\cdot; \theta)$ is parametrized by a (possibly high-dimensional) vector θ, which is optimized based on the training dataset consisting of N pairs of inputs and target outputs $\mathcal{D} := \{(x_i, y_i)\}_{i=1}^N$. In a supervised learning setting, we assume the existence of some θ that controls the dependence between the input and output $p(\mathcal{D}|\theta)$ (i.e., the likelihood of θ). Synthesizing a CT from an MR image is a problem of predictive inference: given a set of data $\mathcal{D}$ and a query x_q, what is the associated prediction $\hat{y}_q$? In the framework of probabilistic machine learning, inference involves several learning and approximation steps, and all the errors and uncertainties incurred at these steps contribute to the uncertainty of the output $\hat{y}_q$. Below, we present a taxonomy of different uncertainty types and explain their differences and interrelations (see Table 26.1).

Predictive uncertainty is a measure describing the degree of ambiguity (or confidence) in the model's output $\hat{y}_q$ for a given input x_q. For example, we may report the 95% confidence interval for each pixel (i.e., capturing two standard deviations on

---

[2] See Abdar et al. [44] for a comprehensive review on uncertainty-aware methods in deep learning; medical image classification, segmentation and registration are also thoroughly discussed.

[3] Although under-explored for image synthesis applications, uncertainty quantification is an important, ongoing research topic within the machine learning community, and, for instance, just recently complementary yet alternative formal definitions (to the ones we provide in this chapter) on model bias, model variance, and aleatoric and epistemic uncertainty have been proposed [50].

Table 26.1 Uncertainty types and their distributional forms. Model **M** denotes one element from model class $\mathcal{M}$, e.g., a neural network $F(\cdot; \theta)$ with the associated parameter vector θ.

Uncertainty Type	Distributional Form	Ambiguity in
Predictive	$p(\hat{y}|x)$	the model's output
Aleatoric	$p(y|x)$	the data formation process
Epistemic – Structural	$p(\mathrm{M}|\mathcal{D})$	the model specification
Epistemic – Parametric	$p(\theta|\mathcal{D})$	the estimation of the model parameters

either side of the mean estimate, under the Gaussian assumption) along with the synthetic image as a measure of predictive uncertainty. The confidence interval can then be used to assess the variability of the prediction (e.g., the smaller the interval, the more certain the model is about the prediction). Predictive uncertainty is represented in, what is known as, the (posterior) predictive distribution $p(\hat{y}_q|x_q)$.

One is often interested not only in quantifying predictive uncertainty, but also in understanding its sources [51,52], which are useful in identifying the factors from which predictive uncertainty arises. In medical image synthesis, Tanno et al. [53] have shown how disentangling the constituents of uncertainty yields a form of interpretation of predictive uncertainty. The sources of predictive uncertainty are typically further categorized into *aleatoric* and *epistemic* uncertainty [54–58].

Aleatoric uncertainty – from the Latin word *alea* meaning a die – refers to the uncertainty inherent to a problem or an experimental setup that cannot be reduced by additional physical or experimental knowledge [59]. It is also referred to as data, intrinsic or irreducible uncertainty in collected measurements caused by the presence of stochasticity (e.g., measurement noise [60], data transmission and storage errors). For instance, when synthesizing CTs from MR images, aleatoric uncertainty stems from the fact that there are multiple plausible CT solutions for a single MR image. Uncertainty of aleatoric nature is summarized by the underlying conditional distribution $p(y_q|x_q)$ of the task, which describes the inherent stochasticity in the system output y_q for the given input x_q. Such uncertainty is irreducible by collecting more data under experimental settings. If we wish to reduce aleatoric uncertainty (e.g., the noise in the acquired data), we might have to switch to a different acquisition protocol.

Epistemic uncertainty – from Ancient Greek "$\epsilon\pi\iota\sigma\tau\eta\mu\eta$" meaning knowledge – refers to the uncertainty arising from a lack of knowledge or statistical evidence (i.e., the "epistemic" state of the decision maker). It is often further decomposed into two sources, namely *structural* and *parametric* uncertainty.

Structural uncertainty (or model inadequacy) refers to the uncertainty about whether the model is structurally correct. It is also referred to as model specification uncertainty or architecture uncertainty [61]. In fact, we might even be uncertain about whether we have chosen the correct model class in the first place. Perhaps, the current model class does not explain the data well, and if it is inadequate, we may need to construct a different one. It is expressed as the plausibility of the true target process to lie in the specified model class $\mathcal{M}$. It is thus described by a distribution $p(\theta \in M|\mathcal{D})$ which quantifies how probable it is that model M (e.g., a neural network $F(\cdot; \theta)$ with the parameter vector θ) is within the model class $\mathcal{M}$, given the data $\mathcal{D}$. Model uncertainty is strictly related to multi-model inference [62], which subsumes Bayesian model comparison, selection and averaging, as there may exist a multitude of model classes that explain the data equally well. Is linear regression appropriate? Or a neural network? If the latter, how many layers should it have? In medical image synthesis, we often assume that the hypothesis space Θ is correctly specified and neglect the risk of model misspecification.

Parametric uncertainty denotes the uncertainty related to the estimation of the model parameters under a given model specification, assuming that the form of the model faithfully captures reality. Consider a scenario in which we choose a complex model (with $\approx$ 60 million parameters) but we lack a sufficient amount of training data (as is often the case in medical image synthesis) to train our model on. In this case, we will likely struggle to constrain the model's parameters. Out of all the "functions" our model can represent, which one should we choose? Parametric uncertainty is described by the posterior distribution $p(\theta|\mathcal{D})$ over the unknown parameters θ of the specified model $F(\cdot; \theta)$, given the data $\mathcal{D}$. The more "peaked" $p(\theta|\mathcal{D})$ is (i.e., the more concentrated the probability mass is in a small region in Θ), the less uncertain the decision maker should be. In other words, high parametric uncertainty arises when the predictions obtained from several "plausible" parameter settings disagree the most.

Many technical and practical problems with uncertainty quantification boil down to estimating these distributions in various settings. For complex models such as neural networks, these distributions are mostly intractable, necessitating the development of efficient and effective approximations. In medical imaging synthesis, the "ground truth" for these distributions of interest, $p(\hat{y}|x_q)$, $p(y|x_q)$, $p(\theta|\mathcal{D})$, and $p(M|\mathcal{D})$ are often not explicitly available, rendering the exact evaluation of uncertainty estimation very challenging [63]. We shall describe efficient strategies for tractable approximations in Section 26.3.

26.2.2 Why should we care?

Uncertainty quantification offers a principled and consistent framework that provides reliability measures of the model's output, which potentially can shed valuable insight for downstream applications. In this regard, we argue that uncertainty quantification could assist the translation of medical image synthesis technologies into clinical practice while improving clinicians' trust [64]. Below we present four use cases of estimated uncertainty information in a variety of settings: quality check, propagating uncertainty, shedding insight and improving predictive performance. We also present the safety implications of deploying machine learning based image synthesis applications in clinical practice.

Quality check

Taking contrast enhancement of CTs as an exemplary synthesis application, one may be interested in whether the model generalizes in new environments. One may want to asses if the model can reliably enhance the CTs of all relevant sub-populations that are not well-represented in the training data. Or, one may want to know how the model would behave if the acquisition parameters of the CT scanner or even its type were to change in the deployment site due to some operational reasons. How would the model perform if the CTs of patients with rare conditions or diseases were to be taken? Ideally, we would collect enough validation data in all these possible scenarios and assess the model's performance. Such an approach, however, is impractical. To make matters worse, several works have shown that deep learning models often overestimate their confidence in the synthesis process. First, Cardoso et al. [4] warn about the "risks" of the model being overconfident, and possibly propagating large errors to downstream analysis. Then, Cohen et al. [34] and Antun et al. [35] warn about the dangers of machine learning models hallucinating image features, and advocate the need for a quality check for image-to-image translation and MR image reconstruction.

To address these questions, we can look at recent works. Tanno et al. [53] have suggested that predictive uncertainty, if quantified correctly, provides a surrogate performance metric that could reliably inform the clinicians when not to trust the model's predictions. They propose a Bayesian image quality transfer via convolutional neural networks (CNNs) [65] and demonstrate the usefulness of uncertainty modeling by measuring the deviation from the ground truth on standard metrics. The standard deviation map highly correlates with reconstruction errors, which shows their potential as a surrogate measure of accuracy. More recently, Tanno et al. [66] show that predictive uncertainty can be used to define a binary classifier, discriminating "risky" predictions from the "safe" ones. In a different synthesis task, Reinhold et al. [67] propose a Bayesian deep learning method that learns how to translate a CT into an MR image and to quantify uncertainty, which is then used as a proxy for anomaly detection. On the basis that high pixel-wise uncertainty occurs in pathological regions of the synthetic CT, Reinhold et al. [68] use uncertainty quantification for unsupervised anomaly segmentation. Klaser et al. [69] propose a novel multi-resolution cascade 3D network for end-to-end full-body MR to CT synthesis yet include uncertainty quantification as a measure of safety. Lastly, Nair et al. [46,70] investigate several uncertainty metrics for quality control in lesion segmentation of multiple sclerosis.

Propagating uncertainty

Clinical researchers may use predictive uncertainty in downstream analysis, or include it in the pipeline of medical image analysis, which generally comprises a sequence of inferential tasks (e.g., synthesis, registration, and segmentation). The uncertainty quantified at the image level is passed to subsequent tasks in the form of an uncertainty map (e.g., pixel-wise variance). Recent works have explored this prospective use. Tanno et al. [53] propagate uncertainty into downstream quantities in the context of diffusion MRI super-resolution, by computing the expectation and variance of mean diffusivity and fractional anisotropy with respect to the predictive distribution. Mehta et al. [71] show how the performance of a downstream task in a medical image analysis pipeline can be improved if uncertainty estimates are propagated: the output of each module (including the associated uncertainty) is used as an input to the subsequent one across cascaded inferential tasks. The paper studies several medical image pipelines, each of which cascades two different inferential tasks (e.g., two-stage MRI synthesis and brain tumor segmentation). Experimental results indicate that propagating the synthesized image along with its associated uncertainty map to the downstream tumor segmentation network improves the downstream performance in comparison to only propagating the synthesized image.

Shedding insight on sources of errors

In a scenario where the synthesis error is consistently high on certain image structures, decomposing predictive uncertainty into aleatoric and epistemic uncertainty provides high-level "explanations" for a model's behavior. For instance, such a decomposition allows quantifying how much uncertainty arises from (i) the inherent difficulty to reconstruct image structures (i.e., uncertainty of aleatoric nature); (ii) the unfamiliarity of such image structures due to their limited representation in the training data (i.e., uncertainty of epistemic nature). If the epistemic uncertainty is high but the aleatoric one is low, this indicates that collecting more training data would be beneficial. On the contrary, if the epistemic uncertainty is low and the aleatoric one is high, then we need to regard such errors as inevitable, and abstain from predictions to ensure safety or account for errors appropriately in subsequent analysis. Data-driven approaches for uncertainty quantification also present an additional technical challenge: the selection and collection of the training data and the evaluation of its completeness and accuracy. Disentangling the constituents of predictive uncertainty may suggest how to collect the training data, and the extent to which it is informative and exhaustive. Tanno et al. [66] show that the decomposition of the effects of aleatoric and epistemic uncertainty in the predictive uncertainty provides additional explanations of the performance of the considered methods.

Improving predictive performance

Bayesian approaches to machine learning models offer a number of theoretical as well as practical advantages. They provide a potential solution to over-fitting, and a principled and automatic way of selecting hyper-parameters [63,72,73]. Many techniques of regularization arise in a natural way in the Bayesian framework as the maximum a posteriori (MAP) estimator of certain posterior probability density functions. The need for regularization is compelling in the context of deep learning based techniques, where nearly all models are severely over-parameterized, due to a lack of abundant high-quality training samples. Bayesian approaches also deliver quantifiable estimates of uncertainty of the model parameters and predictions as well as quantitative comparisons between predictions obtained by alternative models (e.g., different network architectures) within the framework of model selection (e.g., using Bayes factor [74]). Furthermore, these approaches enable developing "optimal" estimators with respect to suitable Bayesian risks within the Bayesian decision theory framework [75].

In order to fully realize these advantages, there remain computational challenges, which we shall discuss in detail in Section 26.3.

26.2.3 Uncertainty quantification in action

Lastly, we would like to end this section by illustrating how uncertainty could be used in image synthesis applications. In fact, there are many scenarios in which uncertainty quantification could be useful to clinicians. Here, we illustrate how positron emission tomography (PET)/MR image reconstruction may benefit from uncertainty-aware attenuation correction in PET. Clinical researchers have improved PET/MR reconstruction by generating a "pseudo-CT" and deriving the attenuation coefficients [3], which, in turn, play a substantial role in PET reconstruction. The synthetic information is implicitly used within the reconstruction pipeline to inform the attenuation coefficients, and it is also customary for nuclear medicine physicians to visualize the pseudo-CT for PET/MRI (CT in case of PET/CT) mainly to check the movement artefact. In theory, one should check the plausibility of pseudo-CTs as obvious artifacts (e.g., air in the middle of the brain because of a segmentation problem) can easily be detected. This is, however, rarely done in practice. What happens if the approach is unable to correctly synthesize a CT from the MR image? This might be the case for patients that have evident bone defects (e.g., low or high bone density). For such an "outlier" patient, a notion of uncertainty over the pseudo-CT could be useful as it would provide a background defensive mechanism that informs the clinician not to use the pseudo-CT and attenuation maps as "too risky" to trust for PET reconstruction. We may want our automated system to abstain from using the pseudo-CT and request the assistance of a clinician when the uncertainty is above a certain threshold.

26.3 Tools for modeling uncertainty

In this section, we delve into the details of practical computational techniques for handling uncertainties within the Bayesian framework [76,77]. The main idea is as follows: all the quantities which appear in synthesis tasks are modeled probabilistically as random variables with corresponding probability distributions (e.g., density for continuous random variables). Within the Bayesian framework, there are two fundamental building blocks, namely the likelihood (of the training data $\mathcal{D}$) and the prior distribution. The training data set $\mathcal{D}$ consists either of a set of available measurements y in data-to-image synthesis or a set of N pairs (x_i, y_i) in the context of supervised learning. The prior distribution $p(\theta)$ of the parameter θ specifies the prior knowledge we have before collecting the measurements. In the context of standard data-to-image synthesis, θ is the target image and $p(\theta)$ encodes the *a priori* knowledge we have about the sought-for image, whereas in supervised learning, we seek to learn the posterior distribution $p(\theta|\mathcal{D})$ over the parameters θ of the model $F(\cdot; \theta)$. Learning consists of updating the prior distribution $p(\theta)$ to the posterior distribution $p(\theta|\mathcal{D})$ defined as

$$p(\theta|\mathcal{D}) = \frac{p(\mathcal{D}|\theta)p(\theta)}{\int p(\mathcal{D}|\theta)p(\theta)d\theta}, \qquad (26.1)$$

where the likelihood function of parameters θ, $p(\mathcal{D}|\theta)$, is the probability of the given training data set $\mathcal{D}$ given θ. The posterior distribution $p(\theta|\mathcal{D})$ over θ is inferred by *deductively* updating the prior knowledge $p(\theta)$ we had, given the data $\mathcal{D}$ we observed [78,79]. Note that, in "machine learning parlance," we usually denote the input by x and the target output by y, whereas in the inverse problem community, y denotes the observations (i.e., measurements that have undergone through a corruption process) and x is the image to be reconstructed (and θ, for instance, is the parameter vector of the neural network). Here we will follow the machine learning notation.

To represent uncertainty about a prediction $\hat{y}_q$, all possible configurations of θ are considered, with each prediction being weighed by its posterior probability $p(\theta|\mathcal{D})$. We compute the posterior predictive distribution $p(\hat{y}_q|x_q)$ as

$$\underbrace{p(\hat{y}_q|x_q)}_{\substack{\text{Predictive} \\ \text{uncertainty}}} = \int \underbrace{p(\hat{y}_q|x_q, \theta)}_{\substack{\text{Aleatoric} \\ \text{uncertainty}}} \underbrace{p(\theta|\mathcal{D})}_{\substack{\text{Epistemic} \\ \text{uncertainty}}} d\theta, \qquad (26.2)$$

which captures both aleatoric and epistemic uncertainty. The final prediction is obtained by Bayesian *model averaging*; or, if stated differently, is made through Bayesian *marginalization* as the predictive distribution of interest no longer conditions on θ. Intuitively, we can think of Eq. (26.2) as a weighted average (i.e., the outcome of a reconstructed image) of many different hypotheses by their plausibility given data—we would like to use every possible setting of θ—rather than a single one. In the supervised learning setting, the challenges in computing the posterior predictive distribution $p(\hat{y}_q|x_q)$ are two-fold: (i) estimating the posterior distribution $p(\theta|\mathcal{D})$; (ii) integrating out θ. Since Bayesian model averaging is often too hard, we either tend to approximate the integral with a simple Monte Carlo (MC) approximation

$$p(\hat{y}_q|x_q) \approx \frac{1}{T}\sum_{t=1}^{T} p(\hat{y}_q|x_q, \hat{\theta}^t), \quad \text{with } \hat{\theta}^t \sim p(\theta|\mathcal{D}),$$

or we adopt only the single prediction with the highest posterior distribution, $\theta^* = \text{argmax } p(\theta|\mathcal{D})$. This estimate is commonly known as the MAP estimate and is computationally more tractable. Even though MAP involves the posterior distribution $p(\theta|\mathcal{D})$ and looks like an application of the Bayes' rule, it is not properly Bayesian. In fact, it would put everything on one single hypothesis, that is, on a single setting of the parameters $F(\cdot; \theta_{\text{map}})$. Accordingly, Eq. (26.2) would be computed by using an approximate posterior distribution $p(\theta|\mathcal{D}) \approx \delta(\theta = \theta_{\text{map}})$, where δ is a Dirac delta distribution with all its mass at θ_{map}, with the likelihood being $p(\hat{y}_q|x_q, \theta_{\text{map}})$. The difference between these two approaches relies on the posterior distribution $p(\theta|\mathcal{D})$, but most importantly on how "sharp" it is. In fact, there would be almost no difference if the posterior distribution happened to be sharply peaked, and the likelihood $p(\hat{y}_q|x_q, \theta)$ did not vary much in the region where the posterior distribution places its mass. A Dirac delta may then be a reasonable approximation of the posterior distribution in Eq. (26.2).[4] If this is not the case, averaging the predictions of many high performing models $\hat{\theta}^t$ (e.g., neural networks) that "disagree" for some input cases can lead to a significant improvement in accuracy [82,81].

26.3.1 Approximation techniques

Although the posterior distribution $p(\theta|\mathcal{D})$ gives a complete probabilistic solution to the synthesis task—it combines both the prior knowledge with the given data—a closed form expression for $p(\theta|\mathcal{D})$ is often unavailable in medical image synthesis. There are several forms of intractable posterior distributions: (i) the normalizing constant is intractable (i.e., "analytically" intractable); (ii) the posterior distribution is intractable due to an intractable likelihood (e.g., the data generating process being too complex due to poorly understood physics). Generally, summary statistics (e.g., mean and variance or correlation) are sought. However, these quantities require computing high-dimensional integrals, which are computationally infeasible for most synthesis tasks. Thus, it is imperative to employ numerical procedures to effectively explore the posterior distribution $p(\theta|\mathcal{D})$. These can roughly be divided into two groups: MC-type methods and approximate inference techniques. MC-type methods include Markov chain Monte Carlo (MCMC), which constructs a Markov chain whose stationary distribution is the posterior distribution, and which uses ergodic averages to approximate the statistics of interest, and sequential MC, which constructs a finite sequence of importance samplers targeting a sequence of distributions with the last being the posterior distribution.

Approximate inference methods include the Laplace approximation using a local Gaussian approximation constructed at the MAP, variational inference (VI) framing the approximation of the posterior distribution as optimizing a lower bound on the evidence with respect to a tractable family of simple distributions (commonly referred to as a variational distribution), and expectation propagation, which iteratively leverages the factorization structure of the target distribution.

Before we proceed further, it is useful to recall that the end goal is to accurately approximate the posterior predictive distribution in Eq. (26.2). To do so, it is important to have an accurate approximation of the posterior distribution in the regions that would contribute most to the Bayesian model averaging integral in Eq. (26.2). Let us imagine one samples two different settings of parameters of the network $F(\cdot; \theta)$, namely $\hat{\theta}^1$ and $\hat{\theta}^2$, but both give rise to similar functions $F(\cdot; \hat{\theta}^1)$ and $F(\cdot; \hat{\theta}^2)$. In this case, the second setting of parameters $\hat{\theta}^2$ would not contribute much to estimating

---

[4] However, this is hardly the case for neural networks, which are highly under-specified by the available data [80,81].

the integral in Eq. (26.2), and we should seek functional diversity for a good approximation of Eq. (26.2) [83].

Monte Carlo methods

In MC-type methods, one generates samples from $p(\theta|\mathcal{D})$, which are then used to produce representative reconstructions or to compute summary statistics. Directly generating samples is generally very challenging. MCMC [84] methods (e.g., the Metropolis–Hastings algorithm or the Gibbs algorithm) generate a Markov chain whose stationary distribution is the target distribution, and is asymptotically exact. These methods can approximate the target distribution arbitrarily well, provided that one can run the chain for sufficiently long, and thus have been established as the gold standard for exploring the posterior state space. In practice, these methods are often easy to implement, but their efficiency relies heavily on various algorithmic parameters (e.g., proposal distribution and step-size). To make matters even worse, the scalability with parameter dimensionality is often not very favorable and the convergence diagnosis remains largely an art rather than a science.

Consequently, despite their impressive progress in recent years (e.g., Hamiltonian Monte Carlo [85]), the use of MC methods in the context of medical image synthesis (including image reconstruction) remains fairly limited. However, there are some exceptions. Pedemonte et al. [86] use a recent Riemann manifold MCMC sampling scheme [85] to sample the posterior distribution of emission rates given the photon counts for PET. The method obtains uncertainty information from all the processes involved in the reconstruction algorithm (i.e., the observed data, the measurement noise and the background signal, the reconstruction process itself, and also possibly the hyper-parameters). Moreover, the tightening of the posterior distribution is also used as a reliability indicator for estimating the required patient scan time. Weir et al. [87] propose an approach for single-photon emission computed tomography (SPECT) that samples the joint posterior distribution of the image and hyper-parameters using a Gibbs prior and the Metropolis–Hastings sampler on simulated and phantom data. Similarly, Barat et al. [88] propose a Gibbs sampler for PET with a nonparametric Dirichlet process mixture prior. However, even for medium-size medical image reconstruction, exploring the posterior distribution with MCMC type methods can incur a prohibitively high computational expense, and thus is not practically feasible. As a rule of thumb, the higher the dimensionality, the more complex the posterior distribution, and the slower the sampling procedure converges. For PET, Filipovic et al. [89] develop a Gibbs type sampler formed from a distance-driven Chinese restaurant process (for clustering). Nonetheless, the procedure remains expensive: "The computation time was 4 days for RCP-GS (30 runs × 250 sampler iterations), compared to 1 h 20 min for MR-MAP and 50 min for OSEM (8 iterations × 27 subsets)" [89].

Approximate inference schemes

Deterministic approximate inference techniques encompass a large variety of methods such as the Laplace approximation [90], VI [91–93] (using mean-field approximation [94], or the variational Gaussian approximation [95,96] and more recently stochastic VI [97]), and expectation propagation [98].

The Laplace approximation is a classical approach to approximate the posterior distribution. It constructs a Gaussian distribution based on the second-order Taylor expansion of the log-posterior $\log p(\theta|\mathcal{D})$ around the MAP estimate θ^*,

$$p(\theta|\mathcal{D}) \propto \exp\left\{-\frac{1}{2}\left(\theta - \theta^*\right)^{\top} H(\theta^*)\left(\theta - \theta^*\right)\right\}, \tag{26.3}$$

where $H(\theta^*) = -\nabla_\theta^2 \log p(\theta|\mathcal{D})|_{\theta=\theta^*}$ denotes the Hessian of the (negative log) posterior distribution estimated at the MAP estimate θ^*. This approach requires good differentiability of the negative log-posterior distribution, and it is thus not directly suitable for non-smooth priors (e.g., sparsity or total variation) which commonly appear in image reconstruction[5]; but most importantly, computing the full Hessian $H(\theta)$ is computationally demanding and memory-wise infeasible, unless further fast approximations (e.g., diagonal + local rank, Kronecker or sparse (inverse) covariance) are employed. The low-rank assumption is reasonable for severely ill-posed imaging problems. It is also worth noting that often more accurate approximations can be obtained using the integrated nested Laplace approximation [100]. Despite its simplicity, it has barely been employed in medical image restoration or synthesis.

Most VI techniques were developed within the machine learning community, where the aforementioned computational challenge is widely acknowledged. VI is often based on approximately minimizing the Kullback–Leibler (KL) divergence[6] [101] between the target distribution and the approximate surrogate one. The divergence KL from q to p is defined by

$$\mathrm{KL}(q\|p) = \int q(x)\log\frac{q(x)}{p(x)}\mathrm{d}x. \tag{26.4}$$

VI then searches for an approximating distribution $q_\psi^*(\theta)$ parametrized by ψ within an admissible family $\mathcal{Q}$ by minimizing the KL divergence,

$$q_\psi^*(\theta) := \underset{q_\psi \in \mathcal{Q}}{\mathrm{argmin}}\, \mathrm{KL}\left(q_\psi(\theta)\|p(\theta|\mathcal{D})\right). \tag{26.5}$$

Introducing a prior distribution $p(\theta)$ and applying the Bayes rule allows us to rewrite the optimization of Eq. (26.5) as the maximization of the Evidence Lower BOund (ELBO) with respect to the variational parameters defining $q_\psi(\theta)$,

$$\mathcal{L}_{\mathrm{VI}} := \int q_\psi(\theta)\log p(\mathcal{D}|\theta)\mathrm{d}\theta - \int q_\psi(\theta)\log\frac{q_\psi(\theta)}{p(\theta)}\mathrm{d}\theta \le \log p(\mathcal{D}). \tag{26.6}$$

---

[5] Various smoothing (e.g., Huber) can be used for non-smooth priors, but it can also significantly hinder the approximation; see [99] an illustration with the anisotropic total variation prior.

[6] Note that the divergence is asymmetric and does not satisfy the triangle inequality, but it vanishes if and only if p equals to q almost everywhere.

The maximizing functional $\mathcal{L}_{VI}$ is a lower bound to the log-evidence (i.e., the normalizing constant or marginal log-likelihood) $p(\mathcal{D})$. Note that the ELBO plus KL$\left(q_\psi(\theta)\,\|\,p(\theta|\mathcal{D})\right)$ equals the marginal log-likelihood $p(\mathcal{D})$, which is constant with respect to the variational parameters ψ.

The computational tractability of VI is achieved by imposing suitable assumptions on the approximating family $\mathcal{Q}$, for instance, a fully-factorized (also known as mean-field) Gaussian $\mathcal{Q}_{FFG}$ defined by

$$\mathcal{Q}_{FFG} = \left\{ q(\theta) = \prod_i \mathcal{N}(\theta_i; \mu_i, \sigma_i^2) \right\},$$

where $\mathcal{N}(\theta_i; \mu_i, \sigma_i^2)$ denotes a Gaussian distribution for the component θ_i with mean μ_i and variance σ_i^2. The parameters μ_i and σ_i^2 are variational parameters that have to be optimized. Then maximization is often carried out by coordinate ascent type schemes, or stochastic gradient type algorithms [97]. The latter requires an MC estimate of the gradient, which often has to be done carefully in order to ensure low bias and low variance. It is worth noting that in a different vein, suitable averaging of the stochastic gradient iterates can also be interpreted as approximate inference [102,103], though the covariance estimate may differ in shape.

In contrast, expectation propagation [98] minimizes the KL divergence defined as KL$(p\|q)$, which mathematically amounts to moment matching, and its practicality relies on a factorized form of the posterior distribution and a possible reduction to low-dimensional (often still delicate) numerical integration. The stability of the implementation relies heavily on the accuracy of the quadrature rules, and an inaccurate quadrature can cause the nonconvergence of the iteration. In this regard, Zhang et al. [99] develop an approximate Bayesian inference technique based on expectation propagation for PET reconstruction (with the anisotropic total variation prior), where the delicate issue of numerical integration is studied in depth and the approach is showcased on medium-size simulated phantom data.

Besides these established approximate inference techniques, there are several others. One notable recent example is Stein variational gradient descent [104], which also performs moment matching but it does so implicitly [105]. Compared with MCMC type methods, deterministic approximations are often computationally more efficient, but may be limited in accuracy (and often with little theoretical understanding [106]), yet they remain expensive for truly large-scale problems arising in medical imaging, especially in the presence of strong correlation between different pixels.

More recently, attention has also been paid to blending start-of-the-art optimization algorithms with uncertainty quantification. For example, Repetti et al. [107] propose a method to analyze the confidence in specific structures in MAP estimates using Bayesian hypothesis testing. The method holds potential for large-scale problems, but remains to be evaluated clinically. In sum, approaches, which aim to quantify uncertainties, are mathematically principled, but there remain computational challenges; various approximations have been developed to address these challenges but a complete mathematical theory of the mathematical-statistical properties of these methods is yet to emerge and their potential in medical image analysis is to be evaluated.

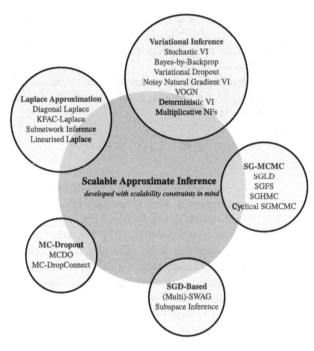

FIGURE 26.4

Scalable approximate inference methods for Bayesian neural networks.

26.3.2 Probabilistic deep learning

With the advent of deep learning, uncertainty quantification has resurfaced as an important framework. In medical image synthesis, Bayesian deep learning can provide the information about uncertainty associated with each prediction [108]. Below, we review the basics of Bayesian neural networks (BNNs), which holds great potential yet remains relatively under-explored in the image synthesis community. We also discuss methods for disentangling predictive uncertainty into the components associated with aleatoric and parametric uncertainty, and briefly mention several alternative approximations. The aforementioned computational challenges are more pronounced in deep neural networks due to the high dimensionality of the parameter space and high degree of nonlinearity. In Fig. 26.4, we provide a diagram that summarizes different approximate inference schemes, which have been developed with scalability constraints in mind.

Bayesian neural networks

BNNs place a probability distribution on the parameters θ (which are now treated as random variables) to encode the uncertainties associated with the prediction [109–111]. We consider the posterior distribution over all possible settings of the model parameters given the observed data. Such probability density encapsulates parametric uncertainty, and its spread of mass signifies the ambiguity in selecting appropriate parameters. In recent years, there have been significant efforts to characterize and approximate the posterior distribution $p(\theta|\mathcal{D})$ [112–114], which, in practice, is intractable due to the difficult-to-compute normalizing constant. It is worth noting that many approximate inference algorithms share the same approximating family $\mathcal{Q}$. For instance, VI, the diagonal Laplace approximation [115], probabilistic backpropagation [113], stochastic expectation propagation [116], black-box alpha divergence minimization [117], Rényi divergence VI [118], natural gradient VI [119], and functional variational BNNs [120] all use a fully-factorized Gaussian family $\mathcal{Q}_{\text{FFG}}$, which itself is largely motivated by computational considerations.

We only review the three most popular schemes used in image synthesis, that is, Laplace approximation, VI, and Monte Carlo dropout (MCDO), and omit to review MCMC approaches to BNNs [121–124], which remain computationally inefficient due to the evaluation of a large ensemble of models for the exploration of the posterior distribution. We also do not review methods that construct Gaussian approximations to the posterior distribution from a few iterates along the optimization trajectory obtained by stochastic gradient descent methods of a deterministic neural network [103]. To the best of our knowledge, these methods have yet to be applied to medical image synthesis.

Laplace approximation

We can use Laplace's method to approximate $p(\theta|\mathcal{D})$. The canonical form of (supervised) deep learning is that of empirical risk minimization, $F(\cdot; \theta)$ is trained to minimize the following (regularized) empirical risk:

$$\theta^* \in \underset{\theta}{\operatorname{argmin}} \left\{ \mathcal{L} := \sum_{i=1}^{N} \ell(y_i, \hat{y}; \theta) + r(\theta) \right\}, \tag{26.7}$$

with $\ell(y_i, \hat{y}; \theta) = -\log p(y_i|x_i, \theta)$ and $r(\theta) = -\log p(\theta)$. Hence, $\exp(-\mathcal{L})$ amounts to an unnormalized posterior. Upon normalization, we obtain

$$p(\theta|\mathcal{D}) = Z^{-1} p(\mathcal{D}|\theta)p(\theta) = Z^{-1} \exp(-\mathcal{L}), \tag{26.8}$$

with $Z := \int p(\mathcal{D}|\theta)p(\theta)d\theta$. Laplace's method employs a second-order expansion of $\mathcal{L}$ around θ^* to construct a Gaussian approximation to $p(\theta|\mathcal{D})$:

$$\mathcal{L} \approx \mathcal{L}_{|\theta=\theta^*} + \tfrac{1}{2} \left(\theta - \theta^*\right)^{\top} \nabla_\theta^2 \mathcal{L}_{|\theta=\theta^*} \left(\theta - \theta^*\right), \tag{26.9}$$

since the first-order derivative $\nabla_\theta \mathcal{L}(\theta)$ vanishes at θ^*. Then we can identify the Laplace approximation as

$$p(\theta|\mathcal{D}) \approx q(\theta) := \mathcal{N}(\theta; \theta^*, \Sigma(\theta)), \quad \text{with} \quad \Sigma(\theta) = -\left[\nabla_\theta^2 \mathcal{L}_{|\theta=\theta^*}\right]^{-1}. \tag{26.10}$$

Hence, to obtain $q(\theta)$, we first need to find a minimizer θ^* of $\mathcal{L}$ (i.e., perform standard deep learning) and then to compute the inverse of the Hessian matrix $\nabla_\theta^2 \mathcal{L}$ at θ^*. Thus the construction is post-hoc to a pretrained network. To compute $\Sigma(\theta)$, we have to compute $\nabla_\theta^2 \mathcal{L}_{|\theta=\theta^*}$ in Eq. (26.9). The prior term is usually trivial to compute, but the likelihood is more involved, which is given by

$$\nabla_\theta^2 \log p(\hat{y}|x, \theta) = H(x; \theta)^\top r(\hat{y}, \theta) - J(x; \theta)^\top \Lambda(\hat{y}; \theta) J(x; \theta), \qquad (26.11)$$

where $H(x; \theta)$ and $J(x; \theta)$ are the Hessian and Jacobian of the log-likelihood per-data point (expressed through the Hessian and Jacobian of $F(\cdot; \theta)$); the residual $r(\hat{y}, \theta) = \nabla_F \log p(\hat{y}|x, \theta)$, and $\Lambda(\hat{y}, \theta) = -\nabla_F^2 \log p(\hat{y}|x, \theta)$ is the per-input noise. The network Hessian is infeasible to construct in practice, and instead the generalized Gauss–Newton (GGN) approximation is commonly used [125,126]

$$q_{\text{GGN}}(\theta) := \mathcal{N}\left(\theta; \theta^*, \left(J(x; \theta)^\top \Lambda(\hat{y}; \theta) J(x; \theta) + S_0^{-1}\right)^{-1}\right), \qquad (26.12)$$

where S_0 denotes the Hessian of the prior $r(\theta)$. The approximation is obtained by assuming $H(x; \theta)^\top r(\hat{y}, \theta) = 0$. To justify this, there are two independently sufficient conditions [127]: (i) the residual term vanishes for all data-points, which is true if $F(\cdot; \theta)$ is a perfect predictor; (ii) the Hessian term vanishes, which is true for linear networks, and can be enforced by linearization. In practice, the GGN approximation is further approximated (e.g., diagonal or block diagonal).

Note that the posterior predictive distribution is still intractable due to the non-linearity of the neural network, and for the Laplace approximation, the most general approximation (i.e., MC integration) can perform poorly [128]. Immer et al. [129] attribute it to the inconsistencies between the Hessian approximation and the predictive one, and suggest to use a linearized predictive distribution. The linearized network $h(\theta)$ around θ^* is defined as

$$h(\theta) := F(x; \theta^*) + J(x; \theta^*)(\theta - \theta^*). \qquad (26.13)$$

Note that $h(\theta)$ is affine linear in the parameters θ, but not the input x. Under a Gaussian posterior $q(\theta)$, the marginal distribution over the network output is again Gaussian [130], and given by

$$p(\hat{y}_q|h(x_q; \theta^*), \mathcal{D}) \approx \int \delta(x^* - h(x_q; \theta^*)) q(\theta) d\theta \qquad (26.14)$$

$$= \mathcal{N}(x^*; F(x_q; \theta^*), J(x_q; \theta^*) \Sigma(\theta) J(x_q; \theta)^\top). \qquad (26.15)$$

This approximation has been extensively used, but only for small neural networks since the per-data point Jacobian is often computationally intractable. Within computational tomography, the Laplace approximation was recently employed for CT reconstruction (together with a probabilistic version of deep image prior) [131].

Variational inference

VI recasts intractable inference as an optimization problem: we replace marginalization with the optimization of Eq. (26.6), which is (unbiasedly) estimated by randomly selecting a mini-batch set $\mathcal{B}$ of M data-pairs and using $T \geq 1$ MC samples (with $\hat{\theta}^t \sim q_\psi(\theta)$) [112],[7]

$$\hat{\mathcal{L}}_{\text{VI}} = \frac{N}{M} \sum_{i \in \mathcal{B}} \frac{1}{T} \sum_{t=1}^{T} \log p\left(y_i^t | x_i^t, \hat{\theta}^t\right) - \text{KL}\left(q_\psi(\theta) \| p(\theta)\right). \tag{26.16}$$

Currently, the most efficient technique to compute the gradients $\nabla_\psi \hat{\mathcal{L}}_{\text{VI}}$ is the so-called reparametrization trick [132], which employs a deterministic dependence of the ELBO with respect to ψ to back-propagate. To this end, we rewrite $q_\psi(\theta)$ using a differentiable transformation $\hat{\theta}^t = g(\psi, \hat{\epsilon}^t)$ with $\hat{\epsilon}^t \sim p(\epsilon)$ and $p(\epsilon)$ being an underlying, parameter-free distribution (e.g., the standard Gaussian distribution). We can then use MC integration over $p(\epsilon)$ to evaluate the expectations, yet the value depends on θ and we can hence propagate gradients through $g(\cdot)$. The reparametrization can be carried out either explicitly [133,134] or implicitly [135]. Once we obtain $q_\psi^*(\theta)$ by maximizing Eq. (26.16), we perform inference on a new query by approximating the predictive distribution in Eq. (26.2) as

$$p(\hat{y}_q | x_q, \mathcal{D}) \approx \int p(\hat{y}_q | x_q, \theta) q_\psi^*(\theta) d\theta := q_\psi^*(\hat{y}_q | x_q). \tag{26.17}$$

In practice, we approximate the optimal variational distribution $q_\psi^*(y_q | x_q)$ with MC integration

$$\hat{q}_\psi^*(\hat{y}_q | x_q) := \frac{1}{T} \sum_{t=1}^{T} p(\hat{y}_q | x_q, \hat{\theta}^t), \quad \text{with } \hat{\theta}^t \sim q_\psi^*(\theta). \tag{26.18}$$

Barbano et al. [136,137] propose a scalable and efficient framework rooted in VI formalism to jointly quantify aleatoric and epistemic uncertainties in unrolled optimization. The framework is showcased on CT reconstruction with both sparse view and limited angle data, and the estimated uncertainty is observed to capture the variability in the reconstructions, caused by the restricted measurement model, and by missing information, due to limited angle geometry.

Monte Carlo dropout

Gal and Ghahramani [114] propose an MCDO method, which approximates $p(\theta | \mathcal{D})$ with a multiplicative Bernoulli distribution. It defines an approximate posterior distribution $q(\theta)$ over a neural network with weight matrices $W_i \in \mathbb{R}^{K_i \times K_{i-1}}$ and bias vectors $b_i \in \mathbb{R}^{K_i}$ for each layer by

$$\begin{aligned} W_i &= M_i \cdot \text{diag}\left(\left[z_{i,j}\right]_{j=1}^{K_i}\right), \\ z_{i,j} &\sim \text{Bernoulli}\,(p_i) \text{ for } i = 1, \ldots, L, j = 1, \ldots, K_{i-1} \end{aligned} \tag{26.19}$$

---

[7] Note that we assume that the KL term can be computed deterministically as a closed form solution might exist; otherwise it can be estimated using Monte Carlo.

where probabilities p_i and M_i are variational parameters and the binary variable $z_{i,j} = 0$ corresponding to the unit j in layer $i - 1$ are dropped as input to layer i. The minimization of the variational objective becomes

$$\mathcal{L}_{\text{MCDO}} := \frac{1}{N} \sum_{i=1}^{N} \|y_i - \hat{y}_i\|_2^2 + \lambda \sum_{i=1}^{L} \left(\|W_i\|_F^2 + \|b_i\|_2^2 \right). \qquad (26.20)$$

MCDO has been interpreted as VI [56]. Although the MCDO objective is not strictly an ELBO [138], we do sometimes refer to it as such. Analogously, other stochastic regularization techniques [139–141] can also be reinterpreted as VI. Schlemper et al. [142] explore the applicability of MCDO to architectures which are commonly used in medical image synthesis to model uncertainty for accelerated MR reconstructions. More generally, the majority of the works in medical image synthesis use MCDO to approximate predictive uncertainty [142,53,71]. Indeed, MCDO is one of the most popular approximate inference schemes for complex deep learning models like CNNs, or recurrent neural networks (RNNs) [143,144]. Nonetheless, despite the impressive progress of BNN techniques, these technologies remain severely under-explored within medical image synthesis.

How to measure predictive uncertainty?

Eq. (26.2) gives the mechanism to synthesize medical images and represents the full information of uncertainty of the imaging task. Here we differentiate metrics that summarize predictive uncertainty. The total uncertainty of the posterior predictive distribution $p(\hat{y}_q | x_q, \mathcal{D})$ is commonly measured by its variance $\mathbf{V}[\hat{y}_q | x_q]$. See Fig. 26.5 for results of a CNN model for diffusion MRI, which show the predictions of mean diffusivity (MD) and fractional anisotropy (FA), and their associated predictive uncertainty maps. The figure displays high correspondence between the root mean squared error (RMSE) maps and the predictive uncertainty on both FA and MD of a test subject, demonstrating the utility of the uncertainty map as a surrogate of prediction accuracy. It also shows strong correlation between the intensity value of the prediction and the predictive uncertainty, being in agreement with the observation that the error map itself correlates strongly with the intensity values.

To elucidate the sources of uncertainty, the total uncertainty can be further decomposed using the law of total variance as

$$\mathbf{V}[\hat{y}_q | x_q] = \underbrace{\mathbf{V}_{q^*(\theta)} \left[\mathbf{E}(\hat{y}_q | x_q, \theta) \right]}_{\Delta_{\text{E}}[\hat{y}_q]} + \underbrace{\mathbf{E}_{q^*(\theta)} \left[\mathbf{V}(\hat{y}_q | x_q, \theta) \right]}_{\Delta_{\text{A}}[\hat{y}_q]}, \qquad (26.21)$$

where $\mathbf{E}(\hat{y}_q | x_q, \theta)$ and $\mathbf{V}(\hat{y}_q | x_q, \theta)$ are, respectively, the mean and variance of the prediction $\hat{y}_q$ according to $p(\hat{y}_q | x_q, \theta)$. The first term $\Delta_{\text{E}}[\hat{y}_q]$ measures epistemic uncertainty since it ignores any contribution to the variance of $\hat{y}_q$ from the stochasticity in the data x_q. In contrast, the second term $\Delta_{\text{A}}[\hat{y}_q]$ represents the average value

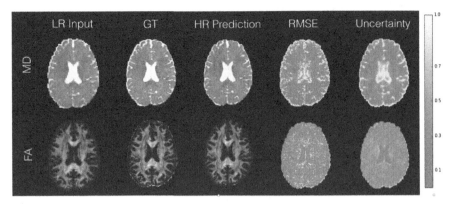

FIGURE 26.5

Comparison between voxel-wise RMSE and predictive uncertainty maps for FA and MD computed on a Human Connectome Project test subject (min–max normalized for MD and FA separately). Low resolution input, ground truth, and the mean of high resolution predictions are also shown. Source: [66].

of $\mathbf{V}(\hat{y}_q | x_q, \theta)$. This term ignores any contribution to the variance of $\hat{y}_q$ from θ and thus models aleatoric uncertainty. The importance of distinguishing between different forms of uncertainty has recently been recognized in deep learning models [57,53]. We describe one approach in this direction by decomposing the predictive variance into aleatoric and epistemic components. The epistemic uncertainty (of parametric nature) can be obtained using BNNs and approximate inference schemes (e.g., VI or MCDO) thus it is encapsulated in the approximate posterior distribution. Meanwhile, quantifying aleatoric uncertainty can be captured by computing the variance of the likelihood. This broad class of models, where the variance is a function of the input, is often termed as input-dependent or heteroscedastic noise models [145,146]. In practice, recent works rely on doubling the network architecture and modeling the likelihood as a Gaussian distribution with input-dependent varying variance (see Fig. 26.6), that is, $p(\hat{y}_q | x_q, \theta) = \mathcal{N}\left(\hat{y}; \mathrm{F}^{\mu}(x; \theta_1), \mathrm{F}^{\sigma}(x; \theta_2)\right)$, where $\mathrm{F}^{\mu}(\cdot; \theta_1)$ and $\mathrm{F}^{\sigma}(\cdot; \theta_2)$ refer to the "mean" and "covariance" networks, respectively, with the approximate posterior distribution being $q_{\psi}(\theta = \{(\theta_1, \theta_2)\})$. Note that predictive uncertainty can be also decomposed by using homoscedastic noise models (i.e., constant variance across all spatial locations), but this approximation is highly unrealistic in medical image synthesis.

One can estimate the variance of a quantity of interest derived from a synthesized image and potentially decompose it into aleatoric and epistemic components. Let $f(\cdot)$ be any reasonably behaved function, which transforms the synthesized image $\hat{y}_q$ into a quantity of interest, and we estimate the variance in the transformed domain (i.e., $\mathbf{V}[f(\hat{y}_q) | x_q]$). If $f(\cdot)$ is an identity map, that is, $f(\hat{y}_q) = \hat{y}_q$, Eq. (26.21) can be approximated using T MC samples:

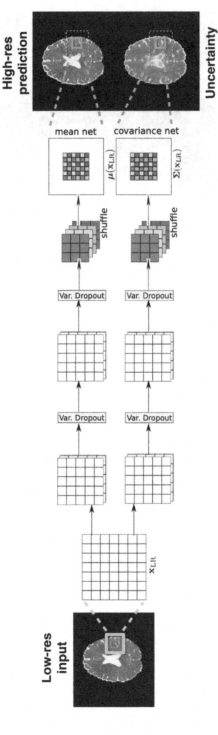

FIGURE 26.6

Illustration of a heteroscedastic network with variational dropout [139], with diagonal covariance. The top 3D-ESPCN estimates the mean and the bottom one estimates the covariance matrix of the likelihood. Variational dropout is applied to feature maps after every convolution, where Gaussian noise is injected into feature maps $F_{out} = \mu_Y + \epsilon \odot \sigma_Y$, with $\epsilon \sim \mathcal{N}(0, I)$. Source: [66].

$$\widehat{\mathbf{V}}[\hat{y}_q | x_q] = \underbrace{\frac{1}{T} \sum_{t=1}^{T} \mathrm{F}^{\mu}(x_q; \theta_1^t) \mathrm{F}^{\mu}(x_q; \theta_1^t)^{\top} - \bar{\mathrm{F}}^{\mu}(x_q) \bar{\mathrm{F}}^{\mu}(x_q)^{\top}}_{\widehat{\Delta}_{\mathrm{E}}(\hat{y}_q)} + \underbrace{\sum_{i=1}^{T} \mathrm{F}^{\sigma}(x_q; \theta_2^t)}_{\widehat{\Delta}_{\mathrm{A}}(\hat{y}_q)},$$

(26.22)

where $\bar{\mathrm{F}}^{\mu}(x_q) = \frac{1}{T} \sum_{t=1}^{T} \mathrm{F}^{\mu}(x_q; \theta_1^t)$ with $\{(\theta_1^t, \theta_2^t)\}_{t=1}^{T} \sim q_{\psi}^{*}(\theta)$. If $f(\cdot)$ is "complicated" again, we need to resort to MC sampling. Following Tanno et al. [53], given $\{(\theta_1^t, \theta_2^t)\}_{t=1}^{T} \sim q_{\psi}^{*}(\theta)$ and $\{f^t\}_{j=1}^{J} \sim p(\hat{y}_q | x_q, \theta_1^t, \theta_2^t)$ we estimate the propagated epistemic uncertainty $\Delta_{\mathrm{E}}[f(\hat{y}_q)]$ and propagated aleatoric $\Delta_{\mathrm{A}}[f(\hat{y}_q)]$ uncertainty as

$$\widehat{\Delta}_{\mathrm{E}}\left[f(\hat{y}_q)\right] := \frac{1}{T} \sum_{t}(\bar{f}^t)^2 - \left(\frac{1}{(J-1)T} \sum_{j,t} f_j^t\right)^2, \qquad (26.23)$$

$$\widehat{\Delta}_{\mathrm{A}}\left[f(\hat{y}_q)\right] := \frac{1}{(J-1)T} \sum_{j,t}(f_j^t)^2 - \frac{1}{T} \sum_{t}(\bar{f}^t)^2, \qquad (26.24)$$

$$\bar{f}^t := \frac{1}{J} \sum_{j} f_j^t. \qquad (26.25)$$

Due to "double sampling," these estimators tend to have higher variance than the case where $f(\hat{y}_q) = \hat{y}_q$.

Instead of the variance of the posterior predictive distribution, we can also use its entropy as a measure of the overall predictive uncertainty [147]. The total uncertainty of the predictive distribution in Eq. (26.2) can then be quantified as $\mathbf{H}(\hat{y}_q | x_q)$, where $\mathbf{H}(\cdot)$ denotes the differential entropy of a probability distribution. This also allows decomposing predictive uncertainty into the two forms of uncertainty. The expectation of $\mathbf{H}\left(\hat{y}_q | x_q, \theta\right)$ under $q_{\psi}^{*}(\theta)$, that is, $\mathbf{E}_{q_{\psi}^{*}(\theta)}[\mathbf{H}(\hat{y}_q | x_q, \theta)]$, can be used to measure aleatoric uncertainty, and the difference between total and aleatoric uncertainty to quantify the epistemic uncertainty,

$$\mathbf{H}\left[\hat{y}_q | x_q\right] - \mathbf{E}_{q_{\psi}^{*}(\theta)}\left[\mathbf{H}(\hat{y}_q | x_q, \theta)\right] := \mathbf{MI}(\hat{y}_q, \theta), \qquad (26.26)$$

which is the mutual information [148] between the posterior distributions of the model parameters θ and $\hat{y}_q$.

This decomposition allows us to separately quantify aleatoric and epistemic uncertainties. We give an illustration in Fig. 26.7 for CT reconstructions [137]. It is observed that in both sparse view and limited angle CT reconstructions, aleatoric uncertainty appears to dominate, with its overall shape close to the mean (but of a smaller magnitude). Epistemic uncertainty is localized to certain regions, capturing artifacts due to limited angle data. Thus, aleatoric and epistemic uncertainties provide complementary information about the reconstructions, and might provide different insights into their reliability.

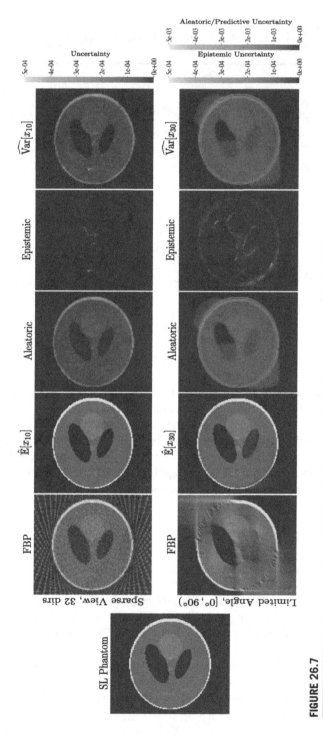

FIGURE 26.7

The reconstructions for sparse view CT with 32 directions (top) and limited angle with [0, 90°] (bottom). Source: [137].

Miscellaneous approximations

Recent deep inferential machinery may also hold potential for the synthesis community. These techniques also employ deep neural networks but often obtain the associated uncertainties differently from BNNs. Below we describe the most influential ones. Adler et al. [149] employ a modified conditional Wasserstein generative adversarial network [150] to generate a high-dose CT from low-dose counterparts. However, the approach was only evaluated on simplified settings. Denker et al. [151] use conditional invertible neural networks which are inferential machinery based on (conditional) normalizing flow [152,153]. Normalizing flow allows learning expressive conditional densities by maximum likelihood estimation. The authors aim to learn a conditional density of images from noisy low-dose CT measurements based on training data obtained from high-dose reconstructions. Tonolini et al. [154] and Zhang et al. [155] concurrently use a conditional variational autoencoder framework [132] for solving Bayesian image reconstruction problems. Zhang et al. [155] provide the theoretical underpinning for approximate posterior inference and demonstrations on Gaussian and Poisson image denoising. More recently, Tezcan et al. [156] propose a hybrid approach for under-sampled MRI reconstruction to overcome the curse-of-dimensionality. The authors introduce a low-dimensional latent space given the acquisition data in k-space modeled via a variational autoencoder, and then apply MCMC for the sampling. In a yet slightly different vein, more recently, Edupuganti et al. [157] propose an approach for uncertainty quantification via variational autoencoders, with uncertainty encoded in the low-dimensional latent variable, and consistency enforced by minimizing a loss based on the Stein unbiased risk estimator, and demonstrate the approach on MRI reconstruction.

Finally, an alternative approach to uncertainty quantification is ensembling (i.e., bootstrap posteriors), where the variance of the predictions of multiple networks (i.e., the ensemble) is used to quantify predictive uncertainty [158]. In a number of settings, deep ensembles are becoming the gold standard approach for obtaining an accurate and well-calibrated posterior predictive distribution [159–161]. Within the machine learning community, the idea that deep ensembles should be regarded as an approximate approach to Bayesian marginalization, instead of a competing (non-Bayesian) method to Bayesian inference, is emerging [83]. Pearce et al. [162] argue that deep ensembles perform approximate Bayesian inference, and Gustafsson et al. [163] also mention that deep ensembles can be regarded as samples from an approximate posterior distribution. Ensemble methods are limited by their computational cost as multiple neural networks need to be trained independently (using different network initializations). Furthermore, ensembling neural networks requires even more significant memory and computational overhead at training and test time. To overcome the computational bottleneck, Huang et al. [164], among others [80,165,166], propose faster methods which train ensembles by leveraging different parameter configurations obtained in one single stochastic gradient descent trajectory. However, these methods come at the cost of reduced predictive performance [160]. There has been growing interest in uncertainty quantification using deterministic neural networks which quantify uncertainty in a single forward pass and therefore have a smaller memory footprint [167–169].

All these approaches hold great potential for medical image synthesis.

Useful GitHub repositories

Training a Bayesian neural network efficiently is highly nontrivial. The current practice in machine learning strongly encourages the sharing of relevant implementations, mostly via GitHub. Instead of listing all existing links on Bayesian neural networks, we would like to mention a few GitHub repositories that provide PyTorch implementations of the approximate inference methods that we have discussed, along with useful Google Colaboratory (Colab) notebooks. We believe that it is preferable to suggest exemplary implementations that are currently available on GitHub, and that have been carefully vetted by many members of the machine learning community. In this regard, we highly recommend the following GitHub repository https:// github.com/JavierAntoran/Bayesian-Neural-Networks, which has been redacted by Javier Antorán, a PhD candidate in the Machine Learning Group at Cambridge University. We include this repository for its richness, as well as its excellent readability. The author also provides Colab notebooks, which can be easily run without any need for expensive hardware, and allow interested readers to better familiarize themselves with different models. We would also like to mention Kumar Shridhar's repository https://github.com/kumar-shridhar/PyTorch-BayesianCNN, which includes Bayesian convolutional layers.

26.4 Open challenges

In the previous sections, we have provided a general exposition of several machine learning techniques available for uncertainty quantification in deep neural networks with no specific applications in mind. In this final section, we bring out attentions back to the synthesis applications and aim to elaborate on a number of outstanding technical and clinical challenges specific to this domain. For instance, we are often forced to opt for restrictive, yet computationally feasible descriptors of reality over more truthful but computationally infeasible ones. In Section 26.4.1 we discuss the implications of the approximations we employ, and identify several possible research opportunities. In Section 26.4.2 we briefly discuss the additional hurdles we face when deploying uncertainty quantification technologies within the complex structure of healthcare, and envision that risk needs to be quantified in the context in which clinical decisions are formulated.

26.4.1 Can we trust uncertainty?

As is with all kind of quantifications, one is naturally interested in assessing whether we can actually trust the obtained uncertainty estimates; even more so if several approximations are taken. So, can we trust uncertainty? To answer the question we first present the sources of "(in)accuracy," putting a major focus on BNNs. We then argue that a quantitative evaluation of the uncertainty estimates would address at least (i) how accurate the estimates are (with respect to the ground-truth posterior distribution); and (ii) how robust they would be with respect to data distribution shift.

Sources of (in)accuracy

Computational feasibility often imposes restrictive approximations, leading to approximate likelihood, prior and posterior distributions, and thereby resulting in inaccurate estimation of aleatoric or epistemic uncertainty. Likelihood misspecification arises when overly simplistic assumptions are adopted for either the forward map or the noise statistics. Due to the high-dimensionality of the output, the likelihood is often assumed to be a Gaussian distribution with a diagonal covariance matrix, which provides only pixel-wise marginal distributions, and thus is unable to capture multi-modality of the predictive distribution (i.e., the presence of multiple modes). Further, the diagonality assumes that the output pixels are statistically independent given the input. Likewise, the prior distribution $p(\theta)$ is prone to misspecification. This is especially true for data-driven approaches, where the parameters θ in neural networks (possibly due to severe over-parameterization) often lack a clear semantic meaning or physical interpretation. This has largely prohibited domain practitioners from constructing hand-crafted priors. Instead of the result of the attempt to capture the modeler's prior knowledge (which is hard to grasp), priors are usually chosen (or at least in part) to ease computation, and as a result, in neural networks, one often contents with simple priors (i.e., the standard Gaussian distribution). Inevitably, this alters an orthodox interpretation of the prior in Bayesian statistics.

Even if the likelihood and the prior were both faithfully constructed to capture the real-world physics, the posterior distribution $p(\theta|\mathcal{D})$ is often approximated by Gaussian distributions with diagonal covariance (sometimes with low-rank or diagonal assumption), to facilitate or enable the requisite computation. Undoubtedly, this is a restrictive assumption. Foong et al. [170,128] study the quality of common approximate inference methods VI and MCDO in approximating the Bayesian predictive distribution. They shed interesting insight into the pathologies of these approximation schemes, which up to now remain poorly understood. The issue of calibrating uncertainty estimates remains a big open question for both approximate inference techniques and deep learning based approaches, and it is currently an active area of research within the deep learning community [171,172].

Practical shortcomings of Bayesian neural networks

Bayesian methods have the potential to fix the shortcomings of deep learning (e.g., over-fitting, robustness, detection of out-of-distribution samples). Yet currently BNNs are often impractical and rarely match the performance of standard methods [173]. The impracticability of such deep inferential machineries can be attributed to several factors including (i) implementation complexity: BNNs are fairly sensitive to hyper-parameter selection and initialization strategies, and the training process can be substantially more challenging [174]; (ii) computational cost: BNNs can take orders of magnitude longer to converge than standard (deterministic) neural networks, or alternatively, deep ensemble models require simultaneous training of multiple networks; (iii) weak performance: BNNs rely on crude approximations to achieve scalability, which often result in limited or unreliable uncertainty estimates [128]. In fact, the approximating family (e.g., Q_{FFG}) may not contain good approximations to the posterior distribution, and even if it does, the method (e.g., stochastic VI) may not be able to find a good approximate posterior within the chosen family. Not surprisingly, BNNs are rarely employed by the medical imaging community due to their complex deployment, which tends to overshadow their theoretical advantages.

The machine learning community proposed several solutions that partially address some of the pitfalls: recent works have largely focused on scalable inference [81,103,119,173,175–177]. However, these have not yet been picked up by the medical imaging community, arguably due to the lack of communication between the two. Undoubtedly, the primary goal of this review is to bridge two different communities to inform the imaging community of the recent exciting developments in the machine learning community.

When it comes to uncertainty quantification, medical image synthesis practitioners often have blindly resorted to simple (as less expressive) Bayesian methods (e.g., MCDO) without a second thought. The machine learning community has recently proposed several solutions, which may have the potential to scale up to truly high-dimensional data regimes, as commonly occurring in practical medical imaging applications. Clearly, we still face a scalability issue. One thus may argue that if many of the available methods (if not all!) are not yet applicable to high-dimensional medical imaging problems, it is then acceptable to resort to MCDO. On the contrary, we believe that it is still worth informing the medical image community of the existence of more "sophisticated" methods, even if those are not yet applicable to medical imaging problems. Addressing the lack of scalability would open a myriad of research opportunities, which the synthesis community should seize. For example, Tezcan et al. [156] propose a novel method, which reveals a mature understanding of the limitations of the current approaches in Bayesian deep learning. Overcoming those led to a novel reconstruction algorithm.

Benchmarking uncertainty estimates

The lack of realistic ground truths has greatly hindered the quantitative evaluation of the accuracy of uncertainty estimates. In practice, it is often highly desirable to validate the accuracy of the approximation via golden standard MCMC, which, however, is infeasible for many real-world synthesis applications, since the distribution of interest $p(y|x)$ (i.e., the underlying data distribution) is almost always unknown or the resulting posterior is simply too costly even for the most advanced MCMC sampling algorithm. Nonetheless, it may be still possible to validate the aleatoric uncertainty by handcrafting a test dataset where the "ground truth" intrinsic noise is known (e.g., passing a set of medical images through a known stochastic transformation). The validation of the parametric uncertainty is by no means less challenging as the target distribution of interest $p(\theta|\mathcal{D})$ (i.e., the posterior distribution over the parameters) is not accessible. However, controllable and realistic means to edit input images (e.g., adding pathological structures or structural perturbations) would enable systematically studying what kinds of "out-of-distribution" structures can be detected through the analysis of parametric uncertainty for different Bayesian approximation schemes to neural networks. There have been various attempts to use distributional shift while bench-marking parametric uncertainty [158,159].

The robustness under data shifts of the uncertainty estimate is as well under scrutiny [159]. Robustness is strictly related to how well-calibrated uncertainty estimates are under domain shifts—in various settings, the test data distribution tends to deviate from the training environment due to sample bias[8] and non-stationarity, which detracts from performance. This unfortunately occurs to uncertainty estimates as well (i.e., non-calibrated as the distribution changes). Robustness under distributional shift (e.g., the presence of out-of-distribution inputs) is necessary for the safe deployment in clinical practice in which distributional shift is widely prevalent. Therefore, predictive uncertainty must be well-calibrated to allow us to quantitatively assess the risk of a possible degradation of the synthesis task while sounding out unknown ground. This is critical since we would like to use uncertainty as a defensive mechanism against failures.

Future work should investigate the benefits of using more complex likelihood models (e.g., the correlations between neighboring pixels may further improve the reconstruction quality) such as mixture models [45], diversity losses [178–180], and more powerful density estimators [181–183], as well as more structured and expressive posterior approximations [184,185]. Moreover, finding answers to the queries above would shed insight on the clinical validation of predictive uncertainty as a measure of practical utility.

26.4.2 How to communicate uncertainty to clinicians?

Last we discuss the challenges with communicating uncertainty to clinicians, and risk-aware uncertainty quantification, where the risk is related to the degree to which the synthesis has to be faithful. These challenges motivate revisiting the development of uncertainty analysis and quantification technologies.

Ideally, the translation of uncertainty quantification technologies from the machine learning community into clinical practice should cause as little disruption as possible to existing clinical workflows. There are several possible ways to convey uncertainty to clinicians. The uncertainty can be either directly handed over to clinicians as visuals by means of pixel-wise reliability scores (e.g., error bars or voxel-wise predictive variance) or summarizing image-wise reliability scores (e.g., overall probability). Conveying uncertainty through visuals via voxel-wise variance appears more

---

[8] Sample bias is of epistemic nature and reflects the fact that the data we observed is only in part representative of the ground-truth data distribution. If we train our model in presence of sampling bias, it is highly likely that it would poorly generalize towards under-represented features.

disruptive to clinical practice than a single reliability score. Having a one-off score is very tempting, but how will we actually go about deriving a single score from voxel-wise reliability maps or directly estimating a single score while foregoing the full Bayesian framework? It should be nothing less than a score that expresses whether the synthetic image is usable or not for the given task. For example, in the context of CT reconstruction, we may wish the score to inform us of the probability that a certain pathology (e.g., tumor or lesion) is present in the synthesized image. This issue can potentially be systematically addressed within the framework of hypothesis testing. Alternatively, uncertainty could play only behind closed doors, either embedded as a background defensive mechanism, or propagated through a pipeline (e.g., a cascade of inferential tasks for downstream decision-making).

How to optimally propagate uncertainty quantification in downstream analysis remains an open question, and is expected to be highly application dependent: different downstream tasks would require uncertainty information of different quality. Indeed, we argue that the uncertainty quantification procedures should take the specifics of the downstream application into account, and we advocate for "granular" risk management as the risk depends on the downstream application.

We take radiation treatment planning as an example to show granularity of the risk-aware decision in image synthesis. For instance, if we had to synthesize a CT, which is often used to guide how to position radiation beams to target a tumor while avoiding healthy areas, we would not mind if there were defects (or high unreliability) in regions outside of the reach of the photon beams. Furthermore, larger or smaller margins could be drawn around the target—which we may want to treat or avoid—based on the reliability of the image. Consider a scenario in which a diagnostic decision is made based on a synthesized image. In order to make such a diagnostic decision, we need to quantify how reliable the image is. Taking Cohen's caricature example [34], which shows how a deep learning based algorithm can "hallucinate" cancer. If the clinician is somehow not investigating the cancer itself, this image might still be useful. Meanwhile, if the downstream task were radiotherapy treatment planning for the cancer, it would be a clear red flag not to use the image. The ideal scenario would be to quantify risk based on the details of the application. However, risk-sensitive uncertainty quantification raises several technical and conceptual challenges about how to apply a threshold to uncertainty (or to define an admissible set) for risk management.

It remains unclear how to use predictive uncertainty appropriately so that we can quantify the risks in the space in which the clinical decisions are made. This remains a completely open question, yet we recognize the enormous importance of future works in this direction, while realizing the full potential of uncertainty quantification technologies in clinical practice. These discussions also have significant implications for technology development (e.g., developing technologies that directly deliver uncertainty estimates for the clinical practice of interest) to optimize the computational expense.

26.5 Concluding remarks

In this chapter we have provided an up-to-date overview of uncertainty quantification for medical image synthesis, including image reconstruction. In recent years, uncertainty quantification has been hailed as a very promising strategy to address the outstanding challenge, i.e., the lack of robustness of many deep learning based techniques, and thus has received much attention. We have described basic concepts in uncertainty analysis (e.g., predictive, aleatoric and epistemic uncertainty) and the potential benefits of providing uncertainty information in image synthesis along with the usual point estimators.

Conceptually, uncertainty reasoning can be carried out elegantly within a Bayesian framework, where all relevant information is represented by probability distributions and different sources of information can be integrated by Bayes' formula. Nonetheless, this poses enormous computational challenges, especially with the complex models, which have arisen in deep learning. We have discussed representative computational techniques, including classical approximate inference strategies (e.g., MCMC, Laplace approximation, and variational inference) along with the more recent Bayesian neural networks and Monte Carlo dropout. We have also pointed out relevant links to open source implementations available on GitHub repositories and discussed how to quantify the sources of uncertainty.

Lastly, we discussed the technical and clinical challenges associated with uncertainty quantification. The technical ones are largely concerned with calibration of the obtained uncertainty estimates. The clinical ones instead involve how to communicate the uncertainty information without disrupting existing medical pipelines.

In sum, uncertainty quantification holds enormous potential for medical image synthesis. However, there remain many outstanding technical and clinical challenges that have to be overcome before these technologies can be routinely deployed in clinical practice. This calls for further research from both theoretical and applied perspectives. Big practical challenges include developing scalable inference techniques, which are as non-intrusive as possible to the current imaging pipelines and providing clinically interpretable metrics for conveying useful uncertainty information. Theoretically, it is important to establish relevant mathematical–statistical guarantees for existing and forthcoming computational techniques.

References

[1] J.E. Iglesias, E. Konukoglu, D. Zikic, B. Glocker, K. van Leemput, B. Fischl, Is synthesizing MRI contrast useful for inter-modality analysis?, in: International Conference on Medical Image Computing and Computer-Assisted Intervention, Springer, 2013, pp. 631–638.

[2] D.H. Ye, D. Zikic, B. Glocker, A. Criminisi, E. Konukoglu, Modality propagation: coherent synthesis of subject-specific scans with data-driven regularization, in: International Conference on Medical Image Computing and Computer-Assisted Intervention, Springer, 2013, pp. 606–613.

[3] N. Burgos, M.J. Cardoso, K. Thielemans, M. Modat, S. Pedemonte, J. Dickson, A. Barnes, R. Ahmed, C.J. Mahoney, J.M. Schott, et al., Attenuation correction synthesis for hybrid PET-MR scanners: application to brain studies, IEEE Trans. Med. Imaging 33 (12) (2014) 2332–2341.

[4] M.J. Cardoso, C.H. Sudre, M. Modat, S. Ourselin, Template-based multimodal joint generative model of brain data, in: International Conference on Information Processing in Medical Imaging, Springer, 2015, pp. 17–29.

[5] A.F. Frangi, S.A. Tsaftaris, J.L. Prince, Simulation and synthesis in medical imaging, IEEE Trans. Med. Imaging 37 (3) (2018) 673–679.

[6] M. Dashti, A.M. Stuart, The Bayesian approach to inverse problems, arXiv preprint, arXiv:1302.6989, 2013.

[7] S. Arridge, P. Maass, O. Öktem, C.-B. Schönlieb, Solving inverse problems using data-driven models, Acta Numer. 28 (2019) 1–174.

[8] H. van Nguyen, K. Zhou, R. Vemulapalli, Cross-domain synthesis of medical images using efficient location-sensitive deep network, in: International Conference on Medical Image Computing and Computer-Assisted Intervention, Springer, 2015, pp. 677–684.

[9] A. Chartsias, T. Joyce, M.V. Giuffrida, S.A. Tsaftaris, Multimodal MR synthesis via modality-invariant latent representation, IEEE Trans. Med. Imaging 37 (3) (2017) 803–814.

[10] S.U. Dar, M. Yurt, L. Karacan, A. Erdem, E. Erdem, T. Çukur, Image synthesis in multi-contrast MRI with conditional generative adversarial networks, IEEE Trans. Med. Imaging 38 (10) (2019) 2375–2388.

[11] D. Nie, X. Cao, Y. Gao, L. Wang, D. Shen, Estimating CT image from MRI data using 3D fully convolutional networks, in: Deep Learning and Data Labeling for Medical Applications, Springer, 2016, pp. 170–178.

[12] D. Nie, R. Trullo, J. Lian, C. Petitjean, S. Ruan, Q. Wang, D. Shen, Medical image synthesis with context-aware generative adversarial networks, in: International Conference on Medical Image Computing and Computer-Assisted Intervention, Springer, 2017, pp. 417–425.

[13] J.M. Wolterink, A.M. Dinkla, M.H. Savenije, P.R. Seevinck, C.A. van den Berg, I. Išgum, Deep MR to CT synthesis using unpaired data, in: International Workshop on Simulation and Synthesis in Medical Imaging, Springer, 2017, pp. 14–23.

[14] A. Ben-Cohen, E. Klang, S.P. Raskin, M.M. Amitai, H. Greenspan, Virtual PET images from CT data using deep convolutional networks: initial results, in: International Workshop on Simulation and Synthesis in Medical Imaging, Springer, 2017, pp. 49–57.

[15] L. Bi, J. Kim, A. Kumar, D. Feng, M. Fulham, Synthesis of positron emission tomography (PET) images via multi-channel generative adversarial networks (GANs), in: Molecular Imaging, Reconstruction and Analysis of Moving Body Organs, and Stroke Imaging and Treatment, Springer, 2017, pp. 43–51.

[16] K. Armanious, C. Jiang, M. Fischer, T. Küstner, T. Hepp, K. Nikolaou, S. Gatidis, B. Yang, MedGAN: medical image translation using GANs, Comput. Med. Imaging Graph. 79 (2020) 101684.

[17] G. Yang, S. Yu, H. Dong, G. Slabaugh, P.L. Dragotti, X. Ye, F. Liu, S. Arridge, J. Keegan, Y. Guo, et al., DAGAN: deep de-aliasing generative adversarial networks for fast compressed sensing MRI reconstruction, IEEE Trans. Med. Imaging 37 (6) (2017) 1310–1321.

[18] T.M. Quan, T. Nguyen-Duc, W.-K. Jeong, Compressed sensing MRI reconstruction using a generative adversarial network with a cyclic loss, IEEE Trans. Med. Imaging 37 (6) (2018) 1488–1497.

[19] Y. Zhang, G. Wu, P.-T. Yap, Q. Feng, J. Lian, W. Chen, D. Shen, Hierarchical patch-based sparse representation—a new approach for resolution enhancement of 4D-CT lung data, IEEE Trans. Med. Imaging 31 (11) (2012) 1993–2005.

[20] Y. Huang, L. Shao, A.F. Frangi, Simultaneous super-resolution and cross-modality synthesis of 3D medical images using weakly-supervised joint convolutional sparse coding, in: Proceedings of the IEEE Conference on Computer Vision and Pattern Recognition, 2017, pp. 6070–6079.

[21] A.S. Chaudhari, Z. Fang, F. Kogan, J. Wood, K.J. Stevens, E.K. Gibbons, J.H. Lee, G.E. Gold, B.A. Hargreaves, Super-resolution musculoskeletal MRI using deep learning, Magn. Reson. Med. 80 (5) (2018) 2139–2154.

[22] K. Sommer, A. Saalbach, T. Brosch, C. Hall, N. Cross, J. Andre, Correction of motion artifacts using a multiscale fully convolutional neural network, Am. J. Neuroradiol. 41 (3) (2020) 416–423.

[23] L. Gondara, Medical image denoising using convolutional denoising autoencoders, in: 2016 IEEE 16th International Conference on Data Mining Workshops (ICDMW), IEEE, 2016, pp. 241–246.

[24] J. Xie, L. Xu, E. Chen, Image denoising and inpainting with deep neural networks, in: Advances in Neural Information Processing Systems, 2012, pp. 341–349.

[25] F. Natterer, F. Wübbeling, Mathematical Methods in Image Reconstruction, SIAM, 2001.

[26] G. Ongie, A. Jalal, C.A. Baraniuk, R.G. Metzler, A.G. Dimakis, R. Willett, Deep learning techniques for inverse problems in imaging, IEEE J. Sel. Areas in Inf. Theory 1 (1) (2020) 39–56.

[27] G. Wang, J.C. Ye, B. De Man, Deep learning for tomographic image reconstruction, Nature Mach. Intell. 2 (2020) 737–748.

[28] P. Putzky, M. Welling, Recurrent inference machines for solving inverse problems, arXiv:1706.04008, 2017.

[29] J. Adler, O. Öktem, Learned primal-dual reconstruction, IEEE Trans. Med. Imaging 37 (6) (2018) 1322–1332.

[30] A. Hauptmann, F. Lucka, M. Betcke, N. Huynh, J. Adler, B. Cox, P. Beard, S. Ourselin, S. Arridge, Model-based learning for accelerated, limited-view 3-D photoacoustic tomography, IEEE Trans. Med. Imaging 37 (6) (2018) 1382–1393.

[31] V. Monga, Y. Li, Y.C. Eldar, Algorithm unrolling: interpretable, efficient deep learning for signal and image processing, arXiv:1912.10557, 2019.

[32] B. Zhu, J.Z. Liu, S.F. Cauley, B.R. Rosen, M.S. Rosen, Image reconstruction by domain-transform manifold learning, Nature 555 (7697) (2018) 487–492.

[33] J. He, Y. Wang, J. Ma, Radon inversion via deep learning, IEEE Trans. Med. Imaging 39 (6) (2020) 2076–2087.

[34] J.P. Cohen, M. Luck, S. Honari, Distribution matching losses can hallucinate features in medical image translation, in: International Conference on Medical Image Computing and Computer-Assisted Intervention, Springer, 2018, pp. 529–536.

[35] V. Antun, F. Renna, C. Poon, B. Adcock, A.C. Hansen, On instabilities of deep learning in image reconstruction-does AI come at a cost?, Proc. Natl. Acad. Sci. USA 117 (48) (2020) 30088–30095.

[36] Y. Bengio, I. Goodfellow, A. Courville, Deep Learning, vol. 1, MIT Press, Massachusetts, USA, 2017.

[37] K. Hammernik, T. Klatzer, E. Kobler, M.P. Recht, D.K. Sodickson, T. Pock, F. Knoll, Learning a variational network for reconstruction of accelerated MRI data, Magn. Reson. Med. 79 (6) (2018) 3055–3071.

[38] L.I. Rudin, S. Osher, E. Fatemi, Nonlinear total variation based noise removal algorithms, Physica D 60 (1–4) (1992) 259–268.

[39] E.J. Candès, J. Romberg, T. Tao, Robust uncertainty principles: exact signal reconstruction from highly incomplete frequency information, IEEE Trans. Inf. Theory 52 (2) (2006) 489–509.

[40] D.L. Donoho, Compressed sensing, IEEE Trans. Inf. Theory 52 (4) (2006) 1289–1306.

[41] E. Begoli, T. Bhattacharya, D. Kusnezov, The need for uncertainty quantification in machine-assisted medical decision making, Nature Mach. Intell. 1 (1) (2019) 20–23.

[42] T.J. Sullivan, Introduction to Uncertainty Quantification, Springer, 2015.

[43] H. Greenspan, R. Tanno, M. Erdt, T. Arbel, C. Baumgartner, A. Dalca, C.H. Sudre, W.M. Wells, K. Drechsler, M.G. Linguraru, et al. (Eds.), Uncertainty for Safe Utilization of Machine Learning in Medical Imaging and Clinical Image-Based Procedures: First International Workshop, UNSURE 2019, and 8th International Workshop, CLIP 2019, Held in Conjunction with MICCAI 2019, Shenzhen, China, October 17, 2019, Proceedings, vol. 11840, Springer Nature, 2019.

[44] M. Abdar, F. Pourpanah, S. Hussain, D. Rezazadegan, L. Liu, M. Ghavamzadeh, P. Fieguth, A. Khosravi, U.R. Acharya, V. Makarenkov, S. Nahavandi, A review of uncertainty quantification in deep learning: techniques, applications and challenges, arXiv:2011.06225, 2020.

[45] S. Kohl, B. Romera-Paredes, C. Meyer, J. De Fauw, J.R. Ledsam, K. Maier-Hein, S.A. Eslami, D.J. Rezende, O. Ronneberger, A probabilistic U-net for segmentation of ambiguous images, in: Advances in Neural Information Processing Systems, 2018, pp. 6965–6975.

[46] T. Nair, D. Precup, D.L. Arnold, T. Arbel, Exploring uncertainty measures in deep networks for multiple sclerosis lesion detection and segmentation, Med. Image Anal. 59 (2020) 101557.

[47] S. Hu, D. Worrall, S. Knegt, B. Veeling, H. Huisman, M. Welling, Supervised uncertainty quantification for segmentation with multiple annotations, in: International Conference on Medical Image Computing and Computer-Assisted Intervention, Springer, 2019, pp. 137–145.

[48] A.G. Roy, S. Conjeti, N. Navab, C. Wachinger, A.D.N. Initiative, et al., Bayesian QuickNAT: model uncertainty in deep whole-brain segmentation for structure-wise quality control, NeuroImage 195 (2019) 11–22.

[49] A.V. Dalca, G. Balakrishnan, J. Guttag, M.R. Sabuncu, Unsupervised learning of probabilistic diffeomorphic registration for images and surfaces, Med. Image Anal. 57 (2019) 226–236.

[50] M. Jain, S. Lahlou, H. Nekoei, V. Butoi, P. Bertin, J. Rector-Brooks, M. Korablyov, Y. Bengio, DEUP: direct epistemic uncertainty prediction, Preprint, arXiv:2102.08501v1, 2021.

[51] S.C. Hora, Aleatory and epistemic uncertainty in probability elicitation with an example from hazardous waste management, Reliab. Eng. Syst. Saf. 54 (2–3) (1996) 217–223.

[52] B.M. Ayyub, G.J. Klir, Uncertainty Modeling and Analysis in Engineering and the Sciences, CRC Press, New York, 2006.

[53] R. Tanno, A. Ghosh, F. Grussu, E. Kaden, A. Criminisi, D.C. Alexander, Bayesian image quality transfer, in: International Conference on Medical Image Computing and Computer-Assisted Intervention, Springer, 2016, pp. 265–273.

[54] H.G. Matthies, Quantifying uncertainty: modern computational representation of probability and applications, in: Extreme Man-Made and Natural Hazards in Dynamics of Structures, Springer, 2007, pp. 105–135.

[55] A. Der Kiureghian, O. Ditlevsen, Aleatory or epistemic? Does it matter?, Struct. Saf. 31 (2) (2009) 105–112.

[56] Y. Gal, Uncertainty in Deep Learning, PhD thesis, University of Cambridge, 2016.

[57] A. Kendall, Y. Gal, What uncertainties do we need in Bayesian deep learning for computer vision?, in: Advances in Neural Information Processing Systems, 2017, pp. 5574–5584.

[58] S. Depeweg, Modeling Epistemic and Aleatoric Uncertainty with Bayesian Neural Networks and Latent Variables, PhD thesis, Technische Universität München, 2019.

[59] H. Wang, D.M. Levi, S.A. Klein, Intrinsic uncertainty and integration efficiency in bisection acuity, Vis. Res. 36 (5) (1996) 717–739.

[60] E. Hüllermeier, W. Waegeman, Aleatoric and epistemic uncertainty in machine learning: a tutorial introduction, arXiv preprint, arXiv:1910.09457, 2019.

[61] U. Bhatt, Y. Zhang, J. Antorán, Q.V. Liao, P. Sattigeri, R. Fogliato, G.G. Melançon, R. Krishnan, J. Stanley, O. Tickoo, et al., Uncertainty as a form of transparency: measuring, communicating, and using uncertainty, arXiv preprint, arXiv:2011.07586, 2020.

[62] G. Claeskens, N.L. Hjort, Model Selection and Model Averaging, Cambridge University Press, 2008.

[63] D.J. MacKay, Bayesian methods for adaptive models, PhD thesis, California Institute of Technology, 1992.

[64] O. O'Neill, Linking trust to trustworthiness, Int. J. Philos. Stud. 26 (2) (2018) 293–300.

[65] D.C. Alexander, D. Zikic, J. Zhang, H. Zhang, A. Criminisi, Image quality transfer via random forest regression: applications in diffusion MRI, in: International Conference on Medical Image Computing and Computer-Assisted Intervention, Springer, 2014, pp. 225–232.

[66] R. Tanno, D.E. Worrall, E. Kaden, A. Ghosh, F. Grussu, A. Bizzi, S.N. Sotiropoulos, A. Criminisi, D.C. Alexander, Uncertainty modelling in deep learning for safer neuroimage enhancement: demonstration in diffusion MRI, NeuroImage (2020) 117366.

[67] J.C. Reinhold, Y. He, S. Han, Y. Chen, D. Gao, J. Lee, J.L. Prince, A. Carass, Validating uncertainty in medical image translation, in: 2020 IEEE 17th International Symposium on Biomedical Imaging (ISBI), IEEE, 2020, pp. 95–98.

[68] J.C. Reinhold, Y. He, S. Han, Y. Chen, D. Gao, J. Lee, J.L. Prince, A. Carass, Finding novelty with uncertainty, in: Medical Imaging 2020: Image Processing, vol. 11313, International Society for Optics and Photonics, 2020, p. 113130H.

[69] K. Kläser, P. Borges, R. Shaw, M. Ranzini, M. Modat, D. Atkinson, K. Thielemans, B. Hutton, V. Goh, G. Cook, et al., Uncertainty-aware multi-resolution whole-body MR to CT synthesis, in: International Workshop on Simulation and Synthesis in Medical Imaging, Springer, 2020, pp. 110–119.

[70] T. Nair, D. Precup, D.L. Arnold, T. Arbel, Exploring uncertainty measures in deep networks for multiple sclerosis lesion detection and segmentation, in: International Conference on Medical Image Computing and Computer-Assisted Intervention, Springer, 2018, pp. 655–663.

[71] R. Mehta, T. Christinck, T. Nair, P. Lemaitre, D. Arnold, T. Arbel, Propagating uncertainty across cascaded medical imaging tasks for improved deep learning inference, in: Uncertainty for Safe Utilization of Machine Learning in Medical Imaging and Clinical Image-Based Procedures, Springer, 2019, pp. 23–32.

[72] D.J. MacKay, A practical Bayesian framework for backpropagation networks, Neural Comput. 4 (3) (1992) 448–472.

[73] C.M. Bishop, Bayesian methods for neural networks, Tech. Rep., Aston University, 1995.

[74] J.O. Berger, L.R. Pericchi, The intrinsic Bayes factor for model selection and prediction, J. Am. Stat. Assoc. 91 (433) (1996) 109–122.

[75] J.O. Berger, Statistical Decision Theory and Bayesian Analysis, second ed., Springer Series in Statistics, Springer, New York, 1985.

[76] A.M. Stuart, Inverse problems: a Bayesian perspective, Acta Numer. 19 (2010) 451–559.

[77] K. Ito, B. Jin, Inverse Problems: Tikhonov Theory and Algorithms, World Scientific, Hackensack, NJ, 2015.

[78] Z. Ghahramani, Probabilistic machine learning and artificial intelligence, Nature 521 (7553) (2015) 452–459.

[79] T. Broderick, N. Boyd, A. Wibisono, A.C. Wilson, M.I. Jordan, Streaming variational Bayes, arXiv preprint, arXiv:1307.6769, 2013.

[80] T. Garipov, P. Izmailov, D. Podoprikhin, D. Vetrov, A.G. Wilson, Loss surfaces, mode connectivity, and fast ensembling of DNNs, arXiv preprint, arXiv:1802.10026, 2018.

[81] P. Izmailov, W.J. Maddox, P. Kirichenko, T. Garipov, D. Vetrov, A.G. Wilson, Subspace inference for Bayesian deep learning, in: Uncertainty in Artificial Intelligence, in: PMLR, 2020, pp. 1169–1179.

[82] P. Izmailov, D. Podoprikhin, T. Garipov, D. Vetrov, A.G. Wilson, Averaging weights leads to wider optima and better generalization, arXiv preprint, arXiv:1803.05407, 2018.

[83] A.G. Wilson, P. Izmailov, Bayesian deep learning and a probabilistic perspective of generalization, arXiv preprint, arXiv:2002.08791, 2020.

[84] J.S. Liu, Monte Carlo Strategies in Scientific Computing, Springer, New York, 2001.

[85] M. Girolami, B. Calderhead, Riemann manifold Langevin and Hamiltonian Monte Carlo methods, J. R. Stat. Soc. B 73 (2) (2011) 123–214.

[86] S. Pedemonte, C. Catana, K. van Leemput, Bayesian tomographic reconstruction using Riemannian MCMC, in: International Conference on Medical Image Computing and Computer-Assisted Intervention, Springer, 2015, pp. 619–626.

[87] I.S. Weir, Fully Bayesian reconstructions from single-photon emission computed tomography data, J. Am. Stat. Assoc. 92 (437) (1997) 49–60.

[88] É. Barat, C. Comtat, T. Dautremer, T. Montagu, R. Trébossen, A nonparametric Bayesian approach for PET reconstruction, in: 2007 IEEE Nuclear Science Symposium Conference Record, vol. 6, IEEE, 2007, pp. 4155–4162.

[89] M. Filipovic, E. Barat, T. Dautremer, C. Comtat, S. Stute, PET reconstruction of the posterior image probability, including multimodal images, IEEE Trans. Med. Imaging 38 (7) (2019) 1643–1654.

[90] Q. Long, M. Scavino, R. Tempone, S. Wang, Fast estimation of expected information gains for Bayesian experimental designs based on Laplace approximations, Comput. Methods Appl. Mech. Eng. 259 (2013) 24–39.

[91] M.I. Jordan, Z. Ghahramani, T.S. Jaakkola, L.K. Saul, An introduction to variational methods for graphical models, Mach. Learn. 37 (1999) 183–233.

[92] M.J. Wainwright, M.I. Jordan, Graphical Models, Exponential Families, and Variational Inference, Now Publishers Inc, 2008.

[93] D.M. Blei, A. Kucukelbir, J.D. McAuliffe, Variational inference: a review for statisticians, J. Am. Stat. Assoc. 112 (518) (2017) 859–877.

[94] M.J. Beal, Variational Algorithms for Approximate Bayesian Inference, PhD thesis, University of London, London, 2003.

[95] M. Opper, C. Archambeau, The variational Gaussian approximation revisited, Neural Comput. 21 (3) (2009) 786–792.

[96] E. Challis, D. Barber, Gaussian Kullback–Leibler approximate inference, J. Mach. Learn. Res. 14 (2013) 2239–2286.

[97] M.D. Hoffman, D.M. Blei, C. Wang, J. Paisley, Stochastic variational inference, J. Mach. Learn. Res. 14 (2013) 1303–1347.

[98] T.P. Minka, A family of algorithms for approximate Bayesian inference, ProQuest LLC, Ann Arbor, MI, 2001, PhD Thesis, Massachusetts Institute of Technology.

[99] C. Zhang, S. Arridge, B. Jin, Expectation propagation for Poisson data, Inverse Probl. 35 (8) (2019) 085006, 27.

[100] H. Rue, S. Martino, N. Chopin, Approximate Bayesian inference for latent Gaussian models by using integrated nested Laplace approximations, J. R. Stat. Soc., Ser. B, Stat. Methodol. 71 (2) (2009) 319–392.

[101] S. Kullback, R.A. Leibler, On information and sufficiency, Ann. Math. Stat. 22 (1951) 79–86.

[102] S. Mandt, M.D. Hoffman, D.M. Blei, Stochastic gradient descent as approximate Bayesian inference, J. Mach. Learn. Res. 18 (2017) 1–35.

[103] W.J. Maddox, P. Izmailov, T. Garipov, D.P. Vetrov, A.G. Wilson, A simple baseline for Bayesian uncertainty in deep learning, in: H. Wallach, H. Larochelle, A. Beygelzimer, F. d'Alché-Buc, E. Fox, R. Garnett (Eds.), Advances in Neural Information Processing Systems, vol. 32, Curran Associates, Inc., 2019, pp. 13153–13164.

[104] Q. Liu, D. Wang, Stein variational gradient descent: a general purpose Bayesian inference algorithm, Adv. Neural Inf. Process. Syst. 29 (2016) 2378–2386.

[105] Q. Liu, D. Wang, Stein variational gradient descent as moment matching, in: S. Bengio, H. Wallach, H. Larochelle, K. Grauman, N. Cesa-Bianchi, R. Garnett (Eds.), Advances in Neural Information Processing Systems, vol. 31, Curran Associates, Inc., 2018, pp. 8854–8863.

[106] Y. Wang, D.M. Blei, Frequentist consistency of variational Bayes, J. Am. Stat. Assoc. 114 (527) (2019) 1147–1161.

[107] A. Repetti, M. Pereyra, Y. Wiaux, Scalable Bayesian uncertainty quantification in imaging inverse problems via convex optimization, SIAM J. Imaging Sci. 12 (1) (2019) 87–118.

[108] A.G. Wilson, The case for Bayesian deep learning, arXiv preprint, arXiv:2001.10995, 2020.

[109] R.M. Neal, Bayesian Learning for Neural Networks, vol. 118, Springer Science & Business Media, 2012.

[110] D.J. MacKay, Probable networks and plausible predictions—a review of practical Bayesian methods for supervised neural networks, Netw. Comput. Neural Syst. 6 (3) (1995) 469–505.

[111] A. Graves, Practical variational inference for neural networks, in: Advances in Neural Information Processing Systems, 2011, pp. 2348–2356.

[112] C. Blundell, J. Cornebise, K. Kavukcuoglu, D. Wierstra, Weight uncertainty in neural networks, arXiv preprint, arXiv:1505.05424, 2015.

[113] J.M. Hernández-Lobato, R. Adams, Probabilistic backpropagation for scalable learning of Bayesian neural networks, in: International Conference on Machine Learning, 2015, pp. 1861–1869.

[114] Y. Gal, Z. Ghahramani, Dropout as a Bayesian approximation: representing model uncertainty in deep learning, in: International Conference on Machine Learning, 2016, pp. 1050–1059.

[115] J.S. Denker, Y. LeCun, Transforming neural-net output levels to probability distributions, in: Proceedings of the 3rd International Conference on Neural Information Processing Systems, 1990, pp. 853–859.

[116] Y. Li, J.M. Hernández-Lobato, R.E. Turner, Stochastic expectation propagation, arXiv preprint, arXiv:1506.04132, 2015.

[117] J. Hernandez-Lobato, Y. Li, M. Rowland, T. Bui, D. Hernández-Lobato, R. Turner, Black-box alpha divergence minimization, in: International Conference on Machine Learning, in: PMLR, 2016, pp. 1511–1520.

[118] Y. Li, R.E. Turner, Rényi divergence variational inference, arXiv preprint, arXiv:1602.02311, 2016.

[119] M. Khan, D. Nielsen, V. Tangkaratt, W. Lin, Y. Gal, A. Srivastava, Fast and scalable Bayesian deep learning by weight-perturbation in Adam, in: International Conference on Machine Learning, in: PMLR, 2018, pp. 2611–2620.

[120] S. Sun, G. Zhang, J. Shi, R. Grosse, Functional variational Bayesian neural networks, arXiv preprint, arXiv:1903.05779, 2019.

[121] T. Chen, E. Fox, C. Guestrin, Stochastic gradient Hamiltonian Monte Carlo, in: International Conference on Machine Learning, 2014, pp. 1683–1691.

[122] Y.-A. Ma, T. Chen, E. Fox, A complete recipe for stochastic gradient MCMC, in: Advances in Neural Information Processing Systems, 2015, pp. 2917–2925.

[123] R.M. Neal, Bayesian learning via stochastic dynamics, in: Advances in Neural Information Processing Systems, 1993, pp. 475–482.

[124] M. Welling, Y.W. Teh, Bayesian learning via stochastic gradient Langevin dynamics, in: Proceedings of the 28th International Conference on Machine Learning, 2011, pp. 681–688.

[125] N.N. Schraudolph, Fast curvature matrix-vector products for second-order gradient descent, Neural Comput. 14 (7) (2002) 1723–1738.

[126] J. Martens, New insights and perspectives on the natural gradient method, arXiv preprint, arXiv:1412.1193, 2014.

[127] L. Bottou, F.E. Curtis, J. Nocedal, Optimization methods for large-scale machine learning, SIAM Rev. 60 (2) (2018) 223–311.

[128] A.Y. Foong, Y. Li, J.M. Hernández-Lobato, R.E. Turner, 'In-between' uncertainty in Bayesian neural networks, arXiv preprint, arXiv:1906.11537, 2019.

[129] A. Immer, M. Korzepa, M. Bauer, Improving predictions of Bayesian neural nets via local linearization, in: Proceedings of the 24th International Conference on Artificial Intelligence and Statistics, in: PMLR, vol. 130, 2021, pp. 703–711.

[130] C.M. Bishop, Pattern Recognition and Machine Learning (Information Science and Statistics), Springer-Verlag, Berlin, Heidelberg, 2006.

[131] J. Antorán, R. Barbano, J. Leuschner, J.M. Hernández-Lobato, B. Jin, A probabilistic deep image prior for computational tomography, arXiv preprint, arXiv:2203.00479, 2022.

[132] D.P. Kingma, M. Welling, Auto-encoding variational Bayes, arXiv preprint, arXiv:1312.6114, 2013.

[133] C. Naesseth, F. Ruiz, S. Linderman, D. Blei, Reparameterization gradients through acceptance-rejection sampling algorithms, in: Artificial Intelligence and Statistics, in: PMLR, 2017, pp. 489–498.

[134] F.R. Ruiz, M. Titsias, D. Blei, The generalized reparameterization gradient, in: Advances in Neural Information Processing Systems, 2016, pp. 460–468.

[135] M. Figurnov, S. Mohamed, A. Mnih, Implicit reparameterization gradients, in: Advances in Neural Information Processing Systems, 2018, pp. 441–452.

[136] R. Barbano, C. Zhang, S. Arridge, B. Jin, Quantifying model uncertainty in inverse problems via Bayesian deep gradient descent, arXiv preprint, arXiv:2007.09971, 2020.

[137] R. Barbano, Ž. Kereta, C. Zhang, A. Hauptmann, S. Arridge, B. Jin, Quantifying sources of uncertainty in deep learning-based image reconstruction, arXiv preprint, arXiv:2011.08413, 2020.

[138] J. Hron, A. Matthews, Z. Ghahramani, Variational Bayesian dropout: pitfalls and fixes, in: International Conference on Machine Learning, in: PMLR, 2018, pp. 2019–2028.

[139] D.P. Kingma, T. Salimans, M. Welling, Variational dropout and the local reparameterization trick, arXiv preprint, arXiv:1506.02557, 2015.

[140] M. Teye, H. Azizpour, K. Smith, Bayesian uncertainty estimation for batch normalized deep networks, in: International Conference on Machine Learning, in: PMLR, 2018, pp. 4907–4916.

[141] Y. Wen, P. Vicol, J. Ba, D. Tran, R. Grosse, Flipout: efficient pseudo-independent weight perturbations on mini-batches, arXiv preprint, arXiv:1803.04386, 2018.

[142] J. Schlemper, D.C. Castro, W. Bai, C. Qin, O. Oktay, J. Duan, A.N. Price, J. Hajnal, D. Rueckert, Bayesian deep learning for accelerated MR image reconstruction, in: International Workshop on Machine Learning for Medical Image Reconstruction, Springer, 2018, pp. 64–71.

[143] Y. Gal, Z. Ghahramani, Bayesian convolutional neural networks with Bernoulli approximate variational inference, arXiv preprint, arXiv:1506.02158, 2015.

[144] Y. Gal, Z. Ghahramani, A theoretically grounded application of dropout in recurrent neural networks, in: Advances in Neural Information Processing Systems, 2016, pp. 1019–1027.

[145] D.A. Nix, A.S. Weigend, Estimating the mean and variance of the target probability distribution, in: Proceedings of 1994 IEEE International Conference on Neural Networks (ICNN'94), vol. 1, IEEE, 1994, pp. 55–60.

[146] C.R. Rao, Estimation of heteroscedastic variances in linear models, J. Am. Stat. Assoc. 65 (329) (1970) 161–172.

[147] S. Depeweg, J.-M. Hernandez-Lobato, F. Doshi-Velez, S. Udluft, Decomposition of uncertainty in Bayesian deep learning for efficient and risk-sensitive learning, in: International Conference on Machine Learning, in: PMLR, 2018, pp. 1184–1193.

[148] C.E. Shannon, A mathematical theory of communication, Bell Syst. Tech. J. 27 (3) (1948) 379–423.

[149] J. Adler, O. Öktem, Deep Bayesian inversion, arXiv preprint, arXiv:1811.05910, 2018.

[150] M. Arjovsky, S. Chintala, L. Bottou, Wasserstein GAN, arXiv preprint, arXiv:1701.07875, 2017.

[151] A. Denker, M. Schmidt, J. Leuschner, P. Maass, J. Behrmann, Conditional normalizing flows for low-dose computed tomography image reconstruction, arXiv preprint, arXiv:2006.06270, 2020.

[152] C. Winkler, D. Worrall, E. Hoogeboom, M. Welling, Learning likelihoods with conditional normalizing flows, arXiv preprint, arXiv:1912.00042, 2019.

[153] G. Papamakarios, E. Nalisnick, D.J. Rezende, S. Mohamed, B. Lakshminarayanan, Normalizing flows for probabilistic modeling and inference, arXiv preprint, arXiv:1912.02762, 2019.

[154] F. Tonolini, J. Radford, A. Turpin, D. Faccio, R. Murray-Smith, Variational inference for computational imaging inverse problems, J. Mach. Learn. Res. 21 (179) (2020) 1–46.

[155] C. Zhang, B. Jin, Probabilistic residual learning for aleatoric uncertainty in image restoration, arXiv preprint, arXiv:1908.01010, 2019.

[156] K.C. Tezcan, C.F. Baumgartner, E. Konukoglu, Sampling possible reconstructions of undersampled acquisitions in MR imaging, arXiv preprint, arXiv:2010.00042, 2020.

[157] V. Edupuganti, M. Mardani, S. Vasanawala, J. Pauly, Uncertainty quantification in deep MRI reconstruction, IEEE Trans. Med. Imaging 40 (1) (2021) 239–250.

[158] B. Lakshminarayanan, A. Pritzel, C. Blundell, Simple and scalable predictive uncertainty estimation using deep ensembles, in: Advances in Neural Information Processing Systems, 2017, pp. 6402–6413.

[159] Y. Ovadia, E. Fertig, J. Ren, Z. Nado, D. Sculley, S. Nowozin, J. Dillon, B. Lakshminarayanan, J. Snoek, Can you trust your model's uncertainty? Evaluating predictive uncertainty under dataset shift, in: Advances in Neural Information Processing Systems, 2019, pp. 13991–14002.

[160] A. Ashukha, A. Lyzhov, D. Molchanov, D. Vetrov, Pitfalls of in-domain uncertainty estimation and ensembling in deep learning, arXiv preprint, arXiv:2002.06470, 2020.

[161] F. Wenzel, K. Roth, B.S. Veeling, J. Świątkowski, L. Tran, S. Mandt, J. Snoek, T. Salimans, R. Jenatton, S. Nowozin, How good is the Bayes posterior in deep neural networks really?, arXiv preprint, arXiv:2002.02405, 2020.

[162] T. Pearce, F. Leibfried, A. Brintrup, Uncertainty in neural networks: approximately Bayesian ensembling, in: International Conference on Artificial Intelligence and Statistics, in: PMLR, 2020, pp. 234–244.

[163] F.K. Gustafsson, M. Danelljan, T.B. Schon, Evaluating scalable bayesian deep learning methods for robust computer vision, in: Proceedings of the IEEE/CVF Conference on Computer Vision and Pattern Recognition Workshops, 2020, pp. 318–319.

[164] G. Huang, Y. Li, G. Pleiss, Z. Liu, J.E. Hopcroft, K.Q. Weinberger, Snapshot ensembles: train 1, get m for free, arXiv preprint, arXiv:1704.00109, 2017.

[165] W.J. Maddox, P. Izmailov, T. Garipov, D.P. Vetrov, A.G. Wilson, A simple baseline for Bayesian uncertainty in deep learning, Adv. Neural Inf. Process. Syst. 32 (2019) 13153–13164.

[166] S. Fort, S. Jastrzebski, Large scale structure of neural network loss landscapes, arXiv preprint, arXiv:1906.04724, 2019.

[167] J. van Amersfoort, L. Smith, Y.W. Teh, Y. Gal, Uncertainty estimation using a single deep deterministic neural network, in: International Conference on Machine Learning, in: PMLR, 2020, pp. 9690–9700.

[168] J.Z. Liu, L. Lin, S. Padhy, D. Tran, T. Bedrax-Weiss, B. Lakshminarayanan, Simple and principled uncertainty estimation with deterministic deep learning via distance awareness, in: NeurIPS, 2020.

[169] J. Mukhoti, A. Kirsch, J. van Amersfoort, P.H. Torr, Y. Gal, Deterministic neural networks with appropriate inductive biases capture epistemic and aleatoric uncertainty, arXiv preprint, arXiv:2102.11582v1, 2021.

[170] A.Y. Foong, D.R. Burt, Y. Li, R.E. Turner, On the expressiveness of approximate inference in Bayesian neural networks, arXiv preprint, arXiv:1909.00719, 2019.

[171] A. Kumar, P. Liang, T. Ma, Verified uncertainty calibration, in: NeurIPS 2019, 2019, arXiv:1909.10155.

[172] J. Mukhoti, V. Kulharia, A. Sanyal, S. Golodetz, P.H. Torr, P.K. Dokania, Calibrating deep neural networks using focal loss, in: NeurIPS 2020, 2020, arXiv:2002.09437.

[173] K. Osawa, S. Swaroop, A. Jain, R. Eschenhagen, R.E. Turner, R. Yokota, M.E. Khan, Practical deep learning with Bayesian principles, arXiv preprint, arXiv:1906.02506v2, 2019.

[174] S. Rossi, P. Michiardi, M. Filippone, Good initializations of variational Bayes for deep models, in: International Conference on Machine Learning, in: PMLR, 2019, pp. 5487–5497.

[175] S. Farquhar, M.A. Osborne, Y. Gal, Radial Bayesian neural networks: beyond discrete support in large-scale Bayesian deep learning, in: International Conference on Artificial Intelligence and Statistics, in: PMLR, 2020, pp. 1352–1362.

[176] E. Daxberger, E. Nalisnick, J.U. Allingham, J. Antorán, J.M. Hernández-Lobato, Expressive yet tractable Bayesian deep learning via subnetwork inference, arXiv preprint, arXiv:2010.14689, 2020.

[177] J. Antorán, J.U. Allingham, J.M. Hernández-Lobato, Depth uncertainty in neural networks, arXiv preprint, arXiv:2006.08437, 2020.

[178] D. Bouchacourt, P.K. Mudigonda, S. Nowozin, Disco nets: dissimilarity coefficients networks, in: Advances in Neural Information Processing Systems, 2016, pp. 352–360.

[179] A. Guzman-Rivera, D. Batra, P. Kohli, Multiple choice learning: learning to produce multiple structured outputs, Adv. Neural Inf. Process. Syst. 25 (2012) 1799–1807.

[180] H.-Y. Lee, H.-Y. Tseng, J.-B. Huang, M. Singh, M.-H. Yang, Diverse image-to-image translation via disentangled representations, in: Proceedings of the European Conference on Computer Vision (ECCV), 2018, pp. 35–51.

[181] X. Huang, M.-Y. Liu, S. Belongie, J. Kautz, Multimodal unsupervised image-to-image translation, in: Proceedings of the European Conference on Computer Vision (ECCV), 2018, pp. 172–189.

[182] A. Odena, C. Olah, J. Shlens, Conditional image synthesis with auxiliary classifier GANs, in: International Conference on Machine Learning, in: PMLR, 2017, pp. 2642–2651.

[183] D.J. Rezende, S. Mohamed, Variational inference with normalizing flows, arXiv preprint, arXiv:1505.05770, 2015.

[184] C. Louizos, M. Welling, Structured and efficient variational deep learning with matrix Gaussian posteriors, in: International Conference on Machine Learning, 2016, pp. 1708–1716.

[185] M.D. Hoffman, D.M. Blei, Structured stochastic variational inference, in: Artificial Intelligence and Statistics, 2015.

Future trends in medical and biomedical image synthesis

27

Ninon Burgos[a], Sotirios A. Tsaftaris[b], and David Svoboda[c]

[a]*Sorbonne Université, Institut du Cerveau - Paris Brain Institute - ICM, CNRS, Inria, Inserm, AP-HP, Hôpital de la Pitié-Salpêtrière, Paris, France*
[b]*School of Engineering, University of Edinburgh, Edinburgh, United Kingdom*
[c]*CBIA, Faculty of Informatics, Masaryk University, Brno, Czech Republic*

The contributions of this book demonstrate a wide variety of image synthesis and simulation methods, from parametric modeling to deep learning, and their application to diverse tasks such as image enhancement or data augmentation. The ultimate goal when developing methods is to design a simulation system that can produce realistic anatomical or biological images for diverse acquisition conditions and that is fully controllable, accurate, robust, simple to use, fast and easily accessible to all. This would ideally lead to simulated/augmented data of high quality, high variability and high fidelity (both spatially and in time). However, several challenges remain. This chapter will highlight current limitations and identify possible future research directions.

Methods used for the processing and analysis of medical imaging data often come from the computer vision field. However, medical images have different characteristics than natural images and therefore standard computer vision methods cannot be directly used for image synthesis. This is, for example, the case of deep learning methods as many imaging modalities are intrinsically 3D, meaning that networks built for 2D images must be redesigned, and the amount of data samples available to train networks is far below that of natural images. Without sufficient training samples, the results are thus suboptimal. This is accentuated by the fact that training still often requires paired data (i.e., pairs of images from different modalities, but also pairs of images and annotations), which are difficult to gather, for instance, because of the invasiveness of a modality or the difficulty to obtain annotations. The development of approaches able to exploit unpaired data, but also of weakly-supervised or unsupervised methods, comes as a natural solution. But such approaches face difficulties due to the residual mismatches or shifts that often exist between domains. For example, generative adversarial networks with cycle-consistency loss allow non-unique unpaired image translation as a one-to-many mapping exists between the source and target domains in the forward cycle, and a one-to-many mapping exists between the target and source domains in the backward cycle. Data-related difficulties are not

Biomedical Image Synthesis and Simulation. https://doi.org/10.1016/B978-0-12-824349-7.00034-7

the only obstacles in medical image synthesis, computational complexity is also of concern.

The attentive reader has surely observed between the lines that computational complexity is indeed an Achilles heel in the world of simulations. The problem of complexity can also be viewed as a scale bar where each tick mark uniquely expresses how difficult it is to design and develop a new simulation engine. On the very left tip of the bar are the complex simulation engines that try to properly model all the physical phenomena, which makes the engines rather complex. Typically, such a kind of simulation can require days or weeks. These methods include, for example, Monte Carlo based approaches. In the middle of the scale are image-based parametric models. These models are significantly simpler because their objective is to offer a good visual imagination of the studied objects whereas the detailed description is intentionally omitted to reduce the amount of parameters. These simulation engines are, nevertheless, still quite complicated and require a good expert knowledge during the initial design. Finally, deep learning based simulation methods, that occupy the right-most part of the bar, do not require as much expert knowledge as the learned model tends to replace it. This, however, comes at the cost of limited controllability. Regardless of the choice of the simulation or synthesis method, we must be aware of high demands for hardware performance. The simulations stand and fall together with the availability of high performance computing. However, the computational complexity of Monte Carlo and living system simulations or of deep learning should become less of an issue with the increased availability of highly-parallel architectures (GPU).

While generative models continue to improve, naturally the utility of synthetic data depends on how they are intended to be used. For example, if synthetic will be used to augment real data, one expects that the synthetic data do not merely replicate what they have seen in the training set but are able to synthesize new and unseen samples. This ability of generative models to generalize remains a topic of active investigation. In fact, there is broad consensus now that generative models tend to faithfully be able to reproduce regions of the underlying distribution that contain the majority of the mass, whereas they find difficulty to learn how to generate rare data (closer to the distributional boundaries and tails). Of course, the ability to generate only the mass and thus replicate what is frequently encountered in the training data may have suitable applications as well. For example, in settings where data cannot be distributed due to privacy concerns, synthetic proxies can (and have been shown to) be suitable stand-ins.

This highlights another limitation preventing the wider use of synthetic images: the lack of extensive validation and comparison of the methods proposed. Synthetic data must be validated qualitatively and quantitatively, as well as for their usability for particular medical or biomedical tasks. The first two are gradually becoming a standard. Usability, however, appears very rarely and has to be tailored to the intended use for the synthetic data. Usability remains hard to demonstrate. One can show that with synthetic data similar decisions can be made or show that by adding synthetic data models can be trained better, but perhaps this is not enough to convince clinical users downstream.

Readers will have noticed that, for many applications, deep learning has supplanted the approaches in place. However, classical methods must not be forgotten. Their combination with deep learning might improve the overall performance. Hybrid solutions combining deep learning and systematic modeling, or deep learning and sparse representation would exploit the advantages from each approach. If we have physical models that we know how to mathematically describe, spending data and deep model parameters to capture these degrees of freedom is not efficient use of resources. Thus, one can imagine the marriage between physical systems capturing degrees of freedom we know with learned (from data) models capturing degrees of freedom that describe physically/mathematically we either do not know how to describe or are intractable. Future methodological developments could also focus on systematic modeling to eliminate magic constants and ad-hoc parameters. The model should be well mathematically and biologically based. The still wider availability of performant computing resources will enable the larger development of synthesis of longitudinal/temporal data. Finally, future simulation frameworks need to be flexible and continually develop as current systems are too task- or data-specific. Harmonization may help reach this goal.

Overall, despite the limitations we identified and the trends which we observe, we are optimistic that synthetic and simulated data will continue to play a considerable role in medical image analysis and beyond.

Index

Printed in the United States
by Baker & Taylor Publisher Services